Real Estate Law and Business

Real Estate Law and Business
Brokering, Buying, Selling, and Financing Realty

George Lefcoe
FLORINE AND ERVIN YODER PROFESSOR OF REAL ESTATE LAW
UNIVERSITY OF SOUTHERN CALIFORNIA LAW SCHOOL

With the Assistance of:
Kaveh K. Heravi USC Gould '16
Taylor Hooks USC Gould '17
Zachary Farbod Molarabi USC Gould '17
Jonathan Rabbanian USC Gould '18 &
Aja-Fullo Sanneh USC Gould '16

CAROLINA ACADEMIC PRESS
Durham, North Carolina

eBook ISBN 978-1-63284-797-3
Print ISBN 978-1-63284-796-6
LCCN 2016948338

Carolina Academic Press, LLC
700 Kent Street
Durham, North Carolina 27701
Telephone (919) 489-7486
Fax (919) 493-5668
www.cap-press.com

Printed in the United States of America

*I dedicate this book to my life partner, Leon Chiu,
the light of my life for over three decades now.*

Contents

Acknowledgments

This text was hugely influenced by the many guest experts who joined me in co-teaching my classes over these past six years.

Mark Alverado
Brian Angel
Dennis Angel
Bruce Batlin
John Briscoe
David S. Brown
Tom Burns
Susan Booth
Paul Carey
Nick Christen
Melissa Clark
Paul Cliff
Patrick Crandall
Steven Daily
Luke Daniels
Jon Daurio
Patricia Diefenderfer
Jim Dillavou
Carol Dillon
Lew G. Feldman
Bill Fishel
Amy Forbes
Jim Friedman
Robert Garrett
Danielle Graf
Dennis Greenwald
Daniel Gryczman
Danny Guggenheim
Elva Harding

Catherine Holmes
Noel Hyun Fleming
Lawrence H. Jacobson
Reza Jahangiri
Nam Joe
Jeff Katz
Kevin Keller
Nancy Kennerly
Rick Kirkbride
Mark Kirkhart
Larry Kosmont
Leanne Lachman
Jaime Lee
Jeff Lerman
Derek Lewis
Daniel K. Liffman
William Lindsay
Jeff Lugosi
Steven R. Maizes
Ryan McBride
Michael E. Meyer
Kevin Miller
Mark Minsky
DJ Moore
Tony Natsis
Jay Newman
Brett Nicholas
Phil Nichols
Leanne Nikaido

Robert J. Odson
L. Mark Osher
Michelle Ouellette
Andrew Ouvrir
Elisa L. Paster
Sonia Plesset
David Rand
Kurt Rappaport
Oscar Sandoval
Luke Scholastico
Kevin Shannon
Jesse Sharf
Noah Shore
David C. Smith
Arthur Spaulding
Martin Steere
David Sudeck
Scott Talkov
Glen Trowbridge
David A. Upshaw
Dan Villalpando
Brian Weinhart
Adam Weissburg
Jack Westergom
Pam Westhoff
Jack Wong
Jan Zemanek

Frequently, leading developers host site visits for the students in my real estate law and business classes. Our site visit hosts, their attorneys, financial consultants, architects, planners and principal executives make formal presentations.

Ron Altoon	Andy Gilford	Tom L. Safran
David Alvarado	Andrew Gross	Peter Schwartz
Sonny Astani	Emile Haddad	Jeremy Selman
Christopher J. Barton	Ephrem Harkham	Carlos Siderman
Rick Caruso	Robert Healy	Patti Sinclair
Ed Casey	Marc Huffman	Arturo Sneider
Jeff Chen	Bryan Jackson	Ryan Spruston
Victor J. Coleman	Randy Johnson	Howard K. Stern
Claire De Briere	Keith Kaplan	Bob Tarnofsky
Victoria Diese-Wilson	Philip S. Lanzafame	Marshall Taylor
Vanessa Delgado	Dominic Lowe	Kay L. Tidwell
Gary Dempster	Jennifer Luong	Mark Weinstock
Mehrdad Farivar	John Manavian	John Whitaker
Chris Forman	Bret Nielsen	John Wong
Mark Frobes	James Phelan	William Yi
James Frost	Wayne Ratkovich	Dick Ziman
John Frost	Alex J. Rose	Kev Zoryan

These site visit hosts and speakers have earned my students' gratitude and my heartfelt appreciation for sharing their time and insights.

Andrew Berman made helpful suggestions, while co-authoring the Teachers' Manual for the sixth edition of Real Estate Transactions, Finance and Development, that I incorporated into this textbook.

I am also grateful to Phil Nichols and Oscar Sandoval. As adjunct professors of law at USC, Phil put together a skill-enhancing course on Negotiating and Drafting Purchase and Sale Contracts. Oscar guided students in selecting and analyzing potential investment properties, determining entitlement requirements and developing realistic project pro formas. Oscar edited some of the text and I have borrowed heavily from the material that Phil prepared for his students.

Over the years, many student researchers worked energetically on this project to whom I am grateful to them for their assistance. The names of the five students who shaped the text into publishable condition appear with mine on the title page. Here are the names of others have contributed significantly over the years:

2014–2015	2013–2014	2011–2012
Justin Bubenik	Ashkan Agahzadeh	Keandra Dodds
Daniel Carper	Katherine Allen	John Flynn
Kevin Javidzad	Jessica Burns	Kaleb Keller
	Laurie Choi	Brady Minter
	Phillip Hyun	Jennifer Phillips
	Shaunt Kodaverdian	Tiffany Stone
	Monica Kohles	
	Sean Ricks	

The USC law school continues to offer an ideal working environment, thanks to our Deans present and past including Scott Bice, Andrew Guzman, Robert Rasmussen, Scott Altman, Alex Capron, and Greg Keating.

Our law librarians provided continuing assistance and instruction, especially Brian Raphael and Paul Moorman, and to our acquisitions librarian, Diana Jaque, for her persistence in finding and acquiring every resource needed for this project.

Fortunately, Keith Moore has been my principal editor once again, ever resourceful, patient, and with a discerning eye for spotting the gaps in footnotes and text that need to be filled. I have also been guided and encouraged over the years by Legal Editor Cristina Gegenschatz and greatly assisted in preparing the final copy for this book by Sara Hjelt at Carolina Academic Press.

None of this would be imaginable without Michael Earnhart, my assistant. He managed the preparation of this text and coordinated the efforts of our guest experts, site visit hosts and student assistants over the years.

I am also grateful for the support I have received from members of my family, starting with my late mother, Edyth (September 3, 1916–November 18, 2014), my first real estate teacher who shared the details of her hotel transactions with me as far back as I can remember. Thanks as well to my sister Judy who has let me share each of her real estate transactions, and to my nephews and their wives, Scott and Kelly, Howard and Ann.

Real Estate Law and Business

Chapter 1

Buying and Selling Realty: An Overview[1]

I. How the Chapters Fit Together

This text is an introduction to the legal infrastructure of brokering, selling, buying and financing of real estate assets. Each chapter can be seen as a separate building block in analyzing the basic legal and financial framework that supports real estate transactions.

Leading real estate transactions lawyers and brokers pride themselves on knowing "what's market" in their respective turfs. "What's market" has both a legal and financial aspect. The legal aspect concerns prevailing contract terms and conditions. The financial aspect is called the "economics" of the deal, starting with valuation and measurements of asset performance.

Chapter 1 is an overview of how the typical commercial purchase and sale transaction is phased from start to finish and the range of issues that buyers and sellers customarily negotiate and resolve by written contract.

Chapter 2 is about the finance terms that real estate investors use to describe what is market. The chapter explains the three main methods of real estate appraisal, how investors measure the success or failure of their ventures, and the factors that buyers and lenders weigh when selecting their debt to equity ratios.

Chapter 3 begins by comparing how sellers can market their properties themselves, by auction, or through contracting with a real estate broker. When sellers contract with a broker, as most of them do, they enter a listing agreement with the broker, the key provisions of which are analyzed critically in this chapter.

Chapter 4 details the many ways available to buyers for holding title to real estate, and the main advantages and disadvantages of each choice of entity—including tax considerations. The chapter includes a section on the questions that joint venture partners, typically a project sponsor and a financial partner, need to address in their joint venture agreement.

---

1. The author is grateful to Nancy Kennerly who appeared in USC law classes as a guest expert on purchase and sale agreements and letters of intent, and whose counsel has shaped this chapter.

Chapter 5 is about the different ways that buyers and sellers can allocate between themselves the risks and responsibilities for the physical condition of the properties being sold and purchased.

Chapter 6 describes the requisites of a deed. A deed is the document that effectuates the seller's transfer of title to the buyer and defines the obligations of the seller/grantor, if any, regarding the use and ownership of the subject property.

Chapter 7 is about the various ways of describing land. Buyers risk boundary disputes and disappointments when the formal legal description in a deed differs from the observable facts on the ground on which the buyer probably relied in purchasing the property. In this chapter, we explain how to read the three main types of descriptions. This is also where we discuss boundary disputes, how they arise and the legal norms that come into play in their resolution.

Chapter 8 features an explanation of the core concepts of our recording system in the U.S., and the publicly kept land records upon which our system of property ownership is based.

Chapter 9 is about title insurance upon which buyers rely heavily for the validity of their titles, and mortgage lenders for their lien priorities. A close examination of the main provisions of title policies reveals precisely what title insurers promise buyers and lenders and, perhaps more importantly, what risks title insurers leave with the policy holder.

Chapter 10 is about real estate closings and escrows. Here, we observe how intermediaries assist buyers and sellers to fulfill the reciprocal promises they made in their purchase and sale agreement, culminating in a closing.

Because some purchase and sale contracts that start out smoothly end contentiously, Chapter 11 describes certain legal norms that figure prominently in real estate transaction litigation, including the presumed right to specific performance. We also compare various alternative dispute mechanisms to litigation.

The last four chapters are about mortgage lending: loan originations, loan prepayments, the transfer of the seller's mortgage to the buyer, and foreclosure.

Chapter 12 is an introduction to mortgage lending where we explain the cash flow consequences and trade-offs implicit in the borrower's choice of loan terms.

Chapter 13 is about the prepayment of mortgage loans, the borrower paying off the loan before its stated maturity date. Prepayment is a major factor for lenders and loan investors in considering what a loan is worth to them and a significant feature of any long-term mortgage loan for the borrower.

Chapter 14 is about due-on-sale clauses. These provisions come into play when borrowers try to keep their mortgage loans in place for the benefit of those to whom they sell the security property without obtaining the prior consent of the mortgage lender.

Chapter 15 is about foreclosure. We analyze the complex multi-phased process, potential borrower defenses to foreclosure, and the main alternatives to foreclosure for loans in default. The last part of the chapter compares the various ways available to investors for acquiring distress properties and purchasing mortgage loans in default from those who are holding nonperforming loans.

II. The Purchase and Sale Process
Scope of the Chapter

Here we describe the eight stages of a typical real estate purchase and sale transaction. Then, we compare three documents used in those transactions: letters of intent, purchase and sale contracts and options. Contracts concerning real estate are subject to the Statute of Frauds unless one of the many exceptions to the Statute applies. The chapter ends with a detailed explanation of the Statute and potential exceptions.

Following chapter 1, we have reproduced one of many forms prepared over the years by the California Association of REALTORS®. This one is labelled *Commercial Property Purchase Agreement and Joint Escrow Instructions*. Throughout the text, we refer to specific sections of the forms to show how they deal with particular issues.

A. The Eight Stages in Buying and Selling Realty

The real estate purchase and sale process goes through these eight stages:

(1) *Searching and Marketing*. The real estate transactions process begins when buyers first consider and then commence searching for properties, and sellers and their real estate brokers devise plans for marketing the properties they would like to sell.

The buyer's search could include not just assembling and reviewing information about potential acquisitions but also beginning to identify possible sources of equity and mortgage capital with which to make the purchase.

Leading commercial real estate brokers often serve as advisors to firms, helping them analyze their present and future needs, engage in strategic planning, conduct market surveys and comparisons, perform financial analyses of alternative uses for their real estate assets, and compare the long-term net costs of meeting their space needs, either by purchasing or leasing.

(2) *Pre-contract*. Sellers and buyers could negotiate the terms of their purchase and sale directly or through intermediaries. Quite often, buyers and sellers of major commercial properties begin the formal acquisition process by negotiating and entering letters of intent and term sheets, described below.

Legal Advice. The best time for buyers and sellers to seek the advice of real estate transactions attorneys is before they sign a purchase and sale contract.

When it comes to home sales, "[b]rokers wish to be able to put together binding deals while the parties' momentum is in that direction. They fear that the doubts that afflict people entering substantial transactions may unravel perfectly good deals while the lawyers pick nits. Lawyers believe that some brokers are inclined to push the parties toward deals that may be against their interests. They believe that lawyers offer valuable advice to people entering real estate transactions. They are frustrated by the limitations on the role they can play if their clients appear for the first time with binding agreements in their hands.

"To mitigate this concern and to avoid claims that real estate agents are engaged in the unauthorized practice of law, many realtors use form contracts that contain 'attorney approval' clauses, giving the parties a specified time to consult with an attorney after signing the document."[2]

"The New York high court (Court of Appeals) ruled that an attorney-approval contingency clause that permits either party to terminate the contract if his or her attorney disapproves of the contract within the stated period of time is absolute, regardless of the reason for the disapproval."[3]

(3) *Contract Formation and Execution.* Generally, purchase and sale contracts are written and signed by both parties. The Statute of Frauds requires the material terms of real estate contracts to be written, and the contracts to be signed by "the party to be charged." (The Statute is fully described in the last section of this chapter.)

(4) *Escrow.* The basic real estate purchase and sale involves the buyer paying the seller money for title. This simple exchange of legal title for cash could be achieved with no written agreement at all. The buyer and seller could agree to a simultaneous, concurrent exchange of cash for deed. For convenience, they often designate a third party — a closing attorney, title insurer, or escrow agent — to intermediate the exchange of "good funds" for a valid, recordable deed.

The closing expediter is also assigned the task of overseeing the fulfillment of other pre-closing promises specified in the purchase and sale contract, including buyer sign-offs on inspections of the property, title reports, financing contingencies, the payment and release of liens and encumbrances on the property, and payment of transfer taxes and the real estate broker's commission. These tasks are usually completed during or at "escrow."

(5) *The Executory Period.* The executory period is usually, though not necessarily, coterminous with the escrow period. Technically, the executory period commences at the precise juridical mini-second when both the buyer and seller have signed a binding purchase and sale contract. The executory period ends when each has fulfilled all its obligations precedent to the valid transfer of title from seller to buyer. Generally, during this interim period, the seller retains possession, the right to rents, and liability for maintenance of the property.

---

2. Alice M. Noble-Allgire, *Attorney Approval Clauses In Residential Real Estate Contracts—Is Half a Loaf Better Than None?* 48 U. Kan. L. Rev. 339, 341 (2000).

3. *Contracts: Attorney-Approval Contingency,* 38-APR Real Est. L. Rep. 2 (April, 2009).

(6) *The Due Diligence Period.* Most purchase and sale contracts extend to the buyer a period of time after the contract is signed to make arrangements for title insurance, inspection of the property for potential defects, and financing.

Often, at the outset of the due diligence period, the seller is obligated to tender certain reports and disclosures to the buyer. For example, see paragraph 11 of the purchase and sale contract at the end of this chapter. Among the seller's transmissions is a statement disclosing all property condition defects, a natural and environmental hazard report (required by California statutes), the property's income and expenses, tenant leases, structural issues, and the like.

The seller is also obligated to provide to the buyer a preliminary report from a title insurance company that describes the seller's title and shows exactly what title risks the insurer is willing to take.

The due diligence period is measured either by the number of days from contract signing or the date that the seller delivers promised reports and other documents to the buyer.

During this time, commercial buyers spend thousands of dollars determining whether buildings are structurally sound, soils are buildable, utilities available, zoning and other land use approvals obtainable, and the exceptions to title policy coverage acceptable.

Residential buyers, too, incur the costs of property inspections, title reviews, and other inquiries.

Under most purchase and sale contracts, whether residential or commercial, buyers have complete discretion to terminate a contract during the due diligence period, for any reason or no reason at all, and to receive a full refund of the down payment, as long as they pull the plug on the contract before the due diligence period expires.

There was a time when buyers risked forfeiting their down payments if they terminated their contracts at the end of the due diligence period without ample justification. Over the years, real estate brokers came to realize the futility of trying to force buyers to complete deals they did not want. Litigation, stress and ill-will absorbed their time and attention to no avail because overwhelmingly, recalcitrant buyers never completed their contracts. Productive brokers found that their time was better spent finding ready, willing and able buyers, though they insisted upon the terminating buyer's irrevocable, written and signed rescission statement.

After the due diligence period, typically, if the buyer elects to go forward with the purchase, deposited funds "*go hard.*" This means that the funds are credited to the purchase price at closing or, if the buyer defaults, the funds belong to the seller. Significantly, modern purchase and sale contracts limit the liability of the buyer who breaches a contract of purchase and sale to the funds the buyer paid on deposit. These monies are *liquidated damages,* the total sum of money the seller is entitled to receive as a result of the buyer backing out of the deal.

(7) *Closing.* Usually, sellers are expected to provide executed and notarized deeds at the same time that purchasers advance the final payments due on their contracts. Ideally, the deed is instantaneously recorded. The buyer and the buyer's lender advance all the funds needed to complete the purchase. The seller's lender executes a recordable release of its lien in exchange for simultaneous repayment of the seller's debt. The seller receives the balance due on the purchase price.

New York and Western Style ("Escrow") Closings. There are two distinct methods of organizing for the performance of concurrent conditions. Under either format, closing attorneys[4] and escrow agents[5] utilize checklists of documents each party owes the other under the contract.

The first is known as the *New York* style. The alternative method is called the *escrow* or *western closing.* The New York style closing takes place in a conference room attended by all the significant players in the transaction. Key documents are signed and, if necessary, notarized. The buyer and the buyer's lender wire funds. Upon confirmation of receipt, the seller authorizes the deed and other documents to be delivered into the buyer's possession. Then, title company representatives rush the deed, mortgage, and other real estate-affecting documents to the recorders' office.

In an *escrow* closing, there is seldom an "all hands" meeting. A neutral third party deals directly with buyers, sellers, and lenders to ensure that all the contract conditions to closing are met by the date set for the closing, the necessary documents have been prepared and executed, and funds are being or have been transferred. The closing agent prepares a financial statement accounting for all revenues, disbursements, costs, and expenses. Provisions are made for prompt recordation of documents that affect the real estate.

Usually, local custom dictates the choice of format. In some states, Illinois for instance, residential closings tend to use the escrow format while commercial closings proceed New York style. In the west, escrows are favored except in complex commercial deals that may be closed in the New York style, especially when attorneys oversee the process directly. Even in these situations, attorneys usually involve commercial escrow agents to perform the routine tasks of accounting, bookkeeping, pro-rations and document execution. Even where face-to-face closings predominate, exceptions are made and escrow closings are used, for example, to accommodate parties who are out of town. Closings will be covered in greater detail in Chapter 10.

---

4. In states where lawyers regularly process residential real estate closings, the state bar association often makes available indispensable "how to" guides. California Continuing Education of the Bar, CALIFORNIA REAL PROPERTY SALES TRANSACTIONS, Vols. 1 & 2 (4th ed. 2012).

5. Escrow agents widely utilize form checklists in states where they perform closings. *See, e.g., Florida Bar Continuing Legal Education,* FLORIDA REAL PROPERTY SALES TRANSACTIONS (7th ed. 2013).

(8) *Post-closing.* Here are two specific examples of typical post-closing events.

First, during escrow, the buyer's inspection may have pinpointed a need for certain repairs that the seller subsequently agreed to finance but that were to be completed under the buyer's supervision after the closing. The buyer and seller would have amended their escrow instructions, authorizing the agent to withhold a specified sum for remission to the buyer upon satisfactory completion certified by the buyer and seller.

Second, the buyer could demand compensation from the seller after the closing for damages resulting from: (a) latent material defects that the seller neglected to disclose, (b) the failure of the seller to provide a natural and environmental hazard disclosure report required by state statute, (c) inaccuracies in the promised income and expense statements, or (d) missing copies of permits and licenses necessary to operate the business being conducted by the owner of the subject property.

B. Pre-Contractual Documents: Letters of Intent and Term Sheets

Many complex commercial transactions begin with the buyer and seller negotiating a letter of intent (LOI), sometimes referred to as a term sheet or deal letter, possibly with the help of a broker or an attorney, and sometimes on their own.[6] This two or three page document lists the key deal points on which they agree.

The LOI enables the buyer and seller to see if they can hammer out a tentative resolution of the main terms of the purchase and sale agreement before investing effort and incurring substantial legal and accounting fees negotiating and drafting a detailed, formal purchase and sale contract. If the negotiations stall, it is often because of insurmountable obstacles that would have killed the deal anyway.

An LOI encourages the exchange of information "necessary to arrive at the essential terms for contract formation."[7] It makes drafting a formal contract much easier, and gives buyer and seller a chance to see if they are sufficiently compatible to eventually complete a purchase and sale.

LOI formats vary considerably. Some cover nearly every aspect of the transaction including how the purchase price is to be financed and when it is to be paid, the length of the "due diligence" period (described below), whether the sale is "as is" (with the seller making no warranties or representations concerning the condition of the property), a detailed itemization and allocation of closing costs, and a provision that negotiations will terminate if a contract has not been executed by a certain date.

---

6. Bradley D. Scheick, *The High Price of Imprecision: An Examination of the Enforcement of Letters of Intent Under California Law*, 23 No. 5 Miller & Starr, Real Estate Newsalert 1 (May 2013).

7. Gregory G. Gosfield, *The Structure and Use of Letters of Intent as Prenegotiation Contracts for Prospective Real Estate Transactions*, 38 Real Prop. Prob. & Tr. J. 99, 166 (Spring 2003). Stable URL: http://www.jstor.org/stable/20785721.

Other LOIs are confined to a page with little more than the names of the parties, the purchase price and when it is to be paid, identification of the subject property, maybe the names of the title or escrow firms to be involved, and a target closing date.

Often, LOI provisions are not just about the substance of the contemplated purchase and sale agreement. They can contain reciprocal covenants of confidentiality, obligations to negotiate in good faith, privileged access to certain information, prohibitions on further marketing or acceptance of offers, negotiation exclusivity (not to "shop" the deal with others), and performance deadlines or agreements to pay for certain pre-agreement costs. This gives the buyer an opportunity to tie up the property while determining its feasibility, and the seller a chance to evaluate a potential buyer's seriousness.[8]

Many real estate lawyers are wary of one participant to an LOI attempting to enforce it as a binding contract against the will of the other. Lawyers drafting LOIs hope to deter such attempts with disclaimers that "this document is not meant to be binding." In addition, they often include *"drop dead"* dates in LOIs — dates by which the chitchat is over and negotiations are to halt unless an agreement has been inked. But these provisions for automatic termination are never entirely beyond judicial tampering because of the well-established norm that a contract results at the instant there has been mutual agreement on all material terms even if one of the participants later contends that the parties never meant to conclude a contract, and tries to repudiate it.

Are LOIs Binding? Overwhelmingly, courts defer to the provisions in the LOI that state it is not meant to be a binding contract, declaring the LOI unenforceable.

Courts have occasionally granted enforcement of LOIs as if they were binding contracts, over the objections of one of the parties,[9] but never when the LOI contained a "clear, unambiguous statement that it was their shared intention that the provisions of the LOI would not be legally binding on either party."[10]

Courts have implied an obligation on the parties to continue negotiating the terms of a letter of intent in good faith. These decisions are often predicated on a court-implied covenant of good faith and fair dealing. Critics of such decisions contend that the implied covenant should only be used by courts to fill in the missing terms in an otherwise complete contract when it is clear what the parties would have done themselves had they considered the issue.[11] They contend LOIs should not be used to create a contract where there was none or add provisions that the parties would not have added themselves had they thought about it.

---

8. Rick Daley, Real Estate Development Law, p. 76 (West 2011).

9. Alan Schwartz & Robert E. Scott, *Precontractual Liability and Preliminary Agreements, 120* Harv. L. Rev. 661 (2007).

10. Rick Daley, Real Estate Development Law, p. 80 (West 2011). What did not work for the reluctant seller was its acceptance of an offer that "a mutually acceptable Purchase and Sale Agreement shall be executed within four weeks of acceptance of this offer." *Goren v. Royal Investments Incorporated,* 516 N.E.2d 173 (1987). After signing the buyer's offer, the seller contracted to sell the property for a higher price to someone else. The jilted buyer was able to persuade a court to order that the seller deliver marketable title of the property to the buyer.

11. The risk that each party assumes by entering into negotiations is that the other party may break off discussions at any time. The motivation of the terminating party and whether it acted in

Summing up what many real estate lawyers conclude about LOIs, "[a]t their best, letters of intent facilitate efficiency, speed and reduce costs of preparing final documents. At their worst, they give rise to a bitter dispute between the parties that ends up in a lawsuit over whether they had actually come to agreed terms, an obstacle to deal making or, heaven forbid, the unintended memorialization of an incomplete agreement between the parties."[12]

C. Purchase and Sale Contracts

Requisite Real Estate Purchase and Sale Contract Formalities. To be valid and enforceable, real estate purchase and sale contracts need to contain all the material terms in writing and be signed by the "party to be charged." Material terms include an offer and acceptance, identification of the parties to the contract, the subject property, and the price. Purchase and sale contracts are regarded as bilateral, the consideration for which is simply an exchange of reciprocal promises—the buyer to buy and the seller to sell. "Material" could extend to anything that the buyer or seller deem essential—financing contingencies, "drop dead" closing dates, whatever.

Formal requirements for contracts pertaining to real estate are embodied in state laws derived from the English Statute of Frauds. These statutes and the many exceptions to them are described in the last section of this chapter.

The Free (and Not So Free) Look. Real estate brokers are particularly eager for buyers and sellers to sign written agreements because a contract signed by buyer and seller is an important milestone to the broker earning a commission. Brokers are compensated on commissions for making deals and are usually paid by the seller from sale proceeds at closing.

In addition, brokers urge prospective buyers to write a deposit check. Buyers feel more committed to the transaction with money down, and sellers don't take offers seriously, unaccompanied by cash or its equivalent. Brokers ease buyers' apprehensions of putting money down by assuring them that they can easily back out of the deal virtually at-will with a full refund of their deposit. This is the "free look," and REALTOR® forms specify "free look" due diligence periods.

There is a catch, revealed by a close reading of the REALTOR® contract form. Usually, the buyer's down payment will be held by a third party, in western states, an escrow agent. The agent will not release the refund unless both the buyer and seller consent in writing. See paragraph 18(G) in the form below. This requirement of mutual consent is necessary to protect escrow agents from becoming embroiled in disputes that may arise between buyer and seller. The escrow agent is designated as the neutral expeditor for the fulfillment of the purchase and sale agreement. Escrow instructions

---

good faith is not material. R. Peter Fontaine, *Letter of Intent and the Obligation of Good Faith Negotiation*, 10 No. 4, ACCA DOCKET 76 (Fall, 1992).

12. *Id.*

are signed by all three parties—buyer, seller and agent. The agent is a deal expeditor, not a financial or legal advisor, a guidance counselor, a mediator, arbitrator, or judge. If disputes arise between buyer and seller, the agent awaits their reaching a final resolution on their own and confirming that resolution in writing, or she interpleads them in a lawsuit and awaits a court order.

Under a purchase and sale contract with a provision like 18(G), close friends of mine, both practicing physicians, sought a refund of their deposit after inspecting the condo they had contracted to purchase. But the seller refused to sign the escrow instructions releasing their funds despite pleas from his own broker who pointed to the statutory penalty mentioned in 18(G) for a wrongful refusal to release the buyer.

After six months of acrimonious wrangling, the buyers acceded to the seller's demand to let him keep half the buyers' deposit because it was less expensive and time-consuming than litigation or arbitration.

Is Due Diligence Before Signing a Contract A Good Idea? Understandably, before signing a purchase and sale contract to acquire a home or income producing property, most real estate buyers are reluctant to spend the money and invest the time in "due diligence" efforts. These could include obtaining the advice of a buyer's broker familiar with market conditions in the area, consulting with a financial advisor familiar with the buyers' resources and objectives, reviewing their financing options with a knowledgeable mortgage broker, contracting with a real estate transactions lawyer to review their purchase and sale contract in light of their personal goals and resources, talking to the seller's tenants and other people with whom the seller has done business, and visiting the subject property at various times of night and day to assess its approximate rate of occupancy, the occupants themselves, the type of visitors it draws, and neighborhood conditions. Some of these explorations will be relevant to any purchase contract they sign. Buyers may suffer last minute "buyer's remorse" who defer all their "due diligence" efforts to the executory period, and wish they had entered an option instead of a purchase and sale contract.

D. Options

Sometimes, a buyer or seller wants to bind the other party to the deal but not be bound themselves. Purchase and sale agreements involve reciprocal promises by buyer to buy and seller to sell. Options are one-sided contracts made by the optionor, *either* the buyer to buy *or* the seller to sell in the sole discretion of the other party, the holder. During the term of the option, at least where the holder has given consideration for the option, the optionor's offer to sell or buy is irrevocable.

To be enforceable, option agreements must satisfy certain parameters:

(1) An option must explicitly confer upon the prospective buyer as optionee the right but not the obligation to buy (known as a *call*), or the right but not the obligation to compel the buyer to buy (a *put*). Overwhelmingly, real estate options are *calls*, rarely are they *puts*.

(2) The agreement must describe the property with the same clarity as is required for the enforcement of a purchase and sale contract.

(3) The time for exercising the option, and any other conditions precedent to its exercise, should be specified, such as an obligation by the optionee to notify the property owner of its intent to exercise the option. Typically, the option itself specifies the steps or procedures necessary for its exercise, including obligations for the optionee to notify the optionor of its intent to exercise the option, and then following through by actually exercising the option on or before the dates specified.

(4) The optionee must have paid specific consideration for the option. Unlike bilateral purchase and sale contracts where reciprocal promises of the buyer and seller count as sufficient consideration, the option is a unilateral contract. The optionor is bound to sell but the optionee or holder of the option is not obligated to do anything. Hence, the optionee must pay consideration for the option, usually money. Since the optionee has no obligation to buy, all the optionee forfeits by electing not to buy is the consideration paid for the option. Usually, if the optionee decides to exercise its right to buy, the consideration for the option is credited towards the purchase price.

Hence, an option has two components: (1) An underlying contract to buy or sell on specific terms that is not binding until accepted by the optionee and (2) the optionor's covenant to hold open to the optionee the opportunity to accept.

Once the option holder exercises it, the option becomes a contract of purchase and sale. At that point, to be enforceable, the contract must meet the strictures of the Statute of Frauds which require identification of the parties, specification of the price, and a description of the subject property.[13]

To avoid squabbles over the contract terms and details after the option has been exercised, the optionor and optionee could attach a complete copy of the purchase and sale contract they propose to use. Alternately, they could select a particular form as their contract, filling in the blanks. (See the REALTORS® form at the end of this chapter.)

The Restatement provides a few default rules for options. Options not specifying the length of time the holder has to exercise them are implied to last for a reasonable time, options are presumed transferable, and the recording acts apply to them.[14]

Examples of When Options Could Be Used.[15]

(1) A land developer may need to assemble a large site for a particular project that is held by many separate owners. Typically, the developer, or surrogate buyers acting on the developer's behalf, negotiate for these parcels one-by-one over considerable time periods. The developer may not know how many of the sites she will be able to

---

13. A real estate broker hired by a property owner to find a buyer has not earned a commission when the owner grants an option until the optionee exercises the option.

14. RESTATEMENT (THIRD) OF PROP. SERVITUDES §§ 1.1, 1.3, 4.3, 7.2, 7.14–.16 (AM. LAW. INST. 2000).

15. Ronald Benton Brown, *An Examination of Real Estate Options*, 12 Nova L. Rev. 147 (1987).

acquire. By using options and letting them lapse, she cuts her losses if she cannot tie up enough of the sites to make the project feasible.

(2) Under rolling options, tract house builders constructing big projects in phases obtain commitments from land owners to sell portions of their parcels at the builder's behest. If the houses built in the early phases sell poorly, builders are not stuck with more land than they can develop profitably, or at land purchase prices that turn out to have been unrealistically high. If early phases go well, the builder will exercise the rolling options. The agreed option price precludes the land owner from hiking land prices later to capture some of the value that results from the builder's early success.

(3) Tenants with lease-purchase options may reserve the right to buy their leased space from their landlords. Knowing the tenant can buy them out deters landlords from raising rents disproportionate to the value of the underlying property, gives tenants a chance to reap any increased land value created by their successful operations, and potentially off-sets the tenant's costs of occupancy when the value of the property rises to exceed the option price.[16]

A Comparison of Options and Purchase and Sale Contracts. The option and the purchase and sale contract have some similarities. Each will have specified a purchase price for the realty, described the property and set a closing or exercise date.

There are also differences. The option will rarely mention the buyer's right to inspect the property, the type of deed the seller is to convey, the allocation of closing costs, and the like. For these items, the buyer and seller will need to have negotiated a complete purchase and sale agreement with all material terms included in writing.

Judicial Review of Late Performance. Options and purchase and sale agreements both specify deadlines by which buyers are to exercise or relinquish their rights to the subject property. *Strict performance* of the conditions for exercise is the norm for options; *substantial performance* is the norm for purchase and sale contracts. Courts hold buyers to a standard of strict compliance with option deadlines but often forgive buyers who are a bit late in notifying sellers of their intent to exercise or terminate their rights under purchase and sale agreements as long as the buyer has performed within what the court determines to have been "a reasonable time."

If a court characterizes the agreement between the parties as an option, the optionee will forfeit its right to purchase if it exercises its right even slightly late. Time is how options are priced; the longer the holder's right to exercise the option remains irrevocable, the greater the burden on the optionor. Otherwise, extending the exercise period beyond the time specified in the contract would confer a gratuitous benefit upon the optionee.

Delays occur in the customary real estate purchase and sale agreement that are often beyond the control of the best efforts of buyers and sellers, as they helplessly and anxiously

---

16. Manning Chris *Leasing Versus Purchase of Corporate Real Property: Leases with Residual Equity Interests,* JOURNAL OF REAL ESTATE RESEARCH: 1991, Vol. 6, No. 1, pp. 79–85. (1991).

await such events as final loan approvals from mortgage lenders, the completion of real estate appraisals, or certificates of occupancy from city building and safety departments.

There is an understandable exception to the rule of strict compliance for options when the optionor promised to improve the property before the optionee has to exercise or relinquish its rights to the option. That is what happened in *224 Westlake, LLC v. Engstrom Props., LLC.*[17] The property owner had promised to remove hazardous and toxic material from the site to the satisfaction of the buyer's experts by the option exercise date. The owner was slow in starting the effort, and then discovered that the most effective removal method was to dig up the soil and transport it to a landfill that would accept it.

The owner proposed just capping the soil with an impervious cover but the buyer had good reasons for rejecting this method. By the time the owner became resigned to the soil removal program, the originally scheduled date for closing had long passed. The buyer was not going to pay for the property until the seller financed the completion of the clean-up.

Opportunistically, the owner seized upon the buyer's refusal to advance the option price to declare the option no longer valid. Although time is usually of the essence for options, the court allowed the optionee to extend the final option exercise date until after the optionor had met its obligation satisfactorily to clean-up the site.

Reading between the lines of the opinion, it looked like the optionor may have hugely underestimated the clean-up cost in setting the option price, and was looking for an excuse to terminate the option so that it could sell the property for a higher price than the optionee had bargained for.

Anti-Forfeiture Limitations on Liquidated Damages Do Not Apply to Option Prices. Purchase and sale contracts often provide for liquidated damages when a buyer breaches, and courts sometimes refuse to honor these if the court concludes that the seller was being greatly overcompensated for its loss. The legal norm is that liquidated damages are unenforceable if they are hugely disproportionate to the actual or anticipated loss that a buyer or seller would experience from the other party's breach.

When it comes to the price that an optionee agrees to pay for the option, the sky is the limit, as far as what optionors can charge. Courts do not second guess the appropriateness of option prices any more than they question the appropriateness of a price specified in a purchase and sale agreement for realty short of fraud or overreaching.

Modern Real Estate Purchase and Sale Contracts Blur the Distinction Between Options and Contracts. Under many form purchase and sale contracts, as we have noted, the buyer has a "due diligence" period within which to rescind the contract for any reason or no reason at all. Further, if the buyer passes up this "free look" exit, and later breaches the contract, the seller's sole remedy is to retain the buyer's deposit as liquidated damages. See paragraph 25 (B) of the REALTORS® form. The buyer has

---

17. 169 Wn. App. 700 (2012).

the right but not the obligation to purchase the subject property, and the seller is limited to liquidated damages if the buyer elects not to buy.

How, then, is such a contract different from an option?

The California Supreme Court, in an opinion that attracted considerable concern among real estate lawyers and brokers, ruled that "free look" purchase contracts were unenforceable options because the contract buyer paid nothing for terminating the contract on or before the due diligence period.[18] The consequence could have been particularly devastating for the buyer in this case.[19] Fortunately for the buyer, the property was development land, and the buyer had spent a considerable sum of money to subdivide the parcel as part performance of its contract obligation. Because the court ruled that this constituted consideration for the option, the buyer was allowed to enforce its purchase and sale agreement.

Following this case, many real estate transactions lawyers in California began to add the payment of nominal consideration (typically, $100) to realty purchase and sale contracts that embody the option-like features of the REALTORS® form.

E. The Statute of Frauds

Real estate purchase and sale agreements are almost always written, and rarely based solely on oral promises and a handshake. There are many good reasons for this. Reviewing a written contract before signing it gives buyers and sellers a chance to reflect, clarify and modify terms, and to achieve a measure of "deliberateness" and a "hoped-for caution" before entering agreements.[20] A signed written contract is also a reliable reference later if recollections differ about the details of the agreement.

If the buyer and seller have a falling out, one of them wants to go through the sale and the other does not, courts will only grant specific performance of contracts embodying all the essential terms in writing—with a few exceptions described below. This norm traces back to the English Statute of Frauds.

What the Statute of Frauds Requires. Under state laws based on the English Statute of Frauds of 1677, many types of agreements, including contracts for the purchase and sale of realty and leases for a period of more than one year must be written and contain sufficient details to enable courts to enforce them. No law prohibits buyers and sellers of real estate from carrying out oral purchase and sale agreements. Oral realty contracts are not void under the Statute of Frauds. They cannot be set aside once they are fully performed. They are voidable in the sense that they cannot be enforced.

The law stops short of requiring that the writing embody absolutely every aspect of the parties' agreement. The only items that must be in writing are these:

---

18. Liana C. Epperson, *Are "Free Look" Provisions In Real Estate Purchase Contracts Still Viable?: An Analysis of Steiner v. Thexton,* 20 No. 6 Miller & Starr, Real Estate Newsalert 1 (July, 2010).

19. *Steiner v. Thexton,* 48 Cal. 4th 411, 226 P.3d 359, 106 Cal. Rptr. 3d 252 (2010).

20. Gregory G. Gosfield, *The Structure and Use of Letters of Intent as Prenegotiation Contracts for Prospective Real Estate Transactions,* 38 Real Prop., Prob. & Tr. J. 99,139 (Spring 2003). Stable URL: http://www.jstor.org/stable/20785721.

(1) The parties to the agreement,

(2) The signatures of the party to be charged, namely, the seller if the buyer files the lawsuit, and the buyer if the seller sues,[21]

(3) The price,

(4) A description of the property sufficient for a judge to identify,

(5) Possibly, all other essential terms of the agreement, as courts interpret what is essential. In California, only price, the parties and the property need to be identified for a court to order specific performance.[22]

The Limited Purpose of the Statute of Frauds. The purpose of the Statute is mainly evidentiary, to protect courts from being misled by a party asserting the existence of an agreement where there was none. That is why the Statute is no barrier to parties honoring their oral real estate agreements if they wish. In litigation, the Statute of Frauds is a defense that must be pleaded or deemed waived, and in most states is ineffectual when invoked by a buyer or seller who admits in court that there was a contract.

Exceptions. The Statute is not meant to be punitive or a handy excuse for the blanket repudiation of promises. Hence, it is subject to many exceptions allowing enforcement of unwritten real estate-related promises.

Part Performance. One significant exception is for oral agreements that are partly performed. This can happen when a property owner allows a prospective purchaser to take possession before they enter a formal purchase and sale agreement, or when a landlord promises to sell the house or condo to a tenant, and the tenant, relying on the seller's oral promise to sell, takes possession and makes valuable improvements to the property.[23] The improvements support the buyer's claim that the landlord had promised to sell her the property. The buyer's possession removes some of the reason for the requirement that there be a written agreement by aiding in the court's identification of the property to be conveyed.

---

21. Cal. Civ. Code § 1624(b)(3)(B) ("There is a note, memorandum, or other writing sufficient to indicate that a contract has been made, signed by the party against whom enforcement is sought or by its authorized agent or broker.").

22. David E. Harris, *California Supreme Court Reduces Terms Necessary to Specifically Enforce a Real Property Sales Contract to Three Ps: Parties, Price, and Property Description*, 19 No. 4 Miller & Starr, Real Estate Newsalert 1 (March, 2009).

23. Michelle L. Evans, *The Part Performance Exception to the Statute of Frauds in Real Estate Transactions*, 55 Am. Jur. 3d. Proof of Facts 441. *See Hunte v. Blake*, 476 So. 2d 75 (Ala. 1985) (holding that the part performance exception requires the purchaser to be in possession and have paid all or part of the purchase price for the property); *Sutton v. Warner*, 15 Cal. Rptr. 2d 632, 636 (1st Dist. 1993) (Purchaser took possession under a lease. Seller then granted purchaser an oral option for which purchaser paid $15,000 to be credited to the purchase price. Purchaser also made minor improvements. Trial court found evidence of the existence of the oral contract based on purchaser's occupancy, payments, improvements, and reliance on the oral contract.).

Equitable Estoppel. Another Statute of Frauds exception is based on the "fairness" principal of equitable or promissory estoppel.[24] Here is a prototypical example:

An elderly woman in fragile health encourages a registered male nurse to quit his full time job and provide her with 24/7 in-home care. The woman lives on a modest pension and social security, and cannot afford to pay the caregiver as much as he was earning as a registered nurse; but she owns her house free and clear. So she promises to leave the house to the caregiver upon her death.

The caregiver accepts and works tirelessly with minimal pay for nearly a year, when the woman passes away. She neglected to make any provision for the caregiver's benefit. Complicating matters even more for the nurse, years earlier, she had willed the house to her now estranged spouse, a person who had not so much as visited her in over a decade.

Suppose the spouse challenges the caregiver's claim to the house, pointing out that the decedent's promise was at most oral, and thus is unenforceable under the Statute of Frauds, assuming it was ever made at all. The caregiver's claim is going to be based on the equitable estoppel exception to the Statute of Frauds.

Courts are likely to favor the nurse although some could decide to limit the nurse's recovery to money damages calculated on the basis of the wages he lost while caring for the woman.

F. Frequently Asked Questions about the Statute of Frauds

Question: Must the "party to be charged" sign the contract personally, or can a designated agent to sign for them?

Answer: <u>The name and signature of an agent will suffice.</u> *Neither party will be prejudiced because the law of agency liberally allows principals to sue or be sued on contracts entered on their behalf by their designated agents. Keep in mind one detail, though. If a party's signature is legally required to be affixed in writing under the Statute of Frauds, the agent's authority to sign the contract must also be in writing. This is sometimes called the* **equal dignities rule.**

Question: If the price is left out of the writing, will a court infer the price?

Answer: Not in real estate transactions, but keep reading.

Question: If a contract makes clear how the buyer and seller intend for the price to be determined, but fails to specify a definitive price, will that do?

Answer: Yes. Farm acreage is often sold at so many dollars per acre with the exact acreage to be determined by a survey after the contract is signed. Similarly, income-producing real estate can be sold without a price tag, and instead be determined by some agreed upon formula such as a gross rent multiplier.

---

24. *See Carvel Corp. v. Nicolini,* 535 N.Y.S.2d 379, 381 (1988) (stating that estoppels is reserved "for that limited class of actions where the result of enforcing the contract would be so egregious as to render unconscionable the Statute of Frauds.").

Question: Does the property have to be identified by reference to a formal legal description, such as a subdivision map or the U.S. Public Land Survey System?

Answer: No. In a purchase and sale contract, a <u>street address usually suffices</u> as a means or key to finding a formal legal description for the property. In a deed, a street address will not suffice to convey title because street addresses do not delineate the precise boundaries of the property being conveyed.

Question: Do electronic contracts satisfy the Statute of Frauds?

Answer: Yes. Federal law prohibits signatures and contracts from being denied enforcement solely because they are in <u>electronic form</u>.[25] Of course, the parties must have <u>intended to contract electronically</u>. For example, a court could infer that the buyer and seller intended to contract electronically when, though a lengthy exchange of emails, they finally reach consensus on the price and other important contract terms.

Questions

Question 1: *Letters of Intent, Purchase and Sale Contracts, or Options?*

The subject property is a 57-unit apartment house in a working class neighborhood of a mid-size California city near the center of the state. The seller has owned the property for over a decade, and is earning a positive cash flow. Apartment house values have risen slowly and steadily over the years, and the seller is hoping to "trade up" into a larger building. The buyer is a recent college graduate and a business major, using borrowed funds from family and friends to become a first-time apartment owner/manager/investor. They happen to meet at an alumni social event at a college they both attended, start talking about apartment investments, and realize they might strike a mutually satisfactory deal for the purchase and sale of the apartment house. The seller has yet to list the property with a broker. Compare the advantages and drawbacks of their negotiating a letter of intent, a purchase and sale contract, or an option for the apartment house.

Question 2: *Alternatives to a Written Agreement for Realty.*

An aspiring sculptor meets the owner of a 10,000 square foot downtown warehouse at a cocktail party, and they start talking about whether the aggregation of homeless people in the area is going to prevent it from ever becoming viable for the millennials who enjoy the edginess and low prices of places like these in other cities. Their casual meeting leads to a serious discussion in which the owner agrees to rent the space to the sculptor on a one year lease at $1,000 a month, a very low rent for the warehouse.

The sculptor moves in, feels very much at home, and would be willing to spend $100,000 to $130,000, installing a designer kitchen, two well equipped bathrooms, lighting similar to that of a four star hotel, and ceramic floors. But the landlord must agree to extend the lease for two more years, holding the rent increases to prevailing

---

25. Federal Electronic Signatures in Global and National Commerce Act, (E-Sign), 15 U.S.C. § 7006(4) (2000).

market rents of comparable units that are unimproved. The owner agrees, and also volunteers that if she should ever decide to sell, she would want the sculptor to have the right to purchase the warehouse at its appraised fair market value, at the pre-improved value of the warehouse.

Fortunately, they have a mutual friend who invests in the area and is willing to serve as their resource for setting the rent and, if necessary, determining fair market value.

The sculptor makes the improvements. One year later, the owner lists the property for sale with a real estate broker. The sculptor only learns of this when the broker knocks on the door one morning to show the property to a prospective buyer

Since the sculptor and the owner had no written agreement, does the sculptor have any basis for remaining in possession another year, and purchasing the warehouse if he can raise the money?

Question 3: *Curbing the Enforceability of Letters of Intent.*

The developer of a new shopping center is negotiating letters of intent simultaneously with a major retailer, a grocery chain and a multinational consumer technology company. The center could use all three. All three would like the option to buy the shopping center at some point during their lease terms. Understandably, the developer wants the negotiations to be confidential and would not want to be bound by any tentative agreements — pending the negotiation, drafting and signing of a complete long-term lease agreement. The developer's attorney has cautioned that occasionally courts have enforced letters of intent despite clear language proclaiming that they are meant to be unenforceable, that a formal agreement is to follow, and that the parties have no obligation to continue negotiating after a date specified in the LOI. Of course, the developer wants its LOI to bind the parties to confidentiality.

The attorney has an idea, knowing that the Statute of Frauds applies to leases for more than a year just as it applies to contracts for the purchase and sale of realty (including options). "Just don't sign the LOI. That way, the LOI language concerning leases and options will be unenforceable. Don't worry about the enforceability of the confidentiality provisions; the Statute of Frauds does not apply to them."

In your opinion, is this good advice?

Question 4: *Back up Offers and "No Shopping" Clauses.*

Quite commonly, letters of intent contain a "no shopping" clause in which the seller promises not to negotiate with anyone else while LOI negotiations are pending. But once sellers enter a purchase and sale contract, they are, typically, free to obtain "back up" offers contingent on the termination of the extant purchase and sale agreement.

Real estate brokers welcome the chance to continue marketing the property. With an accepted offer in hand, it is easier for them to attract a second offer on even better terms for the seller. With a backup offer in hand, the brokers have a chance to earn a commission even if the first deal falls through.

(a) How can a seller justify "shopping" a purchase and sale contract that resulted from a letter of intent with such provisions in it?

(b) Suppose a buyer, having negotiated a letter of intent, insists upon the purchase and sale contract containing the same exclusivity and confidentiality provisions that were used in the LOI. How can the seller reasonably refuse such a request?

Question 5: *Financing Contingencies.*

A prospective buyer has saved $25,000 for a down payment on a house or condo. She has heard that she could afford monthly housing costs of approximately 30% of her income after deducting her student loan and car repayment obligations. She has also found a mortgage loan calculator and figured out approximately the size of a loan she could afford. She finds a house she would like to buy. She would hate to forfeit the down payment as liquidated damages if she cannot finance her purchase.

Does she need to determine exactly how she plans to finance the acquisition before signing the purchase and sale contract, or will the standard financing contingency provision protect her from this risk?

Question 6: *Why the "Free Look" Purchase and Sale Agreement Instead of an Option?*

A thoughtful home seller, reviewing the terms of the standard real estate purchase and sale agreement form, asks why she should enter a contract with a buyer who has several weeks to decide whether to buy or not.

During that time, the buyer and the buyer's inspectors have access to the property. If the buyer discovers anything negative during an inspection and discloses it to the seller, the seller must disclose that information to future buyers, even if the inspecting buyer's information is incomplete or misleading.

She will have to fill out an extensive disclosure form herself concerning the property and emphasizing all of its defects. She will have to contract with a title company to prepare a preliminary title report. She will not be able to sell the house during the time the buyer is deciding whether to purchase.

(a) For all of this effort, the seller receives no compensation at all if the buyer walks. Why should she or any other seller be expected to sign such a one-sided contract form?

(b) Most sellers who list their houses for sale with real estate brokers would be far more wary of accepting an option than a purchase offer, even turning down a non-refundable option fee if the optionor elected not to buy. Why do you suppose this is true?

Question 7: *Comparing The Process of Renting with Buying.*

If you have ever rented an apartment, what were the steps in that process? Why was it so much simpler than what is involved in buying a house?

Question 8: *Comparing New York and Western Style Closings.*

(a) When buyers and sellers live outside the jurisdiction where the property is located, which type of closing will prove most convenient — New York or western?

(b) When one of the parties wants to "re-trade" (that is, re-negotiate) the terms of the transaction, which style of closing facilitates that?

COMMERCIAL PROPERTY PURCHASE AGREEMENT
AND JOINT ESCROW INSTRUCTIONS
(NON-RESIDENTIAL)
(C.A.R. Form CPA, Revised 12/15)

CALIFORNIA
ASSOCIATION
OF REALTORS®

Date Prepared: _____

1. OFFER:
   A. THIS IS AN OFFER FROM _____ ("Buyer").
      ☐ Individual(s), ☐ A Corporation, ☐ A Partnership, ☐ An LLC, ☐ An LLP, or ☐ Other _____ .
   B. THE REAL PROPERTY to be acquired is _____ , situated in
      _____ (City), _____ (County), California, _____ (Zip Code), Assessor's Parcel No. _____ ("Property").
   C. THE PURCHASE PRICE offered is _____
      _____ Dollars $ _____ .
   D. CLOSE OF ESCROW shall occur on _____ (date)(or _____ **Days** After Acceptance).
   E. Buyer and Seller are referred to herein as the "Parties." Brokers are not Parties to this Agreement.
2. AGENCY:
   A. DISCLOSURE: The Parties each acknowledge receipt of a ☑"Disclosure Regarding Real Estate Agency Relationships" (C.A.R. Form AD)
   B. CONFIRMATION: The following agency relationships are hereby confirmed for this transaction:
      Listing Agent _____ (Print Firm Name) is the agent of (check one):
      ☐ the Seller exclusively; or ☐ both the Buyer and Seller.
      Selling Agent _____ (Print Firm Name) (if not the same as the
      Listing Agent) is the agent of (check one): ☐ the Buyer exclusively; or ☐ the Seller exclusively; or ☐ both the Buyer and Seller.
   C. POTENTIALLY COMPETING BUYERS AND SELLERS: The Parties each acknowledge receipt of a ☑"Possible Representation
      of More than One Buyer or Seller - Disclosure and Consent" (C.A.R. Form PRBS).
3. FINANCE TERMS: Buyer represents that funds will be good when deposited with Escrow Holder.
   A. INITIAL DEPOSIT: Deposit shall be in the amount of .... $ _____
      (1) Buyer Direct Deposit: Buyer shall deliver deposit directly to Escrow Holder by electronic funds
      transfer, ☐ cashier's check, ☐ personal check, ☐ other _____ within 3 business days
      after Acceptance (or _____);
      OR (2) ☐ **Buyer Deposit with Agent:** Buyer has given the deposit by personal check (or _____)
      to the agent submitting the offer (or to _____), made payable to
      _____ . The deposit shall be held uncashed until Acceptance and then deposited
      with Escrow Holder within 3 business days after Acceptance (or _____).
      Deposit checks given to agent shall be an original signed check and not a copy.
      (Note: Initial and increased deposit checks received by agent shall be recorded in Broker's trust fund log.)
   B. INCREASED DEPOSIT: Buyer shall deposit with Escrow Holder an increased deposit in the amount of .... $ _____
      within _____ **Days** After Acceptance (or _____).
      If the Parties agree to liquidated damages in this Agreement, they also agree to incorporate the increased
      deposit into the liquidated damages amount in a separate liquidated damages clause (C.A.R. Form RID)
      at the time the increased deposit is delivered to Escrow Holder.
   C. ☐ **ALL CASH OFFER:** No loan is needed to purchase the Property. This offer is NOT contingent on Buyer
      obtaining a loan. Written verification of sufficient funds to close this transaction IS ATTACHED to this offer
      or ☐ Buyer shall, within **3 (or _____) Days** After Acceptance, Deliver to Seller such verification.
   D. LOAN(S):
      (1) FIRST LOAN: in the amount of .... $ _____
      This loan will be conventional financing or ☐ Seller financing (C.A.R. Form SFA), ☐ assumed
      financing (C.A.R. Form AFA), ☐ subject to financing, ☐ Other _____ . This loan shall be at
      a fixed rate not to exceed _____% or, ☐ an adjustable rate loan with initial rate not to exceed _____%.
      Regardless of the type of loan, Buyer shall pay points not to exceed _____% of the loan amount.
      (2) ☐ **SECOND LOAN** in the amount of .... $ _____
      This loan will be conventional financing or ☐ Seller financing (C.A.R. Form SFA), ☐ assumed
      financing (C.A.R. Form AFA), ☐ subject to financing, ☐ Other _____ . This loan shall be
      at a fixed rate not to exceed _____% or, ☐ an adjustable rate loan with initial rate not to exceed
      _____%. Regardless of the type of loan, Buyer shall pay points not to exceed _____% of the loan
      amount.
   E. ADDITIONAL FINANCING TERMS: _____
      _____
   F. BALANCE OF DOWN PAYMENT OR PURCHASE PRICE in the amount of .... $ _____
      to be deposited with Escrow Holder pursuant to Escrow Holder instructions.
   G. PURCHASE PRICE (TOTAL): .... $ _____
   H. VERIFICATION OF DOWN PAYMENT AND CLOSING COSTS: Buyer (or Buyer's lender or loan broker pursuant to paragraph 3J(1))
      shall, within **3 (or ___) Days** After Acceptance, Deliver to Seller written verification of Buyer's down payment and closing costs.
      (☐ Verification attached.)

Buyer's Initials (_____)(_____)   Seller's Initials (_____)(_____)

CPA REVISED 12/15 (PAGE 1 OF 11) Print Date

Property Address: _____   Date: _____

I.   APPRAISAL CONTINGENCY AND REMOVAL: This Agreement is (or ☐ is NOT) contingent upon a written appraisal of the Property by a licensed or certified appraiser at no less than the purchase price. Buyer shall, as specified in paragraph 14B(3), in writing, remove the appraisal contingency or cancel this Agreement within **17 (or ___) Days** After Acceptance.

J.   LOAN TERMS:

(1) LOAN APPLICATIONS: Within **3 (or ___) Days** After Acceptance, Buyer shall Deliver to Seller a letter from Buyer's lender or loan broker stating that, based on a review of Buyer's written application and credit report, Buyer is prequalified or preapproved for any NEW loan specified in paragraph 3D. If any loan specified in paragraph 3D is an adjustable rate loan, the prequalification or preapproval letter shall be based on the qualifying rate, not the initial loan rate. (☐ Letter attached.)

(2) LOAN CONTINGENCY: Buyer shall act diligently and in good faith to obtain the designated loan(s). Buyer's qualification for the loan(s) specified above **is a contingency** of this Agreement unless otherwise agreed in writing. If there is no appraisal contingency or the appraisal contingency has been waived or removed, then failure of the Property to appraise at the purchase price does not entitle Buyer to exercise the cancellation right pursuant to the loan contingency if Buyer is otherwise qualified for the specified loan. Buyer's contractual obligations regarding deposit, balance of down payment and closing costs **are not contingencies** of this Agreement.

(3) LOAN CONTINGENCY REMOVAL:
Within **21 (or ___) Days** After Acceptance, Buyer shall, as specified in paragraph 18, in writing, remove the loan contingency or cancel this Agreement. If there is an appraisal contingency, removal of the loan contingency shall not be deemed removal of the appraisal contingency.

(4) ☐ NO LOAN CONTINGENCY: Obtaining any loan specified above is NOT a contingency of this Agreement. If Buyer does not obtain the loan and as a result Buyer does not purchase the Property, Seller may be entitled to Buyer's deposit or other legal remedies.

(5) LENDER LIMITS ON BUYER CREDITS: Any credit to Buyer, from any source, for closing or other costs that is agreed to by the Parties ("Contractual Credit") shall be disclosed to Buyer's lender. If the total credit allowed by Buyer's lender ("Lender Allowable Credit") is less than the Contractual Credit, then (i) the Contractual Credit shall be reduced to the Lender Allowable Credit, and (ii) in the absence of a separate written agreement between the Parties, there shall be no automatic adjustment to the purchase price to make up for the difference between the Contractual Credit and the Lender Allowable Credit.

K.   BUYER STATED FINANCING: Seller is relying on Buyer's representation of the type of financing specified (including but not limited to, as applicable, all cash, amount of down payment, or contingent or non-contingent loan). Seller has agreed to a specific closing date, purchase price and to sell to Buyer in reliance on Buyer's covenant concerning financing. Buyer shall pursue the financing specified in this Agreement. Seller has no obligation to cooperate with Buyer's efforts to obtain any financing other than that specified in the Agreement and the availability of any such alternate financing does not excuse Buyer from the obligation to purchase the Property and close escrow as specified in this Agreement.

4.   SALE OF BUYER'S PROPERTY:
   A. This Agreement and Buyer's ability to obtain financing are NOT contingent upon the sale of any property owned by Buyer.
OR B. ☐ This Agreement and Buyer's ability to obtain financing are contingent upon the sale of property owned by Buyer as specified in the attached addendum (C.A.R. Form COP).

5.   ADDENDA AND ADVISORIES:
   A.   ADDENDA: _____   ☐ Addendum #_____   (C.A.R. Form ADM)
   ☐ Back Up Offer Addendum (C.A.R. Form BUO)   ☐ Court Confirmation Addendum (C.A.R. Form CCA)
   ☐ Septic, Well and Property Monument Addendum (C.A.R. Form SWPI)
   ☐ Short Sale Addendum (C.A.R. Form SSA)   ☐ Other _____

   B.   BUYER AND SELLER ADVISORIES: ☑ Buyer's Inspection Advisory (C.A.R. Form BIA)
   ☐ Probate Advisory (C.A.R. Form PA)   ☐ Statewide Buyer and Seller Advisory (C.A.R. Form SBSA)
   ☐ Trust Advisory (C.A.R. Form TA)   ☐ REO Advisory (C.A.R. Form REO)
   ☐ Short Sale Information and Advisory (C.A.R. Form SSIA)   ☐ Other _____

6.   OTHER TERMS: _____
_____
_____
_____

7.   ALLOCATION OF COSTS
   A.   INSPECTIONS, REPORTS AND CERTIFICATES: Unless otherwise agreed, in writing, this paragraph only determines who is to pay for the inspection, test, certificate or service ("Report") mentioned; it **does not determine who is to pay for any work recommended or identified in the Report.**
   (1) ☐ Buyer ☐ Seller shall pay for a natural hazard zone disclosure report, including tax ☐ environmental ☐ Other: _____ _____ prepared by _____.
   (2) ☐ Buyer ☐ Seller shall pay for the following Report _____ prepared by_____.
   (3) ☐ Buyer ☐ Seller shall pay for the following Report _____ prepared by _____.

Buyer's Initials (_____)(_____)   Seller's Initials (_____)(_____)

COMMERCIAL PROPERTY PURCHASE AGREEMENT (CPA PAGE 2 OF 11)

Property Address: _____   Date: _____

B. GOVERNMENT REQUIREMENTS AND RETROFIT:

(1) ☐ Buyer ☐ Seller shall pay for smoke alarm and carbon monoxide device installation and water heater bracing, if required by Law. Prior to Close Of Escrow ("COE"), Seller shall provide Buyer written statement(s) of compliance in accordance with state and local Law, unless Seller is exempt.

(2) **(i)**☐ Buyer ☐ Seller shall pay the cost of compliance with any other minimum mandatory government inspections and reports if required as a condition of closing escrow under any Law.

(ii) ☐ Buyer ☐ Seller shall pay the cost of compliance with any other minimum mandatory government retrofit standards required as a condition of closing escrow under any Law, whether the work is required to be completed before or after COE.

(iii) Buyer shall be provided, within the time specified in paragraph 18A, a copy of any required government conducted or point-of-sale inspection report prepared pursuant to this Agreement or in anticipation of this sale of the Property.

C. ESCROW AND TITLE:

(1) (a) ☐ Buyer ☐ Seller shall pay escrow fee _____.
(b) Escrow Holder shall be _____.
(c) The Parties shall, within **5 (or ___) Days** After receipt, sign and return Escrow Holder's general provisions.
(2) (a) ☐ Buyer ☐ Seller shall pay for **owner's** title insurance policy specified in paragraph 17E _____.
(b) Owner's title policy to be issued by _____.
(Buyer shall pay for any title insurance policy insuring Buyer's **lender**, unless otherwise agreed in writing.)

D. OTHER COSTS:

(1) ☐ Buyer ☐ Seller shall pay County transfer tax or fee _____.
(2) ☐ Buyer ☐ Seller shall pay City transfer tax or fee _____.
(3) ☐ Buyer ☐ Seller shall pay Owners' Association ("OA") transfer fee _____.
(4) Seller shall pay OA fees for preparing all documents required to be delivered by Civil Code §4525.
(5) ☐ Buyer ☐ Seller shall pay OA fees for preparing all documents other than those required by Civil Code §4525.
(6) Buyer to pay for any HOA certification fee.
(7) ☐ Buyer ☐ Seller shall pay for any private transfer fee _____.
(8) ☐ Buyer ☐ Seller shall pay for _____.
(9) ☐ Buyer ☐ Seller shall pay for _____.

8. ITEMS INCLUDED IN AND EXCLUDED FROM SALE:

A. NOTE TO BUYER AND SELLER: Items listed as included or excluded in the MLS, flyers or marketing materials are **not** included in the purchase price or excluded from the sale unless specified in paragraph 8 B, C or D.

B. ITEMS INCLUDED IN SALE:

(1) All EXISTING fixtures and fittings that are attached to the Property;
(2) EXISTING electrical, mechanical, lighting, plumbing and heating fixtures, ceiling fans, fireplace inserts, gas logs and grates, solar power systems, built-in appliances, window and door screens, awnings, shutters, window coverings, attached floor coverings, television antennas, satellite dishes, air coolers/conditioners, pool/spa equipment, garage door openers/remote controls, mailbox, in-ground landscaping, trees/shrubs, water features and fountains, water softeners, water purifiers, security systems/alarms.
(3) A complete inventory of all personal property of Seller currently used in the operation of the Property and included in the purchase price shall be delivered to Buyer within the time specified in paragraph 18A.
(4) Seller represents that all items included in the purchase price are, unless otherwise specified or identified pursuant to 8B(7), owned by Seller. Within the time specified in paragraph 18A, Seller shall give Buyer a list of fixtures not owned by Seller.
(5) Seller shall deliver title to the personal property by Bill of Sale, free and clear of all liens and encumbrances, and without seller warranty of condition regardless of value.
(6) As additional security for any note in favor of Seller for any part of the purchase price, Buyer shall execute a UCC-1 Financing Statement to be filed with the Secretary of State, covering the personal property included in the purchase, replacement thereof, and insurance proceeds.
(7) **LEASED OR LIENED ITEMS AND SYSTEMS:** Seller shall, within the time specified in paragraph 18A, (i) disclose to Buyer if any item or system specified in paragraph 8B or otherwise included in the sale is leased, or not owned by Seller, or specifically subject to a lien or other encumbrance, and (ii) Deliver to Buyer all written materials (such as lease, warranty, etc.) concerning any such item. Buyer's ability to assume any such lease, or willingness to accept the Property subject to any such lien or encumbrance, is a contingency in favor of Buyer and Seller as specified in paragraph 18B and C.

C. ITEMS EXCLUDED FROM SALE: Unless otherwise specified, the following items are excluded from sale: _____
_____
_____.

D. OTHER ITEMS:

(1) Existing integrated phone and automation systems, including necessary components such as intranet and Internet-connected hardware or devices, control units (other than non-dedicated mobile devices, electronics and computers) and applicable software, permissions, passwords, codes and access information, are (☐ are NOT) included in the sale.

9. CLOSING AND POSSESSION:

A. Seller-occupied or vacant property: Possession shall be delivered to Buyer: (i) at 6 PM or (____ ☐ AM/☐ PM) on the date of Close Of Escrow; (ii) ☐ no later than ___ calendar days after Close Of Escrow; or (iii) at ____ ☐ AM/☐ PM on _____.

B. Seller Remaining in Possession After Close Of Escrow: If Seller has the right to remain in possession after Close Of Escrow, (i) the Parties are advised to sign a separate occupancy agreement such as ☐ C.A.R. Form CL; and (ii) the Parties are advised to consult with their insurance and legal advisors for information about liability and damage or injury to persons and personal and real property; and (iii) Buyer is advised to consult with Buyer's lender about the impact of Seller's occupancy on Buyer's loan.

Buyer's Initials (_____)(_____)   Seller's Initials (_____)(_____)

Property Address: _____   Date: _____

C. Tenant Occupied Units: Possession and occupancy, subject to the rights of tenants under existing leases, shall be delivered to Buyer on Close Of Escrow.

D. At Close Of Escrow: (i) Seller assigns to Buyer any assignable warranty rights for items included in the sale; and **(ii)** Seller shall Deliver to Buyer available Copies of any such warranties. Brokers cannot and will not determine the assignability of any warranties.

E. At Close Of Escrow, unless otherwise agreed in writing, Seller shall provide keys, passwords, codes and/or means to operate all locks, mailboxes, security systems, alarms, home automation systems and intranet and Internet-connected devices included in the purchase price, and garage door openers. If the Property is a condominium or located in a common interest subdivision, Buyer may be required to pay a deposit to the Owners' Association ("OA") to obtain keys to accessible OA facilities.

10. SECURITY DEPOSITS: Security deposits, if any, to the extent they have not been applied by Seller in accordance with any rental agreement and current Law, shall be transferred to Buyer on Close Of Escrow. Seller shall notify each tenant, in compliance with the Civil Code.

11. SELLER DISCLOSURES:

A. NATURAL AND ENVIRONMENTAL DISCLOSURES: Seller shall, within the time specified in paragraph 18, if required by Law: **(i)** Deliver to Buyer earthquake guides (and questionnaire) and environmental hazards booklet; **(ii)** even if exempt from the obligation to provide an NHD, disclose if the Property is located in a Special Flood Hazard Area; Potential Flooding (Inundation) Area; Very High Fire Hazard Zone; State Fire Responsibility Area; Earthquake Fault Zone; Seismic Hazard Zone; and **(iii)** disclose any other zone as required by Law and provide any other information required for those zones.

B. ADDITIONAL DISCLOSURES: Within the time specified in paragraph 18, Seller shall Deliver to Buyer, in writing, the following disclosures, documentation and information:

    (1) RENTAL SERVICE AGREEMENTS: (i) All current leases, rental agreements, service contracts, and other agreements pertaining to the operation of the Property; and **(ii)** a rental statement including names of tenants, rental rates, period of rental, date of last rent increase, security deposits, rental concessions, rebates, or other benefits, if any, and a list of delinquent rents and their duration. Seller represents that no tenant is entitled to any concession, rebate, or other benefit, except as set forth in these documents.

    (2) INCOME AND EXPENSE STATEMENTS: The books and records, including a statement of income and expense for the 12 months preceding Acceptance. Seller represents that the books and records are those maintained in the ordinary and normal course of business, and used by Seller in the computation of federal and state income tax returns.

    (3) ☐ TENANT ESTOPPEL CERTIFICATES: (If checked) Tenant estoppel certificates (C.A.R. Form TEC) completed by Seller or Seller's agent, and signed by tenants, acknowledging: **(i)** that tenants' rental or lease agreements are unmodified and in full force and effect (or if modified, stating all such modifications); **(ii)** that no lessor defaults exist; and **(iii)** stating the amount of any prepaid rent or security deposit.

    (4) SURVEYS, PLANS AND ENGINEERING DOCUMENTS: Copies of surveys, plans, specifications and engineering documents, if any, in Seller's possession or control.

    (5) PERMITS: If in Seller's possession, Copies of all permits and approvals concerning the Property, obtained from any governmental entity, including, but not limited to, certificates of occupancy, conditional use permits, development plans, and licenses and permits pertaining to the operation of the Property.

    (6) STRUCTURAL MODIFICATIONS: Any known structural additions or alterations to, or the installation, alteration, repair or replacement of, significant components of the structure(s) upon the Property.

    (7) GOVERNMENTAL COMPLIANCE: Any improvements, additions, alterations or repairs made by Seller, or known to Seller to have been made, without required governmental permits, final inspections, and approvals.

    (8) VIOLATION NOTICES: Any notice of violations of any Law filed or issued against the Property and actually known to Seller.

    (9) MISCELLANEOUS ITEMS: Any of the following, if actually known to Seller: **(i)** any current pending lawsuit(s), investigation(s), inquiry(ies), action(s), or other proceeding(s) affecting the Property, or the right to use and occupy it; **(ii)** any unsatisfied mechanic's or materialman's lien(s) affecting the Property; and **(iii)** that any tenant of the Property is the subject of a bankruptcy.

C. WITHHOLDING TAXES: Within the time specified in paragraph 18A, to avoid required withholding Seller shall Deliver to Buyer or qualified substitute, an affidavit sufficient to comply with federal (FIRPTA) and California withholding Law, (C.A.R. Form AS or QS).

D. NOTICE REGARDING GAS AND HAZARDOUS LIQUID TRANSMISSION PIPELINES: This notice is being provided simply to inform you that information about the general location of gas and hazardous liquid transmission pipelines is available to the public via the National Pipeline Mapping System (NPMS) Internet Web site maintained by the United States Department of Transportation at **http://www.npms.phmsa.dot.gov/**. To seek further information about possible transmission pipelines near the Property, you may contact your local gas utility or other pipeline operators in the area. Contact information for pipeline operators is searchable by ZIP Code and county on the NPMS Internet Web site.

E. CONDOMINIUM/PLANNED DEVELOPMENT DISCLOSURES:

    (1) SELLER HAS: 7 (or ____) Days After Acceptance to disclose to Buyer whether the Property is a condominium, or is located in a planned development or other common interest subdivision.

    (2) If the Property is a condominium or is located in a planned development or other common interest subdivision, Seller has **3 (or ____) Days** After Acceptance to request from the OA (C.A.R. Form HOA1): **(i)** Copies of any documents required by Law; **(ii)** disclosure of any pending or anticipated claim or litigation by or against the OA; **(iii)** a statement containing the location and number of designated parking and storage spaces; **(iv)** Copies of the most recent 12 months of OA minutes for regular and special meetings; and **(v)** the names and contact information of all OAs governing the Property (collectively, "CI Disclosures"). Seller shall itemize and Deliver to Buyer all CI Disclosures received from the OA and any CI Disclosures in Seller's possession. Buyer's approval of CI Disclosures is a contingency of this Agreement as specified in paragraph 18B(3). The Party specified in paragraph 7, as directed by escrow, shall deposit funds into escrow or direct to OA or management company to pay for any of the above.

Buyer's Initials (_____)(_____)   Seller's Initials (_____)(_____)

EQUAL HOUSING OPPORTUNITY

Property Address: _____   Date: _____

12. ☐ **ENVIRONMENTAL SURVEY** (If checked): Within _____ **Days** After Acceptance, Buyer shall be provided a phase one environmental survey report paid for and obtained by ☐ Buyer ☐ Seller. Buyer shall then, as specified in paragraph 18, remove this contingency or cancel this Agreement.

13. SUBSEQUENT DISCLOSURES: In the event Seller, prior to Close Of Escrow, becomes aware of adverse conditions materially affecting the Property, or any material inaccuracy in disclosures, information or representations previously provided to Buyer of which Buyer is otherwise unaware, Seller shall promptly Deliver a subsequent or amended disclosure or notice in writing, covering those items. **However, a subsequent or amended disclosure shall not be required for conditions and material inaccuracies disclosed in reports ordered and paid for by Buyer.**

14. CHANGES DURING ESCROW:
  A. Prior to Close Of Escrow, Seller may only engage in the following acts, ("Proposed Changes"), subject to Buyer's rights in paragraph 14B: **(i)** rent or lease any vacant unit or other part of the premises; **(ii)** alter, modify, or extend any existing rental or lease agreement; **(iii)** enter into, alter, modify or extend any service contract(s); or **(iv)** change the status of the condition of the Property.
  B. (1) 7 (or ☐ _____) **Days** prior to any Proposed Changes, Seller shall Deliver written notice to Buyer of any Proposed Changes.
       (2) Within 5 (or _____) **Days** After receipt of such notice, Buyer, in writing, may give Seller notice of Buyer's objection to the Proposed Changes in which case Seller shall not make the Proposed Changes.

15. CONDITION OF PROPERTY: Unless otherwise agreed in writing: **(i)** the Property is sold **(a)** "AS-IS" in its PRESENT physical condition as of the date of Acceptance and **(b)** subject to Buyer's Investigation rights; **(ii)** the Property, including pool, spa, landscaping and grounds, is to be maintained in substantially the same condition as on the date of Acceptance; and **(iii)** all debris and personal property not included in the sale shall be removed by Close Of Escrow.
  A. Seller shall, within the time specified in paragraph 18A, DISCLOSE KNOWN MATERIAL FACTS AND DEFECTS affecting the Property, including known insurance claims within the past five years, and make any and all other disclosures required by law.
  B. Buyer has the right to conduct Buyer Investigations of the property and, as specified in paragraph 18B, based upon information discovered in those investigations: **(i)** cancel this Agreement; or **(ii)** request that Seller make Repairs or take other action.
  C. Buyer is strongly advised to conduct investigations of the entire Property in order to determine its present condition. Seller may not be aware of all defects affecting the Property or other factors that Buyer considers important. Property improvements may not be built according to code, in compliance with current Law, or have had permits issued.

16. BUYER'S INVESTIGATION OF PROPERTY AND MATTERS AFFECTING PROPERTY:
  A. Buyer's acceptance of the condition of, and any other matter affecting the Property, is a contingency of this Agreement as specified in this paragraph and paragraph 18B. Within the time specified in paragraph 18B(1), Buyer shall have the right, at Buyer's expense unless otherwise agreed, to conduct inspections, investigations, tests, surveys and other studies ("Buyer Investigations"), including, but not limited to, the right to: **(i)** inspect for lead-based paint and other lead-based paint hazards; **(ii)** inspect for wood destroying pests and organisms. Any inspection for wood destroying pests and organisms shall be prepared by a registered Structural Pest Control company; shall cover the main building and attached structures; may cover detached structures; shall NOT include water tests of shower pans on upper level units unless the owners of property below the shower consent; shall NOT include roof coverings; and, if the Property is a unit in a condominium or other common interest subdivision, the inspection shall include only the separate interest and any exclusive-use areas being transferred, and shall NOT include common areas; and shall include a report ("Pest Control Report") showing the findings of the company which shall be separated into sections for evident infestation or infections (Section 1) and for conditions likely to lead to infestation or infection (Section 2); **(iii)** review the registered sex offender database; **(iv)** confirm the insurability of Buyer and the Property including the availability and cost of flood and fire insurance; **(v)** review and seek approval of leases that may need to be assumed by Buyer; and **(vi)** satisfy Buyer as to any matter specified in the attached Buyer's Inspection Advisory (C.A.R. Form BIA). Without Seller's prior written consent, Buyer shall neither make nor cause to be made: **(i)** invasive or destructive Buyer Investigations except for minimally invasive testing required to prepare a Pest Control Report; or **(ii)** inspections by any governmental building or zoning inspector or government employee, unless required by Law.
  B. Seller shall make the Property available for all Buyer Investigations. Buyer shall **(i)** as specified in paragraph 18B, complete Buyer Investigations and either remove the contingency or cancel this Agreement, and **(ii)** give Seller, at no cost, complete Copies of all such Investigation reports obtained by Buyer, which obligation shall survive the termination of this Agreement.
  C. Seller shall have water, gas, electricity and all operable pilot lights on for Buyer's Investigations and through the date possession is made available to Buyer.
  D. Buyer indemnity and seller protection for entry upon property: Buyer shall: **(i)** keep the Property free and clear of liens; **(ii)** repair all damage arising from Buyer Investigations; and **(iii)** indemnify and hold Seller harmless from all resulting liability, claims, demands, damages and costs. Buyer shall carry, or Buyer shall require anyone acting on Buyer's behalf to carry, policies of liability, workers' compensation and other applicable insurance, defending and protecting Seller from liability for any injuries to persons or property occurring during any Buyer Investigations or work done on the Property at Buyer's direction prior to Close Of Escrow. Seller is advised that certain protections may be afforded Seller by recording a "Notice of Non-Responsibility" (C.A.R. Form NNR) for Buyer Investigations and work done on the Property at Buyer's direction. Buyer's obligations under this paragraph shall survive the termination of this Agreement.

17. TITLE AND VESTING:
  A. Within the time specified in paragraph 18, Buyer shall be provided a current preliminary title report ("Preliminary Report"). The Preliminary Report is only an offer by the title insurer to issue a policy of title insurance and may not contain every item affecting title. Buyer's review of the Preliminary Report and any other matters which may affect title are a contingency of this Agreement as specified in paragraph 18B. The company providing the Preliminary Report shall, prior to issuing a Preliminary Report, conduct a search of the General Index for all Sellers except banks or other institutional lenders selling properties they acquired through foreclosure (REOs), corporations, and government entities. Seller shall within 7 Days After Acceptance, give Escrow Holder a completed Statement of Information.
  B. Title is taken in its present condition subject to all encumbrances, easements, covenants, conditions, restrictions, rights and other matters, whether of record or not, as of the date of Acceptance except for: **(i)** monetary liens of record (which Seller is obligated to pay off) unless Buyer is assuming those obligations or taking the Property subject to those obligations; and **(ii)** those matters which Seller has agreed to remove in writing.
  C. Within the time specified in paragraph 18A, Seller has a duty to disclose to Buyer all matters known to Seller affecting title, whether of record or not.

Buyer's Initials (_____)(_____)   Seller's Initials (_____)(_____)

Property Address: _____   Date: _____

D. At Close Of Escrow, Buyer shall receive a grant deed conveying title (or, for stock cooperative or long-term lease, an assignment of stock certificate or of Seller's leasehold interest), including oil, mineral and water rights if currently owned by Seller. Title shall vest as designated in Buyer's supplemental escrow instructions. THE MANNER OF TAKING TITLE MAY HAVE SIGNIFICANT LEGAL AND TAX CONSEQUENCES. CONSULT AN APPROPRIATE PROFESSIONAL.

E. Buyer shall receive a standard coverage owners CLTA policy of title insurance. An ALTA policy or the addition of endorsements may provide greater coverage for Buyer. A title company, at Buyer's request, can provide information about the availability, desirability, coverage, and cost of various title insurance coverages and endorsements. If Buyer desires title coverage other than that required by this paragraph, Buyer shall instruct Escrow Holder in writing and shall pay any increase in cost.

18. TIME PERIODS; REMOVAL OF CONTINGENCIES; CANCELLATION RIGHTS: The following time periods may only be extended, altered, modified or changed by mutual written agreement. Any removal of contingencies or cancellation under this paragraph by either Buyer or Seller must be exercised in good faith and in writing (C.A.R. Form CR or CC).

A.   SELLER HAS: 7 (or ____) Days After Acceptance to Deliver to Buyer all Reports, disclosures and information for which Seller is responsible under paragraphs 5A, 6, 7, 8B(7), 11A, B, C, D and F, 12, 15A and 17A. Buyer after first Delivering to Seller a Notice to Seller to Perform (C.A.R. Form NSP) may cancel this Agreement if Seller has not Delivered the items within the time specified.

B. (1) BUYER HAS: 17 (or ____) Days After Acceptance, unless otherwise agreed in writing, to:
(i) complete all Buyer Investigations; review all disclosures, reports, lease documents to be assumed by Buyer pursuant to paragraph 8B(7) and other applicable information, which Buyer receives from Seller; and approve all matters affecting the Property.

(2) Within the time specified in paragraph 18B(1), Buyer may request that Seller make repairs or take any other action regarding the Property (C.A.R. Form RR). Seller has no obligation to agree to or respond to (C.A.R. Form RRRR) Buyer's requests.

(3) By the end of the time specified in paragraph 18B(1) (or as otherwise specified in this Agreement), Buyer shall Deliver to Seller a removal of the applicable contingency or cancellation (C.A.R. Form CR or CC) of this Agreement. However, if any report, disclosure or information for which Seller is responsible is not Delivered within the time specified in paragraph 18A, then Buyer has **5 (or ____) Days** After Delivery of any such items, or the time specified in paragraph 18B(1), whichever is later, to Deliver to Seller a removal of the applicable contingency or cancellation of this Agreement.

(4) Continuation of Contingency: Even after the end of the time specified in paragraph 18B(1) and before Seller cancels, if at all, pursuant to paragraph 18C, Buyer retains the right, in writing, to either (i) remove remaining contingencies, or (ii) cancel this Agreement based on a remaining contingency. Once Buyer's written removal of all contingencies is Delivered to Seller, Seller may not cancel this Agreement pursuant to paragraph 18C(1).

C.   SELLER RIGHT TO CANCEL:
(1) Seller right to Cancel; Buyer Contingencies: If, by the time specified in this Agreement, Buyer does not Deliver to Seller a removal of the applicable contingency or cancellation of this Agreement, then Seller, after first Delivering to Buyer a Notice to Buyer to Perform (C.A.R. Form NBP), may cancel this Agreement. In such event, Seller shall authorize the return of Buyer's deposit, except for fees incurred by Buyer.

(2) Seller right to Cancel; Buyer Contract Obligations: Seller, after first delivering to Buyer a NBP, may cancel this Agreement if, by the time specified in this Agreement, Buyer does not take the following action(s): **(i)** Deposit funds as required by paragraph 3A or 3B or if the funds deposited pursuant to paragraph 3A or 3B are not good when deposited; **(ii)** Deliver a letter as required by paragraph 3J(1); **(iii)** Deliver verification as required by paragraph 3C or 3H or if Seller reasonably disapproves of the verification provided by paragraph 3C or 3H; or **(iv)** In writing assume or accept leases or liens specified in 8B(7); **(v)** Sign or initial a separate liquidated damages form for an increased deposit as required by paragraphs 3B and 25B; or **(vi)** Provide evidence of authority to sign in a representative capacity as specified in paragraph 23. In such event, Seller shall authorize the return of Buyer's deposit, except for fees incurred by Buyer.

D.   NOTICE TO BUYER OR SELLER TO PERFORM: The NBP or NSP shall: **(i)** be in writing; **(ii)** be signed by the applicable Buyer or Seller; and **(iii)** give the other Party at least **2 (or ____) Days** After Delivery (or until the time specified in the applicable paragraph, whichever occurs last) to take the applicable action. A NBP or NSP may not be Delivered any earlier than **2 Days** Prior to the expiration of the applicable time for the other Party to remove a contingency or cancel this Agreement or meet an obligation specified in paragraph 18.

E.   EFFECT OF BUYER'S REMOVAL OF CONTINGENCIES: If Buyer removes, in writing, any contingency or cancellation rights, unless otherwise specified in writing, Buyer shall conclusively be deemed to have: **(i)** completed all Buyer Investigations, and review of reports and other applicable information and disclosures pertaining to that contingency or cancellation right; **(ii)** elected to proceed with the transaction; and **(iii)** assumed all liability, responsibility and expense for Repairs or corrections pertaining to that contingency or cancellation right, or for the inability to obtain financing.

F.   CLOSE OF ESCROW: Before Buyer or Seller may cancel this Agreement for failure of the other Party to close escrow pursuant to this Agreement, Buyer or Seller must first Deliver to the other Party a demand to close escrow (C.A.R. Form DCE). The DCE shall: **(i)** be signed by the applicable Buyer or Seller; and **(ii)** give the other Party at least **3 (or ____) Days** After Delivery to close escrow. A DCE may not be Delivered any earlier than **3 Days** Prior to the scheduled close of escrow.

G.   EFFECT OF CANCELLATION ON DEPOSITS: If Buyer or Seller gives written notice of cancellation pursuant to rights duly exercised under the terms of this Agreement, the Parties agree to Sign mutual instructions to cancel the sale and escrow and release deposits, if any, to the party entitled to the funds, less fees and costs incurred by that party. Fees and costs may be payable to service providers and vendors for services and products provided during escrow. Except as specified below, **release of funds will require mutual Signed release instructions from the Parties, judicial decision or arbitration award.** If either Party fails to execute mutual instructions to cancel escrow, one Party may make a written demand to Escrow Holder for the deposit (C.A.R. Form BDRD or SDRD). Escrow Holder, upon receipt, shall promptly deliver notice of the demand to the other Party. If, within **10 Days** After Escrow Holder's notice, the other Party does not object to the demand, Escrow Holder shall disburse the deposit to the Party making the demand. If Escrow Holder complies with the preceding process, each Party shall be deemed to have released Escrow Holder from any and all claims or liability related to the disbursal of the deposit. Escrow Holder, at its discretion, may nonetheless require mutual cancellation instructions. **A Party may be subject to a civil penalty of up to $1,000 for refusal to sign cancellation instructions if no good faith dispute exists as to who is entitled to the deposited funds (Civil Code §1057.3).**

Buyer's Initials (_____)(_____)   Seller's Initials (_____)(_____)

CPA REVISED 12/15 (PAGE 6 OF 11) Print Date

COMMERCIAL PROPERTY PURCHASE AGREEMENT (CPA PAGE 6 OF 11)

Property Address: _____   Date: _____

19. REPAIRS: Repairs shall be completed prior to final verification of condition unless otherwise agreed in writing. Repairs to be performed at Seller's expense may be performed by Seller or through others, provided that the work complies with applicable Law, including governmental permit, inspection and approval requirements. Repairs shall be performed in a good, skillful manner with materials of quality and appearance comparable to existing materials. It is understood that exact restoration of appearance or cosmetic items following all Repairs may not be possible. Seller shall: **(i)** obtain invoices and paid receipts for Repairs performed by others; **(ii)** prepare a written statement indicating the Repairs performed by Seller and the date of such Repairs; and **(iii)** provide Copies of invoices and paid receipts and statements to Buyer prior to final verification of condition.

20. FINAL VERIFICATION OF CONDITION: Buyer shall have the right to make a final verification of the Property within **5 (or ☐ ___) Days** Prior to Close Of Escrow, NOT AS A CONTINGENCY OF THE SALE, but solely to confirm: **(i)** the Property is maintained pursuant to paragraph 15; **(ii)** Repairs have been completed as agreed; and **(iii)** Seller has complied with Seller's other obligations under this Agreement (C.A.R. Form VP).

21. PRORATIONS OF PROPERTY TAXES AND OTHER ITEMS: Unless otherwise agreed in writing, the following items shall be PAID CURRENT and prorated between Buyer and Seller as of Close Of Escrow: real property taxes and assessments, interest, rents, OA regular, special, and emergency dues and assessments imposed prior to Close Of Escrow, premiums on insurance assumed by Buyer, payments on bonds and assessments assumed by Buyer, and payments on Mello-Roos and other Special Assessment District bonds and assessments that are now a lien. The following items shall be assumed by Buyer WITHOUT CREDIT toward the purchase price: prorated payments on Mello-Roos and other Special Assessment District bonds and assessments and HOA special assessments that are now a lien but not yet due. Property will be reassessed upon change of ownership. Any supplemental tax bills shall be paid as follows: **(i)** for periods after Close Of Escrow, by Buyer; and **(ii)** for periods prior to Close Of Escrow, by Seller (see C.A.R. Form SPT or SBSA for further information). TAX BILLS ISSUED AFTER CLOSE OF ESCROW SHALL BE HANDLED DIRECTLY BETWEEN BUYER AND SELLER. Prorations shall be made based on a 30-day month.

22. BROKERS:

A. COMPENSATION: Seller or Buyer, or both, as applicable, agrees to pay compensation to Broker as specified in a separate written agreement between Broker and that Seller or Buyer. Compensation is payable upon Close Of Escrow, or if escrow does not close, as otherwise specified in the agreement between Broker and that Seller or Buyer.

B. BROKERAGE: Neither Buyer nor Seller has utilized the services of, or for any other reason owes compensation to, a licensed real estate broker (individual or corporate), agent, finder, or other entity, other than as specified in this Agreement, in connection with any act relating to the Property, including, but not limited to, inquiries, introductions, consultations and negotiations leading to this Agreement. Buyer and Seller each agree to indemnify, defend, and hold the other, the Brokers specified herein and their agents, harmless from and against any costs, expenses or liability for compensation claimed inconsistent with the warranty and representations in this paragraph.

C. SCOPE OF DUTY: Buyer and Seller acknowledge and agree that Broker: **(i)** Does not decide what price Buyer should pay or Seller should accept; **(ii)** Does not guarantee the condition of the Property; **(iii)** Does not guarantee the performance, adequacy or completeness of inspections, services, products or repairs provided or made by Seller or others; **(iv)** Does not have an obligation to conduct an inspection of common areas or areas off the site of the Property; **(v)** Shall not be responsible for identifying defects on the Property, in common areas, or offsite unless such defects are visually observable by an inspection of reasonably accessible areas of the Property or are known to Broker; **(vi)** Shall not be responsible for inspecting public records or permits concerning the title or use of Property; **(vii)** Shall not be responsible for identifying the location of boundary lines or other items affecting title; **(viii)** Shall not be responsible for verifying square footage, representations of others or information contained in Investigation reports, Multiple Listing Service, advertisements, flyers or other promotional material; **(ix)** Shall not be responsible for determining the fair market value of the Property or any personal property included in the sale; **(x)** Shall not be responsible for providing legal or tax advice regarding any aspect of a transaction entered into by Buyer or Seller; and **(xi)** Shall not be responsible for providing other advice or information that exceeds the knowledge, education and experience required to perform real estate licensed activity. Buyer and Seller agree to seek legal, tax, insurance, title and other desired assistance from appropriate professionals.

23. REPRESENTATIVE CAPACITY: If one or more Parties is signing the Agreement in a representative capacity and not for him/herself as an individual then that Party shall so indicate in paragraph 40 or 41 and attach a Representative Capacity Signature Disclosure (C.A.R. Form RCSD). Wherever the signature or initials of the representative identified in the RCSD appear on the Agreement or any related documents, it shall be deemed to be in a representative capacity for the entity described and not in an individual capacity, unless otherwise indicated. The Party acting in a representative capacity (i) represents that the entity for which that party is acting already exists and (ii) shall Deliver to the other Party and Escrow Holder, within **3 Days** After Acceptance, evidence of authority to act in that capacity (such as but not limited to: applicable portion of the trust or Certification Of Trust (Probate Code §18100.5), letters testamentary, court order, power of attorney, corporate resolution, or formation documents of the business entity).

24. JOINT ESCROW INSTRUCTIONS TO ESCROW HOLDER:

A. The following paragraphs, or applicable portions thereof, of this Agreement constitute the joint escrow instructions of Buyer and Seller to Escrow Holder, which Escrow Holder is to use along with any related counter offers and addenda, and any additional mutual instructions to close the escrow: paragraphs 1, 3, 4B, 5A, 6, 7, 10, 11D, 17, 18G, 21, 22A, 23, 24, 30, 38, 39, 41, 42 and paragraph D of the section titled Real Estate Brokers on page 11. If a Copy of the separate compensation agreement(s) provided for in paragraph 22A, or paragraph D of the section titled Real Estate Brokers on page 11 is deposited with Escrow Holder by Broker, Escrow Holder shall accept such agreement(s) and pay out from Buyer's or Seller's funds, or both, as applicable, the Broker's compensation provided for in such agreement(s). The terms and conditions of this Agreement not set forth in the specified paragraphs are additional matters for the information of Escrow Holder, but about which Escrow Holder need not be concerned. Buyer and Seller will receive Escrow Holder's general provisions, if any, directly from Escrow Holder and will execute such provisions within the time specified in paragraph 7C(1)(c). To the extent the general provisions are inconsistent or conflict with this Agreement, the general provisions will control as to the duties and obligations of Escrow Holder only. Buyer and Seller will execute additional instructions, documents and forms provided by Escrow Holder that are reasonably necessary to close the escrow and, as directed by Escrow Holder, within **3 (or ___) Days**, shall pay to Escrow Holder or HOA or HOA management company or others any fee required by paragraphs 7, 11 or elsewhere in this Agreement.

Buyer's Initials (_____)(_____)   Seller's Initials (_____)(_____)

Property Address: _____ Date: _____

B. A Copy of this Agreement including any counter offer(s) and addenda shall be delivered to Escrow Holder within **3 Days** After Acceptance (or _____). Buyer and Seller authorize Escrow Holder to accept and rely on Copies and Signatures as defined in this Agreement as originals, to open escrow and for other purposes of escrow. The validity of this Agreement as between Buyer and Seller is not affected by whether or when Escrow Holder Signs this Agreement. Escrow Holder shall provide Seller's Statement of Information to Title company when received from Seller. If Seller delivers an affidavit to Escrow Holder to satisfy Seller's FIRPTA obligation under paragraph 10C, Escrow Holder shall deliver to Buyer a Qualified Substitute statement that complies with federal Law.

C. Brokers are a party to the escrow for the sole purpose of compensation pursuant to paragraph 22A and paragraph D of the section titled Real Estate Brokers on page 11. Buyer and Seller irrevocably assign to Brokers compensation specified in paragraph 22A, and irrevocably instruct Escrow Holder to disburse those funds to Brokers at Close Of Escrow or pursuant to any other mutually executed cancellation agreement. Compensation instructions can be amended or revoked only with the written consent of Brokers. Buyer and Seller shall release and hold harmless Escrow Holder from any liability resulting from Escrow Holder's payment to Broker(s) of compensation pursuant to this Agreement.

D. Upon receipt, Escrow Holder shall provide Seller and Seller's Broker verification of Buyer's deposit of funds pursuant to paragraph 3A and 3B. Once Escrow Holder becomes aware of any of the following, Escrow Holder shall immediately notify all Brokers: **(i)** if Buyer's initial or any additional deposit is not made pursuant to this Agreement, or is not good at time of deposit with Escrow Holder; or **(ii)** if Buyer and Seller instruct Escrow Holder to cancel escrow.

E. A Copy of any amendment that affects any paragraph of this Agreement for which Escrow Holder is responsible shall be delivered to Escrow Holder within 3 Days after mutual execution of the amendment.

25. REMEDIES FOR BUYER'S BREACH OF CONTRACT:

A. **Any clause added by the Parties specifying a remedy (such as release or forfeiture of deposit or making a deposit non-refundable) for failure of Buyer to complete the purchase in violation of this Agreement shall be deemed invalid unless the clause independently satisfies the statutory liquidated damages requirements set forth in the Civil Code.**

B. **LIQUIDATED DAMAGES: If Buyer fails to complete this purchase because of Buyer's default, Seller shall retain, as liquidated damages, the deposit actually paid. Buyer and Seller agree that this amount is a reasonable sum given that it is impractical or extremely difficult to establish the amount of damages that would actually be suffered by Seller in the event Buyer were to breach this Agreement. Release of funds will require mutual, Signed release instructions from both Buyer and Seller, judicial decision or arbitration award. AT THE TIME OF ANY INCREASED DEPOSIT BUYER AND SELLER SHALL SIGN A SEPARATE LIQUIDATED DAMAGES PROVISION INCORPORATING THE INCREASED DEPOSIT AS LIQUIDATED DAMAGES (C.A.R. FORM RID).**

Buyer's Initials_____/_____   Seller's Initials_____/_____

26. DISPUTE RESOLUTION:

A. **MEDIATION:** The Parties agree to mediate any dispute or claim arising between them out of this Agreement, or any resulting transaction, before resorting to arbitration or court action through the C.A.R. Consumer Mediation Center (**www.consumermediation.org**) or through any other mediation provider or service mutually agreed to by the Parties. The Parties **also agree to mediate any disputes or claims with Broker(s), who, in writing, agree to such mediation prior to, or within a reasonable time after, the dispute or claim is presented to the Broker.** Mediation fees, if any, shall be divided equally among the Parties involved. If, for any dispute or claim to which this paragraph applies, any Party (i) commences an action without first attempting to resolve the matter through mediation, or (ii) before commencement of an action, refuses to mediate after a request has been made, then that Party shall not be entitled to recover attorney fees, even if they would otherwise be available to that Party in any such action. THIS MEDIATION PROVISION APPLIES WHETHER OR NOT THE ARBITRATION PROVISION IS INITIALED. **Exclusions from this mediation agreement are specified in paragraph 26C.**

B. **ARBITRATION OF DISPUTES:**

The Parties agree that any dispute or claim in Law or equity arising between them out of this Agreement or any resulting transaction, which is not settled through mediation, shall be decided by neutral, binding arbitration. The Parties also agree to arbitrate any disputes or claims with Broker(s), who, in writing, agree to such arbitration prior to, or within a reasonable time after, the dispute or claim is presented to the Broker. The arbitrator shall be a retired judge or justice, or an attorney with at least 5 years of transactional real estate Law experience, unless the parties mutually agree to a different arbitrator. The Parties shall have the right to discovery in accordance with Code of Civil Procedure §1283.05. In all other respects, the arbitration shall be conducted in accordance with Title 9 of Part 3 of the Code of Civil Procedure. Judgment upon the award of the arbitrator(s) may be entered into any court having jurisdiction. Enforcement of this agreement to arbitrate shall be governed by the Federal Arbitration Act. Exclusions from this arbitration agreement are specified in paragraph 26C.

"NOTICE: BY INITIALING IN THE SPACE BELOW YOU ARE AGREEING TO HAVE ANY DISPUTE ARISING OUT OF THE MATTERS INCLUDED IN THE 'ARBITRATION OF DISPUTES' PROVISION DECIDED BY NEUTRAL ARBITRATION AS PROVIDED BY CALIFORNIA LAW AND YOU ARE GIVING UP ANY RIGHTS YOU MIGHT POSSESS TO HAVE THE DISPUTE LITIGATED IN A COURT OR JURY TRIAL. BY INITIALING IN THE SPACE BELOW YOU ARE GIVING UP YOUR JUDICIAL RIGHTS TO DISCOVERY AND APPEAL, UNLESS THOSE RIGHTS ARE SPECIFICALLY INCLUDED IN THE 'ARBITRATION OF DISPUTES' PROVISION. IF YOU REFUSE TO SUBMIT TO ARBITRATION AFTER AGREEING TO THIS PROVISION, YOU MAY BE COMPELLED TO ARBITRATE UNDER THE AUTHORITY OF THE CALIFORNIA CODE OF CIVIL PROCEDURE. YOUR AGREEMENT TO THIS ARBITRATION PROVISION IS VOLUNTARY."

"WE HAVE READ AND UNDERSTAND THE FOREGOING AND AGREE TO SUBMIT DISPUTES ARISING OUT OF THE MATTERS INCLUDED IN THE 'ARBITRATION OF DISPUTES' PROVISION TO NEUTRAL ARBITRATION."

Buyer's Initials_____/_____   Seller's Initials_____/_____

Buyer's Initials (_____)(_____)   Seller's Initials (_____)(_____)

CPA REVISED 12/15 (PAGE 8 of 11)   Print Date

Property Address: _____   Date: _____

C. ADDITIONAL MEDIATION AND ARBITRATION TERMS:
    (1) EXCLUSIONS: The following matters are excluded from mediation and arbitration: **(i)** a judicial or non-judicial foreclosure or other action or proceeding to enforce a deed of trust, mortgage or installment land sale contract as defined in Civil Code §2985; **(ii)** an unlawful detainer action; and **(iii)** any matter that is within the jurisdiction of a probate, small claims or bankruptcy court.
    (2) PRESERVATION OF ACTIONS: The following shall not constitute a waiver nor violation of the mediation and arbitration provisions: **(i)** the filing of a court action to preserve a statute of limitations; **(ii)** the filing of a court action to enable the recording of a notice of pending action, for order of attachment, receivership, injunction, or other provisional remedies; or **(iii)** the filing of a mechanic's lien.
    (3) BROKERS: Brokers shall not be obligated nor compelled to mediate or arbitrate unless they agree to do so in writing. Any Broker(s) participating in mediation or arbitration shall not be deemed a party to the Agreement.

27. SELECTION OF SERVICE PROVIDERS: Brokers do not guarantee the performance of any vendors, service or product providers ("Providers"), whether referred by Broker or selected by Buyer, Seller or other person. Buyer and Seller may select ANY Providers of their own choosing.

28. MULTIPLE LISTING SERVICE/PROPERTY DATA SYSTEM: If Broker is a participant of a Multiple Listing Service ("MLS") or Property Data System ("PDS"), Broker is authorized to report to the MLS or PDS a pending sale and, upon Close Of Escrow, the terms of this transaction to be published and disseminated to persons and entities authorized to use the information on terms approved by the MLS or PDS.

29. ATTORNEY FEES: In any action, proceeding, or arbitration between Buyer and Seller arising out of this Agreement, the prevailing Buyer or Seller shall be entitled to reasonable attorneys fees and costs from the non-prevailing Buyer or Seller, except as provided in paragraph 26A.

30. ASSIGNMENT: Buyer shall not assign all or any part of Buyer's interest in this Agreement without first having obtained the written consent of Seller. Such consent shall not be unreasonably withheld unless otherwise agreed in writing. Any total or partial assignment shall not relieve Buyer of Buyer's obligations pursuant to this Agreement unless otherwise agreed in writing by Seller (C.A.R. Form AOAA).

31. SUCCESSORS AND ASSIGNS: This Agreement shall be binding upon, and inure to the benefit of, Buyer and Seller and their respective successors and assigns, except as otherwise provided herein.

32. ENVIRONMENTAL HAZARD CONSULTATION: Buyer and Seller acknowledge: **(i)** Federal, state, and local legislation impose liability upon existing and former owners and users of real property, in applicable situations, for certain legislatively defined, environmentally hazardous substances; **(ii)** Broker(s) has/have made no representation concerning the applicability of any such Law to this transaction or to Buyer or to Seller, except as otherwise indicated in this Agreement; **(iii)** Broker(s) has/have made no representation concerning the existence, testing, discovery, location and evaluation of/for, and risks posed by, environmentally hazardous substances, if any, located on or potentially affecting the Property; and **(iv)** Buyer and Seller are each advised to consult with technical and legal experts concerning the existence, testing, discovery, location and evaluation of/for, and risks posed by, environmentally hazardous substances, if any, located on or potentially affecting the Property.

33. AMERICANS WITH DISABILITIES ACT: The Americans With Disabilities Act ("ADA") prohibits discrimination against individuals with disabilities. The ADA affects almost all commercial facilities and public accommodations. The ADA can require, among other things, that buildings be made readily accessible to the disabled. Different requirements apply to new construction, alterations to existing buildings, and removal of barriers in existing buildings. Compliance with the ADA may require significant costs. Monetary and injunctive remedies may be incurred if the Property is not in compliance. A real estate broker does not have the technical expertise to determine whether a building is in compliance with ADA requirements, or to advise a principal on those requirements. Buyer and Seller are advised to contact an attorney, contractor, architect, engineer or other qualified professional of Buyer's or Seller's own choosing to determine to what degree, if any, the ADA impacts that principal or this transaction.

34. COPIES: Seller and Buyer each represent that Copies of all reports, documents, certificates, approvals and other documents that are furnished to the other are true, correct and unaltered Copies of the original documents, if the originals are in the possession of the furnishing party.

35. EQUAL HOUSING OPPORTUNITY: The Property is sold in compliance with federal, state and local anti-discrimination Laws.

36. GOVERNING LAW: This Agreement shall be governed by the Laws of the state of California.

37. TERMS AND CONDITIONS OF OFFER:
This is an offer to purchase the Property on the above terms and conditions. The liquidated damages paragraph or the arbitration of disputes paragraph is incorporated in this Agreement if initialed by all Parties or if incorporated by mutual agreement in a counter offer or addendum. If at least one but not all Parties initial, a counter offer is required until agreement is reached. Seller has the right to continue to offer the Property for sale and to accept any other offer at any time prior to notification of Acceptance. Buyer has read and acknowledges receipt of a Copy of the offer and agrees to the confirmation of agency relationships. If this offer is accepted and Buyer subsequently defaults, Buyer may be responsible for payment of Brokers' compensation. This Agreement and any supplement, addendum or modification, including any Copy, may be Signed in two or more counterparts, all of which shall constitute one and the same writing.

38. TIME OF ESSENCE; ENTIRE CONTRACT; CHANGES: Time is of the essence. All understandings between the Parties are incorporated in this Agreement. Its terms are intended by the Parties as a final, complete and exclusive expression of their Agreement with respect to its subject matter, and may not be contradicted by evidence of any prior agreement or contemporaneous oral agreement. If any provision of this Agreement is held to be ineffective or invalid, the remaining provisions will nevertheless be given full force and effect. Except as otherwise specified, this Agreement shall be interpreted and disputes shall be resolved in accordance with the Laws of the State of California. **Neither this Agreement nor any provision in it may be extended, amended, modified, altered or changed, except in writing Signed by Buyer and Seller.**

39. DEFINITIONS: As used in this Agreement:
    A. "Acceptance" means the time the offer or final counter offer is accepted in writing by a Party and is delivered to and personally received by the other Party or that Party's authorized agent in accordance with the terms of this offer or a final counter offer.
    B. "Agreement" means this document and any counter offers and any incorporated addenda, collectively forming the binding agreement between the Parties. Addenda are incorporated only when Signed by all Parties.

Buyer's Initials (_____)(_____)   Seller's Initials (_____)(_____)

CPA REVISED 12/15 (PAGE 9 of 11)   Print Date

COMMERCIAL PROPERTY PURCHASE AGREEMENT (CPA PAGE 9 OF 11)

Property Address: _____ Date: _____

    C. **"C.A.R. Form"** means the most current version of the specific form referenced or another comparable form agreed to by the parties.

    D. **"Close Of Escrow" or "COE"** means the date the grant deed, or other evidence of transfer of title, is recorded.

    E. **"Copy"** means copy by any means including photocopy, NCR, facsimile and electronic.

    F. **"Days"** means calendar days. However, after Acceptance, the last **Day** for performance of any act required by this Agreement (including Close Of Escrow) shall not include any Saturday, Sunday, or legal holiday and shall instead be the next Day.

    G. **"Days After"** means the specified number of calendar days after the occurrence of the event specified, not counting the calendar date on which the specified event occurs, and ending at 11:59 PM on the final day.

    H. **"Days Prior"** means the specified number of calendar days before the occurrence of the event specified, not counting the calendar date on which the specified event is scheduled to occur.

    I. **"Deliver"**, **"Delivered"** or **"Delivery"**, unless otherwise specified in writing, means and shall be effective upon: personal receipt by Buyer or Seller or the individual Real Estate Licensee for that principal as specified in the section titled Real Estate Brokers on page 11, regardless of the method used (i.e., messenger, mail, email, fax, other).

    J. **"Electronic Copy" or "Electronic Signature"** means, as applicable, an electronic copy or signature complying with California Law. Buyer and Seller agree that electronic means will not be used by either Party to modify or alter the content or integrity of this Agreement without the knowledge and consent of the other Party.

    K. **"Law"** means any law, code, statute, ordinance, regulation, rule or order, which is adopted by a controlling city, county, state or federal legislative, judicial or executive body or agency.

    L. **"Repairs"** means any repairs (including pest control), alterations, replacements, modifications or retrofitting of the Property provided for under this Agreement.

    M. **"Signed"** means either a handwritten or electronic signature on an original document, Copy or any counterpart.

40. AUTHORITY: Any person or persons signing this Agreement represent(s) that such person has full power and authority to bind that person's principal, and that the designated Buyer and Seller has full authority to enter into and perform this Agreement. Entering into this Agreement, and the completion of the obligations pursuant to this contract, does not violate any Articles of Incorporation, Articles of Organization, ByLaws, Operating Agreement, Partnership Agreement or other document governing the activity of either Buyer or Seller.

41. EXPIRATION OF OFFER: This offer shall be deemed revoked and the deposit, if any, shall be returned to Buyer unless the offer is Signed by Seller and a Copy of the Signed offer is personally received by Buyer, or by _____, who is authorized to receive it, by 5:00 PM on the third Day after this offer is signed by Buyer (or by ☐ _____ ☐AM/☐PM, on _____(date)).

☐ One or more Buyers is signing the Agreement in a representative capacity and not for him/herself as an individual. See attached Representative Capacity Signature Disclosure (C.A.R. Form RCSD-B) for additional terms.

Date _____ BUYER _____

(Print name) _____

Date _____ BUYER _____

(Print name) _____

☐ Additional Signature Addendum attached (C.A.R. Form ASA).

42. ACCEPTANCE OF OFFER: Seller warrants that Seller is the owner of the Property, or has the authority to execute this Agreement. Seller accepts the above offer and agrees to sell the Property on the above terms and conditions, and agrees to the above confirmation of agency relationships. Seller has read and acknowledges receipt of a Copy of this Agreement, and authorizes Broker to Deliver a Signed Copy to Buyer.

    ☐ (If checked) SELLER'S ACCEPTANCE IS **SUBJECT TO ATTACHED COUNTER OFFER (C.A.R. Form SCO or SMCO) DATED:** _____.

☐ One or more Sellers is signing the Agreement in a representative capacity and not for him/herself as an individual. See attached Representative Capacity Signature Disclosure (C.A.R. Form RCSD-S) for additional terms.

Date _____ SELLER _____

(Print name) _____

Date _____ SELLER _____

(Print name) _____

☐ Additional Signature Addendum attached (C.A.R. Form ASA).

(_____/_____)
(Initials) **(Do not initial if making a counter offer.) CONFIRMATION OF ACCEPTANCE:** A Copy of Signed Acceptance was personally received by Buyer or Buyer's authorized agent on (date) _____ at _____ ☐AM/☐PM. **A binding Agreement is created when a Copy of Signed Acceptance is personally received by Buyer or Buyer's authorized agent whether or not confirmed in this document. Completion of this confirmation is not legally required in order to create a binding Agreement; it is solely intended to evidence the date that Confirmation of Acceptance has occurred.**

CPA REVISED 12/15 (PAGE 10 of 11)   **Print Date**

COMMERCIAL PROPERTY PURCHASE AGREEMENT (CPA PAGE 10 OF 11)

Property Address: _____   Date: _____

REAL ESTATE BROKERS:
A. **Real Estate Brokers are not parties to the Agreement between Buyer and Seller.**
B. **Agency relationships are confirmed as stated in paragraph 2.**
C. If specified in paragraph 3A(2), Agent who submitted the offer for Buyer acknowledges receipt of deposit.
D. **COOPERATING BROKER COMPENSATION:** Listing Broker agrees to pay Cooperating Broker **(Selling Firm)** and Cooperating
      Broker agrees to accept, out of Listing Broker's proceeds in escrow, the amount specified in the MLS, provided Cooperating Broker
      is a Participant of the MLS in which the Property is offered for sale or a reciprocal MLS. If Listing Broker and Cooperating Broker
      are not both Participants of the MLS, or a reciprocal MLS, in which the Property is offered for sale, then compensation must be
      specified in a separate written agreement (C.A.R. Form CBC). Declaration of License and Tax (C.A.R. Form DLT) may be used to
      document that tax reporting will be required or that an exemption exists.

Real Estate Broker (Selling Firm) _____   CalBRE Lic. #_____
By _____   CalBRE Lic. #_____   Date _____
By _____   CalBRE Lic. #_____   Date _____
Address _____   City_____   State _____ Zip _____
Telephone _____ Fax _____   E-mail _____
Real Estate Broker (Listing Firm) _____   CalBRE Lic. #_____
By _____   CalBRE Lic. #_____   Date _____
By _____   CalBRE Lic. #_____   Date _____
Address _____   City_____   State _____ Zip _____
Telephone _____ Fax _____   E-mail _____

ESCROW HOLDER ACKNOWLEDGMENT:
Escrow Holder acknowledges receipt of a Copy of this Agreement, (if checked, ☐ a deposit in the amount of $ _____),
counter offer numbers _____ ☐ Seller's Statement of Information and _____
_____ , and agrees to act as Escrow Holder subject to paragraph 24 of this Agreement, any
supplemental escrow instructions and the terms of Escrow Holder's general provisions.

Escrow Holder is advised that the date of Confirmation of Acceptance of the Agreement as between Buyer and Seller is _____

Escrow Holder _____   Escrow # _____
By _____   Date_____
Address _____
Phone/Fax/E-mail_____
Escrow Holder has the following license number # _____
☐ Department of Business Oversight, ☐ Department of Insurance, ☐ Bureau of Real Estate.

PRESENTATION OF OFFER: (_____) Listing Broker presented this offer to Seller on _____ (date).
                              Broker or Designee Initials

REJECTION OF OFFER: (_____)(_____) No counter offer is being made. This offer was rejected by Seller on_____ (date).
                            Seller's Initials

Buyer's Initials (_____)(_____)   Seller's Initials (_____)(_____)

Published and Distributed by:
REAL ESTATE BUSINESS SERVICES, INC.
a subsidiary of the CALIFORNIA ASSOCIATION OF REALTORS®
525 South Virgil Avenue, Los Angeles, California 90020

Reviewed by
Broker or Designee _____

CPA REVISED 12/15 (PAGE 11 of 11)   Print Date
COMMERCIAL PROPERTY PURCHASE AGREEMENT (CPA PAGE 11 OF 11)

Chapter 2

Valuing Real Estate[1]

Scope of the Chapter

In setting prices for real estate assets, market participants use a handful of generic terms and methods for valuing, describing and measuring the financial performance of most financial assets including stocks, bonds, commodities, cash and real estate. This chapter describes how these terms and methods apply specifically to real estate.

The terms we describe in this chapter include "net present value," "internal rate of return," "net operating income," "capitalization rates," "the direct capitalization of income," "discounted cash flow," the reproduction/replacement and comparable sales methods of appraisal.

These concepts enable investors to compare options among asset classes, and among offerings within each asset class. They provide promoters and developers a menu from which to allocate between themselves the risks and rewards of jointly undertaken real estate ventures. Mortgage lenders use these in deciding whether and on what terms to finance particular projects and borrowers. Clients expect their real estate transactions lawyers to understand these terms well enough to review and critique financial analysts' assumptions and incorporate provisions based on the parties' financial agreements in purchase and sale contracts, leases, joint venture agreements, mortgage loans, and other legal documents. Real estate buyers and sellers need to appreciate the subjective assumptions that make real estate appraisal as much an art as a science when they decide whether to include an appraisal contingency in their purchase and sale contracts.

Importantly, real estate is capital intensive, and usually heavily financed with layers of equity and secured debt — typically mortgage loans. So we include in this chapter a few pages on the legal and financial distinctions between real estate equity and debt.

A concluding section evaluates the financial factors of possible relevance to an individual's decision of whether to buy or rent a dwelling.

---

1. The author is grateful to Edward Barkett, Nic Christen '11, Terence F. Cuff '77, Nam Joe '03, David Pirnazar '98, and Oscar Sandoval '99 who appeared in USC law classes as guest experts on valuation and related topics, and provided information, insights and advice that have shaped this chapter.

I. Measuring Investment Yields

A. Net Present Value (NPV)

Typically, real estate investors advance funds in the early stages of a project and hope to receive repayment and a return on invested capital later from two potential sources: (1) net lease revenues from the acquired property during the period of ownership, and (2) a profit upon selling the asset, called residual value.

These dual sources of cash flow are not unique to real estate. For example, shareholders buy common stock in hopes of periodic dividends from the firm's operating income and a profit on sale of the stock.

Investors who part with money now in hopes of money later need to consider the time value of money. "Net present value" (NPV) is a prescription for doing that. NPV is the sum of the present values of cash outflows (e.g. investments) and cash inflows (e.g. returns). Present value (and therefore NPV) depends on the particular investor's or borrower's benchmark rate, or desired discount rate. The discount rate is what an investor needs to earn on a given amount of money today to end up with a given amount of money in the future.

Three factors explain why the receipt of money sooner is generally presumed preferable to the receipt of money later: (1) lost opportunity costs, (2) inflation, and (3) the risk of default. (1) At the moment that an investor parts with capital, the investor forfeits other possible uses of the funds. Opportunity cost is what an investor missed out on receiving by choosing to do something else.

(2) Inflation is a nominal increase in the price of goods and services, resulting in cash losing its purchasing power. "For example, suppose that the basket of goods and services on which the official government Consumer Price Index is based cost $100 in the base year, $150 last year, and $154.50 this year. The price level this year is 154.50 ($154.50/$100.00). The inflation rate from last year to this is the percentage increase in the cost of the basket since last year, or 3%."[2] Due to inflation, lenders are repaid in dollars' worth less than the dollars they lent.

(3) The risks to which a long-term investment is susceptible tend to be less predictable than the risks of shorter-term investments, and the long-term investor's funds may be more costly or even impossible to withdraw, depending on the nature of the investment.

These assumptions are based on cash having a positive value and assets increasing in value over time, not deflating. Under the opposite circumstances, during times when asset values are deflating and banks charge investors for the privilege of keeping their cash in a safe institution, money later could be better than money now. Savers

---

2. Measuring the Price Level and Inflation, Ubc. Ca (last visited Jan. 2, 2015), http://courses.land food.ubc.ca/FRE302/Econ202/chapter%206.pdf.

would have avoided the cost of keeping their funds in banks and investors could purchase assets later at deflated values.

The Discount Rate. An individual's discount rate, often referred to as a "hurdle" rate, can be equated to a lender's interest rate. Hurdle rates are an investor's minimum acceptable return. They measure the time value of money to the individual equity investor or lender, and also to the savers whose funds the lender is using.

Consider this thought experiment to compare how individuals differ in their choice of preferred discount rates. Ask a group of your friends what they would pay now for the right to receive $100 from you a year from now. Suppose a friend says $95. You might ask what he or she would have done with the money, in formal terms, his or her *opportunity cost of capital.* Could they have earned $5 by placing $95 in a federally insured bank or savings account for a year?

Besides the opportunity cost of capital, other factors come into play, including the uncertainty of repayment because the promisor might default, and the trade-off between saving the money or spending it now. Investors consider these factors in setting their preferred discount rates: (i) the nominal interest rate for a similar time period; (ii) the perceived inflation rate—because prospectively, anticipated rates of inflation have greater bearing on discount rates than the actual rates of inflation that take place after the investor commits funds to a venture at a specified rate; (iii) the risk of default, that the borrower will not make the promised payments; and (iv) the prevailing supply and demand conditions for money.

Positive and Negative NPVs. To distinguish positive from negative NPVs, consider this simple example. Assume your preferred discount rate is 5%. The net present value of $2,000 ten years from now is $1,227.83. So if someone offered you $1,000 now or $2,000 ten years from now, you'd pick the latter because its net present value at your chosen discount rate is higher.[3]

A positive NPV means the investment has a higher yield than the investor's benchmark discount or hurdle rate, while a negative NPV means the investment yields less than the discount rate. An NPV of zero signals that the investment yield is exactly equal to the investor's benchmark discount rate.

Discount Rates Are Market Determined, Not Idiosyncratic. Knowledgeable investors' discount rates vary with the perceived riskiness of a particular investment. The higher the individual's discount rate for a particular asset, the less the bidder will pay for the asset. So an investor's discount rate on a federally insured savings account is going to be lower than on the acquisition of land for development in an unproven market. Sellers will tend to favor buyers prepared to pay the most for the asset, and these will be the buyers with the lowest discount rates as price and discount rates are inversely proportional. Researchers are able to infer market discount rates for any asset or class of assets by studying price trends. They derive effective market discount rates by com-

---

3. *The Smart Student Guide to Financial Aid*, FinAid (last visited June 29, 2015), http://www
.finaid.org/loans/npv.phtml.

paring what investors paid for particular assets with the total payouts they actually received from those investments through periodic dividends and value appreciation upon sale.[4]

B. Internal Rate of Return (IRR)

An IRR is just a mathematical variation of NPV; it is expressed as a percentage. "It is the rate of return [at which] the *present value* of a stream of cash inflows and outflows [equals] zero."[5] Zero is the investor's hurdle rate. Mathematically, an investment is worthwhile if the IRR exceeds or equals the investor's chosen discount rate; it is not worthwhile if the IRR is lower than the discount rate.

"An IRR calculation answers this question: What rate of return on my investment (cash input) results from the multiple cash flows (cash outputs) from this property over the entire term of the investment? To compute the rate of return that the investment provides over its term, the internal rate of return (IRR) calculation uses (1) the investment amount (such as the property's purchase price) and (2) cash flows the investment produces over its entire term (such as annual NOI and net sale price at the end of the term). Calculating the IRR allows the investor to evaluate the investment in relationship to alternative investments."[6]

Comparing NPV and IRR. To compare NPV and IRR, consider the timing of returns on two investments with a comparable risk of nonpayment, both of which require a $100,000 equity investment and produce a yield of $120,000.

- Investment I: Investor pays the entire $100,000 up front, and receives $50,000 at the end of year one and $70,000 at the end of year two.

- Investment II: Investor pays $20,000 a year in each of the first five years, receiving $70,000 at the end of year five and $50,000 at the end of year six.

Assuming the investor has a 10% desired return, or discount rate, the investor can begin by calculating the NPV of each investment. The investor would calculate the NPV of Investment I by summing the present value of all future payments, and subtracting the present value of outlays.

$$\text{NPV} = \frac{\$50,000}{(1+.10)^1} + \frac{\$70,000}{(1+.10)^2} - \frac{\$100,000}{(1+.10)^0}$$

$$= \$45,454 + \$57,851 - \$100,000 = \$3,305$$

---

4. *See, e.g.,* Andrew Ang & Xiaoyan Zhang, *Price-Earnings Ratios: Growth and Discount Rates* (May 20, 2011). https://www0.gsb.columbia.edu/faculty/aang/papers/PEratio.pdf.

5. Robert J. Rhee, Essential Concepts of Business for Lawyers 346 (2012).

6. Carl Circo, *Real Estate Project Valuation and Underwriting Metrics—A Refresher*, p. 9 (2010). http://www.acrel.org/Documents/Newsletters/April%202010%20News.pdf.

This means Investment I would yield $3,305 more, in today's dollars, than simply investing $100,000 at a 10% annual rate. Therefore, Investment I is worth making. If NPV were zero, the investor would receive exactly 10%.

Now search "net present value"[7] online to find an NPV calculator and compute the NPV for Investment II, using the same 10% minimum rate of return. We use an online IRR calculator by DataDynamica.

NPV =	$70k	+ $50k	− $20k	− $20k	− $20k	− $20k	− $20k
	$(1.10)^5$	$(1.10)^6$	$(1.10)^0$	$(1.10)^1$	$(1.10)^2$	$(1.10)^3$	$(1.10)^4$

The resulting number is negative, ($11,709). Here, the negative NPV means the investment is expected to yield less than 10% annually; thus, the investor would reject Investment II.

Using our IRR calculator, we will see that Investment I yielded an IRR of approximately 12%, and Investment II yielded an IRR of approximately 5%. Both IRR and NPV indicate that Investment I is superior to Investment II. Because IRR calculations are approximate, the result may vary slightly based on the program used. Thus, if a contract includes an IRR, it should specify the use of a particular device and program.

NPV or IRR? Why Use Both? NPV and IRR are both useful as complementary ways of looking at a problem or opportunity; IRR and NPV together give a better economic analysis than either alone.[8] Because IRR is expressed as a percentage, it enables investors and lenders to compare rates of return on projects competing for their investments or loans.[9] Consider the balance sheets of commercial banks. These lenders' cost of funds is the percentage of interest they pay depositors; they cannot lend money at a rate lower than that and survive. Percentages matter to borrowers as well; a borrower whose equity earns only a 5% return will lose money paying a mortgage interest rate of 6%.

Dollar values are also important to lenders, investors and sponsors. As one consultant quipped, "you don't eat IRRs; you eat chunk dollars." NPV and equity multiples are expressed in chunk dollars. As an investor, would you prefer receiving a 20% annual return on a $100 investment ($20), or a $100,000 return on a $900,000 investment? It would take a bundle of $100 deals to yield $100,000 even at 20%, not even counting the actual time and transactions costs of placing the funds.   ⬩

---

7. *See, e.g.,* Google™ the website "hp calculators." *See also* Present Value Calculator (last visited July 10, 2015), http://www.moneychimp.com/calculator/present_value_calculator.htm (last visited July 2015).

8. Ray Martin, *Internal Rate of Return Revisited: Economic Analysis,* (last visited July 10, 2015), http://members.tripod.com/~Ray_Martin/DCF/nr7aa003.html.

9. Gary Anthes, *ROI Net Present Value, available at* (last visited July 10, 2015), http://www.computerworld.com/article/2581461/it-management/roi-guide—net-present-value.html.

Some real estate investors avoid the use of IRRs entirely. The calculations are complicated, different software applications yield different results, many deal participants don't really understand how they work, and using cash dollar amounts adds clarity. Further, the IRR places greater stress on the timing of yields than on the total amount of the yield.

How the IRR Rewards Quick Rates of Return Over Long-Term Cash. In typical real estate joint venture transactions between developer-promoters and passive investors, the developer-promoter earns management fees for overseeing the project and may also earn fees on leases and property acquisitions. In addition, the developer receives a percentage share of the ultimate profit from the transaction calibrated to the IRR received by the investor.[10] This is called a "promote."

> Generally, a "promote" is triggered once the project generates a specified preferred return on the invested capital. Once the project achieves the specified preferred return, the promote rewards the sponsor with a greater proportion of the project's profits. Real estate professionals commonly discuss promotes using industry short-hand, in which they describe the economics as "an X over a Y." For example, the phrase "20% over an 8%" means the sponsor would receive 20% of incremental profits after the project generated an 8% preferred return [the 8% is measured by reference to the IRR].[11]

Investors in real estate funds are usually looking for high IRRs. Because the IRR is such a time-sensitive measure of yield, its use prompts short holding periods, necessitating the fund selling off all of its assets in time to distribute the proceeds to investors as quickly as promised, usually three to five years.[12]

Developer-promoters would often prefer longer holding periods because they earn periodic management and other fees as long as they are overseeing the project. Given a choice, they would usually prefer measuring investor yields in terms of actual cash dollars or net cash flow, not IRRs. Also, developer-promoters are more concerned with total wealth accumulation than with "quick hits." Given a choice between a $10,000 net gain recovered so quickly their rate of return would be 200% and a longer

---

10. *Scion Breckenridge Managing Member, LLC v. ASB Allegiance Real Estate Fund, EBREF Holding Company, LLC*, 68 A.3d 665 (2013). The promoter and the investors sought to modify their original management fee-promote arrangement by giving the developer a larger promote if the investors received a higher IRR.

11. 68 A.3d at 669.

12. Venture capital investors generally seek a specified **internal rate of return** on their investments over a three to five year period. If, for some reason, the investors believe that the company will be unable to achieve an initial public offering at a specified valuation during that period, it may push for a lower valuation in order to improve the **internal rate of return** over the extended holding period. Alternatively, the investors may push for some other type of liquidity event (e.g., a merger or sale of the company) in order to allow them to achieve their investment objectives by shortening the holding period. ALAN S. GUTTERMAN, BUSINESS TRANSACTIONS SOLUTIONS § 156:74 (Database updated June 2015).

term yield of $1,000,000 at a much lower rate of return, they will patiently await the big bucks.

C. Other Investment Performance Measures: Cash on Cash, Rate of Return, Equity Multiples

These measures—cash on cash, rate of return and equity multiple—have the virtue of simplicity. But they are not time sensitive. The investor's yield would appear to be the same regardless of when the investor contributed cash or received a return, as if the investor thought money now was worth the same as money later.

All of them are about annual cash flow and not about possible gain or loss upon sale. For this reason, they are incomplete because most real estate investors anticipate capturing value appreciation through an eventual sale or refinancing. They are useful nonetheless because experienced real estate investors are wary of "pie in the sky" promises that any given property will appreciate wildly in value in the distant future. The volatility of real estate prices eludes reliable prediction. A similar wariness can be found in the decision of some investors in common stocks who avoid purchasing stocks priced at historically high price-to-earnings ratios in anticipation of future valuations that are promised to rival the shooting stars of the social media universe.

Cash on Cash Return on Equity = *net operating income/total equity invested*. Net operating income is gross revenues collected (for example, tenant rents) after subtracting all operating expenses paid by the owner to operate and maintain the project, including real estate taxes, casualty insurance, maintenance and repairs, janitorial fees, utility costs and property management fees.

Imagine an investor paid $1,000,000 to buy a real estate asset. In the first full year of operation, the project produces net operating income of $150,000. The investor's cash on cash return on the total investment in the project is $150,000/$1,000,000, or 15%.

Cash on Cash Return on Total Costs = *net operating income/total assets invested including borrowed sums*. These are two ways of expressing the same outcome: one as a percentage (rate of return) and the other as a fixed amount of money.

Suppose that in the above example, the total cost of the project had been $3,000,000. Two million had been borrowed from a mortgage lender. The cash on cash return would be $150,000/$3,000,000, or 5%.

Equity Multiple = *income distributions (+) sale proceeds/total cash equity contribution*. The equity multiple is the total sum returned to the investor from income distributions and sale proceeds paid out over a specified time period measured as a percentage of the investor's total cash equity contribution.

As an example, say an investor buys an interest in a neighborhood shopping center for $1,000,000. The sponsor compensates the investor from project earnings with $100,000 in each of the first five years of the deal, then sells the asset at the end of year five, returning $1,500,000 to the investor from sales proceeds. In total, the investor received $2,000,000 for $1,000,000 invested—an equity multiple of two.

Equity multiples can also be derived from cap rates described in the following section. Suppose an asset's cap rate is 5%; the resulting multiplier is 20 (1/.05). So, for instance, a property yielding $1 million a year in net operating income with a cap rate of 5% is worth $20 million.

II. Appraisal Methods

Real estate appraisers commonly use four methods of appraisal:

(A) Capitalized Income,

(B) Discounted Cash Flow,

(C) Comparable Sales, and

(D) Reproduction/Replacement Cost

A. Capitalized Income

Investors in rental property—apartments, offices, retail, industrial—look primarily to the capitalized income method of valuation, a simple formula for determining the present value of a property based on its anticipated income. Mortgage lenders are also interested in net operating income since a project's net operating income is usually the primary source of loan repayments. This method is based on two factors: (1) net operating income, and (2) the capitalization rate.

Calculating Net Operating Income. Net operating income (NOI) refers to the annual income generated by an income-producing property after taking into account all income collected from operations, and deducting all expenses incurred from operations. The net operating income formula is as follows:

> **Net Operating Income Formula**
>   Potential Rental Income
> − Vacancy and Credit Losses
>   Effective Rental Income
> + Other Income
>   Gross Operating Income
> − Operating Expenses
>   **Net Operating Income**

Net Operating Income and Lease Analysis. "Before we go over each of the components of NOI, let's first take a quick detour into the world of commercial real estate leases. Lease analysis is the first step in analyzing any income-producing property since it identifies both the main source of income as well as who pays for which expenses. As you can see from the net operating income formula above, understanding this is essential to calculating NOI.

While there are many industry terms for different real estate leases, such as the modified gross lease, triple net lease, or the full service lease, it's important to understand that these terms all have various meanings depending on who you are talking to and which part of the world you are in. It's critical to remember that you must read each individual lease in order to fully understand its structure.

At a high level, leases can be viewed on a spectrum of possible structures. On the one hand you have *absolute gross leases* where the owner pays all of the operating expenses related to the property. On the other hand you have *absolute net leases*, where the tenant is required to pay all operating expenses. Everything else falls in between these two extremes and is considered a negotiated or hybrid lease. A common form of hybrid or negotiated lease is called an *expense stop*. This format calls for the landlord to calculate the operating expenses incurred in the first year of operation. Suppose the expenses were $15 per square foot. In future years, the landlord pays the first $15 of expenses, and the tenants reimburse the landlord for sums above that level.[13]

How to Calculate Net Operating Income (NOI). Calculating net operating income is relatively straightforward once you break out each of the individual components. The components of net operating income consist of potential rental income, vacancy and credit losses, other income, and operating expenses.

1. Add up the total rent due, plus any other income a property may be producing, such as parking revenues or income from signage on the building.

2. Subtract a dollar amount or a percentage of the scheduled rent to account for vacancies or uncollected rent. Deduct a per diem sum equal to the estimated number of days it will take to rent each vacated space after the current leases expire. The amount that results from subtracting (2) from (1) is called the effective gross income (EGI).

3. From EGI, subtract all operating expenses: insurance, real property taxes, utilities, repair/maintenance, administrative costs and salaries, and management/leasing commissions. The resulting amount is the NOI.

Net operating income measures the ability of a property to produce an income stream from operations. Net operating income is positive when operating income exceeds gross operating expenses, and negative when operating expenses exceed gross operating income. For the purposes of real estate analysis, NOI can either be based on historical financial statement data or on forward-looking estimates of cash flow for future years (also known as *pro formas*).

Writing about NOI in his textbook, *Valuation and Common Sense*, Professor Pablo Fernandez observes that: "*A company's net income is a quite arbitrary figure obtained after assuming certain accounting hypotheses regarding expenses and revenues (one of*

---

13. Robert Schmidt, *Understanding Net Operating Income in Real Estate*, PROPERTYMETRICS (last visited, Jan. 2, 2015), http://www.propertymetrics.com/blog/2014/03/05/net-operating-income/.

several that can be obtained, depending on the criteria applied). However, the ex-post cash flow is an objective measure, a single figure that is not subject to any personal criterion."[14]

This statement appears in a chapter called: *Cash flow is a fact. NOI is an opinion.* Professor Fernandez draws a distinction between the undeniable reliability of the difference between a firm's "money spent" and "money received" for any particular time period, and the accounting concept of net operating income as described below.

Definitions of Terms Used in NOI Calculations:

Potential Rental Income: Potential Rental Income (PRI) is the sum of all rents under the terms of each lease, assuming the property is 100% occupied. If the property is not 100% occupied, then a market-based rent is used based on lease rates and terms of comparable properties.

Vacancy and Credit Losses: Vacancy and credit losses consist of income lost due to tenants vacating the property and/or tenants defaulting (not paying) their lease payments. For the purposes of calculating NOI, the vacancy factor can be calculated based on current lease expirations and estimated vacancy rates at comparable properties in the same sub-market area.

In other words, as space becomes vacant in the subject property, the analyst should assume that it will eventually be occupied at about the same rate as similar properties in the same market place. So, for instance, if 20,000 square feet of space is about to become vacant shortly, the building has a total of 50,000 square feet, and comparable properties are experiencing a 20% vacancy rate, the analyst should not assume that all 20,000 square feet will remain permanently vacant or permanently occupied. Instead, the analyst should presume that ten thousand square feet of the 50,000 square foot building will presumptively remain vacant.

Effective Rental Income: Effective rental income in the net operating income formula above is simply potential rental income less vacancy and credit losses. This is the amount of rental income that the owner can reasonably expect to collect.

Other Income: A property may also collect income other than rent derived from the space tenants occupy. This is classified as Other Income and could include billboard/signage, parking, laundry, vending, etc.

Gross Operating Income: This is simply the total of all income generated from the property, after considering a reasonable vacancy and credit loss factor, as well as all other additional income generated by the property.

Operating Expenses: Basically, operating expenses include all cash expenditures required to operate the property and command market rents. Common commercial real estate operating expenses include real estate and personal property taxes, property insurance, management fees (on or off-site), repairs and maintenance, utilities, and other miscellaneous expenses (accounting, legal, etc.).

---

14. Pablo Fernandez, Valuation and Common Sense (6th ed, Nov. 2015), http://papers.ssrn.com/sol3/papers.cfm?abstract_id=2209089.

Net Operating Income: As shown in the net operating income formula above, net operating income is simply gross operating income less operating expenses.

Verifying the Numbers. Over time, rents and operating expenses gravitate toward prevailing market levels. For this reason, appraisers make appropriate adjustments to account for rents or operating expenses that are out of line with the market. For potential purchasers, these divergences from market levels raise a host of questions. Can over-performance be sustained? Does an under-performing property present opportunities for improved operations and profit? In any case, NOI projections are susceptible to unanticipated changes in revenue and expense.[15]

Exclusions from Net Operating Income Calculations:

What's Not Included in Net Operating Income? It's also important to note that there are some expenses that are typically excluded from the net operating income figure.

Debt Service: Financing costs are specific to the owner/investor and as such are not included in calculating NOI.

Depreciation: Depreciation is not an actual cash outflow, but rather an accounting entry and therefore is not included in the NOI calculation.

Income Taxes: Since income taxes are specific to the owner/investor they are also excluded from the net operating income calculation.

Tenant Improvements: Tenant improvements, often abbreviated as just "TI", include construction within a tenant's *usable space to* make the space viable for the tenant's specific use.

Leasing Commissions: Commissions are the fees paid to real estate agents/brokers involved in leasing the space.

Reserves for Replacement: Reserves are funds set aside for major future maintenance items, such as a roof replacement, or air conditioning repair. While the textbook definitions of NOI usually exclude reserves from the NOI calculation, in practice, some market participants actually do include reserves for replacement in NOI. For example, most lenders will include reserves for replacement into the NOI calculation for determining debt service coverage and the maximum loan amount. This makes sense because lenders need to understand the ability of a property to service debt, which of course has to take into account required capital expenses to keep the property competitive in the marketplace.

Capital Expenditures: Capital expenditures are expenses that occur irregularly for major repairs and replacements, which are usually funded by a reserve for replacement. Note that capital expenditures are major repairs and replacements, such as replacing the HVAC system in a property. This does not include minor repairs

---

15. Thomas S. Kaufman, *Understanding Real Estate Economics*, 30 THE PRACTICAL REAL ESTATE LAWYER 50 (Jan. 2014): "[o]nly in hindsight can the actual performance of an asset be judged with certainty."

and maintenance which are considered an operating expense, such as replacing door-knobs and light bulbs.

Stabilized NOI. When a building first opens upon completion or after a major renovation, it may take a while for occupancy and rents to reach the property's anticipated long-term performance. Once it does, NOI is said to be "stabilized." Investors in a well-located, stabilized asset anticipate receiving a steady, reliable cash flow as if they were clipping bond coupons.

Developers tend to be optimistic. In seeking out funds from investors and lenders, they offer rosy projections of the amount of time needed to complete and stabilize a project. And in buoyant real estate markets, developers often succeed in obtaining funds even before they have signed up the solvent tenants willing to pay the rents that will stabilize the project. But real estate markets are volatile, and more than a few lenders and investors regretted relying upon the optimistic assumptions of developers after projects failed to achieve the forecasted rents and occupancy.

Value Added Deals. In a "value added" deal, sponsors become venture capitalists. They acquire an underperforming asset intending to increase its value by making improvements to justify higher rents. Maybe rents were low and vacancy rates were high because the property was in disrepair or was not rigorously marketed to the best possible tenant mix for the location. Once the promoter successfully improves the property and manages to lease it out at higher rents, the property income is regarded as stabilized.

B. Determinants of Capitalization Rates ("Cap Rates")

Cap rates are to property investors what interest rates are to savers. They are a measure of the nominal return on the investment. Cap rates are market driven and fluctuate over time with all the factors that matter to investors.[16] Cap rates fall when demand for real estate outpaces supply, and rise when supply is over-abundant. They fall with growing confidence in the market or the asset, capital availability, and improving local real estate market conditions and general economic trends. Cap rates rise when investors expect inflation and fall when they believe deflation is coming. Cap rates also tend to track market rates of return for investments other than real estate, including rates on risk-free assets.

Cap rates take into account the perceived riskiness of the particular asset, which vary in all the ways that one property differs from all others, including by project type, size, design, and location. Indirectly, cap rates measure the investor's confidence in the amount, certainty, and volatility of the cash flow during the anticipated period of ownership. Cap rates also account for the investor's anticipated sale of the asset,

---

16. Philip Conner, *Cap Rates and Interest Rates—A Conundrum, Or Not,* Predicts that Treasury rate of 5% would push cap rates to 6.5%, due to rising and other improvements in real estate market fundamentals. (last visited July 7, 2015), http://www3.prudential.com/prei/pdf/Conundrum_PRU .pdf.

hopefully at a substantial profit. The factors that influence investors in global financial markets can also affect cap rates.

C. NOI, Price and Cap Rates: Simple Math, Complicated Reality

The formulas used in the capitalized income method of appraisal consist of three variables. Knowing any two of the variables, you can calculate the unknown third one with the following formulas.

<u>Variables:</u>

I = *net operating income*

R = *capitalization rate*

P = *market price (aka V=Value)*[17]

<u>Formulas:</u>

(1) I = R x P:

Net operating income = *Capitalization rate x Price*

(2) R= I/P:

Capitalization rate = *Net operating income/Price*

(3) P= I/R:

Price= *Net operating income/Capitalization rate*

Appraisers often use formula (2) above to determine the cap rate by observing the prices paid for properties in completed transactions, if they know the net operating incomes of those properties. Suppose the recent sales price of a Class A office building in downtown Boston was $20,000,000, and the property had a stabilized Net Operating Income (NOI) of $1,000,000. As you can see, Formula (2) would show that this property had sold at a cap rate of 5% ($1,000,000/ $20,000,000).[18]

Formulas (2) and (3) reveal that cap rates and prices (sometimes referred to as value) move in opposite directions. Like two equally balanced kids riding opposite ends of a see-saw, rising cap rates mean falling prices. Conversely, cap rates down mean prices up.

---

17. Some formulas substitute a V for value in place of P for price. Price refers to the "bottom line" in a purchase and sale transaction, the purchase price. Value represents what something is worth to a particular buyer. Often, property has greater value to a particular buyer than is measured by the purchase price. The difference between value and price is called "consumer surplus."

18. Robert Schmidt, *What Should You Know About the Cap Rate,* Property Metrics (last visited July 2015), http://www.propertymetrics.com/blog/2013/06/03/cap-rate/

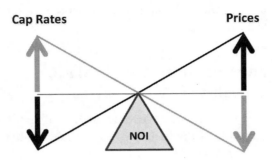

You might have heard the adage "buy low, sell high" in reference to the purchase and sale price of an asset. Sophisticated investors sometimes say they hope to "buy high and sell low." Reconciling these statements can be puzzling until you realize that the first concerns prices, and the second refers to cap rates.

The cap rate/value ratio is essentially the same as bond interest rates and bond values. As the market rates of interest on bonds rises, the value of bonds falls since bond investors need to pay more to attract a given amount of savings, all other things being equal. Similarly, the cap rate is analogous to the inverse of a price-earnings multiple in common stock equities. Stocks trade at higher prices when stock buyers are willing to pay higher multiples of earnings for them.

Formula (3) shows that net operating income and cap rates impact prices in opposite ways. The value of a property tends to increase, all else equal, when its net operating income goes up. But when cap rates go up, its value tends to fall.

While skillful property owners can sometimes improve their net operating income, outperforming comparable properties, there is not much they can do to impact cap rates. To sustain rising cap rates without huge reductions in asset prices, net operating incomes have to rise very steeply. For the price of a rental income property not to decrease when cap rates rose, for example, from 5% to 6%, the property's net operating income would have to jump to 20%; an increase from 4% to 8% would necessitate a 100% increase in NOI for the asset to maintain a stable price.

Using Cap Rates Properly

The Proper Extraction and Use of Cap Rates in Real Estate Valuation

Stan Tish
(September 16, 2011)[19]

Applying the Overall Rate. In direct capitalization, a single year's net operating income (NOI) — typically the income anticipated for the first year after the date of value — is

---

19. Stan Tish, *The Proper Extraction and Use of Cap Rates in Real Estate Valuation*, OPINEXPERTS (last visited Jan. 2, 2015), http://opinexperts.com/journal/2011/09/16/the-use-of-cap-rates-in-real-estate-valuation/.

divided by the overall rate of capitalization. As a single year's income is being converted into a capital sum that is the present worth of all future benefits, the income to be capitalized must be net operating income, a stabilized income based upon market rent net of stabilized operating expenses.

If you capitalize income from a below-market contract rent, you are capitalizing a revenue loss in perpetuity that persists only until the end of the lease term. The situation is similar with above-market rents: you would be capitalizing revenue in perpetuity that is only temporary.

For illustration, let's consider a few examples based upon a 50,000 s.f. building that will produce NOI of $20.00/s.f. or $1 million at stabilized occupancy and market rent (i.e., fully leased at market rent less stabilized expenses). We have selected an overall rate of 10.0% based upon the range of capitalization rates extracted from sales data.

Example 1 — Stabilized Occupancy at Market Rent (Correct Methodology)

Net Operating Income: 50,000 s.f. @ $20.00 = $1,000,000

Overall Rate: 10%

Indicated Value: $10,000,000

The value indicated by direct capitalization is $10 million. Now let's suppose that contract rent is below market, and the income net of expenses generated under the lease is only $15.00 (but that in three years the lease requires an adjustment to market rent). The sale should be analyzed in the same manner as subject, i.e., based upon a pro forma or stabilized operating statement in which NOI from market rent is estimated and capitalized.

A common error is to forego the estimation of NOI and capitalize the actual income from contract rents. In Example 2A, this procedure would indicate a value of $7,500,000.

Example 2A — Capitalizing Income From a Below-Market Contract Rent (Incorrect Methodology)

Contract Net Income: 50,000 s.f. @ $15.00 = $ 750,000

Overall Rate: 10.0%

Indicated Value: $7,500,000.

The methodology is improper and fallacious: the revenue loss from below-market rent lasts for three years but is being capitalized in perpetuity, vastly overstating the adverse impact on value.

The correct procedure is to capitalize NOI from market rent and deduct the present worth of the three-year revenue loss from the capital value, as follows:

Example 2B — Below-Market Rent (Correct Methodology)

Net Operating Income: 50,000 s.f. @ $20.00 = $1,000,000

Overall Rate: 10.0%

Indicated Value, Stabilized Occupancy & Market Rent: $10,000,000

Less: Revenue Loss from Below-Market Rent, 50,000 s.f. @ $5.00, 3 years @ 12.0% = (595,336)

Indicated Value, As-Is (Rounded): $9,400,000

As you can see by comparing the methodology correctly (2B) and incorrectly (2A) employed, capitalizing the income from below-market rents understates market value by $1.9 million in this particular example (which includes neither a very large building nor a very high rent differential from contract to market).

If the lease were expected to turn over in three years, we would also have to deduct a leasing commission and perhaps also a refurbishing cost and a revenue loss from vacancy at turnover, as we shall see in an ensuing example.

For the next case, let's suppose that 20% or 10,000 s.f. of the building is vacant. If you capitalize only the income being produced by the current occupancy, you will again drastically overstate the financial impact of the vacancy.

Example 3A — Capitalizing the Current Occupancy (Incorrect Methodology)

Contract Net Income: 40,000 s.f. @ $20.00 = $ 800,000

Overall Rate 10.0%

Indicated Value: $8,000,000

The methodology is incorrect because it foresees no income from the currently vacant space in perpetuity. It is tantamount to saying the vacant rentable area no longer exists.

What would the value be by this methodology if the building were completely vacant? Let's say that our market research has determined that the lease-up time for 10,000 s.f. at market rent is one year, that the requisite leasing commission is equivalent to 25% of the first year's net operating income, and that the space will have to be refurbished at a cost of $5.00/s.f. to achieve a market rate of rent.

The correct methodology is analogous to Example 2B above:

Example 3B — Partial Vacancy (Correct Methodology)

Net Operating Income 50,000 s.f. @ $20.00 = $1,000,000

Overall Rate: 10.0% Indicated Value

Stabilized Occupancy & Market Rent: $10,000,000

Less: Revenue Loss from Vacancy 10,000 s.f. @ $20.00, 1 year = (200,000)

Less: Leasing Commission $200,000 X 25.0% = (50,000)

Less: Refurbishing Cost 10,000 s.f. @ $5.00 = (50,000) Indicated Value,

As-Is (Rounded) = $9,700,000

Comparing the results of 3A and 3B, we can see that even in this very limited example, the incorrect methodology understates market value by $1.7 million. If the building were completely vacant, the methodology would be the same; only the numbers would change accordingly. A case can be made that the prospective buyer is entitled to an entrepreneurial reward or profit for undertaking the effort to achieve stabilized occupancy at market rent but that, as they say, is another story.

In the case of above-market rents the procedure is still to apply the overall rate to NOI from market rent; if you capitalize the total rent you are attributing value to the property in perpetuity that lasts only as long as the remaining term of the lease.

This same article proceeds to explain how the capitalized income method of appraisal can be applied to reflect a variety of changing cash flows. It does not have to be inflexibly unresponsive as some appraisers make it when they select a single cap rate and a uniform NOI for properties with fluctuating cash flows.

D. Discounted Cash Flow (DCF): An Alternative to Direct Capitalization

For properties where income and expenses fluctuate considerably, appraisers may deploy a discounted cash flow (DCF) analysis. Based on a detailed analysis of the subject property, periodic estimates of income and expenses replace a single NOI.[20]

In an easy case where no lease is shorter than 10 years, the analyst just needs to guess the solvency of the tenant, and study the leases for possible "outs" the tenant could use to exit with impunity before the end of the term. Where there is lease turnover, the DCF analyst estimates future market rent levels. The same foresight is required in estimating operating expenses, inflation, labor contract renewals, utility cost trends and the like.

Understandably, some appraisers prefer confining their DCF analyses to shorter, more predictable terms. This cautious approach has its critics, as the following excerpt shows.

"One of the most common criticisms of DCF models is that any forecast beyond a couple of years is suspect. Investors, therefore, are alleged to be better off using more certain, near-term earnings forecasts. Such reasoning makes no sense, for at least two reasons.

First, a key element in understanding a business's attractiveness involves knowing the set of financial expectations the price represents. The market as a whole has historically traded at a price-to-earnings multiple in the mid-to-high teens. Simple math shows today's stock prices reflect expectations for value-creating earnings and cash flows many years in the future. To make the point more concrete, imagine you are a restaurant industry executive in charge of finding new store locations. When assessing the attractiveness of a prospective site, would you consider only two years of earnings because 'any beyond that is guessing'? Of course not. You'd base your judgment on the location, past results for similar sites, and other value-relevant factors. Intelligent capital allocators take a long-term view.

Second, some investors swear off the DCF model because of its myriad assumptions. Yet they readily embrace an approach that packs all of those same assumptions, without any transparency, into a single number: the multiple.

---

20. Wayne E. Etter, *Direct Capitalization Versus Discounted Cash Flow Analysis*, Appraisal, Fall 1994, Publication 1051, Real Estate Center Journal (last visited July 10, 2015), http://recenter. tamu.edu/pdf/1051.pdf.

Multiples are not valuation; they represent shorthand for the valuation process. Like most forms of shorthand, multiples come with blind spots and biases that few investors take the time and care to understand. John Maynard Keynes famously said, 'I'd rather be vaguely right than precisely wrong.' His message applies here."[21]

Real estate transactions lawyers may understandably question the significance of all these appraisal uncertainties and nuances to their work. The answer comes from Professor Rick Daley, for decades a real estate transaction lawyer for developers until he became a developer himself: "Aspiring real estate development lawyers should be forewarned that the developer often calls upon its lawyer to review and bless the analysts' assumptions as they relate to the various economic rights, obligations and liabilities spelled out in the leases and other legal documents governing the project's operations."[22]

E. The Sales Comparison Approach[23]

Definition. The sales comparison (or "market") approach is the method of appraising single family houses and other frequently traded properties that is most favored by mortgage lenders, real estate brokers, buyers, sellers, property tax assessors, and public agencies acquiring land for public uses. In court, and in privately commissioned valuations, appraisers are asked to formulate an opinion of the subject property based on "market value," which is formally defined as the most probable price a property is expected to bring after reasonable exposure in a competitive market.[24]

The "comps." The challenge in a sales comparison approach is identifying a few truly comparable properties ("comps") to the property that is the subject of the appraisal. This method works better in valuing tract houses in a robust market than it does appraising distinctive properties that are traded infrequently, such as churches, football stadiums, and regional shopping malls.

In deciding whether the price of a "comp" truly indicates what the subject property will bring, appraisers try to consider all the factors that would influence price. These would include the location of the property, views, accessibility, neighborhood qualities and legal constraints on the property's ownership or use. They pay close attention as well to physical characteristics of the building such as age, design features, construction quality, and square footage.

---

21. Tim Koller et al., *Common Errors in DCF Models* (last visited Jan. 2, 2015), http://www3.nd .edu/~scorwin/fin70610/Common%20DCF%20Errors_LeggMason.pdf.

22. Rick Daley, Real Estate Development Law p. 56 (2011).

23. Appraisal Institute (last visited July 6, 2015), http://www.appraisalinstitute.org/myappraisal institute/resources/understand_appraisal_1109.pdf.

24. Appraisers are subject to state licensing requirements. Many appraisers are also certified by the more rigorous qualifications of an industry organization called The Appraisal Institute. Appraisal Institute, The Appraisal of Real Estate 22 (2001).

Comps are rarely identical to the subject property. So appraisers endeavor to place a price tag on each significant element by which they differ—an extra half-bath, three bedrooms instead of four, a swimming pool, a better view, lush landscaping, a corner lot. Valuing each of these items separately is theoretically possible but can be extremely challenging because it is difficult to find properties otherwise identical except for one or another of these features.

Date of sale matters because real estate markets are volatile. A sale that took place thirty days ago is more probative of current value than a sale that closed last year. Appraisers need a cut-off limit, a time frame outside of which they will disregard sales of otherwise comparable properties. For most residential mortgage lenders using the sales comparison approach, the cut-off is six months. Because of the 30 to 90 day time gap between when a purchase and sale contract is executed, and when the sale closes, a buyer who signs a purchase contract today could be relying on sales prices set nine months earlier.

Highest and Best Use: Accounting for Regulatory Uncertainty. Appraisers are often asked to value property in its "highest and best use," and many times the most profitable use differs from the current use. One example would be an orange grove barely covering its operating expenses and located in an area experiencing a population influx where homebuilders are paying generously for large sites they can subdivide for housing tracts. Another could be a long abandoned gas station at an intersection suitable for a neighborhood shopping center with a grocery store.

These changes in use would require extensive approvals from local, state and possibly federal government officials administering and applying numerous land use, environmental, and subdivision laws.

When the owner has obtained all of the requisite discretionary government approvals for the proposed development, a property is said to be "entitled." In estimating the value of the property, the appraiser the likelihood of the owner succeeding in securing all these approvals, and the costs and time it could take to do so.

Shortcomings of Reliance on the Comparable Sales Method of Appraisal. A real estate appraiser using the comparable sales method of value can easily miss broad trends, relying mainly or exclusively on the limited data from a handful of recently completed sales.

More sophisticated analysts of real estate values use richer data to measure housing demand and supply.[25] For instance, during the housing bubble that preceded in house price collapse in many parts of the US in 2007, house prices rose far above the customary ratios of sales prices to rents on comparable houses. Homebuyers were paying

---

25. Glennon, Dennis and Kiefer, Hua and Mayock, Tom, *Housing Value Estimation: An Application of Forecast Combination to Residential Property Valuation* (last visited July 11, 2015), available at SSRN: http://ssrn.com/abstract=2610865 or http://dx.doi.org/10.2139/ssrn.2610865

historically high value-to-rent ratios.[26] Real estate appraisers using the comparable sales method of appraisal missed this although they might have caught it, had they used the capitalized income method of appraisal.

Another blind spot is that the comparable sales approach cannot measure potential demand for product types or features not already available in the market place.

F. The Cost Approach

"This approach has the most validity/reliability when improvements are new or near-new. For older/aged structures, the cost approach may not be relevant due to the greater subjectivity involved in estimating accrued depreciation.

"The cost approach begins with the determination of site value. Sales of vacant land with similar zoning, utility, and acquired for the same or similar use as the subject property being appraised, are analyzed. In markets where site sales are limited, other site sales of varying property type may be considered as long as they have core similarities in legally acceptable use.

"Once site value has been determined, reproduction or replacement costs of the improvements are estimated as if the improvements were new. The estimate is then further adjusted for all elements of accrued depreciation including physical depreciation, functional and/or external obsolescence."[27]

Land value estimates can be challenging in fully built-out areas where there are few or no vacant parcels for sale. The appraiser will then look to either or both of two land residual methods—one based on income capitalization and other on comparable sales of similar property.

In the capitalized income version of finding the land residual value, the appraiser starts with the net operating income of the subject property or of a comparable property (rent less expenses), determines what the improvement cost to build, attributes an annual market rate of return to the construction cost, and capitalizes that portion of the NOI that remains after subtracting the construction cost return. "**Example:** *A property generates $10,000 net operating income ($15,000 rent less $5,000 operating expenses). The improvements cost $70,000 to construct and claim a 12% rate of return (10% interest plus 2% depreciation), which is $8,400. The remaining $1,600 income is capitalized at a 10% rate (divided by .10) to result in a $16,000 land value using the land residual technique.*"[28]

---

26. Glaeser, Edward L. and Nathanson, Charles, *An Extrapolative Model of House Price Dynamics* (last visited July 10, 2015), HKS Working Paper No. RWP15-012, available at SSRN: http://ssrn.com/abstract=2614539 orhttp://dx.doi.org/10.2139/ssrn.2614539

27. http://www.propex.com/C_g_cost.htm#Replacement Cost (Last visited 05/24/2016).

28. https://www.allbusiness.com/barrons_dictionary/dictionary-land-residual-technique-4962044-1.html (Last visited 05/23/2016).

Applying the market value variation of the land residual approach, the appraiser could try to find a comparable existing building, estimate what the labor and materials costs would be to replicate it, and subtract those from its current fair market value. The difference presumably would represent the value of the land.[29] For instance, suppose a house in a fully developed area has a current market value of $500,000 based on recent sales of comparable houses. An appraiser who concludes that such a house could be replicated today for $400,000 will set the land value at $100,000.

When it comes to estimating the reproduction or replacement cost of the structure, there are several ways to do this. One of them involves calculating the cost of construction by multiplying the square footage of the structure by the construction cost for that type of building. Another method would be to aggregate the various components of the building, and determining the labor and materials costs for creating each of its parts, including the foundation, roofing, framing, mechanical systems, and walls and finish work.

As properties age, buildings become increasingly vulnerable to physical deterioration, functional obsolescence and economic obsolescence. Collectively, these factors are elements of depreciation for which the appraiser needs to subtract a percentage of the construction cost or a fixed dollar amount.

Functional obsolescence refers to such items as outdated designs, inadequate wiring, room layouts no longer suitable for current space-users.

Economic obsolescence includes: changing demographics, transportation infrastructure and the like. Selecting the right deduction for the ravages of time can be more of an art than a science, complicated by those special older buildings that are highly valued precisely because of their age and history.

Appraisal Contingencies. Purchase and sale contracts often come with appraisal contingencies that entitle the buyer to cancel the contract within a specific time,[30] based upon a written appraisal by a licensed or certified appraiser at less than the agreed purchase price. (See paragraph 3(I) of the REALTORS® form Commercial Property Purchase Agreement and Joint Escrow Instructions.)

Buyers take comfort in these appraisal contingencies for two reasons. They can cancel if it appears that they could be paying too much, and they may not be able to

---

29. Since land cannot be reproduced, it must be valued using one of the other two appraisal methods described here: either the market or income approach.

30. The buyers may be able to cancel a few days later than specified. *See Harris v. Stewart*, 193 N.C. App. 142, 666 S.E.2d 804 (2008). The buyers had contracted to pay $2,100,000. They received the lender's appraisal of $1,900,000 on December 20, 2005 and that same day, notified the sellers they were cancelling. This was five days after the specified contract cancellation date of December 15, 2005. The court ordered the sellers to refund the buyers' down payment, ruling that the buyers had cancelled within a reasonable time. The sellers sold the property three weeks later for $1,700,000.

borrow as much as they would have preferred if their lender's appraiser concludes that the property is worth less than what they contracted to pay for it.

III. General Distinctions between Debt and Equity

A. Equity: The Risks and Rewards

A purchaser could acquire a real estate asset for 100% cash from personal funds. Or, the purchaser could advance a down payment and borrow the balance of the money needed from a mortgage lender.

Real estate promoters often invest some of their own funds in their projects and obtain additional equity from investors with whom they enter joint venture agreements, usually on a project-by-project basis.

Joint venture agreements between promoters and their equity partners usually contain an arrangement specifying when the equity investor is to advance funds for the venture, and how profits are to be shared between the promoter and the investor.

The project promoter or developer guarantees no fixed return to the investor, although the investor may have the right to displace the promoter and take over the ownership of the project under specific circumstances negotiated in their joint venture agreement.

When the value of the investment falls, equity investors take the first losses ahead of mortgage lenders. Their failure to make their debt service payments can result in losing the project to the mortgage lender through foreclosure.

On the upside, if the value of the project rises, the equity investors capture the increase after paying off their mortgage debt. (Historically, the term "equity" derives from early common law rules prohibiting mortgage lenders from trying to tap into value appreciation in excess of the loan amount.)

B. Debt

Notes and Deeds of Trust or Mortgages. Mortgage lenders usually contemplate periodic payments from the owners or, upon foreclosure and following a default, from tenants of the collateral property. They cushion their reliance on the collateral by lending less than 100% of the fair market value of the property at the date the loan is originated. The percentage they are willing to lend is called the loan-to-value (LTV) ratio. Commercial mortgage lenders also consider the extent to which net operating income exceeds debt service (NOI/Debt service). Called the "Debt Service Coverage Ratio" (DSCR), lenders require a ratio above 1.0, the "break even" point, though often much higher. In cash flow terms, DSCR is the amount by which the net operating income exceeds the payment obligation on the mortgage loan.

When the debt exceeds the value of the collateral, the lender faces an increased risk of borrower default. Stock becomes virtually worthless when a debtor company files bankruptcy; but real estate assets usually retain some value even if less than the balance due on the mortgage loan. On the other hand, a mortgage lender who takes over possession of the security property will need to cover the costs of maintenance and repairs, property taxes and insurance. The operating costs could easily exceed the net operating income, resulting in losses far greater than the amount of the original mortgage loan.

By applying these norms, mortgage lenders hope borrowers will have a financial incentive not to default for fear of losing the property through foreclosure. The difference between the loan-to-value ratio and 100% of the value of the property is the borrower's stake in the property. Mortgage lenders describe this sum as their "equity cushion" against the possibility of their not being able to recover the debt from the security property.

Despite these precautions, mortgage lenders experience defaults that often lead to steep losses. There are many reasons for this including borrower fraud, changing life circumstances (death, illness, divorce), or volatile market conditions. Typically, at the time of default, the loan to value ratio far exceeds 100% and debt service coverage ratio is well below 1.0.

Layering Debt. There is no legal limit to the number of mortgages a home owner can place upon a home.[31] But a senior mortgagee who forecloses wipes out the liens of junior lienors. Junior lienors will then be left with nothing but personal claims against borrowers. These collection claims are based on the borrower's signed promise to repay, and could be subject to discharge in bankruptcy.

Home sellers comprise an important class of junior lienors in the residential market, often taking back notes secured by deeds of trust to facilitate sales. For example, imagine that a bank offers a potential homebuyer a loan with an LTV of 70%. This means that the buyer would need to supply a 30% down payment. If the buyer could only come up with 20%, the home seller could agree to finance the shortfall by accepting a note and junior lien for the remaining 10%. In this way, home sellers become mortgage lenders secured by the houses they are selling. Of course, the bank will require first priority for its lien, so the seller will need to accept a junior lien.

In these situations where a buyer makes a down payment, borrows money from a mortgage lender, and the seller takes back a note and deed of trust for part of the purchase price, there would be three layers of capital at risk. Imagine that on the date of the transaction the property is worth $300,000. The buyer makes a down payment of $30,000. The senior mortgage lender advances 80% of the purchase price, $240,000. The home seller takes back a note and deed of trust for $30,000.

---

31. The reason for this is explained in the chapter on Prepayment. While federal law allows home owners to place more than one mortgage on a one-to-four family dwelling even if the senior mortgage loan prohibits a borrower from doing so without the lender's prior consent, borrowers whose loans are secured by any other type of property are subject to limitations on junior lien financing specified in the note and mortgage or deed of trust of the existing mortgage loan.

Assuming risk and return are proportionate, the rate of interest on the senior debt should be lower than the rate of interest on the purchase money loan. And the buyer's capitalization rate should be the highest of all. If the value of the house falls $15,000, the owner has lost a sum equal to one-half of its down payment.

Providing a purchase money loan can yield a potentially hidden financial benefit for the seller. Imagine the interest rate on the first mortgage loan was 6%, and the contract rate on the purchase money loan was 10%. In transactions like these, the seller has an opportunity to inflate the sales price of the house if the buyer would not otherwise be able to acquire a comparable dwelling without a purchase money loan. For instance, a typical buyer, not needing the additional financing, might only have been willing to pay $295,000. That extra $5,000 extracted from the cash-short buyer could be characterized as an additional cost of the purchase money loan for the borrower (e.g. deferred points) and an additional rate of return for the seller on its loan.

C. Calculating the Weighted Average Cost of Capital

By using debt, real estate investors hope to lower their costs of capital. Suppose an apartment developer needs $10,000,000 for her next project. She has a good track record for producing and operating profitable multifamily buildings. She could find investors willing to advance as much capital as she needs but they would be looking for rates of return on their invested equity of 15%.

Her net operating income before debt service is 20%. If she gave an equity investor the right to the first $1,500,000 of net operating income for putting up all $10,000,000, she would take home $500,000. Not bad for a zero cash investment. But she might believe she was entitled to more than that. After all, she embarked upon an extensive and costly search that came up with the site, she acquired it, obtained land use approvals, negotiated with architects and contractors, built the project, and rented it successfully. She will also capture all the value above $10,000,000 upon a sale—if she does not need to share it with her equity investor. But she could probably boost her financial return by borrowing some of the capital from a mortgage lender at a rate less than the 15% demanded by equity investors.

Suppose she borrows 70% of the money on an interest only loan from a commercial bank at 7%, and strikes a deal with her equity investor for the remaining 30% at an interest cost of 15%. Her weighted cost of capital will be 70% (X) 7% + 30% (X) 15% = 9.4%

D. Leverage

Borrowing a higher percentage of the total purchase price or value of the asset simultaneously increases the borrower's downside risk and upside potential. To see why, compare what happens to a realty buyer who borrows either 60% or 90% of the purchase price from a mortgage lender. How does the equity investor fare in good times and bad?

Suppose the realty loses 15% of its value or appreciates by the same amount. In the loss scenario, with a 60/40 debt-equity ratio, the equity investor loses 37.5% of the value of her investment. In the loss scenario for an equity investor with a debt/equity ratio of 90/10, the investor's equity is wiped out entirely and she owes her mortgage lender more than the shrunken worth of the realty.

The opposite happens in the appreciation scenario. For the equity investor who placed only 10% down, a 15% increase in the value of the realty increases her return on equity a whopping 150%. Had she been more cautious and put 40% down, her return on equity would have been 37.5%. Consider the example below with real numbers.

Formula:

Return on equity = *net income/invested equity*

Example: Investor A and Investor B each decide to purchase identical properties valued at $100,000. Investor A puts down $10,000 (10%) and borrows $90,000, and Investor B puts down $40,000 (40%) and borrows $60,000. If values increased by $15,000 (15%), Investor A would have a 150% return on equity (15,000/10,000), and investor B would have 37.5% (15,000/40,000) return on equity. Investors can increase their nominal yields by borrowing heavily in the short term at rates of interest below their rate of return on the borrowed funds. But this is a risky strategy.

Suppose an investor can earn $10,000 a year on a present investment of $100,000 — a 10% return. Consider what the investor's return would be if she borrowed $99,000 from her Aunt Tillie at no cost at all. She would only have only to invest $1,000 of her own funds and her return would be a staggering 1000%.

Magical? Not really. She paid Aunt Tillie no interest for the use of the $99,000 for a year. Had she paid interest of $10,000, her return would have been reduced to zero because she would have had to spend the entire $10,000 yield to cover the interest payment on the $99,000 loan.

Even worse, suppose Aunt Tillie was counting on her loan being safely returned in full at the end of the year, and the value of the property had fallen by 10% to $90,000. If Aunt Tillie had been relying for repayment solely on the value of the security property, as mortgage lenders often do, she would stand to lose $9,000 — a bitter price to pay for having loaned her favorite niece $99,000 at a zero interest rate.

Here is another example to illustrate both the upside and downside implications of borrowing. Suppose A and B each purchase a home for $500,000. Buyer A makes a down payment of $50,000, and obtains a loan for $450,000 — a 90% LTV ratio. Buyer B makes a down payment of $100,000, and obtains a loan for $400,000 — a LTV ratio of 80%. Now, assume good news, the value of each of their properties rises to $550,000. Buyer A's equity doubles from $50,000 to $100,000. Buyer B's equity increases from $100,000 to $150,000, an increase of one-third. But while leverage can elevate returns in good times, it can crush equity in bad times. Suppose each of their properties declines in value by $50,000. The decline wipes out A's equity completely; B takes a hit, but still has skin in the game to the tune of $50,000 in equity.

E. The Implied "Put"

When property values rise, the borrower, as the equity holder, retains all of the upside. Quite often, in buoyant real estate markets, borrowers—including home owners—can find lenders willing to make junior lien loans enabling the borrower to extract some of the accumulated equity with borrowed funds.

But what happens in falling markets? Borrowers have what economists sometimes call a "put" option. This is the borrower's option of defaulting on a mortgage loan and handing the collateral property over to the lender without being liable for the repayment of the debt. Borrowers tend to do this when: (1) they believe the value of the mortgaged property will remain less than the unpaid balance of the mortgage debt for the foreseeable future; and (2) they believe that they will never be called upon to repay the debt from income or other assets they may own. In many states the borrowers are correct because of state laws shielding them from personal liability on certain types of mortgage loans.[32]

IV. The Choice between Renting or Buying a Home or a Condo

This section is a summary of the factors relevant to anyone on the cusp of deciding whether it is better to buy or rent a domicile. How potential buyers answer that question is important to many professionals involved in real estate, including brokers, mortgage lenders, housing developers, and apartment owners.

A. The Recent Trend

Homeownership rates in the U.S. declined from 69.2% in 2004 to 64.7% in 2014.[33] "Owning a home isn't as popular or feasible as it once was: Since 2004, the home-ownership rate among younger households has plunged. Stagnant income growth,

---

32. A debtor's liability to reimburse the lender for the difference between the balance due on the debt and the value of the foreclosed property is called a deficiency. State laws determine the buyer's vulnerability to deficiency judgments. Commercial real estate operatives can avoid personal liability by borrowing in the name of a limited liability company (LLC) or other entity that has no assets other than the mortgaged realty.

In Switzerland, "Borrowers are subject to full recourse in Switzerland. A bank can claim all assets (there are limited exemptions from bankruptcy) as well as future income until a remaining debt is paid off. The implementation of these rules is typically well-organized and not particularly costly. For example, municipal bankruptcy authorities make sure that regular payments are deducted directly from a borrower's wages." Email to author from Prof. Dr. Martin Brown, Swiss Institute of Banking & Finance. 5/25/2015 12:35 PM.

33. U.S. Census Bureau News, Census.Gov (last visited July 10, 2015), http://www.census.gov/housing/hvs/files/qtr314/q314press.pdf.

high levels of student-loan debt and tighter lending policies—not to mention bad memories of the housing bust—all could push more households toward renting homes, analysts say."[34]

Some analysts see implications for the timing and desirability of home ownership in big changes that have taken place in the economics of marriage and family formation.

With greater wariness of interdependent relationships, both men and women have more options. They can live by themselves, choose an intimate partner with no strings attached, live with roommates of their choice, or move back in with mom and dad. Marriage is optional. A globe-trotting journalist, male or female, is not likely to marry a restaurant owner rooted to one place. This search builds in more uncertainty— the college student who plans to make a killing on Wall Street may enjoy better marital prospects at thirty-two than at twenty-two but only if he succeeds.... Mating and dating have become a higher stakes game that homeownership can only complicate.[35]

B. Aspects of Tenure

Home and condo unit owners enjoy security of tenure. They can decide when and whether to move, and whether to share the space with others as guests or permanent members of the household. A tenant is subject to the landlord's periodic lease renewal decisions, rent increases and rules governing sub-leasing and co-occupancy. Security has significant value to homeowners though a value is seldom actually placed on it. But it could be. Imagine what a tenant would have to pay a landlord for a "security of tenure" option that would confer upon the tenant in perpetuity the same security of tenure prerogatives that a homeowner enjoys.

Landlords and condo HOAs (home owners' associations) may impose limitations regarding pets, parking arrangements, décor, waterbeds and the like. Home owners are free of these. Former renters who buy condo units may find that they have to deal with many of the same use restrictions they hoped to escape by becoming owners.

Another difference between owning and renting is that the process of renting is a lot easier and cheaper than that of buying. Of course, the tenant pays the landlord's costs of acquisition indirectly through rent.

Mobility. The reverse side of security of tenure is home owners have a harder time accepting job offers in other cities. They are confronted with having to sell, becoming absentee landlords, or keeping their homes vacant. Tenants can move without penalty when their leases expire, and even before then, usually with minimal financial loss.

---

34. Sanjay Bhatt, *Wall Street Buyers Snap Up Thousands of Local Homes for Rentals*, Census.Gov (last visited July 10, 2015), http://www.seattletimes.com/business/wall-street-buyers-snap-up-thousands-of-local-homes-for-rentals/.

35. June Carbone & Naomi Cahn, *Marriage Markets: How Inequity is Remaking the American Family*, New York: Oxford University Press, 2014 pp. 258, 124, and 43.

Owners of condominium units wishing to rent their units may be subject to limitations on renting that appear in the condominium recorded Covenants, Conditions and Restrictions. But unlike homeowners, they do not have to worry about maintenance outside the walls of their own unit because the Home Owners' Association is responsible for the upkeep and refurbishment of common areas.

C. The Costs of Housing

Housing Cost Predictability. Housing costs are more predictable for homeowners than for apartment tenants. Homeowners will have a fairly good idea of their monthly mortgage payments, property taxes and insurance premiums; although they may be clueless about the costs of maintenance and repairs. Tenants are vulnerable to periodic rent increases at the end of their lease terms, limited only by generally prevailing supply and demand conditions unless they live in cities with rent control laws.

Default. A tenant who does not pay rent can be summarily evicted in most places even if the reason for her default was an unanticipated decline in income.

Homeowners who cannot afford their mortgage payments will have the option of selling as long as the value of the house is greater than the balance due on the mortgage. Otherwise, they could end up losing the house through foreclosure and be dispossessed thereafter. But defaulting borrowers may enjoy many months of rent-free possession because in most states the mortgage foreclosure and eviction process takes a long time to complete.

Maintenance Costs. All housing requires maintenance and is subject to recurrent property taxes and insurance premiums. These are included in tenant rents. Homeowners need to pay insurance premiums and property tax payments directly as well as to pay for maintenance and repairs. Homeowners on average spend 10–12% of their gross income on maintenance, insurance, utilities, and property taxes.

In condo projects, owners pay monthly maintenance fees to the HOA for the maintenance of the common areas (the hallways, exterior walls, shared garage facility, roof and outdoor space). But owners must maintain their individual units and pay taxes on the value of their units which are separately assessed. The HOA covers insurance premiums for the common areas while unit owners are responsible for insuring the contents and fixtures within their units.

A tenant's rent includes management and maintenance oversight, which accounts typically for 10% to 20% of the rent. Further, the tenant is dependent on the landlord's decisions about how and when to make repairs and improvements. Most homeowners contract directly for and oversee their own plumbing, electrical, roofing, HVAC, and landscaping work.

The Ratio of Rent to Purchase Price. Most buyers making offers on houses they intend to occupy as primary residences never bother figuring out a house's rental value. But buyers can estimate the premium they are paying at any point in time to be owners rather than renters simply by comparing the full costs of ownership including mortgage payments, taxes, insurance and maintenance, with what the rent would be on a house like the one they are buying.

When house prices were rising from 1960–2000, the rent-price ratio was about 5%. In the big house-price surge of 2000–2006, rents fell to about 3% of house prices. During the real estate recession of 2007–2009, that ratio returned to what it had been in earlier years. Prospective home-buyers aware of these ratios would have avoided buying during the years of the housing bubble. The house price bubble is obvious when you compare house prices and rents in the following chart from 2000 to 2014.

Is A Home A Good Investment? The common wisdom for decades was that houses were a great investment, and home mortgage payments were a forced savings plan that helped homeowners build wealth that would otherwise have been squandered in rent and luxuries.[36]

In fact, scholars and investment advisors often pointed out that house prices lagged far behind stock market prices and barely kept up with inflation. Still, comparing the long-term wealth accumulations, homeowners were way ahead of tenants, according to a 2010 Federal Reserve Board Survey of Consumer Finances.

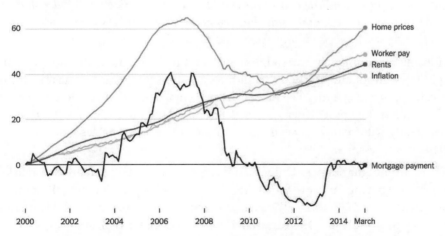

Home Prices Are Looking More Normal

Housing looks more reasonably valued relative to fundamentals than it has in years, and is a bargain when low mortgage rates are factored in.

Percent change vs. January 2000

Home prices = Federal Housing Finance Agency purchase-only home price index; worker pay = average weekly earnings for nonsupervisory private-sector employees; rents = consumer price index for owners' equivalent rent; inflation = consumer price index for all urban consumers; mortgage payment = F.H.F.A. home price index adjusted for average 30-year fixed-rate mortgage rate.

Source: New York Times analysis of data from Bureau of Labor Statistics, Federal Housing Finance Agency and Freddie Mac

36. Todd Sinai and Nicolas S. Souleles, *Housing As A Hedge Against Risk* (last visited July 10, 2015), NBER Working Paper 9462. http://www.nber.org/papers/w9462.

Here is how financial analysts put it:

It's pretty stunning that for all the hidden costs and arguments about better investments, housing makes up more than 60% ($47,500/$77,300) of the median family's cushion against bankruptcy. That's over a 30-to-1 net-worth advantage in favor of homeowners.

Anticipating the sharp readers who will argue that this could be demographics (e.g., older people, more educated people, families, or high-income people are more likely to own houses), I looked further. Households headed by folks under age 35 have a median net worth that's about double the $5,100 median net worth of non-homeowners. Households headed by folks with no high school diploma have saved more than triple what the non-homeowner has. So have single folks with no children. And, yes, even families in the bottom 20% of income have more net worth than the non-homeowner.

As for the hidden costs of homeownership, I think a greater percentage of us than we'd like to admit end up blowing the money anyway—on fancier vacations, or extra glasses of wine on nights out, or living in a more upscale house or neighborhood, or shoes, or playoff tickets, or whatever it is that keeps our median net worth at just $77,300.

This isn't a call to arms for everyone to jump willy-nilly into one of the biggest, most complicated financial decisions of their lives. The harrowing stories from the housing bubble showed us what happens when we buy when we don't have enough income or savings, overpay, or don't do our due diligence. There are also non-financial reasons that buying a house just doesn't make sense for some people.

And nothing I've written should be interpreted as a justification to buy that expensive rug instead of putting a little extra into your 401(k). This is just a reminder that there are many theories on the other side, but the real-world numbers greatly favor buying versus renting when all else is anywhere close to equal.[37]

Housing can ultimately enrich homeowners if they are fortunate enough to have bought low and sold high. Though buildings are subject to wear-and-tear over time, land can appreciate greatly. The higher the percentage of land bears to total housing cost, the better the homeowner's chance of accumulating housing wealth. That ratio varies greatly within and between cities. In the city of Los Angeles it is about 70%; in Detroit it is less than 10%.

There are no guarantees. Unlucky buyers, forced to sell in depressed markets, could end up paying far more for shelter than if they had been renters. Plummeting house prices from 2007 to 2009[38] resulted in many houses being worth less than the mortgages they secured. One researcher concluded that a typical lot in the city of

---

37. *See* Anand Chokkayelu, *Rent vs. Buy: Why Buying a House Generally Wins*, THE MOTLEY FOOL (last visited July 10, 2015), http://www.fool.com/investing/general/2013/09/22/rent-vs-buy-why-buying-a-house-wins.aspx (saying that housing prices barely keep up with inflation, citing a return of "about just 0.2% annually").

38. Bill Conerly, *Should You Buy a House or Rent? The Economics of Homeownership*, FORBES, Nov. 11, 2013; *see also* Global Property Guide, *U.S. housing market's strongest performance since Q1 2006*, Feb. 13, 2014 ((last visited July 10, 2015). http://www.globalpropertyguide.com/North-America/United-States/Price-History.

Los Angeles that would have sold for $121,000 in 1995 became worth $620,000 in 2006 at the height of the housing boom and would have sold for $450,000 in 2009 when house prices leveled off.[39]

The Advantageous Strategy of Buying Young in Volatile and Expensive Housing Markets. Undeniably, housing can be a risky investment. But unlike other risky assets that risk-averse individuals can simply avoid, housing consumption is unavoidable and the vast majority of individuals will eventually own a home.[40] In addition, for most individuals the demand for housing will rise over the life-cycle as family size increases. The combination of these factors results in an insurance role for housing wealth in early adult life. Those who purchase houses when they are young, especially in housing markets that have been historically volatile, are better able to move up the housing ladder into ever larger homes as their families grow, and end up with more housing wealth as they age.[41]

D. Homeownership Tax Advantages and Drawbacks

U.S. federal tax laws encourage home ownership in several ways:

(1) *No Tax on Imputed Rent Value.* Homeowners pay no imputed tax on the value of occupancy while for landlords, rent is taxable income.

(2) *Home Mortgage Interest Deduction.* The law allows the taxpayer to deduct from adjusted gross income all *'qualified residence interest'* on debt incurred to buy, build, or improve a home.[42] Most of the benefit is attributable to the home mortgage interest deduction. In effect, the federal government indirectly subsidizes home mortgage borrowing. The higher the taxpayer's tax bracket, the more the deduction is worth.

(3) *Gain on Sale.* Home sellers aren't taxed on the first $250,000 of gain on sale ($500,000 for a couple filing a joint return in the taxable year of the sale).[43]

---

39. Davis, Morris A. & Michael G. Palumbo, 2007, *The Price of Residential Land in Large US Cities*, 63 J. URBAN ECON. 352–384, data located at *Land and Property Values in the U.S.*, Lincoln Institute of Land Policy http://www.lincolninst.edu/resources/.

40. Banks, James W., Blundell, Richard W., Oldfield, Zoé & Smith, James P., *House Price Volatility and the Housing Ladder*, NBER WORKING PAPER NO. w21255. Available at SSRN: (last visited July, 2015), http://ssrn.com/abstract=2618643.

41. *Id.* at 23

42. For a good policy analysis and review of the history of the home mortgage interest deduction, see Roger Lowenstein, *Who Needs the Mortgage-Interest Deduction*, N.Y. TIMES MAGAZINE (Mar. 5, 2006).

43. I.R.C. § 121. The taxpayer must have owned and used the property as a principal residence for two years or more during the 5-year period ending on the date of the sale or exchange. A residence may be "used as a principal residence" even if vacant. *Gummer v. U.S.*, 40 Fed. Cl. 812 (1998). You calculate gain or loss on a personal residence by: (1) determining the taxpayer's adjusted basis. Adjusted basis is usually the original purchase price (including borrowed sums) plus most closing settlement costs not deductible at the time of origination (*e.g.*, title, escrow, recording and attorneys' fees). Add to adjusted basis capital improvements made during taxpayer's ownership. Subtract any deductions such as for depreciation taken for a home office or casualty loss tax deductions. (2) Calculate adjusted

(4) *Stepped-Up Basis.* If the house appreciates and the owner dies still owning it, the devisee receives a stepped-up basis to the home's fair market value at the date of death.[44] This will reduce the devisee's capital gains tax liability when and if the devisee ever sells the house. However, there could be estate taxes to pay.[45]

(5) *Deduction for Property Taxes.* The homeowner can deduct property taxes from gross income for federal tax purposes.[46]

The tax advantages of homeownership come with drawbacks. For starters, they are only available to taxpayers who itemize deductions, and most taxpayers do not.

Because the biggest tax incentive is tied to mortgage debt, the owner's interest payments will far exceed any tax savings from the mortgage interest deduction. "You're still out of pocket more than you get back in tax savings."[47]

Perhaps most important of all, many economists believe that the value of the home mortgage interest deduction has already been factored in to house prices. If this is true, homebuyers are paying up front for deductions they may not be able to use if federal legislators repeal or limit the home mortgage interest deduction. It confers generous tax benefits on the wealthy that far exceed all direct federal expenditures for low-and moderate-income housing.

Additionally, calculating the value of these tax benefits can be challenging since they depend on the homeowner's tax bracket, life plans, and longevity.

Further complicating the tax picture, landlords, too, receive substantial tax benefits, some of which could result in lower rents, described in Chapter Four.

Questions

Question 1: *Valuing Houses for Mortgage Loans.*

When mortgage lenders determine the maximum loan-to-value ratios they will lend, which of the methods of appraisal is likely to be the one that makes the most sense for them to use?

(net) sales price. Deduct selling costs such as a broker's commission. Include all of the selling price, even that portion of the sale proceeds used to pay off an existing mortgage. (3) Sale price minus adjusted basis equals gain or loss. This is the number from which the qualified taxpayer is entitled to deduct up to $250,000 or $500,000.

See Michael F. Lynch & Marcel G. Hebert, *New Opportunities to Exclude Gain on the Sale of a Principal Residence*, 17 REAL EST. FIN. J. 62 (2001) (describing regs).

44. I.R.C. § 1014. For example, assume that O purchased Blackacre in 1966 for $30,000. At O's death in 1990, the fair market value of Blackacre had increased to $250,000. When O's devisees inherit Blackacre, it is valued at its stepped-up basis of $250,000 rather than its acquisition cost of $30,000. Therefore, when O's devisees sell Blackacre, they will only pay capital gains taxes on the difference between the sales price minus the stepped-up basis ($250,000) rather than on the sales price minus the devisor's original acquisition cost ($30,000).

45. *See generally* IRS Publication 559 (For use in preparing 2012 returns), Survivors, Executors, and Administrators (last visited July 10, 2015), http://www.irs.gov/pub/irs-pdf/p559.pdf.

46. I.R.C. § 164(a).

47. Kelly Phillips Erb, *11 Reasons Why I Never Want to Own a House Again*, FORBES (Sept. 27, 2013).

Question 2: *Valuing Houses As Rental Properties.*

During the 2008 mortgage crises, house values plummeted, and major financial firms including Blackstone and Colony Capital went on a buying spree for distressed properties — properties selling for historically low prices. Each of these entities acquired about 15,000 houses, and pooled their holdings into a joint enterprise. Their business plan was to rent the houses and eventually sell them when housing markets recovered. What method of appraisal would be the most relevant to a potential investor in the funds that these firms created?

Question 3: *The Relevance of the Cost Method of Appraisal.*

Why might the purchaser of a newly built apartment complex care what the reproduction/replacement cost of the complex would be?

Question 4: *Why DCF Instead of a Gross Rent Multiplier?*

A client, the trustee of a large family trust, complains that she is spending a lot of money on a DCF analysis of a shopping center she is about to purchase for the trust. "They can't predict the future," she notes. "Wouldn't I be OK just using a gross rent multiplier to justify my investment decision?" How would you respond?

Question 5: *Appraisal Contingencies.*

What advice would you offer the buyer who posted the following episode online at Trulia?

"Appraisal contingency? I just had an accepted offer on a house and the appraisal came in almost 20 thousand below the agreed offer. Our agent put in the original offer contingent on inspection and appraisal and during the negotiation the seller rejected the appraisal contingency.

"This was NOT mentioned to me by my agent, much of the back and forth was over the telephone. When we agreed on a price my agent had me come in and sign the offer, which at this point had the appraisal contingency removed. Again this was not pointed out to me and initially I made it clear that this contingency be in the offer.

"When the appraisal came in low the seller refuses to negotiate the price. I don't want to overpay and am walking away. The seller is threatening to sue for the earnest money and this is becoming a huge pain.

"I spoke with the appraiser, even went over the comps with him and his number makes sense. My agent is trashing the appraiser and encouraging me to make the deal. I am furious at the agent and once they sort this out will fire them."[48]

Question 6: *Estimating Yields on Real Estate Investments.*

(a) What is the difference between rate of return and return on equity?

(b) What is the difference between NPV and IRR?

(c) What is the point of having two ways to estimate future yields? Would not one or the other suffice?

---

48. http://www.trulia.com/voices/Home_Buying/Appraisal_contingency_I_just_had_an_accepted_off-310233 (last visited 3/28/2016).

(d) Why do some mortgage lenders insist that borrowers set aside reserves for the eventual replacement of major building components, such as the roof, air conditioning and heating systems, and elevators?

(e) Project developers often obtain capital from equity investors. Investors prefer deals in which the developer's returns are based on the financial performance of the project. Hence, developers' returns are often based on NOI and IRR calculations. Why might developers try to keep lender reserve requirements to a minimum?

Question 7: *Income Capitalization Approach.*

(a) How is it possible for an investor to profit from the same project "buying high and selling low" and "selling low and buying high" simultaneously?

(b) An investor acquires a rental property for $5,000,000 producing an NOI of $500,000 a year from short-term leases to mom and pop tenants with a high turnover rate. The investor signs up a NYSE listed retailer willing to rehabilitate the property and occupy all of it on a long-term lease with a starting annual rent of $600,000. Once the property is improved and occupied under the new lease, it would command a cap rate of 5%. What would the property then be worth all other factors being equal?

Question 8: *Applying Valuation Methods to Resolve Purchase and Sale Issues.*

A client who just entered escrow on a purchase and sale agreement to sell an office building for $100,000,000 calls her attorney for advice because the buyer wants an $8,000,000 reduction in the purchase price. One of the building's tenants has just filed for bankruptcy, and the purchase price had been predicated on the estimated future cash flow from rental income. The seller has an accountant and access to an appraiser. But the seller wants the attorney's advice on how she should determine whether the $8,000,000 price reduction is reasonable under the circumstances. What advice should the attorney give?

Question 9: *Finding the Right Debt-Equity Balance.*

You have a chance to buy a very beautiful four-plex constructed in the 1920s. It was recently restored with new plumbing, electrical, roof, window, doors and appliances. You estimate that each unit will rent for $3000 a year. Calculating 30% of your gross income for maintenance, property taxes and insurance, you estimate a net operating income of about $100,000. The firm asking price is $300,000 per unit. You can obtain a mortgage loan for $900,000, interest only for ten years at 7%. Which of the following arrangements would you prefer if you have $150,000 to invest?

The seller will take back a purchase money second deed of trust for up to $300,000 at an annual interest rate of 11% payable monthly, no principal amortization, the entire debt due and payable in three years.

Your distant cousin Ida will lend you $150,000 for 50% of the annual NOI plus 50% of any gain on sale above $1,200,000 plus closing costs. She wants the right to compel a sale any time after the first six years of ownership.

Question 10: *Money Now or Money Later?*

Some methods of valuation are time-sensitive and others are not. Under what circumstances might investors or savers not prefer money sooner than later?

Question 11: *Calculating the Blended Cost of Capital.*

An individual acquires a house with the idea of holding it as a rental property and eventually selling it, hopefully at a big profit. She has $20,000 to invest in this venture. She acquired the house for $400,000. She was able to obtain an acceptable mortgage loan from a private equity fund that specializes in providing mortgage loans for rental homes. That loan was for $280,000 at an interest rate of 7%. A business associate managing a family trust was willing to provide $100,000 as a loan from the trust at an interest rate of 10% if it was secured by a second mortgage on the property. What is the investor's blended cost of capital?

Question 12: *To Own or Rent?*

(a) What factors prompt your personal choice between owning and renting a residence?

(b) Would you feel differently if you believed that rents were going to rise by about 2% annually and house prices by 5% over the next decade in the city where you would like to live and work?

(c) Considering the historic volatility of house prices, do you believe you are better off deferring buying a house and renting until house prices hit a slump, or buying as soon as you can and trading up when you can?

(d) If you bought a house, would you leverage to the max by borrowing as much as you could?

Chapter 3

Real Estate Brokers and Listing Agreements[1]

Realty is not a friendly business. It only seems to be.

—RICHARD FORD, INDEPENDENCE DAY 55 (1995)

Scope of the Chapter

Once property owners decide to sell or lease, they need to consider the best way to market their properties. They could: (1) market the property themselves; (2) auction the property, usually on contract with an auction specialty firm; or (3) contract with a real estate broker. Most property owners contract for the service of a real estate broker.[2]

This chapter highlights the functions that sellers' and buyers' brokers perform for their respective clients, and how potential buyers or sellers should go about finding suitable brokers whether for the sale of a home or commercial property.

We summarize the advantages and disadvantages of homeowners marketing their properties themselves. When sellers contract for the services of a real estate broker, they usually sign a listing agreement which is a contract specifying the main terms of the seller-broker relationship. For home sales, these agreements are typically based on a broker-drafted form. Commercial real estate owners tend to prepare their own more seller-friendly listing agreements. We pinpoint the changes that home sellers might want to consider making in the standard broker listing agreement form.

Brokers vary enormously in their skills and integrity. We describe the minimal legal obligations that brokers owe their own clients and others in the transaction, and present examples of acceptable and inappropriate broker conduct.

---

1. The author is grateful to the following who appeared in USC law classes as guest-expert real estate brokers and whose observations contributed to the material in this chapter: June Barlow, Dennis L. Greenwald, Lawrence H. Jacobson, Derik Lewis, Kurt Rappaport, and Kevin A. Shannon.

2. Brokers are involved in nearly eight out of ten home sales in the U.S. PETER G. MILLER & DOUGLAS M. BREGMAN, SUCCESSFUL REAL ESTATE NEGOTIATION at 231 (Rev. ed. 1994). Websites for FSBO properties may be augmenting FSBO ranks. Kathy M. Kristof, *Looking to Sell the House Yourself? Do Your Homework First*, LOS ANGELES TIMES, Jan. 16, 2000, at C2, col. 1.

A concluding sub-section is about the sometimes subtle line that separates the typical sale of real estate from securities offerings that could be subject to regulation under federal and state securities' laws.[3]

I. Definitions

Listing Agreements. Most broker-client relationships begin with sellers authorizing a broker to act as their marketing agent. The *listing* agreement derives its name from the fact that in it the seller empowers the broker to place the seller's property among those that the broker has listed for sale, and to share that information with other brokers and sales agents. A *listing* is a property description written for marketing purposes, prepared by the seller's broker with the seller's consent.

The listing agreement should be in writing, and in most states must be in writing to be enforceable. It should contain:

(1) The names of the parties;

(2) An identification of the property;

(3) The sales price, including terms of payment;

(4) The amount of broker compensation;

(5) The commencement and termination dates of the broker's employment and the listing period; and

(6) Any additional specific provision, e.g., whether there is an exclusive agency or right to sell.[4]

Real Estate Broker. This is a person licensed to market and, hopefully, find a prospective buyer for the property. A broker acts as the intermediary between the buyer and seller to reach an agreement memorialized in an enforceable purchase and sale contract, and makes provisions for the implementation of the terms of the contract that result in a closing. Brokers' commissions are customarily payable from sale proceeds at closing.

Real Estate Sales Agent. A real estate sales agent is licensed to operate under the supervision of a real estate broker. In the licensing hierarchy, only brokers are entitled to act on behalf of others in purchase and sale, leasing, and financing transactions, and only they are entitled to be paid or to receive commissions for brokerage services.

State legislatures impose more stringent licensing standards on 'brokers' than on 'sales agents,' and sales agents outnumber brokers by a large margin—two to one in

---

3. This definition comes from the National Association of Exclusive Buyer Agents, NAEBA (last visited July 17, 2015), http://naeba.org/resources/first-steps/what-buyers-agent.

4. Richard R. Powell & Patrick J. Rohan, 7 POWELL ON REAL PROPERTY § 938.16[z], at 84C-46 (Supp. 1987). Some statutes mandate listing agreement contents. For instance, D.C. CODE ANN. Section 45-1922(14) requires: (1) specification of price and terms acceptable to seller, (2) broker's promise to use reasonable marketing effort, and (3) a definite termination date.

California. California law requires a broker applicant to have obtained at least two years of agent's experience or its equivalent, or a four-year college degree with a real estate emphasis.[5]

To obtain a sales agent's license, the applicant must be associated with a real estate broker by a written engagement. The agent-broker relationship could be that of an independent contractor or an employee. As employees, they would be entitled to the protection of minimum wage and all the laws that protect employees.

Brokers are legally accountable for the professional conduct of the agents working with them. Generally, only brokers, not sales agents, can sue principals directly for commissions.

Buyer's Broker. A real estate broker or sales agent hired by a prospective buyer is called the buyer's broker, or the "selling" broker since without a "ready, willing, and able" buyer, there would be no sale. Often, buyer's brokers have no written agreement with their clients, and derive their right to compensation from the terms of the seller's listing agreement. There is a lack of consensus on whether a buyer's broker whose status depends entirely on the seller's broker's listing agreement is a sub-agent of the seller or a true fiduciary of the buyer.

Buyer's Exclusive Broker. To preclude confusion about the obligations owed by a buyer's broker to the seller, some brokers declare themselves to align their interests exclusively with buyers. They are able to maintain a constant and pristine fidelity to the buyer's position in every transaction by foregoing the potentially lucrative representation of sellers. In exchange, they expect their clients to sign a pledge to deal only with them, and not to work with other brokers to show them properties.

Dual Agent. A dual agency occurs when a buyer is represented by the same brokerage firm that has the listing.[6] The dual agent must disclose the dual agency to the buyer and seller at the earliest feasible time, and secure their mutual consent. For not doing so, dual agents could jeopardize their rights to a commission even if their efforts result in a sale. Dual agency arrangements are commonplace where large brokerage firms dominate their particular markets, and a seller who lists property with a broker in a dominant firm would not want to be deprived of the efforts of that firm's other brokers and prospective buyers.

Sometimes, to avoid conflicts of interest or the appearance of such conflicts, brokerage firms designate separate agents within the firm to represent each party; these are called *designated agents.* Buyers and sellers must still consent to the dual agency because otherwise, the dual agent would have no legal claim to a commission.

Realtor. A REALTOR® is a federally registered collective membership mark which identifies a real estate professional who is member of the NATIONAL ASSOCIATION

---

5. CAL. BUS. & PROF. CODE § 10150.6 (West 1987).

6. Caruthers, Chrystal, *What is Dual Agency,* REALTOR.COM (last visited July 10, 2015), http://www.realtor.com/advice/dual-agency/.

OF REALTORS® and subscribes to its strict Code of Ethics.[7] Industrial and office real estate brokerage professionals have their own trade association called AIR Commercial Real Estate Association.

Transactions Broker. Typically, a transaction broker is defined as "a broker who assists one or more parties with a real estate transaction without being an agent or advocate for the interests of any party to such transaction."[8] "Essentially, the non agent broker would act very much like a mediator who assists the parties in reaching acceptable terms for their transaction, and this seems to be the concept that underlies non-agency brokerage."[9] Colorado was the first state to authorize transaction brokers, and about twenty states have followed its lead.[10]

Multiple Listing Service. In most U.S. cities (New York is the most notable exception) residential 'realtors'[11] share their listings with independently run organizations, usually set up by the local Board of Realtors.[12] Commercial brokers, too, have organized multiple listing services in some parts of the country, organized by property type and price range.

A residential MLS will provide a form (called a setup or data sheet) which each broker fills out for every new listing. That data sheet will include the asking price, a photo of the listed property, and basic facts about the property, including its location, the number of bedrooms and bathrooms, and the presence of special features such as a pool, air conditioning, or views. Online data sheets also track the number of days the property has been on the market.

Commission splits. By prior agreement with the MLS, listing brokers agree to split their commissions with any member broker who is the first agent to find an acceptable buyer for a listed property. The customary split is 50/50, though some MLS agreements

---

7. *Definition of Realtor*, NAR (last visited July 10, 2015), http://www.realtor.org/membership-marks-manual/definition-of-realtor.

8. 58 KAN. STAT. ANN. § 58-30, 102(s) (2003).

9. Patricia A. Wilson, *Nonagent Brokerage: Real Estate Agents Missing in Action*, 52 OKLA. L. REV. 85, 102 (1999).

10. Walt Albro, *The Law and You: Rewriting Agency Law* (Feb., 1998), http://realtormag.realtor.org/law-and-ethics/law/article/1998/02/law-you-rewriting-agency-law; Vernon L. Jarboe, *Brokerage Relationships in Real Estate Transaction Act*, 68 J. KAN. B.A. 36, 37 (1999) ("In trying to cubbyhole the type of transaction involved, the law did not assign brokers of real estate a niche consistent with how they actually acted").

11. Local boards of realtors operate clearinghouses — there are about 900 of them — called Multiple Listing Services (MLS). The primary mission of a MLS is to serve its members in marketing their listings.

12. The Ninth Circuit has upheld the MLS practice of restricting access to members of the local board of realtors against antitrust challenge. *Supermarket of Homes, Inc. v. San Fernando Valley Bd. of Realtors*, 786 F.2d 1400 (9th Cir. 1986). The exclusion of part-time workers from MLS access was held a violation of California's antitrust law in *Marin Cty. Bd. of Realtors v. Palsson*, 549 P.2d 833, 130 Cal. Rptr. 1 (1976). *See* Comment, *Exclusion From Real Estate Multiple Listing Services as Antitrust Violations*, 14 CAL. WEST. L. REV. 298 (1978); John D. Perovich, Annotation, *Validity, Construction, and Effect of Real Estate Brokers' Multiple Listing Agreement*, 45 A.L.R. 3d 190 (1973).

favor listing brokers with a 60/40 split. Commercial MLS splits usually tilt in favor of the listing broker because of the sizable marketing expenses the listing broker incurs.

Commissions are divided not just between listing and selling brokers but between those individual brokers and the firms in which they work. The firms cover overhead, marketing, and managerial costs. The percentages vary; higher performing brokers are in a position to negotiate retention of bigger percentages for themselves.

The Sealed or Managed Bid Process. These methods of marketing are usually organized by a real estate broker, and are customarily reserved for the sale of prime properties expected to attract numerous offers from qualified, eager bidders.

In a sealed or managed bid process, rather than advertising the property for sale at a fixed price, and then responding to offers one-at-a-time as they are received, the seller or the seller's broker promulgate detailed rules and conditions regarding the format for bids, and the terms on which the property is being offered for sale. Prospective buyers are invited to submit their best offers in writing. Offers are usually placed in individual sealed envelopes and dropped off at the office of the listing agent or with the seller's attorney.

In a sealed bid process, all the bids will be opened at a pre-set time, and the property will be sold to the highest bidder. In a managed bid process, the seller reviews the initial bids, and initiates negotiations with a few of the higher bidders.

There might be one or more additional rounds of biding, with the number of bidders successively narrowed, each of them given a chance to make a "best and final" offer before the seller chooses the bidder with whom to initiate negotiations towards a final deal.

Before submitting binding offers, preselected bidders are provided access to extensive information about the physical condition of the building, title information, copies of the leases and all the other data that any well-informed buyer would require. Sometimes, this information is assembled in what is called a "war room" though much of the informatoin is often available online these days. Physical inspections of the property are organized. By a set date, bidders present their offers.

Bidders are free to present offers on any contract form they choose but competing bidders are well advised to stick with the purchase and sale agreement that the seller will have provided along with a dossier of bidding materials . Varying from the seller's preferred contract terms is a bad idea because sellers are known to have rejected bids from otherwise qualified buyers who seem poised to engage in protracted, contentious negotiations over each of the fine points of the deal.

Auctions.[13] Real property can be sold at a public auction. Owners of distressed or hard to value properties often sell at auctions. One advantage to selling large portfolios

---

13. See, Steven L. Good and Celeste M. Hammond, *Real Estate Auctions—Legal Concerns for an Increasingly Preferred Method of Selling Real Property*, 40 REAL PROP. PROB. & TR. J. 765 (2006) for analysis of legal concerns about using an auction to market real estate.

of property at auction is that instead of disposing of properties one-at-time over many months, and even years, numerous sales of many properties can be concluded in a single day. Professional auction firms are adept at conducting extensive media marketing to spur demand. Buyers at auctions are often motivated by their competitive instincts to outbid others by offering the top dollar.

Auction bidders are usually given extensive pre-sale opportunities for due diligence, certainly more than in most foreclosure sales. To encourage bidding, sellers, through the auctioneers they have hired, provide title details, environmental data,, a survey, financing availability, and other information buyers would want. Sellers are able to dictate the terms of purchase and sale agreements unilaterally. But buyers have the chance to submit their own preferred contract terms, or to accept the seller's contract terms and adjust the offered price according to the risks they would be assuming.

Government agencies customarily sell their holdings through sealed bids or auctions to avoid the appearance of favoritism, encourage competitive bidding and comply with open and competitive bidding statutes and ordinances.[14]

II. Functions

Difference Between Commercial and Residential Brokers. Brokers tend to specialize. The most successful residential brokers only sell homes or condos, and concentrate on properties located within a particular area and price range.[15] Residential brokers of very expensive houses know how to pre-qualify potential buyers for whom they prepare and reserve the expensive brochures trumpeting the special features of the homes for sale and picturing it in its best light.

Similarly, many of the most successful commercial brokers restrict themselves to particular types of property—warehouse industrial, retail, apartments, office buildings and hotels/resorts. Although some brokers confine themselves geographically, others stake out a sub-category (for instance, office buildings above $30,000,000) and might be prepared to represent buyers or sellers of that kind of property in selected cities, regions or nationwide.

Commercial brokers spend thousands of dollars (sometimes reimbursed by the seller) putting together data-rich, glossy, professionally designed sales brochures that display cash flow projections and key information about the current leases and tenants. Listing brokers send out commercial brochures with the expectation that recipients

---

14. Managing the Crisis: The FDIC and RTC Experience, Ch. 13 "Auctions and Sealed Bids" (2005). https://www.fdic.gov/bank/historical/managing/history1-13.pdf (Last visited 07/14/2016).

15. For some basic advice to realtors wanting to cross over from residential and small commercial property sales to the "big time" of commercial real estate, see Cindy S. Chandler, *Getting Started in Commercial Real Estate*, REALTORMAG (last visited July 10, 2015), http://realtormag.realtor.org/commercial/feature/article/2007/01/getting-started-commercial-real-estate.

will sign confidentiality agreements that prevent them from sharing the brochure with others, and bind them to only placing offers through the exclusive agent.

The best commercial brokers know virtually the entire universe of buyers with the resources needed to purchase, say, a $250,000,000 office building or a regional shopping mall. Buyers would mostly be institutions: pension funds, sovereign wealth funds, insurance companies, real estate investment trusts, private equity funds and family trusts. These brokers would be able to arrange personal meetings with the most promising prospects to pitch the property in hopes of procuring an offer.

Functions that Seller's Residential Brokers Perform.

Seller's brokers may:

(1) Offer advice on the best time to put the property on the market;

(2) Review "comparable sales" and other data to help the seller decide the list price;

(3) Prepare a marketing strategy;

(4) Assure compliance with disclosure laws;

(5) Conduct negotiations;

(6) Arrange to show the property;

(7) Pre-qualify potential buyers or bidders;

(8) Assist in opening escrow, procuring a title report, obtaining access for the buyer's property inspections;

(9) Gather all information the seller has regarding the condition of the property such as surveys, geological reports, and the like;

(10) Suggest minor improvements to increase the "curb appeal" of the property.

Functions that a Buyer's Residential Broker Performs.

Buyer's brokers may:

(1) Start by defining the buyer's needs and preferences—type of property, location, price range—identifying potentially suitable properties and arranging to show those to the buyer;

(2) Advise buyers on potential financing and assist in filing out loan applications;

(3) Assist in finding inspectors, reviewing inspection reports, directing buyers to attorneys, accountants, geologists, title insurers, or other professionals as needed;

(4) Negotiate the terms of the contract, including price, and proffer counter-offers;

(5) Help resolve title issues should they arise;

(6) Help determine whether the property is in compliance with building codes, zoning and environmental laws;

(7) Review escrow instructions.

Functions That a Commercial Real Estate Broker Performs.[16]

(1) Investigate the local market of the subject property as to properties of similar size, location, finishes, and amenities and with similar kinds of leases;

(2) Recommend appropriate financial and inducement proposals to compete effectively for a Qualified Prospect in the context of the local market;

(3) Recommend advertising and marketing programs;

(4) Gather contacts for potential Qualified Prospects and recommending offer recipients;

(5) Prepare a written comprehensive Strategic Plan with measurable goals, assemble and produce for the Client review and approval an offering brochure and/or other marketing materials of a type that is customary for similar properties which shall include, as appropriate, property facts, photographs, high-quality graphics, cash flow projections, market competition data, descriptive area and location information, site plan, and other relevant information as available;

(6) Negotiate terms to improve Client's benefits and reduce Client's detriments including, without limitation, [rent holidays, tenant allowances, security deposits, restrictions on increases in basic rent, formulas for increases and restrictions on additional rent];

(7) Identify, interview, and qualify Qualified Prospects, [provided, however, that the Client shall have the ultimate responsibility for determining the financial condition and capabilities of any Qualified Prospect];

(8) Require each Qualified Prospect to execute and deliver to Broker a confidentiality agreement;

(9) Make the necessary arrangements with the Client to physically inspect the Premises;

(10) Tour the Premises with Qualified Prospects;

(11) Maintain records of the identity and contact information for Qualified Prospects.

---

16. Gregory G. Gosfield, *Commercial Real Estate Brokers: Engaging and Disengaging* (January, 2015), pages D-2 and D-3, http://www.klehr.com/?t=3&A=793&format=xml&Gregory%20G.%20Gosfield.

III. Searching for a Good Broker

Good listing brokers add value for their clients by securing timely offers that justify the steep commissions they earn. They keep track of current sales prices, not the seller's hoped for listing price or even the prices at which sales have been concluded recently. In fast-moving real estate markets, today's negotiated contract prices can be months more current than yesterday's contract prices reflected in closings.

Adept brokers understand the markets where they specialize, and frame marketing messages precisely aimed at the features that target buyers are looking for, and deliver their messages in the most cost-effective ways. Once potential buyers come into play, adept listing brokers are skillful at sizing them up. They understand how to maneuver the buyer and seller into a written, signed real estate contract, and how to steer a transaction from contract to closing.

Inept brokers are numerous, particularly in the housing market where inexperienced amateurs, with meager formal training in real estate law or business, often work part-time, lack the managerial finesse needed to conclude sales successfully, know little about the capabilities and reliability of local title insurers, home inspectors, general contractors, mortgage lenders, and other real estate market participants — and the most productive and trustworthy brokers active on the same turf. Property owners waste time and money dealing with clueless brokers. This is also why it is usually a very bad idea to select a broker solely because he or she is a friend or relative.

Owners thinking of listing their homes or other properties can easily identify the leading brokers in any given sub-market area by word of mouth, narrow the field to two or three, and interview them. At those interviews, sellers should ask potential listing brokers about their past sales track records, inspect the volume and quality of their past and current listings, ask specific questions probing the broker's knowledge of the market place, and require a market analysis of the subject property along with a detailed, scheduled marketing program to which the broker commits.[17] Brokers should be asked to specify whether they contemplate print advertisements, direct mail, news releases, company brochures or portfolios or even postings on the company's website.

A good listing broker has ongoing relationships with other brokers but does not depend solely on their bringing potential buyers to the property because she has her own resourceful means of reaching potential buyers directly.

Questions Potential Sellers Should Ask Commercial Brokers. There are far fewer commercial brokers than residential brokers, and more is expected of them. The following is a list of questions for potential brokers prepared by a lawyer who represents commercial real estate owners.[18]

---

17. *See* Robert J. Bruss, *Choosing a Good Real Estate Agent*, Los Angeles Times, Aug. 27, 1989, at 9 (Real Estate Section).

18. Gregory G. Gosfield, *Commercial Real Estate Brokers: Engaging and Disengaging*, Part 2 (February, 2015), B-2 and B-3.

(1) Can you explain to me what distinguishes your services from other brokers that would help bring a higher price sooner for this asset ("Property")?

(2) What strengths, weaknesses distinguishes you from your competitors?

(3) If a buyer is represented by your company, how will I get your aggressive and undivided loyalty?

(4) Please describe your fee structure.

(5) Will you offer a dual-variable commission?

(6) Would you accept a lower commission if there were no cooperating broker and a [___]% commission if there were a cooperating broker?

(7) Please identify any costs (other than typical closing costs for transfer tax and pro rations) you anticipate the seller will incur that are outside that fee structure, for example, signage or marketing expenses.

(8) Who would be the responsible party at your company to conduct the engagement and implementation of the strategic plan?

(9) What is the structure of your team/business and who will I be dealing with on what issues i.e., do you have an assistant, closing manager, buyer agents, etc.?

(10) Please briefly describe the marketing strategy you would plan to use for this Property or a property like this and how you would target prospective buyers.

(11) Who do you think is the "typical buyer" for this property?

(12) Please describe how you would qualify prospective buyers.

(13) Can you describe your experience with sales of similar properties in this geography?

(14) How may properties did you list last year?

(15) What was the average time on the market for your listings of similar properties at similar prices over the past year?

(16) How many properties are you listing currently?

(17) How many properties did you sell last year?

(18) How many properties have you sold over $[___],000,000 in the last two years?

(19) Can you provide 5 examples of similar sales for which you have been responsible?

(20) Can you provide 5 current references of sellers you have represented for sale of similar properties?

(21) At what percentage of the initial listing price do the majority of your listings sell?

(22) How many days do you expect the Property to be on the market?

(23) What is your suggested list price and why?

(24) What is your projected final sale price and why?

(25) Do you think there are any special market conditions affecting the Property?

(26) When would you recommend listing this property and why?

IV. The Advantages and Disadvantages of Not Hiring a Broker at All

Online Competition to Traditional Brokerage Arrangements. Home buyers and sellers can determine a much tighter range for the likely price than ever before. Thanks to *Realtor.com, Zillow.com, Redfin.com,*[19] or *Trulia.com,* home buyers and sellers are no longer dependent on brokers and Multiple Listing Services for house price information. Brokers still play a role but buyers and sellers have considerable pricing information long before contract negotiations ensue.

For commercial properties, there are sites like Co-Star. "In recent years the old system, in which Realtors tightly controlled home listings, searches, and buying, has been confronted by a series of alternative models. Experts predict that these new Internet-based business models could cut commission costs in half, saving consumers $30 billion per year."[20] If buyers and sellers had direct access to information about houses for sale, the buyer could have more control over what they see, while realtors, requiring less time for each client, could handle more of them. By drastically lowering costs per transaction, online operations could lead to huge discounts in brokerage commissions.

"For Sale by Owner" (FSBO): Should Sellers Market Their Own Property Without Listing Brokers? To avoid the expense of a brokerage commissions and save the 5 to 7% of the gross sales price that brokers usually charge, a seller may personally place a "for sale" sign in the yard and show the property to prospective buyers on request. FSBOs hope that potential buyers driving around the neighborhood will spot the sign and call them.

While FSBO sellers are often motivated by the prospect of saving money on brokers' commissions, there are some costs that FSBOs will find unavoidable. The FSBO seller will need to offer commissions, typically 3% of a home's gross sales price, if she expects client referrals from buyers' brokers. Sellers signal their willingness to pay a buyer's broker commission by promising 'courtesy to brokers' in ads and posted 'For Sale' signs. In addition, the FSBO seller incurs marketing and document preparation expenses that would have been paid by a listing broker, had there been one.

---

19. Redfin is a broker operating with an online network of independent sales agents.

20. Susanne Ethridge, *Cannon, Disruption, Disintermediation and Real Estate Crowdfunding*, 43 Real Est.Rev. J, art. 2 (2014).

The FSBO seller must perform many more of the broker's functions than just finding a buyer and making a deal. She must obtain a purchase and sale contract form and make sure it is comprehensive and properly signed to be enforceable under the Statute of Frauds. In California and many other states, sellers must provide a written Transfer Disclosure Statement detailing the condition of the property.[21] California also requires the seller to provide a Natural Hazard Disclosure Statement,[22] a Residential Earthquake Hazards Report,[23] a written certification that all water heaters have been braced, anchored or strapped to resist falling or displacement during an earthquake,[24] and disclosure of deaths that have occurred on the property within the last three years. Many local governments require sellers to disclose information about the applicability of local zoning laws.

The seller will need to enter a contract with an escrow agent or a closing attorney to oversee the accounting details, prepare a deed, arrange for payment of the documentary transfer tax, collect and distribute funds, and assure compliance with all of the contract terms precedent to closing. The seller will also need to contract with a title insurer to prepare a preliminary title report for the buyer's approval and to issue a title policy at closing.

Ideally, the seller should be able to introduce the buyers to a mortgage broker or mortgage lender familiar with local lending parameters.

During the escrow period, the seller will be expected to arrange access to the property for the buyer and the buyer's inspectors. The seller has to secure the buyer's written release of financing, inspection and title contingencies that were written into the purchase and sale contract to avoid the buyer claiming not to have granted those releases.

Some firms offer FSBO sellers complete "Do It Yourself" packages including purchase and sale agreement forms, signs, and marketing tips.

FSBO Risks. Many property owners give self-marketing a chance, but later hire a broker in desperation after their efforts fail to produce a willing buyer at the desired price. Here are some potential risks that a FSBO seller could be taking:

(1) Delaying or losing the deal for lack of knowledge about how to schedule and document a transaction from start to finish;

(2) Pricing the property so far above market value that prospective buyers pass it by;

(3) Selling for too little on unfavorable terms and conditions; or

(4) Incurring liability for failure to comply with myriad public regulations governing closings and disclosures.

---

21. CAL. CIV. CODE § 1102.
22. CAL. CIV. CODE § 1102.6(c).
23. CAL. GOV'T CODE § 8897.
24. CAL. HEALTH AND SAFETY CODE § 19211.

Should Buyers Hire a Broker? Some prospective buyers shop alone, figuring that the buyer's broker is only pointing the buyer to potential properties for sale. They plan to rely on newspaper ads, 'For Sale' signs, online listings, and word-of-mouth.

There are some good reasons for buyers to work with brokers. The seller's broker has no incentive to look out for the buyer's best interests in the transaction. Prospective home buyers who use brokers, and seventy to eighty percent do, see more properties in a shorter time period than those searching on their own.[25] The buyer's broker is going to be the buyer's advocate to acquire the property since she will only earn a commission if the seller accept her client's offer and buys the property. The buyer's broker will probably have had more experience than the buyer in negotiating deals.

Using a broker costs the buyer nothing directly. Generally, the buyer's broker is compensated by receiving a share of the listing (seller's) broker's commission if the buyer's broker becomes the procuring cause of a sale.

The only time where the buyer might be better off without her own broker is when competition is vigorous for the property she wants, and there are multiple offers. The seller's broker may have a tendency to favor buyers who have consented to allow the seller's broker to be a dual agent because they will not have to share the commission.

V. The Listing Agreement

In Some States the Listing Agreement is Only Enforceable if Written. About half the states deny enforcement of listing agreements without a writing signed by the broker and the owner, describing the property to be sold, specifying the amount of the commission, and signed by the seller and the broker.[26] In fact, standard purchase-and-sale contract forms, prepared by state realtors' associations, invariably authorize the escrow or closing agent to pay the broker from sale proceeds.[27] Although few buyers' brokers insist upon buyers signing agency agreements of their own, buyer's brokers satisfy the writing requirement by piggybacking their commission claims onto the seller's listing agreement through contracts that brokers sign on joining an MLS.

Brokers relying solely on oral promises of compensation from sellers who renege after the broker had been instrumental in arranging a real estate purchase and sale

---

25. Harold W. Elder, Leonard W. Zampano & Edward Baryla, *Buyer Search Intensity and the Role of the Residential Real Estate Broker*, 18 J. REAL EST. FIN & ECON. 350, 350–51 (1999).

26. *Marathon Realty Corp. v. Gavin*, 398 N.W.2d 689 (Neb. 1987).

27. *Petrosky v. Peterson*, 859 A.2d 77 (Del. Supr. 2004). Broker's written listing of seller's commercial property was for a sale at $750,000. Seller and potential buyer couldn't agree on price and instead settled on a 20-year lease with two five year renewal options, at $70,000 per year for five years, increasing thereafter. Court held that broker was entitled to quantum meruit recovery since broker's claim was supported by original written listing agreement and the written lease affirmed broker's right to commission.

sometimes invoke the doctrine of *equitable estoppel* to try to collect. They have only been successful in these lawsuits in a few jurisdictions.[28]

A Listing Agreement Is Not an Offer to Sell. The listing agreement defines the terms of the agency relationship between broker and seller. It is neither a contract of sale nor an offer to sell.[29] Prospective buyers have no right to compel the seller to sign a purchase and sale agreement even at the listed price and terms. Brokers lack authority to enter purchase and sale agreements on the seller's behalf.

Three Types of Listings: Open Listing, Exclusive Agency, Exclusive Right to Sell. Listing agreements cover all aspects of the seller-broker relationship. But they derive their characterization from a single feature concerning when the broker becomes entitled to a commission. (a) In an open listing, the listing broker is entitled to a commission only by personally producing the buyer for the property. (b) In an exclusive agency the listing broker is entitled to a commission if she or any other broker finds the buyer. (c) In an exclusive right to sell, the listing broker is entitled to a commission if the property is sold during the listing period or an extension of it, no matter who finds the buyer, even if the seller finds the buyer.[30]

A. Open (Non-Exclusive) Listing

Under an open listing, the seller may list the property with as many brokers as she chooses, placing all of them in direct competition with each other in a race to become the 'procuring proximate cause' of the sale by producing the ultimate buyer.

Brokers shun open listings. As one lawyer-broker explains, "Most real estate agents will work on open listings only if the potential sales commission is large and it is a rainy day with nothing better to do. Rarely will an agent spend money ad-

---

28. E. ALLEN FARNSWORTH, CONTRACTS § 6.11, at 453 (2d ed. 1990).

29. The listing agreement does not authorize the broker to consummate a sale of the property, unless such authority is explicitly stated in the contract with the broker. *Mason v. Mazel*, 187 P.2d 98 (Cal. Ct. App. 1947); RESTATEMENT (SECOND) OF AGENCY § 50 cmt. 6, illus. 1 (1958).

30. Some commentators also include a fourth, the net listing. "Net" describes a type of commission arrangement in which the broker keeps as her commission everything above a fixed 'net' price. However, a net listing could be open, an exclusive agency or an exclusive right to sell. D. Barlow Burke, Jr. lists six types of listings. Besides the open, exclusive agency, exclusive right to sell, and net, he describes the "option" listing—the broker obtains an option to buy at a specific price and exercises it upon locating a buyer. The sixth is the MLS, an exclusive right to sell for the listing broker but an open listing shared by all MLS members among buyers. BURKE, LAW OF REAL ESTATE BROKERS § 2:13-2:36 (2d ed. 1982).

Net listings are generally frowned upon because (1) sellers may not be receiving the highest possible price as net listings give brokers an incentive to 'lowball' the estimate they give sellers of the value of listed property; (2) net listings encourage brokers to use "straws" in order to purchase the property at its net price and resell it later at a handsome profit; and (3) whenever brokers earn more than 5–7% on a net listing, sellers are likely to claim it was because the broker misled the seller into undervaluing the property. Net listings are either prohibited or regulated in Alabama, California, Georgia, Maryland, Michigan, Tennessee, and Utah. ROBERT W. SEMENOW, QUESTIONS AND ANSWERS ON REAL ESTATE 71 (9th ed. 1978).

vertising an open listing, and most multiple listing services will not accept open listings."[31]

While open listings are rare in the residential market, they are more common in the marketing of commercial realty, though the most successful commercial brokers insist upon exclusives.

The Broker's Vulnerability Under an Open Listing: Proof of Procuring Cause. Disputes often arise over which of several buyers' brokers was the procuring cause of a sale. When all the brokers in the dispute are members of the National Association of Realtors, these disputes are customarily resolved through arbitration between the contesting brokers.

Buyers' brokers would prefer that arbitrators award them commissions whenever they can prove that one of their clients ultimately purchased a property. But the NAR rules favor listing brokers by adopting the "procuring cause" norm for resolving competing claims to the buyers' share of the commission between listing and buyers' brokers. Under this norm, what starts out as an "exclusive" for the listing broker ends up becoming an open listing for all the cooperating member brokers. To receive a commission, the buyer's broker must prove that she was the "procuring cause" of the sale just as on any open listing. To be deemed the procuring cause, the broker must prove she was the one ultimately responsible for the buyer's decision to purchase the property.

The Pocket Listing. A pocket listing is a type of open listing which results from sellers informing a favored broker that they would sell for a certain price. The pocket listing broker is loath to share this information about the property potentially being available because she will not be entitled to a commission if another broker introduces a buyer to the seller.

B. Exclusive Agency

Under this arrangement, to earn a commission the listing broker has to prove that the property was sold either through her individual efforts or through the efforts of another duly licensed broker or agent. She receives nothing if the *owner* himself finds a buyer without any broker's help.[32]

Brokers are wary of exclusive agency agreements, worried that the seller will 'eat the broker's lunch' by finding a buyer as an indirect result of the broker's marketing efforts, a fact that will often be difficult for the listing broker to prove.

---

31. Robert J. Bruss, *Open Listing Is Not the Best Route to Go*, Miami Herald, Aug. 7, 1988 (Real Estate Section). There is probably a direct link between the success of brokers in resisting open listings and the existence of multiple listing services. Brokers representing buyers depend on the seller's listing agreement with the seller for their compensation. If that relationship is weak because the seller's broker has only an open listing, affiliated brokers representing buyers may downplay the listing when they come across it in the listing book.

32. *Dorman Realty & Ins. Co. v. Stalvey*, 212 S.E.2d 591, 593 (S.C. 1975) (holding that the "right of an owner to sell his own property is an implicit condition of every contract of agency unless negatived"). Vikas Bajaj, *Five Multiple Listings Services Agree to Equal Treatment for Discount Brokers*, N.Y. Times, 10/13/06, p. C3, Col 1.

Discount brokers such as the firm Help-U-Sell use exclusive agencies, anticipating that sellers will take on many of the tasks customarily performed by full service brokers.

C. Exclusive Right to Sell

Under this arrangement, the broker is entitled to a commission if "the property is sold" during the term of the listing "by broker, by seller, or by another broker, or through any source."[33] The listing broker earns a commission even if another agent finds the buyer without assistance from the listing broker, or if the owner finds the buyer on his own.[34]

The exclusive-right-to-sell is the format that brokers prefer. "Most multiple listing services adopt an exclusive right to sell listing agreement for use by its members. The use of that agreement then becomes, according to its by-laws, mandatory for the membership."[35]

Spot Exceptions to Exclusive Right to Sell. Suppose the seller says to the broker: "An old friend always said he would like to buy this house if I ever decide to sell. I don't want to pay you a commission if he buys it."

The seller could avoid paying a commission on a sale to the friend by selling before entering a listing agreement, after the listing agreement expires or by entering an exclusive agency or open listing. Alternately, most brokers would suggest a modification of the listing agreement to give the seller a few days to conclude a contract with the friend without incurring liability for a brokerage commission. Such modifications are known as spot exceptions.[36]

---

33. *See Flynn v. LaSalle Nat'l. Bank*, 137 N.E.2d 71 (Ill. 1956); *Berven Co. v. Newman*, 281 N.W.2d 268 (S.D. 1979).

34. *See First Fla. Realty & Auction Co., Inc.*, 703 So. 2d 1199, 1200 (Fla. Dist. Ct. App. 1997) (Broker sold some of the 160 acres listed and seller paid 10% commission voluntarily for those transactions. Seller balked at paying a commission for the acreage broker couldn't sell and that seller negotiated to sell to a neighbor. Seller had begun negotiating with neighbor before entering listing agreement.).

35. Burke, Law of Real Estate Brokers § 2:35, at 2.2.6 (2d ed. 1982)

36. The form listing contract prepared by the Minnesota State Bar Association (Rev. 1996), provides:

> Exclusion List: I will not owe You any compensation if I sell the Property to any of the following:
> 1. My parents, children, siblings, grandparents, grandchildren, first cousins, aunts or uncles, nephews or nieces, or any other relatives by operation of law
> 2. Neighbors named here: _____
> 3. Employees of the companies named here: _____
> 4. Other persons named here: _____
> 5. Anyone who responds to my marketing efforts.
> If this provision #5 is deleted, I might owe you a compensation even if I find the buyer.

Few brokers will accept an exclusion list that extends for the full length of the listing period. Brokers

D. Critical Listing Agreement Provisions That Sellers Should Consider

Sellers' Liability for Commissions on Deals That Never Close. Brokerage commissions are based on contingent fees. Commonly, brokers believe they have earned their commissions when they produce a "ready, willing and able" buyer—whether a sale results or not. Conversely, sellers expect to pay commissions from sales prices at closing.

Realtor-drafted forms treat the broker as having earned a commission when the seller receives an offer at the listed price and terms, or the seller accepts a buyer's offer, even though ultimately the deal fails to close through no fault of the seller. Maybe the deal failed because the buyer backed away or the buyer's lender withheld the promised loan funding. Most sellers would be stunned by brokers claiming commissions on failed deals.[37]

In fact, only rarely do brokers actually press such claims against blameless sellers. Most brokers prefer good client relations and are content to re-list the seller's property and try again. Instead of relying passively on the broker's good will in such circumstances, informed sellers insist upon modifying the listing agreement by specifying: *"Broker's compensation will be earned and deemed due if, and only if, escrow actually closes as evidenced by the recordation of a grant deed from the seller to the buyer."*

A commercial real estate attorney's form also specifies "no closing; no commission" with this language: "In the event a Sale Contract is signed, but title is not transferred for any reason whatsoever, Broker shall receive no commission or other compensation regardless of whether or not Client is entitled to retain any down payment made by the purchaser. Client has no responsibility to pay any fee or compensation to Broker (including reimbursement of any costs incurred by Broker in connection with this Agreement), except as specifically provided in this Agreement."[38]

Understandably, brokers balk at the idea of breaching buyers escaping liability for broker's commissions duly earned. The California Association of Realtors' form entitles brokers to share in any recovery including liquidated damages that the seller receives from a breaching buyer.

Suppose the seller receives an offer at the listing price but believes the list price recommended by the broker was too low. It was the seller's broker who may have

---

don't want to waste time and money marketing a property unless the seller's right has expired to sell commission-free to someone on the exclusion list.

37. *See, e.g., Callaway v. Overholt*, 796 S.W.2d 828 (Tex. App. 1990) (broker earns commission when parties enter a purchase-and-sale agreement); Restatement (Second) of Agency § 445 cmt. d (1958); 12 Am. Jur. 2d, Brokers § 192 (1964); George J. Seidel, Real Estate Law 159 (1979); 12 C.J.S. Brokers § 145 (1980); Karl B. Holtzschue, Real Estate Contracts 5 (1985) (but see the 1987 Supplement; a valid contract is required in New York); California Real Property Sales Transactions § 2.87 (Gordon L. Graham, ed., 2d ed. 1993) (stating the general rule for California).

38. G. Gosfield, *Commercial Real Estate Brokers: Engaging and Disengaging* (January 21, 2015), http://www.klehr.com/?t=3&A=793&format=xml&Gregory%20G.%20Gosfield.

pegged the price too low, not the buyer's broker. Why should the buyer's broker not be paid for having found a buyer on the seller's terms? California brokers believed they were entitled to commissions under these circumstances until a California appellate court ruled that they were not. In the litigated case, a broker sued for a commission after a buyer offered to pay the full $17,000,000 asking price, the seller made a counter offer of $19,500,000, and buyer and seller were unable to reach an agreement on the price. Disregarding the plain language of the listing agreement, the California appellate court held that the broker had no right to a commission because there had been no concluded sale.[39]

The court opinion was unclear as to whether the outcome was based on an interpretation of the standard form listing agreement which the seller had agreed to, or on a court-formulated policy that brokers should rarely, if ever, be entitled to commissions on failed deals, no matter why the deal failed to close.[40] To preserve their right to reject full price offers without becoming liable for a commission, sellers should not depend on a "Hail Mary" court victory. Instead, they should draft listing agreements to specify: *"Notwithstanding the list price, seller in its sole and absolute discretion may require a higher purchase price for the property."*

Suppose the buyer agrees to the seller's counter-offer, and then breaches the contract? Standard listing agreements make sellers liable for commissions "provided the Buyer completes the transaction *or is prevented from doing so by Seller."* Sellers should strike the italicized part of this provision. Though it is seemingly plausible that a seller who prevents a sale should compensate the broker, it is problematical for many reasons. Experienced real estate litigators will explain that what counts as a seller's or buyer's 'willful' breach is often subject to varying interpretations, and court or arbitration outcomes are often unpredictable. So instead of wasting time and money in costly, enervating disputes where brokers try to pin the cause of a contract not closing on the seller, brokers are better off just moving on. Successful brokers know this and will agree to the above-suggested deletion. The broker who would be so desperate as to risk litigation or arbitration for a commission is probably not one with whom the seller should enter a listing agreement.

The Typical Duration of a Residential Listing Agreement. Most residential listing agreements end in a sale, or expire at a set date. Residential listing agreements usually come with fixed durations—typically six months—renewable at the seller's option. That is the period of time many brokers believe they need to justify the costs of a conscientious marketing effort. State laws often require that exclusive listings have definite dates of termination. Otherwise, the property owner could be stuck with having to pay a commission to a poorly performing broker whose efforts were ineffectual in producing a sale.

---

39. *RealPro, Inc. v Smith Residual Co.,* 203 Cal. App. 4th 1215, 138 Cal. Rptr. 3d 255 (2012).

40. Roger Bernhardt, *Does It Take a Matching Offer, a Signed Contract, or a Complete Closing Before a Cooperating Broker Earns Its Commission?* CEB RPLR (May 2012). http://www.rogerbernhardt.com/index.php/ceb-columns/328-matching-offers-a-brokers-commissions-realpro-v-smith-residual.

The Ideal Termination Provision for the Seller. Sellers may wish to reserve the right to terminate their listing agreements at will. They may simply change their minds about selling, or their life circumstances may change. For example, the quarreling couple contemplating a divorce may reconcile, the employer may cancel plans to relocate the firm, or the seller may be displeased with the broker's efforts and believe it is time for a change.

The Ideal Termination Provision for the Residential Broker. Most brokers want to be sure their listing agreements will not be terminated precipitously. They may spend serious money producing elaborate sales brochures, reaching out to contact lists, staging "open houses," placing advertisements in magazines and newspapers, and incurring major overhead expenditures for quality office space and skilled support staff. So that they can recoup their costs and earn their fees, they want a fair chance to find a buyer and close a sale.

Withdrawal Clause Remedies. Realistically, though, brokers realize the futility of working with a disgruntled seller who has become uncooperative. So they allow termination with a fee, ranging from actual marketing expenses incurred to the date of termination all the way to the full commission the broker would have earned on a consummated sale.

Withdrawal clause remedies vary. Some designate a fixed sum for the seller's premature termination of the listing, often the same amount the broker would have earned had there been a sale.[41] Other agreements limit the seller's liability for withdrawal to the broker's direct marketing expenditures plus a small fixed fee.[42]

When Listing Agreements are Terminable at the Seller's Will. Some residential brokers' listing agreements allow sellers to terminate at will and without penalty. These are rare. As a matter of policy and good customer relations, many brokerage firms will waive their prohibitions against termination and allow sellers to cancel listings if they believe the seller is acting in good faith. They only draw the line when they believe the seller is canceling the listing to squeeze the broker out of a legitimately earned commission.

The brokers who specialize in houses selling for $10,000,000 and up, and office buildings for $50,000,000 or more, do repeat business with prized clients in circles where reputations matter. In their listing agreements, such firms allow sellers to cancel at will, even during escrow—without liability to their brokers, although they may expect reimbursement for expensive marketing materials they prepared before the agreement was cancelled.[43]

---

41. *CMG Realty of Conn., Inc. v. Colonnade One at Old Greenwich*, 653 A.2d 207, 214 (Conn. App. Ct. 1995) (Court refused to enforce $50,000 withdrawal penalty and held it not to be a contract for alternate performance or a liquidated damage fee because sellers would remain liable for actual damages upon wrongful termination of listing agreement).

42. *Compare Blank v. Borden*, 524 P.2d 127 (Cal. 1974), *with Wright v. Schutt Constr. Co.*, 500 P.2d 1045 (Or. 1972).

43. "Commissions shall be payable hereunder at the close of escrow. Owner reserves the right, in its sole discretion, to discontinue negotiations, cancel escrow and/or remove the Property from the

Protection Periods. What brokers fear most is being cheated out of a commission by a seller cancelling the listing in order to make a secret deal with a prospective buyer the seller met through the broker's efforts. One way brokers try to discourage such chicanery is by reserving a protection period in the listing agreement. A protection period preserves the broker's right to a commission when the seller concludes a sale after the listing expires to a buyer introduced to the property while the listing was in effect.[44] Another prophylactic is the anti-withdrawal clause, a staple of residential listing agreement forms.

Responsibility for Security of the Property. During the time that property is marketed for sale, the broker will usually have access to it. Residential brokers use lock boxes, often give cooperating brokers the lock box code, and conduct "open houses" during which anyone can enter the home with no prior security check and no safeguards against theft during the open house. Prospective buyers on broker-organized tours of office buildings when the offices are vacant could be creating an opportunity to access computers and sensitive information.

In the absence of agreements between the seller and the broker, listing brokers would have substantial responsibilities to the seller both as a fiduciary agent and under tort law mandates to use reasonable care in safeguarding the listed property. Standard residential listing agreements prepared by realtors and widely used by brokers exonerate brokers from any responsibilities along these lines. Here is a typical provision, this one from the California Association of Realtors (CAR) Lease Listing Form, paragraph 8 (11/13). An identical provision appears in the residential sale form:

> *Security and Insurance: Broker is not responsible for loss or damage to personal or real property, or person, whether attributable to use of a key safe/lockbox, a showing of the Premises, or otherwise. Third parties, including, but not limited to, inspectors, brokers and prospective tenants, may have access to, and take videos and photographs of, the interior of the Premises. Owner agrees: (i) to take reasonable precautions to safeguard and protect valuables that might be accessible during showings of the Premises, and (ii) to obtain insurance to protect against these risks. Broker does not maintain insurance to protect Owner.*

Compare the above provision to what a commercial real estate attorney's listing agreement form provides. Basically, the broker is obligated to use "the standard of care and diligence as is customary for professional providers of like services within the commercial real estate services industry."

> *Notwithstanding anything to the contrary contained in this Agreement, Client shall not be liable or responsible for any accident, loss, injury, or damage attributable*

---

market at any time prior to the close of escrow without liability or obligation to Broker." CBRE Exclusive Sales Listing Agreement (on file with author).

44. Protection clauses typically obligate the listing broker to deliver to the seller a list of all those to whom the broker introduced the property, and exempt sales for which the seller owes a commission to another licensed broker. Even if the parties defer their sale until after the protection period, the broker who was the procuring cause of the sale is nonetheless entitled to a commission. *Resort Realty of Outer Banks, Inc. v. Brandt*, 163 N. C. App. 114, 593 S.E.2d 404 (2004).

to the extent arising out of the negligence of Broker, its partners, agents, employees, successors, and assigns, occurring or accruing on the Premises in performing the Services during the Term of this Agreement or in connection with this Agreement.

Broker shall and does fully indemnify, protect, defend, and hold harmless Client, Client's shareholders, venture partners, employees, agents, successors, and assigns from and against all liens, demands, liabilities, causes of action, judgments, costs, claims, damages, suits, losses, and expenses, or any combination thereof, including attorneys' fees or any nature, kind, or description ("Liabilities"), of any person or entity whomsoever or, whatsoever, to the extent arising out of, caused by, or resulting from the negligence [of or violation of the terms of this Agreement by] or [or willful misconduct of] Broker, its partners, agents, employees, successors, and assigns.[45]

Consider the consequences of a situation where jewelry is missing from a closet drawer or a company's computer records are compromised after the listing broker allowed access to the seller's property to a person previously convicted of theft and the broker neither keeps reliable records of the names and identities of the people who have had access to the property nor maintains security oversight while strangers are on the premises.

VI. Broker Licensing Requirements

Even if you have no plan to become licensed as a real estate broker, you may want to know something about state broker licensing requirements for a number of reasons. For one, it is unlawful in California, as in many other states, to pay to an unlicensed person a commission for performing services that require a license. There are important exceptions which entitle unlicensed intermediaries to earn fees for bringing buyers and sellers together.

A. State Licensing Laws

1. When Is a Broker's License Required?

Typically, brokers advertise and show properties, help the parties negotiate the deal terms, and oversee closings. In all states, a person or firm needs a broker's license to engage in the business of assisting realty owners, buyers, tenants or lenders to sell, buy, lease or mortgage realty.[46]

Performing Brokerage Services Without a License. Anyone performing brokerage services without a license runs the risk of the client refusing to pay. To sue, the broker needs a license which is ordinarily deemed an essential element of any claim for a

---

45. G. Gosfield, Commercial Real Estate Brokers: Engaging and Disengaging (January 21, 2015), page D-8, http://www.klehr.com/?t=3&A=793&format=xml&Gregory%20G.%20Gosfield.

46. National Association of Real Estate License Law Officials, 1990 Digest of Real Estate License Laws.

commission.[47] A broker practicing without a license, besides not being entitled to a judgment for recovery of commissions,[48] actually commits a criminal offense.[49]

An unlicensed person or entity performing an array of services can lawfully claim compensation for services that did not require a broker's license. For instance, a property management company could legitimately claim payment for the maintenance and repair of an apartment house; these activities require no broker's license. But, the company would not be entitled to commissions for leasing apartments without a broker's license.[50] A financial consultant would have a right to a judgment against a borrower-client for proffering advice on the best available mortgage loan terms because the consultant did not need a broker's license to provide financial advice. But the consultant would not be entitled to payment for arranging a mortgage loan because mortgage originators need licenses.[51]

When the License Lapses. Sometimes, brokers carelessly allow their licenses to lapse, leaving courts to decide whether they were legally entitled to claim a commission for services performed during the lapse. Resolution often depends on the precise wording of the state's licensing law. In some states, brokers will be granted judgments for their commissions as long as they were duly licensed when they began rendering service to a client. In other states, they might need to have a valid license at the moment when they obtained a signed listing agreement from the seller, at the time they present an acceptable offer to the seller, or at closing.[52]

2. Qualifying for a License

Administrative agencies within each state are empowered to issue applications for real estate licenses, to perform background checks of prospective applicants, and give

---

47. "No person engaged in the business or acting in the capacity of a real estate broker or a real estate salesman within this State shall bring or maintain any action in the courts of this State for the collection of compensation for the performance of any of the acts mentioned in this article without alleging and proving that he was a duly licensed real estate broker or real estate salesman at the time the alleged cause of action arose." WEST'S ANN.CAL.BUS. & PROF.CODE § 10136.

48. *In re Kun*, 868 F.2d 1069 (9th Cir. 1989) (salesman ineligible to sue for earned commissions after leaving brokerage firm); *Shehab v. Xanadu Inc.*, 698 S.W.2d 491 (Tex. App. 1985).

49. "It is unlawful for any person to engage in the business, act in the capacity of, advertise or assume to act as a real estate broker or a real estate salesman within this state without first obtaining a real estate license ..." CAL. BUS. & PROF. CODE § 10130. Violators can be brought by the Commissioner of Real Estate "before any court of competent jurisdiction." *Id.*

50. *MKB Management Inc. v. Melikian*, 184 Cal. App. 4th 796 (2010). Real estate licensing law in California does not prohibit unlicensed broker from claiming compensation for services not requiring a license.

51. *Eaton Associates v. Highland Broadcasting Corp.*, 81 App. Div. 2d 603 (1981) (Eaton's financial advice to defendant's employees and officers fell outside the scope of the licensing requirement.) *Kreuter v. Tsucalas*, 287 App. Div. 2d 50 (2001 (Negotiating a lower payoff figure for an existing mortgage did not come within the Real Property Law because he did not facilitate the sale, transfer, or leasing of the property or negotiate the original mortgage.).

52. In California, the statute requires the broker to be licensed at the time the cause of action arises, usually deemed to be the closing or the time when an unconditional purchase and sale contract was formed. CAL. BUS. & PROF. CODE § 10136 (West 1987).

exams to test for competence. No college or graduate degrees are needed for a broker's license though it is a good idea to take a private prep course before sitting for the state exam.

Courts universally uphold the constitutionality of broker licensing laws, accepting the stated legislative purpose to weed out the "untrustworthy" and test for a general knowledge of agency and real estate law.[53]

Courts sometimes overturn administrative denials of licenses that were made without evidence of applicant dishonesty or incompetence. To be used as a basis for license denials, past felony or misdemeanor convictions must bear directly on a broker's job performance.[54] For instance, a broker convicted of driving under the influence of drugs or alcohol might be deemed unfit because brokers often transport buyers to visit properties listed for sale. On the other hand, failure to pay parking tickets might not be probative of professional incompetence.

State real estate commissions are also empowered to suspend or revoke the licenses of brokers and sales people. Disciplinary proceedings often arise from consumer complaints. Brokers eager to safeguard their reputations may strive to find ways to appease unhappy clients before complaints metastasize into formal administrative or legal actions.

B. Exceptions to the Broker License Laws

1. Owners

Most state real estate licensing laws define a broker as someone trying to sell or lease property for another.[55] By implication, owners marketing their own property ("For Sale by Owner," FSBOs) are exempt from broker licensing laws.

---

53. *Roman v. Lobe*, 152 N. E. 461, 462–63 (N.Y. 1926). Most states require out of state brokers to work with local brokers, splitting commissions between them. A few states ban in-state licensees from splitting commissions with agents licensed out of state, permitting payment of referral fees but not commissions to out of state licensees. A federal court held such a ban in Kentucky to violate the dormant commerce clause. *River Oaks Management, LLC v. Brown*, 2007 WL 2571909 (W.D. Ky. 2007). ("While licensure protects the public from unscrupulous and incompetent brokers, the court cannot discern how prohibiting cooperation between an out-of-state broker and a Kentucky licensed broker reinforces this protection if the Kentucky licensed broker oversees the interstate transaction. Instead, it appears that the prohibitions' main purpose is to ensure that virtually all commissions are kept in Kentucky. This is achieved, however, at an unconstitutional cost to interstate commerce.").

54. A California real estate broker, a certified pilot, flew a small plane from Mexico to the Central Valley that was stocked with nearly 1,000 pounds of marijuana. The broker was caught and pled guilty to felony possession of marijuana for sale. The DRE revoked the broker's license based on the conviction, although he was issued a restricted salesman's license. The reviewing court emphasized the dishonesty aspect of selling drugs in upholding the decision. *Goolde v. Fox*, 98 Cal. App. 3d 167 (1979).

55. *Xarin Real Estate Inc. v. Gamboa*, 715 S.W.2d 80 (Tex. App. 1986). Xarin assigned its contract to purchase an apartment complex to a condo converter. Later, the converter sued Xarin and Xarin's seller, Gamboa, after discovering the complex contained less square footage than promised. Among other claims, Gamboa and the converter contended that Xarin had acted as a broker, without a broker's license. The appellate court ruled that Xarin didn't require a broker's license to sell property it had

The purpose of the licensing laws is to protect the public against amateurs posing as qualified professionals. Owners aren't doing that when trying to market their own houses. They are acting solely for their own benefit. There is also a managers' exception covering home builders' employees showing and selling the firm's houses and apartment managers leasing units for their landlords. A home builder's employees who are promised bonuses based on their sales or leasing success are not barred by broker licensing laws from suing for their promised compensation.

2. Finders

Finders often claim and are sometimes able to collect commissions without a broker's license.[56] A finder, like a matchmaker, is someone who introduces the parties, but leaves them to negotiate and implement the deal on their own. "A more precise designation for a finder would appear to be an 'intermediary' or a 'middleman.'"[57]

Besides being unlicensed, what distinguishes finders from brokers is that after bringing the parties together, they jeopardize their claim to a finder's fee by becoming involved in negotiating the price, or any of the other terms of the transaction, or participating in processing the transaction to closing.

A person who starts out as a finder and strays, however slightly, into negotiating or closing the sale, inadvertently transforms herself into the unenviable status of practicing brokerage without a license.[58] This gives the principal a chance to repudiate her promise to pay a finder's fee even in situations where, had the finder not intervened, the deal would have collapsed.

Another characteristic of finder status is that the principal may change his mind and revoke it at will with impunity anytime before the finder performs the promised feat of producing a ready, willing and able buyer.[59]

Many state courts flatly refuse to fashion a loophole in their brokerage licensing statutes for finders.[60] Other state courts enthusiastically enforce seller promises to pay unlicensed intermediaries finders' fees to prevent their being taken advantage of by

---

acquired for its own account, citing the 'for another' language in the Texas brokers' license law, Tex. Rev. Civ. Stat. Ann. art. 6573a, §2(2) (Vernon Supp. 1987).

56. *Tuohey & Barton v. Anaheim Mem. Hosp.*, 231 Cal. Rptr. 706 (Ct. App. 1986).

57. *Evans v. Riverside Intern. Raceway*, 47 Cal. Rptr. 187, 193, 237 Cal. App. 2d 666, 676 (1965).

58. *Evans*, 47 Cal. Rptr. at 193 (quoting 9 Cal. Jur. 2d §26, 164); *see also* D. Barlow Burke, Law of Real Estate Brokers §4.5.2, at 212–14 (2d ed. 1982).

59. *Evans*, 47 Cal. Rptr. at 193.

60. *Diversified Gen. Corp. v. White Barn Golf Course, Inc.*, 584 P.2d 848 (Utah 1978). The court took this position so that Utah's licensing statute would not be a 'toothless enactment,' allowing unlicensed finders to engage in what they saw as the practice of brokering. *See also Brakhage v. Georgetown Assocs.*, 523 P.2d 145 (Colo. Ct. App. 1974); *First Equity Corp. of Fla. v. Riverside Real Estate Inv. Trust*, 307 So. 2d 866 (Fla. Dist. Ct. App. 1975); *Gregory v. Roedenbeck*, 174 S.W.2d 585 (Tex. 1943); *Swor v. Tapp Furniture Co.*, 146 S.W.3d 778 (Tex. Ct. App. 2004) (finder's fee denied for sale of funeral home since intermediary had no real estate broker's license and no written agreement from seller authorizing payment of a commission for the sale of realty even though the sale also involved items of personal property not covered by real estate license law); *Baird v. Krancer*, 246 N.Y.S. 85 (Sup. Ct. 1930); *Corson v. Keane*, 72 A.2d 314 (N.J. 1950).

knowledgeable buyers or sellers benefitting from their services and then shirking clearly made promises to pay for their assistance.[61] Perhaps courts figure that finders don't need the competence, training, and professionalism required of brokers as long as they haven't stepped over the line into broker territory by negotiating contract terms, drafting the purchase and sale agreement, or closing the deal.

3. Attorneys

Most states do not provide an exemption from brokerage licensing laws for attorneys.[62] Among those few states which do, some totally exempt attorneys from broker licensing laws while others including California only exempt attorneys acting within the scope of their duties as attorneys.[63] Under the total exemption, an attorney could enforce a client's promise to pay a brokerage or finders' fee as long as the attorney only acted as a broker occasionally.[64] Attorneys covered by the more limited exemption can never file suit to compel payment for rendering brokerage services without a broker's license.

In all states, attorneys can become licensed as real estate brokers, but in most states they cannot legitimately represent a client both as an attorney and as a real estate broker in the same transaction. In these states, broker-attorneys must find ways of building and maintaining impervious walls separating their legal from their brokerage services to make sure clients understand and accept the distinct nature of the services being rendered. Some practitioners create literal walls by keeping offices, records and support staff completely separate for legal and brokerage services. Similarly, attorneys expecting to earn finders' fees by introducing buyer and seller need to make clear their role in the transaction is as a finder, not as an attorney.

With the client's informed consent,[65] some states allow attorneys to represent a buyer or seller while acting as the same party's broker in the transaction. In order to

---

61. Don Augustine & Peter Fass, *Finder's Fees in Security & Real Estate Transactions*, 35 Bus. Law. 485, 489 (1980). *Sammarone v. Bovino*, 395 N.J. Super. 132, 928 A.2d 140 (App. Div. 2007). Buyers could be liable for promised commission after unlicensed intermediary introduced them to seller with whom they concluded a sale.

62. *See, e.g., Tobin v. Courshon*, 155 So. 2d 785 (Fla. 1963) (attorney hired to locate land for buyer, though authorized by buyer to share brokerage fee, had no right to a brokerage fee, not being a licensed broker, except as compensation for legal services). In New York, however, an attorney who is not licensed as a real estate broker may act as co-broker with a licensed real estate broker and share the brokerage commission. N.Y. Real Prop. §442(f) ("the provisions of this Article shall not apply to ... attorneys at law"). The attorney exemption in New Jersey has been held only to allow attorneys to perform brokerage services incidental or ancillary to the normal practice of law, never for a brokerage commission. *In re Roth*, 577 A.2d 490 (N.J. 1990) (interpreting N.J.S.A. 45:15-4). New Jersey attorneys have no right to collect brokerage commissions without a broker's license.

63. J.P. Sawyer, *When Does An Attorney Need a Real Estate License?*, 17 J. Legal Prof. 329 (1992).

64. *Atlantic Richfield Co. v. Sybert*, 456 A.2d 20, 295 Md. 347 (1983) (attorney could enforce the seller's promise to pay a customary brokerage commission when attorney found a buyer even though attorney was not licensed as a broker and acted as a dual agent with knowledge and implied consent of both parties).

65. *Iowa Supreme Court Bd. of Prof'l Ethics & Conduct v. John C. Wagner*, 599 N.W.2d 721, 728 (Iowa 1999) (attorneys acting as brokers should insist their clients secure independent counsel).

secure the client's informed consent, the lawyer needs to disclose how his or her business interest in the transaction could inhibit offering the kind of independent, unbiased advice clients might expect. Professor Roger Bernhardt cautions that just because attorneys can earn legal fees and a broker's commission in the same deal does not mean it is a smart thing to do. As a seller's broker, for instance, the attorney would owe a duty to the buyer to disclose known defects in a home sale, a disclosure quite inconsistent with attorney's duty to preserve client confidences.

VII. Examples of Brokers' Legal Duties Owed to Their Clients and Counter Parties

A. Brokers' Fiduciary Obligations to Clients

Brokers are regarded as fiduciaries of their clients. A fiduciary owes his or her principal the highest ethical standard, "utmost good faith, integrity, honesty, and loyalty in her transactions with her principal."[66] Fiduciaries are never supposed to place their own interests above those of their clients, are expected to carry out their responsibilities with appropriate skill and dispatch, and relay promptly to their clients all relevant information.

Here are a few specific illustrations of the broker's fiduciary obligations:

Brokers' Fiduciary Obligation to Offer Accurate Pricing Advice. Sellers look to brokers for advice regarding the price at which the property should be listed for sale. Brokers often respond by preparing a comparative market analysis of recently sold, similar properties. Because of their fiduciary relationship to the seller, brokers must be careful not to over or undervalue the property and may be held accountable to the seller for incompetent advice.[67]

Many brokers cannot resist the temptation to overvalue property when they are pitching a seller for a listing. Naively, sellers assume that the higher the price a broker claims the property to be worth, the higher the price the broker will be able to produce.

Sometimes, just the opposite is true. Prospective buyers tend not to waste their time bidding on properties listed at unrealistically high prices. Prospective buyers and their brokers can easily see how long a property has been on the market, and avoid "stale" properties, figuring the asking price is too high or there are other good reasons the property has lingered on the market for such a long time. "The flavor of the warnings against over-pricing is well-captured by an article from About.com with

---

66. *Perkins v. Thorpe*, 676 P.2d 52, 54–55, 106 Idaho 138 (Ct. App. 1984).

67. *Snead v. McCaskey*, 1997 WL 402396 (Ohio Ct. App. 1997) (Seller's estate overturned summary judgment for agent in listing brokers' office who had purchased "tear down" for $40,000, the listing broker's estimate of value given to the seller, invested $60,000 in repairs and sold it for $142,000. Issues of negligence, intentional misconduct and breach of fiduciary duty raise questions of fact requiring a trial.).

the attention-grabbing headline, 'The Worst Home Selling Mistake.' The article relates the history of a specific house that according to the author never sold due to agent inexperience and seller greed. It is now '... stale, dated, a market-worn home that was over-priced for too long.' "[68] The broker who obtains a listing by overvaluing the property that attracts few if any inquiries or requests to show the property will try to persuade the seller to reduce the asking price later, and most sellers do.

There is some empirical evidence that higher listing prices tend to lead to higher selling prices. This is due to a process called "anchoring." Research suggests that even irrelevant numbers influence buyers' judgments of what a property is worth.

Conversely underpricing would be an effective strategy for the seller due to a phenomenon called "herding." Properties listed at bargain prices tend to attract multiple bidders all looking to bag a good deal, maybe one so good they could re-sell it at a profit. The ensuing excitement can lead to bidding wars—yielding prices higher than the seller would have realized through any other strategy.

"Thus the question of whether a seller ought to price a good relatively high or relatively low in the context of a consequential information-rich market transaction remains very much unanswered."[69] The best recent evidence, though, is that in hot real estate markets, there is no discernible herding effect. Underpriced properties may sell more quickly but they sell at lower prices than if they had been listed higher.[70]

Brokers attempt to deflect the onus of over or underpricing by relying on explicit exoneration language in the form listing agreement.[71]

Brokers' Fiduciary Obligation to Seller When Broker Buys the Property Listed. No rule prohibits brokers from making an offer on properties they list as long as the seller knows the offer comes from the broker, and the broker has divulged to the seller all she knows about the value and other salient characteristics of the property. To avoid claims of undue influence, before buying one of their own listings, brokers should advise the seller to verify the reasonableness of the broker's offer through an independent appraisal made by someone with no connection to the broker.

Once the seller accepts the broker's offer, must the broker relinquish her right to compensation under the listing immediately? It is difficult to see how the broker can

---

68. Grace W. Bucchianeri & Julia Minson, *A Homeowner's Dilemma: Anchoring in Residential Real Estate Transactions.* http://opim.wharton.upenn.edu/DPlab/papers/publishedPapers/Bucchianeri_2012_Home%20buyers%20are%20not%20a%20herd.pdf.

69. *Ibid.* note 69.

70. *Ibid.* note 69.

71. The California Association of Realtors residential purchase agreement: "Buyer and Seller acknowledge and agree that Brokers ... do not decide what price Buyer should pay or Seller should accept." Does this language exonerate brokers from liability for faulty price advice? Doubtful. It isn't clear exculpatory language, appears in a contract to which brokers are expressly not a party, flouts the broker's obligation to inform the seller of comparable sales, and removes from the trier of fact the issue of whether the broker's opinion of value should be characterized as a statement of fact because of the broker's presumed competence.

continue to serve diligently as the seller's fiduciary once the broker has become the buyer. But brokers often do this—and pocket the commissions—because they believe they are acting in the seller's best interest by becoming buyers. Of course, this position is more convincing when the broker buys the property after it has lingered on the market for a long time.

Sometimes a broker purchases underpriced property on which she has taken the listing or arranges for friends, relatives or employees to buy it. Then, the broker promptly resells the property for a quick profit, concealing the bonanza from the seller. Brokers are legally obligated to disclose both ends of these transactions to the seller, their purchase and the resale.[72]

Brokers' Obligation to Avoid Indiscriminate Disclosures. Fiduciaries are supposed to honor their principal's confidences and avoid indiscriminate disclosures,[73] including the willingness of the seller to accept less than the asking price.[74]

There is an exception when the agent discloses confidential information strategically to advance the client's interest in buying or selling. So, for instance, a listing broker would be ill advised to tell a prospective buyer that the seller recently made a counteroffer, ultimately rejected, at 15% off the list price. Instead, the seller's broker might encourage the buyer to make an offer at a price below list so the seller would have the opportunity of considering it.

B. Brokers' Professional Obligations to Counter Parties

Brokers' Obligation Not to Deceive or Mislead Counter Parties. Listing brokers are fiduciaries of the seller but not of the buyer. Exclusive buyers' brokers are fiduciaries of the buyer but not of the seller. But all brokers are bound by professional standards of conduct even when bad behavior might advance their clients' interests. In all their dealings, brokers are always held to professional standards of honesty, trustworthiness, and competence. Not being bound to treat the other party to the transaction as a fiduciary does not free sellers' brokers to mislead buyers, or absolve buyers' brokers from liability for misleading sellers.

A listing broker who owns an interest in the listed property needs to disclose that fact to potential buyers.

---

72. F. G. Madara, Annotation, *Duty of Real Estate Broker to Disclose That Prospective Purchaser Is a Relative*, 26 A.L.R. 2d 1307 (1952). "[W]here the broker effects a sale of the vendor's property to his partner, or to a firm in which the broker himself owns an interest, such fact not being revealed to the vendor, or where the property is sold by an employee of the broker without the knowledge of the broker to a nominal purchaser with the intention of a secret resale later at a profit, the cases have usually been resolved in favor of the vendor, and brokers have been denied commissions." C.E. Basham, Annotation, *Duty of Real-Estate Broker to Disclose Identity of Purchaser or Lessee*, 2 A.L.R. 3d 1119 (1966).

73. Molly Moore Romero, *Theories of Real Estate Broker Liability: Arizona's Emerging Malpractice Doctrine*, 20 ARIZ. L. REV. 767, 774 (1978) (paraphrasing RESTATEMENT (SECOND) OF AGENCY §§ 367–77, 379–81, 383, 387–91, 394–95 (1957)).

74. Jeffrey M. Sharp, *Digest of Selected Articles*, 28 REAL EST. L. J. 368, 370 (2000).

Any broker making an offer to purchase listed property for herself needs to reveal her status as a broker to the seller. So does any broker with an interest in the entity that is making an offer to purchase listed property.

Sometimes, in an overzealous effort to market the seller's property, listing brokers may be tempted to exaggerate or lie about how the sales effort has been going. When they do and are caught, they can end up paying a steep price for their transgressions. For example, a listing broker coaxes a bidder into offering a higher price by claiming there is a competing buyer when, in fact, there is none. Or a leasing broker marketing space in a newly opened shopping mall lures a potential tenant by claiming "available space is going fast" and the center is 85% occupied when, in fact, the center is 70% vacant. The tenant's shop opens up but soon goes dark because there isn't enough foot traffic to justify keeping the place open.

Later, caught in their lies, brokers could be made to disgorge their commissions, and also become liable for the buyers' and tenants' losses.[75] The broker would be liable to the deceived bidder for the excess purchase price paid in the mistaken belief there was a competing bidder.[76]

An entirely different situation arises once the broker manages to snare a legitimate offer. At that point, the listing broker, with the seller's consent, is free to 'shop' the offer by disclosing it to motivate other bidders.[77]

Listing Brokers' Obligation to Alert Buyers of Property Defects. Most states require a listing broker (even though representing only the seller) to tell the buyer any facts "materially affecting the value or desirability of the property offered for sale, facts known or accessible only to him [and his principal], and not within the reach of the diligent attention and observation of the buyer."[78] It may be painful for the listing broker to disclose to prospective buyers serious defects in the seller's property. Even so, listing brokers are generally held accountable to buyers for failing to disclose fully all material, latent, known defects. Brokers are required to disclose information about property defects to buyers, even when the seller instructed the broker not to, because sellers themselves have no right to withhold such information from their buyers.[79]

---

75. *Pancakes of Haw., Inc. v. Pomare Props. Corp.*, 944 P.2d 97 (Haw. Ct. App. 1997).

76. *Beavers v. Lamplighters Realty*, 556 P.2d 1328 (Okla. 1976).

77. *See, e.g., Walter v. Murphy*, 573 N.E.2d 678 (Ohio Ct. App. 1988) (The listing broker owes no fiduciary duty to the buyer. The competing bidder had been the offeror's listing broker on the sale of their house. That broker owed them a fiduciary duty only in fulfilling his obligations regarding that listing. He was free to compete against his former clients on other properties.).

78. *Lingsch v. Savage*, 29 Cal. Rptr. 201, 204 (Ct. App. 1963); *see also Ditcharo v. Stepanek*, 538 So. 2d 309 (La. Ct. App. 1989) (broker owes duty to both parties to relay accurate information about the property).

79. Charles P. Edmonds & Rudolph Lindbeck, *How Brokers Can Reduce Vulnerability to Lawsuits*, 17 REAL EST. REV. 90 (Spring 1987); Carol R. Goforth, *Sales of Structurally Defective Homes: The Potential Liability of Sellers and Real Estate Brokers*, 41 OKLA. L. REV. 447 (1988); Diane M. Allen, Annotation, *Real Estate-Broker's Liability to Purchaser for Misrepresentation or Nondisclosure of Physical Defects in Property Sold*, 46 A.L.R. 4th 546 (1986). Craig A. Peterson, *Tort Claims by Real Estate Purchasers Against Sellers and Brokers: Current Illinois Common Law and Statutory Strategies*, 1983 So. ILL. L. J. 161 (1983).

Listing Brokers Held Obligated to Alert Buyers Before They Signed a Purchase and Sale Contract of Sellers' Financial Incapacity to Convey Unencumbered Title. In *Holmes v. Summers,*[80] prospective buyers contracted to purchase a home for $749,000. The sale was to close in 30 days. Once the buyers signed the contract, they sold their house and made plans to relocate.

Afterwards, the buyers learned that their deal with the seller would never close because the seller's title was subject to three mortgage liens totaling $1,141,000. To deliver the promised title, the seller would have had to come up with $392,000 in cash at closing, or convince the lenders to reduce their liens by that amount.

The sellers' broker in the Holmes case knew this, and was held liable in negligence to the buyers for failing to disclose before they signed the contract.

The seller's broker had argued that the buyers would have had the right to terminate the contract upon reviewing the title information they would have received soon after the contract was signed. The appellate court explained that this was not good enough because brokers should realize that buyers seldom know anything about the liens against the properties they are contracting to buy. They deserve forewarning from the seller's broker who knows the seller is not in a position to fulfill his side of a contract bargain that buyers are about to sign.

C. When Is A Real Estate Offering a Security?

Only a licensed security broker is legally entitled to sell a security. Hence, real estate brokers need to know whether they have become involved in representing clients who are buying or selling securities.

The consequences of violating securities laws can be serious, and ignorance of the law is no defense. Real estate promoters and the professionals who assist them are open to criminal and civil charges brought by government agencies. Also, when deals fail, investors in unregistered securities are entitled to refunds.

Consider these two examples.

(1) A condo buyer asks a real estate broker for help in finding a condo that would be a good investment as a rental with eventual appreciation.

(2) A real estate entrepreneur, hoping to find an investor to provide equity to enable her to acquire a particular commercial rental property, asks a real estate broker to help find an equity investor/partner for the transaction.

Are either the entrepreneur or the condo buyer asking the broker for assistance with a transaction involving a security?

The courts have defined a security or 'investment contract' as an interest with these characteristics: (1) an investment of money; (2) with the expectation of profit; (3) in reliance on the efforts of others to realize that profit; and (4) in a 'common enterprise.'

---

80. 188 CAL. APP. 4th 1510 (2010).

Both the entrepreneur's equity investor and the condo buyer would be investing money with the expectation of profit. But neither of them would be deemed to be relying on the efforts of others to realize a profit if they received title to a particular property which they could sell at will. The condo buyer would almost certainly be taking title. But the equity investor's exit options would depend on the terms of the arrangement with the entrepreneur.[81]

Exemptions. There are many exemptions from securities law registration requirements based on the type of security offered or the nature of the transaction. For most entrepreneurs, the most practical exemption is the one based on Securities Act Section 4(2) for transactions "not involving any public offering."

Although the statute offers no definition of "public offering," SEC regulations and case law fill the void. A and B getting together jointly to invest in a deal are not making a "public offering."

Generally, case law protects offerings acquired by purchasers who are wealthy enough to 'fend for themselves,' and sufficiently sophisticated to evaluate the merits and risks of the deal. Rule 506 of Regulation D provides a 'safe harbor' for promoters relying on the private placement exemption. In any event, each offeree must receive or have access to information comparable to what would be disclosed in a registration statement and the same anti-fraud rules apply as if the offering were registered.

Questions

Question 1: *Decision to Use a Broker.*

(a) Explain to a friend who is about to sell her home, and wants to save money on a brokerage commission, what she would have to do to succeed in a "For Sale By Owner" (FSBO) situation, forgoing the help of a qualified, competent broker?

(b) Why do most home sellers who start out as FSBOs end up selling their properties through a broker?

(c) In addition to the reasons that home owners probably do better with brokers than without them, what other reasons could persuade the owner of, say, a small hotel, to list with a broker?

Question 2: *Broker Licensing Laws.*

(a) How do consumers benefit from broker licensing laws?

---

81. "Some states have adopted special rules for determining whether membership interests in an LLC are to be treated as securities under their blue sky laws. For example, the New Mexico blue sky laws include "any interest in a limited liability company" and "any limited partnership interest" in its definition of a "security." N.M. Stat. Ann. § 58-13B-2(X). See also Uniform Securities Act § 102(28)(E), 7C U.L.A. 28-29 (2002) (including within the definition of an investment contract "an interest in a limited partnership and a limited liability company"). The blue sky laws of the state of residence of each member acquiring a membership interest in an LLC should be reviewed to determine the extent to which they apply to the LLC membership interests being issued." Report, Joint Task Force on Model Real Estate Development Operating Agreement with Commentary, 63 Bus. Law. 385, fn 3 (Feb., 2008).

(b) Why do state laws permit home owners to market their own homes even though they have no real estate licenses?

(c) A second-year law student learns that her landlord wants to sell the apartment building in which she resides, and she happens to know someone who might be interested in buying it. Although she doesn't have a broker's license, under what conditions might she be able to enforce the landlord's oral promise to pay her a fee if she locates a suitable buyer?

Question 3: *Negotiating the Terms of the Listing Agreement.*

(a) What is the main distinction among the types of listings: exclusive rights to sell, exclusive agencies, and open listings?

(b) How can a seller, about to list her home, avoid having to pay a commission if her next door neighbor, who has long expressed a keen interest in acquiring the property, becomes her buyer?

(c) A couple on the verge of dissolving their relationship decide to list the home they own together. Shortly after they sign an exclusive right to sell agreement with a licensed real estate broker, they reconcile and decide not to sell the house after all. Under the terms of California Association of Realtors Listing Agreement, they owe their broker the full commission for withdrawal, even though she has yet to produce a single offer.[82] Under these circumstances, why might a prudent broker decide to waive her rights to a commission under the withdrawal clause?

(d) If you were advising a home or condo owner about what to include in a listing agreement, would you cut and paste the numbered items that appear in the list of functions of residential seller's brokers?

(e) A seller insists upon modifying the listing agreement to insert a "no closing, no commission" clause, applicable even if the seller rejected a full price offer, or signed a purchase contract and later prevented the closing. The broker balks, asking why the seller should not be obligated to pay the broker a commission after the broker did her part by producing a full price offer, or an offer the seller accepted, and then caused the sale not to close. How could the seller possibly justify such a modification?

(f) The seller, a busy accountant, has owned a 20-unit apartment house for seven years. It produces a steady positive cash flow but the seller has never had much luck with resident managers, and is now on his third one. He lists the building for sale and a buyer from out of state makes a full price offer. The buyer had the idea of residing in the building and managing the place herself. Buyer and seller sign a purchase and sale agreement.

During the due diligence period, the buyer presents a long list of improvements she insists upon the seller making. If asked, she would say these are previously undis-

---

82. Available at https://www.pdffiller.com/6961590—Association-realtors-agreement-form-User-Forms. The withdrawal-without-broker-consent provision requiring payment of the full listing price is in the CAR Residential Listing Agreement (11/10 version) at paragraph 4(A)(3).

closed property defects. To take one example, there are hairline cracks at various places in the building. The buyer wants the seller to pay for an engineer to determine if the building is sound. Even if it is, she wants the seller to paint the building. The building was repainted three years ago and looks just fine to the seller. The seller refuses to comply with the buyer's requests or to continue dealing with her.

What language in the listing agreement would the buyer's broker wish to see to preserve the right to a commission if the seller repudiates the purchase and sale contract?

What language would the seller hope to find in the listing agreement to remove any doubt that he has any obligation for a brokerage commission if he calls the deal off because the buyer is too annoying and unreasonable to continue dealing with?

(g) A friend or family member is about to list their home for sale with a broker. The standard form listing agreement calls for payment of the full commission if the property is withdrawn from sale or leased during the term of the listing. The same agreement disavows liability for the negligence of the broker and its agents even though the agreement calls for a lock box allowing any broker or agent with the lock box number to enter the property. You suggest to your friend or family member that they insist upon the listing agreement containing a right to cancel at will, and use the same assumption-of-negligence form for commercial realty that appears in the text. Can you imagine any convincing reasons that would justify a broker refusing to accommodate these requests?

(h) A seller proposes to strike language in the listing agreement making him liable for a commission if he causes a purchase and sale contract not to close. The broker asks why she should forego a commission she earned by finding a "ready, willing, and able" buyer because the seller derailed the sale. Should the seller acquiesce? If not, is there any coherent way to explain his refusal?

(i) Interviewing potential brokers, the seller hears Broker A explain that although the property is worth about $400,000, it should be listed at $350,000 to spur potential buyers into making offers, eventually engaging in a bidding war with each other. Broker B agrees that the property is worth about $400,000 but recommends listing it at $450,000. For one thing, buyers like to haggle over price. For another, the higher the listing agreement pegs the price, the higher the eventual sales price is likely to be. If you believe either broker is right, explain why. If you believe neither is correct, what listing price would you regard as optimal for the seller?

Question 4: *Buyers and Their Brokers.*

Based on what you have read in this chapter, would you recommend to a friend about to look for her first home to contract with an exclusive buyers' broker, sign a dual agency agreement with the listing broker, work with as many brokers as are willing to assist her with no strings attached, or go it alone?

Question 5: *Obligations of Listing Broker to Sellers and Buyers.*

An office building seller, after signing a binding purchase and sale contract, confesses to his broker that the heating and air conditioning system will probably need to be replaced in the next year or two, and the building's major tenant is about to file bankruptcy and go out of business. The seller wants the broker to keep these facts to herself. Does the broker have any obligation to disclose this information to the buyer?

Question 6: *Buyers' Broker's Duty to Buyers and Sellers.*

A buyer's broker knows that her clients, the buyers, have a seriously flawed credit history and may have great difficulty obtaining a mortgage loan. Does she owe the seller a duty to pass along this information?

Question 7: *When Brokers Buy Their Own Listings.*

A seller doesn't realize how much the house is worth, and lists it for sale with a broker at a price considerably below market. Under what conditions is the listing broker free to buy it without having to worry about the seller later suing successfully for the lost profit?

Question 8: *When Is a Realty Sale A Security?*

An architect-developer buys 'fixer uppers' in good neighborhoods, refurbishes them and sells them, usually for tidy profits. To attract equity investors, he solicits friends and from time to time runs ads in newspapers including the Wall Street Journal.

(a) He usually lists his houses for sale with the same real estate broker. He asks the broker to find investors for him. Would the broker need to be licensed to sell securities in order to help in this way?

(b) Would the architect-developer need to comply with federal and state securities laws?

Chapter 4

Entity Selection: Limited Liability, Tax Issues, Operating Agreement Deal Points and Fiduciary Duties[1]

Scope of the Chapter

Real estate promoters and investors select an entity for taking and holding title to real estate. In this chapter we compare these entities:

A. Sole Proprietorship

B. C Corporation

C. General Partnership

D. Joint Venture

E. Tenancy in Common

F. Limited Liability Company (LLC)[2]

G. Limited Partnership (LP)

H. S Corporation

I. Real Estate Investment Trust (REIT)

After reviewing the main features of these entities, we focus on two aspects of particular interest to real estate investors in entity selection: (1) the role of the selected

---

1. Substantial contributions to text and examples in this chapter came from Ed Barkett '91, Terrence F. Cuff '77, Adam Handler, and Tom Muller.

2. Mary Siegel, Publicly Traded LLCs: The New Kid on the Exchange, 68 SMU L. Rev. 885 (2015). For publicly held real estate firms—those that are widely traded on securities exchanges or in secondary markets, the entities of choice are corporations and real estate investment trusts, though some publicly traded real estate equity firms have chosen limited partnership (Blackstone) or limited liability company formats (Fortress, Och-Ziff). Mohsen Manesh, Legal Asymmetry and the End of Corporate Law, 34 Del. J. Corp. L. 465 (2009). As of September 2013, there were 20 publicly-traded LLCs. Suren Gomtsian, The Governance of Publicly Traded Limited Liability Companies 9 (Tilberg Law and Economics Center, Discussion Paper No. 2014-008, 2014).

entity in protecting project promoters and investors from personal liability for entity debts, and (2) entity tax advantages and drawbacks.

To show how these various factors come together, in the concluding section of the chapter, we introduce a hypothetical transaction in which a developer and her equity investor, teaming up to build a multi-family project, work through a list of the main deal points forming the basis for their Limited Liability Company (LLC) operating agreement.

I. Seven Entities Compared

In this section, we compare the first seven entities above. The last two — S Corporations and Real Estate Investment Trusts — we reserve for a later section on tax issues because these entities are purely tax code-created entities.

A. Sole Proprietorship

Description. Sole proprietorships are technically not entities at all; the term refers to owners running their own businesses. They are easy to start and free of the legal constraints applicable to corporations, limited partnerships or limited liability companies.

Fictitious Name Statutes. Still, the sole proprietor needs to comply with minimal local registration, business license, and permit laws. These include registering under state fictitious business name statutes. Depending on the particular state statute, registration may be with a state agency or with each county recorder where the proprietorship does business.

Typical of similar statutes in many states, a Florida statute makes not registering under the fictitious name statute a misdemeanor, and disqualifies a proprietor from maintaining a lawsuit. (Failure to register a fictitious name and obtain a license does not invalidate contracts.[3])

Duration. Sole proprietorships have no fixed duration. The proprietorship enterprise terminates when the proprietor sells, decides to terminate the business, or dies. "This is a striking contrast to the restrictions on duration imposed by other entity choices."[4]

B. C Corporation[5]

Corporate Decision Making Formalities. To protect shareholders against incompetent or dishonest management, legislators promulgated statutory regimens modeled

---

3. 8 Fla. Prac. Constr. Law Manual § 1:2 (2015–2016 ed.).

4. *Choice of Entity for Considerations for Real Estate Investors,* EXETER (last visited May 17, 2016) http://www.exeter1031.com/choice_of_entity_considerations.aspx

5. The name "C Corporation" derives from Subchapter C, 26 U.S. Code. For an introduction to forming a corporation, see Beth Laurence, *How to Form a Corporation, NOLO* (last visited May 17, 2016) https://www.nolo.com/legal-encyclopedia/form-corporation-how-to-incorporate-30030.html

after constitutional democracies. Shareholders were empowered—one vote per share—to elect a board of directors. The directors were to serve at the will of the shareholder-owners and to oversee management in the best interests of the shareholders. Sometimes, though, managers serve their own interests ahead of shareholder interests.[6] As a preventive back-stop, statutes also impose non-waivable *fiduciary duties* upon corporate boards and officers to safeguard a corporation's assets.[7]

Close Corporations. "A close corporation is generally a smaller corporation that elects close corporation status and is therefore entitled to operate without the strict formalities normally required in the operation of standard corporations. Many small-business owners find this benefit invaluable. In essence, a close corporation is a corporation whose shareholders and directors are entitled to operate much like a *partnership.* The close corporation election is made at the state level, and state laws vary with respect to the eligibility of close corporation status and with respect to the rules governing them. Some states do not authorize them."[8]

C. General Partnership

General Characteristics. A general partnership is defined as two or more persons carrying on a business for profit as co-owners. Whether a partnership exists is a *question of fact.* Determinative factors include whether the co-venturers participated in management, agreed to share profits and losses, and contributed something of value in exchange for an interest in the joint enterprise, such as cash, personal services, land, or other assets.

The general partnership is the presumed "default" entity of choice unless the founders explicitly chose another type of entity for doing business together.

Most states have enacted some version of the Uniform Partnership Act (UPA) or the Revised Uniform Partnership Act (RUPA). Generally their provisions only set default rules that the partners are free to modify by agreement.

Partnership Agreements and Statutory Default Rules. Partnership agreements are useful, though not necessary, to the formation of a partnership. "Every *partnership*

---

6. For many publicly traded, large corporations, the governance model has proved flawed. See Lucian Bebchuk & Jesse Fried, Pay Without Performance: The Unfulfilled Promise of Executive Compensation 207-08 (2004); Lucian A. Bebchuk, The Myth of the Shareholder Franchise, 93 Va. L. Rev. 675, 676–87 (2007).

7. See generally, Andrew D. Shaffer, *Corporate Fiduciary—Insolvent: The Fiduciary Relationship Your Corporate Law Professor (Should Have) Warned You About* 8 Am. Bankr. Inst. L. Rev. 479, 499–506 (Winter, 2000).

8. Michael Spadaccini, *What Is A 'Close Corporation'?* Entrepreneur (last visited May 20, 2016) https://www.entrepreneur.com/article/78032 There has been a considerable difference of opinion about whether the fiduciary duties that partners owe each other should be grafted into close corporation law, or whether the fiduciary duties of close corporation shareholders to each other should be the same as those corporate shareholders generally. See Mary Siegel, *Fiduciary Duty Myths in Close Corporate Law,* 29 Del. J. Corp. L. 377 (2004) (contending that the partnership model will and should eventually prevail).

agreement is a compromise between time, patience, money, and the need to consider reasonably expected events in the *partnership's* future."[9] The default rule is that partners share profits equally after repayment of the initial contributions to the partnership and no partner has the right to receive compensation for services performed for the partnership, unless the other partners have specifically agreed in writing.[10]

Sale of Partnership Property. Partnerships may hold title to real property in the name of the partnership. Partnership property may be sold by agreement, upon termination of the partnership, the bankruptcy of a partner or of the partnership, a court order responding favorably to a partner's petition to dissolve the partnership, or the death of a partner.

"A partner is not a co-owner of partnership property and has no interest in partnership property that can be transferred, either voluntarily or involuntarily."[11] The only transferable interest of a partner in the partnership is the partner's share of the profits and losses of the partnership and the partner's *right to receive distributions.* The partnership interest is personal property."[12]

Any partner is deemed empowered to bind the partnership by selling partnership assets *in the usual conduct of the partnership's business.* Suppose a partnership was in the business of selling real estate, as are tract homebuilders. Any partner would presumably be entitled to sell houses. Conversely, if the partnership was in the business of acquiring houses exclusively as rental properties, no partner would have the right to sell the house without all of the partners agreeing to a sale.[13]

A Comparison of Corporate and Partnership "Default" Characteristics. The legal norms governing partnership operations are quite different from those of corporations. Unlike the separation of ownership and control that is characteristic of the shareholder-board-management structure, each partner is presumably entitled to participate directly in all aspects of partnership decision making. Because of their presumed right to participate directly in all aspects of decision making, partners are seen as less needful of the types of protective formal procedures governing corporate decision making.

Besides the rules governing the corporate decision making apparatus, corporate shareholders are also endowed with statutory protections that facilitate their ability to sell their stock because "exit" is their ultimate protection against incompetent management. Among the liquidity-enhancing aspects of corporate governance, a stock purchaser is entitled to succeed to all of the rights that the selling stockholder had in corporate decision-making. Conversely, the partnership default rule bars partners

---

9. See generally, Terence Floyd Cuff, *Drafting Allocation and Distribution Provisions in Partnership and LLC Agreements: What Business Lawyers Should Know*, TSWA09 ALI-CLE 145 (2014).

10. CAL. CORP. CODE §§ 16401(b), 16401(h) cited in EXETER, *Choice of Entity Considerations for Real Estate Investors* (last visited May 31, 2016), http://www.exeter1031.com/choice_of_entity_considerations.aspx

11. CAL. CORP. CODE § 16501

12. CAL. CORP. CODE § 16502.

13. *Elias Real Estate, LLC v. Tseng*, 156 Ca. App. 4th 425 (2007).

from assigning their decision-making prerogatives without the consent of the remaining partners. One of the main reasons for this distinction is that partners share unlimited liability for partnership debts while corporate shareholders are not personally liable for the corporation's debts and other obligations.

Another liquidity protection is that the corporation as an entity is presumed to survive the death of any shareholder while the opposite default rule applies to partnerships. Partnerships are presumed to dissolve on the death of a partner unless the partnership agreement provides otherwise.[14]

D. Joint Ventures

Description. A joint venture arises when two or more persons contemplate a single undertaking or project, to which each contributes money, property, skill or other assets of value, with an agreement to share profits and losses and some degree of control over the venture.

Generally, courts and lawyers have characterized joint ventures as a partnership formed for a single project. The Uniform Partnership Act[15] and Revised Uniform Partnership Act include joint ventures as partnerships.[16]

Historically, the joint venture was a distinct entity at common law, not a type of partnership. True to the historic origins of the joint venture, a few courts and lawyers maintain that disputes among co-venturers should be resolved by reference solely to joint venture agreements and not by reference to the default rules applicable to particular partnerships.[17] Colorado has codified the special status of joint ventures, and enables joint ventures specifically to elect that status, and to designate those who are authorized to sell or mortgage joint venture property.[18]

The subtle but important differences between the majority and minority approach regarding whether partnership law should be the lodestar of judicial opinions in joint venture disputes were highlighted in the 1928 landmark New York Court of Appeals case of *Meinhard v. Salmon*.[19] Meinhard, an equity investor, had been invited by de-

---

14. Events Causing Dissolution and Winding Up of Partnership Business, Rev. Uniform Partnership Act Section 801 (2015–2016 ed.).

15. The language of the Uniform Partnership Law refers in several places to a partnership for a fixed term or particular undertaking. See the Colorado UPA: CRS §§ 7-60-123(1) and 131(1)(a)(I).

16. Revised Uniform Partnership Act § 202 (a) provides, "[T]he association of two or more persons to carry on as co-owners a business for profit forms a partnership, whether or not the persons intend to form a partnership." Comment 2 to Revised Uniform Partnership Act § 202 provides, "Relationships that are called 'joint ventures' are partnerships if they otherwise fit the definition of a partnership An association is not classified as a partnership, however, simply because it is called a 'joint venture.'"

17. Michael A. Sabian and Beat U. Steiner, *Partnership Status Of Joint Ventures In Colorado: Editorial Comments On Crs § 38-30-166*, 25-FEB Colo. Law. 61 (1996).

18. Colo.Rev.Stat.Ann. § 38-30-166. Any co-venturer can record in the local land records an affidavit declaring an entity to be a joint venture and specifying details such as who is authorized to sell or encumber joint venture assets, including real estate.

19. 249 N.Y. 458 (1928.).

veloper Salmon to provide financing for a project in mid-town Manhattan at the corner of 42nd Street and Fifth Avenue. The site was owned by Elbridge T. Gerry who had leased the site to Salomon for a term of twenty years in order to transform a worn-out hotel into upscale shops and offices.

Salmon and Meinhard each contributed half the renovation costs, and entered an agreement to share profits and losses. Salman was to manage, lease and operate the project. In the early years of the lease, Salmon and Meinhard lost money which they more than recouped in the profitable later years.

Less than four months before the end of the lease term, Gerry, the property owner, approached Salmon and initiated negotiations with him for a new lease of not just the corner lot, but of the entire block which Gerry owned. The initial term of the extended lease was for 20 years with renewal options for up to 80 years.

Under the new lease, Salmon promised within seven years to demolish a large building on the property and replace it with a new one.

Salmon never mentioned this transaction to Meinhard; but when Meinhard heard about it, he asked Salmon for a 50% interest in the deal. Salmon turned him down, and Meinhard filed suit. His suit was based on Salmon having breached an implied fiduciary duty to inform Meinhard of the opportunity, and include him in what was an off shoot of their original partnership.

A trial court referee recommended that the court reject Meinhard's petition, after concluding that Salmon and Meinhard had never been partners, just joint venturers in a single transaction, nothing more.

On appeal, Justice Cardozo sided with Meinhard. In a 4–3 majority opinion, Justice Cardozo described the nature of the fiduciary obligations that business partners owe each other:

> Joint adventurers, like copartners, owe to one another, while the enterprise continues, the duty of the finest loyalty. Many forms of conduct permissible in a workaday world for those acting at arm's length are forbidden to those bound by fiduciary ties. A trustee is held to something stricter than the morals of the market place. Not honesty alone, but the punctilio of an honor the most sensitive, is then the standard of behavior ... The trouble about his [Salmon's] conduct is that he excluded his co-adventurer from any chance to compete, from any chance to enjoy the opportunity for benefit that had come to him alone by virtue of his agency.[20]

Justice Andrews, on behalf of the three dissenters, rooted his opinion in joint venture law. The dissenting opinion disregarded partnership law entirely because there had been no partnership between Salmon and Meinhard, "merely a joint venture for a limited object, to end at a fixed time."[21] In short, the dissenters thought joint venture

---

20. 249 N.Y. at 463–66.
21. 249 N.Y. at 478.

disputes should be resolved on the basis of the particular features of each joint venture transaction, not upon general principals of partnership law.

In this case, the new lease was entirely different from the one underlying the Salmon-Meinhard transaction. It covered additional property, with many new terms and conditions, and a possible duration of 80 years. Because of that, it was more like a purchase of the reversion than a typical lease.

Most US courts have followed the Cardozo precedent in *Salmon v. Meinhard*, and characterized joint ventures as partnerships.[22]

The Programmatic Joint Venture. Participants in arrangements known as programmatic joint ventures can anticipate and clarify the scope of their reciprocal obligations, and head off costly subsequent disputes, by reaching agreement at the outset on the sorts of issues that led to *Salmon v. Meinhard*.

In a programmatic venture relationship, Sponsors and Equity Investors go beyond striking a deal for a single transaction and establish a system through which they can invest together as a part of a common plan. Most programmatic joint venture relationships will fall under one of two types of general structures, being either: a) a holding company structure; or b) a framework or deal sharing agreement structure.

In a holding company structure, the parties enter into a joint venture agreement at an upper tier level and acquire properties through subsidiaries of the holding company. In a deal sharing or framework agreement, the parties enter into a contract that sets forth the framework under which the parties will enter into various individually and independently documented and executed transactions. A typical framework agreement will provide for some obligation to present deals and form documentation and terms that are attached as exhibits to the framework agreement pursuant to which each of the deals will be carried out. Less formal framework and deal sharing agreements are often employed as well.

In programmatic relationships there is typically some level of exclusivity and one or more parameters on such exclusivity. Such parameters may include: Time, Size, Asset Class, Dollar Amount and Geography.

An example using all of such referenced parameters would be: Sponsor and Sponsor's Affiliates shall be obligated to present all Qualified Transactions to Equity Investor until the earlier to occur of: (x) the third anniversary of the Closing Date; and (y) the date Equity Investor has made or committed to make Capital Contributions to the Joint Venture equal to or in excess of $200,000,000.00 in respect of investments presented to it by Sponsor or Sponsor's Affiliates. As used herein the term "Qualified Transaction" shall mean any real estate development project for the construction of multifamily rental housing with a minimum equity requirement of $5,000,000.00 and a maximum equity

---

22. "Courts have many varied techniques for handling conflicts within joint ventures. The underlying theme, however, is that joint ventures are almost always subject to partnership principles. This is true no matter how the courts have couched their decisions. In that sense, the joint venture is treated as a pseudopartnership." Adam B. Weissburg, *Reviewing The Law On Joint Ventures With An Eye Toward The Future*, 63 S. Cal. L. Rev. 487, footnote 8. (1990).

requirement of $40,000,000.00 located in any of the following States: California, Oregon, Nevada, and Washington.[23]

Rights of Joint Venture Participants to Sell Joint Venture Property. In jurisdictions where partnership law applies to joint ventures, any co-venturer would be entitled to sell joint venture assets, including real estate, as long as the sale was in line with the business of the partnership. This is a *question of fact* that usually eludes an indisputably clear answer.

Where courts differentiate joint ventures from partnerships, the best practice is for all the co-venturers to sign the deed or mortgage. That way, none of them will be in a good position to challenge the sale later. Buyers, mortgage lenders and title insurers often insist upon all the co-venturers signing a deed or mortgage to joint venture realty. The Colorado joint venture statute was enacted specifically to provide a reliable procedure for fewer than all of the co-venturers having authority to sign a deed or mortgage. The founders of the joint venture need to record an affidavit in the county land records where the property is located, listing the names of those who are authorized to convey or mortgage joint venture realty.[24]

E. Tenancies in Common

The Essential Nature of TIC Interests. A tenancy in common is not an entity. It is a term describing the direct undivided ownership of real or personal property by two or more individuals.

Imagine, for instance, that A and B own undivided equal shares of a duplex as tenants in common. They could decide to allocate to A the exclusive use of Unit 1 and to B the exclusive use of Unit 2. They would hold equal title to the common areas—the backyard, the driveways, the exterior walls of the units.

Without an explicit understanding, neither A nor B would have the right to lease either unit separately. Either of them would own an undivided interest in the entire property which they could occupy, lease, sell or mortgage. Of course, undivided possession of a house or apartment by different households can be problematic, a primary challenge implicit in the tenancy in common form of ownership. Unanimous consent is the hallmark of a tenancy in common.

Complicating matters even further, fractional interests in a co-tenancy need not be equal in quantity or duration. In the above example, Uncle Alex could have deeded the duplex 75% to A and 25% to B, or 50% each to A and B for a term of five years, and then fee simple ownership to B. Each co-tenant would be entitled to a pro rata

---

23. Josh Kamin, John Mallinson, and Vytas Petrulis, The Programmatic Real Estate Joint Venture, THE PRACTICAL REAL ESTATE LAWYER 53 (last visited May 31, 2016), http://www.kslaw.com/ imageserver/KSPublic/library/publication/2015articles/05-01-15_The-Practical-Real-Estate-Lawyer_Kamin.pdf

24. "The affidavit may set forth a statement that fewer than all of the joint venturers are authorized to act on behalf of the joint venture in any acquisition, conveyance, encumbrance, lease, or other dealing with an interest in property in the name of the joint venture." C.R.S.A. §38-30-166.

share of any income produced from the property, offset by a proportionate share of the co-tenancy expenses.

Examples of Co-tenancy Property:

(1) A vacation resort developer who sold designated suites in a hotel to different households, each of them entitled to occupy a particular suite or type of suite for a specified time period each year.[25]

(2) Co-tenancies often result from familial gifts, wills, and trusts. "Tenancy in Common (TIC) is the main form of non-spousal, collective property ownership."[26] For instance, Uncle Alex gifts each of his three grandchildren an undivided one-third interest in a beach house.

(3) Close friends and family members decide to acquire property as tenants in common that they intend to share for a long time to come.

(4) Despite the complexities, commercial real estate investors sometimes decide to take title as tenants in common, or convert their ownership interest to a TIC after acquiring title, especially when motivated by the wish to avail themselves of the benefits of the "like kind" exchange provision of Section 1031 of the Internal Revenue Code,[27] described later in this chapter.

(5) Condo Conversions. Sometimes unrelated households may pool their financial resources, and form a tenancy in common specifically with the idea in mind of acquiring a multi-family dwelling in which they will allocate a particular unit to each household in their group.

Why would sensible people bother crafting similar documentation to what would be found in standard condominium declarations, CC&Rs, and by-laws when they could purchase a condominium and benefit from well-established condominium laws and procedures extant in every state?

Well, in San Francisco and other cities with rising demand for housing, local governments endeavor to protect an affordable rental housing inventory from being depleted by demolition or conversion into condominiums. They attempt to deny condo converters the right to obtain recordable subdivision maps that would enable them to sell individual apartments in older buildings. By using the tenancy in common format combined with TIC agreements that allocate separate apartments to individual

---

25. Daniel T. Engle, *Legal Challenges to Time Sharing Ownership*, 45 Mo. L. Rev..423 (1980).

26. J. William Callison, *Nine Bean-Rows LLC: Using the Limited Liability Company To Hold Vacation Homes and Other Personal-Use Property*, 38 Wm. Mitchell L. Rev. 592. 599 (2012).

27. In 1995, a San Diego attorney came up with the idea of using the tenancy in common format to allow investors to acquire fractionalized interests in real estate that they could eventually exchange, tax deferred, under IRC § 1031. In 2002, the IRS sanctioned this arrangement, issuing guidelines, Revenue Procedure 2002-22. A multi-billion dollar industry was born, that soon crashed and burned in the real estate downturn. Jason W. Armstrong, *Rise and Fall of a Real Estate Market Niche*, Daily Journal (Supplement to Los Angeles and San Francisco), October 27, 2010. http://documents.jdsupra.com/b82c88e9-a2f0-4bd6-8118-9ed1c44d02fb.pdf; see also. Bradford Updike, *Exploring The Frontier Of Non-Traditional Real Estate Investments: A Closer Look At 1031 Tenancy-In-Common Arrangements*, 40 Creighton L. Rev. 271 (2007).

occupants, condo converters are able to achieve *de facto* condominiums through co-tenancy agreements.[28]

"What is the difference between a tenancy in common and a condominium?

In a condominium, property has been legally divided into physical parts that can be separately owned. Each condo owner owns a particular area of the property that is delineated on a map recorded in the public records, and has a deed which identifies the area which is individually owned. By contrast, TIC owners own percentages in an undivided property rather than particular units or apartments, and their deeds show only their ownership percentages. The right of a particular TIC owner to use a particular dwelling comes from a written contract signed by all co-owners (often called a "Tenancy In Common Agreement"), not from a deed, map or other document recorded in county records. The difference between physical division of ownership in county records (as in a condominium) and an unrecorded contract allocating usage rights (as in a tenancy in common) is significant from both regulatory and practical standpoints."[29]

The Right to Partition the TIC. Stalemates among co-tenants sometimes lead them to seek a court-ordered partition of the co-tenancy property. Although the right to petition for a partition is *waivable,* if it has not been waived, courts have the option of dividing the property physically, or ordering a sale of the co-tenancy property, and dividing the proceeds among the co-tenants.

In some situations, like the duplex example mentioned above, a partition in kind might be feasible. A court could grant each of the co-tenants a separate unit. For other types of real estate, such as a single-family house, splitting the property into two distinct ownerships might be impractical, and even illegal under local zoning and building codes. Courts are empowered to use their best judgment to maximize the value of co-tenancy property, of either ordering a sale of each co-tenant's interest separately, or of the entire property as a whole, and then splitting the sale proceeds among the co-tenants.

F. Limited Liability Companies (LLC)

1. General Considerations

LLC: A Creature of Statute. "*Like corporations and limited partnerships, LLCs are creatures of statute. It is simply impossible to create an LLC without expressly and properly invoking a specific LLC statute; those who err in this threshold step risk personal liability and unenforceable contracts.*

"All **LLC** statutes have certain characteristics in common. They all ...

(1) provide for the creation of **LLCs** through filing of public documents;

---

28. See Andy Sirkin, *Clear Answers and Explanations on Tenancy in Common (TIC)* (last visited May 31, 2016), http://www.andysirkin.com/HTMLArticle.cfm?Article=1.

29. Andy Sirkin, *Clear Answers and Explanations on Tenancy In Common (TIC)* (last visited May 31, 2016), http://www.andysirkin.com/HTMLArticle.cfm?Article=1

(2) recognize the **LLC** as a legal person separate from its **members**;

(3) establish a liability shield for the **members**;

(4) provide some default rules for the governance of the entity;

(5) provide some default rules for the financial rights of the **members**;

(6) establish restrictions on the transferability of membership interests; and

(7) provide for the dissolution of the entity."[30]

Despite the common characteristics of LLC statutes, there are greater differences among state LLC statutes than among state partnership statutes.[31]

2. Buying Realty from an LLC Seller

Frequently, for each of their real estate assets, investors form a single-purpose LLC to be designated as its nominal owner.[32] Some buyers form LLCs to hold title to their residences, thus insulating themselves from personal liability for claims arising from their owning homes or condos. By taking title in a specially formed LLC, investors are also able to shield their personal identity from public view since state laws do not require the names of LLC members to be made public.[33] Availing themselves of this opportunity for anonymity, white-collar criminals use LLCs to defraud homeowners out of their titles, evade local taxes, hide stolen assets, and escape liability for flouting building codes.

Buyers from LLCs may not have any idea who they are actually dealing with unless they require disclosure of the names of the LLC members as a condition to entering purchase and sale agreements for LLC-owned property. At a minimum, buyers should

---

30. Robert R. Keatinge and Naomi M. Baez Amos, *Duties Of Managers, Managing Members, And General Partners In Unincorporated Organizations,* TSWA06 ALI-CLE 1 (September 4, 2014).

31. Two professors who teach LLC law note "the lack of uniformity in the laws of LLCs compared to the laws of partnerships or corporations. The Revised Uniform Partnership Act (RUPA) has achieved significant uniformity in partnership laws. For corporations, Delaware law is somewhat of a quasi-national corporation law, and the Model Business Corporation Act (MBCA) has been influential with many states ... For LLCs there is not a similar gravitational pull. The uniform statutes have not had the same degree of penetration and influence as RUPA. Outside of the minority of states that have adopted one of the two uniform statutes, there are significant state-by-state differences." Michelle M. Harnera and Robert J. Rhee, *Teaching LLCs Through A Problem-Based Approach,* 71 Wash. & Lee L. Rev. 489, 492 (2014).

32. One reason is to assuage the concerns of mortgage lenders that their ability to enforce their rights as mortgage lenders could be impeded if the developer/owner held title directly to the asset that secured their mortgage loan, and the developer/owner became bankrupt. These single purpose LLCs are favored for their presumed "bankruptcy remoteness."

33. See, e.g., Stephanie Saul, *Real Estate Shell Companies Scheme to Defraud Owners Out of the Homes: Relying on the secrecy of limited liability companies, white-collar thieves are targeting pockets of New York City for fraudulent deed transfers, leaving the victims groping for redress,* N.Y TIMES (last visited May 31, 2016), http://www.nytimes.com/2015/11/08/nyregion/real-estate-shell-companies-scheme-to-defraud-owners-out-of-their-homes.html?_r=0

Louise Story, *A Mansion, A Shell Company, and Resentment in Bel Air,* N.Y TIMES (last visited May 31, 2016), Dec. 14, 2015. http://www.nytimes.com/2015/12/15/us/shell-company-bel-air-mansion.html

purchase title insurance policies to protect themselves against forged titles, and should use reliable intermediaries as escrow agents or closing attorneys so as never to entrust funds to anonymous LLC members until they have become title-insured owners of record of the property they contracted to purchase.

3. Selling Realty to an LLC Buyer

Capacity to Perform the Contract. Home sellers should also be wary of signing purchase and sale contracts with LLCs. They would be better off to contract with individuals whose personal financial statements they could review. Cautious sellers entering contracts with LLCs as buyers insist upon a large cash deposit being placed for safe-keeping with a reliable escrow agent that will become liquidated damages for the buyer's failure to perform the contract.

Mortgage lenders making loans to LLCs often require personal guarantees from the individual members of the LLC.

4. Operating Agreements and Statutory Norms

Anyone forming or doing business with an LLC needs to view the LLC operating agreement, the equivalent of a partnership agreement, the "constitution" of the LLC entity. LLC "due diligence" cannot stop there, however, because state LLC statutes contain mandated norms that cannot be overridden by an LLC operating agreement. For example, state statutes vary considerably in the extent to which they allow LLC operating agreements to abrogate statutory and common law norms applicable to how LLC members are allowed to deal with each other and third parties.

Consider a Utah case in which three individuals formed an LLC to purchase and develop a particular parcel of real estate. They designated one of them to be the manager of the LLC. But the other two members preferred not to entrust too much power to the manager-member. So their operating agreement stipulated that "No loans may be contracted on behalf of the [LLC] ... unless authorized by a resolution of the [m]embers."

The worst fears of the two non-managing members came to fruition. Flouting the above-quoted provision in the operating agreement by not obtaining the authorization of the two members, the designated manager-member borrowed $25,000 secured by the LLC-owned real estate and absconded with $20,000 of the $25,000 loan proceeds (the lender kept $5,000 in fees). No payments were ever made on the loan, the lender foreclosed, and only then did the other two LLC members learn they had been cheated.

The two members filed suit to invalidate the loan. They argued that since the operating agreement precluded any one member from mortgaging LLC realty, the loan was invalid. They contended the lender deserved no sympathy, not having read the operating agreement before making the loan. At a minimum, the lender could have obtained a security interest in that percentage of the property that was owned by the member who agreed to the loan. The non-managing members petitioned the court to partition the property so that they could at least retain a two-thirds interest in the realty.

In support of their argument, the two members cited this statute: "If the management of the limited liability company is vested in a manager or managers, any manager has authority to bind the limited liability company, *unless otherwise provided in the articles of organization or operating agreement.*"[34] Clearly, the operating agreement had provided otherwise, stripping the member-manager of the authority to bind the LLC in this situation.

The court turned them down,[35] based on another statute which the court perceived as more directly applicable to the facts of the case at hand: "*Instruments and documents providing for the acquisition, mortgage, or disposition of property of the limited liability company shall be valid and binding upon the limited liability company if they are executed by one or more managers of a limited liability company having a manager or managers* or if they are executed by one or more members of a limited liability company in which management has been retained by the members."[36]

LLCs can be managed by its members or a designated manager. This case demonstrates one of the risks that LLC members take when they elect to designate a manager.

G. Limited Partnerships (LP)[37]

Description. Unlike the general partnership which is an entity of common law origin, the limited partnership is purely a statutory creation.[38] An alternate form of business enterprise to the corporation, it enables investors to entrust their funds to professional managers without risking personal liability for entity obligations.

---

34. UTAH CODE § 48–2b–125(2)(b).

35. *Taghipour v. Jerez,* 52 P. 3d 1252 (2002).

36. UTAH CODE ANN. § 48–2b–127(2) (1998).

37. Limited Liability Partnerships. "Another kind of partnership, called a limited liability partnership (LLP) or sometimes called a registered limited liability partnership (RLLP), provides all of its owners with limited personal liability. LLPs are particularly well-suited to professional groups, such as lawyers and accountants. In fact, in some states LLPs are only available to professionals. Professionals often prefer LLPs to general partnerships, corporations, or LLCs because they don't want to be personally liable for another partner's problems—particularly those involving malpractice claims. An LLP protects each partner from debts against the partnership arising from professional malpractice lawsuits against another partner. (A partner who loses a malpractice suit for his own mistakes, however, doesn't escape liability.) Forming a corporation to protect personal assets may be too much trouble, and some states (including California) won't allow licensed professionals to form an LLC." Peri Pakroo, Limited Liability Partnerships. http://www.nolo.com/legal-encyclopedia/limited-partnerships-limited-liability-partnerships-29748.html (last visited June 5 , 2016).

38. The two major uniform laws have been the Uniform Limited Partnership Act (ULPA) of 2008 and the Revised Limited Partnership Act (RULPA). California replaced The Uniform Limited Partnership Act of 2008 (Re-RULPA) (Cal Corp C §§ 15900–15912.07) with the former California Revised Limited Partnership Act (CRLPA) (Cal Corp C §§ 15611–15723), the latter of which applied to limited partnerships formed after July 1, 1984 and before January 1, 2008.

Every limited partnership needs to have at least one general partner and one limited partner. A general partner has plenary authority over limited partnership operations. "General partners take the role of corporate officers in supervising the employees, making business decisions, planning the direction of the business, hiring and firing, purchasing equipment, plotting business strategy, and other similar matters. If the partnership delegates management functions to particular committees, it is likely that general partners will be on those committees."[39]

"One of the distinct differences between a general and a limited partnership is that general partners own the partnership while in a limited partnership, the actual ownership of the partnership assets is in the limited partnership.

'The limited partners have merely a right to a designated return on their capital and a share of the profits generated by the partnership."[40]

"Like general partnerships, limited partnerships typically provide that the profits, losses and distributions of the partnership are allocated in proportion to the partners' respective contributions to the partnership, unless the partnership agreement has provided for preferential distributions."[41]

"A limited partnership is essentially a contractual relationship. A lawyer is usually involved in the formation of a limited partnership, and a written contract almost always is prepared to govern the relationship. The agreement typically contains provisions that make it clear that the general partner has the exclusive power of management of the business of the limited partnership with certain limited exceptions."[42]

Before drafting a limited partnership agreement, understanding the rules that apply to issues not covered by an agreement seems to be a good idea, although there are obvious drawbacks in relying on the sometimes convoluted or ambiguous provisions of a statute.[43]

---

39. J. Cary Barton, *Role of General Partners*, Tex. Prac. Guide Bus. Entities § 23:288 (updated 2015).

40. Cal. Corp. CODE § 15671.

41. The Revised Uniform Limited Partnership Act provides: "The profits and losses of a limited partnership shall be allocated among the partners in the manner provided in the partnership agreement. If the partnership agreement does not otherwise provide, profits and losses shall be allocated in the same manner as the partners share distributions."

"A distribution by a limited partnership must be shared among the partners on the basis of the value, as stated in the required records when the limited partnership decides to make the distribution, of the contributions the limited partnership has received from each partner."

42. Robert W. Hamilton, *Corporate General Partners Of Limited Partnerships*, 1 J. Small & Emerging Bus. L. 73 (1997).

43. California adopted its own ULPA (2008), drawing provisions from both the RUPA and the RULPA to avoid prior conflicting case law involving these statutes, and because neither of those statutes addressed the special problems of (1) sophisticated, manager-focused commercial deals whose participants commit for the long term; and (2) estate planning arrangements (primarily family limited partnerships).Lynn M. Fisher and David J. Hartzell, Real Estate Private Equity Performance: A New Look (May 2013). http://areas.kenan-flagler.unc.edu/finance/PERC/REPE%20Performance%20May%202013%20v2.pdf (last visited May 31, 2016), https://www.investmentlawgroup.com/overview/

Why Private Equity Funds Utilize the Limited Partnership Structure. Private real estate equity funds are a conduit for major investors such as pension funds and high-net worth individuals to invest in real estate. Real estate private equity funds have been attracting unprecedented amounts of capital with assets under management (or AUM) reaching an all-time high of $724 billion.[44]

Utilizing the limited partnership structure, these funds often join forces with private real estate developers and owners. The equity fund becomes the limited partner, typically investing 90% of the equity.

The developer/promoter is the general partner, putting up 10% of the required equity, and assuming responsibility for finding, acquiring, underwriting, financing, and selling assets, and delivering promised investment returns. The general partner is rewarded, if the venture proves successful, with a generous slice of the earnings, called a "*promote*." When things go well, the limited partner receives a return of its capital usually in two to five years, and a high rate of return on its investment. Sometimes, the private equity fund also acquires a percentage interest in the general partner (called "a GP co-investment"), as a way of sharing in the general partner's "promote."[45]

II. Liability Issues

A. Sole Proprietorship

Limitless Personal Liability. All of a sole proprietor's personal assets are at risk to pay the proprietorship's debts. In addition, agency law imposes upon the sole proprietor legal responsibility for the actions of the entity's agents and employees when they are acting within the scope of their actual or apparent authority for the proprietorship.

Limiting Liability by Contract. Sole proprietors can achieve a measure of limited liability protection by contract. For example, the sole proprietorship can use *liquidated damage clauses* in leases and purchase and sale contracts to place a dollar cap on the proprietor's personal liability arising from these transactions.

Along similar lines, sole proprietors can negotiate "*non-recourse*" mortgage loans, barring the mortgage lender seeking repayment of the debt from the proprietor's personal assets. As Professor Greg Stein has explained, "Non-recourse loans have become a staple of commercial real estate."[46] Real estate lenders agree to non-recourse loans to compete for borrowers. Mortgage lenders hope that even if they have to foreclose,

---

44. Arthur Penn, *All You Need to Know About Real Estate Private Equity,* MARKET REALIST (last visited May 31, 2016), http://marketrealist.com/2015/05/need-know-real-estate-private-equity/."Most private equity houses typically look for investors who are willing to commit as much as $25 million. Although some firms have dropped their minimums to $250,000."

45. Ian Formigle, *The Beauty of the GP Co-Investment Structure,* CROWDSTREET (last visited May 31, 2016), https://www.crowdstreet.com/education/article/beauty-gp-co-investment-structure/

46. Gregory M. Stein, *When Can A Nonrecourse Lender Reach The Personal Assets Of Its Borrower?* 17 No. 2 PRAC. REAL EST. LAW. 33, 38 (2001).

by not lending more than 70 to 80 percent of the value of the security property, they will be able to sell the property for at least as much as they loaned against it.

Insurance. Insurance policies can offer the sole proprietor a degree of protection from personal injury claims due to accidents and casualty losses. For a nominal premium, the proprietor can purchase additional coverage in the form of an umbrella policy.

Still, insurance coverage leaves gaps. Some risks (such as indemnity for criminal conduct) are uninsurable; most policies come with high deductibles and numerous exclusions and exceptions to coverage.

Other Entity Options. To hedge against personal liability an individual proprietor could also elect to do business as a corporation or a single-member Limited Liability Company (LLC).

B. C Corporation

Limited Shareholder Liability for Corporate Debts. Corporations have the well-known attribute that individual shareholders are immune from personal liability for corporate obligations. Even if the corporation fails, and the stock becomes worthless, shareholders ordinarily risk no more than the money they paid for their stock.[47]

Piercing the Corporate Veil. Courts possess the authority to "pierce the corporate veil," and hold the corporation's owners and operators personally liable for bad acts they perpetrated in the name of the corporation.[48]

Individuals with decision-making authority in a corporation could become personally liable for entity obligations by using their control for personal gain, commingling personal and corporate funds, not maintaining the formal statute-dictated decision-making procedures, disregarding the articles of incorporation, or engaging in practices that are criminal, fraudulent, abusive or environmentally hazardous.

Inadequate capitalization is also an often-cited criterion for exposing corporate owners and operators to personal liability for corporate obligations, though "the appropriate test for capital adequacy has long befuddled the courts."[49]

Protection of Entity Assets from Shareholders' Creditors. The corporation as a legal entity is totally distinct from the individuals involved in it. Hence, creditors have no direct access to the corporation's assets to repay the personal debts incurred by indi-

---

47. Limited liability was not always the norm until governments, eager to stimulate economic development, instituted special laws conferring limited liability upon corporate shareholders to ease their reluctance to assume the limitless array of risks inherent in large-scale enterprises. For a history of the evolution of corporate limited liability, see Phillip I. Blumberg, *Limited Liability and Corporate Groups,* 11 J. Corp. L. 574 (1985–1986); Frank H. Easterbrook & Daniel R. Fischel, *Limited Liability and the Corporation,*" 52 U. Chi. L. Rev. 89 (1985).

48. Robert B. Thompson, *Piercing the Corporate Veil: An Empirical Study,* 76 Cornell L. Rev. 1036 (1991),

49. Thomas K. Cheng, *Form And Substance Of The Doctrine Of Piercing The Corporate Veil,* 80 Miss. L.J. 497 (2010).

vidual shareholders, corporate officers, managers, and employees. Of course, an individual shareholder's judgment creditors can access the debtor's stock, and in that way become entitled to assert the rights that the debtor-shareholder would have had in the corporation.[50]

C. General Partnership

The Personal Liability of General Partners for Partnership Debts. General partners are "jointly and severally" liable for partnership debts; "several" means that each of them is liable for the entire debt, "jointly" means they are both liable for the entire debt. In a partnership of two individuals, each of them is potentially liable for 100% of partnership obligations even though each partner is only entitled to 50% of partnership gains.

"While the partners may agree among themselves to disproportional allocation of losses and debts, those internal negotiations are not binding on the rights of creditors and/or other claimants who are at law entitled to recover in full from any one or more of the partners as membership in a general partnership."[51]

General Partnership Interest Can Be Held in an LLC. Partners have a means of insulating themselves from personal liability for partnership obligations by holding their partnership interests in an entity with limited liability, such as a corporation or an LLC.

Consider this example: Jack and Jill form a general partnership to purchase and renovate old houses in prime neighborhoods. To minimize their tort and contract liability for partnership obligations, neither holds their general partnership interest individually. Jack forms an S Corporation and Jill a LLC to be the general partners of their general partnership. For this strategy to succeed, the S corporation or LLC must be adequately capitalized. Further, Jack and Jill must conduct the business and make decisions through the entity. If they act as if the entity does not exist, creditors may convince courts to do the same, and disregard the entity as a sham.

Liability of Partnership for Personal Obligations of Individual Partners. An individual partner's creditors have no rights to seize and sell partnership assets to repay anything but partnership debts. "A partner has no right by one's promise to bind the other members of the partnership to pay the partner's own private debt from the partnership assets without the consent or ratification of the other partners to satisfy the personal creditor."[52]

---

50. "Generally, a creditor or bankruptcy trustee of a stockholder can seize stock. The creditor's rights will then depend on what rights the stock carries and what restrictions and agreements govern the stock. In certain cases, shareholders' agreements may provide some protection." Kathryn G. Henkela and Judith K. Tobey, Est. Plan. & Wealth Pres. ¶ 20.10 (2016).

51. Exeter, *Choice of Entity Considerations for Real Estate Investors* (last visited May 16, 2016),http://www.exeter1031.com/choice_of_entity_considerations.aspx

52. Christine M. G. Davis, Robert F. Koets, and Ferdinand S. Tinio, *Payment of Individual Debts*, 29 Ill. Law and Prac. Partnership § 66 (May 2016 update).

To protect entity assets, the remedies of an individual partner's personal creditors against the entity are limited to a "charging order."[53] A charging order directs the partnership to remit to the judgment creditor any distributions due to the debtor partner whose interest is subject to the order.[54] The court order instructs the partnership not to divert or deny the creditor any such distributions. The partnership retains full control over the right to make distributions as long as the partnership does not use its plenary authority to engage in subterfuge distributions, for example, disguising distributions as wages and then remitting them only to non-debtor partners, or borrowing money from non-debtor partners on excessively generous repayment terms.[55]

D. Joint Ventures

Liability of Co-Venturers for Joint Venture Obligations. As mentioned above, courts generally apply partnership norms to the resolution of disputes arising from joint ventures. Generally, participants in a joint venture, like general partners, are held jointly and severally liable for joint venture obligations.

The default rules under the UPA and the RUPA link partner liability for losses to each partner's right to share in profits from the partnership: "Profits are shared equally and losses, whether capital or operating, are shared in proportion to each partner's share of the profits. Thus, under the default rule, partners share profits per capita and not in proportion to capital contribution as do corporate shareholders or partners in limited partnerships."[56] Unless the co-venturers establish a different formula, the partnership default rules are likely to apply.

Rights of Co-Venturer's Creditors. The creditors of an individual in a joint venture are treated as subject to the same "charging order" limitations as the creditors of individual partners.

E. Tenancies in Common (TIC)

Personal Liability of Tenants in Common for Obligations Arising from Ownership of the Common Areas. Tenants in common are personally liable for the maintenance and ownership of areas owned in common.

---

53. Elizabeth M. Schurig, Amy P. Jetel, *A Charging Order Is The Exclusive Remedy Against A Partnership Interest,* 17-DEC Prob. & Prop. 57 (November/December 2003).

54. Daniel S. Kleinberger, Carter G. Bishop, and Thomas Earl Geu, *Charging Orders and the New Limited Partnership Act: Dispelling Rumors of Disaster,* PROPERTY AND PROBATE 30 (July/August 2004). Charging order provisions can also be found in every LLC statute except Nebraska's. In most states, the creditor can foreclose on the LLC member's interest in the LLC or a limited partner's interest in a limited partnership.

55. Chad J. Pomeroy, *Think Twice: Charging Orders And Creditor Property Rights,* 102 Ky. L.J. 705 (2013–2014). The author makes a case for allowing creditors to foreclose debtor membership interests in LLCs.

56. Official comments, Rev. Uniform Partnership Act, Section 401 (2015–2016 ed.).

This norm has proven problematical when applied to the owners of condominiums. They rely on HOAs (home owners' associations) to manage, maintain and insure the common areas, even though the individual condo unit owners are tenants in common of the project hallways, elevators, recreational facilities, exterior walls and roofs. The implication is that each condo unit owner could be held personally liable for personal injury claims attributable to hazardous conditions in the common areas.[57]

"Courts are unclear as to what extent they should impose liability on individual unit owners for injuries arising from the negligent maintenance of the common elements." Citing state laws regarding "common interest developments" and other sources of authority, some courts have immunized condo unit owners from liability for claims arising from the common areas.[58]

Condo owners and other tenants in common have several ways to ameliorate their potential liability. For starters, they can obtain ample insurance coverage. Also, instead of holding title as tenants in common, they could vest their ownership in a specially formed C corporation or LLC.[59] Addressing this problem head on, some states have enacted statutes barring tort actions against individual condo unit owners as long as the owners' association maintains adequate insurance coverage.[60]

The Rights of a Co-tenant's Creditors to Levy Upon and Foreclose Co-tenancy Property.

"Although a TIC owner cannot bind the other co-owners to his or her creditors, the tenant's creditors can wreak havoc, for example, by threatening to seek a partition of the property sufficient to force the co-tenants to deal with it."

A mortgage lender could foreclose on a defaulting co-tenant's undivided interest in the property. Upon obtaining title through foreclosure, the lender could sell or lease an undivided interest in the property as long as the sale or lease did not oust other co-tenants by making their occupancy impracticable.[61] But the sale or lease price would probably be far less than half of what the property undivided would have yielded. For this reason, mortgage lenders seldom extend a loan on co-tenancy property without all the co-tenants signing the mortgage or deed of trust.

---

57. See *Pekelnaya v. Allyn,* 25 A.D.3d 111, 808 N.Y.S.2d 590 (1st Dep't 2005) (holding that unit owners are not liable for injuries that an individual has sustained as a result of a defect in the common elements of the condominium complex). Daniel L. Stanco, *The Proper Extent Of Liability A Condominium Unit Owner Should Have For Injuries Caused By A Limited Common Element,* 19 St. John's J. Legal Commentary 637, 638 (Summer, 2005).

58. Richard Siegler and Eva Talel, *Personal Liability of Condominium Unit Owners,* 235 N.Y. L. J. 1 (Jan. 4, 2006); Daniel L. Stanco, *The Proper Extent Of Liability A Condominium Unit Owner Should Have For Injuries Caused By A Limited Common Element,* 19 St. John's J. Legal Commentary 637, 638 (Summer, 2005).

59. J. William Callison, Nine Bean-Rows LLC: Using the Limited Liability Company To Hold Vacation Homes and Other Personal-Use Property, 38 Wm. Mitchell L. Rev. 592 (2012).

60. See, e.g., West's Ann.Cal.Civ.Code § 5805. (Tort actions against owner of separate interest; tenant-in-common in common area; association liability; insurance requirements).

61. J. William Callison, *Nine Bean-Rows LLC: Using the Limited Liability Company To Hold Vacation Homes and Other Personal-Use Property,* 38 Wm. Mitchell L. Rev. 592, 599 (2012).

Nonetheless, commercial mortgage lenders in San Francisco have advanced multi-million-dollar purchase-money loans to large groups of tenants acquiring formerly rent-controlled apartments through tenancies in common. Sophisticated commercial mortgage lenders, documenting their transactions carefully, have loaned millions of dollars secured by tenancy in common interests in regional malls and other significant commercial real estate.[62]

F. Limited Liability Companies (LLC)

Limited Liability for Entity Obligations. LLC statutes confer upon LLC members the same limited liability protections from LLC debts and obligations as corporate shareholders from corporate debts, and limited partners from limited partnership obligations.

Even so, the designated managers or member-managers of LLCs are subject to the same potential exposure to personal liability as corporate managers and controlling shareholders are under the amorphous concept of "piercing the corporate veil."

Member Creditors Are Relegated to "Charging Orders" to Receive Distributions. Creditors of individual LLC members are limited to the same "charging orders" process that keeps creditors of an individual partner at arms' length from reaching partnership assets. The creditor of an individual member has no claim against LLC-owned assets. With a court order, the judgment creditors of an individual LLC member can become entitled to receive distributions that would otherwise have belonged to the debtor-member, but only of LLC-approved distributions.

The Charging Order and Single Member LLCs. LLC statutes contemplate the possibility of there being single-member LLCs. Judgment creditors, pursuing an individual debtor who is also the only member of a single-member LLC, have occasionally succeeded in being granted the right to foreclose on LLC assets to collect an obligation that was incurred by the debtor personally.[63] They were able to persuade judges that a debtor who is the only member of an LLC has no legitimate justification to shirk creditors' claims to LLC assets since there are no non-debtor interests to protect in the entity's assets. (A California court in such a case required that the judgment creditor must show that it was unable to collect the debt through a charging order or a levy against the debtors' other personally owned property.)[64]

---

62. Ken Swenson and Mary L. Dickson, *Common Ground:T he Recent Trend Toward Financing Tenancies in Common Poses Substantial Challenges to Lenders,* 28-SEP L.A. Law. 40 (2005). This article describes the underwriting requirements of a commercial lender making a $92,000,000 loan to thirty tenants in common to acquire the 1.2 million square feet Puente Hills Mall in the City of Industry, California, in 2003 for $148,000,000. The lender required each co-tenant to sign the note and deed of trust and waive the right to partition the co-tenancy, and the co-tenancy had to designate a manager to operate and lease the acquired property and represent them in their dealings with the lender.

63. Herrick K. Lidstone, *Single-Member LLCs and Asset Protection,* 41-MAR Colo. Law. 39 (2012); Robert R. Keatinge, R, *Single Member LLC: Now You See It, Now You Don't Regarding Disregarded Entities*, VCWA0217 ALI-CLE 169 (February 17, 2015).

64. *Evans v. Galardi,* 16 Cal.3d 311, 128 Cal. Rptr. 25, 33 (1976).

G. Limited Partnerships (LP)

Unlimited Liability of the General Partner. State statutes require that in a limited partnership there must be at least one limited partner and one general partner, and the general partner is held personally liable for limited partnership obligations.

The general partner need not be an individual. By making the general partner a corporation or an LLC, entrepreneurs utilizing a limited partnership are able to shield their personal assets from the limited partnership's environmental, tort and contract liability. Of course, they incur the cost of forming, documenting and maintaining two entities—the limited partnership and the LLC or corporation that becomes the general partner of the limited partnership.

The Limited Liability of Limited Partners for Entity Obligations. Limited partners enjoy the same limited liability protection as corporate shareholders and LLC members. The limited partners in a limited partnership are usually only liable for losses up to the amount of their individual contributions to the partnership. Nonetheless, in an excess of caution, limited partners copy the strategy of general partners and hold their limited partnership interests in a specially formed LLC, S or C corporation.

At one time, limited partners risked forfeiting their limited liability status if they participated in the management and control of the limited partnership. Under the latest version of the *Uniform Limited Partnership Act (ULPA, 2001),* this potentially worrisome source of personal liability was eliminated. A limited partner is now able to retain limited liability status even while participating in the *management and control* of the limited partnership.

Beware The UFTA and UVTA. In surveying the extent to which partners, members or shareholders are free of personal liability for entity obligations, it is important to be mindful of the Uniform Fraudulent Transfers Act (UFTA), now replaced by the Uniform Voidable Transactions Act (UVTA).[65]

Summarized briefly, these laws allow judgment creditors to set aside distributions of entity assets previously made to entity owners at a time when the entity lacked sufficient funds to pay all its debts. Besides clawing back distributions, judgment creditors may also be able to set aside completed sales of entity property made to buyers who paid less than full value, with knowledge that the partnership lacked sufficient assets from which to pay all of its debts.[66]

---

65. Gary A. Foster and Eric C. Boughman, *The Uniform Voidable Transactions Act: An Overview of Refinements to the uniform Fraudulent Transfer Act,* 29 PROBATE & PROPERTY, The UVTA replaced the necessity of the creditor, as a condition to reclaiming the distributed payments or rescinding property sales, having to prove "constructive" fraud with the more objective norm that at the time of the transaction, the entity's debts probably exceeded its ability to pay them (last visited May 31, 2016), http://www.americanbar.org/publications/probate_property_magazine_2012/2015/july_august_2015/2015_aba_rpte_pp_v29_3_article_foster_boughman_uniform_voidable_transactions_act.html

66. Thomas J. Hall, Janice A. Payne, *The Liability Of Limited Partners For The Defaulted Loans Of Their Limited Partnerships,* 122 BANKING L.J. 687, 693–95 (2005). The creditors of a corporation

III. Tax Factors in Selecting an Entity to Buy and Hold Title to Commercial Property

In this section, we compare the key tax features of sole proprietorships, corporations, limited liability companies, general partnerships, limited partnerships and tenancies in common, starting with the "double tax" and the use of partnerships and LLCs to avoid it.

Then, we introduce the concepts popularly referred to as phantom income and phantom expenses (aka phantom losses). These are traceable to several tax code provisions. One of them prescribes that taxpayers deduct business expenses in the year they are incurred but requires that taxpayers amortize their capital investments over the period when those improvements will remain in use.

Another aspect of the tax code is that borrowers who incur debts for business purposes are allowed to deduct their mortgage interest payments from taxable income as paid, but they are not allowed to deduct repayments of mortgage principal.

Perhaps the most notable and controversial of the "phantom" expense is the depreciation deduction.

An additional option available to investors in real and personal property, detailed later in this section, is the tax-deferred exchange.

The section concludes with descriptions of two entities created by the tax code, the S Corporation and the Real Estate Investment Trust (REIT).

A. Avoidance of Entity Level Taxation

Gains. The "double tax" is exemplified by corporations, which are subject to tax at the entity level when they earn profits, and then again when corporate shareholders are taxed on what remains of those profits after being taxed once, if the corporation distributes the profits to shareholders as dividends. The "double tax" is a logical consequence of the tax code treating the corporation as an entity totally distinct from its shareholders even though the shareholders are the nominal owners of the corporation.

Conversely, partnerships are disregarded entities for tax purposes. A partnership's profits and losses are "passed through" directly to the individual partners in the year the profits are earned or the losses incurred, often putting the taxpayer in a quite different after tax position than if the gains and losses had been accounted for at the entity level.

Suppose two investors form a corporation to own and operate an apartment house that earns an annual net rental income of $1,000,000. The corporation pays tax on

---

have a similar prerogative, though they may have to bring suit to prod the corporation into suing the shareholder for a refund of distributions made in violation of the Uniform Fraudulent Transfer Act.

that income, currently at a rate of 35%. After paying the tax, the corporation's net earnings on the apartment shrunk to $650,000.

Now, suppose the corporation distributes the $650,000 to its two shareholders as a dividend.[67] Each of the shareholders will be taxed at his or her ordinary income tax rate (currently up to 39.6%). Assume these two shareholders were subject to combined state and federal income taxes at an average rate of 50%. Their combined personal after tax yield will have been reduced to *$325,000.*

> Had the two investors chosen a "pass through" entity, a partnership, limited partnership, or LLC—the partners or LLC members would have received $1,000,000, not $650,000, just as if they had owned the apartment house directly, like sole proprietors or tenants in common.

Losses. Losses, like income, belong to the corporation. The Internal Revenue Code allows corporations to offset its taxable income gains against losses either in the current tax year or in previous or future years. Partnership losses "flow through" to the individual partners' tax returns in the year incurred.

The Benefit of Taxation at the Entity Level. Taxation at the entity level has one advantage. It entitles entity managers or directors to decide whether to distribute earnings to shareholders as dividends or retain those earnings in the corporation, as long as retention has a defensible business purpose other than tax avoidance. Retention benefits shareholders indirectly because, generally, retained earnings enhance the book value of a corporation, and its liquidation value. Also, in a closely held corporation, dividend distributions can be scheduled to complement the financial needs and personal net tax situations of the major shareholders.

State Taxation of Pass through Entities. State tax regimes replicate the federal "double tax" format. To escape it, many firms have reduced their state tax obligations when they converted from corporations into LLCs. Legislators pushed back in some states by imposing new taxes on LLCs.[68] California levies on LLCs a state level franchise fee and gross receipts tax.[69] Some entrepreneurs may consider forming an LLC in a nearby state with no gross receipts tax, but California will lay claim to tax the LLC on its income earned in California.[70] A better option for a California resident not

---

67. A dividend is defined by IRC § 316(a) as any distribution of cash or property by a corporation to its owners, but only to the extent that it was paid out of earnings and profit. A distribution not paid out of earnings and profit would be a return of capital.

68. Bruce P. Ely, Christopher R. Grissom, and William T. Thistle II, *State Taxation Of Pass-Through Entities And Their Owners Continues To Evolve*, Journal of Multistate Taxation and Incentives (September 2012).

69. In California, each LLC licensed to do business in California is subject to an $800 franchise fee plus a tax based on its gross receipts (last visited May 19, 2016),
http://www.incorporatefast.com/filingfee.asp.

70. Loeb & Loeb, *California Launches campaign to collect taxes from out-of-state entities*, Lexology (last visited May 31, 2016), http://www.lexology.com/library/detail.aspx?g=d29c2a6b-4422-490f-addc-1044c5c0358e

wanting to pay these LLC levies would be to select another entity, such as a Limited Partnership. Limited Partnerships are not subject to the LLC special franchise fee and annual gross receipts tax.[71]

B. Phantom Income and Phantom Expense: The Benefits of Loss "Pass Throughs"

Definitions. The terms "phantom income" and "phantom expense" or "phantom loss" are shorthand references to the relationship between a taxpayer's actual cash flow and the taxpayer's taxable income. A phantom expense is an allowable deduction from adjustable gross taxable income that requires no cash outlay from the taxpayer claiming the deduction. In other words, it is tax-free cash flow. Phantom income is taxable income that exceeds the taxpayer's actual cash flow.

Three Main Sources of Phantom Income. (1) *The distinction between currently deductible expenses and capital expenditures.* The owner of commercial rental property who calls a plumber to fix a leaky pipe can deduct the cost of the repair in the year she pays the plumbing bill. That is a good thing for the taxpayer but no free ride. She will need to have paid the plumber a dollar for every dollar she deducts as an operating expense.

The taxpayer's cash flow situation is less favorable if she decides instead of patching the leak to re-pipe the building. She figures that the pipes are worn and rusted, and recurrent leaks will be disruptive to her tenants. The piping job will be costly, fifty times more than what the plumber charged to patch the leak.

Although the plumber will expect to be paid in full once the pipe replacement work is completed, the apartment owner will not be able to deduct the entire cost in the year she pays for the work. The Internal Revenue Code is written to require taxpayers to amortize their capital expenditures over the useful life of the improvements.[72] In this way, the Code synchronizes the deduction for the expenditure with the long-term benefits the apartment owner will receive in rents over the life of the improvement. Assuming the plumber's warranty was for five years, the apartment owner will probably be limited to claiming a deduction of one-fifth of the cost over a five-year amortization period.

(2) *Investors Could Be Taxed on More Cash Than a Pass Through Entity Distributes to Them.* When real estate is owned by a general partnership, limited partnership, tenancy-in-common or an LLC, entity level gains and losses flow directly to the

---

71. Jared R. Callister, *Single Member Limited Partnerships: A Tool to Get Around the CA Gross Receipts Tax* (last visited May 31, 2016), http://flcz.net/2014/12/single-member-limited-partner ships-tool-get-around-ca-gross-receipts-tax

72. IRC § 263 expressly disallows immediate deductions of capital expenditures made primarily for the acquisition, development, or improvement of an asset, interest, or income producing status. "when either the asset acquired or the benefit derived will last beyond the close of the taxable year."

tax returns of the individual owners. The individual owners owe income tax on entity gains in the year they are earned—whether or not the entity distributes those gains to its individual partners or members. If the entity retains the gains, the partners or members will need to find cash from some other source to cover their tax obligations.[73]

So, for instance, imagine that an LLC has five members each owning equal one-fifth shares of a professionally managed LLC. The parking garage earned a net income of $1,000,000 in the most recently completed tax year. Instead of distributing the earnings to the five LLC members, the manager of the LLC decides that the money should be spent refurbishing the garage, improving the lighting, installing new security cameras, replacing the decrepit, moldy elevator and re-striping the parking spaces. Each of the five members will be liable for $200,000 of income they did not actually receive. But the $1,000,000 expenditure will be amortized as a deduction against income in each of the years of its useful life.

To avoid taxation on phantom income, investors in "pass through" entities need to contract for minimum cash distributions that are at least sufficient to cover their share of entity-generated tax liability.

Had the asset been held in a corporation, the corporation would have been taxed on the $1,000,000 of earned income but the investors, as shareholders, would not have incurred any tax liability until the income was distributed to them as dividends.

(3) *Repayments of Mortgage Principal.* When a commercial property owner borrows money for business purposes, to acquire or renovate real estate, the loan proceeds are being used for a business purpose, so the interest is deductible as an ordinary and necessary business expense under IRC § 162.[74] Because taxpayers receive loan proceeds tax-free (on the assumption they will eventually repay them), they are not entitled to deduct their repayments of principal. Of course, the tax law could have taken the reverse tack, taxing borrowers upon receiving borrowed money and allowing deductions when they repaid their loans. Principal repayments not being deductible results in what is called phantom income because the borrower typically allocates after tax income to the repayment of mortgage principal.

---

73. Diana Fitzpatrick, *How LLC Members Are Taxed*, Nolo (last visited May 31, 2016), Taxes assessed on entire distributive share. "However members' distributive shares are divvied up, the IRS treats each LLC member as though the member receives his or her entire distributive share each year. This means that each LLC member must pay taxes on his or her whole distributive share, whether or not the LLC actually distributes all (or any of) the money to the members. The practical significance of this IRS rule is that, even if LLC members need to leave profits in the LLC—for instance, to buy inventory or expand the business—each LLC member is liable for income tax on his or her rightful share of that money." http://www.nolo.com/legal-encyclopedia/how-llcs-are-taxed-29675.html

74. IRC § 162 allows current deductions for ordinary and necessary business expenses and requires that capital expenditures, if deductible at all, must be amortized over the useful life of the asset which they enhanced.

When the Lines Cross. Homes mortgage loans are usually repaid in equal monthly installments so that on the loan maturity date when the time of the final payment is made on the loan, the mortgage principal has been amortized and all outstanding interest has been fully paid.

Since borrowers are only liable for interest on the unpaid balance due on their loans, most of the early payments on a fully amortizing loan consist of interest payments, which are deductible. With each monthly payment, the loan balance due is reduced. Consequently, the interest component shrinks and the non-deductible principal repayment expands.

There comes a time when more than half of each monthly payment is a non-deductible repayment of principal. This is when the "lines cross." For the borrower, this presents a challenge. The borrower's cash outlay to repay the principal amount due on the loan is not a deductible expense. So the borrower must find a source of income to cover the repayment, and any federal and state taxes that the borrower had to pay upon earning the money with which to make that repayment of principal. This would have been taxable income that exceeded the taxpayer's actual net cash flow after paying taxes and mortgage principal.

To avoid phantom income, some commercial borrowers prefer "interest only" loans, or loans with no repayments of principal in the early years. They pay a steep price in additional interest payments for the avoidance of phantom income, much greater amounts of interest than if they had repaid the principal sooner. Also, just to escape phantom income, some borrowers refinance their loans when the "lines cross." This keeps them running on the mortgage repayment treadmill a lot longer than if they had not refinanced their loans.

The Phantom Expense: The Depreciation Deduction.[75] Consistent with a tax on income, the owner earning income from an asset that is subject to wear and tear is allowed to deduct a portion of the asset's cost from the earnings it produces each year. Some of those earnings represent a return *OF* the investment, not *ON* the investment. This is called a depreciation deduction.

For example, a rental car company can offset the cost it incurred in acquiring its automobiles from the income it earns from car rentals. Similarly, when an investor acquires an apartment house for $1,000,000, on which it earns a net operating income of $50,000 by renting apartments, some of that rent is actually a return of the $1,000,000 to the extent the building is wearing out.

Land Is Not Depreciable. The rationale for the depreciation deduction is that part of the taxpayer's net income was not a return *ON* capital; it was a return *OF* capital because the apartment building is subject to physical wear-and-tear. But land is not going to wear out. So the investor is only going to be able to depreciate that portion

---

75. I.R.C. § 167: "There shall be allowed as a depreciation deduction a reasonable allowance for the exhaustion, wear and tear (including a reasonable allowance for obsolescence) (1) of property used in the trade or business or (2) of property held for the production of income."

of the $1,200,000 purchase price attributable to the value of the building when she bought it. (Sometimes, buyers and sellers specifically allocate the purchase price between land and buildings. The local property tax assessor's apportionment of land and building value is also probative.)

A consequence of land not being depreciable is that developers acquiring land for redevelopment must add the costs of demolishing buildings on those sites to their basis. The cost will not produce any tax benefit until the land is sold.[76]

Calculating the Deduction Amount. The depreciation allowance is deducted from the rental income in calculating the gross adjustable revenue subject to taxation. For most commercial real estate, the cost of the building must be deducted equally over a 39 year recovery period which works out to be 2.56% per year of the total depreciable cost, and for residential rental property, a 27 ½ year recovery period, 3.63% annually.[77]

Cost Segregation. In addition to the depreciation deduction on the building, realty owners are also entitled to segregate costs allocable to items of personal property within the building, such as carpeting and telecom systems. They can offset gross taxable income with depreciation allowances for these items, typically subject to depreciation schedules of three to ten years.[78]

Acquisition Expenditures Must Be Capitalized and Depreciated, Not "Expensed." Most investors would prefer to deduct the money they spend acquiring property in the year they spend it. Otherwise, the expenditures result in phantom income—cash flow not retained but subject to tax in the year it was earned.

Instead, the purchaser only has the option of adding the expense to the cost of acquiring the property bought, and depreciating it over the life of the building. These would include legal and escrow fees and title insurance.[79]

Inclusion of Borrowed Funds in Depreciable Basis. An important feature of the depreciation allowance is that investors can claim depreciation on more than the cash they actually invested in their properties. Suppose an investor pays $1,200,000 to acquire an apartment house, borrowing $900,000 secured by a mortgage on the property acquired. Assume the value of the land is $300,000. As along as she borrowed this

---

76. Stephan F. Tucker, *Acquisition, Construction, Operation And Ownership Of Real Estate: Capitalized Expenditures, Amortizable Expenses And Deductible Expenses*, SX008 ALI-CLE 695 (2015).

77. I.R.C. § 168(c).

78. To use a separate depreciation schedule for personal property, the realty owner needs a cost segregation study identifying all elements of personal property within the building. The Code definition of tangible personal property specifically excludes inherently permanent or structural components–for example, heating and air conditioning systems and ducts, wall partitions, windows, doors, sprinkler systems and elevators. Despite these limitations, one CPA estimates "savings can be as high as five percent" of the owner's cost of acquiring the realty. David Grant, *How Cost Segregation Offers Substantial Tax Benefits to Real Estate Owners & Investors in Real Estate*, 25 REAL ESTATE ISSUES 1, 2 (Summer 2000).

79. Stephan F. Tucker, *Acquisition, Construction, Operation And Ownership Of Real Estate: Capitalized Expenditures, Amortizable Expenses And Deductible Expenses*, SX008 ALI-CLE 695, § 14:3 (2015).

money from an institutional lender (in tax parlance, in the form of a "qualified" mortgage), she is entitled to depreciate the value of the building over 27.5 (but not the land), $900,000/27.5 years equals $32,760.36 per year.

The Benefit of the Loss Pass Through from Depreciation. To appreciate the practical significance of the depreciation deduction for the owners of "pass through" entities, consider two possibilities: (1) the net operating income exceeds the annual depreciation; and (2) the depreciation deduction exceeds the net operating income. In the first scenario, the individual partner or member in the "pass through" entity will be able to off-set her adjustable gross taxable income by the amount of the depreciation deduction. In the second scenario, the investment in the entity has resulted in a loss which the individual partner or member can use to off-set income from other sources (subject to the passive activity loss rules described below.)

Depreciation Deduction Is Only Available to Certain Types of Taxpayers. The depreciation deduction is only available for property used in the taxpayer's business (a grocer's store) or held for the production of income (all rental property). Property held for personal use, including a home, is not depreciable.

I.R.C. § 469–was aimed directly at passive investors in rental real estate. The regulations under I.R.C. § 469 divide all sources of income into three categories: active, portfolio and passive.

Active income includes salaries, fees and profit or loss from a trade or business in which the taxpayer materially participates.

Portfolio income includes investment income and losses such as interest, dividends, royalties and securities sales.

Passive income encompasses income and deductions attributable to a trade or business in which the taxpayer does not materially participate. Income from rental property is defined as passive income no matter how actively the taxpayer oversees the rental property. Passive income also includes gain from the sale of property held for investment.

Each year individuals can only deduct losses from passive activity against gains from the operation of similar passive activity, as defined by the Code and regulations.[80] If the taxpayer lacks sufficient passive gains in any one year to offset that year's passive losses, the taxpayer carries the losses forward to offset passive activity gains in future years. The losses become fully deductible upon a taxable sale of the activity. An investor losing money on a rental real estate investment can only deduct the loss from gains generated by an investment made mainly for the generation of passive income, or PIGs, as they are called.

There are two exceptions to the passive activity loss rules under IRC § 469:

(1) A *partial exemption* is available for individuals or other taxpayers who actively participate in rental real estate activity. The exemption allows the first $25,000 of

---

80. IRS Publication 925 (January, 2010) details the passive activity loss rules.

losses each year to offset non-passive income. The taxpayer must own at least 10% of the property and can't have income above certain qualifying levels. The $25,000 allowance is phased out by 50 percent of the amount by which the taxpayer's adjusted gross income for the year exceeds $100,000, thus disappearing entirely at $150,000. This provision invites middle-income taxpayers to enjoy a modicum of tax shelter from rental property investments without opening the door to wholesale tax avoidance by the wealthy.

(2) *Full-time real estate professionals* (*e.g.*, brokers, leasing agents) may deduct the passive losses from rental real estate activities against their active income from other sources, subject to some very precise guidelines and limitations.[81]

What Is Left for Realty Investors of the Passive Loss Tax Shield. Realty investors benefit by being able to use passive losses from realty to shield gains that would otherwise be taxable and were able to lobby Congress successfully to retain much of that benefit.[82] For starters, the law still allows investors to shelter all their earnings from a particular property by paper tax losses from the same property. For another, individuals are still entitled to use passive losses from one activity to shelter passive gains from another. Also, most C corporations aren't bound by these rules. They can use passive losses from one of the corporation's activities to shelter active gains from other corporate endeavors–provided the C corporation isn't closely held, as the Code defines that term.

Finally, investors can often structure their activities to generate active or passive income, whichever suits their tax planning needs. For instance, suppose A and B purchase a profitable parking garage. They could choose between hiring a management company to operate the garage on their behalf for active income, or leasing the garage to the operator for a fixed or percentage rent, passive income.[83]

Depreciation Recapture on Sale. The investor's "basis" for tax purposes is reduced each year by the depreciation deduction taken. Someday, when the investor sells the building, she will be subject to tax on her gain as measured by subtracting her "basis" from the ultimate net selling price (the sales price less brokerage, escrow and other costs of sale). The consequence is that the taxpayer is going to be taxed at the point of sale on the depreciation allowances she claimed each year that she owned the property. Currently, the "depreciation recapture" rate is 25%. One way to look at this is that the taxpayer avoided being taxed on the depreciation allowance at her average federal income tax rate in exchange for eventually paying tax on that sum at the depreciation recapture rate.

The Actual Value of the Property Will Probably Exceed the Taxpayer's Basis. Critics of the depreciation deduction label it "ostensible depreciation" since "the point of

---

81. *See* REG. § 1.469-9; Richard M. Lipton, *Passive Loss Audit Guidelines Highlight Issues for Taxpayers*, 72 TAXES 606 (1994).

82. *See* Jeffrey H. Birnbaum & Alan S. Murray, SHOWDOWN AT GUCCI GULCH: LAWMAKERS, LOBBYISTS, AND THE UNLIKELY TRIUMPH OF TAX REFORM 219–222 (1987).

83. *See generally* Mona L. Hymel, *Tax Policy and the Passive Loss Rules: Is Anybody Listening?*, 40 ARIZ. L. REV. 615 (1998).

owning buildings is that they generally appreciate."[84] While it is true that the value of real property often greatly exceeds the owner's depreciated basis in the property, buildings inevitably wear out. But land often appreciates so that upon sale, the owner receives a net sales price far greater than his depreciated basis in the property.

Consequences of Pass Through (Flow Through) Gains and Losses for LLCs and Partnerships. As previously mentioned, entities taxed as partnerships (including LLCs) avoid tax at the entity level.[85] All of their gains and losses are passed through to the individual partners or LLC members. Each partner's share of entity income and loss is reported on the partner's separate income tax return.

These shares are established at the entity level based on allocation provisions in the partnership or operating agreement. Within limits, the partnership form allows flexibility so that losses may be allocated to some partners and gains to others, or operating income to some and capital gains to others.

Gains and losses can be allocated to different partners in different amounts as long as the allocation has a 'substantial economic effect' other than tax savings. 'Substantial economic effect' test has two requirements. First, the allocation of gains or losses must have economic effect. This means that the partner to whom the allocation is made must bear the economic burden of the allocation. Second, the economic effect must be substantial. The general rule for substantiality is that an economic effect of allocation is substantial if there is a reasonable possibility that the allocation (or allocations) will substantially affect the dollar amounts to be received by the partners from the partnership, independent of tax consequences.

The allocation of tax gains and losses follow the ratio of capital or the agreed upon fair market value of land or other non-cash contributions that each partner or member contributes to the partnership or LLC. Contributions made to a partnership by a partner (whether in cash or in-kind) are generally made tax-free.[86]

A partner's contributed capital becomes part of the partner's basis in the partnership. No partner can deduct a tax loss greater than her basis in the partnership. Distributions made to a partner are taxed that exceed the partner's basis in its partnership interest.[87] Profits and losses allocated in a way that lacks substantial economic effect will be reallocated by the Internal Revenue Service for tax purposes according to the partners' interests in the partnership.

With respect to recourse debt to an entity (debt for which the entity can be liable), the right to include a pro rata share of that debt in basis belongs to individual members of that entity who would in reality bear the economic risk of loss if the debt weren't

---

84. See, e.g., Steven Rattner, *Trump and the Art of the Loophole*, NY Times, 05/13/2016, p.A23, col. 2.

85. Internal Revenue Code §§ 701–777.

86. Internal Revenue Code § 721 (a).

87. Internal Revenue Code § 731((a) (1).

paid. A partner cannot claim a share of partnership debt if that partner is *not* liable on the mortgage if any other partner is personally liable. If, however, the partnership debt is non-recourse as to all the partners, then each of them may include a proportionate share of the debt in his or her basis.

Hypo: G and L are general partners in a partnership formed to acquire an apartment building costing $1,000,000. Each makes a cash contribution of $100,000 and the partnership obtains a mortgage in the amount of $800,000 to fund the balance of the construction costs. Under the terms of the partnership agreement they are to share profits equally, but L's liabilities are limited to the extent of his contribution. Neither the partnership nor either of the partners assumes any personal liability on the mortgage, and the loan is obtained from a 'qualified' lender who regularly makes loans and who is not related to the partnership or the partners. *Results*: The basis of G and L for their partnership interest is increased from $100,000 to $500,000, since each partner's share of the partnership liability has increased by $400,000.

Pass Throughs (Flow Throughs) of Gains and Losses for Tenancies in Common. All tenancy-in-common gains and losses are passed directly to the individual co-tenants. Each co-tenant pays tax on rents, profits and capital gains from her undivided share of the co-tenancy property. Each co-tenant may deduct her proportionate share of co-tenancy expenses, whether paid by her or on her behalf, as well as mortgage payments, insurance premiums and property tax payments owed by and advanced on behalf of her co-tenants, unless it is reimbursed. Unlike partners, co-tenants may not reallocate income and depreciation deductions in ratios different from their share in the co-tenancy property.

C. The Tax Free Exchange

A bright spot for a commercial real estate investor is the opportunity to defer paying capital gains tax on a property sale, *the relinquished property*, by re-investing the sale proceeds into *a replacement property* of "like kind."[88] As the Internal Revenue Service explains Section 1031 of the Code: "*Whenever you sell business or investment property and you have a gain, you generally have to pay tax on the gain at the time of sale. IRC Section 1031 provides an exception and allows you to postpone paying tax on the gain if you reinvest the proceeds in similar property as part of a qualifying like-kind exchange. Gain deferred in a like-kind exchange under IRC Section 1031 is tax-deferred, but it is not tax-free.*

---

88. It is also permissible under Section 1031 to acquire the replacement property first under a reverse exchange.

"A reverse exchange is somewhat more complex than a deferred exchange. It involves the acquisition of replacement property through an exchange accommodation titleholder, with whom it is parked for no more than 180 days. During this parking period the taxpayer disposes of its relinquished property to close the exchange." IRS, *Like-Kind Exchanges Under IRC Code Section 1031*, FS-2008-18 (last visited May 31, 2016), https://www.irs.gov/uac/Like-Kind-Exchanges-Under-IRC-Code-Section-1031

"Virtually any kind of rental real estate, as long as the sale and subsequent purchase qualify as an 'exchange' under the strict rules of Section 1031 of the Internal Revenue Code. To qualify as a Section 1031 exchange, a deferred exchange must be distinguished from the case of a taxpayer simply selling one property and using the proceeds to purchase another property (which is a taxable transaction). Rather, in a deferred exchange, the disposition of the relinquished property and acquisition of the replacement property must be mutually dependent parts of an integrated transaction constituting an exchange of property. Taxpayers engaging in deferred exchanges generally use exchange facilitators under exchange agreements pursuant to rules provided in the Income Tax Regulations.

"Be careful in your selection of a qualified intermediary as there have been recent incidents of intermediaries declaring bankruptcy or otherwise being unable to meet their contractual obligations to the taxpayer. These situations have resulted in taxpayers not meeting the strict timelines set for a deferred or reverse exchange, thereby disqualifying the transaction from Section 1031 deferral of gain. The gain may be taxable in the current year while any losses the taxpayer suffered would be considered under separate code sections."[89]

Strict time limits apply; the taxpayer needs to identify potential replacement properties within 45 days, and take title to the replacement property within 180 days of the relinquished property sale closing.

"Both the relinquished property you sell and the replacement property you buy must meet certain requirements. Both properties must be held for use in a trade or business (e.g., a welder's shop) or for investment (e.g., undeveloped acreage, or the production of income, e.g., rental units). Property used primarily for personal use, like a primary residence or a second home or vacation home, does not qualify for like-kind exchange treatment. (If the owner of rental property occupies one of the units as her personal residence, and exchanges the property for an apartment house where she does not plan to reside, that portion of the gain or loss attributable to the personal residence is ineligible for 1031 treatment.)

"Both properties must be similar enough to qualify as 'like-kind.' Like-kind property is property of the same nature, character or class. Quality or grade does not matter. Most real estate will be like-kind to other real estate. For example, real property that is improved with a residential rental house is like-kind to vacant land. One exception for real estate is that property within the United States is not like-kind to property outside of the United States. Also, improvements that are conveyed without land are not of like kind to land."[90]

An owner could consolidate her holdings and free herself of the burden to attend personally to tenant needs by exchanging, say, three single-family rentals for one

89. IRS, *Like-Kind Exchanges Under IRC Code Section 1031*, FS-2008-18 (last visited May 31, 2016), https://www.irs.gov/uac/Like-Kind-Exchanges-Under-IRC-Code-Section-1031

90. IRS, *Like-Kind Exchanges Under IRC Code Section 1031*, FS-2008-18 (last visited May 31, 2016), https://www.irs.gov/uac/Like-Kind-Exchanges-Under-IRC-Code-Section-1031

apartment complex large enough to support a resident manager. She could exchange vacant land producing no income for an office building generating substantial rental income. Desiring to diversify her holdings, the owner of a portfolio of apartment houses in New Jersey could sell some of them to reinvest the proceeds in a Virginia warehouse, a Los Angeles grocery store and a Florida citrus grove.[91]

Real property and personal property can both qualify as exchange properties under Section 1031; but real property can never be like-kind to personal property. In personal property exchanges, the rules pertaining to what qualifies as like-kind are more restrictive than the rules pertaining to real property. As an example, cars are not like-kind to trucks.

Finally, certain types of property are specifically excluded from Section 1031 treatment. Section 1031 does not apply to exchanges of:

- *Inventory or stock in trade*
- *Stocks, bonds, or notes*
- *Other securities or debt*
- *Partnership interests*
- *Certificates of trust"*[92]

Owners of investment and business property may qualify for a Section 1031 deferral. Individuals, C corporations, S corporations, partnerships (general or limited), limited liability companies, trusts and any other taxpaying entity may set up an exchange of business or investment properties for business or investment properties under Section 1031.[93] However, the owning entity must engage in the exchange, not the individual shareholders, partners, or LLC members. Individually, they have no right to exchange their particular ownership interests except as part of a transaction involving the entire entity. The statute specifically excludes exchanges of corporate shares, partnership interests, or LLC memberships from the benefits of 1031 deferred tax treatment.

When the controlling entity owners reject the idea of exchanging an entity asset for another, dissenters are stuck. Dissenter's options are available in a tenancy in common because each co-tenant owns a direct interest in tenancy in common property. The tenancy in common is not an entity; it is simply a description of how title is held. This is why LLCs sometimes convert into tenancies-in-common, and why some developers and investors prefer the tenancy-in-common form. As previously noted, the tenancy in common is not an entity.

---

91. http://www.investmentnews.com/article/20080211/REG/546590174/1031-exchanges-yield-income-write-offs

92. IRS, *Like-Kind Exchanges Under IRC Code Section 1031*, FS-2008-18 (last visited May 31, 2016), https://www.irs.gov/uac/Like-Kind-Exchanges-Under-IRC-Code-Section-1031

93. IRS, *Like-Kind Exchanges Under IRC Code Section 1031*, FS-2008-18 (last visited May 31, 2016), https://www.irs.gov/uac/Like-Kind-Exchanges-Under-IRC-Code-Section-1031

Tenants in Common Can Exchange Interests in One TIC for Interests in Another TIC

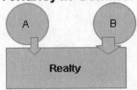

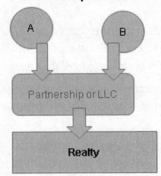

Boot. Only rarely will exchanged properties have identical values. The owner of the less valuable property will need to pay additional consideration to make-up for the difference. Anything a taxpayer receives through a 1031 exchange that is not property of 'like kind' is taxable, called 'boot.'

'Boot' can take the form of cash, mortgage debt or personal property. Receipt of boot does not necessarily destroy an exchange but the owner is taxed on boot at the point of sale. Gain or loss will be recognized (*i.e.*, subject to tax) on the exchange "but only to the extent of the boot received."[94]

The IRC calls for the recipient of the additional consideration to be taxed on the cash received in excess of the taxpayer's adjusted basis in the relinquished property. The taxpayer owes no tax on the cash received to the extent it just equals or is less than the taxpayer's adjusted basis, though the recipient's basis is reduced dollar for dollar by the amount of cash received.

Example: Taxpayer exchanges real estate worth $100,000 that has a tax basis of $60,000 for real estate worth $80,000 plus $20,000 in cash. Gain on the transaction is $40,000 ($100,000 minus $60,000), but only $20,000 of it is recognized, the amount of the boot.[95]

When each side gives and receives cash in addition to the qualified property, only the net amount is treated as boot. Liabilities assumed, and liabilities on property taken subject to liabilities, are treated as cash received. The transferor who assumes the liability or who takes the property subject to a liability is the one giving the boot. The transferor whose liability is assumed or the one who transfers property subject to a liability is the one receiving the boot.

---

94. Michael P. Dunworth, *Comparisons and Consequences: A Primer on Like Kind Exchanges*, Business Law Today 52,56 (July/August 2002).

95. 2 Ill. Forms Legal & Bus. § 1C:10

Example: Blackacre has a value of $230,000, a basis of $80,000, and a mortgage of $120,000. It is exchanged for cash of $10,000 and Whiteacre, valued at $200,000, with a $100,000 mortgage. Gain on the transaction is $150,000, made up of $100,000 for Whiteacre ($200,000 minus $100,000), the mortgage of $120,000, $10,000 cash, minus the $80,000 basis. Only the **boot** of $30,000 is recognizable gain. That is determined by subtracting the $100,000 mortgage on the property received (Whiteacre) from the mortgage on Blackacre ($120,000) and adding to that result ($20,000) the $10,000 cash received.[96]

The Advantage of the Tax Deferred Exchange. A like kind exchange allows the taxpayer the use of pre-tax dollars rather than after-tax dollars for reinvestment. By deferring tax, an investor is left with more after tax dollars to invest than if she had paid taxes on her gain.

Suppose an investor has a cost basis in real estate of $250,000 that she sells for $750,000. Her realized gain will be $500,000, taxed at a rate of 15%, resulting in a tax liability of $75,000. She deducted $100,000 in depreciation deductions, subject to a tax rate of 25%, adding $25,000 to her total tax bill on sale. She also had a mortgage of $450,000 that must be repaid upon sale. This leaves her with $300,000 subject to a $100,000 tax upon sale, a net amount of $200,000.

By utilizing a tax deferred exchange, she will be able to earn income on an investment of $300,000 instead of $200,000. Tax on the $100,000 will be deferred. For most real estate investors, this benefit is multiplied by the use of borrowed funds.[97]

In the following example, the taxpayer borrows two dollars for every dollar of invested equity, earns a 5% annual return on the total amount invested and pays an annual interest rate of 4% on the borrowed funds. Her annual net income without using 1031 would have been $16,000. Utilizing 1031, it is $36,000.

The Consequences of Using Pre Tax Dollars to Acquire Real Estate

POST TAX LEVERAGE	PRE TAX LEVERAGE
▪ 200,000 (equity)	▪ 300,000 (equity)
▪ 400,000 (debt)	▪ 600,000 (debt)
▪ -----------------------	▪ -------------------------------
▪ 600,000 (acquisition price) x 5% annual return =$30,000 [less cost of debt @4%=$16,000]	▪ 900,000 (acquisition price) x 5% annual return =$45,000 [less cost of debt @4%=$36,000]

---

96. 2 Ill. Forms Legal & Bus. § 1C:10.

97. However, researchers have found that investors utilizing 1031 use some of the deferred gains to increase the size of their investment in subsequent properties, and use less leverage than ordinary investors to acquire replacement properties and hold their replacement properties for shorter periods of time. David C. Ling and Milena Petrova, *The Economic Impact of Repealing or Limiting Section 1031 Like-Kind Exchanges in Real* Estate (last visited May 31, 2016), http://taxprof.typepad.com/files/ling-petrova.pdf

Many of Those Eligible Do Not Avail Themselves of 1031.

Here are some of the reasons that well over half of those who are eligible to utilize 1031 do not avail themselves of it.

(1) They were selling because they needed the cash.

(2) They wished to disinvest or reduce their holdings of real estate assets.

(3) They wanted to avoid the administrative costs of a tax deferred exchange— fees for tax or accounting advisors, and for "qualified intermediaries" to administer the exchange.

(4) They were unable to identify replacement properties or close on the acquisition within the statutory time limits.

(5) They could not find an acceptable replacement property at what they regarded as a reasonable price.

(6) They were unaware of the statute.

(7) They decided to recognize their gains at the point of sale instead of deferring them because they believed that capital gains tax rates would never be lower.

(8) They sought to preserve the depreciation deduction based on the purchase price of the newly acquired property, instead of carrying forward their already deeply depreciated basis from the relinquished property.

To elaborate on this last point, in complying with 1031, a property seller is required to carry forward into the replacement property the basis she had in the relinquished property. *"The resulting depreciable basis is generally lower than what would otherwise be available if the replacement property were acquired in a taxable transaction.*[98] In a tax-deferred exchange, the taxpayer is trading the deferral of tax at capital gains tax rates for the right to set a new depreciation schedule based on the value of the acquired property to off-set earnings taxable at higher ordinary income rates. Currently, the capital gains tax rate is 23.8 percent, and the ordinary income rate 39.6 percent.

Tax Credits Compared to Depreciation Deductions. Governments also make tax credits available to draw investors to projects they regard as being of special public benefit. Presently, there are two significant tax credit programs. One is for low-income housing[99] and the other for the rehabilitation of certain historic buildings.[100] Deductions reduce taxable income and their value thus depends on the taxpayer's marginal tax rate, which rises with income. Credits reduce taxes directly, dollar for dollar, and the extent of the cash benefit does not depend on the taxpayer's particular tax rate like the depreciation deduction.

---

98. 26 C.F.R. § 1.1031(a)-1(b)

99. Low-Income Housing Tax Credits, Hud.Gov (last visited May 31, 2016), http://www.huduser.gov/portal/datasets/lihtc.html

100. Rehabilitation Tax Credit, Irs.Gov (last visited May 31, 2016), http://www.irs.gov/Businesses/Small-Businesses-&-Self-Employed/Rehabilitation-Tax-Credit-Real-Estate-Tax-Tips

D. The S Corporation: Tax Advantages and Disadvantages

An S corporation is a corporation that elects to be taxed under the provisions of Subchapter S of the Internal Revenue Code[101] instead of Subchapter C.

An S corporation shareholder has the same limited liability protection as a C corporation shareholder.

The main tax advantage is that an S corporation shareholder avoids double taxation because the corporation is not taxed on earnings at the entity level.[102] Shareholders of S corporations report the flow-through of income and losses on their personal tax returns, and are taxed at their individual rates on their proportionate share of corporate earnings, whether distributed as dividends or not.

Compared to other "pass through" entities—partnerships or LLCs, the S corporation has several disadvantages described next.

Statutory Criteria for S Corp Status. In order to elect Subchapter S status, a corporation must meet the statutory definition of a 'small business corporation':[103]

(1) a corporation created or organized in the U.S.;

(2) which is an eligible corporation;

(3) has 100 or fewer shareholding individuals;

(4) has no nonresident alien shareholder; and

(5) has only one class of stock.[104]

Compare the above restrictions with the flexibility of the partnership format. A *partner* can be an individual, corporation, trust, estate, or partnership. With few exceptions, S corp shareholders can only be individuals, not entities. Also, while nonresident aliens are barred from being S corp shareholders, they can be general or limited partners in a partnership. Again, unlike the S corp with its strict limit on the number of permissible shareholders, there are no restrictions on the number of partners in a partnership.

S Corp Shareholder Basis Limitations. Tax losses (phantom expense) passed to S corporation shareholders cannot exceed each shareholder's adjusted basis in her shares. *That basis excludes the corporation's non-recourse mortgage debt.* "In other words, while a partner is able to obtain a step-up in its adjusted basis equal to its share of mortgage liabilities, a Subchapter S shareholder cannot."[105]

---

101. INTERNAL REVENUE CODE §§ 1361–1379.

102. S-Corporations, IRS. Gov (last visited May 31, 2016), https://www.irs.gov/Businesses/Small-Businesses-&-Self-Employed/S-Corporations

103. I.R.C. §§ 1361(a) and 1362(a).

104. S-Corporations, IRS. Gov (last visited May 31, 2016), https://www.irs.gov/Businesses/Small-Businesses-&-Self-Employed/S-Corporations

105. In one circumstance the S corporation shareholder may treat a loan to the corporation as part of the shareholder's basis: when the shareholder guarantees the loan and "the lender looks primarily to the shareholder as the primary obligor." Just guaranteeing the S corp debt is insufficient if the lender expects repayment from a primary obligor other than the shareholder guarantor.

Hypo: G and F formed an S Corporation to acquire an apartment building worth $1 million. Each makes a cash contribution of $200,000 and the Corporation obtains a mortgage in the amount of $600,000 for the remainder of the purchase price. Neither the Corporation, nor G or F, assume any liability on the mortgage. G and F each have a tax basis of $200,000 in the asset. Had they elected limited liability or partnership status, each of them would have had a tax basis of $500,000.

E. The Real Estate Investment Trust (REIT)

Congress created REITs in 1960 to make accessible to average investors the opportunity to invest in passively held investments in income-producing real estate equities, mortgages or both.[106] As with mutual funds that invest in stocks and bonds, the main REIT tax advantage is the avoidance of tax at the entity level. To maintain this privileged tax treatment on its income, REITs must comply with a number of requirements described below, primarily concerning distributions of earnings, portfolio limitations and equity ownership limitations.[107]

Distributions. REITs must pay at least 95 percent of their taxable income to their shareholders.

Distributions made to a REIT's shareholders are generally treated as ordinary dividends. Long-term capital gains of the REIT, when distributed, are taxable to the beneficiaries as long-term capital gains if the REIT has designated such distribution as a capital gain dividend.

Because of this distribution requirement, REIT shareholders avoid the risk of becoming liable for taxes on "phantom income." Investors in partnerships, limited partnerships, LLCs or S corporations will be taxed on entity gains due to their "pass through" tax status, whether or not the entity actually passes those gains to its partners, members or shareholders.

The taxable income considered in the minimum distribution requirement does not include capital gains income. A REIT is not required to distribute capital gains income, but capital gains are taxed to the shareholders whether distributed or not. If a REIT retains capital gains income, the shareholder reports the amount of capital gain on their income tax return for the year in which the gain is realized. The shareholder may then increase their basis in their shares to the extent of per share funds withheld by the REIT on which the shareholder paid taxes.

---

106. See generally, A. Overton Durrett, The Real Estate Investment Trust: A New Medium for Investors, 3 Wm. & Mary L. Rev. 139 (1961).

107. Thomas A. Jesch, *The Taxation Of "Opportunistic" Real Estate Private Equity Funds And U.S. Real Estate Investment Trusts (REITs)—An Investor's Comparative Analysis*, 34 Real Est. L. J. 275, 283–84 (2005).

REIT distributions can only be made pro rata among all shares of the same class. Any other method of distribution is dubbed 'preferential' and would trigger taxation at the entity level.

The majority of REIT dividends are taxed as ordinary income up to the maximum rate of 39.6 percent, plus a separate 3.8 percent surtax on investment income. However, REIT dividends will qualify for a lower tax rate in the following instances: when the individual taxpayer is subject to a lower scheduled income tax rate; when a REIT makes a capital gains distribution (20 percent maximum tax rate, plus the 3.8 percent surtax) or a return of capital distribution; when a REIT distributes dividends received from a taxable REIT subsidiary or other corporation (20 percent maximum tax rate, plus the 3.8 percent surtax); and when permitted, a REIT pays corporate taxes and retains earnings (20 percent maximum tax rate, plus the 3.8 percent surtax).

Due to the distribution requirement, REITS are severely limited in their options for managing and reinvesting their profits. Unlike C corporations, REITs cannot tap into retained earnings to grow their businesses in good times, and accumulate reserves to cover losses in bad times. REITs can increase their capital only by issuing stock, borrowing money or accumulating cash as a result of depreciation allowances. (Shareholders add basis to REIT distributions of depreciation deductions.)

Portfolio Limitations. So that REITs veer away from unfairly competing with real estate firms that are subject to tax at the corporate level, they must derive at least 95% of their income from long-term "passive" activities such as collecting rents, mortgage interest payments and dividends. REITs jeopardize their tax exempt status at the entity level by earning income from subdividing land; developing real estate; constructing projects; buying, renovating and "flipping" property for sale within two years of acquisition; selling property as "stock in trade" (as homebuilders do); or offering real estate-related services such as brokerage, title, escrow and mortgage lending.

REITs are allowed to a limited extent to form subsidiaries that earn "active" income through specially created entities called Taxable REIT subsidiaries that are subject to the same corporate taxes at the entity level as C corporations.[108]

Equity Ownership Dispersal Tests. REITs must be widely held to preclude their becoming a tax dodge for wealthy individuals instead of a sort of mutual fund for real estate available to ordinary investors. To encourage small investors, REIT ownership is widespread, precluding five or fewer individuals from owning shares that represent more than 50% of the REIT's value. A REIT must have at least 100 shareholders during at least 335/365ths of a taxable year.[109]

---

108. Thornton Matheson, *The Development of Taxable REIT Subsidiaries, 2001–2004, Statistics of Income*, Bulletin (2008).http://66.77.0.238/pub/irs-soi/01-04coreitbul.pdf

109. Some REITs, however, are organized with nominal accommodation shareholders designated by a handful of principals to reach the 100 shareholder level *Ibid.*

Equity, Mortgage or Hybrid REITS. An equity REIT acquires commercial properties, such as office buildings, shopping centers and apartment buildings—and leases the space to rent-paying tenants. Equity REITs invest in and own real properties of all kinds. Their revenues come principally from rents and property appreciation and assume the customary downside risks associated with real estate assets. After paying the expenses associated with operating their properties and managing their companies, Equity REITs must distribute the bulk of their income annually to their shareholders as dividends.

Mortgage REITs deal in the investment and ownership of mortgages on real property. They loan money to owners of real estate, purchase existing mortgages or mortgage-backed securities, and issue mortgage backed securities secured by the loans they originate. Mortgage REITs, like banks, earn profits from the spread between the rates they pay to borrow funds from warehouse lenders or in short-term bond markets and what they earn by investing in longer term mortgages or mortgage backed securities. Thus, their earnings are greatly dependent on the spread between short and long term mortgage rates.

There are two broad types of Mortgage REITs: *residential* and *commercial*. Residential REITs focus on buying securities backed by government guaranteed mortgages, which seek to provide returns based on high leverage and minimal credit risk. They may also accumulate mortgages in order to sell them as privately issued mortgage backed securities. Commercial REITs focus on commercial properties rather than residential, seeking to create returns by sound underwriting practices combined with prudent leverage.

Hybrid REITs combine the Investment Strategies of equity REITs and mortgage REITs by investing in both properties and mortgages. All three attempt to provide shareholders with consistent dividends.

About 10 % of REITs are mortgage REITs; the other 90% are equity REITs.[110]

Publicly Traded or Private (Non-Traded) REITs. REITs typically pay relatively high annual dividends based on stock prices, and the stock can be bought and sold easily in stock markets.[111] The downside is that, like all publicly traded stock, REIT share prices are subject to the whimsical ups and downs of instantaneous market pricing that can be unrelated to the actual performance of the particular REIT or the actual value of its assets.

A REIT that is not publicly traded on a securities exchange has constrained liquidity for its investors, and often offers them far less information than is available to shareholders of publicly traded REITs. Front-end fees paid to sponsors, real estate brokers

---

110. *Understanding the Basics of REITs*, REIT.COM (last visited May 31, 2016), https://www.reit.com/investing/reit-basics/faqs/basics-reits

111. As of Jan. 29, 2016, there were 198 REITs listed on the New York Stock Exchange. These REITs have a combined equity market capitalization of $857 billion. Internal Revenue Service shows that there are about 1,100 U.S. REITs that have filed tax returns. *Understanding the Basics of REITs*, REIT.COM (last visited May 31, 2016), https://www.reit.com/investing/reit-basics/faqs/basics-reits

and other intermediaries can be exorbitant, and it is difficult, if not impossible, to sell the securities before they become publicly traded.

Summary. The REIT investor obtains a conduit tax treatment on the one hand and limited liability and liquidity on the other. Still, the REIT does not allow the investor to deduct losses personally, has restrictions on its investment portfolio options, and cannot build cash reserves from retained earnings.

IV. Drafting LLC Operating Agreements

A. A Joint Venture Hypothetical

In typical real estate joint ventures, project sponsors seek equity funding from investors. Consider this example: Alisia (A), an aspiring apartment operator and developer, has successfully completed the construction of two apartment buildings (12 and 16 units) with cash from family and friends. She is in her early 30s with two children to support, a boy three years old and a girl of two. She has retained ownership of the buildings because the net operating income from them is her sole source of financial support.

Now, she feels ready to take on a larger project, a 100 unit multifamily building not far from her first two ventures, in a somewhat more expensive area. The site is on a walkable street with considerable pedestrian traffic so she plans to include 50,000 square feet of ground floor retail space.

She has prepared a *pro forma* showing that the project will produce a significant cash flow when the units are rented at levels comparable to those in the area.

Her estimated project cost is $25,000,000. She is fairly confident of being able to borrow $20,000,000 through the same mortgage broker who helped arrange financing for her first two projects. In that mortgage broker's opinion, A's chances of obtaining favorable financing would be greatly enhanced if she could raise $5,000,000 of equity capital.

When her husband was killed by a drunk driver just over a year ago, A obtained an insurance settlement of $2,500,000. She plans to invest $1.0 million of that money in this venture.

Carlos (C) is in his early 50s. A few years after graduating from law school, he and two classmates founded a law firm that specializes in consumer and tort litigation, and now employs 20 lawyers. (He met A through a friend.)

C is an avid saver because he and his co-founders have established a mandatory retirement age of 65 at the firm to nurture advancement opportunities for younger associates. He has placed most of his savings in ETF mutual funds with Vanguard. He would like the diversification of owning an income producing asset in the neighborhood that A has selected for her next project. He is willing to invest $4 million into this project.

Before they pool their resources and begin their venture, A and C will probably meet to work out the major details of their business relationship. At some point, they may decide they are close enough to a consensus on the major issues to hire counsel to draft a formal LLC operating agreement, either selecting one attorney to represent "the entity" or separate attorneys to represent each of them.[112]

The operating agreement governs the members' relationships to each other and to the LLC. This is the document which memorializes the members' understanding of their business arrangement and their respective rights and duties.[113] Here are some of the issues that they will need to address.

1. How Is Decision Making and Management Oversight to Be Allocated Between Alisia (A) and Carlos (C)?

Should either A or C, acting alone, be entitled to make crucial decisions binding the other—land acquisition, construction contracts, financing and re-financing? Quite often, while equity investors are content to allow the project sponsor to make day-to-day operating decisions, subject to periodic financial reporting and compete access to project books and records, they insist upon the right to participate in "major decisions" with significant financial consequences, such as the development of a business plan, decisions to buy land, sell the project or borrow against it, approve the budgets for construction and annual operations, take in additional partners, or modify the underlying agreement.

C might insist upon the right to make these decisions since his cash investment is four times A's. But the concept for the project and its ultimate success depend on A's capabilities and commitment.

What will be the respective roles of A and C in hiring the architect and general contractor, and negotiating agreements with them? Selecting a management company and replacing it? Negotiating compensation for the manager? Deciding on the amount and types of insurance for the project and the LLC, and the "deductibles"? Setting rent levels, granting rent concessions, and choosing tenants? Establishing the amount of replacement reserves to be for the building's major components? Picking the project and LLC accountant?

2. Who Contributes How Much Capital and When?

Will C be required to contribute all $4,000,000 at once even before A obtains an option on the site, or actually acquires title to the site with her own funds? Should

---

112. "Representing an entity: Who is the client? The Rules provide that the lawyer's loyalty is to the entity itself, not the individuals comprising the entity. New York courts have long adhered to this principle, absent a lawyer's affirmative assumption of the duty of representation." Stewart D. Aaron, Ethical Issues in Commercial Cases, 4B N.Y.P Com. Litig. in New York State Courts § 70:6 (4th ed.) (updated September 2015).

113. Carter G. Bishop and Daniel S. Kleinberger, *Operating Agreements*, Limited Liab Co.. ¶ 5.06 (2016). See generally, Terence Floyd Cuff, *How To Compromise Partnership And LLC Agreements*, 27 No. 3 Prac. Tax Law. 5 (Spring, 2013).

C's cash contributions be phased to become due only when A procures the necessary land use approvals to build a 100-unit apartment house on the site, draws plans and obtains a building permit, or signs a note and deed of trust for a construction loan, and begins construction?

3. How About Additional Capital Calls?

What should the agreement provide regarding who can initiate additional capital calls, for what reasons, and in what amounts? Additional funds might be needed to complete the project, pay the mortgage loan, property taxes, insurance premiums, utilities and maintenance. A stalemate could sink the project, leading to dissolution of the LLC.[114]

4. What Should Be The Sanctions For An Individual Failing to Contribute As Required?

Common alternatives result in the dilution of the non-contributing member's share of future distributions from the LLC (called a "squeeze down"), or the contributing member making a loan to the non-contributor or the LLC.[115]

5. What Preferred Return Are Cash Investors Entitled to Receive?

"Historically, the rate of the annual preferred return rate on real estate development deals has run somewhere between 8% and 12% of the contributed capital."[116] This return is rarely guaranteed; it is contingent on there being sufficient cash flow to pay it. Frequently, investors are able to insist upon their preferred returns being cumulative, so that shortfalls in cash flow are made up in later years.

A related issue is whether the investor first becomes entitled to its target return on the date it contributes its capital, only when the project is completed, or not until the project attains its "stabilized" projected rents or achieves its anticipated net operating income.

6. When Is Cash To Be Distributed from the Project to the Members, and How Is It To Be Split Between A and C?

The operating agreement should specify how the cash flow is to be used, including how much of it is to be used for capital improvements and replacement reserves, and

---

114. The Uniform LLC Act provides the HOW TO COMPROMISE PARTNERSHIP AND LLC AGREEMENTS at upon dissolution, the assets of the LLC, after paying creditors, are to be distributed to the former members on the basis of the fair market vale of their interests on the date of dissolution. ULLCA §§ 701, 702 (1996). These are default provisions subject to change by the terms of the operating agreement.

115. See Stevens A. Carey, Daniel B. Guggenheim, and Michael Soejoto, *Contribution Default Remedies in a Real Estate Venture*, 53 Business Entities 4 (last visited May 31, 2016), http://www.pircher.com/media/publication/53_business%20entity%20article.pdf

116. Rick Daley, Real Estate Development Law p. 243 (2011).

the basis on which A is to be compensated in development/construction fees, management fees, and disposition fees if they sell the project.

The agreement should also prescribe the priorities among members for receiving cash distributions. A typical sequence would be: (1) The equity investor's promised preferred percentage return on its invested capital; (2) The equity investor's return of its contributed capital; (3) The promoter's return *on* its invested capital; (4) The promoter's return of its invested capital; (5) The promoter's return based on an imputed interest in the cash flow or the project.

This last item depends on how A, the developer in our example, is to be rewarded for having successfully developed and leased the project. These payments are called "promotes." The amount of the "promote" is usually contingent on the investor's actual returns.

Operating agreements also allocate the rights among members to distributions from the sale or refinancing of LLC assets. "The typical LLC Operating Agreement requires that the proceeds of the sale or refinancing of the LLC's assets (i.e., Capital Proceeds) first be used to return the members' capital contributions."[117]

The customary sequence is that first each cash investor receives any previously promised but unpaid rate of return on the capital it contributed. Then, the cash investors receive a payment equal to the current rate of return on their invested sums. Next, their capital is returned to them.

All of these payments are made *before* the developer or promoter receives it's "promote."

You might imagine that in a situation like this one, it would be in best interests of the developer-promoter to insist on detailing her right to a "promote" in the Operating Agreement. Not necessarily. State LLC statutes fill in the blanks left by Operating Agreements. While some statutes divide profits and losses among members based on the agreed *value* of each member's contribution to the LLC, other statutes entitle each member to an *equal* share of LLC profits and losses.[118]

7. Under What Conditions Can the Management Authority Be Shifted?

Typically, money partners like C would prefer the option of replacing A as the manager without having to demonstrate to an arbitrator or a court that A's decision was "reasonable." In our example, C has $4,000,000 at stake, a major piece of his future retirement fund. Unfettered, he would probably like to treat A as if she were a junior associate in his law firm, someone he could dismiss for unsatisfactory per-

---

117. Rick Daley, Real Estate Development Law p. 246 (2011). By including this provision, the developer who is granted a profits interest will not be taxed on the date that the LLC first grants the developer the right to a share of future LLC profits.

118. On March 1, 2014, the New Jersey Revised Uniform Limited Liability Company Act ("RULLCA") switched from a default rule calling for the allocation of profits and losses based on the agreed value of each member's contribution to the LLC to a system of equal shares per member. Patrick Convery, *Important Changes that LLC Members Should be Concerned About Regarding New LLC Law in New Jersey* (April 28, 2014).

formance without having to specify detailed reasons. After all, why would C do this if A were performing well?

Of course, A would push back. She might accept a provision terminating her management of the project upon proof that she stole money or committed other unlawful acts. At a minimum, she might insist that if C no longer appreciates her involvement in the project, she should have the option of finding a buyer for his 80% share at its present value or retaining her 20% interest for the greater of $1,000,000 or whatever she reasonably believes its present value to be.

C might take a fallback position, that he should have the right to remove A if she fails to achieve a promised cash flow on-time or on-budget project completion. But A will want to retain her management control if market conditions or other factors beyond A's control explain why her efforts so far have been a disappointment.

8. What Happens If the Members Deadlock on Major Decisions or One Wants to Sell and the Other Does Not?

In our hypothetical, both A and C would probably reserve the right to veto a sale or re-financing of entity assets. Even if A is principally responsible for managing the LLC operation, C would want the option of blocking a move that could imperil his financial stake in the LLC. Quite possibly, their not seeing eye-to-eye on a decision as fundamental as whether to sell or re-finance could lead to dissolution of the venture. A Delaware LLC statute cracks open the court room door for the LLC to be dissolved in situations like this. "The Court of Chancery may dissolve an LLC if one of its members claims that it is not 'reasonably practicable to carry on the business' in accordance with the purpose of the LLC agreement."[119]

Quite often, when one LLC member wants to sell and another does not, instead of risking a deadlock that could result in dissipating the equity value they created together, the Operating Agreement contains provisions for an amicable sale through Buy-Sell Agreements, Rights of First Refusal or Rights of First Offer. These are not mutually exclusive; an Operating Agreement could accommodate all three.

Buy-Sell Agreements allow either member to notify the other of a price at which it is willing to either buy the other member's interest or sell its own interest. These are called buy-sell agreements.[120] The member who initiates this process sets a price

---

119. Meghan Greubner, Delaware's Answer to Management Deadlock in the Limited Liability Company: Judicial Dissolution, 32 J. Corp. L. 641 (Spring, 2007).

See, e.g., Delaware Limited Liability Company Act, Del. Code Ann. tit. 6, § 18-802 (2005) (an LLC will be dissolved: (1) when the LLC operating agreement specifies a certain time for dissolution; (2) when the LLC operating agreement specifies a certain event for dissolution; (3) when the members consent in writing, unless otherwise provided; (4) when all members cease to exist, unless the personal representative of the last remaining member gives written consent to continue the LLC and is admitted to the LLC as a member within 90 days, unless otherwise provided; and (5) by court order).

120. Stevens A. Carey, *Buy Sell Agreements in Real Estate Joint Venture Agreements*, 39 Real Property, Prob. & Trust J. 651 (2005) (last visited May 31, 2016), http://www.pircher.com/media/publication/47_BuySellProvSAC.pdf

on both interests at which she is willing to buy or sell either or both membership interests. This works very well when the two owners have similar information about the value of the asset in question, and comparable abilities to finance the buy-out. Otherwise, it can be a disaster for the one who is ill-informed or under-capitalized.[121]

From the facts of our hypo, it is hard to imagine A consenting to any arrangement like this because she probably wants to operate the apartment house for its operating income and to participate in its eventual capital appreciation though she lacks the capital to buy out C.

Rights of First Refusal (ROFR.) A property owner may grant to a tenant, joint venture partner, or mortgage lender a right of first refusal. Unlike a buy-sell agreement, a ROFR is neither an offer to buy or to sell. It is a limitation on the property owner's right to conclude a sale to a third-party without extending to the holder, the grantee, a chance to match the terms that the grantor would accept from a third party. This gives the grantee the chance to match the precise terms of any offer that the grantor would accept from a third party. The grantor decides whether, how and when to put the property on the market, and what counts as an acceptable offer. Passively, the grantee awaits word from the grantor that she has received an acceptable offer that the grantee now has the chance to accept or reject. Acceptance should lead to the grantor and grantee entering a purchase and sale agreement. The grantee's declining to match the third-party bid frees the grantor to conclude a contract with the third party.

"The ROFR agreement normally designates the duration of the right, the manner in which the grantor must notify the holder of the opportunity, the length of time the holder has to exercise the right after receiving the notice, and the process the holder must follow to exercise the right. More comprehensive ROFR agreements address many other contingencies and nuances, including what specific events and circumstances will or will not trigger the right whether the holder's exercise may deviate in certain respects from the terms of the third party offer, whether and under what circumstances the grantor may sell the property to someone other than the specified third party. If the holder does not exercise the right, whether the holder's right will revive if the grantor's deal with the third party does not close, and more."[122]

Professor David Walker concludes that, all in all, a ROFR thins the ranks of potential bidders, thereby driving down the price for the grantor, while imposing significant negotiating, drafting and dispute related costs.[123] Third-party bidders risk losing the benefit of their search and negotiating efforts to the holder of the right if their offers are below market. As an insider, the holder of the right is likely to know the true value. Once the holder exercises its option, the bidder will have gained nothing from

---

121. Stevens A. Carey, *Buy/Sell Provisions in Real Estate Joint Venture Agreements*, 39 REAL PROP., PROB. & TR. J. 651 (Winter, 2005).

122. Carl J. Circo, *Purchase Options, ROFRs, and ROFOs: Theory and Practice* 287, 292–93 (The ACREL Papers, Spring 2016, San Diego)

123. David I. Walker, *Rethinking Rights of First Refusal*, 5 STAN. J.L. BUS. & FIN. 1 (1999).

its efforts in negotiating for a bargain price. When the holder of the right steps out of the bidder's way, the bidder will be haunted by the thought that she overpaid.

Rights of First Offer (ROFO). If the property owner, the grantor of a ROFO, decides to consider selling the property, she is obligated to make an offer to the grantee on terms she would accept. Alternately, a ROFO could put the burden on the grantee or holder of the right to make an offer first—though ROFOs are seldom drafted this way. The holder can either accept the grantor's terms, or negotiate a mutually acceptable alternative. Either way, a purchase and sale contract should follow.

When the holder of the right declines, the grantor is free to put the property on the market, though only on terms identical to those that were offered and rejected, or not materially more favorable to the buyer. The disputes and drafting issues are pretty much the same as with ROFRs. One significant difference, though, is that the property owner could conclude a transaction under a ROFO with the grantee without having to market the property.

9. Under What Conditions Can A Member Sell or Transfer Its Interest?

If A and C cannot reach agreement to sell, under what conditions may either of them sell their membership interest in the LLC?

"In all states, the assignment of a membership interest in a LLC only transfers the assignor's economic interests in the LLC. An assignee can acquire the full management and participatory rights of members only with the non-transferring members' consent ... or, in some states, as provided in the operating agreement." [124]

10. Is this a One-Time Venture with a Fixed Duration, or Do A and C Envision a Continuing Collaboration?

Would A or C benefit the most from their relationship having been drafted as a programmatic joint venture?

11. Should Either A or C Owe Each Other the Fiduciary Duties that Partners Owe Each Other?

Fiduciary Duties. "*The specific requirements of these duties can be intricate, but the basic duties can be described as follows:*

The fiduciary **duty of care** *requires managers to refrain from gross negligence and to consider all information reasonably available to them in making business decisions on behalf of the firm.*

The fiduciary **duty of loyalty** requires managers to put entity interests ahead of self-enrichment and to avoid any conflicts of interest. This includes not competing with the entity, not engaging in self-dealing with entity assets, not taking advantage

---

124. J. William Callison and, Maureen A. Sullivan, *Limited Liability Companies: A State-by-State Guide To Law And Practice*, Ltd. Liability Co. § 4:4 (2015).

of a business opportunity that arose because of the manager's position within the entity."[125]

The court-imposed *duty of good faith and fair dealing* has proven susceptible to varying and contradictory interpretations. Under one view, this phrase invites courts to determine whether an LLC member or manager acted in a way that was contrary to the reasonable expectations of the aggrieved party. Under another, the phrase is simply an elaboration of the concept of "fiduciary duty," the implied commitment that managers or members of an entity will subsume their individual best interests to the fulfillment of entity objectives in their dealings with each other or in contracts with others on behalf of the entity. A third more restrictive, interpretation is that this covenant seeks to enforce the parties' contractual bargain by implying only those terms that the parties would have agreed to during their original negotiations if they had thought to address them. This is the position taken by the Delaware courts.[126]

Finally, the fiduciary, and the least understood of the fiduciary duties, prohibits managers from intentionally abdicating their responsibilities to the entity.

B. Fiduciary Duties and The Delaware LLC Statute

"Unlike in corporations and partnerships, the duties owed by governing persons and owners (known as members) in a limited liability company (LLC) remain unsettled in most jurisdictions. The reason for the unsettled law seems to stem from the relatively new existence of limited liability companies as business entities. In fact, the emergence of LLCs did not occur until the late 1970s."[127]

"Delaware is becoming the jurisdiction of choice for the formation of limited liability companies, particularly those conducting business in multiple states. One attractive aspect of the (Delaware LLC) Act is found in its policy of maximizing the principle of 'freedom of contract.' The Act provides a framework within which parties are free to establish the precise perimeters of their business relationship through the vehicle of the LLC Agreement."[128]

Generally, project sponsors and developers hold themselves to extremely lax standards when left to draft operating agreements on their own without the active participation

---

125. Mohsen Manesh, *Legal Asymmetry and the End of Corporate Law*, 34 Del. J. Corp. L. 465, 474 (2009). Separate statutes were draft for closely held corporations though there is considerable divergence of opinion and practice about whether closely held corporations should be subject to the same 'fiduciary duty' regimes as publicly held corporations, "who owes fiduciary duties to whom, whether that duty resembles the corporate or partnership model, and whether the corporation is adjudged a close corporation even if it did not elect that status formally. Mary Siegel, *Fiduciary Duty Myths in Close Corporate Law*, 29 Del. J. Corp. L. 377 (2004).

126. Larry E. Ribstein and Robert R. Keatinge, *Concept of Good Faith*, 1 Ribstein and Keatinge on Ltd. Liab. Cos. §9:7 (updated December, 2015).

127. Debra Hatter, Rikiya Thomas, *Swimming in Unsettled Waters; Fiduciary Duties and Limited Liability Companies*, 49-AUG Hous. Law. 22 (July/August 2011).

128. Steven A. Waters and Robert R. Nix II, *Letting The Statute Be The Deal: The Delaware Statutory LLC Default Rules* (last visited May 31, 2016), http://www.acrel.org/Documents/Seminars/2004%20 Waters%20-%20DE%20LLC%20default%20rules.pdf

of other LLC members.[129] However, publicly traded LLCs tend to provide investors with fiduciary obligations comparable to those of publicly traded corporations.[130]

Putting aside the question of what "fiduciary duty" default rules would apply if our hypothetical co-venturers A and C gave no thought to the matter in framing their transaction, consider the following four questions.

(1) Do you see any legitimate reason why C should object if A acquires land for their project from a seller who promises her a kickback of 50% of any sale price above $2,500,000 that she is able to negotiate on behalf of the A-C LLC without C's prior knowledge and consent?

(2) Would you want to place any limitations on A's constructing other projects similar to this one in the same market area in the next few years?

(3) Suppose you learned that A had contracted with a real estate investment fund to develop projects comparable to this one in four cities over the next 18 months. Would C have any cause for concern if A neglected to disclose that before he invested in this project?

(4) Suppose that A had contracted to assign her $1,000,000 stake in the LLC to an off-shore investment fund for $1,200,000 as soon as she raised $4,000,000 or more from an investor. Should C have the right to withdraw from the LLC and get back his money if he only learned about this by chance from a friend who knew the manager of the off-shore investment fund?

When confronted, developer A explains that her project will increase land values far above the LLC's purchase price; it is only right for her to participate directly in this land value increase.

Developer A admits that she plans to build a comparable project two blocks from the one contemplated by the A-C LLC. She believes that the market area can sustain both projects and that each will contribute to improving the image of the neighborhood, benefitting both.

She also believes that her credibility as a developer will be enhanced by the work she is doing in other cities. She is creating a sort of apartment "brand" that will accrue to C's benefit.

As for selling her interest to the fund, this will free up her capital. It also demonstrates that C's interest has already appreciated in value by 20%.

(5) Would A's position be vindicated by the following language in their operating agreement?

Freedom to Engage in Other Business Ventures and Activities. *The Manager and each Equity Owner (and their Affiliates) may engage, or acquire and retain an interest, in any*

---

129. Harner, Michelle M. and Marincic Griffin, Jamie, The Naked Fiduciary (2012). Arizona Law Review, Vol. 54, 2012, pp. 879–937; U of Maryland Legal Studies Research Paper No. 2012-19. Available at SSRN: (last visited May 31, 2016), http://ssrn.com/abstract=2034928

130. Suren Gomtsian, *The Governance Of Publicly Traded Limited Liability Companies,* 40 Del. J. Corp. L. 207, 270 (2015).

*other business ventures (including future ventures), transactions, or other opportunities
of any kind, nature, or description (independently or with others), regardless of whether
those ventures, transactions, or other opportunities are competitive with the Company's
Business or whether any of the operations or properties of those ventures are transacted
or located in the vicinity or market area of the Property or any other real property owned
or leased by the Company, without having any fiduciary duty or other obligation: (a) to
notify the Company or the Equity Owners of any aspect of those opportunities; (b) to
pursue or undertake those opportunities on behalf of the Company or the Equity Owners;
(c) to offer (or otherwise make available to) the Company or the Equity Owners any
interest in those opportunities; or (d) to share with the Company or the Equity Owners
any of the income, profits or rewards derived by that Equity Owner, Manager or other
Person from those opportunities. The fact that the Manager or an Equity Owner (or any
of their Affiliates) takes advantage of any opportunity described in the preceding sentence,
either alone or with other Persons (including Entities in which the Manager or that Equity
Owner has an interest), and does not offer that opportunity to the Company or the Equity
Owners, will not cause the Manager or that Equity Owner to become liable to the Company
or to the Equity Owners for any lost opportunity of the Company.*[131]

Questions

Question 1: *Entity Selection and Member Liability for Entity Debts.*

A real estate broker specializing in home sales and a general contractor who builds
custom houses decide to become co-venturers in the business of buying houses in
bad repair, and renovating them for sale or rent. They each plan to contribute $250,000
to the entity, and to borrow additional funds as needed from "bridge" lenders who
provide short-term loans for co-venturers like them.

Neither of them wishes to be liable for entity debts for more than their initial
$250,000 contribution, nor to have their venture side-tracked by the other's creditors.

They plan to share decision making authority, profits and losses equally, and to
come up with a fair way of compensating each other for services rendered to their
new enterprise—the broker a commission for finding properties and then selling
them, the contractor a fee for organizing the renovation.

(a) Which of the entities described in this chapter would be suitable for them,
and why?

(b) Which should they avoid, and why?

(c) Which would you recommend, and why?

(d) They choose an LLC. The operating agreement specifies that both of them are
to approve any property acquisitions, financing, construction contracts, and sales or
rentals. They agree on their first acquisition, set a fixed price budget for the renovation,

---

131. Joint Task Force of Committee on LLCs, Partnerships and Unincorporated Entities and the
Committee on Taxation, *Model Real Estate Development Operating Agreement with Commentary*, ABA
Section of Business Law, 63 Bus. Law. 385, 413 (2008).

and a contractor's fee of 5% on satisfactory and timely completion at or below the budget. During construction the contractor orders a number of upgrades without consulting the broker which add 25% in excess of the project budget.

The market softens and the two LLC members recoup only 90% of their invested capital.

Do you believe the general contractor has breached the duty of care it owed the broker by ordering the upgrades without the broker's approval?

The contractor believed that the upgrades would spark interest in the house and lead to a rapid sale at a price higher than the two had thought they could achieve based on the original renovation plans.

(e) Would your answer depend on whether the statutory standard of care was defined as "gross negligence"[132] or a duty to act "with the care an ordinarily prudent person would exercise in similar circumstances."[133]

Question 2: *An LLC Assignability Hypothetical.*

The seller was a family trust contracting to sell a "B" quality office tower in downtown Los Angeles for $120,000,000[134] that it had owned for decades. The trust was liquidating all its real estate assets. This is one of the reasons the trust had not invested the funds it would have taken to upgrade the property to "A" quality.

The purchaser was a real estate investment fund with substantial cash to invest, and a great interest in renovating properties in prime locations that are underperforming for their locations but could produce considerably improved net operating income with the right major upgrades.

Both the family trust and the private equity investment fund were LLCs. Each of them had three members who managed their respective LLCs.

The seller's board is extremely interested in closing a sale as quickly as possible. The Board responded favorably to the private equity investment fund because of its substantial access to equity and debt capital.

The Board is wary of buyers who are eager to "flip" the property instead of improving it because all of the property's major systems (HVAC, elevators, public areas) are outdated. They are looking for a buyer who understands that the price is fair but the buyer will have to make substantial investments in the building for this acquisition to make financial sense. The Board would not enter a contract with a buyer lacking the competence and resources to transform this "B" asset into an "A" one.

Consider the provisions that the Trust should place in its purchase and sale contract to preclude its buyer from assigning its interest in the contract to an LLC that lacks comparable resources and incentives.

---

132. Revised Uniform Partnership Act (1997) (RU.L.A.) §404(c).

133. Tex. Bus. Orgs. Code Ann. §152.206(a).

134. This example and all the supporting documents come from Phil Nichols, Adjunct Professor, USC Law School, which he used in his fall 2015 course in Negotiating and Drafting Purchase and Sale Agreements.

Would the following assignability provision protect the seller?

"Purchaser may not assign or transfer its rights or obligations under this Agreement without the prior written consent of Seller. In the event of a transfer, the transferee shall assume in writing all of the transferor's obligations hereunder, but such transferor shall not be released from its obligations hereunder (and hereby waives any suretyship or guarantor defenses that might otherwise apply). No consent given by Seller to any transfer or assignment of Purchaser's rights or obligations hereunder shall be construed as a consent to any other transfer or assignment of Purchaser's rights or obligations hereunder. No transfer or assignment in violation of the provisions hereof shall be valid or enforceable."

The buyer had deposited with a neutral third party $1,000,000 at the time that the purchase and sale agreement was signed. The contract called for the buyer to deposit an additional $4,000,000 at the end of the "due diligence" period. Until that time, the buyer has the option of terminating the contract virtually at will simply by notifying the seller in writing that it wishes to cancel the contract, and executing appropriate termination documents. The terminating buyer is entitled to a prompt return of all of their deposited funds except for nominal fees incurred for services performed by third parties, including the stakeholder. Terminate after that date, and the contract labels the buyer in breach and obligated to relinquish all the monies it had previously placed with the neutral stakeholder as liquidated damages. In this transaction, that sum would be $5,000,000.

(a)   Does the agreement allow the purchaser or the seller to dispose of their membership interests in their respective LLCs?

(b)   What language should the seller have placed in the assignment provision to make sure the original buyer did not assign its interest to a less qualified buyer, leaving the seller at risk if the value of the asset declined during the executory period?

Question 3: *Avoiding Double Taxation in Entity Selection.*

(a)   Which entities are subject to double tax?

(b)   Can you imagine any reason why a real estate developer, sponsor, promoter or equity investor would ever consider doing business as a C Corporation?

(c)   How could an S corp manage to avoid forfeiting its privileged tax status as would happen if a shareholder sold her shares to a nonresident alien or divided her shares among several individuals, pushing the total number of S corp shareholders above 100?

Question 4: *Inclusion of Borrowed Funds in Basis; Loss Pass Throughs.*

(a)   Which of the entities allow the inclusion of entity-borrowed funds into the basis of individual entity members, partners, co-tenants or shareholders—partnerships general and limited, C and S corporations, tenancies in common, LLCs?

(b)   Why do LLC members or partners regard the pass through of losses from the entity to themselves individually to be a good thing?

Question 5: *Restrictions on REIT Ownership, Portfolio Composition and Earnings Distributions.*

(a)   A REIT avoids tax at the entity level only by observing certain limitations on ownership, portfolio composition and earnings distributions listed in I.R.C. §856. Generally, what is the purpose of these restrictions?

(b)   Despite distributing almost all their taxable income to their shareholders, how do REITs manage to accumulate cash flow to facilitate growth?

(c)   A REIT cannot protect its distributed income from taxation unless most of its earnings are from 'passive' sources. Income earned from operating hotels, casinos and racetracks is characterized as active for tax purposes. How, then, can REITs profit from the ownership of such assets without jeopardizing their privileged tax status?

Chapter 5

The Condition of the Subject Property, Fixtures, and Risk of Loss during the Executory Period[1]

Scope of the Chapter

This chapter highlights the allocation of risks and responsibilities between buyers and sellers of real estate for: (1) the physical condition of the property being sold and purchased; (2) the fixtures to be included as part of the sale, and (3) exposure to losses caused by man-made or natural disasters that occur after the contract is signed but before the closing.

Imagine the deep disappointment of a first-time buyer moving into her newly acquired home who notices that the seller has replaced all the designer appliances with cut-rate brands, an exterior wall is covered in graffiti, and windows apparently broken in a recent windstorm have yet to be repaired.

Consider the chagrin of the new owners of a 30-story glass curtain-wall office building on their first day in possession encountering disruptive failures in six elevators,[2] the building's signature 40 foot high sculpture inexplicably having been removed from the lobby wall, and two upper floors completely unusable, charred in a recent fire.

Here we see how buyers and sellers allocate these risks by contract, and the default rules that apply when they do not.

---

1. The author is grateful to Paul Cliff '90 who is the guest expert for my USC law classes on fixtures, fixtures financing and risk of loss issues at the USC law classes and shared his insights his highly useful scholarship on these topics prompted by his work for clients who would have been ill-served by the customary default rules.

The author is also grateful to Melissa Clark '08, Dennis Greenwald, and Elva Harding who are the guest experts for my USC law classes on the Seller Responsibilities Regarding the Condition of the Subject Property.

2. This is what happened in the John Hancock Building. *See* Jacob Feld and Kenneth L. Carper, *Construction Failure, Failure Case Study: John Hancock Mutual Life Insurance Company, Boston, Massachusetts*, 10.1.3 (Wiley, 1997).

I. The Physical Condition of the Subject Property

A. Risk Allocation Arrangements

There are five ways of addressing issues concerning what the condition of the property should be when the realty buyer takes title and possession.

(1) Buyer Inspections;

(2) Seller Disclosures;

(3) Negotiated Seller Representations and Warranties;

(4) Home Builder Warranties Implied by Courts or Statutes; and

(5) "As Is" Clauses.

1. Buyer's Inspections

Purchase and sale contracts grant buyers an inspection contingency period. Under some of these, buyers may have the right to terminate their obligations with complete impunity and full refunds.[3] Other contracts *require* buyers to pinpoint unacceptable defects, and give sellers a meaningful chance to cure.

Advice for Residential Property Buyers on Hiring an Inspector. Prompted by an inspection opportunity, and to avoid purchasing a "lemon" property, an overwhelming majority of home buyers incur the cost of hiring professional inspectors[4] to check out the property during the "due diligence" period.[5] Buyers should arrange to meet the inspector at the site, and learn as much as they can about the property's condition.

Before hiring an inspector, a buyer should review a typical report prepared by that inspector. Some reports contain little more than warmed-over boilerplate and unexplained conclusions consisting of check lists of each building component marked as either functional or non-functional without further explanation or the probable cost of cure. In drafting an agreement with a chosen inspector, buyers need to specify

---

3. Under the California Association of REALTORS® form, a buyer who wants to walk away need not do anything; only a buyer desiring to proceed with the purchase must give the seller notice in the form of a written contingency waiver.

4. Buyers should use inspection licensing laws where they exist by only hiring licensed inspectors, and prefer members of the National Institute of Building Inspectors (www.nibi.com) or the American Society of Home Inspectors (www.ashi.com). These organizations administer their own membership tests, expect continuing education, and promulgate Codes of Ethics. A cautionary note: don't take an inspector's word regarding membership. Check with the organization directly.

5. A nationwide study by the National Association of REALTORS® and the American Society of Home Inspectors found that seventy-seven percent of homebuyers had inspections done before buying, with that percentage on the rise. Donna Halvorsen, *Disclosure Law: New State Law Compels Disclosing; Starting Jan 1, Sellers Must Reveal Problems, But Buyers Still Will Have Few Remedies*, STAR TRIBUNE (Mpls.-St. Paul), June 1, 2002, 2002 WL 5375981.

that the inspection be concluded and a report prepared before the buyer's option of cancelling the contract expires.

For properties with substantial defects, buyers will need to decide on a course of action. They could ask the seller to repair the problem before closing, request a purchase price reduction so that they could solve the problem after the closing, cancel the contract if the seller refuses, or just live with the property "as is."

Responsible real estate brokers caution buyers to use their inspection opportunity well. For example, the California Association of Realtors (CAR) residential purchase agreement comes with a one-page Inspection Buyer's Advisory. This document explains that the seller and broker have no responsibility regarding the physical condition of the property under the CAR form. It cautions buyers that they have "an affirmative duty to exercise reasonable care" to protect themselves against post-closing discoveries of horrific problems with the property. At the same time, the form warns buyers that inspections are imperfect and necessarily incomplete. The page specifies many things that can be wrong with a property, and urges buyers to check these out. The list includes the possibility that the buyer has been misinformed about the square footage of the property, unstable soils, termites, environmental hazards, water and utilities issues, earthquakes, flooding, lack of building permits, possible rent control ordinances, security and safety gaps, and so on. As a condition of entering the contract, buyers are expected to sign the advisory, confirming that they read and understood it.

You may rightly wonder why brokers—whose compensation is based on deals closing—are pointing to potential hazards that could scare buyers away. Maybe it is due to a history of California courts holding brokers liable to buyers for property defects that brokers knew or should have known about, and said nothing.

Scope of Inspections. Customary physical inspections of dwellings cover only defects that are visible and located in readily accessible areas. Owners prohibit invasive inspections, inspectors boring holes in walls, ceilings, roofs or foundations. Owners also resist water pressurized testing of roofs, windows, doors, and shower pans that could drench interiors. Sellers resist the removal of furniture, appliances, or wall hangings. Home inspections generally exclude geotechnical soil or foundation issues.

Construction defect mediator Matt Argue advises buyers willing to spend the money to find an expert capable of reading building plans, someone who would know how to build a house like the one the buyer plans to purchase, such as an architect, engineer, or general contractor.[6] Home owners could also consider assembling a team of the major building trades, including an electrician, an expert in heating and air conditioning systems, a geologist and a structural engineer for properties built on unstable hillsides or in flood plains.

Inspections do not cover neighborhood conditions. Home buyers are seldom in a position to compel sellers to pay for the detailed environmental audits commonly commissioned in sales of commercial realty.

---

6. Interview with author, 06/18/07.

Question: How can homebuyers avoid buying near a landfill, contaminated underground water, or a leaky gas tank at a service station down the street?

Answer: Consumer advocates caution home buyers to "give your potential new neighborhood an 'environmental scan.'" A consumer could hire a company to search local, state and federal environmental databases for "eco-trouble" within a radius.[7]

A more practical, though less comprehensive approach would be to chat with prospective neighbors for the wealth of information they may be willing to share. Local residents often know which houses sold lately and for how much, why houses are on the market, how long they have been for sale, what the local schools are like, if new projects are slated for construction nearby, if toxic dumps or gang violence haunt the area, if traffic and freeway access are a problem, and the lifestyles of area residents. Of course, some neighbors may downplay the negative, having learned to live with adverse conditions, out of solidarity with the seller, or in order to maintain high neighborhood "comps."

Buyers' Limited Recourse for Faulty Inspections. Buyers have little recourse if the report is inadequate. Inspection contracts often limit inspector liability to the inspection fee amount, often less than $1,000. Some courts enforce the caps as written, absent gross negligence.[8] A majority of courts hold them unenforceable as contrary to public policy; they can be miniscule compared to the costs of repairing defects overlooked.[9] Still other courts insist on explicit waivers of negligence liability, and

---

7. Site-specific information about environmental hazards can be found on websites maintained by environmental groups and government agencies responsible for monitoring toxic chemical releases and air quality management districts. *See, e.g.*, http://scorecard.goodguide.com (last visited July 12, 2015) and www.rtknet.org (last visited July 12, 2015). *See* Alan & Denise Fields, *Tips for Saving on New Built Homes*, LA TIMES at K1 (May 14, 1995).

8. New York enforces limits on inspector liability. *See, e.g.*, *Rector v. Calamus Group, Inc.*, 794 N.Y.S.2d 470, 471 (2005); *Kogan v. Fenster*, 744 N.Y.S.2d 628, 630 (2002); *Peluso v. Tauscher Cronacher Professional Engineers, P.C.*, 704 N.Y. S.2d 289, 290–91 (2000); *see also Gladden v. Boykin*, 402 S.C. 140 (2013) (finding limitation of inspector liability not contrary to public policy if "not so oppressive that no reasonable person would make it and no fair and honest person would accept it."); *Head v. U.S. Inspect DFW, Inc.*, 159 S.W.3d 731, 748 (Tx. Ct. App. 2005).

9. *See Finch v. Inspectech, LLC*, 229 W. Va. 147 (2012); *Glassford v. BrickKicker*, 191 Vt. 1, 14 (2011) (holding that a limit of liability to the inspector's fee was "not a reasonable estimate of the customer's likely damages."); *Pitts v. Watkins*, 905 So. 2d 553, 555–57 (Miss. S. Ct. 2005); *Russell v. Bray*, 116 S.W.3d 1, 8 (Tenn. Ct. App. 2003); 68 PA. CONS. STAT. ANN. § 7507(a) (2004) (providing for the performance of home inspections that limit the liability of the home inspector for gross negligence or willful misconduct are contrary to public policy and are void); Cal. Bus. & Prof. Code § 7198 (West 2005) (invalidating any contractual term purporting to waive the duty or limit the liability of a home inspector to the cost of the inspection report); ALASKA STAT. ANN. § 08.18.085(d) (West 2003) ("CONTRACTUAL PROVISIONS THAT PURPORT TO LIMIT THE LIABILITY OF A HOME INSPECTOR TO THE COST OF THE HOME INSPECTION REPORT ARE CONTRARY TO PUBLIC POLICY AND VOID."); MASS. GEN. LAWS ANN. Ch. 112 § 225(6)(v) (allowing denial, suspension, or revocation of inspector's license upon "attempting to limit liability for negligent or wrongful errors or omissions by use of a clause within a performance contract that limits the cost of damages" therefor.); WIS. STAT. ANN. § 440.976 (West 1997) (PROHIBITING THE USE OF A TERM OR CONDITION IN A HOME INSPECTION AGREEMENT TO LIMIT THE LIABILITY OF THE INSPECTOR FOR "FAILURE TO COMPLY WITH THE STANDARDS OF PRACTICE PRESCRIBED IN THIS SUBCHAPTER OR IN RULES PROMULGATED UNDER THIS SUBCHAPTER").

won't enforce caps on inspector liability unless the inspector gave the buyer the option of full tort coverage for a price.[10]

Inspectors' guarantees, even if pursued, are seldom collectible. Inspectors tend to be uninsured and undercapitalized which is why plaintiffs' attorneys in construction defect suits often do not even bother naming inspectors as defendants unless they happen to have meaningful insurance coverage.[11] Buyers expecting to be covered against losses from faulty inspections should verify the scope and insured amount of the inspector's liability (errors and omissions) policy.

*Question: Should home sellers hire inspectors? Inspections are usually ordered by buyers under contract. But is it a good idea for **home sellers** to order inspections before listing the property for sale?*

Answer: Many real estate brokers say it is, observes California real estate attorney John O'Reilly. They urge sellers to pay for home inspections, and show buyers inspection reports before marketing their property and certainly before signing purchase contracts. While sellers are legally obliged to share adverse information revealed in the report, brokers nonetheless see enormous advantages to the seller doing so.

Early information about property shortcomings gives sellers a chance to remedy defects before showing the property to potential buyers who might not make offers on obviously flawed property. Disclosures also increase buyer comfort levels, encourage informed, competitive bidding, and reduce the likelihood a deal will fall out of escrow later if the buyer discovers previously unmentioned shortcomings. A buyer may adjust a purchase offer before signing a contract, instead of waiting to re-negotiate the purchase price later based on problems revealed by their own professional inspection reports.[12]

The seller cannot expect the buyer to forego her own inspection. A buyer would be naïve to rely on the seller's inspection instead of contracting for her own. Buyers understand that sellers could be tempted to seek inspectors with reputations for leniency.

Commercial Property Inspections. Buyers of commercial property take physical inspections very seriously. Some firms have in-house staff fully competent to analyze potential acquisitions. Other firms, and most institutional lenders, look to professional due diligence service providers, typically structural engineering firms.

Inspections can be performed by a single expert—a general contractor, architect, or engineer, or by a team of experts, which could cost the buyer five to ten times more. But not hiring experts specifically for the elevators, curtain walls, roofing, HVAC systems, or security systems can eventually prove disastrously expensive.

Commercial inspection standards are promulgated by the American Section of the International Association for Testing Materials. Commercial inspections are often in-

---

10. *Ricciardi v. Frank*, 620 N.Y.S.2d 918 (City Ct. 1994).

11. Statement by Tim Truax, construction law attorney, El Segundo, California, to author, Sept. 22, 2008.

12. E-mail to author from John O'Reilly, May 5, 2004.

tended to estimate the reserve funds building owners will need to replace or upgrade major mechanical systems in the foreseeable future. Firms specialize in the business of performing reserve studies to recommend how much to set aside each month for the eventual replacement of roofs, HVAC (heating, ventilation, and air conditioning), asphalt surfaces, building paint jobs, and other items.[13]

The commercial buyer's inspection will include examination of building permits to verify that no improvements have been made without the proper permits. "A set of building plans will help the inspector locate the various components and establish the type and date of construction. HVAC and elevator maintenance records will help determine the extent of any previous repairs and ongoing maintenance."[14] Buyers could consult with the building's current maintenance contractors and examine the building insurer's records for claims related to defective building systems.

Buyers want assurance that the building complies with seismic safety standards and the accessibility requirements of state and federal disabilities laws. If the exterior walls are concrete tilt-up or reinforced masonry, they want proof that the wall-to-roof connections have been reinforced according to the 1991 Uniform Building Code.

Quite often, lenders insist upon an environmental assessment report (Phase I audit). They know that they could be liable for cleanup costs greatly exceeding the loan amount if the soil beneath the property contains contaminants, the borrower defaults on the mortgage loan, and the lender forecloses and takes over the management of the property. The U.S. Environmental Protection Agency promulgates standards for environmental audits. Buyers and sellers must decide which of them will assume primary responsibility for obtaining these reports.

2. Seller Disclosures

Most states require home sellers to disclose material defects they know about. Even in the few states without mandatory seller disclosure laws, brokers importune sellers to make such disclosures in order to avoid post-closing disputes with unhappy buyers that could lead to litigation, insurance claims and bad public relations for the broker. Some home sellers may hesitate to "tell all," figuring that buyers will be put off by extensive descriptions of property defects in a disclosure statement. Also, buyers could seize upon disclosed defects to whittle down the agreed purchase price, or extract commitments from the seller to cure defects as a condition to closing.

Sellers may feel especially justified in skimping on disclosures when buyers agree to purchase property "as is," in its present condition with no seller representations or warranties regarding its physical condition. Buyers are amply forewarned in the pur-

---

13. *See, e.g.*, McCaffery Reserve Consulting. http://www.mccafferyreserveconsulting.com (last visited July 13, 2015); Association Reserves, http://www.reservestudy.com/ (last visited July 14, 2015).

14. David V. Tran, *What You Should Do During Due Diligence Period for Commercial Properties?* (last visited, July 14, 2015), http://ezinearticles.com/? What-You-Should-Do-During-Due-Diligence-Period-for-Commercial-Properties?&id=458594.

chase and sale contract to check out the property themselves and not to rely on seller representations and warranties because there are none in an "as is" contract. The seller's obligation is to deliver the property at closing in its condition on the date the contract was signed. Buyers are free to study, inspect, survey, and inquire during the "free look" "due diligence" period, and rescind the contract if they do not like what they discover.

Though the reluctance of sellers to disclose defects is understandable, full disclosure of a property's flaws makes optimal use of the buyer's inspector's time. It also immunizes the seller from post-closing liability for any of the property defects that were disclosed. As a Wisconsin appellate court explained in a case involving that state's mandatory disclosure law: "These provisions are intended to afford a buyer the opportunity to discover actual or potential defects in the property so that the buyer can then make an informed choice whether to proceed with the transaction, whether to seek amendments to the terms of the contract, or whether to abort the contract. Thus, these provisions avoid the prospect of future disputes and possible litigation."[15]

What Must Be Disclosed? Wisconsin's law also provides a useful definition of what would count as a material defect that sellers are obligated to disclose. It would be a defect with "a significant adverse effect on the value of the property; that would significantly impair the health or safety of future occupants of the property; or that if not repaired, removed or replaced would significantly shorten or adversely affect the expected normal life of the premises."[16]

In California, home sellers are obligated to provide a statutory *Transfer Disclosure Statement* (TDS) detailing every aspect of the house itself, including all major systems (foundation, roofing, air conditioning, plumbing, electrical). Sellers are asked about the condition of the appliances, and any past damage or lawsuits. The form appears in California Civil Code 1102.6. Home buyers outside California should consider using this form unless they have a more comprehensive one for the seller to complete.

Specific Disclosure Content. Sellers should not breathe a sigh of relief when they scan the disclosure form and see that a known defect was overlooked. This is no excuse for not disclosing it. Sellers remain obligated under their common law duties to disclose all defects they knew or are presumed to have known about the property that would be significant (material) to a reasonable buyer, unless the buyer actually knew about the defects, or the defects would have been obvious to a buyer upon a casual viewing of the property. Nor do disclosure laws shield sellers from claims of fraud, misrepresentation, or deceit in the transaction.

Stigma Factors. Statutory disclosure obligations in most states only pertain to physical defects, not to psychological ones, such as houses allegedly haunted, previously occupied by the contagiously ill, or the scenes of recent rapes, murders, or deaths.[17]

---

15. *Lambert v. Hein*, 218 Wis. 2d 712, 729, 582 N.W.2d 84, 91 (Ct. App. 1998).

16. Wis. Stat. §709.03.

17. Ronald Benton Brown & Thomas H. Thurlow III, *Buyers Beware: Statutes Shield Real Estate Brokers and Sellers Who Do Not Disclose That Properties Are Psychologically Tainted*, 49 Okla. L. Rev. 625, 626–28 (1996); Paula C. Murray, *AIDS, Ghosts, Murder: Must Real Estate Brokers and Sellers Dis-*

California buyers have a cause of action against brokers who fail to disclose deaths that occurred within the house in the previous three years, unless the cause of death was AIDS, which receives protected status as a disability.[18]

Some statutes explicitly relieve sellers and brokers from revealing information regarding "psychologically tainted" properties. These statutes either declare such information immaterial, barring misrepresentation claims against sellers, or they hold sellers accountable for truthful disclosure only if asked.

Notably, "Since 1996, federal legislation, commonly known as *Megan's Law*, has required state law enforcement agencies to notify communities where convicted sex offenders choose to reside."[19]

Termites. In termite-prone areas, buyers diminish the risk of buying an infested and damaged house by providing for a termite inspection report. A buyer should not rely on a general house inspector, but should instead insist upon a licensed pest control company.[20] Pest control inspectors are specialists. Pest control companies have an enormous incentive to charge modest inspection fees in hopes of finding termites and being hired to do the extensive remedial and suggested preventive work detailed in their reports.

Question about the extent of the seller's disclosure obligations: "Not sure whether you need to mention to potential buyers that your basement once flooded because your neighbor's swimming pool cracked? Or about the summer you had to call exterminators to get rid of termites? Is the nearby presence of a gas station important? What about the fact that every Saturday morning at 7 a.m. the fire station 2 blocks away holds 30 minutes of fire drills, including testing sirens?"

Answer: "Disclose it all. In some states you are legally obligated to give such information to potential buyers. More than 30 states now have home seller disclosure laws explicitly

---

close? 27 Wake Forest L. Rev. 689, 707 (1992) ("A 'defect' must be defined by focusing on the property's physical condition, not a buyer's unusual sensitivities and prejudices.... The fear and prejudice of some buyers should not be allowed to influence the market unilaterally."); Daniel M. Warner, *Caveat Spiritus: A Jurisprudential Reflection Upon the Law of Haunted Houses and Ghosts*, 28 Val. U. L. Rev. 207, 240 (1993) ("Psychologically impacted real estate evaluation is irrational and harmful, and it should be legally unacceptable"). *But see* Houston Association of REALTORS® Seller's Disclosure Notice, Jan. 19, 2002 ("Death on the Property other than death caused by: natural causes, suicide, or accident unrelated to the Property's condition").

18. Cal. Civ. Code § 1710.2. *See* Beverly Bird, *Laws Regarding Death Disclosures in Real Estate Transactions in California*, SF Gate, http://homeguides.sfgate.com/laws-regarding-death-disclosures-real-estate-transactions-california-46748.html. Texas also gives AIDS protected status. Ryan Campbell, *Death Disclosure in a Texas Property*, https://www.facebook.com/permalink.php?story_fbid=200663 173425391&id=138819152943127.

19. Nat'l Institute of Justice, *About Megan's Law* (Jan. 22, 2009), http://nij.gov/topics/corrections/community/sex-offenders/Pages/about-megans-law.aspx (last visited Mar. 21, 2014). All fifty states and the District of Columbia have now enacted such notification requirements.

20. The California Residential Purchase Agreement and Joint Escrow Instructions (11/14), paragraph 12A, specifies that "Any inspection for wood destroying pests and organisms shall be prepared by a registered Structural Pest Control company ... and shall include separate sections for evident infestations and conditions like to lead to infestation."

describing what sellers need to disclose to buyers. But even if you're not required by state law to describe past structural problems or the Thursday evening rehearsals of the garage band across the street, you should do it anyway."[21]

Question about concealment: the seller's duty to disclose repaired damage: *Should the seller disclose not only that the basement leaked from time to time but that they repaired the cracks and re-paint?*

Answer: Absolutely. In one case, the sellers admitted that they knew that the basement walls had twelve-foot long, three-eighths-inch wide cracks, which they caulked and painted over. An appellate court remanded the case because a reasonable jury could find that those cracks and the attempted efforts at remediation should have been disclosed.[22]

Question about Buyer's lack of due diligence as a defense for Seller's failure to disclose known, material defects: *Our house overlooks a beautiful creek that overflows and floods our basement from time to time. Everyone around here knows that the creek overflows. On the basement wall, plainly visible watermarks evidence past flooding. We contracted to sell our house "as is"; the buyers had ample inspection opportunity but decided not to hire an inspector. They waived the contingency concerning the condition of the property. In the late spring, the creek overflowed and they want us to pay for waterproofing the basement — something we never did during our 25 years in the house because we regarded it as ultimately futile and a waste of money. To these buyers too cheap even to pay for an inspection, do we owe anything?*

Answer: One line of reasoning answers: "Absolutely not." Buyers should look out for themselves since they know best their personal preferences and their plans regarding the property. There is an exception for hidden material defects known to the seller that could elude a reasonable inspection.

Courts have summarized the seller-friendly position: "Misrepresentations are not actionable unless the complaining party was justified in relying thereon in the exercise of common prudence and diligence."[23] *"The law does not afford relief to one who suffers by not using the ordinary means of information, whether the neglect is due to indifference or credulity. When the means of knowledge are at hand and equally available to both parties, and the subject of purchase is alike open to their inspection, if the purchaser does not avail himself of these means he will not be heard to say, in impeachment of the contract of sale, that he was deceived by the vendor's representations."*[24]

A different line of reasoning reaches the opposite result, predicated on an information efficiency norm, that sellers are in a better position to know the condition of the property, having lived there, and so they should disclose known material defects to save buyer time and focus inspector attention.

---

21. *Tell All-Disclosure for the Seller,* ZILLOW.COM (last visited July 10, 2015), http://www.zillow.com/wikipages/Tell-All-Disclosure-for-the-Seller/.

22. *Malzewski v. Rapkin,* 296 Wis. 2d 98, 723 N.W.2d 156 (2006).

23. *Brown v. Mack Trucks,* 111 Ga. App. 164, 167, 141 S.E.2d 208 (1965).

24. *Miller v. Clabby,* 178 Ga. App. 821, 344 S.E.2d 761 (1986).

Disclosure of Natural Hazard Conditions. The differing norms described in the preceding paragraph are evident in attitudes regarding whether sellers should have an obligation to disclose public information regarding natural hazards that are as accessible to buyers as to sellers.

In Georgia, buyers are expected to search local data bases for natural hazards like flooding. In a landmark case, the buyers had purchased land which the seller had told them stayed dry and was suitable for raising horses.

During the buyers' first week of ownership, the land flooded twice in heavy rainstorms. Though the pasture drained in 24 hours, it remained muddy and useless for raising horses for quite a long time.

When the buyers confronted the seller to take back the property, he admitted having known about the periodic flooding but refused to do anything since the sale was a done deal.

Infuriated, the buyers filed suit, claiming fraud-and-misrepresentation, and seeking rescission, actual and punitive damages, and attorneys' fees.

In dismissing the buyers' suit, the court pointed out that they had ample access to information about the condition of the property had they bothered to find it. There had been "affidavits from federal and county officials showing that the subject property lies within an identified flood hazard area and that maps showing this were at all pertinent times a matter of public record in Cobb County." The buyers also had access to a survey map with a notation that "the property is partially located in an identified flood hazard area."[25]

The burden is upon sellers in California and a half dozen other states to disclose to their buyers if property is located in areas within statutorily defined Natural Hazard areas, including areas prone to flooding, fire danger, and earthquakes. Sellers cannot rely only on what they actually know, and few sellers are in a position to gather information from every one of the vast networks of "natural hazard" data sources.

To comply with the Natural Hazard Disclosure law, California sellers rely on firms that specialize in preparing Natural Hazard Disclosure Statements. The logic of this requirement is obvious enough. It is far more efficient for sellers to contract for a single report that they can present to any potential buyer rather than for each potential buyer to pay for a separate, identical report.

The firms providing these reports rely on data from maps prepared and periodically revised by numerous federal, state and local agencies. Precision mapping matters greatly; the consequences of a property boundary lying within or just outside of a designated earthquake fault zone or high risk fire danger area can be enormously significant to buyers, mortgage lenders and insurers.

Unfortunately, these public agencies do not share the same geographic information systems, nor do they check the precise boundaries of each property in their data base.

---

25. *Miller v. Clabby*, 178 Ga. App. 821, 822, 344 S.E. 2d 761 (1986).

Publicly available maps and records are not necessarily coterminous with the property boundaries of the sellers paying for these reports. The California Natural Hazard Disclosure Statute lists many maps prepared by public agencies to delineate flood, fire and earthquake hazard areas. The statute itself prescribes a specific disclosure form, urges recipients to consider obtaining professional advice, and cautions that the public agency maps are only estimates of where natural hazards exist, not definitive indicators of whether or not a property will be affected by a natural disaster.[26]

Home sellers, acting upon the advice of their brokers, typically contract for a Natural Hazard Disclosure Report with one of the many private firms offering them for sale. It becomes the responsibility of the firms that prepare Natural Hazard Disclosures to create their own geographic information systems and superimpose government data upon them.

Preparing this data is not a one-time event. Periodic updating is important. The public agencies responsible for mapping flood, fire and earthquake fault zones continuously revise their data. Natural Hazard Disclosure form preparers need to incorporate these changes into their systems.

A few firms specializing in the preparation of Natural Hazard Disclosure Statements do their work very well; many others do not.[27] The California disclosure statutes free home sellers of liability for the errors and omissions that experts may make on whom sellers rely to provide the information required by law.

Seller Liability to Brokers for Incomplete or Inaccurate Disclosures. Property owners listing their properties for sale are obliged to disclose any information that could be relevant to a potential buyer. For home sellers this could include everything from leaky roofs to noisy neighbors. For sellers of commercial rental property, financial information would be added to the batch of items specified in transfer disclosure statements.

Broker-prepared listing agreements also obligate sellers to indemnify brokers for costs they incur defending claims by buyers based on misinformation that sellers supplied.

Post-Closing Liability: Competing Considerations of Buyer and Seller. Sellers and listing brokers aspire to create a disclosure regime that facilitates certainty once a buyer and seller ink a purchase and sale contract. They give the buyer ample opportunity to check out the property during escrow, and hope that by the scheduled closing date the contract is either fulfilled, or has been terminated, thus freeing the seller and broker to find a willing buyer in the marketplace. Real estate brokers and property owners want prospective buyers to make up their minds before the scheduled closing date about whether they are in or out. After the juridical mini-second when the sale closes, sellers want no later obstacles to their using the entire sale proceeds to pay off their creditors, distribute promised returns to their investors, cash their own checks and

---

26. CAL. CIVIL CODE §§ 1103, 1103.2.

27. George Lefcoe, *Property Condition Disclosure Forms: How The Real Estate Industry Eased The Transition from Caveat Emptor to "Seller Tell All,"* 39 REAL PROP. PROB. & TR. J. 193 (2004).

move on. To the extent that sellers get stuck with post-closing obligations, they would probably be required to set aside reserves from the sale proceeds in order to cover those liabilities. Even when sellers make warranties and representations that are meant to survive the closing, as they sometimes do, they negotiate purchase and sale contract provisions calling for strict time and dollar limits to their post-closing liabilities.

Buyers have the opposite view about the need for finality at closing. Buyers want to be sure that they receive the property in its promised condition, and would prefer to hold sellers to their unmet promises even after the closing.[28] Some property defects, may not even become evident until after the closing.

Reilly v. Richards.[29] Despite the best efforts of sellers, buyers sometimes manage to unravel real estate purchase contracts after closing. For instance, in this Ohio case, the buyer (a lawyer but not a real estate lawyer) was acquiring a site near a stream where he planned to build a house. According to the terms of his purchase and sale contract, he had "sixty days from acceptance of this contract to satisfy himself that all soil, engineering, utility and other site related considerations are acceptable." Well before closing, he learned that the site was in a federally designated flood plain, and during the executory period, had his builder inspect the property.

He closed, and took title. Only after the buyer had become the owner of the property did his builder obtain drawings showing exactly on the site the location of the flood plain and the flood hazard zone. After re-visiting the site with these drawings in mind, the builder concluded that he could not warrant the property for one year, as is standard building practice. So he declined to build a house for the buyer on this site, prompting the buyer to unwind the contract, re-convey title back to the seller, and obtain a full refund of the purchase price. The seller objected. He believed under the contract the buyer had ample opportunity to have hired engineers, and determined whether the site was suitable.

At trial, the court agreed with the seller; but the court of appeals reversed, labeling the buyer negligent for not rescinding during escrow. The Ohio Supreme Court decided in the buyer's favor, declaring that the buyer and seller had been mutually mistaken from the very beginning about the impact of the flood plain designation.

Sandbagging. A buyer "sandbags" a seller by asserting a post-closing claim for damages or rescission although fully aware before closing of the defect.[30] Consider the following three potential "sandbagging" situations.

(1) The seller of a commercial rental property presents the buyer with financial information. The buyer believes the information exaggerates the property's net op-

---

28. Stuart M. Saft, COMMERCIAL REAL ESTATE TRANSACTIONS 254 (2d ed. 1995).

29. *Reilly v. Richards*, 69 Ohio St.3d 352 (1994). But see *Maruschak v. Schafer*, 2015 WL 9304700. This was an "as is" sale where buyers had waived their right to rescind, taken title and then brought suit for damages after closing, claiming there was mold in basement due to continued water intrusion that sellers had failed to disclose. Their complaint was dismissed at trial, upheld on appeal, for lack of any evidence that sellers knew about the mold and failed to disclose it.

30. Charles K. Whitehead, *Sandbagging: Default Rules And Acquisition Agreements*, 36 DEL. J. CORP. L. 1081 (2011).

erating income, and questions the seller who adamantly insists that the numbers are correct. The buyer closes. Six months after taking over the property, the buyer realizes that his suspicions were correct all along. The seller had overstated the income and understated the expenses. The buyer files suit for a price reduction.[31]

(2) The buyers pay top dollar for a house the sellers advertise as having been designed by legendary architect Julia Morgan who designed the Hearst Castle in Santa Barbara. During escrow, the buyers consult a relative of Julia Morgan's who expresses doubts that she actually designed that house they were buying. On the other hand, a historian whom the buyers consult says he thought she had designed it.

After closing, the buyers sue the seller for negligent misrepresentation, and are allowed to proceed to trial because they had relied on the sellers' promotional material about the "Julia Morgan-designed house" at the time of purchase.[32]

(3) The seller of an office building warrants that the roof and all mechanical systems are in good working order. Based on these warranties, the buyer makes an offer which the seller accepts. During escrow, the buyer learns through its due diligence efforts that the air conditioning system is corroded and will soon need to be replaced. Eager to place its funds quickly, the buyer closes anyway. After the closing, the buyer demands that the seller make good on its warranty by paying for a new air conditioning system.

The buyers in the above situations can be said to be "sandbagging." (Similar situations arise in contexts other than realty purchase and sale transactions, particularly in corporate mergers and acquisitions.)

Case law is largely unsettled.

Equally compelling arguments can be raised by sandbaggers and their opponents. Sellers can point out that buyers who proceed to complete a purchase, despite knowing that the seller is certain to breach a warranty, or has materially misrepresented facts about the property, cannot be said to have *relied* on those warranties or representations at the time of closing. Nonetheless, many courts do not limit buyers to their pre-closing remedies for property defects despite the buyers having observed those defects during escrow. They believe sellers should make good on what they promise.

Why do some courts allow this? Because "(1) it should encourage sellers and their representatives to investigate and learn the 'true facts' pertaining to real property before it is offered for sale, and (2) it will avoid the 'extraordinarily difficult choice that the defrauded buyer would otherwise be required to make,'"[33] either to close on a deal not as good as the buyer had been promised, or rescind. Neither of these choices preserves the buyer's "benefit of the bargain."[34] The buyer invested time and effort in

---

31. *Cf. CBS Inc. v. Ziff-Davis Publishing Co.*, 75 N.Y.2d 496 (1990).

32. *Jue v. Smiser*, 28 Cal. Rptr. 2d 242 (Cal. Ct. App. 1994).

33. Miller and Starr California Real Estate 3D, Contract Law Applicable to Real Estate Transactions, **Section 1.1: Waiver After Discovery of Fraud;** *Jue v. Smiser*, 23 Cal. App. 4th 312, 28 Cal. Rptr. 2d 242, 1994 Cal. App. 237, 94 Cal. Daily Op. Service 1953.

34. *CBS Inc. v. Ziff-Davis Publishing Co. et. al.*, 75 N.Y.2d 496 (1990). The court determined that the primary issue was "not whether the buyer believed in the truth of the warranted information, as

finding an acceptable property, negotiated a binding contract with the seller, took possession of the newly acquired property, and should be entitled to enforce her contract against the breaching seller.

On the anti-sandbagging side of the debate, sellers contend that courts allowing sandbagging give sellers have little incentive to be completely candid, and open their files to buyers during escrow, if buyers are allowed to close and then sue sellers for damages based on what they learned during the pre-closing due diligence effort. Courts barring sandbagging would encourage sellers to be more forthright in calling defects to the attention of their sellers during escrow to explore amicable resolutions. Buyers, too, are usually better served by resolving all outstanding issues during escrow but sometimes they are left with little choice when sellers only supply corrective disclosures once the buyer's "due diligence" period has expired.

Contracting For or Against Sandbagging. Buyers and sellers could avoid the uncertainties and costs of sandbagging litigation by adding pro-sandbagging or anti-sandbagging provisions to their purchase and sale contracts. This would be easy to do.

A sample pro-sandbagging provision is: 'The right to indemnification based upon any breach of any representation or warranty will not be affected by any investigation conducted, or any knowledge acquired at any time, with respect to the accuracy or inaccuracy of such representation or warranty.'[35]

An anti-sandbagging provision would be: 'No party shall be liable for any losses resulting from any breach of any representation or warranty if the party seeking indemnification for such losses had knowledge of such breach before closing.'[36]

Disclosure Obligations of Commercial Property Owners. In a few states the sellers of commercial property are held to the same obligation as home sellers to disclose all "known material defects."[37] Some courts only hold commercial sellers responsible for latent defects they lie about or conceal.[38]

[the seller] would have it, but 'whether [it] believed [it] was purchasing the [seller's] promise [as to its truth].'" Daniel Avery, Goulston & Storrs, PC, and Daniel H. Weintraub, Audax Group, Trends in M&A Provisions: "Sandbagging" and "AntiSandbagging" Provisions, Bloomberg Law Reports, Mergers and Acquisitions, 2011. http://www.goulstonstorrs.com/portalresource/sandbag_provisions.pdf (Last visited, 5/30/2016).

35. Negotiating "Sandbagging Clauses" in the M&A Context (Apr. 25, 2013), https://www.you tube.com/watch?v=BhO2fQ2IHe8&feature=youtu.be. (Last visited 05/30/2016).

36. https://www.youtube.com/watch?v=BhO2fQ2IHe8&feature=youtu.be. (Last visited 05/30/2016).

37. Duke Chen, Disclosure Requirements for Commercial Sales and Leases in Other States, (Aug. 27, 2013). "We found eight states (California, Maine, Michigan, New Hampshire, Minnesota, Tennessee, Texas, and Washington) with specific disclosure requirements that apply to commercial property. Washington is the only one of these states that has a mandatory commercial disclosure form, similar to a residential disclosure form, which requires sellers to disclose a wide range of information. This includes information on the property title; water rights; building structure, systems and fixtures; and environmental issues ... Although other states may not have specific commercial disclosure requirements, many, including Connecticut, have requirements prohibiting misrepresenting material facts (Conn. Agency Reg. § 20-328-5a)." https://www.cga.ct.gov/2013/rpt/2013-R-0317.htm (Last visited 05/30/2016).

38. Kathleen Tomcho, *Commercial Real Estate Buyer Beware: Sellers May Have the Right to Remain Silent*, 70 S. CAL. L. REV. 1571, 1573 (July 1997). *Id.* at 1573-75; *Shapiro v. Hu*, 233 Cal. Rptr. 470

Floors and Ceilings on Representation and Warranty Liability. Commercial purchase and sale agreements sometimes set both floors and ceilings on the buyer's post-closing claims. The floor is a minimum amount that any claim must exceed before the seller could be held liable, and insulates sellers from having to defend against claims for paltry sums. The ceiling or cap sets a maximum dollar amount above which the seller has no further monetary liability. This frees the seller to distribute the balance of the sales proceeds after closing above a reserve account.

3. Negotiated Seller Representations and Warranties

The Knowledge Standard in a Seller's Representation. Buyers of commercial real estate often extract a representation that their seller has disclosed all KNOWN material facts and defects, updated through closing. After the closing, a representation will not be worth much from a seller that is a limited liability company (LLC) owning no asset except the property to be conveyed to the buyer at closing. The buyer would be better served by representations from each individual LLC member, manager, and employee. The negotiator for the LLC might offer a particular named individual to make the representations, perhaps the property manager or maybe someone quite new to the firm with scant knowledge to share. Buyers will want as designated "knowers" those individuals who are most familiar with the firm.

When the term "knowledge" is used, it is very important to determine whether "knowledge" is limited to what the person is aware of at that moment, or whether it applies to what that person knew at any time, or whether it extends to what the person had the ability to find out, or even if it includes what other people may know.

Using a qualifier with "knowledge" can substantially change the meaning of the term.

"Actual knowledge" typically includes only the information of which the person whose knowledge is at issue is consciously aware. It refers to what the person recalls knowing when the statement is made. It does not include facts or information that the person forgot or is in old files or records.

"Constructive knowledge" includes matters that a person is supposed to know or could have found out. Partners of a partnership have constructive knowledge of the partnership agreement, even if they have not read it. As another example, people are deemed to have constructive knowledge of the existence and contents of documents in the public records, such as the land records in the applicable jurisdiction.

"Imputed knowledge" means knowledge of one person attributed to another person. For example, the knowledge of an agent may be imputed to the principal, the knowledge of an employee or officer to the employer or company, and the knowledge of a partner to other partners and the partnership.

(Ct. App. 1987) ('As is' clause; seller didn't know about a latent defect–a bulging basement wall evidencing water seepage, but materials stored against the wall so neither seller nor buyer knew about the water seepage problem. Held, buyer not entitled to rescission or damages).

"Best knowledge" is reflected in a statement such as "the following is true to the best of my knowledge," or when a written statement or representation begins with "to the best of the knowledge, information, and belief of the undersigned."

Many commercial lawyers believe that representation in a transactional document to that person's "best knowledge" is based on more information than had that person used the phrase "the following is true to the knowledge of the undersigned." Those lawyers believe the phrase "best knowledge" implies knowledge based on research, due diligence, or investigation done shortly before the time that the representation is made. But most reported cases about the meaning of "best knowledge" have reached the opposite conclusion and hold that if a person uses the term "best knowledge" in an affidavit, application, or representation, the term embodies a level of uncertainty.

A statement made to the "best knowledge" of a person does not mean that the person asserts the truth or accuracy of the statement or that the statement is based on that individual's personal knowledge.[39]

The Challenge of Collecting on Breached Warranties. Buyers relying on seller warranties and representations need to determine whether the seller and the insurer will be in a financial position to make good on such promises post-closing. Individual home sellers could relocate to other jurisdictions, retire, or go broke.

Commercial real estate sellers will often be a limited liability company, a specially-formed entity with no assets except the particular project. Post-closing, the entity distributes all proceeds to its lenders and investors and dissolves, leaving no assets to pay damages.

4. Court-Implied, Statutory, and Builder Warranties

Consumers who purchase newly built homes from professional homebuilders are often protected from construction defects by state deceptive trade practices laws, and by statutory and judge-made implied warranties of workmanlike construction (IWWC) to merchant homebuilders, analogous to product liability norms applied to automobile manufacturers and other mass producers of consumer goods.

In these IWWC cases, courts rejected the notions of caveat emptor that had long protected real estate sellers. Generally, defects that make a house unsafe or unlivable readily qualify for implied warranty protection. Whether the implied warranty should cover less than cataclysmic failures (e.g., uneven flooring or mismatched tiles) is decided case-by-case and state-by-state with judges reaching conflicting outcomes on similar facts. "The IWWC stands for the proposition that should a builder fail to deliver a residence that conforms with community standards due to latent defects, the buyer has a legal remedy, as accepted and defined by a history of cases, and in

---

39. *Edward J. Levin, "Best" Is Not Always Best When It Comes to Knowledge*, 30-FEB Prob. & Prop. 44 (2016).

some instances, by statute."[40] In an effort to clarify litigation standards in construction defect cases brought by home buyers, some states codified the Implied Warranty of Workmanlike Construction (IWWC).[41]

The Fine Print. Many builders see warranties primarily as marketing tools and a way to contain repair costs. They insert fine print to narrow the duration and scope of the builder's post-closing liability. Consumers are not represented when homebuilders draft their warranties–although state legislators and common law courts sometimes insist upon certain non-waivable protections for the benefit of homebuyers.[42]

One purpose of these warranties is to induce home buyers to waive completely their rights under statutory or court imposed implied warranties, to place time limits within which buyers may lawfully initiate claims for construction defects, to limit the definition of what counts as a defect, and restrict buyer remedies. State courts differ on the extent to which they will enforce waivers or limitations regarding home builder warranties. Often, in litigation the legitimacy of waivers depends on how clearly they were written, whether they seemed reasonable in scope, and whether they were explained to buyers who actually understood them before buying.

Some of the state statutes codifying the implied warranty prescribe detailed standards regarding the procedures and extent to which home buyer waivers will be enforceable. The Minnesota statute is among the most protective of home buyers: "Minnesota's statutory IWWC may be waived only by full oral disclosure of the defect prior to the sale of the dwelling with a writing that explains the defect, states the "difference between the value of the dwelling without the defect and the value of the dwelling with the defect, as determined and attested to by an independent appraiser," explains the amount of the price reduction, and has the witnessed signature of the home buyer. Minnesota's statutory IWWC may be modified only if certain conditions are met: (1) in a writing, signed with consent by the homeowner, (2) printed in bold type of at least 10 point font, and (3) the writing provides a substitute warranty with "substantially the same protections" as afforded under the statute."[43]

Homebuilder Liability Statutes. By 2002, construction defect claims were crowding court dockets in many states, and increasing insurance costs for builders, contractors, architects, and engineers, especially for those involved in building tract homes and condos. Largely due to efforts by homebuilders who were beset by rising litigation costs, thirty-one states have enacted statutes requiring homeowners to give their

---

40. Wendy B. Davis, *Corrosion By Codification: The Deficiencies In The Statutory Versions Of The Implied Warranty Of Workmanlike Construction,* 39 CREIGHTON L. REV. 103, 104 (2005).

41. "These statutes fall far short of the protection afforded by the common law. The statutes fail to protect the homeowner victim of shoddy work with restrictive and confusing statutes of limitations and expirations, arbitrary exclusions from coverage, and the ability for the contractor to disclaim the warranty." 39 CREIGHTON L. REV. 103, 105 (2005).

42. *See* Elizabeth Birge, *A Warranty is only as Good as the Builder Behind It,* CHIC. TRIB. (Nov. 11, 1995), at HG1 (citing William Young, Director of Consumer Affairs, NAHB).

43. Minn. Stat. Ann. § 327A.04 (West 2004 & Supp. 2005).

homebuilders notice of claimed defects before filing suit,[44] and entitle the homebuilder to make repairs even if the homeowner would have preferred that another contractor remedy the defect.[45]

These statutes imposed non-waivable warranty obligations upon homebuilders in exchange for instituting statutes of repose. A statute of repose sets a fixed period of time within which a home buyer must file a defect claim. Claims subject to statutes of repose are easier for builders to insure because of being measured from the date of substantial completion, less fuzzy than the statute of limitations date which is when the buyer discovered or could reasonably have discovered the defect.[46]

The California "Right to Repair" Act was negotiated between consumer advocates and homebuilding interests. The Act provided a uniform definition of construction defects, prescribed minimum warranty standards, defined measures of damages, protected initial homebuyers and as well as later purchasers, gave homebuyers access to all relevant construction information and details, required homeowners to co-operate with homebuilders in effecting repairs, and shortened the statute of limitations for some types of claims. Unfortunately, the Act has failed to achieve many of its objectives, starting with the fact that the Act seems not to have forestalled litigation but instead has merely changed the nature of the issues raised.[47]

5. "As Is" Clauses

Sellers contract to convey property "as is," "where is," thus negating any obligation regarding the condition of the property or its fitness for use. The mantra of the "as is" seller to the buyer is: "What you see is what you get."

Typically, the "as is" clause is accompanied by a generous inspection opportunity and a right of the buyer to rescind along with a recitation that the buyer is relying on its own inspection and observations, and not upon the seller or seller's agents in any way, or upon representations they may have made.

Preponderantly, state courts interpret "as is" clauses as neither relieving home sellers of the duty to disclose known, material, latent defects, nor as shielding them from post-closing liability for their disclosure flubs, whether intentional or inadvertent.[48] Quite the contrary; in an "as is" contract where the buyer assumes the re-

---

44. Denis Binder, *The Duty to Disclose Geologic Hazards in Real Estate Transactions*, 1 Chap. L. Rev. 12, 13-15 (1998).

45. Robert Miller, et al., *MCLE Self-Study Article: The Ten Year Anniversary of SB 800: "Mission Accomplished or Missed Opportunity*, 30 Cal. Real Prop. J. 3 (last visited July 12, 2015), *available at* http://www.andersonschoech.com/CaliforniaRealPropertyJournal.pdf (Last visited 05/30/2016).

46. *The American Institute of Architects. Statute of Repose*, (last visited July 14, 2015), http://www.aia.org/aiaucmp/groups/aia/documents/pdf/aias078873.pdf.

47. Robert Miller, et al., *MCLE Self-Study Article: The Ten Year Anniversary of SB 800: "Mission Accomplished or Missed Opportunity*, 30 Cal. Real Prop. J. 3,7 (last visited July 12, 2015), *available at* http://www.andersonschoech.com/CaliforniaRealPropertyJournal.pdf (Last visited 05/30/2016).

48. *See Realmuto v. Gagnard*, 110 Cal. App. 4th 193, 201 (4th Dist. 2003), *citing Loughrin v. Superior Court*, 15 Cal. App. 4th 1188 (4th Dist. 1993). Vendor who withheld foundation defect information was held liable despite the Purchaser's having signed a statement that the seller "shall have

sponsibility for acquiring the property subject to its physical condition, the seller's disclosure obligation is heightened because of the seller's presumed greater opportunity to learn about it. A corollary implication of this is that in most states, "a seller may not attempt to sell property that he knows needs some rehabilitation by discounting the price and selling the property 'as is' without disclosure."[49] In a number of states the same "truth in property selling" disclosure laws apply to commercial sellers.

Disclosure omissions can prove just as costly to the seller to cure as a post-closing warranty of the undisclosed item. There is a practical reason for this. Before the closing, a buyer who becomes aware of a property defect is often (though not always) put to a "take it or leave it" choice. She can cancel the contract or risk being held to have waived any objections based on the disclosed defect. But when the buyer only learns of the defect after the closing, it is too late for the seller to just undo the sale. The buyer has the right to have the defect cured, however costly that might be. It is too late for rescission. The buyer has relocated, maybe furnished the new place, and organized her life accordingly. Rescission would mean moving out, undoing the sale, finding another place to live, and paying off the new mortgage. This is too high a price to ask the unsuspecting buyer to pay. Instead, the seller will have to pay what it costs to cure the defect, a cost the seller could have avoided by timely disclosure.

Questions regarding "as is" sellers' obligation to deliver property at closing in same condition as it was in when the purchase and sale contract was signed: Suppose sellers stop caring for the lawn the day they sign the purchase and sale agreement. By the time of closing the grounds are a mess; plants have died and a miscreant has painted vulgar language on a side wall. The sellers figure that they have no liability since they have contracted to sell "as is." Are they right?

Answer: Absolutely not. "As is" buyers aren't contracting for property in whatever condition the seller might happen to leave it on the closing date. "As is" refers to the condition of the property on the day the contract was executed or the property was inspected. The seller remains liable on an "as is" clause to maintain the property in that condition. This includes the burden of cleaning up damage due to vandalism occurring during the executory period.[50] The buyer who discovers that the seller has allowed the property to de-

---

no responsibility or liability whatsoever to Buyer ... and Seller has made no representation or warranty with respect to the physical condition or compliance with state or local building codes and ordinances.... Buyer has relied solely upon Buyer's inspection and evaluation of the property.... Buyer accepts the property in its 'AS IS' condition and waives any claim ... against Seller and Brokers." David Harris & Joel Ring, *The Duty to Disclose—"As Is" Clause Has Little Effect*, MILLER & STARR REAL EST. NEWSALERT 53 (Nov. 1993). *But see Teer v. Johnston,* 60 So. 3d 253(Ala. 2010) (Seller sold house on flood-prone lot "as is," after submitting false property disclosure statement to buyer that there were no "flooding, drainage or grading problems." Alabama Supreme Court held that "as is" buyers could not rely on the truthfulness of seller's disclosure statement.).

49. Florrie Young Roberts, *Disclosure Duties in Real Estate Sales and Attempts to Reallocate Risk,* 34 CONN. L. REV. 1, 2, 37 (2001); Florrie Young Roberts, *Let the Seller Beware: Disclosures, Disclaimers, and "As Is" Clauses,* 31 Real Est. L.J. 303 (2003).

50. *Approved Props. v. City of N.Y.,* 277 N.Y.S.2d 236, 238 (1996).

teriorate since the time it was first inspected has every right to insist on full restoration. However, the buyer who discovers major defects after, but that were evident prior to, the relevant "as is" date, is probably too late to compel redress.[51]

Question regarding commercial sellers' liability for misrepresentations when sale is "as is": *The chef-owner of a restaurant is selling the business, the building — a historic wood structure, and the subjacent land. On a walk-through with the buyer, the owner assures the buyer that the kitchen equipment is all in good condition and the building is sound. The contract specifies that the buyer will be relying on its own inspection and that the sale is "as is."*

After the sale, the buyer discovers that the refrigerators need extensive work, and the seller had contracted with an exterminator to rid the building of wood-boring beetles who had not yet succeeded in doing so. Is the buyer's claim for damages subject to a summary judgment based on the "as is" clause?

Answer: *In most states, even for commercial property, the buyer's suit would survive a summary judgment motion based on the seller's misrepresentations. Refrigeration and infestation problems are both material. The seller knew about the beetle infestation and probably about the refrigeration problems as well. The buyer may have been responsible for checking out the kitchen equipment but would not have been expected to detect the beetles unless they or the damage were visible.*

Question regarding whether "as is" clause shifts risk of hazardous waste clean up to buyer: *The Comprehensive Environmental Response, Compensation, and Liability Act (CERCLA),*[52] *a law commonly known as Superfund, authorizes the EPA to respond to releases, or threatened releases, of hazardous substances that may endanger public health, welfare, or the environment. Government agencies can require owners to contribute to clean-up efforts if the pollutants were released during the time they owned the property even after they sell. Buyers, too, can be liable unless their careful environmental audits showed no signs of toxic or hazardous wastes to be present.*

Would a straight-forward clause that the buyer takes title "as is" shift the risk of potential seller liability under CERCLA to the buyer?

Answer: *An "as is" clause typically provides that the buyer is accepting the property in its current condition, subject to any defects, without any representation by the seller as to the condition of the property and without any obligation of the seller to repair/ remediate any defects.*

The enforceability of such a clause with respect to a seller's environmental hazards liability is unsettled. [The clause would not impede federal or state governments from holding sellers accountable under applicable statutes. But an "as is" clause might serve

---

51. *See, e.g., Lucero v. Van Wie*, 598 N.W.2d 893, (S.D. 1999); *Shapiro v. Hu*, 188 Cal. App. 3d 324 (1st Dist. 1986); *C. Lambert & Assocs. v. Horizon Corp.*, 106 N.M. 661, 662 (1988).

52. 42 U.S. Code chapter 103.

to obligate the buyer to reimburse the seller for clean-up costs that resulted from government enforcement measures.]

"Early cases held that an 'as is' clause operates only as a disclaimer of warranties and would not preclude a buyer's suit against the seller with respect to environmental issues. However, a growing trend of authority holds 'as is' clauses to be enforceable in effectively releasing sellers from environmental hazards liability to their buyers where the provision specifically references that actual or potential environmental hazards are among the conditions as to which the buyer is taking the property 'as is' and without warranty." The best advice is to combine an "as is" clause with an environmental release and indemnity agreement.[53]

Question about whether buyers can waive recourse against sellers for non-disclosure: *Should buyers be able to waive any recourse they might have against sellers for not disclosing defects whether known to the seller or not?*

Answer: Courts and commentators disagree. Some disclosure statutes allow sellers to opt out unilaterally, some require buyers' consent, and some prohibit waivers and disclaimers entirely. Unfortunately, few statutes actually specify whether a pre-closing waiver would be enforceable and whether a waiver must take a particular form.

Oregon REALTORS® lobbied successfully for the repeal of a disclaimer option in their disclosure law.[54] The option was confusing because it only applied to statutory disclosure obligations. The legislature didn't remove the seller's common law obligation to disclose known, material, latent defects. Yet, many sellers and some brokers were misconstruing the disclaimer election as if it had. REALTORS® were troubled because sellers received conflicting advice from real estate agents and attorneys about whether to disclaim or disclose. Attorneys tended to recommend disclaimers to narrow the seller's post-closing exposure to liability. Real estate agents tended to advise disclosure as a tool that instilled buyer confidence. REALTORS® observed that some buyers perceived a disclaimer as signaling a seriously defective property or an untrustworthy seller.

Are "As Is" Clauses a Good Idea for Sellers? "As is" dampens buyer enthusiasm and can drive down offer prices. Sellers' real estate brokers caution clients not to sell "as is" unless the home is a "fixer-upper," lest potential buyers perceive the clause as a tacit warning of hidden defects.

On the other hand, "as is" clauses reduce post-closing problems from property defects. Some brokers have championed "as is" clauses as a means of cutting back on opportunistic or picky buyers raising frivolous complaints after closing. Lawyers commonly advise aggrieved "as is" buyers that their chances of prevailing in court in a

---

53. Dennis L. Greenwald, Steven A. Bank & Contributing Editor, Carol M. Clements, Cal. Prac. Guide Real Prop. Trans. Ch. 5: 221.

54. Interview by Robert Cooper with Matt Farmer, Associate General Counsel, Oregon Association of REALTORS®, July 17, 2003.

defect case against the seller or the broker are slim. Technically, the seller's "as is" clause or disclaimer protects only the seller against suits by the buyer, not from buyer's suits against the seller's broker.[55] Yet, despite this, anecdotal evidence points to a significant decline in lawsuits by buyers against brokerage firms listing properties "as is."

B. Ownership within Common Interest Developments

While estimates vary, about one-fifth of the U.S. population resides in "common interest developments" (CIDs) of one sort or another. These are characterized by individual ownership of a house or unit, combined with shared ownership or rights to use common areas. CIDs can take the form of condominiums, tenancies-in-common, cooperatives, planned unit developments, or gated communities.

Local governments typically favor CID developments because within the project boundaries, the residents undertake the cost of repairing and replacing the streets, parks, sewage lines, and the like, even though they share the same property tax burdens as owners outside the project who live on city streets maintained at public expense.

In a condominium building, condo buyers take title to the airspace inside the walls, coupled with a tenancy in common interest in the building and land—the hallways and lobby, the stairs and elevators, the roof and garage.

In all CID types, the common areas are maintained by a homeowners' association (HOA) to which all unit owners belong. Home or condo owners elect the HOA directors or board members from their ranks.

What Is the Cost to Own? "In addition to mortgage payments, condominium owners are responsible for property taxes, insurance, monthly maintenance or homeowners association fees and any special assessments."[56] Buyers should pay especially close attention to homeowners' dues or fees, as these can be subject to increase. Also, condo owners cannot prevent the HOA from levying special assessments against unit owners to cover the costs of large-scale repairs or planned improvements.[57]

What Are the Rules? Condo ownership is subject to a recorded declaration. This document will contain a legal description of the project. It will also show the dimensions of the site, the individual units, the common areas, and each unit owner's fractional share of the common areas. It will designate "exclusive use common areas," including parking spaces, storage lockers and balconies. As the name suggests, these are common areas, portions of which have been dedicated to individual unit owners. There will also be operating by-laws governing day-to-day operations.

---

55. *See, e.g., Troiano v. Tuccio,* 643 N.Y.S.2d 157, 157 (1996), *citing Wittenberg v. Robinov,* 173 N.E.2d 868, 869 (N.Y. 1961).

56. *What Buyers Should Know About Condominiums,* Realtor.com (last visited July, 13, 2015) http://www.realtor.com/Basics/Condos/ShouldKnow.asp.

57. Monica Dillon, *The Maintenance Fees in Buying a Condo Vs. Renting an Apartment* (last visited July, 13, 2015), http://everydaylife.globalpost.com/maintenance-fees-buying-condo-vs-renting-apartment-16959.html.

Prospective buyers will find the answers to a number of questions in a condo project's governing documents: Are pets allowed? Can owners rent out their units? Are there restrictions on remodeling? What are the rules and hours of the recreational facilities? Are there limits on the number of people who can live in each unit? How many assigned parking spaces are there per unit? What are the procedures for electing Board members? Is barbequing allowed on balconies or patios?

What Amenities Do Homeowners' Dues Cover? While homeowners' dues or fees typically cover insurance costs and maintenance of the common areas, building services vary. Since the costs are shared among homeowners, there can be disputes over which amenities the project should have, such as a concierge, security guards, or a doorman. Prospective buyers can easily see on a walk-through whether there is a fitness center or a swimming pool. They can only guess whether in years to come the owners will vote to install a fitness center or close one down, add a swimming pool or demolish one.[58]

Prospective buyers need to know if HOA dues have been set at a high enough level to repaint the building periodically, replace elevator components as needed, or resurface or replace the roof.[59] Some state laws require HOAs to contract with independent auditors for periodic *reserve studies* that show whether the condo association is collecting and setting aside sufficient money to meet anticipated needs for capital improvements.[60] In projects where monthly dues fall short of accumulating sufficient reserves for capital improvements, buyers can expect whopping special assessments eventually, unless the unit owners are prepared to stand by and do nothing as the building deteriorates.

Apartment dwellers moving into condos can no longer count on the landlord fixing the broken refrigerator or taking care of plumbing or window leaks. Unlike apartment tenants, condo owners are often responsible for maintaining their own units;[61] "In many buildings the condo association's responsibility stops at the midpoint between the walls of your unit."[62] This can lead to serious and complicated disputes among condo owners when the newly installed Jacuzzi tub in the unit upstairs floods the unit below. The HOA is responsible for the space between the units, but the upstairs unit owner is responsible for her own Jacuzzi malfunctioning. Sorting out their respective liabilities for the flooding becomes a multi-party transaction that is likely to be joined by the insurers for each of the parties involved.

Documents Buyers Should Review. Buyers depend on the HOA for maintenance of the common areas and become co-owners of the common areas. As tenants-in-

---

58. *See* Melinda Fulmer, *Your Condo-Buying Cheat Sheet*, http://www.ehomes.com/blog/your-condo-buying-cheat-sheet/.

59. *See* Adam Verwymeren, *5 Tips for Condo Buyers* (last visited July, 13, 2015), http://www.fox news.com/leisure/2013/10/11/5-tips-for-condo-buyers/.

60. *See, e.g.* California Dep't of Real Estate, *Reserve Study Guidelines for Homeowner Association Budgets* (last visited July, 13, 2015), http://www.dre.ca.gov/files/pdf/re25.pdf.

61. Dillon, *supra* note 55.

62. Verwymeren, *supra* note 57.

common of the common areas, they should look closely at the last twelve-month operating budget. Are all the unit owners paying dues on time? Are the dues covering an appropriate level of operating costs? Is there a monthly surplus or a deficit? Is a project running an operating deficit? Sooner or later, operating deficits will have to be covered through special assessments. A condo buyer purchasing into a project running at a deficit may end up being assessed for operating expenses that pre-dated her ownership.[63]

As potential residents, they might want the "inside scoop" on a condo community. For this, buyers should review the board's meeting minutes, which can provide clues about disputes among unit owners, major maintenance issues, pending litigation, and the board's or management's responsiveness to owners' concerns.[64]

All of the unit owners are tenants-in-common of the land; if the entire building were destroyed in a fire, flood or earthquake, absent an agreement to the contrary or a vote to rebuild by a supermajority of unit owners, any unit owner could petition a court to order a sale of the land and divide the proceeds among the unit owners.[65] The sale of the land is less likely when ample insurance proceeds are available to reconstruct the building because some of the owners might otherwise lack the cash or borrowing ability to cover their share of the reconstruction costs. Prospective buyers should review the HOA's insurance policies, which usually cover the building structure, as well as common areas.[66]

Question: A condo buyer is purchasing the largest unit in the building. Does this mean that if the building were destroyed in a flood, fire, or earthquake that she would own the largest share of the land?

Answer: California's default rule is that the common areas are owned in equal shares, one unit, one share. Since this is a default rule, the Declaration can specify any reasonable allocation, such as using the square footage of units or the method prescribed for allocating assessments among unit owners for common area maintenance.[67]

Who Will My Neighbors Be? It is a good idea to consider the age and family composition of condo building inhabitants. For instance, if you value tranquility, you

---

63. *What about the CC&Rs?* Realtor.com (last visited Jan. 2, 2015), http://www.realtor.com/basics/condos/ccr.asp.

64. *See* Verwymeren, *supra* note 57.

65. *See, e.g.,* Mass. Gen. Laws Ch. 183A, §17(b)(1) (a failure to obtain the necessary vote to rebuild may automatically trigger a sale of the property and redistribution of the proceeds according to percentage of ownership.); *What Happens to a Condo after a Catastrophe,* Tampa Bay Times, (last visited July, 13, 2015) http://www.tampabay.com/news/weather/hurricanes/what-happens-to-condo-after-a-catastrophe/508382.

66. *What Buyers Should Know About Condominiums,* Realtor.com (last visited July, 13, 2015), http://www.realtor.com/Basics/Condos/ShouldKnow.asp; *see also* http://www.bankrate.com/finance/real-estate/know-before-you-buy-condo-2.aspx; http://www.investopedia.com/articles/pf/07/buy-condo.asp.

67. *Cebular v. Cooper Arms Homeowners Ass'n,* 142 Cal. App. 4th 106, 47 Cal. Rptr. 3d 666 (2006).

might want to think twice before buying a unit facing the pool in a condo complex brimming with small children.[68] It is also worth noting whether the complex is comprised mostly of owners or renters; "renters may be less respectful of the association rules, and the state of the building and its facilities may suffer as a result."[69] Condo buyers need to know if their co-owners have the same financial capacity and similar tastes for the condition and appearance of the building. In older buildings, this can be obvious. In newer ones, it might be useful to speak with the brokers handling the sales to get an idea of the types of buyers who are being attracted to the project.

Question: The condo buyer would prefer to be in an "adult only" project. Can she take comfort in a provision in the Declaration prohibiting anyone under the age of 18 from residing in the project?

Answer: Just such a provision was held to be a violation of California's Unruh Civil Rights Act in O'Connor v. Village Green Owners Association.[70]

II. Fixtures

"Multi-million dollar deals on Manhattan condos have come close to falling apart when buyers and sellers squabble over a $150 ceiling fan. It's the real estate version of road rage."

—Paula Del Nunzio of Brown Harris Stevens[71]

A. The Fixtures Default Rule

A fixture is an item of personal property that becomes part of the realty by being attached to it, a thought captured in the Latin maxim: *quicquid plantatur solo, solo cedit* (whatever is affixed to the soil becomes part of the soil). When realty changes hands, fixtures remain in place for the buyer,[72] and sellers take personal property with them—unless the parties make another arrangement.

Three non-exclusive factors are considered in characterizing items as fixtures: "(1) the manner in which it is physically attached or installed, (2) the extent to which it is essential to the permanent use of the building or other improvement, and (3) the

---

68. Ben Apple, *Condos: What You Should Know When Buying* (last visited July, 13, 2015), http://www.realtor.com/home-finance/homebuyer-information/condos-what-you-should-know-when-buying.aspx.

69. *Id.*

70. 33 Cal. 3d 790, 191 Cal. Rptr. 320, 662 P.2d 427 (1983). The Unruh Act bars discrimination based on "sex, race, color, religion, ancestry, or national origin." The California courts apply it to any arbitrary discrimination, including age.

71. Robin Finn, *How Fights Over Fixtures Can Derail a Closing*, THE NY TIMES (Aug. 23, 2013).

72. An important exception applies to "trade fixtures," discussed in depth in subpart C, this section.

objective intention [not necessarily the actual stated intention] of the parties who attached or installed it" at the time of affixation."[73]

Physical Attachment. An item so embedded that removal would damage the item or the property to which it is attached is refutably presumed to be a fixture *per se*.[74] A portable dishwasher attached only by a cord is probably personal property, while a dishwasher built into a cabinet is probably a fixture.[75] Some items, attached to the realty but not so firmly as to be practically unmovable, straddle the line.

Essential to the Permanent Use. Under this second factor, courts have defined the term "essential" in various ways: an item the removal of which would cause physical injury to the realty, such as a support beam; something "integral," for instance, custom fitted window coverings; or the removal would cause "economic loss," for example, seating in a movie theater bolted in place.

Many items of personal property loosely attached to realty and easily removable have been characterized as "constructively attached" if it appears they have been incorporated permanently into the annexor's use.[76]

In the sale of commercial rental property, buyers and sellers contract for "personal property used in the operation of the property."[77] In a restaurant, for instance, these items would include chairs and tables, dishware, flatware and glasses. A hotel sale would typically include all furnishings and linens.

Objective Intent of Annexor. The inquiry for determining the objective intent of the annexor becomes a question of fact. For example, what would a reasonable person have thought she was doing when she installed cabinets, hooked up a stove, or bolted in a mobile home?

Question about the Removal of Signature Art from a Commercial Office Property: *We purchased an office building on a busy thoroughfare in a growing, walkable suburban area. The city government required that the developer provide public art equal to one percent of the construction cost of the building. So the developer hired a local artist who painted a brightly colored work on cardboard and stone for the building lobby.*[78]

---

73. This test is applied in most jurisdictions. *See, e.g., In re Thomas*, 362 B.R. 478, 485 (10th Cir. 2007). For a critical assessment of how courts apply the traditional fixtures test, see Ronald W. Polston, *The Fixtures Doctrine: Was It Ever Really the Law?* 16 Whittier L. Rev. 455 (1995).

74. *In re Appeal of Sheetz, Inc.*, 657 A.2d 1011, 1015 (Pa. Commw. Ct. 1995) (involving gas station owner's tax appeal challenging assessor's finding that canopies were 'fixtures' and, as such, taxable as real property).

75. *Sanders v. Butte Motor Co.*, 142 Mont. 524 (1963).

76. *Marsh v. Boring Furs, Inc.*, 551 P.2d 1053, 1055 (Or. 1976).

77. *See, e.g.*, CAR Commercial Purchase Agreement, Section 8(B)(3). The seller provides a list of these items in advance of the closing.

78. Removal could be subject to the federal Visual Artists Rights Act of 1990. "Independently of the author's economic rights, and even after the transfer of the said rights, the author shall have the right to claim authorship of the work and to object to any distortion, mutilation or other modification of, or other derogatory action in relation to, the said work, which would be prejudicial to his honor or reputation." *See* Edward J. Damich, *The Visual Artists Rights Act Of 1990: Toward A Federal System Of Moral Rights Protection For Visual Art*, 39 Cath. U. L. Rev. 945 (1990). It could also be subject to

Since then, the artist has become world-renowned. People tend to refer to the building by the artist's name. The art work has given the building a certain local cache with prime local law firm and accounting tenants.

We acquired the building recently for $38,000,000. On the day after the closing, on taking possession, we discovered that the painting was gone; the wall had been re-surfaced. We never imagined the seller would go to the trouble of hauling this sizable object away until we heard a rumor that the piece was worth $3,000,000.

The seller is uncooperative, and told us: "The art work was personal property; there was nothing about it in the contract. So it became mine at closing." (a) Do we have a good claim against the seller for its return? (b) How should we modify our purchase and sale agreements to deter sellers from removing art work from buildings we acquire in the future?

Answer: *(a) With no contract provision about the art work, you would have no right to the art work if a court determined that the art was personal property. Too bad you did not include the art on an exhaustive list of all the personal property that the seller was to have left with you at closing.*

Unless the seller promised the art work as part of the deal, your claim to it would depend on its being characterized as a fixture. It was not imbedded enough to be classified as a fixture per se. But you could claim it had been constructively attached, having become an inherent part of the marketing, use and commercial rental value of the office building. You could probably find support for alleging that when the seller installed it, he probably intended the art to remain permanently in place, especially since it was commissioned for this specific location and installed to satisfy the local government's "one percent for art" requirement. This is not a position easily vindicated. A claim of "constructive attachment" is always a question of fact. Besides, I would contend that you had a reasonable expectation that the property would be delivered to you in the same condition as on the contract date, and the painting was a material aspect of the physical condition of the property because of its intrinsic importance to the tenants.

Even if you are lucky enough to find a sympathetic judge or arbitrator, if the seller has already sold the art for fair value to a purchaser unaware of your potential claim, you will have no chance to recover the art work, just money damages from the seller, probably limited by a dollar cap for seller breaches that was written into the purchase and sale agreement.[79]

(b) In your future office building acquisitions, you could define the "property conveyed" to include: "the land, all buildings, fixtures and improvements on the land, and all personal property owned by Seller and located upon the land or within the improvements, including, without limitation, art work, sculpture, appliances, carpeting, and tools and supplies used in connection with the operation of the Property." (The seller will probably insist upon an exclusion of computer hardware and software.)

---

limitations upon removal imposed by the city's zoning code "percent for art" ordinance. *See* Steven R. Miller, *Percent for Art Programs at Public Art's Frontier*, 35 No. 5 ZONING AND PLANNING LAW REPORT 1 (May 2012).

79. Thanks to Stan Iezman, CEO, American Realty Advisors, for suggesting this.

B. Practical Advice for Home Buyers and Sellers Regarding Fixtures

Sellers bear the risk of ambiguity for items that could be characterized either as personal property or fixtures.[80] Sellers should explicitly except from the conveyance articles that could be considered fixtures and that the seller intends to remove or that belong to tenants or others. Buyers must include in the conveyance articles that could be considered personal property that they intend to acquire along with the realty.

For example:

> Suppose a house or condo has beautiful draperies and attached wood window blinds. Those draperies hang by hooks from a drapery rod that is screwed into the wall. The law of fixtures says the draperies are personal property because they can be easily removed without damage, but the drapery rods are fixtures included in the home sale. The wood window blinds, if permanently attached to the structure, are considered fixtures, which are included in the home sale. But the printed sales contract can change the result. Most well-written home sales contract forms specify "window coverings" are included in the sales price (unless otherwise excluded).[81]

One disappointed buyer recounts:

> I think we were swindled by our seller and the real estate agent on an expensive house we bought. The house was vacant, but it had very expensive appliances — a Sub-Zero refrigerator, KitchenAid dishwasher, Wolf professional stove. We assumed these items were included in our offer price because they were listed in the information sheet the broker gave us. After closing, when we got the keys to the house, we were dismayed to see all these appliances had been removed.[82]

As this example shows, sellers could remove even items featured in marketing brochures for the house.

Fixtures in Pre-Owned Houses. Sellers who don't want to leave the antique chandelier behind should take it down and put up one they are willing to part with before

---

80. *See, e.g., In re Carson*, 95 Cal. App. 3d 123, 133 (2d Dist. 1971); *Batcheler v. Lally*, 66 Pa. D. & C. 25, 28 (1948). This legal presumption appears lost on some sellers. "When the McMahons took the keys to their new home, they discovered several items missing, including garden paving slabs, a heated towel rail ... and the electric pump from the ... water feature. The items, deemed the judge, were included in the agreed selling price and, therefore, the McMahons were due compensation." In another instance, brokers reported nearly losing the sale of a $4 million dollar home because the buyers and sellers couldn't come to terms over a washer and dryer. To save the sale, the brokers bought the machines from the sellers and gave them to the buyers. Ross Clark, *Contents Not Included: Just how mean can vendors get?*, SUNDAY TELEGRAPH, May 26, 2002, at 18, col. 1.

81. Robert Bruss, *You Can't Always Take It With You*, CHIC. TRIB. (last visited July, 13, 2015), http://articles.chicagotribune.com/2006-05-05/business/0605050102_1_dining-room-chandelier-condo-sale-sales-contract.

82. Robert Bruss, *Should Personal Property Stay or Go? Spell It Out in Sales Contact*, LA TIMES ("[I]t appears you have a very strong case against the seller and realty agent").

showing the house to prospective buyers. Why invite arguments and possibly lose a deal? But sellers willing to part with some fixture-like goodie for a price should by all means keep it in place, specify in the contract that it will be removed at closing, and wait for the buyer to ask about it. The seller then may either try to sell it to the buyer, or be magnanimous and make a gift of it to sweeten the deal.

C. Fixtures and Trade Fixtures: A Snapshot of the Rights of Mortgage Lenders, General Creditors, Fixtures Financiers, Landlords and Tenants

Security Interests in Fixtures: The Owner's Mortgage Lender v. the Owner's General Creditors. The security interests of mortgage lenders are generally regarded as superior to the claims of a borrower's general creditors to fixtures that the borrower installs in an industrial or commercial property as part of the operation. When the owner of a plant installs equipment bolted to the realty or so heavy that it is difficult to remove, there is a presumption that the owner planned to use the equipment as an integral part of its operation within the realty,

The mortgagee's right to include the fixtures as part of its lien is virtually indisputable for loans made after the equipment was in place since the mortgage lender would have presumably observed the item and presumed it was part of the realty when inspecting the property in underwriting the mortgage loan. Courts generally find the mortgagee's claim nearly as convincing when the mortgage loan pre-dates the installation. For starters, most mortgages explicitly cover "after acquired" property affixed to the realty. Even without such provisions, because mortgagors install equipment in a commercial facility to use there, courts usually conclude that such equipment becomes a fixture, part of the realty, and hence subject to a foreclosing mortgagee's lien.[83]

Purchase Money Fixtures Financiers. An equipment vendor or lender who advances the purchase money for an owner or tenant to acquire fixtures can perfect a security interest in those fixtures by placing a fixtures filing in the county land records where the realty is located. The filing must indicate that it covers fixtures, and must describe the real property to which it relates. If the debtor does not have a recorded interest in the realty, the filing document must identify the record owner of the property.[84]

A fixture filing takes priority over later recorded real estate interests in fixtures. If filed to perfect a purchase-money security interest, the fixture filing even takes priority over earlier recorded interests as well. U.C.C. §9-334(a) allows a purchase money fixtures financier to establish a priority over a prior realty mortgage lender on the fa-

---

83. Alphonse M. Squillante, *The Law of Fixtures and the Uniform Commercial Code—Part I: Common Law of Fixtures*, 15 Hofstra L. Rev. 191 (1987).

84. Brennan Posner, *Fixated on Fixtures: An Overview of Perfecting and Ensuring Priority of Security Interests in Fixtures* (last visited July, 13, 2015), http://apps.americanbar.org/buslaw/blt/content/2012/01/0003c.pdf.

miliar notion that but for the fixture financier providing credit, the fixture would probably not have been there anyway to benefit the realty mortgage.

A fixture filing is effective for five years from the date of recording. The effectiveness can be extended for additional five-year periods by filing continuation statements.

Trade Fixtures in Commercial Landlord-Tenant Law. A trade fixture is a piece of equipment on or attached to the real estate that is used in a trade or business such as a physician's X-ray machine or a restaurateur's huge ovens and built-in refrigerators. Usually, commercial landlords and tenants negotiate the ownership and disposition of major items of personal property the tenant intends to install that could be regarded as fixtures. Some leases specify that personal property affixed to the site for use in the tenant's trade or business remain the personal property of the tenant when the lease ends. Other leases characterize the personal property as fixtures once they have been installed for use in the tenant's trade or business, and remain with the landlord.

Question: Who owns trade fixtures during and at the end of the lease term if the lease makes no provision regarding them?

Answer: When the tenant installs items of personal property used in its trade or business, the tenant owns them even if they would have been regarded as fixtures and part of the realty if the landlord had installed them. Thus, tenants have the right and the obligation to remove trade fixtures at the end of the lease term as long as removal does not damage the realty. Tenants are liable for restoring the premises to their condition before the trade fixtures were installed.[85]

Question: Suppose a kitchen appliance vendor sells on credit all the equipment the restaurateur requires and secures its purchase money chattel mortgage with a UCC financing statement. The equipment vendor records UCC fixture filings in the county where the equipment is placed. If the restaurant venture goes broke, as restaurants sometimes do, who has the first lien on the kitchen equipment—the warehouse owner's mortgage lender or the restaurateur's equipment vendor?

Answer: The equipment vendor's UCC fixture lien has priority over the liens of any deeds of trust on the restaurant realty but only upon the kitchen equipment.[86] *The equipment regarded as a trade fixture remains the personal property of the restaurateur subject to the lien of the unpaid supplier.*

Question: A commercial landlord places a mortgage upon tenant-occupied realty. The mortgage purports to cover all fixtures then or later affixed to the realty. The lease made no provision regarding trade fixtures. The landlord defaults; the landlord's mortgagee forecloses. Does the foreclosure sale purchaser become entitled to the trade fixtures?

---

85. *"trade fixtures"*, LEGAL-DICTIONARY.COM (last visited July 11, 2015), http://legal-dictionary .thefreedictionary.com/trade+fixture.

86. *See, e.g.,* *FGB Realty Advisors v. Bennett*, 44 Conn. Supp. 156, 159, 161–63 (1995); *GCI GP, LLC v. Stewart Title Guar. Co.*, 290 S.W.3d 287, 295 (2009).

Answer: No. The trade fixtures belong to the tenant or the tenant's fixtures' financier. They are personal property not belonging to the landlord. Hence, the landlord had no right to pledge them as security for a mortgage on the realty.

III. Casualty Losses during the Executory Period

A. Common Law Default Rule on Executory Period Risk of Loss

Property under contract can be damaged or destroyed by casualties such as fire, flooding, earthquakes, tornados and landslides. A difficult question to resolve in any realty purchase-and-sale agreement is who bears the risk of loss if the property is damaged or destroyed during the *executory period*—the time from when the parties first enter the contract to the precise moment when the deal closes and the buyer becomes the legal owner of the property.[87]

Before contracting to sell, the seller as homeowner bears the risks of a casualty loss. After closing, the burden of a casualty loss is the buyer's. But courts and jurisdictions in the United Kingdom and the United States have differed over time as to who should bear the risk of loss when, for example, before the scheduled closing date, the house burns to the ground, blows apart in a hurricane, or is dislodged from its foundation in an earthquake.

Presently, legal commentators tend to believe the "majority rule" in the U.S. is that the buyer bears the loss. As a practical matter, this means that the seller has the right to insist that the buyer take the property in its damaged condition with no price reduction. Defenders of the majority rule contend that placing the risk of casualty loss upon the buyer is only fair as the corollary of the buyer's right to specific performance at the original contract price if the property value increased during escrow.[88]

Critics of the majority rule point out that the seller in possession during the executory period is in the best position to safeguard the property and is probably insured

---

87. The tax codes take a bit of the sting out of some casualty losses. To the extent casualty losses are uninsured, Internal Revenue Code § 165(c)(3) allows deductions. Taxpayers are obliged to file timely insurance claims or lose their tax deductions. Section 262 precludes deductions for upkeep, insurance, and wear and tear, and the IRS disallows asserted deductions for slowly advancing damage such as from corrosion, termites, and erosion.

88. The majority rule was a feature of the doctrine of equitable conversion under which the seller is said to hold bare legal title during the executory period for the benefit of the buyer who is characterized as the equitable owner by virtue of having the right to specific performance. Though widely followed, this ancient doctrinal relic is fading. *See, e.g., Brush Grocery Kart Inc. v. Sure Fine Market, Inc.*, 47 P.3d 680 (2002) (rejecting equitable conversion and refusing to hold purchaser responsible for uninsured hailstorm loss.); *Rochelle v. Carr*, 418, S.W.2d 710, 711 (Tx. Ct. App.1967) ("We cannot impute to a vendor and purchaser an intention that, in case of injury to the premises during the temporal gap between the making of the contract and the delivery of the deed, the purchaser should be entitled to recover damages from the wrongdoer even though the contract, by mutual consent of the vendor and purchaser, is abandoned.").

against fire and casualty losses while buyers have difficulty obtaining comprehensive coverage during escrow because insurers worry about creating what is euphemistically called "moral hazard."

Preponderantly, U.S. courts (and parliament in the U.K.) make the majority rule more palatable to buyers by granting them the benefit of a constructive trust on the seller's insurance proceeds.[89] In an age when consumers can reject damaged goods, the majority rule seems anomalous, forcing home buyers to accept badly damaged houses with no price abatement when they could reject a damaged kitchen appliance. Further, the buyer's right to insurance proceeds will often be subordinate to that of the mortgage lender as a named co-insured under the policy.

In some states, the lender will have the right to allocate the proceeds to a reduction of the seller's mortgage debt. This will be small comfort to the buyer unless the buyer is acquiring the property subject to the seller's loan. More fortunate buyers are those who will be allowed to use the proceeds to repair the damaged property.[90]

Since most insurance policies are subject to deductible amounts, the buyer and seller will need to negotiate a risk of loss provision that specifies whether the buyer or the seller is liable for repair costs up to the deductible limit.

That issue is anticipated and resolved in the following risk of loss provision for use in multifamily dwellings. This form provision contemplates the use of insurance proceeds to cushion transferring the risk of a casualty loss during the executory period to the buyer as long as the seller is insured.

"Section 12. Risk of Loss

*(a) Except as provided in any indemnity provisions of this Agreement, Seller shall bear all **risk** of **loss** for the Property up to the earlier of either the date of possession or the date title is transferred to Purchaser in accordance with this Agreement.*

*(b) However, if the Property is damaged by fire or other **casualty** prior to the Closing Date and is **insured** under one or more fire or **casualty insurance** policies maintained by Seller, and if repair of the Property would cost less than[amount] ("**Loss** Threshold"), as determined by Seller in good faith, Purchaser may not terminate this Agreement. However, Seller may elect to either (i) repair and re-store the Property to its condition immediately preceding the fire or **casualty**, or (ii) **proceed** to close this transaction without reduction in the Purchase Price, but assign and transfer to Purchaser on the Closing Date all of Seller's right, title, and interest to the **insurance proceeds** paid or payable to Seller under the policy covering the damage and pay to Purchaser the amount of Seller's deductible under the **insurance** policy.*

---

89. Roger A. Bixby, *The Vendor-Vendee Problem: How Do We Slice the Insurance Pie?*, 19 Forum 112 (September, 1983). The most difficult situations involve allocating insurance proceeds when vendor and purchaser each have their own insurance policies.

90. Patrick A. Randolph, Jr., *A Mortgagee's Interest In Casualty Loss Proceeds: Evolving Rules And Risks*, 32 Real Prop. Prob. & Tr. J. 1 (1997).

*(c) However, if the Property is damaged by fire or other **casualty** prior to the Closing Date and is **insured** under one or more fire or **casualty insurance** policies maintained by Seller, and if the repair of the damage would cost in excess of the **Loss** Threshold, as determined by Seller in good faith, Purchaser may either (i) terminate this Agreement and have the Title Company return the Earnest Money and all interest; or (ii) **proceed** to close this transaction, without reduction in the Purchase Price, and have Seller assign and transfer to Purchaser on the Closing Date all of Seller's right, title, and interest to the **insurance proceeds** paid or payable to Seller under the policy covering the damage and to pay to Purchaser the amount of Seller's deductible under the **insurance** policy.*

*(d) Immediately after Seller obtains. notice of any fire or **casualty**, Seller shall notify Purchaser in writing, including Seller's determination of the repair cost. If the repair cost, as determined by Seller, exceeds the **Loss** Threshold, Purchaser shall notify Seller within ten (10) days of Purchaser's receipt of Seller's Notice whether Purchaser elects to terminate this Agreement in accordance with Section 12(c)(i) hereof.*

Closing shall be delayed, if necessary, to allow Purchaser to make the election. If Purchaser fails to make the election within ten (10) business days, Purchaser shall be deemed to have elected the rights under Section 12(c)(ii) hereof, and Closing shall be delayed, if necessary, until the later to occur of (i) the Closing Date or (ii) five (5) business days after the expiration of the ten (10) business day period."[91]

B. The Uniform Vendor and Purchaser Risk Act (UVPRA)

At least thirteen states including California and New York have enacted the UVPRA,[92] first adopted by the commissioners on Uniform State Laws in 1935.[93] It places the risk of loss on the party in possession when the executory period loss occurs, *usually* the seller. The rationale is that the party in possession is best able to prevent, mitigate, and insure against such losses.

The UVPRA:

Any contract hereafter made in this State for the purchase and sale of real property shall be interpreted as including an agreement that the parties shall have the following rights and duties, unless the contract expressly provides otherwise:

---

91. 1 Cal. Real Est. Forms § 1:27 (2d ed.), Miller & Starr California Real Estate Forms; Alexander E. Hamilton, Chapter 1. Real Property Purchase and Sale Transactions, III. Forms, E. Seller-Oriented Purchase and Sale Agreements.

92. Alvin L. Arnold, *Purchase and Sale: As Is Clause*, 40 No. 2 MORTGAGE & REAL ESTATE EXECUTIVES REPORT 6 (March 15, 2007).

93. The twelve states that have adopted the UVPRA in full or in part are: California, Hawaii, Illinois, Michigan, Nevada, New York, North Carolina, Oklahoma, Oregon, South Dakota, Texas, and Wisconsin.

(1) If, when neither the legal title nor the possession of the subject matter of the contract has been transferred, all or a material part thereof is destroyed without fault of the purchaser or is taken by eminent domain, the vendor cannot enforce the contract, and the purchaser is entitled to recover any portion of the price that he has paid;

(2) If, when either the legal title or the possession of the subject matter of the contract has been transferred, all or any part hereof is destroyed without fault of the vendor or is taken by eminent domain, the purchaser is not thereby relieved from a duty to pay the price.

C. Contracting out of Risk-of-Loss Default Rules

Unless the parties provide otherwise, the UVPRA allocates to the seller the casualty risk of loss during the executory period. What this means is that the seller cannot enforce the contract and must return the buyer's down payment when the property is totally destroyed or materially damaged.

Up to the moment when either the title passes to the buyer or the buyer takes possession, the seller cannot enforce the contract and must refund the buyer's down payment. Presumably, once the buyer takes possession or acquires title, the buyer will have gained effective control of the property, responsibility for managing the property, and will be in a position to purchase casualty insurance coverage. At that point, the seller has the option of enforcing the contract.

Is the "As Is" Buyer Entitled to Reject the Property on Final Inspection? Purchase and sale agreements typically allow the buyer the right to make a final verification of the condition of the property to determine that it is in the same condition as when the contract was signed. Does this give the buyer the option of rescinding the contract because due to the casualty loss the seller was not able to convey the property in its "purchase date" condition? Some courts have thought so.[94]

Can the Buyer Compel Specific Performance Despite the Casualty Loss? Suppose the seller would prefer to retain title to the property, and pocket the insurance proceeds. Or the buyer is prepared to accept title to the property despite the damage or destruction. Why would either party ever wish upon themselves title to damaged or destroyed property? Sometimes, property is worth more if the building upon it were demolished. Perhaps the property was not being put to its "highest and best" use because it was a protected historic building. Or maybe the buyer had obtained the approval of local government to demolish the structure and replace it with a more lucrative one.

Notice of Loss. Risk of loss contract provisions require sellers to notify buyers of any loss and set the requirements for doing so.

Buyer's Option. In the case of substantial or material loss, buyers are often given the option to rescind or go forward and close at the agreed purchase price. A well-

---

94. *Bishop Ryan High School v. Lindberg,* 370 N.W.2d 726 (N. Dak 1985).

drafted risk of loss provision also allows a buyer to rescind if the buyer's mortgage lender refuses to fund the acquisition because of a casualty loss.[95]

Insurance Coverage. Sellers may be required to maintain ample insurance coverage for the benefit of their buyers during the executory period, and to assign their insurance proceeds, along with a credit against the sales price for any deductible amount. The seller could designate the buyer as an "additional insured" for the duration of the executory period. Buyers relying on the seller's insurance must make sure the seller maintains the policy until closing and that the coverage is adequate for the buyer's needs.

Buyers can obtain their own policies in states where they bear the risk of executory period casualty losses.

When the Buyer Plans to Demolish the Existing Structure. For buyers who purchase property for development, intending to demolish the improvements immediately after taking title, an assignment of the seller's insurance proceeds could be a pure windfall. Of course, the same could be said of a seller who stands to receive the full purchase price for property (land and buildings) plus insurance proceeds for the destroyed building.

There are situations in which a developer-buyer intending to demolish all the buildings on the site could suffer a loss due to a casualty during the executory period: "A natural disaster, such as an earthquake or levy failure, could render the unimproved portions of property unsuitable for development." A risk of loss contract provision could be drafted to define this possibility as a material part of the property to be acquired, and any other damage or destruction could be defined as immaterial.[96]

Defining Material Losses. The UVPRA only applies when "all or a material" part of the property is destroyed without fault of the vendor or purchaser. But the statute fails to define "material." Risk of loss provisions often fill this void by specifying definitions of "material" in terms of the estimated cost of repairs, the time likely needed for restoration, or the percentage of the structure damaged.

Special Problems of Buyers Acquiring Commercial Rental Property. Buyers of commercial rental property are dependent on the rent to cover their mortgage and tax payments. For such buyers, a "substantial" or "material" loss is one that gives tenants the right to stop paying rent until repairs are completed, or to terminate their leases. Rent interruption insurance would be a good antidote, but might be prohibitively expensive.

Purchase Price Abatements. When it comes to the purchaser's right to specific performance with abatement for a *material* loss, one UVPRA state has granted a purchaser this right; another has denied it.[97] Commercial buyers who need to close

---

95. Paul Cliff, *Catastrophe Planning for Real Estate Practitioners: Traps for the Unwary Contained in Risk of Loss and Premises Damage Provisions in Real Property Purchase and Lease Documents*, 25 CAL. REAL PROP. J. 23 (2007).

96. *Id.* at 24.

97. California courts have denied this remedy; New York courts have granted it. *Compare Lucenti v. Cayuga Apts. Inc.*, 48 N.Y.2d 886 (1979) (allowing purchaser specific performance with abatement),

on or before a specific date for tax or other business reasons might want to consider contracting for the right to specific performance with a price abatement or an assignment of the seller's insurance proceeds in the event of a casualty loss during escrow.

A developer contracting to construct a special purpose building to suit a particular buyer to be delivered upon closing might want the right to compel the buyer to take an incomplete or damaged building subject to the seller's obligation to repair or complete the building within a reasonable time after the casualty delayed closing date.

Protecting the Buyer in Possession. Suppose the seller allows the buyer to take possession of the property on a two month lease coterminous with the escrow period. During that time, the house is badly damaged in an earthquake, flood or fire. Under the UVPRA, the buyer in possession would bear the risk of loss. The buyer would be well advised to make sure the purchase and sale agreement specifies that the parties intend for the UVPRA to apply as if the buyer were not in possession.

Questions

Question 1: *Inspections.*

(a) Why should buyers pay for inspections before purchasing when they will have the benefit of builders' warranties for newly-built houses and seller disclosures of defects for pre-owned homes? Anyway, buyers will have no practical recourse against inspectors who fail to disclose important defects because inspection companies usually have minimal resources and seldom carry errors and omissions coverage.

(b) Why is the seller better off with a contract allowing buyers to back out of their purchase agreements in their sole discretion following the inspection contingency time period, or should buyers be obligated to demonstrate reasonableness in backing out by pointing to "substantial defects" and giving the seller a chance to cure them?

(c) Is it a good idea for sellers to commission a physical inspection of the property's condition when the seller must share the report with potential buyers, even if it reveals horrific defects previously unknown to the seller?

Question 2: *Seller's Post-Closing Liability for Defective Conditions.*

Buyer exercises an option to buy a house in August and closes in September. The first seasonal rains pour down a week after closing; the roof leaks badly. Buyer spends $10,000 on roof repairs.

(a) Is the seller liable at common law, assuming he is not a merchant builder or developer, to deliver the house in a habitable condition?

(b) Is the seller liable in a disclosure state if he said nothing about the roof leaking in the disclosure statement because he didn't know it would leak?

---

with Dixon v. Salvation Army, 142 Cal. App.3d 463 (4th Dist. 1983) (disallowing specific performance with abatement).

(c) If the seller had known all along that the roof was leaky, and the buyer can prove it, would an "as is" clause have exonerated the seller?

(d) Would the seller be liable if he had promised the buyer he would have the roof repaired before closing, and four days before the closing the seller had paid a roofer to fix the leak, and has a receipt to prove it?

Question 3: *Are "As Is" Clauses a Good Idea for the Seller?*

What are the main advantages and disadvantages of an "as is" clause for the seller in a jurisdiction where an "as is" clause negates any implied warranties and representations, but offers no excuse to the seller for not disclosing material, known, latent defects?

Question 4: *Seller Disclosure of Pre-Existing Defects.*[98]

This question is about the seller's obligation to disclose that she repainted the exterior of her home because the exterior wall was cracking in various places and it looked terrible. The house in is Los Angeles.

Melissa, the seller, would prefer not to disclose that there were various cracks in exterior walls of the house. Everything is good now. The house was very recently repainted. The cracks are no longer visible. The seller has no idea whether those cracks suggest structural instability of the house. She knows nothing about engineering or soils stability.

She is convinced that the buyer should be happy that the house has a new paint job.

(a) Should Melissa disclose the existence of those (now invisible) cracks?

Melissa decides not to disclose them. The buyer's inspector informs the buyer that it looks like there had been some cracks in the wall but nothing very serious. The buyer signs the form required by their purchase and sale agreement indicating acceptance of the condition of the property as a contingency of closing.

---

98. This question was prepared for a USC law school class session September 17, 2015, by Dennis Greenwald and Melissa Clark '08.

Six weeks after closing, the buyer notices that cracks are appearing on the concrete outside the house. A geologist explains that the house is slipping off its foundation. The problem was evidenced by the painted-over cracks. Further soils test will be needed to determine if this is a serious problem or not. The testing will cost $10,000.

(b) Is the seller liable for: (1) the cost of testing;, (2) implementing the recommendations of the geologist for shoring up the site, or (3) the difference between what the buyer paid and what a reasonable buyer would have paid had the cracked walls been disclosed?

(c) Is Melissa vulnerable to a claim of fraud?

The California Transfer Disclosure Statute and The Elements of Fraud are described below.

The California Transfer Disclosure Statute. A California statute (Cal. Civ. Proc § 1102(a) requires sellers of one to four family dwellings (with some limitations) to provide Transfer Disclosure Statements to prospective buyers as soon as practicable and before closing.

The buyer has three days after delivery of the TDS if delivered in person; or five days after delivery by mail, *to terminate his or her offer by delivery of a written notice of termination to the transferor or the transferor's agent.* The obligation to provide a transfer disclosure statement is not waivable and applies to "as is" contracts.

However, the transferor is not liable for any "error, inaccuracy, or omission of any information delivered pursuant to [a TDS] ... if such information was "not within the personal knowledge of the transferor...." (CAL. CIV. CODE § 1102.4). Unless the transferor has personal knowledge regarding a disclosure, the transferor is entitled to rely on the expert options of others (e.g., local government officials, geologists, et al.).

Besides not disclosing known, material defects, sellers can be liable for concealing or lying about material defects (fraud, provided all of the other elements can be proved).

As part of the standard statutory seller disclosure form, sellers are required to answer this questionnaire:

California Transfer Disclosure Statement, Cal. Civ. Code 1106.2.

Are you (Seller) aware of any of the following: ___ Yes   ___ No

1. Substances, materials, or products which may be an environmental hazard such as, but not limited to, asbestos, formaldehyde, radon gas, lead-based paint, mold, fuel or chemical storage tanks, and contaminated soil or water on the subject property

2. Features of the property shared in common with adjoining   ___ Yes   ___ No landowners, such as walls, fences, and driveways, whose use or responsibility for maintenance may have an effect on the subject property

3. Any encroachments, easements or similar matters that may   ___ Yes   ___ No affect your interest in the subject property

4. Room additions, structural modifications, or other alterations or repairs made without necessary permits   ___ Yes ___ No

5. Room additions, structural modifications, or other alterations or repairs not in compliance with building codes   ___ Yes ___ No

6. Fill (compacted or otherwise) on the property or any portion thereof   ___ Yes ___ No

7. Any settling from any cause, or slippage, sliding, or other soil problems   ___ Yes ___ No

8. Flooding, drainage or grading problems   ___ Yes ___ No

9. Major damage to the property or any of the structures from fire, earthquake, floods, or landslides   ___ Yes ___ No

10. Any zoning violations, nonconforming uses, violations of "setback" requirements   ___ Yes ___ No

11. Neighborhood noise problems or other nuisances   ___ Yes ___ No

12. CC&Rs or other deed restrictions or obligations   ___ Yes ___ No

13. Homeowners Association which has any authority over the subject property   ___ Yes ___ No

14. Any "common area" (facilities such as pools, tennis courts, walkways, or other areas co-owned in undivided interest with others   ___ Yes ___ No

15. Any notices of abatement or citations against the Property   ___ Yes ___ No

16. Any lawsuits by or against the Seller threatening to or   ___ Yes ___ No
affecting this real property, claims for damages by the Seller pursuant to Section 910 or 914 threatening to or affecting this real property, claims for breach of warranty pursuant to Section 900 threatening to or affecting this real property, or claims for breach of an enhanced protection agreement pursuant to Section 903 threatening to or affecting this real property, including any lawsuits or claims for damages pursuant to Section 910 or 914 alleging a defect or deficiency in this real property or "common areas" facilities such as pools, tennis courts, walkways, or other areas co-owned in undivided interest with others.

If the answer to any of these is yes, explain. (Attach additional sheets if necessary.)

The Elements of Fraud[99]

*"A prima facie case in an action against the **seller** of real property for intentional **fraud**:*

---

99. Richard J. Link, *Cause of Action Against Seller for Intentional Fraud or Deceit in Sale of Real Property*, 32 Causes of Action 2d 659 (originally published in 2006). Database updated November 2015.

*(1) The **seller** made a false representation of existing fact concerning the condition of the property requires proof that:*

*(2) The **seller** concealed or **failed** to **disclose** a material fact about the property which the **seller** had a duty to **disclose**;*

*(3) The **seller** made a false promise in connection with the sale with no intent of keeping it;*

*(4) The false representation or fact not **disclosed** was material;*

*(5) The **seller** knew of the true condition of the property and made the representation with knowledge of its falsity or with reckless disregard as to its truth;*

*(6) The **seller** acted with the intention of deceiving the purchaser as to the true facts about the property and with the intention of inducing the purchaser to rely on the false representation, promise, or nondisclosure;*

(7) The purchaser relied on the false representation, promise, or nondisclosure;

(8) The purchaser's reliance was justified or reasonable and (9) the purchaser suffered loss as a proximate result of reliance on the false representation, promise, or nondisclosure.

There will be no liability if:

*(1) The **seller's** representation was true, or was opinion or speculation and not one of existing fact concerning the property, or the **seller** had no intention of not performing a promise.*

*(2) The **seller's** false representation, failure to **disclose**, or false promise was immaterial to the sale.*

*(3) The **seller** had no duty to **disclose**.*

*(4) The **seller** had no knowledge that the representation was false or that facts allegedly not **disclosed** existed, or intended to perform the promise.*

*(5) The **seller** did not intend to deceive the purchaser as to the condition of the property or did not intend to induce the purchaser to act in reliance on the representation, promise, or nondisclosure.*

*(6) The purchaser did not actually rely on the **seller's** representation, promise, or nondisclosure in purchasing the property.*

*(7) The purchaser was not justified or reasonable in relying on the **seller's** representation, promise, or nondisclosure as to the condition of the property.*

*(8) The purchaser did not suffer loss as a proximate result of the **seller's** representation, promise, or nondisclosure.*

(9) A contract term bars recovery."

Question 5: *Seller Disclosure of Changed Conditions Between the Contract Date and the Closing.*

The events depicted in this question take place in the same jurisdiction as the one in the previous question. At the time the buyers and sellers sign a contract of purchase and sale for a home, the neighborhood is quiet at night. During the executory period, a home across the street sells to a family with three raucous teenagers whose parents are often out of town. The kids' "all-nighters" draw scores of young party-goers so noisy and messy that the neighbors called the police three times last week to halt the disturbance.

(a) Must the sellers report this development to the prospective buyers?

(b) If they do report it, what pre-closing options are available to the buyers— restitution and rescission? Specific performance with a price abatement? Rescission and forfeiture of their down payment?

(c) If the sellers close without disclosing, what remedies, if any, would be available to the buyers against the sellers if the noise persists after the closing?

Question 6: *Home Seller Warranties.*

(a) Why have courts tended to impose implied warranties of habitability on home-builders, but not on sellers of used housing?

(b) What types of provisions that frequently appear in homebuilder warranties should buyers recognize as severely limiting the usefulness of the warranty to the buyer?

Question 7: *Commercial Seller Representations and Warranties.*

An apartment developer is selling its newly constructed 50-unit building in a prime location. The buyer is acquiring the property for a family trust, and wants assurances that the building complies with all building and zoning codes and has no known defects. What is the seller likely to offer in response to this request, assuming it is quite satisfied with the price and other terms of the buyer's offer?

Question 8: *Buyer's Remedies After Closing for a Faulty Representation.*

Buyer and seller conclude a sale for a 200-unit apartment house for $20,000,000. During the "due diligence" period the chief financial officer (CFO) of the seller provided the last two years' financial statements, representing them to be true to the best of the knowledge of her knowledge.

After taking possession, the buyer learned from the landlord's project manager that tenants were often given three months' free rent. Many of those tenants are not renewing their one-year leases. The CFO had over-stated rent collections considerably. Had the buyer known this, it would have reduced its price by $1,000,000.

(a) What remedies would you suggest that the buyer consider for breach of the seller warranty?

(b) How do you suppose this dispute is likely to be resolved?

Question 9: *Fixtures.*

(a) The kitchen cabinetry is original and beautifully detailed. The old O'Keefe and Merritt[100] stove is working perfectly. What facts about the stove and cabinets are rel-

---

100. To see O'Keefe and Merritt stoves, go to (last visited July 13, 2015), http://www.okeefe-merritt .com/pages/okeefe.html (last visited 06/18/08).

evant to whether the home buyer gets to keep the stove or the kitchen cabinets, assuming the buyer and seller leave their status unresolved in the contract?

(b) A restaurateur bought the same type of stove on credit for the kitchen in his newly opened rented space. When the lease expires, who owns the stove — the landlord, the tenant restaurateur, or the landlord's mortgage lender following the mortgage lender's foreclosure of the defaulting landlord's interest in the space?

(c) The lobby of an office building is adorned with a thirty-foot long painting by a prominent artist valued at $10,000,000 and a sculpture garden with museum quality work. These art objects add to the status of the building as the premier location for major law, accounting, and business firms in the area. They could all be removed without permanently damaging the building but the value of the property might be diminished by their removal.

A buyer contracts to purchase the property under which the seller reserves the right to remove personal property that it owns, including the furniture in the building owner's office. The contract also specifies that fixtures are to remain in place after the closing.

The seller removes the painting and sculptures on the evening before closing. The purchase and sale contract has a limit of $100,000 in damages if the seller breaches any warranties and representations.

Has the buyer any meaningful recourse for the art and sculpture removals? Had they become fixtures?

Question 10: *Allocating Risk of Loss by Contract.*

The seller in this transaction would not want a casualty loss to derail her scheduled closing because she has contracted to take title and possession to her new home on the same day that she sells her old one.

(a) Which of the three risk of loss default rules would best suit the seller — the majority rule, the minority rule, or the UVPRA?

(b) For the seller, what would be the ideal contract provision concerning risk of loss consistent with not penalizing the buyer for the mishap?

(c) If you were the buyer's representative asked to sign the seller-friendly risk of loss provision reprinted earlier in this chapter, what changes would you suggest to remove the most buyer-unfriendly language of that prepared form?

Question 11: *Probing the Viability of the Buyer Possession Provision Under the UVPRA.*

A devastating fire destroys 700 houses in a California city. Several of the homes were in escrow at the time. Most of the sellers were in possession. But Seller A had agreed to allow Buyer B to take possession sixth days before the closing so that Buyer B's children could enroll in the local school. They increased the purchase price to account for the seller's increased costs for mortgage payments, property taxes, insurance and maintenance (gardener, security service, pool service).

Before the closing, the house burned to the ground through no fault of the buyer or seller.

Under the UVPRA would the seller have the right to specific performance, or to retain the buyer's down payment designated as liquidated damages in the purchase and sale contract? After all, the buyer was in possession during the executory period and the UVPRA clearly places the risk of loss on the buyer if the buyer has taken title or possession before closing.

The buyer claims that the UVPRA only applies in the absence of a contract provision to the contrary, and the final inspection gives the buyer the right to terminate the contract since the property is not what it was when the purchase and sale contract was signed. The purchase and sale contract had a standard provision for a final walk through so that the buyer could determine whether the house was in the same condition as on the day the contract was entered. But the provision also contained in capital letters: THIS INSPECTION IS NOT A CONTINGENCY OF THE CONTRACT. Is the buyer right?

Chapter 6

Deeds and the Quality of Title

Scope of the Chapter

A deed to real estate is an important document because it effectuates the seller's conveyance of legal title to the buyer. The seller becomes the deed grantor and the buyer, the deed grantee.

Deeds are not transmitted from one owner to the next. Each owner executes a new deed for delivery to her grantee. Deed language may be copied from printed from books or statutes. They can also be drafted by attorneys, escrow agents, real estate brokers, title companies or mortgage lenders.

Because deeds convey interests in land, they must satisfy the Statute of Frauds, unless an exception to the statute applies.

This chapter begins with the requisites for a deed to be valid. Then, we consider how buyers usually assess the quality of title from a preliminary title report and, at closing, purchase a policy of title insurance based on that report, possibly with negotiated modifications and endorsements in response to buyer or mortgage lender concerns about the title.

A later chapter details the contents of title reports. Here we lay the foundation for title insurance by discussing in detail the legal default norm called "a marketable title." This is the same norm that title insurers have adopted as the basis for their standard policy coverage.

Then, we discuss the seller's promises regarding the quality of the title. The chapter concludes by explaining why deeds need to be recorded, and because only acknowledged deeds will be accepted for recordation, what a proper acknowledgement is.

I. The Requisites for a Valid Deed

(1) The grantor must be competent or represented by a guardian.

(2) The proper grantor depends on how title is held.

(3) The grantor or an authorized agent must sign the deed.

(4) The deed need not be "for valuable consideration."

(5) The grantor must explicitly transfer title by present words of transfer.

(6) The grantee must be named in the deed but need not sign it.

(7) The deed need not be dated.

(8) The deed must be delivered to the grantee.

(9) The grantee must accept the deed.

(10) The conveyed property must be accurately described but not the improvements.

(1) The grantor must be competent or represented by a guardian.

To be bound by a deed, the grantor must be of legal age,[1] of sound mind, and possess the mental capacity to understand the nature of the transaction and its consequences on her rights and interests. Incompetent grantors, whose property is being administered by a court-appointed guardian, no longer possess the right to convey title by deed. Only their guardians have that right.[2]

What about deeds that were signed by grantors before guardians were appointed for them, but who were incapable of understanding the consequences of deeding the property? Courts defer to subsequently appointed guardians regarding whether such deeds should be affirmed or set aside. A grantor's guardian or heirs may elect to affirm a sale despite the grantor's incompetence. A grantor may do the same upon recovering from a mental disability.[3] This is what courts and commentators mean when they describe incompetence as making deeds voidable, not void.

Deeds by temporarily disqualified grantors may be resuscitated once the grantor recovers from her disability or a minor reaches the age of consent. At common law, incompetent grantors were estopped from denying the validity of their own deeds. Most states have rejected this absolute approach and prefer a case-by-case analysis based on the equities. Though courts sometimes side with bona fide purchasers and mortgagees,[4] they have also invalidated deeds to bona fide purchasers by legally incompetent grantors.[5]

Various factors such as old age, illness, ignorance or weakness, incline courts to find mental capacity lacking.[6] A typical challenge arises when a widower who is too

---

1. Minors may be *grantees*. Beneficial gifts to minors will be upheld; detrimental ones are voidable even if previously accepted.

2. *The National Conference of Commissioners on Uniform State Laws has promulgated a Power of Attorney Act to deal with the possibility of future incapacity*, UNIFORM LAW COMMISSION (last visited July 13, 2015), http://www.uniformlaws.org/Act.aspx?title=Power+of+Attorney.

3. 1 MASS. PROOF OF CASES CIV. § 11:9 (3d ed.).

4. 2 PATTON AND PALOMAR ON LAND TITLES § 336 (3d ed.).

5. *Shepard v. First Am. Mortg. Co.*, 289 S.C. 516, 520 (S.C. App. 1986).

6. Laura M. Wolfe, Comment, *A Clarification of the Standard of Mental Capacity in North Carolina for Legal Transactions of the Elderly*, 32 WAKE FOREST L. REV. 563 (1997). In North Carolina, "if a deed is executed for consideration, the proper test of capacity to deed is not testamentary capacity … [but] the capacity to contract." *Id.* at 579. "[A] greater contractual capacity is required to make a deed for consideration, while a lesser testamentary capacity is required for a gift deed." *Id.* at 580. In Cal-

infirm to care of himself hires a nurse who moves in and takes care of him for three years. The widower grows senile. The nurse prepares a deed of the widower's house to herself and urges him to sign it just before his death, perhaps even bringing a notary public in to take the widower's acknowledgment. Shortly after the funeral, the widower's children file a suit to show he was too senile to understand what he was doing when he signed the deed, and want the court to set the deed aside. "Cases of this sort occur by the thousands."[7]

In California, such a deed drafted by a caregiver would be invalid unless an attorney issued a certificate of independent review. To issue such a certificate, the attorney would have to determine that the transferor understood and approved the transfer and had not been unduly influenced or defrauded.[8] In most states, courts engage in a fact-driven examination of the relationship between testator and caregiver to probe for undue influence or clear and convincing evidence of donative intent.

(2) The proper grantor depends on how title is held.

Frequent ownership options are: (a) sole ownership; (b) marital property; (c) tenancy in common; (d) joint tenancy; (e) general partnership; (f) limited partnership; (g) limited liability company; (h) corporation; or (i) trust.

(a) *Sole Ownership.* Suppose a grantee is acquiring title from Barry Buyer, the sole owner of the property, an unmarried person living alone, not in a domestic partnership. The grantor should be identified as: "Barry Buyer, a single man." With Barry's signature on the deed as grantor, Barry's grantee has good title.

Had Barry been married at the time he acquired the property, he should have taken title as: "Barry Buyer, a married man, as his sole and separate property." The mention of Barry being married when he acquired or when he sells property will almost always prompt the grantee's title insurer to insist on Barry's spouse signing a quitclaim deed to the property unless he or she had previously recorded a document relinquishing any claim to the property.

(b) *Marital Property.* When a married couple acquires property the ownership of which they intend to share, state laws dictate various presumptions about their title unless they specify otherwise. In most states married couples are presumed to take title as either *joint tenants* or *tenants in common.* In nine states, there

---

ifornia, a grantor who lacks all understanding or a prior judicial determination that the grantor was of unsound mind makes the grantor's conveyance void. However, a conveyance is voidable, but not void, if made by a person of "unsound mind, but not entirely without understanding." A rebuttable presumption of unsound mind arises when a person "is substantially unable to manage his or her own financial resources or resist fraud or undue influence. Substantial inability may not be proved solely by isolated incidents of negligence or improvidence." CAL. CIV. CODE § 39 (West 1982).

7. ROBERT KRATOVIL & RAYMOND J. WERNER, REAL ESTATE LAW 63 (9th ed. 1988).

8. CAL. PROB. CODE §§ 21350, 21351.

is a presumption that marital property is held as *community property*.[9] This means that each spouse holds concurrent and equal interests in the property.

Community property status is reserved for married couples or domestic partners, and implies equal and concurrent ownership. Each spouse owning community property can pass his or her share by will.

Alternately, the couple can elect to take title in *community property with right of survivorship*. In this format, when one spouse passes away, the surviving spouse becomes the sole owner of the community property.

The "Form of Title" Presumption in Marital Property Disputes: In re Marriage of Brooks.[10] Precisely how a grantor is identified in a deed can have a significant bearing on who is deemed to be the owner. A married man or woman takes title to real property by a deed that identifies the property as his or her *separate property, or which identifies the grantee as a single person* is rebuttably presumed to be free to sell or mortgage that property without the consent of the other spouse.

Sometimes, a non-consenting spouse later decides to challenge the sale or mortgage, and contends that the property retained its presumptive status as community property and never became separate property.

In a landmark California case involving such a challenge, a husband and wife, Michael Brooks and Anita (short for Annikkawa) Robinson, bought a house with Michael's earnings. Even though they were searching for a home together, they placed the title exclusively under Anita's name. They did this on the advice of their real estate broker in order to facilitate financing.

Michael knew that title was to be taken in Anita's name. He did not know that she would be identified in the deed "as a single woman."

While they were living in the house together, the wife took out two mortgage loans on the property without Michael's consent. Neither lender contacted Michael. They each had relied on the recorded deed naming the wife as a single woman and the sole owner of the house.

For a time, Michael made mortgage payments from his earnings but eventually stopped. Five years after the loans had been originated, the loans were deeply in default and foreclosures were initiated. At about the same time, the marriage faltered, Anita moved in with a friend (Geneva), and Michael filed for dissolution of the marriage. Michael remained in sole possession, along with their seven-year-old son.

---

9. Arizona, California, Idaho, Louisiana, Nevada, New Mexico, Texas, Washington and Wisconsin. Couples living in Alaska can "opt in" for community property, and Puerto Rico is a community property jurisdiction.

10. *In re Marriage of Brooks*, 169 Cal. App. 4th 176, 191, 86 Cal. Rptr. 3d 624 (4th Dist. 2008) (holding that a third party transferee could rely upon the "form of title" presumption without regard to knowledge of the marital relationship and despite the effect of Fam. Code, §852). *See also In re Marriage of Valli*, 195 Cal. App. 4th 776, 783, 124 Cal. Rptr. 3d 726 (2d Dist. 2011), review filed (June 24, 2011).

With foreclosure imminent, Anita contracted to sell the house to a firm that specialized in acquiring distressed properties. She netted about $42,000 cash from the sale after $100,000 of the sale proceeds were used to pay off the two mortgage loans. She soon disappeared.

The buyer had inspected the property before the closing. Michael was in possession and claims to have told the buyer that his wife had no right to have mortgaged or sold the house without his consent. The buyer denied ever hearing this.

Once the buyer acquired title, it sought possession. Michael refused to leave. He asserted that the house had been acquired with his funds and was community property. He sought a declaratory judgment to set aside the sale because he never agreed to the sale or the mortgage loans.

The court ruled against Michael because title to the house had been vested in Anita as a single woman. The court predicated this outcome on a presumption in the California Evidence Code Section 662: "The owner of the legal title to property is presumed to be the owner of the full beneficial title. This presumption may be rebutted only by clear and convincing proof."

Even though Michael showed that the entire down payment and the mortgage payments came from his earnings, the court rejected this offered evidence as "clear and convincing" proof sufficient to rebut the "form of title" by which the wife had acquired the house, as "a single woman."[11]

(c) *Tenants in Common.* A tenancy in common is a means of holding title. Tenants in common own undivided interests in real estate. They can sell, give away or mortgage what they own — but no more than that. Since they cannot decide by themselves how to partition property among the co-owners, they can only convey undivided interests in it.

Each co-tenant has a right of contribution from the others for necessary operating expenses including ordinary maintenance and property taxes. One co-tenant making improvements without the consent of the others has no right to reimbursement except to the extent that the improvements increase the property's value upon sale.[12]

---

11. Even when the property is actually community property, couples who hide their marital relationship while one of them purports to sell property as his or her own, cannot benefit from their lack of candor and set aside the sale after deeding it to a purchaser in good faith who has no knowledge of the marriage relationship." MILLER & STARR, 3 CAL. REAL EST. § 8:39 (3d ed.).

12. In California, "If the improvements were necessary and enhanced the value of the property, on receiving notice of the cost of the improvements, the other cotenants must elect either to contribute proportionately to the cost or to relinquish all claim to the increased value and rentals resulting from the improvements. If the non-contributing cotenant has not received notice of the improvements and their cost, he or she is not obligated to make such an election." MILLER AND STARR, 5 CAL. REAL EST. § 12:8 (3d ed.) (2006).

The tenancy in common is widely used not only for holding title to marital property but also for holding title to real estate and other assets.[13]

Example: A and B own a 50-unit apartment building as tenants in common. B lists her interest for sale with a real estate broker who finds a potential buyer, C. The broker is careful to explain that B owns the building in a co-tenancy with A, who has an equal and undivided interest in the 50 units.

C understands that he and A could end up disagreeing about everything including tenant selection, maintenance and improvements, financing, insurance and the payment of property taxes.

The best way out of a tenancy in common is by petitioning a court to partition the property. Unless the tenants in common have waived this right, a court could divide the property physically among the co-tenants or if the property cannot be split up fairly and without impairing its total value, the court can order the property to be sold and the proceeds shared among the co-tenants according to their respective interests. (Co-tenancy shares are a matter of contract and can be unequal.)

(d) *Joint Tenants.* Joint tenancies are similar in many ways to tenancies in common except that joint tenants must have acquired *equal interests* in the ownership and *equal rights of possession* of the joint tenancy property at the *same time* by the *same conveyance*, in a document with an express declaration of the parties' *intent to create a joint tenancy estate*.[14]

A surviving joint tenant becomes the owner of the deceased joint tenant's interest in the joint tenancy property by operation of law.

Example: A and B had owned Blackacre as joint tenants; B passes away and A wants to sell all of Blackacre to C. Perfecting individual ownership of joint tenancy property after the death of one of the joint tenants requires the recordation of a document, the contents of which depends on state law.

"In some states, a surviving joint owner can simply file a certified copy of the deceased co-owner's death certificate. In other states, the surviving co-owner must also sign and file a statement setting out the facts and explaining that he or she is now the sole owner. The statement may need to be notarized (in which case it's called an affidavit) or merely signed 'under penalty of perjury' without a notary (in which case it's usually called a declaration). It never hurts to file such a statement, even if it's not the custom in your state."[15]

Joint tenancy property is not subject to disposition by will although a joint tenant can pass title separately to his or her heirs or beneficiaries by conveying title to herself or anyone else as a tenant in common. This will terminate the joint tenancy. Thereafter, each co-tenant's property will pass separately to his or her heirs or beneficiaries.

---

13. B. Joseph Krabacher, *Tenancy-in-Common: Financing and Legal Issues*, 33-JUN COLO. LAW. 89 (2004).

14. First year law students are taught these as the four unities, leaving out a declaration of intent.

15. *How Joint Owners Can Transfer Survivorship Property After Death*, NOLO (2010).

Courts differ on whether a joint tenancy is severed when any of the joint tenants contracts to sell joint tenancy property, or only when the sale is executed.[16]

About half the states recognize a marital property status called *tenancy by the entirety*, which is like a joint tenancy except that neither spouse can impair the right of survivorship unilaterally.[17]

(e) *General Partnership Property.* A partnership is an entity of two or more people to conduct a business. The Uniform Partnership Act (UPA) sets the parameters regarding property transfers. Any partner can transfer partnership property in a way that is consistent with the purposes of the partnership as specified in the partnership agreement. The situation is simple if all the partners sign the deed, or a partnership agreement has been recorded empowering the partner who signed the deed to convey partnership property.

A grantee who accepts a deed not signed by all the partners is at risk of a nonconsenting partner challenging the sale. The matter could end up in court where the judge will have to decide whether: (1) the grantor-partner was empowered to transfer partnership property unilaterally, and (2) the grantee knew the signing partner had no right to be disposing of partnership property under the circumstances.

(f) *Limited Partnership Property.* General partners in a limited partnership have the same rights and liabilities as general partners in a general partnership. So they can convey title to real estate that the partnership owns. Limitations can be placed in the certificate of partnership which, depending on the state, is recorded in the county where the limited partnership is formed, or placed with the state secretary of state. Quite often, the general partner in a limited partnership is a limited liability company (LLC) or a corporation. In either case, the "grantor" will be the person(s) empowered to convey LLC or corporate assets.

(g) *Limited Liability Company.* Some LLCs are member managed and others have a designated managing member. The members must approve the sale usually by a formal resolution with the deed signed by a duly authorized member of the LLC.

Instead of acquiring the asset directly from an LLC, a buyer could acquire the interests of the members in the LLC. Many LLCs are specially formed entities that own a single asset. When that asset is real estate that a buyer would like to acquire, instead of acquiring the realty directly by a deed from the LLC, the buyer could achieve the same result by acquiring all the membership interests in the LLC.

Buying the LLC memberships instead of buying the real estate sometimes avoids taxes that state and local governments levy on real estate transfers but not on transfers

---

16. Sara Johnson, *Contract of sale or granting of option to purchase, to third party, by both or all of joint tenants or tenants by entirety as severing or terminating tenancy*, 39 A.L.R. 4th 1068 (originally published in 1985).

17. "The right of survivorship continues until there is a divorce, a mutual agreement to sever, or joint conveyance of the property." 1 Patton and Palomar on Land Titles § 224 (3d ed.).

of personal property interests, such as LLC memberships. Over time, legislators and regulators have become aware of this method that buyers use to avoid real estate transfer taxes and recording fees. Some jurisdictions have enacted anti-tax-avoidance measures by declaring that a change in the majority control of a real estate-owning entity is for transfer tax or property tax re-appraisal purposes the same as the acquisition of the real estate itself.[18]

Even where the acquisition of an LLC has state and local tax advantages, buyers are wary of acquiring the membership interests in an LLC because they know that they will be acquiring not only the LLC's assets but all the LLC's liabilities as well, including contract obligations and tort claims.

(h) *Corporate Property.* Designated officials of the corporation are empowered to convey title to corporate-owned realty, subject to proper procedures such as board approval or resolutions.

Mortgage lenders often require that a borrower corporation have its counsel prepare an opinion for the lender's benefit covering these four items: (1) the corporation validly exists and is in good standing in the jurisdiction where the mortgage agreement is entered; (2) all authorizations and actions by the corporation and its shareholders that are necessary to bind the corporation to the transaction have been taken or obtained; (3) the corporation has duly executed and delivered all the requisite transaction documents; and (4) the transaction is legal, valid, binding, and enforceable against the corporation in accordance with its terms.[19] Grantees of property held by a corporation should seek verification of these four items.

(i) *Revocable Trusts.* For estate planning purposes, property owners sometimes create revocable trusts, often naming themselves as trustees though designating a co-trustee who can manage the trust assets when the settlor dies. The trust names as beneficiaries the persons who are to acquire the trust assets at the death of the trustor.

Typically, a declaration of trust will list all of the properties that the trustor or settlor intends to pass at death to his or her beneficiaries. Sometimes, the declaration of trust is placed in the public land records, sometimes not.

Quite often, the trustor retains title to real estate that he or she intends to leave to the beneficiaries at death. One reason property owners prefer revocable to irrevocable trusts is their wish to retain control over their real estate assets. Once the property owner lists a particular property as an asset of the revocable trust, and then contracts to sell it, the property owner should sign the deed along with any co-trustees of the revocable trust.

---

18. *See, e.g.,* New York State Department of Taxation and Finance, PUBLICATION 576, TRANSFER OR ACQUISITION OF A CONTROLLING INTEREST IN AN ENTITY WITH AN INTEREST IN REAL PROPERTY (last visited Sep. 21, 2015), http://www.tax.ny.gov/pdf/publications/real_estate/pub576.pdf.

19. Kelly A. Love, *A Primer on Opinion Letters: Explanations and Analysis,* 9 TRANSACTIONS: THE TENNESSEE JOURNAL OF BUSINESS LAW 67, 83 (2007).

Revocable trusts become irrevocable when the person holding the right to revoke passes away. At that point, only a designated, living trustee of the revocable trust is authorized to convey title to the trust property.

The beneficiaries should sign the deed as well to deter them from challenging the sale later. The beneficiaries, when asked to sign the deed, should insist that the sales proceeds be held by a neutral third party escrow and remitted directly to them at closing. The grantee should insist upon this being done to avoid post-closing challenges by the beneficiaries.

(3) The grantor or an authorized agent must sign the deed.

Preserving the Chain Title. In voluntary transfers, yesterday's grantee is tomorrow's grantor. To validate a claim of ownership, the present owner of record traces his or her title back through time through an orderly succession of deeds from one owner to the next, each one recorded in the public land records.

Suppose A once owned a property and sold it to B who is now purporting to sell the same property to C. There should be a deed on record from A as grantor to B as grantee. As the most recent grantee in the chain of title, B is positioned to convey good title of Blackacre to C.

There could be an apparent gap in the chain of title if B changed her name before she deeded title to C without indicating the name change in her deed by adding to her new name an indication that she was "formerly known as B."[20] Without an indication that C's grantor is the person formerly known as B, C would lack record title.

Grantors Can Authorize Others to Sign Deeds On Their Behalf: Powers of Attorney. Grantors do not necessarily have to sign deeds personally. They can execute and record a "power of attorney" empowering a designated agent to take certain actions on their behalf. C could grant a power of attorney to D. D would sign C's name as the true grantor on the deed, and her own name beneath that. By placing in the public land records C's power of attorney to D, signed and acknowledged by C, there will be link of record connecting C's ownership to D's right to sign on C's behalf.

Forged and Fraudulently Obtained Deeds. A deed signed by a forger does not convey the grantor's title even to a purchaser who had no way to know the grantor's signature had been forged. A deed which the grantor is fraudulently tricked into signing may or may not be valid in the hands of a bona fide purchaser unaware of the fraud.

The distinction between forged and fraudulently obtained deeds is not as subtle as it may first appear. There is not much a victim can do when someone forges their name to a deed and sells the property without their knowledge. Like victims of identity theft, the true owner can reclaim title to realty wrongfully conveyed by a forged deed.

---

20. Mary Randolph, The Deeds Book: How to Transfer Title to California Real Estate 6:15–6:16 (1987).

Forgery is a fraud in the factum. A bona fide purchaser unfortunate enough to pay for a deed from the forger takes no title.[21]

By contrast, deeds procured by 'fraud in the inducement' are voidable because in these situations, had the duped owner been more cautious, he or she had a chance to prevent the mishap. One example is a home improvement contractor who persuades a homeowner to sign what the perpetrator claimed to be a contract for a new roof but that turned out to be a deed or a mortgage. Fraudulent inducement is legalese for the skill mastered by proficient con artists. Another example, a perpetrator pays for a property with a check that bounces. Because the grantor could have prevented the fraud by waiting until the check cleared before signing the deed, the deed will be deemed voidable. The trier of fact must decide whether to award title to a bona fide purchaser or the cheated grantor.

Some situations elude easy classification. A perpetrator slips a deed into a batch of innocuous papers the grantor is signing and the grantor doesn't notice it. A court might label the deed void if the grantor was "old, illiterate, disabled, confused."[22] Courts are more likely to declare the deed 'voidable' to protect a bona fide purchaser when the grantor was competent and alert, just a bit careless. Courts may even call the grantor negligent for failing to examine the documents more closely before she signed them.[23]

Foreclosure Scams and the Validity of Fraudulently Procured Deeds. Scam artists descend on defaulting homeowners facing foreclosure. In a typical scam, a perpetrator promises to make the homeowner's mortgage payments if the homeowner deeds the property to the scam artist and leases the property back with an option to repurchase.

The trusting homeowner expects to remain in possession and reacquire title once the perpetrator magically transforms the unmanageable mortgage debt into an obligation the homeowner could pay. Lease terms are shorter and more onerous than the homeowner realizes. The lease expires, or if the homeowner stops paying rent, the new buyer terminates the lease, evicts the former owner, and obtains possession. This scam only works when the homeowner has substantial unrealized equity in the home. The con artist sells the home to an unsuspecting buyer who pays off the homeowner's loan from the proceeds of a new purchase money loan.

In another scam, the rescuer promises to bail out the homeowner by arranging a new loan. The scam artist shows up with a pile of documents on a clipboard for the homeowner to sign. Surreptitiously, the con artist includes a deed among the documents. Not bothering to read the pile of documents, the homeowner inadvertently signs a deed of the property to the con artist. After recording the deed from the homeowner, the con artist sells the house to a bona fide purchaser, pays off the mortgage and pockets the equity.

---

21. Similarly, purchasers of stolen goods must return the goods to the true owner.
22. GRANT S. NELSON & DALE A. WHITMAN, REAL ESTATE TRANSFER, FINANCE, AND DEVELOPMENT 169 (4th ed. 1992).
23. *Id.*

The lease-with-option scheme involves fraud in the inducement. The deed-substituted-for-a-mortgage represents fraud in the factum. In a contest between the duped owner and a bona fide purchaser to whom the perpetrator sold or mortgaged the property, an owner victimized by fraud in the inducement is generally regarded as more culpable than an owner misled by fraud in the factum.

Both types of schemes can lead to a difficult inquiry notice question under the recording acts: whether continued possession by the homeowners after deeding the property to the perpetrator should be deemed sufficient to alert subsequent purchasers to ask the homeowners about the nature of their retained interests in the property.

(4) Deeds need not be "for valuable consideration."

Consideration is not necessary to pass title from one owner to the next. A gift deed is a deed given without valuable consideration. Property owners can gift property to whomever they choose unless they are hiding assets from creditors or are on the brink of bankruptcy.

Whether the grantor is conveying title as a gift or "for valuable consideration," most form deeds contain a recitation of "valuable consideration." The reason is that the recitation of valuable consideration entitles the grantee to the presumed status of a bona fide purchaser (BFP), and burdens a competing claimant with having to prove otherwise.

(5) The grantor must explicitly transfer title by present words of transfer.

The following deed language would be sufficient to transfer owner A's title to grantee B: *"I, A, quitclaim to B property described in Exhibit X."* The "operative word of grant" in the above deed is "quitclaim." By using the present tense, the grantor evidences an immediate transfer; a grantor's promise that she *will transfer* title could be interpreted a promise to make a future transfer. There is no harm, though, in the grantor using both present and perfect tenses, i.e., *"X grants and has granted."*

Depending on the type of deed, the operative verb could be: "convey and warrant," "grant," or "quitclaim." These variations are quite important as they signal whether the grantor is making warranties of good title, assuming liability only for title defects he created or agreed to, or is only relinquishing whatever title he happens to own in the property.

(6) The grantee must be named in the deed but need not sign it.

The grantee needs to be an identifiable person. Nicknames are OK. So is a grant to someone utilizing a fictitious name. But a grant to a fictitious person ("Donald Duck") is void.

Some grantee identifications are impermissibly vague. One example would be a grant to two or more persons using the disjunctive "or" ("To A *or* B") since there would be no way to tell which of them the grantor intended to designate as the transferee. A deed to "the community styling itself the German Roman Catholic Saint Bonifazius Church Community" was too indefinite to transfer the title. So was a conveyance to "Louis Blanchard & Co." The deed transferred the title to Louis Blanchard but the court held that no one received any interest in the property by the designation "& Co." because it was a vague and an unidentifiable group.[24]

(7) Deeds need not be dated.

A deed need not be dated to be valid. But deeds have to be delivered, and a date on a deed creates a refutable presumption of delivery.

(8) The deed must be delivered.[25]

The requirement that there be a delivery harks back to the manual transfer of land ownership required centuries ago in pre-literate England. The legal concept of delivery has two components:

(1) a physical transfer of the deed,

(2) coupled with the grantor's intent to transfer title to the grantee.

A grantor may revoke a deed any time before the deed is deemed to have been delivered. For example, an impatient nephew snatches from his aunt's desk drawer a signed deed naming him as the grantee to a family summer house that the aunt inherited from her parents. She had often mentioned her intention eventually to give him the house. Because he took the deed without the aunt's consent, the deed has not been delivered. It remains revocable.

In most transfers by sale, delivery is presumed to have occurred when the deed is actually passed from seller or the seller's agent to the buyer or the buyer's agent.[26] The agent could be a real estate attorney, a real estate broker, a title insurer or an independent escrow agent.

The grantor's continued possession of a deed made out to a specific grantee implies that the grantor intends to retain ownership, and has yet to relinquish title. The

---

24. Miller & Starr, 3 Cal. Real Est. § 8:26 (3d ed.).

25. George Chamberlin, *Cause of Action to Invalidate Deed for Failure of Delivery*, 5 Causes of Action 2d 471 (originally published in 1994, updated 2015).

26. *See Martinez v. Martinez*, 101 N.M. 88 (1984), in which parents handed a deed to their son and daughter-in-law to hold until the kids performed their obligations under a real estate contract. When they defaulted, they were required to reconvey title back to parents. The son was willing to reconvey, but the daughter-in-law was not. Parents sued and got back the title.

In *Evans v. Waddell*, 689 So. 2d 23 (Ala. 1997), a deed was delivered although the grantor retained it in her safe deposit box until her death. She gave the grantee a copy and told him the property was his. The grantee had taken possession upon receipt of the copy.

grantor giving the grantee possession of a deed raises the opposite inference, raising a presumption that the grantor intended to transfer title by tendering possession of the deed to the grantee.

Many common sense factors evidence delivery or lack of it:

- The grantor remaining in possession of the property and continuing to pay taxes and operating expenses shows a lack of intent to deliver unless the grantor intended to retain only a life estate. Conversely, the grantee taking possession points toward delivery.

- The grantor mortgaging or selling the property weighs against an alleged delivery. The grantor seeking the signature of the grantee on a re-conveyance in order to mortgage, lease, or sell the property suggests the grantor believed delivery had taken place.

- The grantor devising the property by will undermines a claim of prior delivery, while the grantor leaving the property out of the will suggests the grantor believed title had previously been delivered to the grantee.

- The grantor permitting the recordation of the deed is proof of delivery, conclusive in some states because grantors don't usually allow their titles to be clouded by recordation unless they mean to convey.

(9) The grantee must accept the deed.

Usually, grantees evidence their acceptance of title by accepting physical possession of a deed. But sometimes grantees resist title to a "hot potato" property that is thrust upon them. That happened in a case that reached the Iowa Supreme Court.[27] The property was in very bad condition and worth less than the property taxes levied against it. The owner, Vince Jorgenson, offered the property to the County Board of Supervisors, and the Board accepted a deed from him because at the time, it looked like the local American Legion post might want to acquire the property.

Soon thereafter, the Legion decided the property was beyond repair, and decided not to buy it. So the Board of Supervisors tried to convey title back to Jorgenson by mailing him a quitclaim deed. He declined. The Board sued, claiming that once the deed was placed in Jorgenson's post office box, he should be deemed to have accepted the return of title from the County. The court thought otherwise. Acceptance is a question of intent, not just physical possession.

"After stating on direct examination his version of the facts, Jorgenson concluded his testimony: Q. Did you ever *accept* delivery of any such *deed* as Exhibit D? A. No." That was determinative; Jorgenson never accepted delivery. The county of Worth got stuck with a property they should never have accepted.

---

27. *County of Worth v. Jorgenson*, 253 N.W.2d 575 (Iowa 1977).

(10) The property must be described in the deed but not the improvements.

The deed must come with an accurate description of the land being conveyed—land descriptions are the topic of the next chapter. Often, a formal legal description is placed in a separate exhibit, referenced in the deed and appended to it. But deeds rarely identify specific buildings on the site except with a vague phrase such as, "including all structures thereon." This is because buildings are presumed to belong to the owner of the subjacent land. Under the time-honored law of accession, what is attached to the land goes with the land.

Cautious buyers and mortgage lenders can purchase title policy endorsements against loss or damage if the owner of the site turns out not to own the improvements. Such an endorsement could be important to the purchaser of land subject to a long term ground lease because often the improvements are constructed and owned by the ground lessee until the end of the lease term.

II. The Buyer's Title Review during the Executory Period

Prospective buyers and mortgage lenders need to know whether their sellers and borrowers actually own the property free of the interests of others which could be either possessory or non-possessory in nature. The interest of a tenant is possessory; a mortgage lender's interest usually is not—at least until there is a default and foreclosure.

Prospective buyers can visit the property to see if they spot evidence of any visible possessory interests. For non-possessory interests, buyers, or those acting on their behalf, usually have no choice but to rely primarily on public land records or the title plants of title insurers.

A. The Title Company Role

Typically, purchase and sale contracts empower an escrow agent or closing attorney to order a search of the title from a title company on the buyer's behalf.[28] Title insurance policies promise marketable title, subject to specific exclusions and exceptions that buyers have an opportunity to review before closing.[29] These are the title flaws

---

28. Jana Armstrong, *Searching for and Examining Title, Florida Real Property Title Examination and Insurance*, RPTE FL-CLE 3-1 (The Florida Bar 2012).

29. John C. Murray, *Title Insurance Coverage for 'Unmarketability of the Title'*, 524 PLI/REAL 47 (Jan.–Mar. 2006). Typical marketable title glitches arise from incorrect deed descriptions, paid off mortgages unreleased of record, unsigned deeds in the chain of title, encroachments, easements, or disputed boundary locations.

for which the title insurer declines to take responsibility. Whatever interests the title insurer declines to cover, the buyer or lender is left to deal with.

Often, if the buyer objects to certain exceptions in the preliminary report or title commitment, the seller or the seller's attorney meets with the title insurance underwriter to find a way to cure these defects or delete them as exceptions to coverage under the policy.

B. The Marketable Title Standard and Contract Modifications of It

Most property transfers go from contract to closing without a hitch. But when title issues arise, they can become quite complicated to sort out. The common law presumption is that sellers will provide buyers with a marketable title, absent an agreement to the contrary. Typically, marketable title disputes arise after buyers and sellers have entered a purchase and sale contract, and the buyer wants to terminate the sale with a full refund of any deposit because the seller's title is defective.

The customary definition of "marketability" is whether a buyer would have difficulty in the foreseeable future selling the land to a "reasonable purchaser, well informed as to the facts and their legal bearings, willing and anxious to perform his contract."[30] This seems a bit circular though it would not have been in an era when privately employed title examiners in each community were the ultimate arbiters of whether a title was marketable or in states and localities where bar associations promulgated detailed marketable title standards.

Contract Modifications of the Common Law Standard. Buyers' objections based on marketable title have to be "reasonable." And yet, many purchase and sale contracts allow the buyer virtually unfettered discretion to rescind a contract whether other buyers would have done so or not.

> (1) *"Buyer's Satisfaction."* Some courts interpret the "buyer satisfaction" standard as what a reasonable buyer would require.[31] Other courts allow the buyer a greater degree of subjectivity, but limit the buyer's discretion by invoking concepts of good faith and fair dealing.[32]

---

30. *Hocking v. Title Ins. & Trust Co.*, 37 Cal. 2d 644, 649 (1951) (failure of developer to comply with *subdivision map act did not make title unmarketable giving rise to claim by subsequent purchaser under a title* policy). Sellers can only compel buyers to purchase a title "so far free from defects as to enable the holder, not only to retain the land, but possess it in peace, and, if he wishes to sell it, be reasonably sure that no flaw or doubt will arise to disturb its market value." *Mertens v. Berendsen*, 1 P.2d 440, 441 (Cal. 1931) (encroachment of a fraction of an inch is too small to render title unmarketable).

31. *See, e.g., Kniep v. Templeton*, 185 N.C. App. 622, 633 (2007); *Caselli v. Messina*, 567 N.Y.S.2d 972, 974 (1990); *Liberty Lake Sewer Dist. No. 1 v. Liberty Lake Utilities Co., Inc.*, 37 Wash. App.809, 817 (1984).

32. *See, e.g., Plimpton v. Mattakeunk Cabin Colony*, 9 F. Supp. 288, 310 (D. Conn. 1934).

(2) *Buyer's Sole and Absolute Discretion.* In effect, buyers can obtain rescission by rejecting title in their sole and absolute discretion. The California Association of REALTORS® Residential Purchase Agreement form gives buyers an unrestricted right to cancel the agreement at will without cause or penalty.[33] Apparently, California brokers see no point in wasting their time trying to coax recalcitrant buyers into completing an acquisition when their time could be spent more productively finding a willing buyer.

(3) *Insurable Title.* Some contracts call for insurable title. The distinction between a marketable and an insurable title will often be negligible because title policies insure "marketable title."

There can be a big difference between a title that is marketable in fact and a defective title for which the seller can arrange title insurance. Title insurers will sometimes take calculated risks for a price, especially if a seller who happens to be a frequent title customer agrees to indemnify the insurer against loss.

So, for example, a developer-seller's title might be subject to recorded mechanics' liens that arose out of a dispute with a contractor. The seller could promise to reimburse the title insurer for any mechanics' lien claims it has to pay on the title policy. But the buyer might have trouble securing bank mortgage financing because legally any mortgage would be subordinate to the prior recorded mechanics' liens, and bank regulators could find this unsettling.

C. What Makes a Title Unmarketable and What Does Not?

Marketable title issues arise from varied sources. Ideally, the present owner could trace the provenance of its title back through a long series of transfers to an accepted original title in a grant from a sovereign. Depending on the state, that original title could be based on a grant from the U.S. government,[34] royal charters from the English Crown as confirmed by state legislatures or the original colonies,[35] Spanish and Mexican land grants confirmed in the southwest and west,[36] and Indian treaties (often abrogated by force).[37] The recording acts are the primary source of information re-

---

33. California Residential Purchase Agreement (PRA-Ca page 5 of 8), Paragraph 14(B)(3) and 14(F).

34. The Federal Government inherited a substantial public domain from its predecessor, the government under the Articles of Confederation. By Article IV, Section 3, Clause 2 of the Constitution, Congress was empowered "to dispose of and make all needful Rules and Regulations respecting the Territory or other Property belonging to the United States." National Archives (last visited July 8, 2015), http://www.archives.gov/research/guide-fed-records/groups/049.html. *See, e.g.*, W.W. ROBINSON, LAND IN CALIFORNIA (1948); ROY H. AGAKI, THE TOWN PROPRIETORS OF THE NEW ENGLAND COLONIES (1924).

35. ROY H. AGAKI, THE TOWN PROPRIETORS OF THE NEW ENGLAND COLONIES (1924).

36. CHARLES E. GILLELAND, DAVID CARCIERE & ZACHRY DAVIS, TEXAS TITLE TRAILS (2006).

37. U.S. Department of State, Office of the Historian, Indian Treaties and the Removal Act of 1830 (last visited July 10, 2015), https://history.state.gov/milestones/1830-1860/indian-treaties.

garding an owner's "chain of title." The title gaps that result in this process are described in the chapter on the public land records and the recording laws.

Other title problems arise from title surveys or the lack of them. These are mentioned in the next chapter on surveying.

Here we describe marketable title issues raised by encumbrances, easements, leases, and liens. We also explore why publicly enacted land use controls are not regarded as title-impairing, and the arrangements buyers need to make when they plan to develop or change the uses on the properties they acquire.

Encumbrances. Encumbrances are "any right of a third person in real property that diminishes the value to the [owner], but does not prevent the passing of the [owner's] interest."[38] These could be leases, mineral reservations, easements, restrictions on the right to sell or lease, and covenants, conditions and restrictions (CC&Rs).

Buyers are entitled to encumbrance-free titles unless either "the purchaser can suffer no harm from the encumbrance or ... defect," or the purchaser expressly accepted the burden as part of the deal, as when a purchaser agrees to take "subject to" the seller's existing mortgage.[39]

Easements. An easement is a type of encumbrance that confers upon its recipient a right to use a specific portion of someone else's land for a particular purpose such as for a right-of-way, or to place utility lines above, at or below ground level. The easement beneficiary does not have the right to exclusive possession.

Some easements never impair marketability of title because they have become unenforceable due to changed conditions or widespread disuse. Others are so trivial that no reasonable investor would care.[40] Others increase the value of the land or are necessary for the use and enjoyment of the property. Examples include easements granted for streets, utility service, cable TV, and the like.[41]

Leases. A lease is a type of encumbrance for which the tenant pays the landlord rent in exchange for the right to exclusive possession of the property for a specified period of time.

Buyers are presumed to take title free of existing leases in most states. This includes the right to vacant possession, which means that the property is vacant and the buyer will be the sole occupant at closing. These related concepts are not identical. Crafty sellers have sometimes argued that as long as the buyer has good legal title, which includes the legal right to terminate the lease, the buyer can have the tenant removed

---

38. JOYCE D. PALOMAR, TITLE INSURANCE LAW § 5.05, at § 5.11 (1994).

39. *Regan v. Lanze*, 354 N.E.2d 818, 823 (N.Y. 1976). A buyer's breach was not excused on marketable title grounds because the title was subject to covenants restricting property in the area to minimum setbacks, building and structure types, and residential use. The property under contract conformed to all existing CC&Rs. *Caselli v. Messina*, 598 N.Y.S.2d 265 (S. Ct. 1993).

40. *Mucci v. Brockton Bocce Club, Inc.*, 472 N.E.2d 966 (Mass. App. Ct. 1985) (structure slightly encroaching on neighboring property does not make title unmarketable where encroachment would not concern prudent investor).

41. Ohio Standards of Title Examination.

by operation of law. So there is no need for the seller to deliver vacant possession by filing an unlawful detainer action and having the sheriff forcibly remove the former tenant.

In *Watson v. Calvin*,[42] vendors Tom and Rebecca Watson contracted to sell Blanche Calvin a duplex for $110,000, with possession to be delivered at closing. Calvin put up an $11,000 deposit, which would become liquidated damages if she breached the contract.

Because the duplex was occupied by a tenant on the closing date, the buyer refused to go through with the sale. The sellers claimed this was a breach despite the tenant's possession at closing. While admitting that they had not delivered actual possession at closing, they claimed they had provided constructive possession because the buyer would have had the right to possession once she took title.

Not so, the court explained. A tenant has the right to possess leased property against the landlord and anyone claiming through the landlord, including purchasers of the landlord's ownership interest. However, unlike in the sale of an office building or shopping center, where a buyer might actually prefer tenants to remain in possession, a duplex buyer contracting for possession is expecting actual possession. So a buyer is not in breach for refusing to close without it.

In a few states, buyers are presumed to take title subject to the interests of tenants whose presence is evident on the date the contract is entered unless the buyer contracts for "vacant possession" at closing.[43]

Well-considered form brokerage contracts deal with this issue explicitly. For example, under the California Association of REALTORS® Residential Purchase Agreement, there is a provision enabling the parties to make clear either that the tenant is to remain in possession at closing or that the seller is to deliver the property vacant "five or [ ] days prior to close."[44] In bold type, sellers are warned: "If you are unable to deliver Property vacant in accordance with rent control and other applicable Law, you may be in breach of this Agreement."[45]

As the Arkansas court noted in the case of *Watson v. Calvin*, when buyers acquire income-producing property such as office or retail, they usually expect to find tenants in possession. Because they are taking title subject to those leases, they need to know the precise lease terms, verify that the tenants will remain in possession under their leases at closing, pledge to pay rent to the buyer as the new owner, and have no claims against their former landlord for which the buyer will become liable.[46] To do this, buyers expect their sellers to produce copies of all leases coupled with lease verification

---

42. 69 Ark. App. 109 (2000).

43. *Lieb v. Roman Development Co.*, 716 S.W.2d 653 (Tex. App. 1986).

44. Cal. Ass'n of REALTORS® Residential Purchase Agreement (RPA-CA Revised 4/10), ¶ 5(C), page 3 of 8.

45. *Id.*

46. Scott W. Dibbs, *Estoppels, SNDAs and Other Lease Provisions That Can Make or Break a Sale*, 22 PROP. & PROB. 49 (Sept.–Oct.2008).

statements signed by the tenants.[47] These are called *estoppel certificates* because courts will hold tenants accountable to buyers who rely on the tenants' certificates.

Of course, knowledgeable tenants may balk at signing estoppel certificates at all or may seek to limit their potential exposure with exculpatory language. Landlords who anticipate such reactions, and are eager not to end up losing a potential sale because of a missing or incomplete estoppel certificate, will include in all leases the exact language of the estoppel certificate along with a period of time by which tenants are expected to complete them. They might even include monetary penalties for late or non-compliance.

Liens. Liens concern defaults on obligations to pay money, a charge against property as security for a debt such as federal or local tax liens, mechanics' liens, liens of decedents' estates, mortgages and deeds of trust.

Mortgages and Deeds of Trust. In a mortgage, the mortgagor is the owner of specifically described property that serves to secure a specific debt. Usually, the repayment terms are detailed in a note. The mortgagee is the creditor.

In a deed of trust, the owner of the security property is the trustor, and usually but not necessarily the debtor because one person can pledge his or her property as security for someone else's debt. The lender, the beneficiary of the deed of trust, appoints a trustee (usually a bank or title company) to hold legal title to enforce the beneficiary's security interest in the debtor's property.

In the event of a default on the obligations specified in the note, foreclosure will be initiated by the mortgagee or the trustee on instructions from the beneficiary. They are required to comply strictly with the notice and other provisions regarding the conduct of the foreclosure sale.

Liens and Marketable Title. Quite often, a prospective buyer learns during the escrow or due diligence period that the seller's title is subject to various monetary liens. Does this give the buyer an immediate justification to rescind the sale and obtain a refund of any deposit the buyer advanced?

The answer depends on whether the liens can be repaid from the purchase price simultaneously at closing since the seller does not need to tender marketable title until the closing.

Liens do not make titles unmarketable when the vendor is in a position to tender lien-free title because the vendor's net sale proceeds at closing are sufficient to pay off the lien and the lienors agree to sign recordable releases once they are paid in full. Those releases take the form of satisfactions of mortgages signed by the mortgagee and reconveyances of deeds of trust signed by the trustee. Hence, a condo developer who owed mechanics' lienors $950,000 could not force a prospective buyer to complete

---

47. Gregory M. Stein, Morton P. Fisher, Jr., & Gail M. Stern, A Practical Guide to Commercial Real Estate Transactions 78 (2003).

the sale of a condo unit in the liened property for $545,000.[48] On the other hand, a buyer could force a recalcitrant seller to convey good title on a $175,000 purchase option despite the property being subject to a mortgage lien held by the seller's former wife to secure alimony payments because the wife was willing to release her claim for somewhere between $45,000 to $55,000, a settlement price well below the $175,000 purchase price the buyer would have had to pay upon exercising the option.[49]

Publicly enacted land use controls are not title-impairing encumbrances. Buyers who require zone changes to legitimize contemplated changes in the use of property need to condition their obligation to purchase on local government approval.[50]

> In general, the mere existence of local building codes, zoning laws, subdivision laws, or other governmentally imposed land use controls do not render title to real property unmarketable. Those laws, in and of themselves, are not treated as encumbrances [that make title unmarketable].[51]

There are several reasons why sellers' obligations to convey marketable titles rarely include promises concerning whether a buyer's contemplated use of the property conforms to publicly enacted land use controls. First, information about public laws and regulations are equally available to every member of the public, not just to property owners. Second, buyers planning to change the use of the acquired property know their own plans better than the seller and hence are in the better position to determine exactly what public approvals they might need.

In *Glaser v. Minnesota Savings and Loan Association*,[52] Kenneth C. Glaser hoped to open a family restaurant on a parcel of land he contracted to purchase from the Minnesota Savings and Loan Association. Prudently, he conditioned his obligation to purchase on his being able to obtain the necessary rezoning for his restaurant. In this case, the seller was careful to promise marketable title *subject to an exception for building and zoning laws, ordinances, state and federal regulations.*

This exception may have seemed redundant but it was not. Sometimes, after being informed of a buyer's plans, sellers opine that the contemplated changes comply with existing ordinances and regulations or would not be difficult to procure. This contract made it clear that it was the buyer's problem to secure the requisite re-zoning, and the seller's obligation to convey a marketable title did not include the buyer being granted a re-zoning.

---

48. *Venne v. 96 Rockwell Place LLC*, 2010 N.Y. Misc. LEXIS 2056.

49. *Grieg v. Goetzinger*, 2001 WL 35923628 (Pa. Com. Pl.).

50. Lefcoe, George, *How Buyers and Sellers of Development Land Deal with Regulatory Risk*, USC Legal Studies Research Papers Series No. 97-19. SSRN (last visited July 13, 2015), http://ssrn.com/abstract=58121.

51. Charles B. Sheppard, *Assurances of Title to Real Property Available in the United States: Is a Person Who Assures A Quality of Title to Real Property Liable for a Defect in the Title Caused by Conduct of the Assured?*, 79 N. Dak. L. Rev. 311 (2003).

52. 389 N.W.2d 763 (1986).

As it turned out, the buyer obtained the requisite rezoning. But the buyer needed more than zoning approval. Another set of land use controls came into play, known as the state subdivision map act. The buyer needed the local government to approve a subdivision map splitting the portion of the site that the buyer was to purchase from the larger site that the seller owned and planned to retain.

Sellers can only dispose of portions of a larger holding if they obtain prior government approval of a map subdividing the property into two or more separate parcels. Upon receipt of local government approval, a property owner can place in the public land records a map showing the division of land. In most states, the sale of a portion of a larger parcel by reference to a subdivision map is only legal when the map has been recorded.

Subdivision map approval is often quite costly because local governments usually condition their approval on the sub-divider making substantial improvements or land dedications for the benefit of the public. Approval is often also conditioned on the sub-divider paying fees to finance new public infrastructure such as roads, schools, and parks that are needed to accommodate new development.

The dispute between buyer Glaser and the seller, Minnesota Savings and Loan Association, was which of them should pay the subdivision fees, a matter not covered in their contract. So the case was remanded to trial where buyer and seller could each testify about their conversations and expectations regarding payment of those fees.

Code Violations Are Sometimes Held to Make Titles Unmarketable. The marketable title situation is quite different when it comes to property that is presently in violation of building or zoning codes. Case outcomes vary when buyers cite such violations as justification for rescinding their contracts. Buyers usually prevail when the seller has received official notification of the violation coupled with a threat of enforcement. They look particularly bad when they had not disclosed the notification to the buyer. At the other extreme, when a buyer cites a trivial violation of a sort that is rarely if ever pursued, courts have denied the buyer's petition to rescind the contract as unreasonable.

Title policies specifically exclude liability for violations of publicly imposed land use controls. They write policies based on public land records, not government imposed land use controls that could only be located, if at all, in the offices of state and local governments. Buyers and lenders desiring such coverage can contract for it. Before signing off on a special "land use" endorsement, title insurers sometimes outsource the underwriting task to lawyers familiar with local land use controls. If the law firm is willing to stand behind an opinion letter that the project is in full compliance with all land use laws and regulations, title insurers will go along, figuring that if the firm is wrong, the firm's errors and omissions carrier will become the ultimate guarantor-in-fact and cover any resulting losses.

D. Promises That Survive Closing: The Rebuttable Presumption That Promises about Title Merge in the Deed

Sellers often make promises that are not fulfilled by the time of the closing. Whether the buyer can compel the seller to make good on those promises after the closing depends on whether the promise is about the condition of the subject property (for instance, about termites or a leaky roof) or about title (for instance, a lien or a tenant in possession).

In allocating the risks of title defects between grantor and grantee, deeds are presumed to supplant any title guarantees mentioned in the purchase and sale contract that are not repeated in the deed. This is known as the doctrine of merger; contract promises are subsumed by the terms of the deed. Merger is only a presumption, not a rigid rule of law. It can be rebutted by evidence of whether the parties meant for the promise to be enforceable after the closing. Deed warranties become particularly important for promises made in purchase and sale contracts that are deemed not to survive closing.

III. Types of Deeds: Quitclaim, Grant and Warranty

A. General Warranty Deed

A grantor signing a general warranty deed guarantees good title free of any liens and encumbrances, but for the ones that are specifically *excepted* or reserved in the deed itself. The grantor promises to defend title against all challengers and to compensate the buyer for any disturbance of 'quiet enjoyment' arising from title defects.

A general warranty deed contains the broadest warranties, five of which are highlighted below:

> *Grantor, for itself and its heirs, hereby covenants with Grantee, its heirs, and assigns, that Grantor is* **lawfully seized in fee simple** *of the above-described premises; that it has a good* **right to convey;** *that the premises are* **free from all encumbrances;** *that Grantor and its heirs, and all persons acquiring any interest in the property granted, through or for Grantor, will, on demand of Grantee, or its heirs or assigns, and at the expense of Grantee, its heirs or assigns, execute any instrument necessary for the* **further assurance** *of the title to the premises that may be reasonably required; and that Grantor and its heirs will* **forever warrant and defend** *all of the property so granted to Grantee, and its heirs, against every person lawfully claiming the same or any part thereof.*[53]

---

53. Such language as this is standard in grant deed forms.

B. Grant Deed

Alternately, sellers could promise to convey by grant deed—by far the most popular form of conveyance in California and other western states. In these states, the grantor only promises that she has not previously conveyed title to anyone else and has not "done, made or suffered" encumbrances.[54] Thus, a grant deed grantor is only responsible for her own title-impairing moves. She bears no responsibility for defects her predecessors in title may have created.

The seller's title liability exposure ends at closing as long as she discloses any liens, defects, or encumbrances she placed against the property, and specifies in the deed that she is conveying title subject to them. In some states special warranty deeds, similar to grant deeds, are used. The precise differences between grant and special warranty deeds are state-specific, derived from statutes and precedent setting court opinions.

C. Quitclaim Deed

A quitclaim deed is one in which the seller conveys only whatever right, title, or interest she happens to own in a particular property. The grantee takes nothing if the grantor owns absolutely no interest in the property at the effective moment of transfer, even if the grantor acquires the property at a later date. Since the quitclaim grantor makes no title warranties or representations, it is entirely up to the grantee to figure out what interest, if any, the seller has.[55]

Quitclaim deeds are seldom used when buyers pay fair market value in arms' length sales transactions. They are used mostly as an accommodation to extinguish or release dormant, doubtful, or non-existent claims. For instance, if a married person in a community property state is selling separate property, a title insurer might insist that the spouse sign a quitclaim deed as a way of relinquishing any community property claim.

Joint and Several Liability. An accommodation grantor should never co-sign anything but a quitclaim deed because if she were to sign a grant or warranty deed, she could become jointly and severally liable for her co-grantor's breach of the covenants contained in such deeds. For example, a husband who co-signed a grant deed with his wife ended up being held jointly and severally liable to an unsuspecting buyer for a mortgage loan the wife had placed on the property before they were married.[56]

Title Insurers, Grantors and Equitable Subrogation. Title insurers will often accept grant deeds, but not quitclaim deeds. The reason is related to the doctrine of equitable

---

54. *See, e.g.,* CAL. CIV. CODE § 1113.

55. *Dickinson v. Moore,* 468 So. 2d 136 (Ala. 1985) (Ambiguous deed could have been interpreted as a warranty or a quitclaim, but didn't matter because of misrepresentation by grantor. Grantor purported to sell property as his exclusively. His son owned an interest in the property. Buyers were awarded damages presumably equal to the value of the son's interest.).

56. *Evans v. Faught,* 231 Cal. App. 2d 698 (1965).

subrogation. This is the right of someone who pays off another's debts to collect the obligation from the debtor as if he had been the original creditor. When a title insurer is called upon to compensate an insured buyer for a title defect the seller created, the insurer is entitled by the doctrine of equitable subrogation to the same debt collection rights against the grantor as the grantee would have had.

Suppose a grantor surreptitiously mortgages the property just before closing. The mortgagee records its mortgage or deed of trust and the title insurer overlooks it. After closing, the mortgage lender threatens to foreclose unless mortgage payments are forthcoming. The aggrieved buyer will tender a claim to the title insurer. The insurer will almost certainly arrange for the mortgage to be paid and released of record. And then the insurer will seek reimbursement from the dishonest seller-grantor who had no business mortgaging the property on the eve of the sale closing.[57] The insurer may have tort based claims against the seller. But the insurer's right to equitable subrogation will depend on the deed promises the seller made to the insured buyer.

Had the grantor signed a quitclaim deed, the title insurer would have no right to recoup its losses on the basis of the seller-grantor's deed warranties because there were none. However, the grantor would have breached the implied covenant of a grant deed not to have previously encumbered or sold the property.

D. Involuntary Deeds

The deed types in this sub-section are forced sales without warranties of title. Bidders at these sales need to determine for themselves whether their acquisitions will be subject to superior liens or to challenges by the owners whose interests are up for sale.

Trustee's Deed Upon Sale (TDUS). A "deed of trust" trustee, designated by a lender, may issue a TDUS. Under a deed of trust, the borrower is the trustor and the lender is the beneficiary. If the trustor defaults, the beneficiary — the lender — will instruct the trustee to hold a public auction sale of the property. Proceeds of the sale go first to pay trustee's fees and other costs of sale, and then to the trust deed beneficiary to repay the borrower's debt. The trustee conveys title to the winning bidder.

The bidder acquires the title as it existed on the date the borrower executed the deed of trust being foreclosed. Hence, the winning bidder takes title subject to deeds of trust that were executed and recorded before the security interest being foreclosed. But the winning bidder takes title free of deeds of trust that were executed and recorded after the foreclosing beneficiary first acquired its security interest. These subordinate security interests are wiped out and that is why subordinate trust deed beneficiaries are entitled to any surplus foreclosure sale proceeds after the costs of sale and the foreclosing beneficiary are paid in full.

Sheriff's Deed. A sheriff's deed is given to the winning bidder at a sheriff's public auction sale to satisfy a creditor's judgment lien against a property owner.

---

57. *Castleman Constr. Co. v. Pennington*, 222 Tenn. 82 (1968).

Tax Deed. A tax deed is given when a tax collector sells property at public auction to satisfy unpaid property taxes. Property tax liens have priority over all private liens and encumbrances, including mortgage loans executed and recorded before the unpaid property taxes were levied. To keep from losing their interest in the property to a purchaser at a property tax foreclosure sale, mortgage lenders often contract with independent firms called tax services to alert them to any unpaid property taxes.

IV. Acknowledgment and Recordation

Once a deed has been properly signed by the grantor, and the grantor has acknowledged his signature before a notary, the deed should be promptly brought for recordation to the administrator of the public land records.

Recording the deed enables anyone thinking of buying or lending against the property to learn of the seller's or grantee's interest. Whether they checked the public records or not—as long as the deed was properly recorded, they take title subject to prior adverse interests, including deeds. Recorders impose certain formalities as conditions of accepting deeds for recordation. One of these is to identify where the recorder should mail the deed once it has been copied into the official records. Owners who misplace their deeds can obtain a certified copy from the county recorder's office.

Acknowledgments are important because unless a deed is acknowledged, the administrator of the public land records will probably refuse to place it in the public land records. The practical impact of a deed not being placed in the public records is that the former owner could sell the property again to another purchaser unaware of the seller's interest. And under some circumstances, that purchaser would have the better title.

An acknowledgment is a declaration made by a person who has signed or witnessed a deed, mortgage, or other instrument. The declaration is made before a public officer, usually a state-licensed notary public.[58] The notary takes the acknowledgment. The grantor, mortgagor, or witness "acknowledges" to the notary that she signed the deed or mortgage voluntarily or that she witnessed the grantor sign it.

An acknowledgment is not the same as an affidavit, which notaries are also sometimes required to certify. An affidavit is a written statement made under oath, signed by the person making the statement. "An affidavit is not acceptable as a substitute for an acknowledgment. The two serve different purposes. The acknowledgment merely makes the prima facie showing that the instrument was duly executed. The affidavit or verification goes to the truth of the matters there set forth."[59] Notaries

---

58. Someone from out-of-state who needs an acknowledgement must consult the applicable statute to see what is required. The Uniform Recognition of Acknowledgments Act, 14 Uniform Laws Ann. 233 (1990), enacted in sixteen states. *See* 1A Am. Jur. Legal Forms 2d § 7:440.

59. Robert Kratovil & Raymond J. Werner, Real Estate Law 81–82 (9th ed. 1988).

may also take jurats, which are certifications by the notary that she administered an oath or affirmation to the identified signatory.[60]

Notary publics taking acknowledgments from grantors must keep journals of all their official acts, and provide copies upon request to the parties to the transaction. The journals contain the signatures of witnesses and identifying information upon which the notary relied, such as the grantor's passport or driver's license. In California, to discourage and detect forgeries, if the document is a deed or deed of trust, "the notary shall require the party signing the document to place his or her right thumb print in the journal."[61] However, notaries often make mistakes when taking acknowledgments.[62]

Another frequent problem is that some firms handling closings notarize all documents at once, outside the presence of the grantors and mortgagors whose acknowledgments are being notarized. Though easier, it leaves the notary in the position of averring that the signatories personally appeared before the notary when they did not. Blame doesn't stop at the supervisor's door; it reaches the over-obedient notary too.

The holder of an unacknowledged mortgage or deed of trust can enforce it against the mortgagor in most states. But the mortgage holder's interest could be subordinated to that of a bona fide purchaser as if the mortgage had never been recorded. If the debtor becomes bankrupt, and challenges the lien created by the flawed security instrument, the bankruptcy court could allow the debtor to classify the mortgage loan as an unsecured claim. When this happens, unpaid mortgage holders could seek reimbursement from the notary, who blundered, or the closing attorney, title company, or escrow agent who was supposed to be overseeing the transaction. But that is not the security interest that the mortgage lender was counting on when it made the loan.

Consequences of A Faulty or Missing Acknowledgment. Unless notarized and acknowledged, a deed does not convey a marketable title because the recorder of deeds probably will not accept it for recordation. Nonetheless, an unacknowledged deed is valid between buyer and seller; only a few states condition the validity of a deed on a proper acknowledgment.[63]

Critique and Defense of the Acknowledgment Requirement. Critics of the acknowledgement requirement contend that acknowledgment is an imperfect anti-forgery protection. Anyone bent on mischief needs simply to visit the local recording office, search the title of the target property, find the name of the present owner, and forge her name to a new deed.[64] Someone willing to forge the owner's name to a deed can't

---

60. Cal. Gov't Code § 8202 (West 2005).

61. Cal. Gov't Code § 8206 (West 2005).

62. Martin B. Cowan, *Introducing Twentieth-Century Technology Practices to Real Estate Recording Practices (Before the Twenty-First Century)*, 28 Real Est. L.J. 99, 106 (1999).

63. Ariz. Rev. Stat. Ann. § 33-401(B) (West 2005); Ohio Rev. Code Ann. § 5301.01 (2005).

64. *Id.*

have qualms about forging a notary's signature to an acknowledgment.[65] They conclude that deed formalities prevent little harm and cause much distress; the acknowledgment requirement levies a heavy price on honest people,[66] and penalizes "grantors and grantees who retained inept lawyers or no lawyers at all."[67]

Title insurance executives and escrow agents experienced in real estate transactions disagree. They like the formality of requiring grantors to come to the title or escrow office to sign deeds or mortgages and have their signatures acknowledged there. They meet the person signing the deed or mortgage, have a chance to chat with them about the transaction, and assess whether the transaction seems legitimate. Often, title companies and escrow agents will not process transactions with sellers or borrowers who refuse to appear in person, or insist upon using their own notaries.

Below is an example of a Notary Public Acknowledgement in California.

All-Purpose Certificate of Acknowledgment[68]

State of California
County of Los Angeles

On [date] before me, [name of notary taking acknowledgment], personally appeared [name of person making acknowledgment], who proved to me on the basis of satisfactory evidence to be the person(s) whose name(s) is/are subscribed to the within instrument and acknowledged to me that he/she/they executed the same in his/her/their authorized capacity(ies), and that by his/her/their signature(s) on the instrument the person(s), or the entity upon behalf of which the person(s) acted, executed the instrument. I certify under PENALTY OF PERJURY under the laws of this state of California that the foregoing paragraph is true and correct.

WITNESS my hand and official seal.

Signature [signature of person taking acknowledgment] (Seal)

Questions

Question 1: *Community vs. Separate Property.*

You are working for a title insurance company underwriter trying to decide whether to insure the prospective grantee of a deed to property that had been acquired during a marriage but conveyed to only one of the spouses. That spouse would be the grantor. The other spouse refuses to sign a release. Under what circumstances, if any, would you be comfortable recommending that the company insure the prospective grantee's title?

---

65. James C. Smith, *Markets and Law Reform: The Tension Between Uniformity and Idealism*, 20 Nova L. Rev. 1165, 1176 (1996).
66. Robert D. Brussack, *Reform of American Conveyancing Formality*, 32 Hastings L.J. 561 (1981).
67. Paul Goldstein, Real Estate Transactions 133 (2d ed. 1985).
68. Cal. Civ. Code § 1189(a)(1) (West 2005).

Question 2: *Acquisition of Property Held by a Tenancy in Common.*

Brother and sister acquire a summer home as tenants in common. They and their families enjoy its use for many years. Sister relocates abroad and decides to sell her interest in the property, hoping her brother will join in the sale. The prospective buyer contracts to acquire the sister's interest. She promises to use her best efforts to persuade her brother to join in the sale. But as the closing date nears, it becomes clear brother intends to continue using the vacation home.

(a) Is the buyer entitled to specific performance against the sister?

(b) Will he acquire the right to use the entire property?

(c) If the buyer and the brother have difficulty sharing the house, what options are available to them to resolve their disagreements peacefully regarding the use and improvement of the property?

Question 3: *Assuring the Buyer a Marketable Title.*

Practically, how do realty buyers in the U.S. avoid getting stuck with unacceptably defective titles?

Question 4: *"Defects, Liens and Encumbrances."*

During the executory period, the buyer learns certain things she had not known about the commercial property she contracted to buy.

Would any of the following make title legally unmarketable?

(a) To serve the site, there is a recorded easement for cable TV.

(b) The property is zoned for single family use and the buyer had hoped to construct a small house, "a grannie flat," in the spacious back yard for her grandmother. Under local zoning ordinances, "grannie flats" are allowed. But the house is located in a subdivision subject to privately recorded covenants, conditions and restrictions put in place by the original subdivider. These CC&Rs limit each lot to one dwelling unit. This restriction has never been violated in the history of the subdivision.

(c) The property is fully leased to a single tenant and the lease is set to expire one day before the scheduled closing date. But the tenant remains in possession on the date set for closing.

(d) The property is subject to a deed of trust secured by a note under which the seller still owes the beneficiary $100,000 and a federal tax lien of $50,000.

Question 5: *Modifying the Marketable Title Standard.*

(a) What objection could a mortgage lender possibly have if the seller prefers to convey an insurable title instead of a marketable title since the title policy insures "marketability" of title?

(b) How can a buyer reserve for herself the right to judge whether the seller's title is acceptable?

(c) Why do you suppose any seller would ever accept the uncertainty of closing that such an open-ended way out of the contract provides the buyer?

Question 6: *Reserving the Right to Rescind if the Buyer Cannot Use or Develop the Property as Hoped.*

Buyer A is acquiring a downtown parking lot where she hopes to construct a hotel. Buyer B is acquiring 20 acres of previously undeveloped land where he hopes to construct 40 townhouses for sale to homebuyers. They have both determined that their intended uses will require zone changes. Buyer B will need to record a subdivision map. Their sellers are willing to grant purchase contracts for six months but want to be compensated for having to hold title longer than that unless assured of compensation to offset their holding costs (property taxes, insurance, and maintenance). Neither A nor B want to forfeit their 10% down payment deposits as liquidated damages if they are not granted the land use approvals they require. Sellers do not want to be bound to any changes in land use rules or subdivisions of their parcels if the buyers do not complete their acquisitions.

(a) Will buyers A and B have the right to a refund of their deposits because denial of their needed land use approvals would be evidence that their sellers lacked marketable titles?

(b) What provisions would you propose on behalf of A and B to avoid your clients forfeiting their deposits if they cannot obtain the land use approvals they seek, and that would compensate the sellers adequately for extensions of the six month purchase and sale agreement if land use approvals take longer than that to process?

Question 7: *Tenants in Possession.*

The purchaser of a neighborhood shopping center based its purchase price on the income tenants are paying to cover operating costs and produce a small profit. Instead of relying solely on the landlord's estimate of the rent roll, how might the buyer confirm that the tenants agree with the landlord's representations regarding the leases and the rents?

Question 8: *Drafting a Valid Deed Between the Parties.*

Test your mastery of the fine points of drafting short-form deeds by preparing the most minimal document that would validly transfer your interest in the Brooklyn Bridge to a classmate.

Before putting pen to paper, consider: (a) whether to convey by warranty, grant or quitclaim deed, (b) the operative words for each type of conveyance, (c) whether the deed needs to be dated, acknowledged, and/or recite "valuable consideration," (d) whether it needs to identify the grantor and grantee, and either or both of them need to sign it, and (e) how the subject property needs to be described.

Question 9: *Delivery.*

What useful purpose does the deed delivery requirement serve?

Question 10: *Grantor Competence.*

A widower is too infirm to care for himself. He hires a nurse who moves in and takes care of him for three years. The widower grows senile. The nurse prepares a deed of the widower's house to herself and urges him to sign it just before his death, perhaps even bringing a notary public in to take the widower's acknowledgment.

Shortly after the funeral, the widower's children file a suit to show he was too senile to understand what he was doing when he signed the deed. They want the court to set it aside.

If you had been representing the nurse, and anticipated the possibility of the children filing suit, what would you have done to improve the chances of a favorable outcome for the nurse?

Question 11: *Acknowledgments.*

(a) In a typical transfer by deed who acknowledges what to whom, and why do they bother?

(b) A busy law firm handles dozens of closings each day. It has adopted the efficient practice of having the firm's in-house notary affix the acknowledgment form to all the deeds at the end of each day after most grantors have left, instead of taking each acknowledgment separately while the grantors are still present.

Do you see anything seriously wrong with this practice? If you had a notary license and were working as a summer intern in this law firm, would you be willing to affix the acknowledgment forms at the end of the day in the absence of the grantors? If not, how would you explain your refusal to a senior partner?

Question 12: *Deed Covenants.*

(a) Which covenant in a warranty deed will a precocious eleven-year-old grantor have breached at closing?

(b) Which covenants, if any, in a grant deed, will the grantor have breached when the grantee learns soon after closing that the grantor acquired title by a forged deed?

Question 13: *Grant Deeds and Title Insurers.*

Why do title insurers accept grant deeds but seldom accept quitclaim deeds? What is equitable subrogation and why does it matter to title insurers?

Question 14: *Trustees' Deeds Upon Sale.*

On January 4, 2008, the borrower signs a note and executes an accompanying deed of trust to Lender A on property at 222 Glorious Lane. On March 1, 2008, the borrower signs another note and executes an accompanying deed of trust to Lender B on the same property. On December 2, 2008, the borrower signs a third note and executes an accompanying deed of trust to Lender C secured by the Glorious Lane property. All of the deeds of trust are recorded in the order they were executed. Two years later, the borrower defaults on the note to Lender B. The beneficiary under the accompanying deed of trust instructs the trustee to foreclose. X is the winning bidder at the sale.

(a) How would the foreclosure sale proceeds be allocated?

(b) Is the trustee's deed in the nature of a quitclaim, grant or warranty deed?

Chapter 7

Land Descriptions, Surveys and Boundary Disputes[1]

Scope of the Chapter

This chapter begins with a discussion of the various ways of describing land: by street address, property tax assessors' parcel numbers, metes and bounds, recorded subdivision maps, and the public land survey system (PLSS).

Then, we turn to the topic of surveys. "A comprehensive land survey and physical inspection of the property is the only efficient and reliable means of delineating the physical limits of the property and locating the improvements on it."[2] We explain the different types of surveys available and the role of surveys in title insurance. "Every commercial land transaction is anchored with a land survey and a title insurance policy."[3]

Ambiguous land descriptions and survey errors often give rise to boundary disputes—the final topic covered in this chapter. When attempts at peaceable resolution fail, and litigation follows, boundary disputes are resolved by reference to a well-established set of potentially applicable legal doctrines examined here.

I. Types of Land Descriptions

Land descriptions may be broadly divided into two groupings: informal and formal.

Informal Descriptions. Informal methods are *street addresses* and *property tax assessors' parcel numbers (APNs).*[4] Everyone uses street addresses, and anyone can find an area map showing the location of nearly any property of interest identified by APN on their local tax assessor's website.

---

1. Paul G. Carey of Dickenson, Peatman & Fogarty, and John Briscoe, founding partner of Briscoe, Ivester and Bazel made valuable suggestions included in this chapter.

2. Mitchell G. Williams and Harlan J. Onsrud, What Every Lawyer Should Know about Title Surveys, in Land Surveys: A Guide for Lawyers and Other Professionals, p. 3 (2d ed. 1999).

3. John V. Mettee III, *The Role of Surveys in Boundary Dispute Resolution*, (last visited July 08, 2015), http://c.ymcdn.com/sites/www.marylandsurveyor.org/resource/resmgr/imported/SurveysBoundaryDisputeResolution.pdf.

4. In some jurisdictions these are also referred to as assessor's identification numbers (AIN) or property identification numbers (PIN).

Though easy to use, neither APNs nor street addresses are ever proper legal descriptions for deeds. They are not the product of careful title searches or surveys, do not identify the true boundaries of the property, are not necessarily coterminous with legally subdivided lots,[5] and do not describe the size or quantity of the property being conveyed. Cities and counties have limitless authority to change street names, and they sometimes do.[6]

Formal Descriptions. The formal methods commonly used to describe parcels of realty are: (1) "bounds" or "*metes and bounds*" (also sometimes called *courses and distances*), (2) *subdivision or plat map* (sometimes called 'lot and block' descriptions), and (3) the *U.S. government survey*. These are the land descriptions that should be used in deeds, mortgages or deeds of trust, as they are proper legal descriptions.[7]

In sparsely settled areas, land tends to be described either by metes and bounds or government survey. As cities expanded into previously undeveloped areas, most states for many decades have required owners to process and record subdivision maps if they wished to sell or lease their large sites into smaller ones. Subdivision maps are superimposed upon earlier metes and bounds or public land surveys.[8]

A. Metes and Bounds

Metes and bounds describe the boundaries of a parcel of land by lengths or distances. "Metes" means measure; "bounds" means the limits or boundaries of a tract of land. A metes and bounds description "has a defined point of beginning and travels around the parcel in a clockwise or counterclockwise direction, recites courses, distances, monuments and abutting parcels as they are encountered, and returns to the point of beginning."[9] Many lawyers and surveyors refer to a courses-and-distances description as a metes-and-bounds description.[10]

---

5. Assessors often use recorded subdivision maps when available but not exclusively.

6. *See In re Hill*, 2010 WL 3927060 (S. Dist. Ga. Bankr. 2010) (holding that mortgagee had a security interest only to the debtor's unimproved lot identified in the formal legal description in the mortgage, and not to the parcel with the debtor's home on it, identified by street address in the granting clause of the mortgage but completely omitted from the formal legal description of the security property).

7. None of these three types of descriptions apply to rights of ways or other types of easements. For those, "point descriptions" and "centerline descriptions" (topics well beyond the scope of this limited introduction) are often employed.

8. For example, the following description contains both an identification of the site from a government survey and a recorded subdivision map description: "Situated in Marion County, Ohio, and in the north-easterly quarter of Section 36, Township 5 South, Range 15 East, and bounded and described as follows: Being Lot #44 of University Heights 1st Subdivision, as shown on plat of same by Stults and Associates, dated April 4, 1970, and recorded in Map Book 27 at Page 39 in the County Recorder's Office of Marion County, Ohio." Lewis M. Kanner, *What You Should Know About Surveys*, 5 Prac. Real Est. L. 9, 19 (1989).

9. Donald A. Wilson, *Reading, Interpreting, and Writing Land Descriptions in* Mitchell G. Williams (ed.) Land Surveys: A Guide for Lawyers and Other Professionals, p. 3 (2d ed. 1999).

10. Kathleen J. Hopkins & Evan L. Loeffler, Real Estate Closing Deskbook (ABA Solo, Small Firm and General Practice Division, 3d ed. 2012 Copyright © 2012) (last visited Jan. 2, 2016),

Metes-and-bounds descriptions identify land by reference to (1) natural or artificial boundaries such as streets, roads, or creeks, or (2) the land of adjoining owners, such as Smith on the south, Williams on the west. The description must establish all sides of the property by either specifically identifying what constitutes the respective boundary or providing enough information to calculate the size and shape of the land from the boundaries given. Therefore, a description that includes the size of the tract and three of the four sides will suffice.[11]

Metes and Bounds Illustrated. What follows is an example of a metes and bounds description:[12]

> Beginning at a point on the south side of Crickettown Road at an iron stake at the northwest corner of the property now or formerly of William Malloy, continuing South 15° 50' 10" West along the line of the said property now or formerly of William Malloy a distance of 51.89 feet[13] to an iron stake; thence South 20° 00' 00" West a distance of 109.00 feet to an old oak tree; thence North 89° 21' West along the line of the property now or formerly of Forrest Rose a distance of 167.23 feet to an iron stake; thence North 20° 00' 00" East a distance of 109.00 feet to the northwest corner of a well; thence North 15° 50' 10" East a distance of 51.89 feet to a point on the south side of Crickettown Road; thence along the south side of said road to the point or place of beginning.[14]

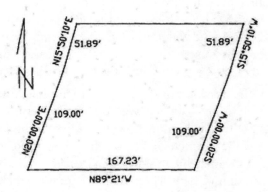

To draw a metes and bounds description, you need a compass either clearly in mind or at hand. So we have put one here so you see precisely how the detailed diagram of the above diagram was drawn.

---

http://www.americanbar.org/publications/gpsolo_ereport/2012/november_2012/real_estate_legal_descriptions.html.

11. *Id.*

12. You can find web sites on compass bearings and YouTube descriptions as well.

13. To indicate dimensions of less than a foot, surveys use tenths and hundreds of a foot, not inches .0833 foot = one inch.

14. Robert G. Natelson, Modern Law of Deeds and Real Property 152–154 (1992) *citing* Curtis M Brown, Walter G. Robillard, & Donald A. Wilson, Brown's Boundary Control and Legal Principles 47–48 (1992).

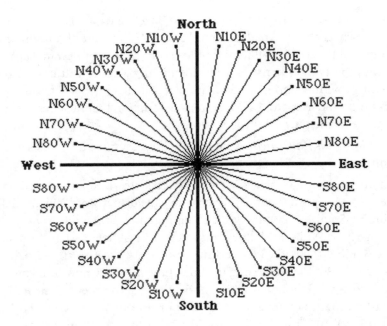

[T]he first course is South 15 degrees 50 minutes 10 seconds (15° 50' 10") West. (A minute is 1/60 of a degree and a second is 1/60 of a minute.) This means that if one were to draw a line due south from the surveyor's starting point on the property (somewhere on the south side of Crickettown Road), then shift the line 15° 50' 10" to the west, it would correspond with the boundary of the property. Thus, the boundary in that area runs approximately south-southwest. One walks along that boundary for a distance of 51.89 feet to a point where the surveyor has planted an iron stake.

At the iron stake, the direction of the perimeter shifts slightly and begins to run 20° 00' 00" west of true south—slightly over four degrees further west than the first course. It continues in that direction for 109.00 feet, where the surveyor has marked an old oak tree. There, the perimeter shifts to a direction approximately westward—North 89° 21' West. One can define this direction by taking a line pointing due north from the oak tree, then shifting it 89 degrees and 21 minutes to the west. The boundary runs in this direction for only 167.23 feet, where the surveyor has planted another iron stake. The description continues until one has reached the beginning point.[15]

Land Description Discrepancies: The Property You Contract to Buy May Not Be What You Get: Cautionary Tale. Karen and Terry Lee contracted to purchase a vacant parcel of land along Steamboat Slough in Solano County, California, identified as Assessor's Parcel Numbers (APN) 9 and 22. Their preliminary title report described the site in two ways, by a metes and bounds description, and with an assessor's parcel map with an arrow pointing to Lots 9 and 22. Like most buyers, they had no idea whether the property conformed to the metes and bounds description. They did not bother to have a surveyor draw the metes and bounds description and walk the site

---

15. *Id.*

with them to be sure that their title policy and, ultimately, their deed, described the site they thought they were acquiring.

Lot 22 was especially important to the buyers because they were avid boaters, and from certain portions of Lot 22, they would have lakefront access. Waterfront access was so important that the listing broker would not have taken a listing on Lot 9 alone because it had minimal value without waterfront access. She always told prospective buyers that Lot 22 came with Lot 9.[16]

After they took title, the Lot 21 property owners claimed title to all of Lot 22. This surprised the Lees because the Solano county tax assessor's maps since 1978 had treated Lots 9 and 22 as being in single ownership.

The Lot 21 owners alerted the county tax assessor to this emerging dispute. After a close review of the actual land descriptions of the affected lots, the assessor's office concluded that it had been mistaken all these years. In fact, Lot 22 belonged to the owner of Lot 21, not the owner of Lot 9.

Stunned and disappointed, Karen and Terry Lee filed contract and negligence claims against their title insurer and escrow agent. Their preliminary title report and their final title policy had described the property by metes and bounds. Both the preliminary and final title policies reprinted the assessor's parcel map that appeared to confirm their title as including Lots 9 and 22. The title insurer cautioned prospective buyers not to rely on the assessor's map. A disclaimer stamped onto the map stated: "This is a Diagram for Location purposes only. And it is not a part of the policy or report to which it is attached."[17]

Although Karen and Terry Lee skipped over the metes and bounds description without attempting to see if it included waterfront access, in fact, the metes and bounds description was entirely accurate. Unfortunately, for many years, the assessor's office had gotten things wrong. Upon further inquiry, it turns out that part of Lot 22 belonged to the owner of Lot 21 and part to the owner of Lot 9 but that part of Lot 22 had no lakefront access at all.

The trial court granted summary judgment for the title insurer since the metes and bounds description had been accurate; the Lees had exactly the title that the policy and their deed described.

The Lees appealed and the appellate court remanded. On retrial, the trial court instructed the jury to decide if the Lees had reasonably believed they had acquired title to waterfront access. The jury answered no. Both Karen and Terry Lee were real estate brokers, quite familiar with the fact that assessor's parcel maps are not formal legal descriptions. The trial court agreed with the jury's conclusion. The Lees actually did own a portion of Lot 22 as their title policy had provided, just not the portion they really wanted. The appellate court affirmed, in an unpublished opinion.[18]

---

16. *Lee v. Fidelity National Title Insurance Company*, 188 Cal. App. 4th 583 (2010).
17. *Id.* at 588.
18. 2013 WL 6191866 (2013) (Not Officially Published).

The facts in this case show why buyers and lenders should not rely on assessors' parcel maps. Those maps for Lots 9, 21 and 22 had not been created from a careful study of the metes and bounds descriptions contained in the recorded deeds in the chains of title to those lots. The assessor's map of Lots 9 and 22 did not describe and then mark the boundaries of those lots with sufficient clarity so that a buyer or lender could walk the site and, by matching the monuments in a land description, identify the true boundaries of each lot. In this situation, a timely survey would have been beneficial to all involved.

B. Subdivision Tract Maps

As areas urbanize, they are often subdivided into salable, buildable lots. Subdividing is largely undertaken by real estate developers, usually working with licensed surveyors.

The Regulatory Process for New Subdivisions. The process of regulating new subdivisions is central to city and county growth controls because new subdivisions can accommodate increased population and result in enhanced demands for schools, parks, libraries, flood control, water and sewer systems. Local governments oversee the approval of subdivisions under state-enabling laws called *Subdivision Map Acts.*

Subdivision maps delineate the size, shape and configuration of lots consistent with local zoning laws, show street locations, dimensions, and designs that adhere to local planning and public works standards, show the location of easements for utilities, storm drains, water and sewerage, and dedicate sites for schools and parks.

To prevent new development from becoming an undue burden upon the taxpayers of the community,[19] local governments condition their approval of subdivision maps on the subdivider contributing significant sums to the mitigation of regional growth transportation, schools, water supplies, or wildlife habitat preservation.

From Tentative Approval of a Tract Map to Final Map Recordation. In the first stage of the subdivision approval process, a subdivider or developer files a proposed map for review by the local government's technical experts — fire, police, public works, water and power suppliers, zoning and planning authorities, and tentative approval by local officials. Local officials grant tentative approval with extensive conditions for physical improvements on the site and financial contributions to the local government. Final map approval is granted when the developer complies with those conditions either by installing all the required infrastructure, or obtaining bonds to cover those costs if the developer fails to do so.

With final approval, the subdivider can record subdivision tract maps in the local public land records and sell individual lots by numbered blocks and lots. The referenced map becomes part of land description of the property being conveyed by each

---

19. *Subdivisions and Other Public Controls,* California Division of Real Estate Reference Book, (last visited July 10, 2015), http://www.dre.ca.gov/files/pdf/refbook/ref17.pdf.

deed. The description can also include the book and page number where the map can be found in the public land records.

Legal descriptions by subdivision lot and block numbers avoid the lengthy and confusing descriptions of metes and bounds and the public land survey system.[20] Because the maps are a matter of public record, buyers are presumed to be on notice of what they could have learned if they had examined the map.

Subdivision Maps Are Subordinate to Earlier Recorded Interests in the Chain of Title. A surveyor preparing a subdivision map should start with copies of all the recorded interests in the chain of title of the new subdivision and should note these in the map. The interests conveyed in those earlier recorded documents remain valid even when a surveyor fails to note them in a newly recorded subdivision map.

Buyers in a new subdivision acquire their titles subject to these earlier interests of record whether the surveyor who prepared the map shows them or not. Unless those earlier interests are clearly shown on the map, a typical buyer by lot and block number in a new subdivision may be greatly distressed when confronted by claimants with superior rights. Such a situation is described near the end of this chapter involving homeowners named Crossman. The Crossmans had acquired a lot with a big back yard that they thought was usable, only to learn that it had been subject to three oil pipeline easements recorded before the property had been subdivided. Those easements precluded their building an in-ground swimming pool in their back yard.

Standard Title Insurance Policies Do Not Cover Non-Compliance with Subdivision Map Laws. Naïve buyers may rely on title insurers to inform them if they are about to purchase a lot that has not been legally subdivided. This is not just a technical matter; the owner of an illegally subdivided lot will probably not be able to build anything on it. A lot that has not been legally subdivided cannot be occupied, developed, leased, sold or financed.

The leading case on this topic was brought by buyers of two adjoining lots in Palm Springs, California.[21] A visit to the site would have revealed that the lots were just part of a vast open desert, nothing but sand in all directions. There were no road or other improvements of any kind.

The subdivider had sold to the Hockings by lot and block number referencing a recorded subdivision map. The county recorder probably should not have accepted the map for recordation because the subdivider had never graded and paved the roads the city of Palm Springs required for new subdivisions, or bonded for the road costs.

Without those road and other subdivision improvements, the Hockings would never be able to obtain a building permit. Improvement costs for the entire subdivision far exceeded what the Hockings had paid for their lots.

---

20. Jeanne Philbin, *Boundaries* § 5, 12 Am. Jur. 2d (Database updated May 2004).
21. *Hocking v. Title Ins. and Trust Co.*, 37 Ca. 2d 644 (1951).

The Hockings sued their title insurer since their title policy had insured them against loss or damage for their title not being marketable, and they could not see how anyone could seriously claim they had a marketable title for two legally unbuildable lots.

The California Supreme Court decided in favor of the title insurer by distinguishing legal title from practical utility. No one disputed the Hockings' lawful title, and title policies exclude coverage for "laws or governmental regulations relating to occupancy of use, character or location of improvements, a separation of ownership or change in dimensions of the land, or environmental protection."[22] For protection against government land use regulations, title insurers offer special endorsements that the Hockings had not purchased.

C. U.S. Public Lands Survey System (PLSS)

Origins. The federal government's present system for surveying publicly owned lands is called the Public Land Survey System (PLSS).[23] It was originally proposed by Thomas Jefferson, and in 1785 it was enacted by the Continental Congress. Both Jefferson and his father were land surveyors. The federal government was broke after the Revolutionary War and had to depend on voluntary contributions from the states even to pay veterans the money that they had been promised. The PLSS was an integral part of a political program to finance the federal government by selling newly acquired lands to settlers as the country expanded to the west and south. For this plan to succeed, the federal government needed a system for surveying the public domain, dividing it into saleable parcels, and mapping those parcels with sufficient clarity to avoid endless squabbles when the federal government conveyed it piecemeal.

The PLSS was a great improvement over the metes and bounds descriptions. It divided the new federal domain into rectangular and square grids of equal size,[24] called townships and sections. The federal government only conveyed land after it had been surveyed and a plat of the survey had been filed with and approved by the General Land Office. The plat became part of the original government grants or deeds. There were exceptions for titles traceable to foreign governments that predated the time that these lands had become territories of the United States. The gov-

---

22. *See, e.g.,* *Nishiyama v. Safeco Title Ins. Co.,* 85 Cal. App. 3d (1978)

23. The system was initially designed to facilitate the U.S. Government's disposal of lands acquired in the Northwest Territory (now Indiana, Illinois, Ohio, Michigan and Wisconsin). The founding fathers hoped that the federal government could earn enough from the sale of these lands to provide U.S. troops to safeguard the ownership rights of federal grantees against Indian tribes and squatters, pay the creditors who had financed the Revolutionary War, and distribute parcels to Revolutionary War veterans to reward their service.

24. The U.S. PLSS mapped all states except the original colonies, their off-shoots (West Virginia, Vermont, Maine, Tennessee, and Kentucky), Texas, and Hawaii. Metes and Bounds (last visited July 10, 2015), www.tngenweb.org/tnland/metes-b.htm; *The Public Land Survey System (hereinafter "PLSS"),* USGS (last visited July 10, 2015), http://nationalatlas.gov/articles/boundaries/a_plss.html.

ernment survey included Alabama, Florida, Mississippi, all states north of the Ohio River, and all states west of the Mississippi River except Texas.[25]

The rectangular, linear U.S. public land survey system was facilitated by a special chain to measure distances and areas, designed in 1606 by the English mathematician and investor Edmund Gunter, a professor of astronomy.

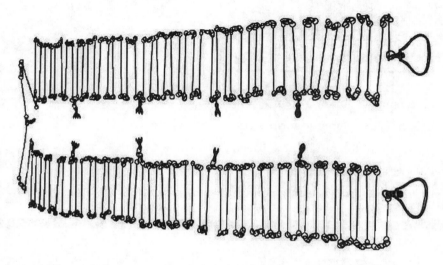

Gunter's Chain

The chain was made of straight metal pieces, and did not stretch, shrink or tear. It was more convenient, accurate, and consistent than other measuring devices in use at the time. Though it has been replaced with a steel tape that is still in use, it gave rise to a new standard of surveying measurement called "the chain." A mile, or 5,280 feet long, contained exactly 80 chains of 66 feet each. One square chain, 1 chain on a side, or 66 feet in length, contained 4,356 square feet; since one acre contains 43,560 square feet, it could be measured by exactly 10 square chains.[26]

According to the U.S. Department of Agriculture, almost four-fifths of the U.S. land subdivisions have been influenced by the systematic rectangular land survey. In the past two centuries, the Bureau of Land Management (BLM), U.S. Department of Interior, has surveyed almost 1.5 billion acres. It maintains the official records of past government surveys, continues to make new ones, and restores obliterated or lost original survey monuments.

25. 1 PATTON AND PALOMAR ON LAND TITLES § 116 (3d ed.).
26. ERAN BEN-JOSEPH, THE CODE OF THE CITY 33–34. (MIT Press 2005).

The rectangular survey system:

- Uses imaginary lines to form a grid to locate land
- North-south longitude lines, called meridians
- East-west latitude lines called baselines
- Intersect to form a starting point from which distances are measured.

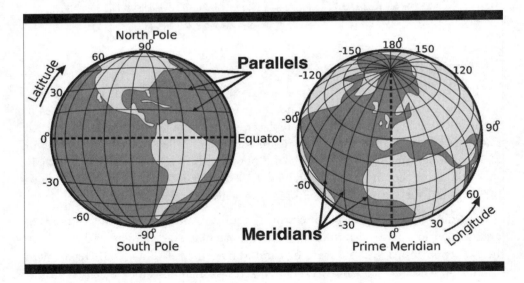

The Primacy of Government Surveys. Even though property rights are generally regarded as a matter of state law,[27] courts defer to the federal authorities that implement the PLSS. This deference was meant to avoid the confusion and litigation that would have stemmed from allowing state and federal courts "to interfere and overthrow the

---

27. Lewis M. Kanner, *What You Should Know About Surveys*, 5 PRAC. REAL EST. L. 9, 19 (1989).

public surveys on no other ground than an opinion that they could have the work in the field better done, and divisions more equitably made, than the department of public lands could do."[28] Unfortunately, the physical difficulties of making these surveys were enormous once surveyors left the flat lands of the plains for the mountainous west. Errors were compounded by a lack of government supervision, and a system of surveyor compensation that rewarded the quantity of land surveyed over the quality of the work.

The Mechanics of the PLSS. The PLSS divided most of the country outside the original colonies into (1) tracts or quadrangles, areas 24 miles square, bounded by baselines running east and west, and meridians running north and south. (2) These huge squares were further divided into 16 areas each six miles square called townships. (3) Every township was subdivided into 36 sections. Each section was both one mile square and one square mile.[29]

The Congressional decision to divide the public domain into these dual layers — sizable townships *and* smaller sections — resulted from a compromise between those who wanted to sell off the newly-acquired territory in vast tracts to investors, promoters, and plantation owners and those who preferred parceling it out to homesteaders and small farmers.

The Continental Congress contemplated the further subdivision of sections that could only be subdivided into smaller portions of land by following the precise template shown below.

Sections may be subdivided into four quarters of 160 acres each, and each quarter section may be further subdivided into quarter-quarters. A quarter-quarter section would contain 40 acres — each side 1320 feet in length (1/4 of a mile), 1,742,400 square feet. By closely scrutinizing the SE 1/4 of the graphic depiction below of a section, you will see that quarter sections and quarter-quarter sections can be halved north, south, east or west. Also, quarter-quarter sections can be subdivided into quarter-quarter-quarter sections.[30]

---

28. *Haydel v. Dufresne*, 58 U.S. 23, 30 (1855). Courts protect titles derived from original patent grantees by not allowing the accuracy of the PLSS to be questioned. By contrast, privately prepared surveys for subdivision maps or metes and bounds descriptions — which don't form the root of title from the state — are challengeable for inaccuracy. State and local surveys are less sacrosanct, so much so that the California Supreme Court took judicial notice of the shortcomings of the early survey of downtown Los Angeles, and remanded a downtown boundary dispute case back to the trial court which had based its decision on extrapolations from the downtown survey instead of hearing testimony regarding how the site was actually being used and where people at the time believed disputed boundary to have been. *Hellman v. Los Angeles*, 125 Cal. 383, 387, 58 P. 10 (1899).

29. One mile square is a square one mile on each side, and has an area of one square mile. One mile square is any shape that has an area of 1 square mile. A section is both one mile square and one square mile. The difference between one mile square and one square mile is this: an object one mile square is shaped so that each side is one mile long. One square mile refers to an object with an area of one mile. It could be any shape — circle, square, a rectangle, triangle.

30. American Right of Way Association, Principles of Right of Way 72 (1972).

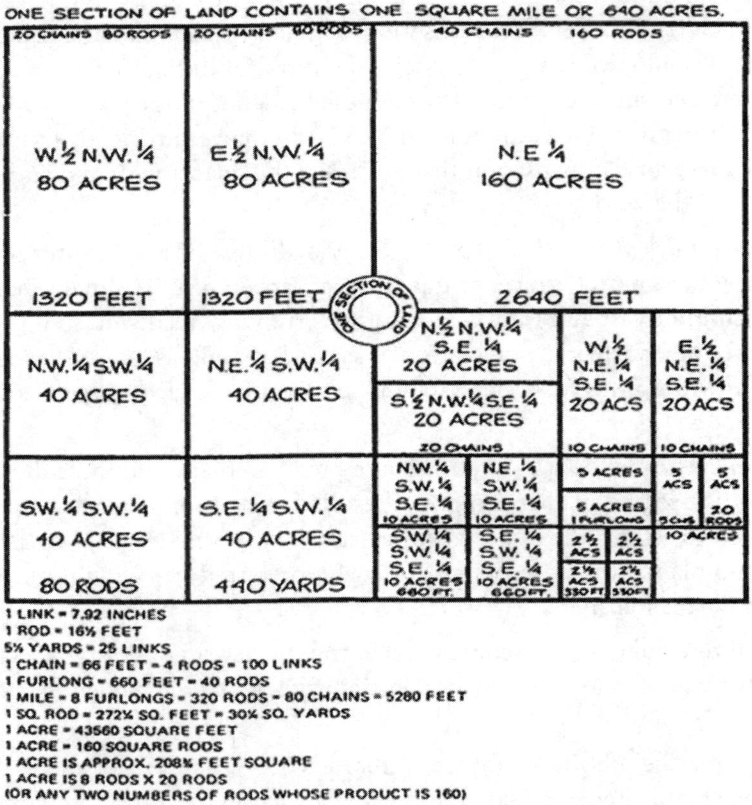

ONE SECTION OF LAND CONTAINS ONE SQUARE MILE OR 640 ACRES.

20 CHAINS 80 RODS	20 CHAINS 80 RODS	40 CHAINS 160 RODS
W.½ N.W. ¼ 80 ACRES	E.½ N.W. ¼ 80 ACRES	N.E ¼ 160 ACRES
1320 FEET	1320 FEET	2640 FEET

(Central diagram showing subdivisions:)

N.W. ¼ S.W. ¼ 40 ACRES

N.E. ¼ S.W. ¼ 40 ACRES

N.½ N.W.¼ S.E. ¼ 20 ACRES

S.½ N.W.¼ S.E. ¼ 20 ACRES — 20 CHAINS

W.½ N.E. ¼ S.E. ¼ 20 ACS

E.½ N.E. ¼ S.E. ¼ 20 ACS — 10 CHAINS / 10 CHAINS

S.W. ¼ S.W. ¼ 40 ACRES

S.E. ¼ S.W. ¼ 40 ACRES

N.W. ¼ S.W. ¼ S.E. ¼ 10 ACRES	N.E. ¼ S.W. ¼ S.E. ¼ 10 ACRES	5 ACRES 1 FURLONG	5 ACS	5 ACS
S.W. ¼ S.W. ¼ S.E. ¼ 10 ACRES	S.E. ¼ S.W. ¼ S.E. ¼ 10 ACRES	5 ACRES 1 FURLONG	20 RODS 10 ACRES 2 CHS	
S.W. ¼ S.E. ¼ S.E. ¼ 10 ACRES 660 FT.	S.E. ¼ S.E. ¼ S.E. ¼ 10 ACRES 660 FT.	2½ ACS 2½ ACS 330 FT	2½ ACS 2½ ACS 330 FT	

80 RODS

440 YARDS

1 LINK = 7.92 INCHES
1 ROD = 16½ FEET
5½ YARDS = 25 LINKS
1 CHAIN = 66 FEET = 4 RODS = 100 LINKS
1 FURLONG = 660 FEET = 40 RODS
1 MILE = 8 FURLONGS = 320 RODS = 80 CHAINS = 5280 FEET
1 SQ. ROD = 272¼ SQ. FEET = 30¼ SQ. YARDS
1 ACRE = 43560 SQUARE FEET
1 ACRE = 160 SQUARE RODS
1 ACRE IS APPROX. 208¾ FEET SQUARE
1 ACRE IS 8 RODS X 20 RODS
(OR ANY TWO NUMBERS OF RODS WHOSE PRODUCT IS 160)

A PLSS Property Description:

Example: "The S/W 1/4, NE 1/4, Section 28, T.4N.-R.2 E., San Bernardino P.M."

The description starts with the section, then the township, range and principal meridian. The above description is of the Southwest quarter of the Northeast quarter of Township 4 North, Range 2 East of the San Bernardino Principal Meridian (SBPM).[31] To determine where the property is, identify each of these items in reverse, starting with the last and most general item, and working to the first item, which is the smallest and most specific.[32]

Land Development Effects of the PLSS. The effects of the PLSS are apparent in the grid-like rectangular layout of farms and subdivisions readily visible from the air.

This facilitated agriculture, and was good for developers and development. Most U.S. cities that were developed after the PLSS were laid out in rectangular grids which made them easily divisible into uniform building lots. In fact, compared to properties described by metes and bounds, properties described by rectangular survey were more readily and frequently traded, brought higher prices; engendered far fewer

---

31. ERAN BEN-JOSEPH, THE CODE OF THE CITY 33 (MIT Press 2005).
32. ROBERT G. NATELSON, MODERN LAW OF DEEDS AND REAL PROPERTY 601, fig. 23-1 (1992).

boundary disputes over time; eased the conversion of farmland into more productive urban uses, stimulated economic activity, facilitated the location of roads and utilities, which could be placed along the grid lines that linked every lot within the area to every other lot in town.[33]

Unfortunately, this obliviousness to local conditions, while facilitating economic development, mandated some subdivisions horrifically insensitive to the local terrain and environment.[34] The road networks completely disregarded natural features such as streams and rivers. Unlike the early settlers in Virginia and Massachusetts, who sited trails and roads according to the lay of the land and minimized river crossings, most of the surveyor's roads along the systemic rectangular survey areas crossed the same streams and hills repeatedly, increasing the costs of construction and sometimes needlessly adding to local travel times.[35]

Some observers see the grid layout as an aesthetic disaster compared to European pre-industrial cities. Streets in those towns and cities were carefully laid out in irregular shapes to enhance the experience of the viewer approaching the cathedrals and important public buildings located within central squares and town plazas.[36]

II. Contracting for Surveys

"Survey" Defined. **What Is a Survey?** The word survey is derived from an old French word meaning "to look over," and refers to the process of evaluating real property evidence in order to locate the physical limits of a particular parcel of land.

The real property evidence considered by the surveyor typically consists of physical field evidence, written record evidence, and field measurements. The surveyor, after evaluating such evidence, forms an opinion as to where he believes the lines would be located if fully adjudicated in a court of law.[37] The surveyor produces a map or plot of the survey to communicate his opinion based on the available evidence as to where a parcel's boundaries are located. But the surveyor's map and accompanying notes are a report of the survey. The survey itself is a measurement and evidence evaluation process. In other words, surveying often involves the exercise of judgment; highly competent surveyors may reach different conclusions about the boundaries and dimensions of the same property. This will become more apparent when issues of surveyor liability are discussed at the end of this chapter.

---

33. Gary D. Libecap & Dean Lueck, *The Demarcation of Land and the Role of Coordinating Institutions*, 119 J. POL. ECON. (last visited July 10, 2015), http://ideas.repec.org/p/nbr/nberwo/14942.html; JOHN REPTS, THE MAKING OF URBAN AMERICA: A HISTORY OF CITY PLANNING IN THE UNITED STATES 217, 298–99, 314 (1965).

34. ERAN BEN-JOSEPH, THE CODE OF THE CITY 34–35 (MIT Press 2005).

35. *Id.*

36. See, *e.g.*, CAMILLO SITTE, CITY PLANNING ACCORDING TO ARTISTIC PRINCIPLES (1889).

37. Mitchell G. Williams & Harlan, J. Onsrud, *What Every Lawyer Should Know About Title Surveys,* LAND SURVEYS: A GUIDE FOR LAWYERS (American Bar Association 1989).

Most states only allow licensed surveyors to prepare property descriptions[38] because only surveyors can locate boundaries, calculate actual acreage, and relate the boundaries to the location of physical improvements.[39]

When Do Buyers Order Surveys? Developers almost always commission surveys before purchasing prospective building sites for development. Commercial lenders often insist upon an American Land Title Association (ALTA) survey so as to secure full title insurance coverage of site dimensions and the location of improvements and easements.

Surveys are more likely to be useful to home buyers acquiring property described by metes and bounds than property in recently recorded subdivisions. Similarly, it may be more important to stake the boundaries of properties situated on hillsides or rugged terrain than of properties on flat lands. Buyers contemplating major new construction might also want to re-assure themselves that their assumptions about the site—its dimensions, topography, the location of easements, and access routes— are as they had expected.

When a yard is fenced, buyers often assume they own everything within the fence and nothing beyond it. Yet, the title described in the deed could convey considerably less or more land than is bounded by the fence. Without a surveyor staking the property boundaries and matching them to the legal description, buyers have no way of knowing for sure what they are getting, or that their improvements are all securely within their own property boundaries, into which none of the neighbor's improvements protrude.

Surveys May Reveal Title Problems. They Do Not Change Titles. Title surveys may identify problems that could impact the marketability of title or the use and enjoyment of property. They could show that A's building encroaches on B's land or that the fence separating the two holdings is twenty feet into A's property. These are important facts. But surveys "do not create or convey title." They match information concerning the recorded title to conditions on the ground.[40]

A. Three Possible Types of Survey Conditions for Buyers in Purchase-and-Sale Contracts

A buyer wishing to condition her obligation to purchase on the preparation of a survey may choose one of three quite different survey-related contract conditions.

---

38. *See, e.g.*, Cal. Bus. & Prof. Code § 8726 (West 1995); Fla. Stat. Ann. § 472.005 (West 2001); N.Y. Educ. Law § 7208e (McKinney 2001) (only surveyors can determine real property boundaries).

39. C. Michael Jackson, Descriptions, Florida Real Estate Property Sales Transactions § 7.11 at 240 (1994). Requiring the surveyor to measure and report the exact acreage is particularly useful when the recorded title appears to create more land than the surveyor actually measures on the ground. For instance, a metes and bounds description might call for 100 feet separations between each of the various natural and artificial monuments marking the corners of the property. But the monuments might actually have been located slightly closer to each other than 100 feet, resulting in the measured parcel being somewhat smaller than the record would have suggested since monuments prevail over distances in construing survey discrepancies.

40. David E. Snediker, *Surveys and Title Insurance, in* MITCHELL G. WILLIAMS (ED.), LAND SURVEYS: A GUIDE FOR LAWYERS AND OTHER PROFESSIONALS, p. 163, 166 (2d ed. 1999).

First, she might condition her contract by agreeing to take *"subject to any state of facts* an accurate survey may show." For the seller, this survey condition is ideal because it creates no new basis upon which the buyer may object to title other than what was already in the contract. The "subject to any state of facts" exception doesn't erase, modify or expand upon the seller's promises in the contract. These words obligate the buyer to purchase the property no matter what the survey shows. The seller is still obligated to convey a marketable title to the property, but only to the property described in the contract.

Second, a buyer could reserve the right *to disapprove the title* based on what the survey reveals. The buyer with this survey condition has the right to back out of a deal for *title* problems such as the neighbor's fence encroaching into the property being acquired the seller can cure the title defects to the buyer's reasonable satisfaction. The buyer would not have the right to back out because the survey showed that an office building on the site could not be fully leased because it was short of the number of parking spaces required by the local zoning code.

Third, the buyer's *approval of the survey could be made a condition to the buyer's obligation to purchase the property*. This survey condition gives the buyer wide leeway to back out of the sale. The buyer could withhold approval for something in the survey totally unrelated to title issues. A surveyor might plot the location of oak trees protected by local or federal law from removal. The laws dedicated to the preservation of the trees could frustrate the buyer's plans to develop. This would be a reasonable basis for buyer disapproval.

B. Ordering the Right Survey

Clients contracting for a survey should: (1) describe the subject property by legal description (usually taken from the deed by which the present owner acquired title), street address and property tax assessor's parcel number (APN), (2) identify the owner, if different from the client, (3) set a delivery date for the survey, (4) specify the form of the desired product (e.g., digital drawing, blueprint, etc.), number of copies, size of drawing, and scale, (5) define and allocate the surveyor's "errors and omissions" insurance coverage, (6) determine the fee and time for payment, and (7) specify the survey content and methodology, for there is no universally agreed upon standard.

Clients unfamiliar with the broad range of survey options should have the surveyor explain them and specify the best one for their situation.[41]

An ALTA/ACSM (American Congress on Surveying and Mapping) Survey.[42] Commercial investors and lenders often insist upon this type of survey as a condition to

---

41. *See* Vanessa L. Washington, *What You Should Know About Survey Certificates*, 9 Practical Real Est. Law 21 (March 1993).

42. Bernard M. Rifkin, "Land Surveys and the Law of Real Property," *Minimum Standard Detail Requirements for ALTA/ACSM Land Title Surveys*, Land Surveys: A Guide for Lawyers 42–48 (American Bar Association 1989). The ALTA/ACSM standards require more than some state standards, and vice-versa, so it is becoming common for surveys to be ordered that meet both the state and

investing or lending because it is the only one for which the insurer will remove its "survey exception."[43] The survey exception frees the title insurer from liability for "any state of facts an accurate survey may show." Even after a survey has been completed, the title insurer circumscribes the scope of its potential liability in language referred to as a survey reading which carefully excepts from insurance coverage each and every one of the specific defects the survey reveals.

Despite this, the survey can be worthwhile for the insured because the survey reading is a list which highlights the problems the survey revealed. Although the title insurer disclaims liability for the items on that list, and for the surveyor's errors and omissions, the title insurer assumes liability for its own errors, omissions and ambiguities in its description of the defects that it specifically mentions as not being covered by the policy,[44] and for inaccuracy in the survey.[45]

Surveyors are not title searchers. They are title plotters. Their job is to map the site and verify that conditions on the site conform to the paper record supplied by the title insurer. Hence, title insurers are indirectly exposed to survey errors resulting from errors or omissions in the recorded documents affecting title supplied to the surveyor by the title insurer.

On the survey map, the surveyor shows precisely the property boundaries and the location of all improvements. This enables buyers, lenders and their counsel to observe whether any buildings encroach into the surveyed estate, or buildings from the surveyed estate encroach on neighboring properties. The surveyor also indicates if the record description forms a mathematically closed figure on the ground. A *gap* is a red flag warning of a faulty or incomplete description.

The surveyor notes the character and location of any possession; structures and easements of record; driveways; cemeteries and burial grounds; and ponds, lakes, springs or rivers on or bordering the site. The surveyor calls out discrepancies between the presumed location of any easement based on recorded documents and actual location of pipes, drains, wires or other indication of the easement.

Among its important details, the surveyor's map should show the names of record owners and the recorded lot or parcel numbers of adjoining properties. It also identifies setback or building restriction lines recorded in subdivision maps, and evidence of all monuments.

Table "A" of the 1997 ALTA Standards lists optional items to be negotiated between client and surveyor. Among them are flood zone designations; identification of set-

---

ALTA/ACSM standards. Ross E. Payne, *What Every Real Estate Lawyer Should Know About Surveys*, 70 FLORIDA BAR J. 65, 66 (July/Aug. 1996).

43. This was a combined effort of ALTA, ACSM and the National Society of Professional Surveyors.

44. Ambiguities in the survey exception are read against the insurer. For a case where lack of clarity caused the survey exception NOT to exonerate the insurer from liability, see *Amidano v. Donnelly*, 615 A.2d 654 (N.J. Super. Ct. 1992).

45. *Enright v. Lubow*, 493 A.2d 1288, 202 N.J. Super. 58 (1985). The title insurer would, of course, have a claim against the negligent surveyor.

back; height and bulk restrictions according to applicable zoning and building codes; square footage of buildings; land area; visible improvements; parking areas and number of parking spaces; location of utilities; and observable evidence of earth moving work, building construction, or building additions within recent months.[46]

Many types of surveys are less extensive than the ALTA/ACSM survey:

(1) **A lot or simple boundary survey.** The surveyor stakes the boundaries of the property, so the owner can build its project within the true boundaries. This survey may be marked on the ground with monuments set at the corners or along property lines, or mapped showing precise distances from walls, curbs, or other features.

(2) **An encroachment survey.** The surveyor determines the precise boundaries of the site and then maps all improvements, showing their dimensions and whether they are within or outside the owner's boundary lines. The surveyor may set new boundary monuments or refer by map to existing ones.

(3) **A record of survey map.** The surveyor prepares a map which meets local or state surveying standards and files it with the appropriate local agency. In some states, surveyors placing monuments on the ground must tag them with their surveyor license number and file a record of survey map with a designated local official.

Many surveys are associated with construction,[47] including:

(4) **Topographic or architect's design survey.** The surveyor locates all nearby roads, railroads, utility installations, sewers, and adjacent buildings, and depicts precisely the elevation and topography of the site. The resulting map is called a *plot plan.*

(5) **Construction survey.** Before constructing improvements, a surveyor will be called to set stakes for the project to be built. Relying on a boundary survey, the construction surveyor makes sure the proposed building lies within the legal boundaries of the site and also complies with local zoning setback and side yard ordinances. The building contractor will be relying on this survey in positioning the project.[48]

(6) **As-built survey.** When a project is completed, the permanent lender will seek an "as built" survey to confirm that the project lies entirely on its own site, to make sure the setbacks, height and bulk of the building conform to zoning and building codes, and so on.

---

46. Table A was modified by the ALTA in 1999. *See Organizations Adopt New ALTA®/ACSM Land Title Survey Standards,* AMERICAN LAND TITLE ASSOCIATION (last visited July 10, 2015), https://www.alta.org/publications/titlenews/00/0002_04.cfm.

47. JACK B. EVETT, SURVEYING 183 (2d ed., Prentice-Hall 1991).

48. Not having a surveyor perform this task can lead to a building being constructed contrary to the zoning setback. This happens because quite often more land has been acquired for the street right of way than has actually been improved with a road. Amateurs, not knowing this, may for instance measure a twenty foot setback line from the public right of way by starting at the point where the improved road appears to abut the private property line. If the public right of way is actually located closer than the improved roadway to the private property line, the property owner relying on the erroneous information may construct the building partially within the proscribed setback line. Tearing down the building will cost a lot more than an accurate construction survey would have cost.

C. Attorney's Scope of Work in Reviewing a Survey

A Los Angeles real estate transactions attorney, Tom Muller, offered this advice concerning how to ensure that the buyer is getting what the buyer is expecting to buy and the seller is selling what it is expecting to sell:

> "EVP for acquisitions calls her favorite lawyer: 'We're buying Three Rivers Shopping Center, so get going on due diligence.'
>
> Favorite lawyer immediately calls title company: 'I need a title report on Three Rivers Shopping Center, ASAP,' and surveyor: 'I need a survey of Three Rivers Shopping Center, ASAP.'"

In due course the title company produces a title report naming the owner, giving an eight-page metes and bounds property description indecipherable to normal humans, and a list of covenants, easements and liens affecting the property. Soon thereafter, the surveyor produces a survey showing many parcels of land, the buildings located on them and plots of the various easements affecting those properties.

How do the lawyer, the title company and the surveyor know that the property described in the eight-page property description is the same as the property shown on the survey? How do all three of them know that that property is the same thing as what EVP for acquisitions meant when she said she was buying Three Rivers Shopping Center?

More often than you'd think, they don't. As a result, either too many or too few parcels of land get conveyed, resulting in embarrassment, financial loss, and sometimes lawsuits against lawyers, title companies and surveyors.

Even though the eight-page metes and bounds property description is very hard to read by those untrained in deciphering property descriptions—"*commencing at a point in Franklin Street distant 342.06 feet easterly of the northwest quarter corner, thence N76°44'32"W 26.77 feet, thence S13°15'28"W a distance of 531.06 feet more or less, thence ...*"—any good proofreader can usually confirm that the description in the title report is the same as the land shown on the survey, because the survey also contains a description of the property shown thereon, and so that description should exactly match the one in the title report.

Sometimes they don't, because the same parcel of land can be described in several different ways. If the descriptions don't match, the surveyor should be asked to confirm that they both describe the same parcel of land. And, of course, sometimes they don't actually describe the same parcels of land. The parties' lawyers, the title company and the surveyor should all take the time to confirm that the land in the title report is the same as the land on the survey.

In reviewing the survey, an attorney for buyer or lender will see if the deed description of the surveyed site conforms to the boundaries described in the survey, verify that all physical structures and easements are located properly in the survey, that there are no encroachments either of the acquired structures into neighboring sites or of neighboring properties into the subject site, ascertain whether any easements would interfere with the buyer's contemplated development or intended use, and investigate unexpected possessory interests that show up in the survey but were not previously shown in any recorded document by identifying and contacting the holders of those interests.

San Francisco real estate attorney John Briscoe adds that the surveyor and the client join him in actually walking the site with the survey in hand to compare what is on the ground with what the survey shows. Seeing the location of easements, encroachments and boundaries is better than trying to envision them on a map.

D. Liability for Faulty Surveys

Surveyors' Liability to Client and Successive Purchasers. Buyer, seller, or both can establish an agency relationship by contracting directly with the surveyor, authorizing the work and paying for it. Like most mortals, surveyors sometimes make mistakes. When they do, their clients may have contract claims against them. Successive purchasers who buy in reliance upon earlier surveys that prove defective have no contract claim against the original surveyor. However, they may have statutory-based claims against the surveyor[49] and claims based on negligence when their reliance on the survey is reasonably foreseeable, as it would be when the surveyor prepares a subdivision map.

Grantors' Liability to Successive Purchasers. Property owners who hire surveyors are not directly liable to successive purchasers for the surveyor's errors when, as is customary, the surveyor works as an independent contractor. However, a seller may breach her warranty deed covenants by purporting to deed more land than she actually owns.[50]

Successive purchasers are usually barred from suing remote grantors for breach of the covenant of seisin.[51] Courts have long regarded this as a "present covenant." A present covenant is breached if at all at the moment of issuance.

---

49. *See* Dag E. Ytreberg, Annotation, *Surveyor's Liability for Mistake in, or Misrepresentation as to Accuracy of Survey, of Real Property*, 35 A.L.R. 3d 504 (1971). Some courts have predicated a third party private right of action based on state statutes regulating surveyors and surveys.

50. *See Kendall v. Lowther*, 356 N.W.2d 181 (Iowa 1984) (holding seller liable to purchasers for breaching warranty deed covenants after conveying each of the adjoining lots to separate purchasers based on an inaccurate survey the seller had commissioned before subdividing the property. The surveyor carelessly interpreted the legal description in the chain of title so that the property the purchasers were shown, based on the surveyor's stakes, wasn't coterminous with the property as described in their deeds. Seller wasn't exonerated even though the court established a boundary line almost identical to the one the surveyor had mistakenly delineated. Basing its decision on the equities, the court refused to honor the true legal description because it bisected a farmhouse that had been improved to become the principal residence on one of the lots.).

51. The *covenant of seisin* is essentially a covenant that the grantor owns the estate that the deed says it conveys to the grantee. This covenant promises that no one else has any conflicting possessory interests, present or future. If someone else owns some part of the described land, that would violate the covenant of seisin.

Likewise, if a deed says it conveys a fee simple absolute, but someone else owns a future interest in the property, that future interest would violate the covenant. DUMMIES.COM (last visited July 10, 2015), http://www.dummies.com/how-to/content/the-various-covenants-of-a-deed.html.

On future covenants, successive purchasers can sue remote grantors; these are actionable whenever they cause damage regardless of the date of the original survey. Future covenants include the covenant to warrant and defend or the covenant of quiet enjoyment.

Grantors of *grant* deeds will not have made any future covenants. All of their covenants are breached if at all on the date the deed is delivered. They only promise that at the time of the grant, they have not previously conveyed the property to anyone else, or "done, made, or suffered" encumbrances against the title. Sometimes, sellers make title promises in their purchase and sale agreements. Under a norm known as "merger," contract promises that concern title are presumed to be supplanted by title covenants in the deed or, possibly, in the land description contained in a grant deed.

Case Study: Hanneman v. Downer

No case depicts the hardship that a defective survey can cause better than *Hanneman v. Downer*.[52] The saga began when Jacobsen decided to subdivide some acreage he had bought fifteen years earlier in order to sell it off in smaller parcels. Jacobsen retained Downer, a surveyor, to prepare and record a subdivision map.

Downer had just left his long tenure at the state highway department to open his own firm and this was one of his first jobs as a self-employed surveyor.

Jacobsen recorded a subdivision map based on Downer's survey and sold one of the lots to Frazier. Frazier sold the lot to Swenson, who sold it to Eldon and Patricia Hanneman. The Hannemans financed their purchase by giving Swenson a note for the $35,000 purchase price and a deed of trust secured by the property, which everyone assumed consisted of 5.88 acres.

Eldon Hanneman, a carpenter, reconstructed the dilapidated and uninhabitable house on the property and moved in. Then, Eldon learned that much of the site he thought he owned actually belonged to the federal government according to a recently concluded survey. Downer's survey had been wrong. Everyone tracing their titles back to Jacobsen had a problem.

Eventually, the source of Downer's error surfaced. In making his survey, Downer had relied on field notes from an 1881 survey but decided to disregard four felled trees with clear survey markings, two of which University of Arizona scientists later dated back to 1881, authenticating the field notes. He had also disregarded a stone monument marking the SW corner of a section. The field notes had denoted "a trachyte stone $24 \times 18 \times 12$." By 1982, that stone measured $22 \times 17 \times 9$. Downer figured the smaller stone couldn't be the same one mentioned in 1881. The Bureau of Land Management disagreed, contending that normal weathering explained the reduced size. The result was that Jacobsen's site was 20 acres smaller than depicted in Downer's survey. Unfortunately, Downer had never bothered to note and explain these issues in the survey.

---

52. *Hanneman v. Downer*, 871 P.2d 279 (Nev. 1994).

Unfortunately for the Hannemans, part of the shortfall encompassed all the habitable portions of their site—over four acres, including the house Eldon had carefully reconstructed. The remaining 1.5 acres were practically inaccessible. Faced with a near total loss of their life savings and hard work, the Hannemans stopped making payments on their purchase money loan from Swenson and sued everyone in sight.

The Hannemans had no difficulty obtaining a judgment against Downer for negligence. Their potential liability for the omission of approximately four acres exceeded $100,000. But the judgment proved uncollectible because Downer was broke. He had left his job with the state and after the judgment in this case, he could not draw clients to his new surveying business.

The Hannemans had no basis for recovery against the original subdivider Jacobsen since he had conveyed to Frazier by grant deed. While Swenson, too, had conveyed by grant deed, the Nevada Supreme Court held her liable based in part on the terms of her purchase-and-sale agreement and in part on her deed's land description. Both purported to convey 5.88 acres. The court concluded that the Hannemans had rebutted the presumption that contract provisions concerning the quality of title are trumped by the provisions concerning title that appear in the deed because "no one would have paid $35,000 for only 1.5 [inaccessible] acres."

Following this decision, Swenson foreclosed and took title to the 1.5 acres. Because of the prohibitive cost of grading to connect the site to the nearest road, the property was virtually worthless. Through no fault of her own, she ended up being held accountable for Downer's error.

The judgment against Swenson is hard to justify as a matter of law since grant deeds contain no covenants of seisin. The grantor in a grant deed only promises that she has not previously conveyed the property to anyone else or done, made or suffered encumbrances to be placed on the property. Clearly, Swenson had not breached the covenants in a grant deed because she was unable to convey the promised acreage to the Hannemans. The case has never been cited for that proposition, either.

Perhaps the Court was just trying to spread the loss occasioned by the faulty survey between the Hannemans who had built a house on land they did not own and Swenson who now held legal title to an inaccessible acre and a half.

III. Boundary Disputes

The typical boundary dispute between adjoining neighbors often begins when a new owner decides to improve recently acquired property, orders a survey, and learns that the true property lines are not where they were expected to be.[53]

---

53. Robert G. Cochran & Andrew F. Macfarlane, *Boundary Disputes*, FLORIDA REAL PROP. LITIGATION, § 2-1 (Florida Bar 2001). *See e.g., Otley v. McCarthy*, 2003 WL 23112729 (Conn. Super. Ct. 2003).

By far the best way to resolve boundary disputes is by mutual agreement—written, properly executed, recorded, and with title insurance of any property the agreement transfers. Adjoining owners who elect to negotiate a mutual boundary agreement have the chance to provide for sharing of maintenance and repair costs, and to restrict their respective uses of the previously disputed turf.

Another way that adjoining neighbors can memorialize a peaceful resolution of a boundary issue would be just to exchange quitclaim deeds confirming their resolution. This approach could entangle them in the planning bureaucracies of local governments if the resulting deeds altered the lot lines in previously recorded subdivision maps. They might need some form of local government approval for a lot line adjustment unless they use reciprocal easements instead of altering fee titles.

Boundary disagreements can turn into nasty and expensive lawsuits over inconsequential strips of shrubbery, far exceeding the market value of the contested turf with unpredictable outcomes not fully satisfying to either party.[54]

In a litigated boundary dispute, a number of doctrines may come into play: (1) trespass; (2) adverse possession; (3) prescriptive easements; (4) boundary by agreement; and (5) boundary by acquiescence.

Because boundary disputes elude consistency, doctrinal purity, or predictability,[55] litigator Paul Carey cautions: "Plead all potentially applicable causes of action. Counsel can never know in advance what a trier of fact will find to be more important, or what an appellate court might choose to hang its hat on to uphold a judgment on appeal."[56]

A. Trespass Statute of Limitations: Encroachments

Good Faith Improvers and the Doctrine of Relative Hardship. Property owners need to safeguard their turf from encroachments. Courts have ordered encroachers to tear down the offending structures.[57] These suits take many forms: quiet title, trespass, ejectment, or to establish a boundary line. They need to be brought within the statute of limitations "for trespass upon injury to real property,"[58] typically three to

---

54. R.H. Helmholz, *The Saga of Van Valkenburgh v. Lutz: Animosity and Adverse Possession in Yonkers*, PROPERTY STORIES 57, 69 (Gerald Korngold & Andrew P. Morriss eds., 2004).

55. *See generally* Lawrence Berger, *Unification of the Doctrine of Adverse Possession and Practical Location in the Establishment of Boundaries*, 78 NEB. L. REV. 19 (1999); James H. Backman, *The Law of Practical Location of Boundaries and the Need for an Adverse Possession Remedy*, 1986 B.Y.U. L. REV. 957. For practical guidance, *see* CORA JACKSON, NEIGHBOR LAW: FENCES, TREES, BOUNDARIES AND NOISE (3d ed., Nolo Press 1998).

56. Paul G. Carey, Boundary Line Presentation (on file with author).

57. *Amkco, Co. v. Welborn*, 985 P.2d 757 (N.M. Ct. App. 1999) (ordering removal of encroaching truck stop because it intruded 58 feet into adjoining owner's property, consuming 9% of that owner's usable land).

58. *See, e.g.*, CAL. CIV. PROC. CODE § 338(b) (West 1982) (three years). *Field-Escandon v. DeMann*, 251 Cal. Rptr. 49 (Ct. App. 1988) (Refusing to order neighbor to remove underground sewer line in place over 25 years. Trespass statute ran 22 years ago even though buyer had neither actual knowledge nor constructive notice.).

five years from when the encroachment first became permanent and obvious.[59] Courts show little sympathy for true owners who stand by silently watching a neighbor building an elaborate encroaching structure in hopes of recovering serious compensation when the improvement is completed.

As long as the encroacher built on the wrong lot out of ignorance of the true boundary,[60] courts sometimes allow a "good faith" improver to retain the encroaching structure, labeling it an *equitable easement.* A homeowner who inadvertently constructs a swimming pool just slightly into a neighbor's lot might be allowed to keep the pool where it is. Balancing the hardships, courts sometimes require the encroaching improver to compensate the true owner.[61]

Here is what a title insurance consultant concluded about one of the few California cases[62] where the encroaching party won: "look at what he got for spending a fortune in attorney's fees: He was forced to pay the full market value of the land affected by the encroaching improvements but he did not even get the fee ownership. He received only a temporary easement that the court called an 'equitable easement.' Rumor had it that the parties were so dissatisfied with the outcome of this case that they got together after appeal and entered into some kind of settlement anyway."[63]

B. Adverse Possession

There is a long-standing tension between ownership based solely on recorded legal descriptions and the rights of parties in possession inconsistent with record ownership. An adverse possessor may be able to transfer marketable title if she can deliver to her

---

59. A fence constitutes a permanent trespass since the injury to the impacted owner remains the same as long as the fence is in place. The statute of limitations doesn't bar a cause of action for a continuing trespass. A gas station leaking oil into a subjacent aquifer would constitute a continuing trespass and the statute of limitations wouldn't bar the ground water owners from protesting fresh violations.

60. *See Goulding v. Cook,* 422 Mass. 276, 278 (1996) (Encroacher needed a leach field for a failed septic system and built it despite pending injunction in suit brought by neighbor to halt the project because the neighbor believed it was being built on his land. The state Supreme Court rejected "relative hardship" balancing test: "[t]he concept of private property represents a moral and political commitment that a pervasive disposition to balance away would utterly destroy.").

61. *Hirshfield v. Schwartz,* 91 Cal. App. 4th 749 (2001) (The appellate court sustained a trial court decision denying an injunction to prevent encroachment because removal would cause substantial hardship. Improvements consisted of a rebar-reinforced concrete block wall, pool and waterfall motors, and extensive underground utility lines. The encroachers were ordered to pay damages of $22,825 as compensation for their use of the neighbor's property and to remove all encroachments upon selling or relinquishing possession of their home. In effect, the encroacher is granted an easement as if it had exercised a private right of eminent domain, with the court ordering the encroacher to pay 'just compensation' to the true owner). For a formal argument supporting results like this one, allowing encroachments with compensation, see Thomas W. Merrill, *Property Rules, Liability Rules, and Adverse Possession,* 79 Nw. L. Rev. 1122 (1984).

62. *See Hirchfield v. Schwartz,* 91 Cal. App. 4th 749 (2001), described in footnote 63.

63. Lawrence Lacombe, *Disputes over the Location of Existing Walls or Fences in California,* CALIFORNIA LAND TITLE ASSOCIATION (last visited July 10, 2015), http://www.clta.org/for-members/legal-center-articles-and-case-summaries.html.

buyer convincing and usable evidence to support her claim without having recorded any notice of the transfer. But the title will be clouded until a court confirms the possessor's new boundary, and the adverse possessor records the judgment in the jurisdiction where the property is located.

The Elements of Adverse Possession. "The majority of adverse possession cases involve boundary disputes between neighbors."[64] To establish title by adverse possession, possession must be *open and notorious,* so as to alert the true owner that someone else is claiming ownership of her property.[65]

Someone taking possession with the owner's consent is by definition not taking possession adversely.[66] Even in the absence of express consent, an innocuous use does not give rise to a claim of adverse possession. In one such case, adverse claimants placed their garbage bins for collection weekly for a period of over fifty years on an unused patch of the true owner's land bordering an alley way. In response to the true owner's plan to create a condominium parking place on that spot, the garbage bin owner objected, asserting a claim of adverse possession. The deciding judge concluded that storing garbage bins temporarily on trash collection days was no clear indicator of a hostile adverse claim.[67]

Color of Title and Claim of Right. An adverse possession claim may be either a *claim of right* (i.e., based entirely on possession), or a *color of title* (based on a written, defective instrument which causes the claimant to hold a good faith belief of legal title).

Three consequences follow from this distinction. First, the trespasser's possession must be "*actual*" as evidenced by fences, roads, or structures. For a claim based on color of title derived from a written deed, courts look to the deed description in setting the boundaries of the adverse use, not the possessor's actual occupancy.

Second, some courts insist that a claim of right must be "*hostile*," with the adverse claimant taking possession as a trespasser intending to exercise exclusive dominion over the occupied terrain.[68] Other courts lack sympathy for claimants who consciously

---

64. Jeffery Stake, *The Uneasy Case for Adverse Possession*, 89 Geo. L.J. 2419, 2457 (2001).

65. The user "must unfurl his flag on the land, and keep it flying, so that the owner may see, if he will, that an enemy has invaded his domains, and planted the standard of conquest." *Wood v. Davidson,* 62 Cal. App. 2d 885, 890 (1944). However, the requirement of apparent hostility is often relaxed in neighbors' disputes over the use of a common driveway commenced with mutual consent, as evident in *Barber v. Peringer,* 877 P.2d 223 (Wash. Ct. App. 1994).

66. *See, e.g.,* CAL. CIV. CODE § 813 (West 1982) (entitling the record title owner to record a notice granting consent to use all or any portion of the owner's property). The recorded notice constitutes conclusive proof that any use by the public or any person is permissive. But the owner cannot thereafter block or obstruct any public use prior to recording a revocation notice. Even if the owner hasn't recorded a consent to use, actually giving consent for public use will suffice to protect the owner against claims of adverse possession or prescriptive easements.

67. Patrick A. Randolph, E-mail to BrokerDirt@umkc.edu.

68. *See Ballard v. Harman,* 737 N.E.2d 411 (Ind. Ct. App. 2000) (Holding that land was adversely possessed by Harman, who planted 50 cedar trees on a five-foot strip of neighboring land, thinking it was his in reliance on the land description in his deed which was based on an erroneous survey. By watering the trees for 18 years, he met Indiana's ten-year adverse possession period.). Other courts have reached contrary results on similar facts.

trespass and try to piggyback their original wrongdoing into absolute title. This is challenging for trial lawyers who may not be sure which position the judge is going to take until after the presentation of all the evidence concerning intent.[69]

Third, some state legislators have voted to limit adverse possession claims to color of title in order to discourage claimants from asserting title to land they know they don't own.[70]

Payment of Property Taxes in Acquiring Title by Long or Short Term Adverse Possession Periods. Payment of taxes is always powerful evidence of an adverse possessor's claim of right, though not required to establish adverse possession under the twenty-year common law period.[71]

Adverse possession statutes modify the common law doctrine in two significant ways. (1) They shorten statutory periods to three, five, seven, or ten years.[72] (2) The adverse possessor has to prove he or she paid all property taxes actually assessed on the disputed parcel.[73]

Of all the elements necessary to prove adverse possession, the requirement that the claimant have paid property taxes for the statutory period is the one that most often proves fatal to adverse possession claims based on "claim of right" and not "color of title." Remember, someone claiming adverse possession based on color of title is usually relying on a legal description in a recorded document. A "claim of right" is based on facts on the ground, not record ownership. Local property taxes are usually assessed based on record ownership, not physical possession.[74]

---

69. Lawrence Berger, *Unification of the Doctrines of Adverse Possession and Practical Location in the Establishment of Boundaries*, 78 NEB. L. REV. 19, 20 (1999).

70. State Senator Elizabeth O'C. Little, Introducer's Memorandum in Support, S.7915-C/A.11574-A (2008) (supporting New York's recently modified adverse possession statute).

71. *Ewings' Lessee v. Burnet*, 36 U.S. 41 (1837).

72. "It is three years in Texas; five years in California, Montana, and Nevada; seven years in Alaska, Arkansas, Florida, Georgia, Tennessee, Utah, and Washington; ten years in Alabama, Iowa, Mississippi, New Mexico, New York, Oregon, and Rhode Island; fifteen years in Connecticut, the District of Columbia, Kansas, and Michigan; eighteen years in Colorado; twenty years in Delaware, Idaho, Illinois, Maine, Maryland, North Carolina, North Dakota, and South Dakota; twenty-one years in Pennsylvania; and thirty or sixty years in New Jersey depending on whether the land is cultivated (thirty) or not (sixty)." Susan Lorde Martin, *Adverse Possession: Practical Realities and the Unjust Enrichment Standard*, 37 REAL EST. L.J. 133 (2008).

73. The following states have short-term adverse possession statutes that condition adverse possession on payment of property taxes: Arizona, Arkansas, California, Florida, Idaho, Illinois, Montana, Nevada, New Mexico, Utah, Washington and Wisconsin. *See, e.g.*, FLA. STAT. ANN. § 95.18 (West 2002) (adverse possession claimant lacking color of title must fill out a form with the tax assessor containing a proper legal description "within 1 year after entering into possession" and then must pay "all taxes and matured installments of special improvement liens levied against the property by the state, county, and municipality").

74. In the absence of an agreed boundary marked by a fence or wall, property owners are presumed to be paying taxes only according to the land described in their deeds. But where neighboring owners set a boundary by agreement, they are presumed to be paying taxes to the agreed boundary line regardless of where the deed appears to locate the boundary. *Townsend v. Koukol*, 416 P.2d 532 (Mont. 1966).

Tax assessors usually send tax bills to the owners of record. They seldom determine ownership by visiting the site and concluding that boundaries follow the lines of walls, fences, or cultivation patterns.

C. Prescriptive Easements

Encroachers can seldom meet the payment-of-taxes requirement because tax assessors rarely value easement interests separately. They rely on assessors' parcel maps, not on-site inspections. Easement holders typically do not record their interests because their rights derive from their actual, visible possession.

In an attempt to circumvent the payment-of-taxes requirement, encroachers often claim prescriptive easements since property tax assessors rarely value easements separately. They assume that the value of the easement is incorporated in the ownership of the adjoining "dominant" tenement. Assessors usually include the value of the right of way in the assessment of the benefitted property.

A prescriptive easement is a claim established by the usual indicia of adverse possession but not a claim of exclusive use. These claims of prescriptive easement will fail whenever they would give the claimant exclusive use of the property. A prescriptive easement boundary marked by a wall or fence effectively precludes the owner on the far side of the wall or fence using the disputed strip of land at all. Compare this to a true claim of prescriptive easement as when hikers claim a prescriptive right to use a country road located on private property. The hiker will not end up with an exclusive use that bars the true owner from sharing the easement.

Claims based on prescriptive easements are resolved by a close look at the facts of the use. When strips of land are shared by adjoining owners, disputes can easily arise over the extent, terms and conditions of the easement—its exact dimensions, the apportionment of obligations to repair and maintain the easement, speed limits, and the permissible uses or the intensity of permitted uses. The resolution of such disputes will turn on evidence of how the easement was used during the time the right to its use was being established.[75]

Sometimes, it becomes apparent that the tax assessor had not relied on a legally recorded deed description in making an assessment. For instance, in one case an entire subdivision was built out in disregard of the deed descriptions. Every owner occupied land technically belonging to his neighbor. An adverse possessor claimed one owner's property, having paid taxes based on the formal legal property description. Technically, the owner was being assessed for the vacant lot next door, not for the property he was actually occupying, yet his tax bill was for an improved parcel although the property described in the tax receipt was of a vacant lot. The court ruled that the home owner was paying taxes on the improved parcel regardless of the deed description and hence no adverse possessor could be legitimately claiming to have paid taxes on that same lot. *Sorensen v. Costa*, 196 P.2d 900 (Cal. 1948).

75. *See, e.g., Lloyd v. Purnell*, 61 Va. Cir. 463 (2003) (since the original prescriptive claim was based on a 12-foot right of way, court declared that easement claimants had no right to 15 feet right of way).

Protecting Private Owners Who Allow Hikers to Use Their Property from Claiming Prescriptive Easements. Law book publisher Nolo provides the following warning to landowners: "If hikers have been using a trail through your backyard for ten years and you've never complained, they probably have an easement by prescription through your yard to the trail."[76]

California legislation gives owners multiple ways to avoid losing control of their property to hikers and bikers claiming adverse possession or prescriptive easements without having to bring a court action to keep them away:

(1) They can record a notice that public use is by permission and subject to the owner's control.[77]

(2) They can preclude claims of prescriptive easement by posting at each entrance to the property, or at intervals of not more than 200 feet along the boundary, a sign reading substantially as follows: "Right to pass by permission, and subject to control, of owner: Section 1008, Civil Code."[78]

(3) Regardless of whether the owner has recorded under 813 or posted under 1008, no public use shall ripen into an adverse claim by the general public or a governmental body unless the owner has made an irrevocable written offer of dedication, which the local government has accepted.[79]

D. The Doctrine of Agreed Boundaries

This doctrine enables adjoining owners to modify a boundary by oral agreement, creating an exception to the Statute of Frauds requirement of a written, signed agreement to alter a boundary.[80] Attorneys with experience in boundary disputes will invariably recommend a signed agreement that precisely describes the physical location of the agreed boundary line. Owners may have misunderstood each other, could forget what they agreed, or be succeeded by uncooperative subsequent owners At a minimum, they would be hoping the agreed boundary could be evidenced by a fence, wall, or line of trees.

---

76. *Nolo's Plain-English Dictionary*, Nolo (last visited July, 10 2015) https://www.nolo.com/ dictionary/prescriptive-easement-term.html. *See also*, Ann M. Simmons, *L.A. Developer Ordered to Let Hikers Use Trail on His Land*, LA Times (last visited July 20, 2015), articles.latimes.com/2012/oct/ 19/local/la-me-hastain-trail-20121019 (reporting on a judge's ruling that hikers had a prescriptive easement to a path crossing nearly half of 97 acres neighboring a park).

77. Cal. Civ. Code § 813.

78. *Id.* at § 1008.

79. *Id.* at § 1009.

80. *Mehdizadeh v. Mincer*, 46 Cal. App. 4th 1296 (1996) (appellate court overturned trial court's attempt to compromise a dispute between two adjoining neighbors over a strip of land that their predecessors had fenced for convenience, never intending to displace the boundary of record.). *But see Orton v. Carter*, 970 P.2d 1254 (Utah 1998) (Court sanctioned continued use of common driveway originally established by mutual consent of adjoining owners. Prescriptive easement O.K. despite consensual origin of driveway use. Title by acquiescence sanctioned despite no uncertainty over location of true boundary.).

In California, courts only honor claims of agreed boundary under three conditions. (1) The owners must convincingly demonstrate that was uncertainty about the location of the boundary line. (2) To resolve the uncertainty peaceably, the owners reached an agreement to locate a new property boundary line. (3) They each accepted and acquiesced in the new property boundary line for at least five years.[81]

E. Boundary by Acquiescence[82]

Suppose the owners of two adjoining hillside properties construct a fence meandering across the true boundary so as to run along the flat portions of the site because it was easier to build the fence that way. Such a fence could be seen as the establishment of a boundary by acquiescence or could have resulted in response to an owner accommodating a neighbor's request to plant trees or construct a fence — with no intent of altering the true boundary lines. Jurisdictions differ.

In California and Washington, the idea has been rejected that long acquiescence in a fence or other barrier represents the true property line.[83] For a fence to mark the true boundary in these states without a written, signed agreement, courts require evidence that the boundary was uncertain and the owners agreed to locate the fence as their boundary.

In other states, Utah and New York among them, a long established fence or other barrier can become the true boundary if the adjoining owners act in a way that evidences their acceptance of it as the boundary.[84]

Questions

Question 1: *Understanding Legal Descriptions.*

(a) *Informal Descriptions.* What is wrong with using the postal street address as the land description in a deed? If it's good enough for MapQuest™ why isn't it good enough for a deed? What is wrong with assessors' parcel numbers?

(b) *Metes and Bounds.* Draw this description: "Beginning at an iron stake where Old Oak Tree Road intersects Plum Avenue, then continuing south 15 degrees west for a distance of fifty feet to an iron stake, then south 20 degrees east 105 feet to a

---

81. CAL. CIV. PRAC. REAL PROPERTY LITIGATION § 11:20.

82. In Pennsylvania, this is called "recognition and acquiescence." Boundary by agreement in Pennsylvania is known as boundary by "dispute and compromise." Email from William J. Maffucci to BROKERDIRT@listerv.UMKC.edu, (Aug. 4, 2013).

83. MILLER & STARR, 6 CAL. REAL EST. § 14:41 (3d ed.); James R. Ellis, *Boundary Disputes in Washington*, 23 WASH. L. REV. & ST. B. J. 125 (1948)

84. *See* 1 N.Y. JUR. 2d Adjoining Landowners § 144 ("A practical location of boundaries which has been acquiesced in for a long number of years will not be disturbed"); *RHN Corp. v. Veibell*, 96 P.3d 935, 942 (Utah. 2004) ("Courts have looked at various landowner actions as evidence of acquiescence in a visible line as a boundary").

maple tree, then north 89 degrees west for a distance of 167 feet to stone monument, then north 45 degrees east 200 feet."[85] Does the description form a fully enclosed area?

(c) *Government Survey.* What is the approximate acreage of this site: N 1/2 SE 1/4, SW 1/4, S24, T32N, R18E.[86]

(d) What could a grantee learn by studying the details of a subdivision map that was incorporated into the legal description of her deed?

Question 2: *Types of Survey Language in Realty Sales Agreements.*

(a) What type of survey condition should a home buyer place in her purchase and sale agreement if she wants to be sure her swimming pool does not encroach on the neighbor's land?

(i) "Subject to any state of facts a survey would reveal."

(ii) "Buyer may disapprove title based on the survey."

(iii) "Buyer's approval of survey is a condition of buyer's obligation to buy."

(b) Which of the above conditions would the seller prefer?

Question 3: *Ordering the Right Survey.*

An institutional lender, as a condition to funding a real estate investor's acquisition of a downtown office tower, insists upon the investor commissioning a survey.

(a) What questions need to be answered in the investor's contract with the surveyor?

(b) What type of survey will the lender probably require of the investor?

(c) Why won't a boundary survey suffice?

Question 4: *Liability for Faulty Surveys.*

How can the purchaser of a lot in a new subdivision make sure she doesn't become liable to her buyer years from now for a survey error made by the original subdivider?

Question 5: *Resolving Boundary Disputes.*

(a) An attorney observes in a blog:[87] Every year, I get calls from clients who need help resolving boundary disputes with their neighbors. One such dispute involved an adjacent neighbor who built a wall on the client's property. Another involved a neighbor who built a barn partially over the client's property line. And another involved a client who owned property on which a neighbor constructed storage sheds. What questions would you ask each of these clients before deciding whether to take the case, and what advice would you give them?

---

85. For a website where you can generate the map for this description, *see Platting Deeds in Metes and Bounds,*(last visited Mar. 6, 2008), http://www.genealogytools.net/deeds.

86. With this example comes a good place to learn how to map descriptions from government surveys: (last visited Feb 19, 2016), http://dnr.wi.gov/topic/forestmanagement/documents/plss tutorial.pdf.

87. Tony Buchignani, *Boundary Disputes Between Neighbors — The Basics*, Los Angles Real Estate Lawyers Blog, (last visited Jan. 2, 2016), http://losangelesrealestatelawyerblog.com/index.php/2014/10/02/boundary-disputes-between-neighbors-the-basics/.

This question appeared in a "Real Estate: Questions and Answers" column in the Los Angeles Times:[88]

(b) We bought our home about 25 years ago. Last year, the house next door was sold. The nice young couple who bought it had a survey made. It says my garage is located about one foot on their side of the property line. This garage was built almost 35 years ago when our house was constructed. The new neighbor is a lawyer and he said I will have to move my garage off "his" property because he doesn't want me to acquire title by adverse possession. What should I do?

Consult a lawyer, you say, but if you are the lawyer, what advice should you give?[89]

Question 6: *Preventing the Casual Location of a Fence from Changing the Boundary.*

(a) When your neighbor asks whether it's OK to construct a fence between your yard and hers, are you potentially forfeiting title to property that belongs to you if the fence is built on your side of the boundary?

(b) How can you avoid inadvertently surrendering title to any of your land and still allow the neighbor to build her fence without incurring the cost of a survey?

Question 7: *Preventing Hikers from Becoming Easement Holders.*

What advice would you offer to the owner of a pristine open space, enjoyed by hikers, who welcomes sharing the terrain but would like someday to develop it, free of adverse possession or prescriptive easement claims?

---

88. Dec. 17, 1989, at K4.

89. *See Faulconer v. Williams*, 936 P.2d 999 (Or. Ct. App. 1997) (Quieting title to innocent possessor based on adverse possession, long use of a portion of the property which a prior grantor had once conveyed for a road easement but which had never been used for that purpose. No evidence that the owners of the adversely possessed strip ever realized it was their property being used).

Chapter 8

Recording Laws and Public Land Records[1]

Scope of the Chapter

This chapter is about the role of recording laws and public land records in facilitating the orderly ownership and transfer of real estate. It contains:

(1) A general overview of the recording system of title assurance and a definition of the terms necessary to understand it;

(2) A description of the main gaps in the recording system, and how title insurance fills them;

(3) A comparison of the three main types of recording statutes that states have enacted;

(4) An explanation of the mechanics of how public land records systems work, focusing on the distinction between when a document is presented to a clerk in the recorder's office ("*filed*") for record and when it becomes functionally accessible to the public by being *indexed*;

(5) An important exception to the usual recording act priorities rules called equitable subrogation, when a mortgage lender is entitled to the priority of an earlier recorded mortgage by paying it off.

I. An Introduction to the Links between the Recording System and Title Insurance

Buyers and mortgage lenders need to know, before they pay for their properties or make their loans, that their titles and security interests will be what they bargained for. In the U.S., we rely on a combination of public land records and private title insurance, working in tandem. The state-enacted recording acts and locally maintained public land records are nothing new in the U.S.; they date back to colonial times.[2]

---

1. The author is grateful to Scott Talkoff for his invaluable contributions to this chapter as a perceptive scholar and an effective litigator.

2. The system of publicly recording land title documents started in the United States in 1640, in the Plymouth and Massachusetts Bay Colonies. Jesse Dukeminier, et al., Property 559 (2006).

Without a system of public land records, buyers, mortgage lenders, other lien creditors, and title insurers would be dependent solely on what they could learn about ownership and other interests in a particular site by what they could deduce physically inspecting the property and reviewing the documents that property owners retained to establish proof of ownership. *Buyers and lenders would be taking substantial risks because many interests in land are not visible on a physical inspection of the property, including mortgages and tax liens, underground utility easements, and the claims of absentee owners.*

Relying on privately kept records would also be problematic. Property owners could retain deeds and other real estate documents tracing their ownership back in time, but there would be no way to verify that the documents retained were authentic, complete, and comprehensive.

Ancient Greek Horoi (mortgage stone) set up on mortgaged lands and homes to convey public notice of mortgages.[3]

The recording system provides a safe place where all the written documents pertaining to the ownership of each parcel of real estate within the jurisdiction are received, copied, indexed, and publicly accessible. The system is designed to protect buyers and mortgage lenders from prior secret "liens, conveyances, or encumbrances" that could invalidate or de-value their interests.[4]

Recording System Drawbacks; Recordation Is No Guaranty of Validity. This system has significant drawbacks. Public land records are like libraries. Members of the public have free access to these records but are on their own when it comes to determining the validity or title implications of what they find there. Recording office indexes are complicated, and searching them can be laborious.

---

3. http://www.ascsa.edu.gr/pdf/uploads/hesperia/146892.pdf.

4. Ronald C. Wescott, *Recording Acts,* (last visited July 2, 2015), http://www.ascsa.edu.gr/pdf/uploads/hesperia/146892.pdf

Recordation does not guaranty the validity of a seller's deed or a lender's mortgage or deed of trust.[5] Recording office personnel are not empowered to identify the true owner of any particular property, or to verify the authenticity of the liens recorded against it. Recorders do not look beyond the four corners of the document itself to safeguard against deeds that are forged, fictitious, or otherwise fraudulent.

Recorders' offices in California have instituted measures to deter fraud. They require notaries to take the fingerprints of grantors and mortgagors, and they notify home-owners when mortgages are recorded against their properties. Nonetheless, county recorders are not responsible for the authenticity or legitimacy of the documents they record. Their job is just to collect recording fees, notify the tax assessor of where to send the new owner's property tax bill, and require that certain formalities appear to have been met, such as that the documents were properly notarized. When recorders err in their limited assigned tasks, those who suffer a loss may have a statutory or common law cause of action in negligence against the recorder.[6] However, negligence claims can be costly to pursue, and are often denied.

Owners whose titles have been compromised by forged or fraudulently obtained documents can sue the perpetrators for slander of title, obtain court decrees of quiet title to re-establish the marketability of their ownership,[7] and seek felony prosecutions of the offenders. But meanwhile, forged or fraudulently obtained deeds remain of record with no way for prospective buyers or mortgage lenders to know that the recorded deed could be invalid, unless the owner has filed a law suit and recorded a notice of it in the public land records.

How Title Insurance Fills the Gaps Left by The Recording System. Title insurance fills some of these gaps. For a one-time premium, title insurers promise to indemnify the owner or mortgage lender against loss or damage from the title being different from what the title policy insured.

The title insurance process begins, typically, when an intermediary—an escrow agent, closing attorney, or title insurer, requests that a title company prepare a title insurance policy. "When a title company receives a request for a title insurance policy, the first step is an examination of the public records."[8] Based on what their search of the public records shows, title companies prepare documents for prospective buyers and mortgage lenders that are called *preliminary reports* or *policy commitments*.

---

5. Barlow Burke, Law of Title Insurance 2.01[B], 17 (3d ed., Aspen L. & Bus. 2000); *see also* Charles Szypszak, *Public Registries and Private Solutions: An Evolving American Real Estate Conveyancing Regime*, 24 Whittier L. Rev. 663 (2003).

6. Cal. Govt. Code § 27203 (West 1988). *See also* Annotation, *Recording Officer's Liability*, 94 A.L.R. 1301 (1935).

7. Wayne S. Bell & Summer B. Bakotich, *What Should You Do If you Learn That a Forge and/or Fraudulent Deed Has Been Recorded Against Your Property?*, Dre.Ca.Gov (last visited July 22, 2015), http://www.dre.ca.gov/files/pdf/ca/2012/ConsumerAlert_ForgedFraudulentDeeds.pdf.

8. Charles J. Jacobus & Bruce M. Harwood, Georgia Real Estate 108 (1995).

In the course of searching the history of a title, the title company may come across indications of defects, liens or encumbrances. Title companies may be able to cure some defects, perhaps by having someone with a potential interest sign a document releasing that interest to the present owner, buyer or mortgage lender, and recording the curative document. Title companies sometimes assume the risk of loss for defects they believe are unlikely to result in loss, for example, a restrictive covenant placed on the property during the era of prohibition that bans the sale of alcohol in a neighborhood now known for its fashionable drinking and dining establishments. A title insurer would exclude or except[9] from insurance policy coverage the interest of a spouse in a community property state who refused to sign the deed.

In these situations, the title company will disclose the defect to the insured in a preliminary title report or commitment. For instance, the policy might except from coverage any loss or damage arising from the non-consenting co-tenant ever claiming an interest in the property. A prospective buyer or lender will have to decide whether to close the deal anyway and live with the risk posed by the excepted co-owner or terminate the transaction and get back the down payment.

Most documents affecting real estate are recorded promptly after being signed. Timing is important because unrecorded interests, with few exceptions, are legally unmarketable and susceptible to being subordinated to competing claims recorded earlier.[10]

II. Key Concepts, Definitions, and Descriptions

A. Registration

The Difference between Registration and Recording Systems. Once you buy a car, you register your ownership with the Department of Motor Vehicles (DMV) which maintains a computerized database of ownership and auto loans.[11] Unlike the public land records systems in most states that are basically just libraries for collecting real estate-related documents, state law requires the DMV to determine the "genuineness, regularity and legality of the application,"[12] and to reject any car ownership application when it has "reasonable ground to believe the issuance of a certificate of title would constitute fraud against the rightful owner or other person having a valid lien upon such vehicle."[13]

---

9. Exclusions are of general applicability while exceptions arise from issues affecting a particular property.

10. *See* Benito Arruñada, *A Transaction Cost View of Title Insurance and Its Role in Different Legal Systems*, GENEVA PAPERS ON RISK INS. 582–88 (2002) (stating that rights of unrecorded parties in possession are commonly excepted from title insurance policies).

11. CAL. VEH. CODE § 1800 (West 2014).

12. *See, e.g.*, Mich. Comp. Laws Ann. § 257.209 (West 2014).

13. *Id.* § 257.219.

In some states and many other countries, there are similar *registration systems* for land ownership.[14] Before accepting a document for inclusion in such a system, a public official verifies the validity of the claimed title or lien,[15] and issues a confirming certificate of title which becomes proof of ownership.[16] Title passes to the grantee at the moment of registration, in the absence of fraud by the purchaser.

In Minnesota where both a recording and a registration exist side-by-side, "the registrar will not only inspect the documents for compliance with recording standards, as the county recorder must do, but also will inspect the document's validity. Is the document made by the registered owner or another party with an interest shown on the certificate? Does it accurately describe the land? Have all necessary parties joined in making the instrument? If all requirements are met the registrar will accept the instrument for registration and 'memorialize' it on the certificate of title."[17]

New owners report to the registrar any changes affecting the title, along with a memorandum of transfer executed by the registered proprietor. Then, the registrar enters the changes into the certificate of title. When the certificate of title is full, the registrar issues a new certificate. Anyone who examines the current certificate, and the memorials added to it, can easily determine the current state of the title.

Opinions differ on whether there is any need for private title insurance where registration systems are the norm.[18] Not wanting to risk that the need for their services could be diminished or even eliminated entirely, title insurers in the U.S. have strongly opposed efforts to create state-managed registration systems. Still, registration systems leave enough uncertainty that title insurers operate successfully even in jurisdictions that use registration systems.[19] One reason is that registration systems are seldom funded sufficiently to assure full compensation to property owners who fall prey to

---

14. Terminology may vary from place to place. In Ontario, Canada, for instance, "land registries" are comparable to U.S. recording systems. Their "registration" equivalent is called the Land Titles System. "As of March 2011, approximately 99.9% of properties in Ontario were recorded under the Land Titles System and had been automated from paper-based to electronic form." http://www.teranet.ca/land-registration-system-ontario?popup=1

15. The limits on the Registrar's authority to accept or reject proffered transfers for registration have given rise to considerable litigation. *See* Douglas J. Whelan, The Torrens System in Australia 145-53 (1982).

16. Australia's registration system is among the best, often referred to as the 'Torrens' system, a tribute to its earliest, most effective designer and advocate, Robert Richard Torrens, appointed Registrar-General of the State of South Australia in 1852. Douglas J. Whelan, The Torrens System in Australia 12 (1982) ("Torrens system law owes its origins and success to the magnificent efforts of Robert Richard Torrens").

17. Kimball Foster, Certificates of Possessory Title: A Sensible Addition to Minnesota's Successful Torrens System, 40 William Mitchell L. Rev. 1, 114 (2013).

18. Michael Ziemer, *The Good, Title Insurance—The Bad and The Ugly: Does Victoria Need It?* 2011 APLJ Lexis 10.

19. Shaun Watchie Perry, Outline of the Torrens System, GP/Solo Law Trends and News, Real Estate (ABA Aug 2005). http://www.americanbar.org/newsletter/publications/law_trends_news _practice_area_e_newsletter_home/torrenact.html

adverse claims based on forgery, fraud, or negligent administration despite their certificates of title.

Iowa's Registration System: An Alternative to Title Insurance. At one time, attorneys were prominent participants in real estate sales. Property owners had to depend on specially commissioned "abstracts of title" which were essentially copies or originals of all the documents affecting the history of a particular ownership. Local attorneys then prepared opinion letters based on a review of the documents in the abstract. Besides being expensive and cumbersome, the system required clients who incurred a loss due to a flawed lawyer's opinion to prove that the lawyer had been negligent, and to prove it in a forum dominated by other lawyers. Even after obtaining a favorable judgment, collecting on the judgment could be a challenge.

In most states, title insurers working hand-in-hand with real estate brokers (and their printed forms) have dislodged real estate attorneys from their dominance in closing real estate transfers—though attorneys have often rigorously defended their turf in residential real estate closings with mixed results.[20]

In Iowa, attorneys found a way to retain their hegemony in the real estate transfer business. They created a state title guaranty system based upon land registration to prevent title insurers from edging lawyers out of the real estate transactions business. Sealing their dominance, in 1947, Iowa banned the in-state sale of title insurance, though some Iowa lenders can and do purchase title insurance out-of-state.

Iowa attorneys contend that widespread dependence on title insurance tends to diminish the quality of titles and takes the pressure off of state and local authorities to update their recording systems. The state of Iowa has raised funds from recording fees for a statewide electronically-accessible system of public land records.[21] This makes it unnecessary for anyone to look to private title plants for the efficient management of land records.[22]

Iowa's titles have been called the cleanest in the country,[23] which is part of the reason Iowa's title guaranty fund earns millions of dollars each year, which is earmarked for various state-sponsored housing programs.[24] Title guarantees cost Iowa homeowners about 10% of what title insurers charge homeowners in other states for comparable coverage.[25] "While the Iowa system has merit, it is not easy to replicate.

---

20. Melissa K. Walker, *Sharing Their Piece of the Real Estate Pie: An Analysis of the Necessity of Lawyers at Residential Real Estate Closings in the Context of the Adoption of Recent Opinions of the North Carolina State Bar*, 26 CAMPBELL L. REV. 58 (April 2004).

21. IOWA LAND RECORDS, (last visited July 10, 2015), http://iowalandrecords.org/portal/.

22. As we will see later in this chapter, tract based indices are far superior to grantor-grantee indexes—though both types of indices are needed. Private title plants usually have both types. Most public land records only have the more cumbersome grantor-grantee indices. Not Iowa.

23. *See* Melynda Dovel Wilcox, *Home Buyers Beware: You Pay the Price for Title Insurance Coverage. But Everyone Else Reaps the Benefits*, KIPLINGER'S PERS. FIN. 97, 98–100 (Oct. 2001) (classifying Iowa's title system as unique).

24. Shannon S. Strickler, *Iowa's Title Guaranty System: Is It Superior to Other States' Commercial Title Insurance?*, 51 DRAKE L. REV. 385, 391 (2003).

25. Scott Wooley, *Inside America's Richest Insurance Racket*, FORBES, p. 148, Nov. 13, 2006.

It would have to be adopted state by state, and some would surely muck it up [by designing their systems poorly and not staffing them well]."[26]

The Iowa system has a few drawbacks. It takes far longer to process a title in Iowa than in most states that depend on title insurance. Also, the system has no mechanism for providing title coverage against minor off-record risks. Further, while lenders avail themselves of the bargain title assurance available in Iowa, homeowners are less informed and tend to buy neither state-offered title guarantees nor out-of-state title insurance.[27] But to the extent that Iowa's registration system is reliable and no problems arise in a particular transaction, buying neither a title policy or a state title guarantee may benefit most buyers and sellers by reducing their total transaction costs.

B. Key Definitions

Abstract of Title. An abstract of title is a chronological account of all the documents affecting title to a particular property or estate.

The abstract could be drawn up either by an attorney or a specialist known as an abstractor. The abstractor might certify the accuracy of his own work, and the abstract could also be accompanied by a legal opinion confirming that the supporting documents prove the current ownership of the property. In some places, title companies issue policies based on abstracts. "Abstracts do not show hidden items, such as the contractual capacity of a grantor, a forged or altered document in the chain of title, an unknown spousal interest, failure of delivery, or unrecorded documents."[28]

Chain of Title. A complete chain of title would depict the provenance of the present holder's claim of ownership. At the present owner's root of title would be a conveyance from an original source of title, perhaps from the sovereign, through a succession of intermediate owners, each connected to its predecessor in the chain. The basic format of a chain of title is as simple as this: Public grant of ownership to A, A to B, B to C, C to D, D to the present owner. The chain would only be as strong as its weakest link. So, for instance, a forged deed anywhere in the chain invalidates all the conveyances that came after it.

Although such elaborate chains of title traced back to the sovereign are rarely required in day-to-day practice, they are theoretically possible to construct under the recording systems in the U.S. The fact that they could is an ultimate assurance of title legitimacy. Otherwise, just about anyone could record a series of bogus deeds, with "made up" grantors and grantees, portraying a seemingly unbroken succession of titles supporting a present claimant with absolutely no legitimate basis for claiming ownership of the property.

---

26. The Mortgage Professor, *What's Wrong With the Title Insurance Industry?* (last visited July 8, 2015), http://www.mtgprofessor.com/A%20-%20Title%20Insurance/what's_wrong_with_the_title_insurance_industry.htm

27. Shannon S. Strickler, *Iowa's Title Guaranty System: Is It Superior to Other States' Commercial Title Insurance?*, 51 Drake L. Rev. 385,398-99 (2003).

28. William A. Pivar & Roobert J. Bruss, California Real Estate Law 463 (8th ed. 2013).

Wild Deeds. A person's entire chain of title must be recorded before she can be a protected party under the recording acts. The term "wild deed" refers to a gap in the chain of title. This happens when Grantor A conveys Blackacre to Grantor B, but there is no record of any deed by which A acquired title. A's title would be unmarketable and so would B's. As soon as the title insurer for A or A's buyer discovers this problem, it will take the measures necessary to establish a recorded provenance of A's ownership. What the title insurer needs to do can range from simply recording an affidavit to bringing a suit to quiet title—depending on how the gap in the chain of title occurred.

These gaps can originate when a landowner dies and nothing is placed of record concerning future ownership—no probate court decree, no affidavit of death and heirship, no will, no transfer-on-death deed, nothing.

A change of name can also lead to a wild deed situation. Here is one way a wild deed can pop up. Sally acquired title to her home as Sally Jones. Many years after marrying Len Choy, she conveyed title as Sally Choy. She did not give a second thought to how she should sign the deed because she had been using the name Sally Choy for decades. Inadvertently, she broke her chain of title by neglecting to record any document showing the connection between Sally Jones and Sally Choy. With nothing of record to substantiate that Sally Jones was Sally Choy, the deed from Sally Choy would be a wild deed. She should have conveyed title as "Sally Choy formerly known as Sally Jones, *and the two names refer to the same person.*"

Disputes over slight name discrepancies can also result in wild deeds although it is challenging to predict how courts might resolve such disputes.[29] Try these yourself:

(1) Is "Martin A. Harrison III" also "Martin Harrison III"?[30]

(2) Are "James J. Johnson" and "James Johnson" the same person?[31]

---

29. *See, e.g., J.I. Case Credit v. Barton*, 621 F. Supp. 610 (E.D. Ark. 1985). Judgment creditors had filed and recorded notice of their lien in the county where the debtor inherited property. He had signed financing statements as "Bill Barton." He acquired title and contracted to sell the real estate as "William Franklin Barton, Jr." The abstract company was held liable for not searching, finding and showing the recorded abstract of judgment against "Bill Barton." The court reasoned thusly: "Bill" is more than a mere nickname for "William." "In the Southern highlands ... diminutives are widely used and 'any highlander is lucky if he escapes with his original first name.'" *Id.* at 612. (Court quoting H.L. Mencken quoting Dr. Josia I. Combs). The "Jr." is dropped because Bill's parents were both dead. Omission of the middle name is not dispositive because the common law did not recognize middle names or middle initials.

30. Yes. *Voelkel v. Harrison*, 572 So. 2d 724 (La. 1990).

31. No. *First Fin. Bank, F.S.B. v. Johnson*, 477 So. 2d 1267 (La. 1985).

Louisiana lawmakers have since adopted a statute preserving the lien priority of mortgages despite their failure to include middle initials or "any reasonable variation of the mortgagor's name...." (LA. REV. STAT. ANN. §9:2728 (West 1991). The Louisiana legislature only reconciled the discrepancy between judicial districts' treatment of slight name differences for mortgages. The old disparities could arise for leases, deeds, easements, and all other documents.

In some computerized digital data systems, title searchers could be able to access all the documents pertaining to a particular parcel. But they will still have to decide whether John Jones, John J. Jones, and J.J. Jones are the same person.

Wild deeds can arise by forgery. The forger records to himself a deed of the true owner's property, either using the record owner's name as grantor or simply deeds the property from himself to himself.

In a recent variant of these all-too-common schemes, the felons had the idea of taking advantage of the five-year period for establishing adverse possession with payment of taxes. They knew that the tax assessor would probably mail the tax bills to them, relying on their names having appeared as grantees on deeds to themselves that they forged from incapacitated or deceased owners of record. When caught, such perpetrators are prosecuted.

Gaps in title can arise from documents, though actually recorded, not being regarded as part of the legally recognized chain of title to a particular parcel of land. For example, tract developers usually draft reciprocal easements and covenants meant to govern all the lots in a subdivision. Such documents should be referenced in each deed that the subdivider grants as houses are sold. But sometimes subdividers only reference or include these easements and covenants in the deed to the first lot conveyed and recorded. Purchasers of lots created or sold later would only learn about these earlier easements and covenants by chance, or if informed by their title insurers. Are those later purchasers bound by the covenants and easements appearing only in the title to Lot 1 of the subdivision in which their lot is located? According to one learned authority, maybe, maybe not.

There are two more or less equally balanced views on whether the recording and indexing of the first conveyance gives notice to the subsequent purchasers of other lots in the subdivision.[32] When all of the houses in a tract share a uniform appearance, buyers may be regarded as having been put on "inquiry" notice that the uniformity might not be just coincidence but could have resulted from recorded restrictions meant to apply to the entire tract.

The oracular "black letter law" is that chain-of-title rules are based on what a diligent title searcher would find in a reasonable, chronological search. Disputes arise in the confusing shadows of terms like reasonable and diligent. They are legal conclusions, not clear behavioral guidelines for title searchers.

Big changes to chain of title rules may be coming with computerized digital access, which allows non-chronological, expeditious, expansive title searches parcel by parcel,

---

32. Richard Powell, POWELL ON REAL PROPERTY 82-91 (1993). For a case consistent with the first view, see *Citizens for Covenant Compliance v. Anderson*, 906 P.2d 1314 (Cal. Ct. App. 1995) (Holding that CC&Rs for a subdivision could be enforced against an owner even though not in his deed, where the subdivision plan is recorded before execution of the contract of sale. The court held that this rule would be applied retroactively).

and also obviates the need for a trip to the recorder's office to pull old volumes from the shelves to find the copy of a particular deed or mortgage. The best public recording offices are moving to digital, on-line recordation of documents, augmented by high-speed scanning, the use of digital signatures and notary seals, acceptance of recording fees by wire transfer, and public accessibility via Internet.

Online access may be free or fee based. Where records are unavailable online, they need to be obtained in person or by written request.[33]

How Far Back Must the Title Search Be? The number of years varies from state to state that must be searched back in the public records to verify the present owner's chain of title.

In states with *Marketable Title Acts*, forty years is the predominant norm.[34] An owner having an unbroken chain of record title going back forty years or longer is considered to have marketable title. Marketable title acts also validate titles based on proof of continuous possession for forty years by the present owner and the present owner's claimed predecessors in title. The Marketable Title Acts conclusively presume that a reasonable inquiry of the possessor would have revealed the identity of the fee simple owner from whom the possessor derived its interest.[35]

Government-held realty is exempt from the requirements of marketable title acts.

Sometimes, in tracing that title back past forty years, it turns out that the root of title was a wild deed. As discussed earlier, a wild deed anywhere in a chain of title invalidates every later conveyance. Despite this, many courts have confirmed titles as marketable upon wild deeds.[36]

A serious trap for the unwary holder of a non-possessory interest in real estate appears in every marketable title act. "Owners whose non-possessory interests are based on an instrument recorded earlier than the requisite statutory period risk losing their interests unless they record a timely Notice of Intent to Preserve."[37] Suppose an environmentally minded owner of undeveloped open space grants a conservation easement over Blackacre to an environmental organization to prohibit construction in perpetuity. Forty-one years later, the owner passes away, leaving the "residual" of his

---

33. Land Records and Deeds Resources, http://publicrecords.onlinesearches.com/Land-Records-and-Deeds.htm

34. *State v. Hess*, 684 N.W.2d 414, 427 (Minn. 2004).

35. *See, e.g.*, CAL. CIV. CODE § 880.240, exempting: "The interest of a person in possession (including use or occupancy) of real property and the interest of a person under whom a person in possession claims, to the extent the possession would have been revealed by reasonable inspection or inquiry."

36. *See, e.g., Esterholdt v. Pacifico*, 301 P. 3d 1086 (Wyo. 2013).

37. The requirement that the holders of future interests re-record was subject to repeated challenges as a violation of the Contract Clause of the U.S. Constitution. It was upheld in California, Iowa, Kentucky, and Nebraska, and invalidated in New York. At the inception of a Marketable Title Act, the holders of interests, potentially terminable under the Act, are given a period of years during which to preserve their claims by re-recording a notice of intent or forfeit for failure to re-record, forfeit. This opportunity at the inception of the law in each state to preserve dormant interests of record older than the statutory period contributed significantly to the statutes surviving attacks as unconstitutionally confiscatory of property rights.

estate to Cousin Ida, a vacation resort developer. She could possibly claim title to the property and develop it free of the easement unless the environmental organization had re-recorded the conservation easement.[38]

The Uniform Simplification of Land Transfers Act recommends 30 years but states enacting it have varied the time periods, ranging from 22 to 50 years. In other states, the search is limited to the period for establishing title by adverse possession.[39]

Title insurers usually look no further than the last time the title was insured.

Bona Fide Purchasers. The term 'purchaser' includes tenants, mortgagees, easement holders, and "anyone who acquires any interest in property for a valuable consideration."[40] A bona fide purchaser ("BFP") (1) pays valuable consideration for property and (2) has no inkling or notice of any prior adverse claim. The significance of this status will become apparent in the next section describing the three distinct types of recording acts.

Valuable Consideration. "Valuable consideration" need not equal "fair market value." Any reasonable price will do, just so long as the purchase price is not so much of a bargain that it looks like the seller's title is probably bogus: "Hey pal, wanna buy this genuine Rolex watch for twenty bucks — all cash?"

The requirement of "valuable consideration" denies gift recipients (donees) the status under the recording acts of being treated as BFPs–at least until they take possession and improve the property. Similarly, charitable organizations receiving gifts of real estate cannot be sure that the donor had not earlier given or sold the same property to someone else. Donees would not be protected by the recording acts against prior grantees even after recording the gift. At most, their recording protects them from subsequent purchasers from the donor. This is why many donees rush to sell donated realty quickly.

Example: Owner deeds Blackacre to Save the Pets Foundation, then to Save the Children Fund. Which has better title? If the Pets Foundation records before the owner deeds the property to anyone else, it has good title. Suppose the Pets Foundation doesn't record. No matter. Save the Children Fund is not a BFP and cannot claim the benefit of most recording acts which only confer priority to subsequent purchasers over the holders of prior unrecorded interests. Hence, this dispute between the two charities will be resolved by the common law priority rules. Basically, first in time is first in right — with one wrinkle.[41] In this example, the title would belong to the Pet Foundation even though it never recorded it's interest.

---

38. Jennifer Cohoon McStotts, *In Perpetuity Or For Forty Years, Whichever Is Less: The Effect Of Marketable Record Title Acts On Conservation And Preservation Easements,* 27 J. LAND RESOURCES & ENVTL. L. 41 (2007).

39. Wendy Lathrop, Record Research: Paper Versus Ground Truth in Mitchell G. Williams, Land Surveys 193,195 (2d ed. 1999).

40. 6A POWELL ON REAL PROPERTY 82-9 (1992 ed.).

41. There is some authority for an exception when the earlier interest is equitable in nature and the later interest is legal and held by a BFP.

Notice. A prospective purchaser with any type of "notice" of a prior adverse interest is not a bona fide purchaser (BFP). Notice can be: (1) actual knowledge, (2) inquiry notice, (3) imputed notice, or (4) constructive notice.

Actual Knowledge. 'Actual knowledge' is what the buyer really knows. Even if the buyer denies knowledge, the finder of fact can conclude otherwise based on circumstantial evidence.[42]

Inquiry Notice (aka Implied Actual Notice).[43] To qualify for BFP status, a person cannot be willfully obtuse. Prospective buyers, lenders, or others need to pay attention to "such facts as would lead any honest man, using ordinary caution, to make further inquiries."[44] They need to ask pointed questions regarding any apparent facts that cast sufficient doubt on the grantor's claim of ownership,[45] and perhaps to make a more thorough investigation.[46] A potential purchaser acquires title subject to the interests that such an inquiry would have disclosed, by neglecting to make what a judge or jury later decides would have been a reasonable inquiry.

Inquiry notice sometimes leads to very costly, fact-based litigation. Here are examples:

(1) Someone other than the record owner occupies a house that a buyer contracts to purchase. Neighbors tell the prospective buyer that the occupant was a tenant because that was the word around the neighborhood, and what the listing broker told the buyer. So the trusting buyer made no direct inquiries. In fact, the occupant was in possession under an earlier purchase-and-sale contract. The seller was either trying

---

42. *Uccello v. Laudenslayer,* 44 Cal. App. 3d 504, 514 n.4 (Ct. App. 1975).

43. It can be difficult to distinguish between inquiry and constructive notice. For a case where the notice could be easily classified as either constructive or inquiry, see *Port Arthur Towing Co. v. Ownes-Ill., Inc.,* 352 F. Supp. 392 (W.D. La. 1972), *aff'd,* 492 F.2d 688 (5th Cir. 1974) (where recorded lease indicated that it was subject to five options to renew and lease was still in effect after initial 10-year term had expired, purchaser had constructive notice from recorded instruments of potential burden of lease and took subject to it).

44. *Tibble v. Wells,* 455 B.R. 648, 655(2011).

45. Richard Powell, POWELL ON REAL PROPERTY 82-57 (1992 ed.).

46. Purchasers aren't expected to detect adverse claims absent suspicious circumstances. For instance, apartment house owners sometimes lease laundry space to firms who provide and maintain coin operated washers and dryers with the parties to the lease splitting the 'take.' A buyer wouldn't be on inquiry notice of the seller's having entered such a lease by the presence of a small sign in the laundry room stating whom to call for repairs, naming the laundry machine lessee. *Pepe Coin Laundries, Inc. v. Catovest Int'l, Inc.,* 820 So. 2d 947 (Fla. Dist. Ct. App. 2002). On the other hand, the buyer of a golf course surrounded by homes had a duty to inquire of the adjoining homeowners whether they claimed rights to the continued existence of the golf course–even though there was nothing in the chain of title to the golf course land itself limiting its use to golf course purposes. All the recorded documents restricting use of the golf course appeared in the title of the dominant tenements. The court held the golf course buyers to have been on inquiry notice of the abutting homeowners' rights. The court explicitly noted that the seller had refused to warrant that there were no restrictions on the development of the site, and the purchase price was based on the assumption that the land would remain as a golf course. *Shalimar Ass'n v. D.O.C. Enterprises, Ltd.,* 142 Ariz. 36 (Ct. App. 1984).

to sell the same house twice or just wanted a "back-up" offer if the first sale fell through. The occupant vehemently denies having ever told anyone anything about why she was in possession.

If the second buyer has inquiry notice of the prior contract, she takes title subject to it. If the second buyer closes escrow without notice of the occupant's prior purchase contract, she would have priority and could evict the occupant.

(2) A 200-acre vacant site, visible from a well-traveled road, contains 30 billboards. Would a prospective buyer need to contact each of the billboard lessees to make sure the site owner has correctly portrayed the provisions in the 30 leases?

(3) Is the prospective buyer of a 160-unit apartment building on inquiry notice that the landlord had granted one of the tenants an option to purchase the building for a price 20% lower than the buyer's contract price?

Would the purchaser's inquiry notice obligation be different, had there been only one billboard on the vacant site, or the property under contract was a duplex? Whether the buyer would be expected to collect signed statements describing their interests (called estoppel certificates) would be a matter of general local real estate transactions practice.

Imputed Notice. Suppose a buyer is about to take title to property that is subject to an unrecorded mortgage. The buyer knows nothing about the mortgage. But if one of the buyer's agents does—it could be the buyer's escrow agent, real estate broker, or mortgage broker, the buyer would take title subject to the mortgage. Anything a buyer's agent knows is imputed to the buyer. Imputation is a harsh legal fiction. It is counterfactual since the principal is treated as knowing something she did not actually know. In this situation, the buyer would either have to pay off the mortgage or risk losing the house through a foreclosure sale.

Imputation does not bar principals from demanding reimbursement from agents who expose them to claims from innocent third parties.

The conventional justifications for imputation are to incentivize real estate buyers, mortgage lenders, lessees and other principals to select honest agents, encourage candor, and avoid conspiring with sleazy agents. In any event, when an agent's bad conduct inflicts a loss on several innocents, there is some justice in allocating the loss to the person who selected the agent.

Constructive Notice. The recording acts hold subsequent purchasers responsible for what they could have reasonably learned from a diligent search of public records. This is properly referred to as "constructive notice." Generally, the public records deemed to impart constructive notice are the land records maintained by the register of deeds and a collection of the plat maps recorded for each new subdivision in the jurisdiction.

Constructive notice has its limits. Not every recorded document imparts constructive notice. For a lease to be valid, it must be signed by the lessor and the lessee.

Neither one acting alone can create a valid lease even though the document is indexed and copied in the public land records. Only a grantor can deed property. So a deed signed only by the grantee conveys nothing. The same goes for a mortgage. A mortgagee cannot encumber the mortgagor's property without the mortgagor's signature on the mortgage instrument.

During the mortgage boom and bust of 2005–2008, over-worked and understaffed mortgage lenders — too frazzled to pay attention to properties' legal descriptions — sometimes recorded satisfactions of mortgages that had not actually been repaid. Upon discovering their error in releasing the liens of the lenders they were working for, some employees hurriedly recorded affidavits documenting their mistakes. A mortgage lender would have recourse against a mortgage borrower who knew perfectly well that the recordation of the satisfaction of mortgage was a mistake.

Property Tax Records Do Not Impart Constructive Notice. The concept of constructive notice does not extend to property tax records. This is unfortunate in a way because property tax records are readily accessible by street address. Most searchers would have an easier time identifying the street address than knowing the full name of the present owner. Sometimes, though, assessor parcel numbers are accurate because they are based on recorded subdivision maps prepared by surveyors. Even so, because street addresses do not reliably define the exact boundaries of any particular parcel, this mitigates against their inclusion as a part of the official public land record system.

Indexing Norms Vary Among Recording Offices. The U.S. has 3,600 locally maintained recording systems. Those using name indices have much in common, but each office has its own rules regarding what names to index, how to key in the names, and how to present that information to users.

Consider the challenge of indexing names. For instance, should the surname "de la Hoya" be indexed delahoya, DE LA HOYA, Hoya, or La Hoya? Each recording office develops its own rules. Another example: some places, Los Angeles County among them, merge the grantor/grantee indices into one table as shown above. These indices would be more useful if they reserved a column for a property description, as many grantor/grantee indices do. But each additional entry slows down the indexing process and increases its costs.[47]

Tract Indexes. A tract index arranges all documents affecting a particular parcel based on its physical location. Parcels may be identified by short legal descriptions based on government surveys or subdivision maps.[48]

---

47. *Indexing of Grantor/Grantee Names by Land Recording Offices,* Joint Task Force of the Property Records Industry Association, (last visited July 10, 2015), http://www.pria.us/files/resource_library_files/Business_Processes_and_Procedures/Grantor_Grantee_IndexingReportFinal.pdf.

48. Dale A. Whitman, *Digital Recording of Real Estate Conveyances,* 32 J. Marshall L. Rev. 227, 230 (1999).

Grantor-Grantee Index in a Race-Notice State
(Los Angeles County, California)

Off. Use Only	Title	Grantors-Grantees(*)	Other Party	File Date	Document No.
02699	Deed	*Delaplaz Teresa	Alou Developers	7-28	87-1193270
179898	Recon[1]	*Delarosa Ramon & Socorro		7-28	87-1196053
10500	Substn Tr[2]	Delcastillo Fernando W & Randi S		7-28	87-1197312
00123	Abst. Jdgt.[3]	*Deleon Margaret	Sec Pac Fin Corp	7-28	87-1191861
16176	Req Nt Dflt[4]	Delgado Luis G		7-28	87-1200498
17237	Tr. D & Asgt[5]	*Delgado Mario A	Sunders Mtg Crop Amer	7-28	87-1200499
00960	Tax Lien	Delgado Teresa	Ca St Franchise Tax	7-28	87-1192353
14493	Deed	*Delgaudio Salvatore Jr	Delgaudio Salvatore Jr & Camerina	7-28	87-1199286

[1] Recon is a reconveyance of a deed of trust by the trustee.

[2] Substn Tr a substitution of trustee. Lenders contemplating foreclosure often substitute in-house trustees for a professional trustee hired to conduct the foreclosure.

[3] Abst. Jdgt. is an abstract of judgment.

[4] Req Nt Dft is a request for a notice of default, a statutory prerogative usually exercised by junior lienors wishing to be notified that a senior has initiated foreclosure and recorded a notice of default as required by law.

[5] Tr. D & Asgt is a trust deed and assignment (usually an assignment of rents), which commercial property lenders often demand of commercial borrowers.

Tract indexes are easier to use than grantor-grantee indexes but require much higher skill levels to create and maintain accurately. In the public sector, grantor-grantee indices far outnumber tract indices.[49]

Title insurers use both tract and grantor-grantor indices in their private title plants. They need grantor-grantor indices for such potentially title-impairing information as the liens of judgment creditors. These liens attach to any property the judgment debtor owns or later acquires in the jurisdiction, so they can only be found by searching periodically under the name of the judgment debtor.

---

49. "Nebraska, North Dakota, Oklahoma, South Dakota, Utah and Wyoming are the only states with tract indexes in all counties. Kansas, Ohio, Wisconsin and Minnesota permit tract indexing at the option of the individual county. In other states, individual counties may operate tract indexes unofficially. New York City has a block index system." 1 Patton and Palomar on Land Titles § 67 n.3 (3d ed. 2002–2014) (updated by pocket part).

Grantor Index to Real Estate Conveyances

Date Filed	Grantors			Grantees	Kind of Instrument	Recorded Book	Page
1/16/92	Lang	Betty L	Jack B	W David Sumpter, III, Tr	Deed Tr	643	60
2/3/92	Lang	Constance M	Raymond Paul	William A Hoover, Jr., Tr	Deed Tr	646	6
2/3/92	Lang	Constance M	Raymond Paul	William A Hoover, Jr., Tr	Cancellation Deed Tr	646	7
7/4/92	Lang	Betty L	Jack B	Robert Gentry, Tr	Deed	652	85
6/2/92	Williams	John		John C. Kovacs	Deed Tr	652	87

Grantee Index to Real Estate Conveyances

Date Filed	Grantees			Grantors	Kind of Instrument	Recorded Book	Page
1/16/92	Lang	Betty L	Jack B	Janice Renee Helton	Deed	644	201
6/2/92	Lang	Betty L	Jack B	Robert Gentry Tr.	Deed	652	86
6/2/92	Kovacs	John C		Williams John	Deed Tr	652	87
7/4/92	Anders	Brady		Woodhead Matt	Easement	657	91
8/3/92	Allen	Thomas		Barnes Lisa	Lis Pendens	661	3

Parcel Index: Lot 13, Block A. Somewhere Estates Subdivision

Type of Instrument	Grantor, etc.	Grantees, etc.	Doc. No.	Date Filed	Book & Page #
Subdiv. Plat	Bayview Devel. Co.	———	36272	3-15-1999	13-17 Plat Bk.
Deed of Trust	Bayview Devel. Co.	First Bank of Ohio	37339	10-10-1959	114-62
Reconv.	First Bank of Ohio	Bayview Devel. Co.	38960	5-30-1960	129-88
Deed	Bayview Devel. Co.	Shaw, Irwin & Gertrude	38961	7-12-1960	130-19
Deed of Trust	Shaw, Irwin & Gertrude	Bank of America	38962	8-11-1960	130-20
Lis Pen.	Shaw, Irwin & Gertrude	Schaeffer Greg	43964	9-30-1962	134-55

Wild Deeds. A wild deed, illustrated in the following diagram, is one of several paradigmatic flaws that can appear in a chain of title.

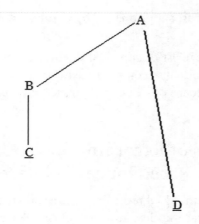

In the above diagram, the length of the line shows the relative time periods when the deeds were recorded. Underlining indicates that the deed was recorded.

Atsumi (A) was the record owner of vacant land (Blackacre) which she deeded to Bennie (B) for valuable consideration. B never bothered recording A's deed to him. B not recording has no bearing on the validity of A's deed to B. Under the recording acts, B's deed is vulnerable to D if D is a bona fide purchaser. D lacks constructive notice of the A to B deed because it was never recorded. C should never have accepted a deed from B since the public land records would show that title is still with A.[50]

In states using grantor-grantee indexes, virtually all of the cases dealing with wild deeds have concluded that C's deed must be treated as unrecorded and D's title as superior to C's.[51] On the other hand, D will almost certainly come across the B-C deed in a tract index. Also, in counties that have computerized their indexes so that the B-C deed will appear with all instruments affecting the particular parcel that B deeded to C, subsequent purchasers like D would probably be held to be on inquiry notice of B's interest.

To fulfill an inquiry notice obligation, D would be expected to make some effort to discover the authenticity of the B to C deed. Diligent inquiry might include (1) visiting the site for clues such as parties in possession, and (2) asking B about how he acquired title.[52]

Private Title Plants. In most big, populous jurisdictions in the western U.S., especially where the public records are indexed by grantor-grantee and not by tract or parcel numbers, the title search is performed at a company's own plant or a plant shared among title insurers. In the eastern part of the U.S., title insurers tend to rely

---

50. Joyce Palomar, 1 PATTON AND PALOMAR ON LAND TITLES § 69 (3d ed. 2012-2014) (updated by pocket part).

51. *See* Rufford G. Patton, PATTON ON TITLES § 69 (2d ed. 1957); IV AM. L. PROP. § 17.17 (1952).

52. *See Miller v. Hennen*, 438 N.W.2d 366 (Minn. 1989). *But see Leeser v. Kibort*, 243 Ill. App. 258 (1927) (because tract index is not required to be kept, it is a mere convenience and does not impart constructive notice).

on the public land records, supplemented by summary abstracts of title prepared by private firms.

Private title plants consist of copies of documents made daily from the public records. Private title plants use computerized tract indices and also maintain their own copies of the recorder's office general grantor-grantee index.

III. Types of Recording Statutes Compared: Notice, Race-Notice, and Race Statutes

Despite similarities among all recording statutes, there are three different types of statutes: (1) race, (2) race-notice, and (3) notice.[53] A close reading of the statutes reveals significant differences among them.[54]

States divide nearly equally between notice and race-notice statutes, except for three states with a race-type statute as their general recording act. The states with race-type recording statutes are Delaware, Louisiana and North Carolina. However, a number of states use a race-type statute for mortgages. Hawaii's land registration system also embodies race-type norms.

Notice Statute. In notice states, only BFPs prevail against the holders of prior unrecorded interests.[55] Here is the wording of a typical notice statute: "No conveyance or mortgage of an interest in land is valid against any subsequent purchaser for value without notice thereof, unless it is recorded."

Under a notice statute, if O conveys Blackacre first to A and then to B, A can only prevail under the statute by recording before B acquires title from O. But B must be a BFP to invoke the statute. In this example, neither A nor B have a good statutory

---

53. For a multistate bar-oriented explanation of how to recognize the three statutes, see (last visited July 10, 2015), http://mbetutorial.blogspot.com/2010/10/note-1-recording-acts.html

54. 'Period of grace' statutes constitute a fourth type of recording statute, often layered on top of a race, notice or race-notice format. These allow a claimant a period of time–a grace period–to record. If the claimant manages to make it to the recorder's office within the grace period, document in hand, her priority under the recording acts relates back to the time the instrument was executed or delivered. In California, for example, when property is sold at foreclosure by private power of sale, the trustee's deed at the sale "shall be deemed perfected as of 8:00 a.m. on the actual date of sale if the trustee's deed is recorded within 15 calendar days of the sale...." CAL. CIV. CODE § 2924h(c) (West 2014). A foreclosure sale trustee needs time to verify that the statutory sale procedures were followed, to deposit the auction winner's check, and to prepare a deed for the auction winner, the foreclosure sale purchaser.

55. Many recording statutes translated "bona fide" literally from the Latin as "good faith" and, as is often the case, something was lost in translation. The concept of "bona fides" comes from 18th and 19th century negotiable instruments law. The term was not an adjective modifying "purchaser," but an adverb modifying "for value and without notice." U.C.C. Art. 8 (Revised), Investment Securities, Appendix 1, proposed final draft (April 5, 1995). "Bona fide" meant "genuine." The phrase "bona fide Rembrandt painting" makes sense; "good faith Rembrandt painting" does not. Recording statutes are redundant when they use the phrase "bona fide purchaser for value in good faith."

claim against the other. So the common law priorities rule prevails. A was first in time and is therefore first in right.[56]

Race-Notice Statute. Here is the wording of the typical race-notice statute: "No conveyance or mortgage of an interest in land is valid against any subsequent purchaser for value without notice thereof, whose conveyance is first recorded." In short, race-notice statutes only protect subsequent takers who are BFPs and who have won the race to the recorder's office.

In a race-notice jurisdiction, O deeds Blackacre first to A and then to B. B has a better title than A under the statute only if (1) B records before A, and (2) B is a BFP, having paid valuable consideration and having been without notice of A's prior interest.

Race Statute. Race statutes encourage prompt recordation. In situations where two adverse claimants derive title from the same grantor, the one who records first has the better title. However, this protection only applies if the second taker was a "creditor or subsequent purchaser." The race statute specifies: "No conveyance or mortgage of an interest in land is valid against any subsequent purchaser whose conveyance is first recorded."

Suppose O conveys Blackacre first to A and then to B. Under a race statute, the first to record wins title to the property. It makes no difference if B actually knew about the O to A deed. But in order to be a "purchaser," B would have had to pay "valuable consideration" for the property, and would have had to derive a legitimate title from O. B would not qualify as a subsequent purchaser by forging O's name to a deed. Further, the deed from O would have to satisfy the requirements for recordation.[57]

The Doctrine of Shelter. A familiar maxim of equity, codified in some states, is that between two innocent claimants to the same property, the one who could most easily have prevented the loss should bear the brunt of it. The best preventer loses title to the property, though she retains the right to compensation from the wrongdoer who defrauded both claimants.

---

56. There is a subtle and often overlooked exception to the common law default rule of "first in time is first in right." Under this exception, a BFP who holds a later legal interest has priority over the holder of an earlier equitable interest. A purchaser under an executory purchase and sale contract has only an *equitable* interest. After closing, a grantee holds *legal* title. But in order to benefit from this rule, the grantee must be a BFP. She would not be a BFP if she had inquiry notice of the occupant's interest under a purchase-and-sale contract. Under the above facts, how would you decide?

57. "Contrary to the announced goals of a pure race recording statute, there are many potential claims to real estate that are not shown by the public records. Purchasers, title examiners, and title insurers must investigate other records and other circumstances to be sure a real estate title is what the owner represents it to be." "The [North Carolina] courts have made a number of important exceptions to recording priority that are not reflected in any statute's text. An owner will be held subject to rights described in an unrecorded instrument if the unrecorded instrument is incorporated by reference into the owner's deed or another recorded instrument in the chain of title." Charles Szypszak, *North Carolina's Real Estate Recording Laws: The Ghost Of 1885*, 28 N.C. Cent. L.J. 199, 206, 207 (2006).

Try creating a diagram that portrays this scenario. O owns Blackacre and deeds it first to A and then to B. A doesn't record its deed from O until many months after B acquires title and records instantaneously. B is a BFP completely unaware of the earlier O-A conveyance. Meanwhile, B had listed the property for sale. By the time B strikes a deal to sell to C, A has recorded his deed from O. Is C on constructive notice of the O-A deed? If A's very tardy recordation taints C with constructive notice of the O-A deed, B's once-superior title will have become unmarketable in spite of the fact that the recording laws are written explicitly to favor B over A.[58]

The doctrine of shelter serves to protect C in order to protect B. It allows a later claimant, even if not a BFP, to acquire "all title which his transferor had or had the power to transfer."[59] The integrity of a land title system necessitates this rule.

Another reason to support this outcome is that recording acts are intended to resolve the competing adverse claims of successive grantees *from the same grantor*. In the above example, the recording act norms only apply to the successive deeds to A and B from O. They do not invalidate the deed from B to C.[60]

A Grantee's Rights May Depend on Whether the Grantor's Title Was Taken by Forgery or Fraud. Here is another sad story from the annals of cheated property owners. To appreciate the outcome when courts are faced with deciding between two innocent victims of the same miscreant, it is important to appreciate the subtle though legally significant distinction between property owners who are victims of forgery and those who are defrauded.

Compare these two scenarios: Scenario (1): A trusting person by nature, Aunt Lizzie hands her nephew an executed and notarized deed to a ski lodge she has owned for many years and seldom uses, instructing him to record the deed only upon her death. Impatient for his inheritance, he records the deed and sells the ski lodge for its fair market value to a total stranger. A law school classmate of the nephew is an escrow agent and handles the sale. Aunt Lizzie only learns about the nephew having sold the ski lodge two years later when a cousin happens to visit the area and meets the ski lodge buyer.

Scenario (2): The nephew knows Aunt Lizzie owns a ski lodge the family seldom uses. With the help of a former law school classmate, he markets the ski lodge for sale, finds an unsuspecting buyer who pays fair market value for the property, and forges Aunt Lizzie's signature to a deed. Several years later, Aunt Lizzie discovers what happened.

---

58. In a jurisdiction with a traditional grantor-grantee annual index, a court could well conclude that the O-A deed was outside C's chain of title. In a tract index or a recording system with an expansive online search engine, the searcher might well have come upon the O-A deed.

59. U.C.C. §2-403-1.

60. One court, not grasping the importance of the doctrine of shelter, wrongly favored a claimant like B in a case involving personal property decided under the U.C.C. *See Aircraft Trading & Servs., Inc. v. Braniff, Inc., 819* F.2d 1227 (2d Cir. 1987). The decision was sharply faulted in Permanent Editorial Board Commentary on the Uniform Commercial Code, Commentary No. 6, §9-301(1) (1990).

In a suit between Aunt Lizzie and the BFPs in these two scenarios, courts often cite the maxim that as between two innocent parties, the one who could best have prevented the fraud should bear the loss.[61] On that rationale, the buyer in Scenario (2) has a better claim to the property than the buyer in Scenario (1) because Aunt Lizzie chose to entrust her nephew with a deed she had executed well before she meant for it to become effective.

Aunt Lizzie's defense will be that the deed was invalid because it was never actually "delivered"; the nephew was holding the deed in trust. She could have revoked it at any time before her death. Still, she could have kept her nephew from temptation by being less trusting. There is nothing much Aunt Lizzie could have done to prevent the nephew's misconduct in Scenario (2), and buyers take nothing from a forged deed.[62]

IV. How Land Record Systems Work

A. Frequent Reasons Recorders Reject Documents Presented for Recordation

The Salt Lake County Recorder's Office lists the following bolded items[63] as the most frequent reasons it rejects documents presented for recordation:

(1) **Missing legal description**, crucial to a tract index, and usually referenced in grantor-grantee indices as well;

(2) **Missing parcel identification number**, which is needed for the tax assessor to begin sending property tax bills to the new owner;

(3) **Incorrect fee**, because the system is supported by user filing fees;

---

61. "Where litigants assert conflicting claims and, hence, a loss or prejudice must be borne by one of them, the decision, in the event that they are shown to have been equally 'innocent' or ignorant of the harmful consequences of their acts, must be rendered against the party whose conduct brought about the prejudicial situation." 55 N.Y. Jur. 2d Equity § 114.

62. *See Strekal v. Espe*, 114 P.3d 67 (Colo. 2004). A naïve property owner deeded his house to a duplicitous friend who promised to clear the owner's title after the owner's wife died, and then to reconvey the property back to the owner. Instead, the untrustworthy friend mortgaged the house, pocketed the loan proceeds, and defaulted on the mortgage. The mortgagee foreclosed and sold the property to a person who had no knowledge of the history of the title. By the time of the mortgagee's sale, the true owner had come to realize that he had been duped. He filed suit to reclaim title from the friend and recorded a *lis pendens*. The notice was too late to have constituted constructive notice of the owner's claim to the mortgagee. But the notice was placed of record before the mortgagee conveyed the property to a bona fide purchaser. In seeking to wrest title from the mortgagee's purchaser, the original owner claimed that the *lis pendens* gave the mortgagee's purchaser notice of the fraud. The court disagreed, and held for the purchaser under the doctrine of shelter. If the owner's *lis pendens* constituted notice to the mortgagee's purchaser of the fraud, the mortgagee would have been divested of its title retroactively. The court left title with the mortgagee's purchaser.

63. *Recording Requirements and Fees*, Salt Lake County Recorder (last visited July 10, 2015), http://www.slcorecorder.org/slcr/RecorderServices/RecordingFees.aspx.

(4) **Grantor's signature different than typed name**, because the recorder has no business guessing who is the true grantor — the one who signed the deed or the one whose name is typed in the first line on the deed;

(5) **Missing grantee address**, because after copying each submitted document into the official records, the recorder returns the original to the person designated on the face of the document to receive it. All copies are collected in bound volumes or placed on microfilm and noted in an official index;[64]

(6) **Missing document return address**;

(7) **Illegible documents**; and

(8) **Inadequate space for recorder's stamp (4 1/4" x 3" in upper right corner of first page of document**), because the time stamp, calibrated to the minute, establishes the lien priority date priority between successive claimants to the same title from the same grantor. In a race-notice state, it is the first to record. In a notice state, the determinant is whether the first of the two claimants recorded before the second taker acquired its interest.

B. Unacknowledged Documents

In all but a few states, documents with faulty acknowledgments do not impart constructive notice to subsequent purchasers.[65] But anyone who views a copy of the instrument has actual knowledge of its contents.[66]

Three rules limit the number of casualties that could otherwise result from lack of an acknowledgment or a defective acknowledgment. First, even though the document does not impart constructive notice, it could create an inquiry notice obligation of its contents to anyone who happens to see it.

Second, a majority of states put subsequent purchasers on constructive notice despite defective acknowledgment unless the defects are latent, that is, not obvious on the face of the recorded document itself.[67] The idea behind the patent-latent distinction is that a subsequent purchaser who can plainly see the instrument is defectively acknowledged is forewarned not to rely on it.

---

64. Some of these practices may yield to the electronic recording of documents by title insurers.

65. IV Am. L. Prop. §§ 17.27, 17.31 n.66 (1962); *but see In re Wonderfair Stores, Inc., of Ariz.*, 511 F.2d 1206 (9th Cir. 1975) (holding that an improperly recorded instrument imparts constructive notice under Arizona law).

66. *But see Amoskeag Bank v. Chagnon*, 572 A.2d 1153 (N.H. 1990) (Holding that an attaching creditor, unlike a subsequent purchaser, is not charged with actual knowledge even if he sees a defectively acknowledged mortgage of record. The subsequent purchaser would insist that the mortgage be released, even if improperly recorded. A judgment creditor would have no choice but to accept title as he finds it, figuring any security for the judgment debt is better than none.).

67. H.D. Warren, Annotation, *Record of Instrument Without Sufficient Acknowledgment as Notice*, 59 A.L.R. 2d 1299, 1316. Not all state courts accept the patent-latent defect distinction. *Messersmith v. Smith*, 60 N.W.2d 276 (N.D. 1953) (acknowledgment held invalid because notary took grantor's statement by phone and not in person).

Examples of latent defects would include that the notary's license had expired, the signatory never actually appeared before the notary, or the notary had no plausible reason to believe the person appearing before her had actually signed the document she was notarizing.

Examples of patent defects include a grantor acting as his own notary,[68] the form being for a witness rather than the main signatory of the document, an undated acknowledgment, a document signed by someone other than the person making the acknowledgment, or the absence of an acknowledgment. In some states only patent acknowledgment defects imperil the constructive notice statutes of an instrument.

Third, most states have curative acts that function, essentially, as statutes of limitations. These laws bar challenges to documents because of technical irregularities after they have been of record for a prescribed statutory period.[69]

C. The Filing Process: The Difference Between Recordation and Indexing

Imagine you want to record a document in the public land records. In Los Angeles County, you bring the document in person or mail it in,[70] and pay a recording fee. You also must comply with certain formal requirements prescribed by statute.[71] Local requirements may vary, although they are mostly meant to give recorders the information they need in order to index documents properly.

The Gap between Recordation and Indexing. A document is filed for record when it is delivered to the recorder's office and accepted. The clerk collects the recording fee and places a time stamp on it. There is always some interval, or gap, between when the recorder receives, accepts and time stamps a document, and when the document is placed in an official index. Searchers will have great difficulty locating documents before they have been indexed because the recorder receives a huge volume of documents each day. The time interval or gap between when a document is accepted for recordation and time stamped by the receiving clerk, and when it is actually copied and indexed can be as short as an hour or as long as several months. A title searcher

---

68. *Metro. Nat'l Bank v. U.S.*, 716 F. Supp. 946 (S.D. Miss. 1989).

69. *See* Richard A. Powell & Patrick J. Rohan, LAW OF REAL PROPERTY 82-96 to 82-119 (1992); *see, e.g.,* CAL. CIV. CODE § 1207 (West 1982) (1 year); FLA. STAT. ANN. § 95.281 (West 1999) (5 years). Illinois allows unacknowledged deeds to be recorded but not to be admissible as evidence except upon proof of execution. 765 ILL. COMP. STAT. § 5/31 (2005). Some acts cleanse all defects in instruments recorded before a certain date. These laws need to be reenacted periodically. 21 PA. STAT. ANN. § 281.1 (West 2014) (defects cured in instrument bearing a date prior to 2013). A bankruptcy court interpreted the Pennsylvania curative act as curing only minor defects, not major defects such as the notary never having met the party giving the acknowledgment. In re Rice, 133 B. R. 722 (E.D. Pa. 1991).

70. General Recording Information, LOS ANGELES COUNTY REGISTRAR-RECORDER/COUNTY CLERK (last visited July 10, 2015), https://www.lavote.net/Recorder/Document_Recording.cfm.

71. CAL. GOVT CODE §§ 27201-27211.

would have to sift through a mountain of documents to find one that had been filed for record but not yet indexed.

In many cities, title insurers have worked out an arrangement with the keepers of public land records to copy instruments as soon as the public recorder accepts and time stamps them. The "gap" between the time of recordation and the appearance of a document in efficiently managed private title insurance records can be as short as half an hour and seldom longer than the following morning.

Allocating the Risk of Late or Faulty Indexing. Among the potential shortcomings of the recording system, recording office employees might neglect to index a document that had been time stamped and accepted for recordation, or could misindex a document in such a way that a subsequent purchaser could never find it — perhaps by misspelling the names of the parties or inserting the wrong site description.[72] Sometimes, title insurers notice that a deed or mortgage has been improperly indexed and inform the county recorder quickly enough to correct the error before anyone is misled by it.[73]

When the indexing omission or error is not quickly corrected, a property owner could create multiple interests in the same property with each of several grantees or mortgagees believing her interest is the only one the grantor created.[74] But for the indexing error, the second of the two claimants would have had constructive notice of the prior deed or mortgage and terminated their purchase or loan at once. Each of them has claims against the duplicitous grantor or mortgagor.

There is no consensus answer on who should bear the loss attributable to an indexing problem: the first-in-time claimant or the subsequent purchaser.[75] Favoring the first to record, some advocates believe that when the recording system fails, courts should revert to the priority rules that applied at common law where first in time was first in right (except that a prior legal interest bested a later equitable one). Thus, as between the two innocent grantees or mortgagees, the one whose interest arose first would prevail. Others favor the subsequent purchaser on the notion that the first

---

72. With increased funding, recorders' offices can reduce key-in error rates. The error rate on unverified key entries is 3-5%. A system of visual verification reduces the error rate to about 1%. Errors can be further reduced to 0.1-0.2% by a double blind entry system. Two operators independently key in each entry and a computer program detects inconsistencies for referral to a third person for resolution. Joint Task Force of the Property Records Industry Association, *Indexing of Grantor/Grantee Names by Land Recording,* PRIA (last visited July 22, 2015), http://www.pria.us/

73. One-Third of all Real Estate Transactions have Title Issues, According to Survey, CAL. LAND TITLE ASS'N (last visited, July 08, 2015), http://www.clta.org/news-and-media/media-kit-documents/alta-survey.pdf, The American Land Title Association took the survey in 2005.

74. *Tibble v. Wells,* 455 B.R. 648, 654 (2011) ("The person presenting an instrument for recording must bear the burden of making sure that it is properly recorded, not the register of deeds to whom it is presented. The person presenting the instrument bears the risk of any clerical errors.").

75. George W. Thompson, THOMPSON ON REAL PROPERTY 92.12 (I) at 28 (Thomas ed. Supp. 2000). The prevailing view has been rejected by courts in California, Florida, Iowa, New York, North Carolina, Pennsylvania, Washington, and Wisconsin, where a document is not deemed recorded until properly indexed.

to record is the best preventer. Between the two of them, only the first to record could have prevented the mishap by examining the public records to make sure his or her document had been properly indexed, and if it had not been, making sure the error was promptly corrected.

This is more than a hypothetical question. Such disputes arose quite frequently in California in 2009 as a result of "*mortgage shotgunning*" or "mortgage slamming." Real estate attorney Scott Talkov explains this phenomenon. It is a form of fraud that occurs "when a homeowner obtains multiple loans secured by the same home in order to receive loan proceeds that, in combination, greatly exceed the value of the real property. The homeowner commits fraud by failing to inform each lender that she has obtained multiple loans secured by the same property. The homeowner then absconds with the proceeds of the multiple loans."[76]

Fraud perpetrators are often quite familiar with the real estate transactions process and use multiple title insurers, notaries, escrow companies and lenders to minimize the chance of their being detected before they are able to cash out and run. At other times, they conspire by bribing notaries and employees in title and escrow companies.

Each lender believes it has a first lien on the property at the time it makes its loan. It searched the public records and found no adverse claims before it filed its mortgage for record. Because of the customary gap between when documents are accepted for recordation and when they appear in the official public recording index, victimized lenders find themselves in disputes with each other over which of them has first-lien priority.

California appellate courts have reached opposite results in these cases, some looking to the date each document was indexed, others relying on the recorder's time stamp indicating when the document was "filed for record." The courts that prefer basing priority on a document being indexed explain that until it is indexed, no subsequent purchaser or mortgagee should be deemed to be on constructive notice of it.

Attorney Talkov disagrees with this analysis. He contends that whether a subsequently recorded lienholder has constructive notice of an earlier lien on the same property is beside the point in these disputes. California Civil Code 1214 grants priority to the claimant whose document is "first duly recorded." All that should matter in a race-notice state like California is which claimant recorded first.

His viewpoint has indirect support from an appellate court opinion dealing with a dispute between two lenders, each of whose loans were secured by deeds of trust on the same property, and bore exactly the same time and date stamp from the recorder's office, 8:00 a.m.[77] The 8:00 a.m. time stamp is not unusual. In exchange for doing all the county's title work free of charge, the Los Angeles county recorder's office places an 8:00 a.m. time and date stamp on all documents received from title insurers before 8:00 a.m.

---

76. Scott Talkov, *Mortgage Shotgunning and the Priority of Trust Deeds*, 32 Cal. Real Prop. J. 9 (2014).

77. *First Bank v. E.W. Bank*, 199 Cal. App. 4th 1309 (2011).

Both loans were indexed two days after recordation, one four hours earlier than the other. Predictably, the lender whose deed of trust was first indexed claimed priority. The appellate court decided that the time of indexing was irrelevant for these reasons: (1) Indexing depends capriciously on when a staff member happens to retrieve a particular document from the batch that falls out of the mail bag, not when a document is readied and presented for recordation; (2) The recorder makes no note of the time and date a document is indexed, just when it is submitted and accepted for recordation; (3) State law requires recorders to time-stamp documents within two days of receipt;[78] there is no state law timing requirement for indexing.

Since neither lender could claim the benefit of the recording act, the court could have decided the case in favor of the holder of the deed of trust that was created first, based on first-in-time is first-in-right, the common law priority rule when both of the competing interests are equitable or legal. But this would require the court to answer the question, when is a deed of trust created? Is it when the deed of trust is duly executed? Funded? Delivered? In many situations, the date of creation will be a question of fact evidenced by loan participants well aware of the consequences of their testimony. No wonder the court chose to set priorities based on those county-affixed time and date stamps which have the virtue of objectivity.

V. Equitable Subrogation and Lien Priorities under the Recording Acts

Because the doctrine of equitable subrogation is a "wild card" in recording act priority disputes, it deserves special mention here. Equitable subrogation concerns the relative lien priorities among mortgage lenders.

An Equitable Subordination Scenario. Suppose property owner V arranges to buy a house for $500,000 with a mortgage loan from Lender A of $400,000 for a term of 10 years at a fixed interest rate of 5%. The loan is interest-only with no amortization of principal. The full $400,000 is due when the loan matures in ten years, at the end of the loan term. Lender A recorded its deed of trust promptly.

During the next year, local property values increase, and the value of V's house rises to $600,000. V needs $100,000 to invest in a business venture and decides the best way to raise money would be with the proceeds of a second mortgage loan secured by the house.

So V borrows $100,000 from Lender B for a term of five years at an adjustable interest rate. Lender B was well aware of Lender A's first lien but figured that its lien was well-secured with an equity cushion of $100,000 — a total of $500,000 borrowed against a $600,000 fair market value. Lender B secured its loan with a recorded deed of trust on the borrower's home.

---

78. "The recorder shall endorse upon it in the order in which it is deposited, the year, month, day, hour, and minute of its reception, and the amount of fees for recording." CAL. GOVT. CODE 27320.

Not long thereafter, V needed another $50,000 urgently to keep the new business venture afloat. One of the principals in that venture was also in the business of making mortgage loans. She offered to provide a new loan to V of $550,000 for a term of five years at a rate of interest of 9% interest-only, thus becoming Lender C.

The C loan was conditioned on an escrow agent using $500,000 of the loan to pay off Lender A in exchange for a reconveyance of Lender A's deed of trust, releasing V's property from Lender A's mortgage lien.

Then, V's business venture failed, property values plummeted, V lost his job and defaulted on all the loans. Lender C initiated foreclosure at a time when the house was worth $450,000.

Applying the common law priority rules as modified by the recording acts, Lender B has the first lien. First in time is right in right[79] as long as the lender who was first in time promptly records its interest.[80] Lender A once had the first lien but its lien had been fully re-paid by the C loan, and the A lien had long been released of record.

Lender C could have avoided being subordinated to Lender B by acquiring Lender A's loan. But then, Lender C would have been limited to the precise terms of the Lender A loan for $500,000. That transaction would not have met the purposes of the refinancing which was to enable the borrower to obtain $50,000 in additional cash.

Under the doctrine of equitable subrogation, Lender C would acquire A's lien priority over subsequent lienors including Lender B up to the amount and on terms no more onerous than those of the A loan that C had repaid. The rationale is simple; B is no worse off being subordinate to C than to A as long as the two loans were equivalent.

The Disparate Court Decisions on Equitable Subrogation.[81] Claims of equitable subrogation by lenders in C's position are petitions to the equitable jurisdiction of courts to do the right thing based on the facts of each case.

Court outcomes vary. Some courts are quite reluctant to upset the A-B-C lien priority. They would prefer that lenders in C's position negotiate subordination agreements directly with lenders in B's position, if they wish to cloak themselves in A's lien priority. Not only would this strategy keep C and B out of court; B and C could tailor the exact terms of the subordination to fit situations in which C's loan differed somewhat from the A loan.

This "negotiate; don't seek to subrogate" norm would not fit situations in which C had no knowledge of the B loan. Reasoning along these lines, some courts have reserved their equitable authority of subrogation for cases in which C lacked actual knowledge of Lender B's deed of trust. Other courts deny subrogation to C if C had at least constructive notice of the B loan.

---

79. Cal. Civ. Code § 2897: Priority of Liens. Other things being equal, different liens upon the same property have priority according to the time of their creation.

80. *Id.* at § 1214.

81. John C. Murray, *Equitable Subrogation: Can a Refinancing Mortgagee Establish Priority Over Intervening Liens?*, 45 Real Prop., Tr. & Est. L.J. 249 Summer 2010.

There is a different approach that almost always favors C's claim for lien priority over B. The rationale of this approach is that Lender B knew or had constructive notice of A's prior secured loan before making its loan. Most probably, Lender B even received an interest rate and terms predicated on the known risk of a loan. To award B more than the benefit of its bargain with V unjustly enriches Lender B at Lender C's expense. Also, it seriously prejudices the V's options for refinancing the A loan, even though an equitably subrogated Lender B would be no worse off than if the A loan had not been refinanced by C.

The basic equitable subordination norm is well expressed as follows: *Restatement (Third) of Property*: "one who fully performs an obligation of another, secured by a mortgage, becomes by subrogation the owner of the obligation and the mortgage to the extent necessary to prevent unjust enrichment."[82] Subrogation empowers a subsequent mortgagee to "step into the shoes" of a prior mortgagee.

The Split Priority. Equitable subrogation safeguards the intervening lienor from ending up worse off because it only applies 'to the extent necessary to prevent unjust enrichment.'[83] To see how this might play out in practice, imagine that in the above scenario, the value of the house slips to $450,000 and prevailing interest rates decline to 4%. Lender A might be willing to accept a pay-off of $400,000 to $450,000 to allow a new buyer to acquire the house for $450,000 with a loan from Lender C. But Lender C would only agree to make a loan in this situation if its lien was superior to Lender B's.[84] Lender C's lien priority would be limited to the terms of the Lender A loan— $500,000 at 5%; not $550,000 at 9%.

As a result of these adjustments, Lender C would actually have a *split priority:* a first lien for $500,000 at 5%, and a third lien for the balance due on the Lender C loan. Also, the court would need to make an adjustment because Lender C's loan became due and payable in five years, not the ten years of Lender A's deed of trust.

Equitable subrogation has no place in mortgage shotgunning situations because none of the defrauded lenders ever expected to have been making junior liens.

Questions

Question 1: *Consequences of Not Recording a Purchase and Sale Contract.*

The purchaser is unable to record a realty purchase and sale agreement because the vendor refuses to acknowledge it. What legitimate reason could the vendor have for preventing the purchaser from recording the purchase and sale contract?

---

82. Restatement (Third) of Prop.: Mortgages § 7.6(a) (1997).

83. David L. Boyette, *Whose Shoes to Use: Achieving a Subrogation Footing in the Wave of Foreclosures,* 87 Fla. Bar J.8 (2013); Christopher Smart, *Equitable Subrogation and Mortgage Lien Priority in Florida* (last visited Oct. 3, 2015), http://www.cfjblaw.com/equitable-subrogation-and-mortgage-lien-priority-3-8-2012. *See also Velazquez v. Serrano*, 43 So. 3d 82 (Fla. 3d DCA 2010) (Lender entitled to be repaid from more than adequate sale proceeds when the loan contained a due on sale clause.).

84. Glenn R. McGillivray, *What's Your Priority? Revitalizing Pennsylvania's Approach to Equitable Subrogation of Mortgages After First Commonwealth Bank v. Heller,* 58 Vill. L. Rev. 301 (2013).

Question 2: *Consequence of Not Recording a Lease.*

A family owned "Dry Bar" leases space in a neighborhood shopping center for a term of five years, and spends $500,000 on improvements to the interior. The family would not want to risk the landlord selling to a subsequent purchaser who could possibly evict them, claiming no knowledge of their lease terms. Do you see any reason for the family to incur the cost of recording its lease? As a practical matter, could the family record it without the landlord's consent?

Question 3: *Marketable Title Acts.*

(a) What is the purpose of marketable title acts, and how does it affect the length of a title search?

(b) Under a Marketable Title Act, what does the holder of a non-possessory interest accomplish by recording a notice of intent to preserve?

Question 4: *Title Insurance and Recording Acts.*

(a) How does title insurance fill the gaps of recording systems and public land records?

(b) What aspects of a land registration system obviate the need for title insurance?

Question 5: *The Language of the Statutes.*

(a) Is this Florida statute a race, race-notice, or notice statute?[85]

Fla. Stat. Ann. § 695.01 (2013):

Conveyances to be Recorded. No conveyance, transfer or mortgage of real property, or of any interest therein, nor any lease for a term of 1 year or longer, shall be good and effectual in law or equity against creditors or subsequent purchasers for a valuable consideration and without notice, unless the same be recorded according to law; nor shall any such instrument made or executed by virtue of any power of attorney be good or effectual in law or in equity against creditors or subsequent purchasers for a valuable consideration and without notice unless the power of attorney be recorded before the accruing of the right of such creditor or subsequent purchaser.

(b) Is the California statute a race-notice or notice statute?

Cal. Civ. Code § 1214 (West 2014):

Unrecorded Conveyance Void as to Subsequent Purchaser or Mortgagee. Every conveyance of real property or an estate for years therein, other than a lease for a term not exceeding one year, is void as against any subsequent purchaser or mortgagee of the same property, or any part thereof, in good faith and for a valuable consideration, whose conveyance is first duly recorded, and as against any judgment affecting the title, unless the conveyance shall have been duly recorded prior to the record of notice of action.

---

85. The Florida statute is dissected in Powell on Real Property 82-24 (1992 Revision). Distinguishing notice from race-notice statutes can be hard work. *See* Charles G. Rogers, *The Colorado Recording Act: Race-Notice or Pure Notice?*, 51 Denv. U. L. Rev. 115 (1974).

(c) Is the Delaware statute a race, race-notice or notice statute?

25 DEL. CODE ANN. § 153 (West 2014):

Priority of deed concerning lands or tenements. A deed concerning lands or tenements shall have priority from the time that it is recorded in the proper office without respect to the time that it was signed, sealed and delivered.

Question 6: *Donees' Rights Under Recording Acts.*

(a) In a race-notice state, O donates land to a private university and then mortgages it to M. The university records before M makes its mortgage loan to O. Who has priority to the realty, O or M?

(b) In a race-notice state, O mortgages land to M and subsequently donates the land to a private university without informing the university of M's prior mortgage. M neglects to record until after the university records its deed from O. Who has priority to the realty, O or M?

Question 7: *The Doctrine of Shelter.*

Suppose O, the record owner of a vacant parcel of land known as Blackacre, deeds the property first to A and then to B. Both pay valuable consideration to O. B knows nothing of A's claim, and pays the full purchase price before A records. But A records before B. Then, A sells to C and soon thereafter, B sells to D. C records before D.

(a) In a race-notice state, who has the superior claim to Blackacre, C or D?

(b) In a notice state, who has the superior claim to Blackacre, C or D?

Question 8: *Lien Priorities, Recordation and Equitable Subrogation.*

In 2008, Seller S closed a sale of her 10-unit apartment house to Buyer B for a purchase price of $1,500,000. Buyer B agreed to take subject to Seller S's existing $1,000,000 mortgage loan from a local bank that Seller S had obtained when she acquired the property two years earlier. The term of the loan was 15 years, interest at 6%, fully amortized.

To facilitate the sale, Seller S took back a $400,000 loan secured by a deed of trust on the apartment house, interest only at 10%, all of the principal to be repaid in a lump sum in ten years. The deed of trust was recorded on the closing date along with the deed from S to B. Buyer B paid $100,000 in cash at closing.

In 2011, Buyer B arranged a refinancing of the balance due on Seller S's original purchase money loan from a private lending consortium which by that time had been reduced to $900,000. The new loan was for $1,400,000. All the terms were the same as those of the mortgage being repaid. The new loan was written so that it became due on the same date as the re-financed loan would have become due. The re-financed deed of trust was promptly recorded. The trustee on the repaid loan executed a reconveyance of title which was recorded. Buyer B retained the $500,000 cash difference between the old and new loan.

Due to increased competition from newer buildings, Buyer B had to reduce rents to a point that she could no longer make payments on her two mortgage loans. The lending consortium initiated foreclosure which would eliminate Seller S's lien. She hired an attorney who sought a court order that Seller S had first priority to the fore-closure sale proceeds to the extent of the unpaid balance on her loan because as against the consortium's deed of trust, under the state's race notice recording statute, her lien was "first duly recorded."

(a) Was Seller S correct?

(b) How would the consortium justify its having a first lien priority?

(c) What would be the correct outcome according to existing applicable legal norms?

Chapter 9

Title Insurance[1]

Scope of the Chapter

Title insurance has become the predominant means by which realty buyers and mortgage lenders in the U.S. protect their financial interests in real property against losses due to sellers' and borrowers' titles being flawed.[2] This chapter begins with a brief comparison of title insurance to casualty insurance, and then focuses on the scope and limits of the basic title insurance coverage, the types of claims covered, and the claims process.

Many property owners follow property value trends in their neighborhoods but few will know much about title insurance and how to deal with title problems unless they previously became entangled in one. Generally, property buyers and sellers leave title matters to title companies, real estate brokers, real estate attorneys, and county recorders.

The following excerpt explains the importance of title insurance to property owners.

Many properties have a long and convoluted history of previous owners and transactions, and you cannot tell by looking at the property and the current deed whether the title is good, flawed or invalid.

For all you know, the people you bought the house from might have slipped out and gotten a second mortgage on the property two days before closing, or neglected to pay a $5,000 special assessment for the new sewer.

Perhaps the swimming pool is located right on the electric company's easement for underground lines. Maybe the prior owner decided not to tell you that her ex-husband has a lien on the house for half the proceeds of sale.

Title insurance is like a stockade fence around your property, protecting it from pirates who might creep out of the past. Chances are you'll never file a claim, but you'll be mighty glad to have title insurance if you do.[3]

---

1. The author is grateful to Gary A, Bregman, Old Republic Title; Partner, Garrett & Tully; Glen M. W. Trowbridge, First American Title; and Randall Scott, First American Title, for their many useful suggestions for this chapter.

2. Tammy L. Ortman, *Title Insurance–A Comprehensive Look Into the World of Title Insurance Today*, 34554 NBI-CLE 27 (2006).

3. *Defending your title*, AMERICANBAR.ORG (last visited July 25, 2015), http://www.americanbar.org/content/dam/aba/migrated/publiced/practical/books/home_ownership/chapter_3.authcheckdam.pdf

I. The Scope of Basic Coverage

A. Pricing and Competition: Comparing Title to Casualty Insurance

After every major disaster—be it floods, landslides, fires, hurricanes, earthquakes—a few homeowners call their title insurers seeking indemnification for the casualty losses. They are wasting their time because these disasters are not listed among the title policy's 'covered risks.'[4]

Natural disasters have been known to knock houses off their foundations, but have never dislodged legal title. Other claims not covered by title insurance include construction defects, poorly compacted fill, toxic or hazardous waste, sinkholes, failed septic tank systems and owner misrepresentations that the property is connected to city sewer and water systems. Title insurance covers none of these because none of them are directly about the ownership of the property even though liens could eventually be placed against the property for the owner's failure to remedy some of these conditions.[5]

Upon taking title, a property owner could contract with a title insurer to provide notice of any subsequently recorded document which could result in a lien against a property owner—a "recorded document guarantee."[6] But the title insurer would decline coverage protecting the owner against potential liability and eventual foreclosure arising from such liens not being paid unless the owner obtained title insurance coverage concurrent with purchasing the property.

Title and casualty insurance are quite different. Casualty and auto insurers levy periodic premiums based on an actuarial risk assessment. They try to minimize their exposure by inspecting properties for basic fire and casualty safety precautions, and

---

4. What kinds of defects does title insurance protect you from?

It protects you against loss due to title defects, liens, or other similar matters. Title insurance protects you from claims of ownership by other parties. It protects you against losses from problems that arose before you bought the property. The title company will defend you in court if there is a claim against your property, and will pay for covered losses." Texas Department of Insurance, Title Insurance Frequently Asked Questions. http://www.tdi.texas.gov/title/titlefaqs.html (last visited Feb. 2, 2016).

5. Under the Comprehensive Environmental Response, Compensation, and Liability Act (CERCLA) a 1980 law commonly known as Superfund, the EPA is authorized to respond to releases, or threatened releases of hazardous substances that may endanger public health, welfare, or the environment. States have enacted similar laws. Property owners can become liable for the extensive costs of cleaning up contaminated sites, and remain liable even after they sell. Government agencies are empowered to impose liens against the titles of potentially responsible parties which can include buyers and mortgage lenders. Those liens would affect the title of property owners and mortgage lenders. Hence, in the early days of these laws, property owners sought recovery under their title polices. They lost these cases; courts cited provisions in title policies disclaiming liability for government imposed restrictions and limitations on the use of property.

6. California Title Insurance Practice, 2d. 2015 Update, § 9.17. Insurer liability is limited to $10,000. But buyers purchasing such coverage enhance their claims of being good faith purchasers without prior knowledge of CERCLA issues.

adjust their premiums periodically to track their loss experience. Their largest expenses are for paying claims on behalf of policy holders. Both title and casualty insurers have profit margins of about 5% on gross sales. Of their premium dollars, title insurers spend *90% for expenses* and *5% for claims;* casualty insurers spend *25% for expenses, 70% on claims.* The largest of a title insurers' expenses go to collecting and examining title information before issuing policies.

Casualty insurance and title insurance do share a common attribute. Neither of them insures that bad things won't happen. They promise only to indemnify the insured for the loss or damage when they do.

Title insurers are reported to find defects in one in three transactions for which they are asked to write title insurance, and in about 25% of home sales. Spotting these defects not only puts title insurers in a position to warn buyers and mortgage lenders of potential title problems. Title insurers also improve the quality of many documents in the public land records system by curing defects before issuing policies. For instance, mortgage lenders often neglect to record a satisfaction of mortgage or a reconveyance of a deed of trust after the borrower has repaid the loan. The lien clouds the title of the present owner until the curative satisfaction of mortgage or reconveyance of the deed of trust is recorded. The title insurer can arrange for these title-clearing documents to be recorded.

Similarly, a deed in the chain of title may never have been properly recorded. In a recorded deed, the name of the grantor or grantee could have been misspelled or the property description may be wrong. Curing these defects by recording corrective deeds is far more efficient than allowing them to impede or derail future transactions in perpetuity. Title insurers have also become adept at instituting preventive measures to detect the ever increasing volume of attempted forged and fraudulent transactions.

Reverse Marketing Makes Title Insurance Pricing Less Competitive Than Casualty Insurance Pricing. Price competition is inhibited because while consumers take the trouble to price auto and home casualty coverage, few home buyers shop around for title insurance. Until the closing, most home buyers and sellers have no idea what title insurance will cost them. A handful of carriers insure most of the nation's properties, and some economists believe that this also severely stifles price competition.

Title companies vary in their rates, integrity, quality of their title searches, how fairly and quickly they respond to claims, creativity in solving title problems, adeptness in curing title defects and insurer solvency. These are the factors that buyers and lenders should consider in choosing their title company.

Commercial buyers and sellers involved in multiple transactions are generally more attentive to the quality of service provided and the price of title insurance than most home buyers. They are also in a better position to know when paying a higher price is justified by better quality service. Many real estate brokers, closing attorneys and escrow agents base their selection of title companies and title insurers on how responsive they are to requests for title information, assistance in clearing title problems, and processing claims.

In sharp contrast to title insurers, casualty insurers engage vigorously in price competition because they market directly to consumers on the basis of price. Title insurers engage in "reverse" competition,[7] marketing to real estate intermediaries — real estate brokers, mortgage bankers, mortgage lenders, and home builders — hoping for business referrals, sometimes in exchange for kickbacks and referral fees despite federal and state laws.

Title insurance pricing is heavily regulated in many states, and many state regulators require title insurers to file price schedules for different types of coverage from which they may not deviate. State regulation of title insurance premiums has produced mixed results for consumers.[8] Regulators are prone to becoming captives of the industries they regulate, and title insurance regulators are no exception.[9]

Comparative shopping for title insurance would be futile in states that ban price competition altogether through rate-fixing regulatory regimes — New Mexico, New York and Texas among them.[10] Another indication of capture is when regulators prevent competition by denying casualty and life insurance companies the right to offer title coverage.

On the other hand, some state officials have intervened on behalf of consumers to lower title policy rates.[11] An encouraging example comes from Pennsylvania. There, regulators understood that title insurers ran title searches only back to the last insured search. So they mandated discounted premiums in the "repeated coverage" situations as when properties recently changed hands or been refinanced.[12]

---

7. Birny Birnbaum, *An Analysis of Competition in the California Title and Escrow Insurance Industry, EntitleDirect (last visited July 22, 2015),* http://www.entitledirect.com/static/entitle/Birnbaum _report.pdf.

8. Scott Wooley, *Inside America's Richest Insurance Racket,* Forbes LLC, Nov. 13, 2006, p. 148.

9. Student Note, Protecting Title in Continental Europe and the United States-Restrictions of a Market, 7 HASTINGS BUS. L.J. 411, 431 (Summer 2011); "Title Insurance Hearings, supra note 146, at 235 (testimony of Rande K. Yeager, President & CEO of Old Republic Nat'l Title Ins. Co. on behalf of the Am. Land Title Ass'n) ("virtually all states require that title insurance rates must not be excessive, inadequate, or unfairly discriminatory").

10. It costs approximately nine times more to insure an office building in New York where title insurance charges are subject to rigorous state administrative control as in Washington, D.C., where rates are unregulated, according to Randall Scott, President, U.C.C. Division, First American Title Company, Washington, D.C. Lecture at U.S.C. Law School, 04/08/04. The costs of title insurance in Texas would probably fall 40% if the state deregulated rates. Interview by author with Dennie Rowland, Executive Vice President, First American Title Insurance Company, 07/16/01. For title insurance rate regulation to be exempt from the antitrust laws as state action, a state agency must exercise comprehensive, independent oversight over rates. *See Fed. Trade Comm'n v. Ticor Title,* 504 U.S. 621 (1992) (striking down a regulatory system in which private title insurance companies submitted rates to state rate bureaus which became effective after thirty days unless the state bureau objected. States must exercise greater control than this to claim the state action exemption to the antitrust laws.).

11. In 2006, as attorney general of New York, Eliot Spitzer pressured title insurers in the southern district of New York to accept a 15% reduction in fee schedules for insuring residential owners' and lenders' policies. Joseph W. Eaton and David J. Eaton, The American Title Insurance Industry: How A Cartel Fleeces the American Consumer, p. 1 (New York University Press, 2007).

12. There were three possible rates — Basic, Reissue and Refinance. The Basic rate was the highest. Depending on when the purchaser previously bought tile insurance, the purchaser could be entitled

B. Title Companies, Title Underwriters, and Title Insurers

Basically, title insurance is a two-part transaction undertaken by two types of firms: title companies and title insurers. The title insurance process begins with a title company conducting a search of the property to determine whether the purported seller or borrower has good title. Based on the search, the title company prepares a template of the policy it is prepared to issue. Then, the title company presents its findings and proposed policy to a title underwriter for a title *insurer,* the ultimate source of payment on claims.

To a commercial real estate attorney involved in a complex transaction, the competence of the title company determines the quality of title service provided in the course of the title search and ensuing negotiations regarding the scope of coverage. Title company counsel can provide valuable advice to transactions lawyers in achieving their clients' goals. The title insurer, and there are only about two dozen of them in the U.S. will actually defend the policy holder's title if it is challenged, and will pay the policy holder for loss or damage resulting from an insured policy on a title that proved defective.

To major real estate investors and mortgage lenders requiring title insurance for very large sums at risk, the solvency of the title insurer or title underwriter is crucial, as well as the fairness and efficiency of how it handles claims. The claims-paying ability of title insurance underwriters is evaluated by the major Wall Street credit rating firms (e.g., Standard & Poor's).[13] Insurers often share risks through reinsurance or co-insurance.[19]

Some title insurers perform both functions as full service providers. They search titles, offer escrow and closing services, negotiate policy terms and endorsements, and provide title insurance policies. They may also offer underwriting contracts to local title insurance agents.

Other title insurers enter Title Insurance Agency Agreements with local title companies for the purpose of issuing title insurance commitments, policies and endorsements. The title insurer underwrites (stands behind) the policy and is obligated on the insurance contract. But it relies on the title company (the title agent) to perform title searches and oversee escrows and closings. Title standards are set by title underwriters and title insurers because they are responsible for paying claims. They also prepare policy forms, oversee the issuance of special endorsements, and have the final word on handling claims.

Some title company agents only represent one title insurer; others represent many. The title company agent actually issues and disseminates the title policy. The rela-

---

to discounts of 70-90% of the Basic rate. *See Levine v. First Am. Title Ins. Co.*, 682 F. Supp. 2d 442, 2010 U.S. Dist. LEXIS 2876.

13. S&P's title insurance credit ratings appear at: *Fitch and A.M. Best ratings of title insurers are also available online*, STANDARD AND POORS (last visited July 20, 2015), http://www2.standard andpoors.com/portal/site/sp/en/us/page.topic/ratings_fs_ins/2,1,5,0,0,0,0,0,0,0,3,0,10,0,0,0.html

tionship between title companies and title insurers is such that the title insurer or underwriter may not even know the policy was issued, except when the policy is so large that the insurer's prior approval was required in the contract between the insurer or underwriter and the agent.

In California, title agents are licensed to issue policies on a county-by-county basis, and need a license for each county in which they operate. An underwriter may issue policies directly in any county, but usually will do so only when it does not have agreements with local title companies to be its agents.

While title insurers are liable to their policyholders, many reserve the right by contract to back charge the title-agent for claims of title defects based on the agent's gross negligence or violation of specific instructions in issuing a policy.[14]

C. Policy Coverage

Title Policies Are Not All Alike. Title policy coverage varies enormously, starting with major differences between owners' and lenders' policies, described later in this chapter. A buyer or lender needs to be aware that the form that is promised in the preliminary title report or title commitment may not necessarily be the same as the policy actually insured.

The list of policies is daunting and sure to evolve. In all states, there are forms issued by the American Land Title Association (ALTA). ALTA is a national trade association for the title industry, responsible for promulgating and updating title insurance policy forms which serve as models nationally. There are also state-specific forms. For instance, in California, forms issued by the California Land Title Association (CLTA) are popular. Because the terms of title coverage vary considerably, forms are named and dated: for example, CLTA Standard 1990; CLTA homeowners 1998; ALTA residential 1987; ALTA standard residential 1998; ALTA Lenders 1992 replaced by ALTA Lenders 2006. Policies from the 1970s and 1980s are still in use because clients request them.

Available Coverage Options. Though title insurers are reluctant to assume the risks inherent in a known title defect, they do take some title risks on an actuarial basis.[15]

A few of the most important are:[16]

---

14. To appreciate the difference between title companies and title insurers, consider the case of *Fidelity National Title Insurance Co. v. Washington Settlement Group (WSG)*, 2013 Va. Cir. LEXIS 136. The WSG owners stole $4 million placed with them in escrowed funds to pay off existing liens by mortgage lenders insured by Fidelity. The title insurer had to cover the losses of the insured mortgagees, and seek whatever they could from the WSG owners who had defrauded them.

15. Dena M. Cruz and Paul L. Hammann and Scott Rogers, THE NEW 2006 ALTA POLICIES: THE INDUSTRY LISTENS!, SP002 ALI-ABA 1613 (2008).

16. *70+ Ways to Lose Your Property,* First American Title Company (last visited July 22, 2015), http://www.firstam.com/title/resources/reference-information/title-insurance-reference-articles/70-ways-to-lose-your-property.html

1. Forgery, fraud, undue influence, incompetency, incapacity or impersonation;

2. Lack of authority of any person or entity executing on behalf of the actual Owner;

3. Failure of any document affecting title or of the insured mortgage to be properly created, executed, witnessed, sealed, acknowledged, notarized or delivered;

4. Failure of an electronic document to properly comply with applicable state and federal legislation pertaining to the creation of electronic documents;

5. The invalidity of a document due to an invalid or unenforceable power of attorney;

6. Failure of a document to be properly filed recorded or indexed;

7. Losses resulting from any defect in any judicial or administrative proceeding through which title or the lien of the insured mortgage derived.

Sometimes, new title policies contain highly explicit and technical expansions of coverage just to avoid disputes that arose when policyholders were denied claims based on crabbed title insurer interpretations of language in earlier policies.

Here is one example: "The 2006 definition of the insured additionally includes a grantee of an insured under a deed delivered without payment of actual valuable consideration. This clause is important in preventing the substantial amount of litigation that has occurred when parties conveyed title by deed without consideration to a solely-owned LLC or corporation for estate-planning or liability-protection purposes."[17]

D. The Title Commitment or Preliminary Report

The Commitment, Report, or Binder. Once a buyer or lender requests title coverage, the first title document the potential buyer or lender will receive is called a preliminary report, title commitment, or a binder, depending on local custom.[18] This written report, usually based on a completed title examination, is a template of the title policy the insurer is willing to issue.

Despite minor differences, these preliminary documents are all signed and dated and they detail the conditions of title, list the required submissions from the insured that are necessary for issuance of a title policy, and indicate the terms of eventual coverage. Only the named insured will be protected by the policy. So the person named in the title commitment should be exactly the same as the grantee's name on the ensuing deed or the mortgagee's name on the mortgage.

Among the most important provisions of the preliminary title report are carefully worded exclusions and exceptions to coverage, which substantially reduce the title

---

17. Joyce Palomar, The 2006 ALTA Title Insurance Policies: What New Protection Do They Give? 42 Real Prop. Prob. & Tr. J. 1, 26 (2007).

18. Linda M. Green, *Preparing the Title Opinion and Issues in Title Insurance,* 15438 NBI-CLE 45 (5/4/2004).

insurer's exposure to liability under the policy.[19] Title insurers will only be liable for adverse interests they neglect to except or exclude.[20] Typical exceptions include unsatisfied mortgages or deeds of trust, notices of pending litigation that could affect the right to title or possession to the property (*lis pendens*), federal tax liens, mechanics liens, unpaid property taxes, encumbrances, and breaks in the chain of title.

The exceptions are noted briefly in Schedule B of most title insurance forms, and are usually displayed by order of priority. A complete assessment of the condition of the title requires studying copies of all the documents mentioned in the special exceptions part of Schedule B. For instance, the buyer might understandably assume that a specific exception of a "right of way for existing roads" refers to the plainly visible 15-foot private road the buyer saw while inspecting the property. The underlying document could be a court decree establishing a 40-foot county right of way.[21]

Disputes often arise over whether the language in the exception was clear enough to warn a diligent buyer or lender of the risk lurking within it. Title insurers are accountable for inaccurate or misleading portrayals of recorded interests excepted from coverage. Nonetheless, buyers and mortgage lenders should not rely on the cryptic description of excepted items in Schedule B. They should request and study a copy of each document excepted from coverage.

Removing Exceptions to Policy Coverage or Writing Endorsements Over Them. The knowledgeable buyer or lender will scrutinize and even reject unacceptable exceptions and exclusions.

Title insurers may agree to delete some exceptions once convinced the chances are negligible that they could ever result in loss or damage to the insured. For instance, a restaurateur learns that the property she is about to acquire is subject to a prohibition-era covenant barring the sale of alcohol. The street is now renowned for several fashionable cocktail bars and a popular brew pub.

Relying on the doctrine of changed conditions, the title insurer might agree to remove the exception for the no-alcohol-sales prohibition. Thus, the restaurateur will be insured against loss or damage resulting from the enforcement of the covenant, and the insurance company will be obligated to provide a legal defense to any enforcement efforts. A more cautious insurer could require an opinion of counsel on the legal issue, expecting the seller to pay for it. The fee charged by the law firm writing the opinion could include a risk premium based on the diminished value of

---

19. Sometimes, instead of characterizing these as either exceptions or exclusions, they are described as pre-printed exceptions or specific exceptions.

20. Fidelity title offers the example of a single mother, a waitress, who bought a house she could barely afford and then discovered her first property tax bill was for $9,000, not the $2,000 she had expected it to be. The difference was due to a special assessment the title insurer had failed to mention and exclude from coverage. Fidelity paid the bill. *Aligning our Title and Real Estate Related Services to Enhance your American Dream*, Fidelity National Title (last visited July 20, 2015), www.fntic.com

21. *Shotwell v. Transamerica Title Ins. Co.*, 588 P.2d 208 (Wash. 1978) (language of insurer's exception for existing right of way held inadequate to put insured on notice of county's interest).

the property if the right to sell alcohol had to be defended in a lawsuit, taking into account the chances of anyone filing a suit and prevailing.

Endorsements. Title companies offer additional coverage in the form of policy endorsements.[22] Title company menus of standard endorsements vary from state to state. In California, title insurance regulators have approved language for over 100 special endorsements. In Texas very few are permissible. Insurers prefer writing special policy endorsements when they can earn fee income rather than removing exceptions or exclusions to coverage free of charge.

Oral promises are unenforceable. Standard policy conditions require endorsements to be written and signed by an authorized signatory of the title insurer.

Buyers and lenders of commercial properties routinely seek special endorsements, often negotiated by their lawyers.[23] Here are two examples: (1) Legal descriptions in deeds are based on two-dimensional surveys and rarely mention the street address or improvements on the property (ten-story office building, tilt-up warehouse, 30-apartment complex). Commercial property owners can obtain an endorsement confirming the accuracy of the address, the nature of the improvements, and the location of the insured property according to the public records. (2) Title policies don't cover losses arising from the realty not having been legally subdivided under state law; developers and home builders will often purchase endorsements guaranteeing the insured loss if the property had not been legally subdivided.[24]

The Policy Pro Forma. Increasingly, commercial borrowers and lenders are dissatisfied relying only on a title commitment before closing. They prefer seeing a copy of the exact policy that the insurer proposes to issue. These 'templates' are called 'pro formas' (not to be confused with financial projections for a project– the more common use of the term 'pro forma' in real estate transactions). Title policy *pro formas* enable counsel to preview the exact wording of the final policy, double check that all the unwanted exceptions were removed and all desired endorsements had been included.

E. Is There Title Insurer Liability for a Faulty Search or Preliminary Report?

Are title insurers liable for harms or damage resulting from their negligence in preparing the commitment or preliminary report even if the recipient of the report never actually purchases a title policy, and paid nothing for it? Where this issue has

---

22. Ted D. Disabato, *Endorsements and Exceptions*, 37282 NBI-CLE 47 (2007).

23. Dena M. Cruz and Scott Rogers, *Commercial Title Insurance Endorsements (The Basics for Owners and Lenders)*, 22 Ca. Rea. Prop. J. 1015 (2004).

24. *See, e.g., CLTA Endorsement 116.7:* "The Company hereby insures the insured against loss or damage which the insured shall sustain by reason of the failure of the land described as Parcel in Schedule to constitute a lawfully created parcel according to the Subdivision Map Act (Section 66410, et seq., of the California Government Code) and local ordinances adopted pursuant thereto."

been considered by courts or statutes, jurisdictions are almost evenly divided with a slight tilt in favor of no liability.[25]

Here are two examples of how claims may arise based on preliminary reports:

(1) A prospective buyer decides against completing an otherwise highly advantageous realty purchase after being scared off by title defects noted in the commitment and excepted from title policy coverage. The insurer was wrong; there were no title defects.

(2) An investor decides to complete its contract to buy without title insurance, relying upon the preliminary report that showed a flawless title. But in fact, the seller's title was deeply flawed.

States allowing liability claims for defective searches or preliminary reports respect the reasonable consumers' expectations of sellers, lenders and prospective buyers who rely on the accuracy of the insurer's title search.[26] Indeed, title insurers invite reliance by emphasizing the importance of preliminary title reports in marketing their products.

In those states which have enacted statutes requiring insurers to conduct reasonable title searches before issuing policies, some courts regard purchasers as the intended beneficiaries of such statutes while other courts interpret the statutory mandate to conduct a title search as having been enacted solely to dissuade title insurers from unwittingly taking excessive risks, not to enlarge the scope of insurer liability for imperfect title searches.[27]

Jurisdictions precluding liability observe that the commitment or preliminary title report was made free of charge and specifically disclaimed liability based on it unless the same error or omission re-appeared in a purchased policy of title insurance. Many insurers offer sellers, buyers and lenders a chance to purchase coverage against errors in preliminary reports.

---

25. "The rule that a title insurer has no duty to carefully search or to disclose all record title defects is definitely a 'bare majority' rule. Approximately 16 jurisdictions say or suggest no duty to search and disclose, but approximately 14 jurisdictions say or suggest the title company has a duty to search carefully and disclose matters of record. I say approximately because a couple of decisions are open to construction. A number of jurisdictions have not yet ruled on the issue." Professor Joyce D. Palomar, E-mail to BrokerDirt@umkc.edu, 04/26/05.

26. "When members of the public purchase policies of insurance they are entitled to the broad measure of protection necessary to fulfill their reasonable expectations. They should not be subjected to technical encumbrances or to hidden pitfalls and their policies should be construed liberally in their favor to the end that coverage is afforded' to the full extent that any fair interpretation will allow." *Danek v. Hommer*, 76 A.2d 198, 28 N.J. Super. 68 (App. Div. 1953), *affirmed*, 105 A.2d 677, 15 N.J. 573 (1954)." Fred I. Feinstein, *Non-contractual Claims Against Title Insurers*, 412 PLI/REAL 459, 473 (1995). Among states that have held title insurers liable for negligent errors in preliminary reports are: Alabama, Alaska, Kansas, Nebraska and New Mexico. A New Mexico statute exonerates title insurers from liability for negligent title searches but New Mexico courts hold that the statute only applies when no title policy has been issued. *See, e.g., Barrington Reinsurance Ltd. v. Fidelity Nat'l Title Ins. Co.*, 143 N. M. 31, 172 P. 3d 168 (2007).

27. Robert T. Edwards, *Solving Problems with Residential and Commercial Title Examinations and Reports*, 34498 NBI-CLE 73, 78 (2006).

At one time in California, Kansas and Montana, courts held title insurers liable for negligent preparation of preliminary reports. Legislatures in these states enacted statutes eliminating tort liability by declaring that preliminary reports were not to be deemed representations or abstracts of title.[28]

II. An Overview of the Title Policy

A. The Three Parts of the Title Policy

Conceptually the title policy is divided into distinct components. On the first page, Schedule A shows the amount of insurance, the premium, the effective date of the policy, the name of the insured, the interest or estate being insured, how title is to be vested and contains a legal description of the insured property. Schedule B lists general exclusions and specific exceptions from coverage. A final section of conditions and stipulations outlines the process for initiating and resolving claims.

B. Schedule A: What the Title Insurer Insures

Title coverage is no guarantee of good title, and no assurance that the title is free of defects. It is insurance against *loss or damage* up to the insured amount resulting from: (1) title being vested other than is shown in Schedule A, (2) unmarketable title, (3) defects, liens and encumbrances, or (4) lack of a right of access to and from the insured land.

Suppose the buyer acquires a home for $500,000, buys a policy of title insurance in that amount, and several years later, discovers a previously undetected forgery in the chain of title that completely invalidates the buyer's title. By then, the value of the property had risen to $700,000. Under the policy, the insured's maximum claim will be for $500,000. *The title insurer does not promise free and clear title. It promises damage for loss or damage resulting from title not being as insured, <u>up to the insurance policy limit</u>.*

1. Access to a Public Road

Title policies insure against losses resulting from a lack of access to a public road. Lack of access would usually result in a title being characterized as unmarketable "ap-

---

28. Cal. Ins. Code § 12340.11 (West 1988); Mont. Code Ann. § 33-25-111 (1995). A real estate investor who bid on foreclosed properties often obtained information from a friendly title insurer about whether the lien being foreclosed was a first lien or not. The insurer provided this information free of charge because when the investor acquired property, he would purchase title insurance from the insurer. On one occasion, the title insurer got it wrong, and told the investor he was bidding on a first lien when, in fact, the lien being foreclosed was a second. He sued the title insurer and lost since California by statute insulates title insurers against suits based on negligence in preliminary reports. The promise of future business is no substitute for purchasing a title policy. *Soifer v. Chicago Title Co.*, 187 Cal. App. 4th 365 (2010).

parently because the purchaser would would need to file and win a lawsuit to gain a right of access perhaps establishing an easement by necessity."[29]

Courts differ on how much legal access it takes for a title to qualify as marketable, sanctioning everything from a "goat path" traversable on foot or horseback[30] to vehicular access.[31]

To be sure of compensation for inadequate access, buyers and lenders can purchase a special endorsement insuring both actual vehicular and pedestrian access to and from a specifically identified street or road, insuring that the street or road is physically open and publicly maintained. "The endorsements provide much broader coverage than the policy alone."[32]

2. Effective Date of Coverage

With a few exceptions noted below, the insured is only protected against title defects existing at the effective date of the policy. The date in the policy will be set at the precise time the title company concludes its record search. Title insurers and title companies are detectives, not fortune tellers. Title defects first originating after the effective date of the policy are not covered.[33] Thus, an insured purchaser is protected against past forged deeds that preceded her acquisition of title but not against an identity thief who tries to forge her signature to a deed or mortgage after she acquired title unless she purchased a premium homeowners' policy that explicitly covered selected post-closing risks including post-closing forgery.[34]

The Gap Risk. Another post-closing risk is that documents could have been filed for record but not indexed before the effective date of the policy. This is sometimes called the "gap" risk, a reference to the gap in time between when a document is brought to a recorder's office to be placed in the public records, and when that document is actually indexed so that someone searching the public records could plausibly be expected to find it.

To appreciate the significance of the gap between the time of closing and the time of recordation, suppose an insured sale or financing closes at 10:00 AM and the title company records rushes the deed or mortgage to the recorder's office where the document is time stamped at 11:30 AM.

Meanwhile, a judgment creditor recorded a notice of its judgment against the grantor at 11:00 AM, duly time stamped. Because the judgment creditor's interest was recorded thirty minutes ahead of the insured grantee or mortgagee, its lien would

---

29. *Stewart Title Guar. Co. v. West*, 676 A.2d 953, 965 (Md. Ct. Spec. App. 1996).

30. *Gates v. Chi. Title Ins. Co.*, 813 S.W.2d 10 (Mo. Ct. App. 1991).

31. Tammy L. Ortman, *Title Insurance—A Comprehensive Look Into the World of Title Insurance Today*, 34554 NBI-CLE 27,32 (2006).

32. Ted D. Disabato, *Endorsements and Exceptions*, 37282 NBI-CLE 47 (2007).

33. Palomar, *supra* note 32, §4.03 at 4-8.

34. For instance, the North American Title Insurance CLTA/ALTA Homeowners Policy which carries an extra premium of 10 to 20 percent, NATIC (last visited July 23, 2015), http://www.natic.com/SiteFeaturePage.asp?Id=583

have been "first duly recorded" and superior to the insured deed or mortgage. Gaps would be rare in a world of instantaneous online digital recordation.

Title policies can be written to cover this risk explicitly. Under the 2006 ALTA policy, this "gap" risk is now covered. Earlier versions of the ALTA policy did not cover it, including the one released in 1992. Some states require title insurers cover buyers and mortgage lenders against the gap risk.

Savvy insureds achieve the same result by specifying that recordation is a condition of the closing, and the effective date of the policy is concurrent with the moment of recordation. The problem arises because recordation is a manual operation.

C. Schedule B: Exclusions and Exceptions

The exclusions and exceptions in a preliminary title report are particularly important to a buyer or mortgage lender because these are the items not covered by the policy. The function of exceptions and exclusions is to shift specified risks from the title insurer to the insured. Since the policies are drafted by the title insurers, in a dispute over the scope of an exclusion or exception, the burden of proof is on the insurer to prove that an otherwise covered claim falls within an exception.[35]

The difference between an exclusion and an exception is that usually, exclusions appear on the policy jacket and are not property specific. Examples would be defects arising after the effective date of the policy, defects "assumed, suffered, or created" by the insured. Exceptions can be general or specific. The specific ones pertain uniquely to the insured property, such as a prior lien, encroachment, or easement. General exceptions could include unrecorded mechanics' liens or mineral or water rights.

Buyers and their attorneys may have questions about the meaning of particular exceptions or the scope of exclusions. Naively, they might assume that title company staff would be more than willing to answer questions and offer examples of how the exceptions and exclusions might apply to situations of special concern to the buyer.

They will usually be disappointed because title company attorneys caution staff members not to offer their opinions about the scope of policy coverage. Not only are title insurers wary of buyers misconstruing what they are told, but also if litigation ensues, a title company staffer's casual comment could be construed as enlarging the scope of coverage beyond the precise language of the printed policy. Instead of being advised about the meaning of policy language, potential insureds will be told to seek the advice of their own attorneys to answer their questions about the scope of title coverage.

The Exception for Defects 'Created, Suffered, Assumed or Agreed by Insured.' Title insurers routinely exclude from coverage defects created, suffered, assumed or agreed

---

35. *Golden Sec., Thrift & Loan Ass'n v. First Am. Title Ins. Co.*, 61 Cal. Rptr. 2d 442, 444 (Ct. App. 1997).

by the insured—whether recorded or not.[36] This is a variant of what most insurers do in disavowing liability for the insured's own bad acts in order to deter 'moral hazard.' Moral hazard occurs when a person becomes indifferent to risks because of knowing someone else will pay the costs.

'Created' by the Insured. The word 'create' implies an affirmative act on the part of the insured though not necessarily taken with an intent to cause loss or damage.[37] For instance, a construction lender sought compensation from its title insurer when a borrower was able to set aside the construction lender's mortgage lien for lack of consideration because the lender mistakenly deposited the construction loan proceeds in someone else's account.[38] By failing to put the loan proceeds into the borrower's account, the lender created the invalidity of its own lien. So the title insurer was relieved of liability for the lender's lien being invalid due to the insured's improvident conduct.

Foreclosure Bidders Whose Title a Court Lets Aside for Price Inadequacy Created Their Own Title Defect. An example of an insured not being entitled to collect on its title coverage due to a self-created defective lien occurred in early 2005, when property values were falling rapidly. The purchasers submitted a winning bid of $3,500 at a sheriff's foreclosure sale for a house that was worth between $300,000 and $400,000. They insured their title for $400,000 as soon as they became the winning bidders.

The foreclosed homeowners persuaded a court to set aside the forced sale for gross inadequacy of consideration. Having had their title declared invalid, the purchasers sued their title insurer on the $400,000 policy. The Arizona Supreme Court held in favor of the insurer.

The title insurer refused to pay the claim because the title had been adjudged invalid solely for gross inadequacy of consideration, due to the purchaser's deep underbid at the sheriff's sale.[39] The title insurer was held not liable since it was the insured purchaser's low bid at the sheriff's sale that was the reason the sale was invalidated.

'Suffered, Assumed or Agreed To.' The most commonly 'assumed' or 'agreed to' liens arise when buyers *contract to take title subject to existing mortgage loans or other liens.*[40] A buyer who accepts a deduction from the purchase price in the amount of the lien will be deemed to have agreed to take title subject to the mortgage.

'Suffered' means 'allowed, permitted.' It implies that the insured had the opportunity to prevent the defect from arising but chose not to. The most common class of liens

---

36. *See* Joel E. Smith, Annotation, *Title Insurance: Exclusion of Liability for Defects, Liens, and Encumbrances, Created, Suffered, Assumed, or Agreed to by the Insured,* 87 A.L.R. 3D 515 (1978).

37. Louis Kushner, *When Has an Insured 'Created' the Loss? New York State Courts Address the Question,* N.Y. L. J. at S-3 (Aug. 30, 1993). Courts differ on whether the insurer must establish that the insured intended by its misconduct to bring about the defect that resulted in the failure of title. Leopold Z. Sher and Kerry J. Miller, *Interpreting the Term 'Created' in Policy Exclusion 3(a),* 434 PLI/ Real 347 (1998).

38. *Mark Twain Kansas City Bank v. Lawyers Title Ins. Corp.,* 807 F. Supp. 85 (E.D. Mo,1992).

39. *First American Title Ins. Company v. Action Acquisitions, LLC,* 218 Ariz. 394, 187 P.3d 1107 (2008).

40. Palomar, *supra* note 32, § 6.04[2] at 6-37.

"suffered" by an insured buyer come from the buyer's judgment creditors. Had the buyer paid her debts, those liens would never have come into existence.

A buyer who acquires property with profits from illegal drug sales, later seized by the Drug Enforcement Agency, has no title insurance claim, having created or suffered the forfeiture by acquiring title with illegally obtained funds. (Drug forfeitures also fit within the exclusion for government laws described below.[41])

Between 2005–2008, a national home-price bubble burst. For years, banks had been making loans to borrowers on houses they clearly could not afford. As buyers defaulted, massive foreclosures ensued as buyers defaulted.

Scam artists saw an opportunity to persuade vulnerable, desperate homeowners who had missed mortgage payments to deed them property by promising to refinance or otherwise stave off the imminent foreclosure. Once they became the owners of record, they sold these houses, sometimes using bloated appraisals to borrow more than enough money to refinance the existing loans and pocketing the surplus. Then, they and their accomplices disappeared. They often used specially formed limited liability companies to avoid being traced.

Courts set aside these fraudulently procured deeds and mortgages. Defrauded mortgage lenders then sought reimbursement on their title policies.[42] Title insurers denied coverage, contending that mortgage lenders had 'suffered, assumed and agreed to' the risks resulting from their own careless underwriting practices.[43]

Unrecorded Defects Known to the Insured and Not Disclosed to the Insurer. Standard title insurance policies also exclude from coverage defects, liens, encumbrances, adverse claims or other matters not known to the Company, and not recorded in the public records at date of policy, but known to the insured.[44]

This exclusion is meant to give the insured a strong incentive to disclose problems to the title insurer before closing, of which the insured has actual knowledge.[45]

---

41. J. Donald Cole & Robbie J. Dimon, *Risky Business: Dealing with Forfeiture Titles,* 12 Prob. & Prop. 8 (1998).

42. For a stunning depiction of how bank executives pushed underwriters into approving shockingly bad loans on penalty of losing their jobs, see Gretchen Morgenson, *Was There a Loan It Didn't Like?,* N.Y.Times, (last visited July 22, 2015), http://www.chicagotribune.com/business/chi-sun-title-insurance-fraud-aug17,0,1998638.story.

43. Susan Chandler, *Title firm ready to do battle: Suit over Chicago house could set up national showdown,* Chicago Tribune.com.

44. Exclusion 3(b) is "not Known to the Company, not recorded in the Public Records at Date of Policy, but Known to the Insured Claimant and not disclosed in writing to the Company by the Insured Claimant prior to the date the Insured Claimant became an Insured under this policy."

45. Conditions Section 1(f) defines " 'Knowledge' or 'Known': Actual knowledge, not constructive knowledge or notice that may be imparted to an Insured by reason of the Public Records or any other records that impart constructive notice of matters affecting the Title."

See, e.g. Eller Media Co. v. DGE, Ltd., 2004 WL 2002449 (Ohio Ct. App. 2004) (Insurer held liable to insured purchaser for grantor's billboard tenant's unrecorded three-year lease. Title insurer removed from the policy the survey exception and exclusion for rights of parties in possession. Policy excused insurer from liability for unrecorded defects of which buyer possessed actual knowledge. Buyer could

Sometimes, these disputes turn on whether sketchy information the seller passed along to the buyer before closing amounted to anything specific enough so that the buyer had an obligation to relay it to the title insurer.[46] Suppose the buyers mentioned to the sellers before closing that they intended to build a swimming pool in the back yard, and the sellers promptly cautioned them that a pool might be precluded by the existence of backyard underground utility easements. Do the buyers need to let the title insurer know this before closing?

Suppose they do not, then after taking title, the city denies the buyers a permit because the pool will impede the utility company from reaching its recorded underground utility easement to make repairs. Does the buyer's title insurer have a good defense because the buyers never mentioned what the sellers had told them about the utility easements?

It is important to note the insured has no obligation to disclose *recorded* defects. Title insurers recognize they have the obligation to search the public land records, and bear any losses arising from an inadequate search.[47] "Thus, if an instrument is 'recorded,' whether the insured has knowledge of an instrument is inconsequential."[48]

When title insurers overlook a recorded defect, they may contend that because the insured knew about the defect, this was tantamount to the insured agreeing to take title subject to it. But knowledge is not acquiescence. The fact is that the insurer had not excepted the defect from coverage.

In a typical case of this sort, the buyer or lender knew of prior recorded liens and proceeded to fund the loan or close the sale anyway after reviewing a title report that did not except these liens from coverage. Title insurers usually lose these cases because courts figure that buyers and lenders are justified in presuming that if there had been recorded liens, their title insurer would have identified and excepted them.

Defects Revealed by Inspection: The Exclusion for Inquiry-Notice-From-Possession. Although standard owner's title policies exclude coverage for "rights or claims of parties in possession not shown by the public records," owners can purchase coverage for defects that an inspection would reveal. To obtain title protection against the rights of parties in possession, buyers will have to pay for a survey. Based on the completed survey, the title policy will be drafted to except coverage for any defects that

---

see the plainly visible billboard, inquired of owner and could rely on owner's statement that billboard lease was month to month. Under the actual knowledge standard in the policy, buyer had no duty to make inquiry directly of billboard tenant.).

46. If the title insurer pays the buyer's claim, it may decide to proceed in subrogation against the seller for not disclosing to the insurer those tidbits of information concerning the right of way it revealed to the buyer. In jurisdictions where the title insurer has no obligation to search title and no liability on its preliminary report or commitment, the seller won't be entitled to defend based on the insurer's negligence in failing to find and except the recorded defect from policy coverage. *Transamerica Title Ins. Co. v. Johnson*, 693 P.2d 697 (Wash.1985).

47. *L. Smirlock Realty Corp. v. Title Guar. Co.*, 418 N.E.2d 650, 654, 52 N.Y.2d 179, 189 (1981) (*insured* under no duty "to disclose to the insurer a fact which is readily ascertainable by reference to the public records").

48. Palomar, *supra* note 32, §6.05[3] at 6-49.

the survey shows. While the buyer not having acquired title coverage for these, at least the buyer would have been told about them. Once informed, the buyer could have refused to take title unless these flaws were cured before closing or insisted upon being compensated by an appropriate reduction in the purchase price.

Suppose under a recorded long-term lease a tenant occupies property the owner is about to sell. But the buyer's title company overlooks the tenant's recorded lease. Will the title insurer be liable to the insured buyer for failing to disclose or except the recorded document, or will the title insurer prevail under the general exclusion for the interests of parties in possession? Case outcomes vary.[49]

The Exclusion for Defects Created by Public Laws. Title policies routinely exclude coverage of defects created by public laws, although there is a homeowners' policy that covers many risks arising from *recorded* violations of subdivision, zoning or building codes.[50] The key word here is "recorded." A restriction on the use of a property that is recorded in the chain-of-title of an insured property would customarily be classified as an "encumbrance," and would be covered by title policies unless they were specifically identified and excepted from coverage in the policy.[51] Most zoning ordinances would not appear in the public land records and hence fall under the general title policy exclusion for publicly imposed land use controls.

On occasion, though, local governments record within a property's chain of title certain types of land use controls that are specifically applicable to a particular property. Such controls typically arise from conditional use permits or contracts between local governments and apartment developers, such as those which grant zoning density bonuses for the maintenance of "affordable" units, subject to occupancy or rent controls. These would turn up in a search of the public land records, and be classified as "encumbrances"

---

49. *See Lipinsky v. Title Ins. Co.*, 655 P.2d 970, 975-76, 202 Mont. 1, 12 (1992), *discussed in*, D. Barlow Burke, Jr., Law of Title Insurance at 308-09 (1986). The court held that a broad exclusion enabling the title insurance company to take away the coverage for which the insured has already bargained contravenes public policy. *But see Horn v. Lawyers Title Ins. Corp.*, 557 P. 2d 206, 89 N.M. 709 (1976) (insurer held entitled to rely on the general exception for the rights of parties in possession even though adverse occupant held title by a recorded deed which the title insurer neglected to find or specifically except from coverage).

50. ALTA Homeowners' Policy (10/17/98), Owner's Coverage Statement, paragraphs 14-18. *But see Elysian Inv. Group v. Stewart Title Co.*, 129 Cal. Rptr. 2d 372 (Ct. App. 2002). The city recorded a notice that a garage had been illegally converted into a dwelling unit and if the owner failed to correct the condition, the city would do the work and bill the owner for it, placing a lien against the owner's title if the city's bill wasn't promptly reimbursed. This notice was held not to impair title because enforcement was not imminent.

51. *1119 Del. v. Cont'l Land Title Co.*, 16 Cal. App. 4th 992 (1993) (recorded occupancy restriction imposed by CUP held to be an encumbrance). *See* Cal. Govt. Code § 27281.5 (West 1988) requiring local governments to record in the chain of title of affected properties all government imposed restrictions affecting owners' ability to convey. *But see Elysian Inv. Group v. Stewart Title Guar. Co.*, 129 Cal. Rptr. 2d 372, 105 Cal. App. 4th 315 (2002) (Title insurer not liable to buyer for failure to disclose or except notice which city recorded in the buyer's chain of title that premises were substandard under city building code and if owner failed to bring property up to code, city could do the work and assess the cost as a lien against the property. Court held that since the notice pertained only to the physical condition of the property, buyer's title was not impaired by it.).

upon the owner's title. To avoid liability under them, title insurers would customarily disclose their existence, and explicitly except them from coverage in Schedule B.

In turn, the law firm asked to render such an opinion would probably contract with a planning consultant to study whether the insured property was in full compliance with minimum side yards, setbacks, height limits, parking requirements, and the like.

Title insurers explicitly except coverage for loss or damage arising because the insured's lot has been illegally subdivided.[52] But they will write special endorsements that the insured's lot has been legally subdivided.

Gratuitously Acquired Interests: The Exclusions for Losses That Would Not Have Occurred 'If the Purchaser Had Paid Value.' Title insurance policies inevitably exclude coverage for "loss or damage, which would not have been sustained if the insured claimant paid value." This exclusion shows how title insurers tailor their policies to the detailed provisions of state recording statutes. In states with notice or race-notice type recording statutes, the exclusion limits the title coverage of anyone who acquired an interest by gift or devise.

Does this mean those who receive gifts of realty would be wasting money buying title insurance? Certainly not.

First, the title report conveys important information to everyone acquiring an interest in realty, however they acquired their interest.

Second, an insured in a notice or race notice state would have a good claim against her title insurer if the holder of a prior legal interest in the same property recorded, and the title insurer failed to disclose and except that interest from the policy. That prior interest holder of a recorded interest would have had superior title even against a subsequent bona fide purchaser.

Also, the insurer might be tempted to claim that the insured suffered no loss, having been gifted the land. But as anyone can explain who has ever been robbed of a valuable gift, the loss is real, measurable by the cost of replacing it.

Third, a donee, as soon as her interest is recorded, will be protected against later purchasers from her grantor. Recording acts protect the first-in-time 'conveyance,' whether it acquired for valuable consideration or not.

D. Conditions and Stipulations for Asserting Policy Claims

The conditions and stipulations are the sections of the policy pertaining to the processing of claims.

---

52. Endorsement, OldRepublicTitle (last visited Jan. 2nd, 2016), http://www.oldrepublic title.com/newnational/resources/CLTAForms/116.7.pdf

"The Company hereby insures the insured against loss or damage which the insured shall sustain by reason of the failure of the land described as Parcel in Schedule to constitute a lawfully created parcel according to the Subdivision Map Act and local ordinances adopted pursuant thereto."

1. The Insured Beneficiary of the Title Policy

Owner's and Lender's Policies. With few exceptions, only the named insured is protected by the policy no matter who paid for it. Often, buyers pay for their lenders' policies.

Buyers need their own policies because they are not regarded as beneficiaries of their lenders' policies.[53] "To avoid duplications of title insurance premiums, the title insurance agent can issue an owner's title insurance policy simultaneously with the lender's at little additional cost."[54]

LLCs and Title Coverage. Sometimes, title to realty is held by an entity such as a limited liability company (LLC) or a corporation. An LLC retains coverage under the title policy even when individual members sell their LLC memberships. But an LLC's title policy expires *when the LLC transfers its realty title to another individual or entity.*

In one litigated case, a married couple formed a limited liability company to develop a single family home which they acquired in 2004. The husband and wife were the only members of the LLC, each holding a 50% interest.

Later, they put their development plan on hold because of a protracted dispute with a neighbor over an easement and decided instead to live in the house. Once they took possession, they transferred title from the LLC to a family revocable trust in which the husband and wife were the sole trustees. At that point, they asked their title insurer to deal with the neighbor over the easement dispute.

The insurer denied coverage because when the title policy was issued, the insured was an LLC. Once title shifted to the revocable trust, title was no longer insured under the LLC's policy.[55]

This was the relevant policy language in the *Kwoks'* CLTA standard policy: "The coverage of this policy shall continue in force as of Date of Policy in favor of an insured

---

53. Palomar, *supra* note 64, at 644. *See Siegel v. Fid. Nat'l Title Ins. Co.*, 54 Cal. Rptr. 2d 84 (1996). The Siegels bought out their half-brother's one-third interest for $150,000 in a duplex left them by their mother. During the brief time the half-brother held title, a recorded judgment lien for $100,127 against the half-brother's interest attached to the property. The title insurer failed to note this judgment lien on the preliminary title report. The Siegel's' attorney ordered a lender's title policy for the Siegel's' lender, but not an owner's policy for the Siegel's. The Siegels paid $662.50 for the lender's policy. For another $198.75 the Siegels could have purchased an owner's policy which would have covered them against the lien. The Siegels didn't purchase a policy for themselves because the title report indicated there was nothing to insure against. The court held the preliminary report was not meant to be a representation of the state of the title, only an offer to issue a policy, which the buyers hadn't purchased for themselves. *See also, Klickman v. Title Guar. Co. of Lewis County*, 716 P.2d 840, 842 (Wash.1986) (vendor had no right to indemnity from buyer's title insurer for insurer's failure to disclose document of which insurer had actual knowledge, obligating vendor to remit one-third of sale proceeds to a prior owner).

54. Donna M More, Attorneys Concerns In Real Property Sales Transactions, RPST FL-CLE 1-1, § 1.14 (2013).

55. *Kwok v. Transnation Title Ins. Co.*, 170 Cal. App. 4th 1562 (2009).

only so long as the insured retains an estate or interest in the land or holds an indebtedness secured by a purchase money mortgage given by a purchaser from the insured,
or only so long as the insured shall have liability by reason of covenants of warranty
made by the insured or any transfer or conveyance of the estate or interest."[56]

Do you see how they could have easily preserved their title coverage? They should
have transferred their membership interests in the LLC to their revocable trust instead
of transferring title to the realty to the revocable trust.

Another alternative would have been for them to request an endorsement from
the title company that would have been issued for a nominal premium, $75 or so.[57]

This would have been unnecessary under the ALTA 2006 policy. "The 2006 Policy
provides for continuation of coverage for transferees by deed between parent and
subsidiary entities and other 100 percent affiliated individuals and entities as well as
when the grantee is the trustee or beneficiary of a trust created by the insured for
estate planning purposes."[58]

2. Notice of Claim

Title policies require the insured to tender claims promptly to the insurer by written
notice followed by a signed and sworn formal proof of loss. The policy itself will
specify where to submit claims.

It can be important for the insured to retain proof of notice of the claim. In one
case, a client lost the benefit of its title insurance coverage when the title insurer
insisted it never received a notice of the claim, and the attorney could offer no proof
of delivery.[59]

The late notice will be no defense for the insurer unless the insurer can establish
that the insured's failure to tender prompt notice of the claim impeded the insurer's
ability to defend against the adverse claim. However, the insured will forfeit reimbursement for sums it spent to cure a title defect before it notified the insurer, if
the insurer proves that those costs could have been avoided by timely notice of the
claim.

3. Insured Amount

The most the insured can recover under the insurance contract is the insured
amount of the policy, not to exceed fair market value of the realty at date of loss. Insureds become under-insured when the value of the realty rises above the original

---

56. *Id.* at 1565.

57. Email to author from Robert Garrett (Garrett Tully was the firm that represented the title
insurer in this case), 07/14/15.

58. Joyce Palomar, The 2006 ALTA Title Insurance Policies: What New Protection Do They Give?
42 Real Prop. Prob. & Tr. J. 1, 22 (2007).

59. *Swanson v. Safeco Title Ins. Co.,* 925 P.2d 1354 (Ariz. Ct. App. 1995).

contract price. They could contract for an automatic inflation adjustment,[60] or an increase in the insured amount. Most insureds do none of these things.

In a falling market, the insured's loss will be capped by the current market value. In a rising market, the insured will be under compensated by being limited to the original insured amount.

4. The Duty to Defend as Modified by the Policy Being One of Indemnity, Not Warranty

Title insurers, under standard ALTA policies, have three options for dealing with valid claims based on defects covered under their policies. (1) They can choose to settle a claim by paying the lesser of the full amount insured under the policy or the insured's actual loss.[61] (2) They can take affirmative action to clear the defect and establish the title as insured. (3) They can defend the title in litigation.[62]

"Sometimes, to avoid conflicts, as many as three attorneys may be needed—one to represent the insured equity owner, a second for the insured mortgagee and a third to look after the interests of the title insurer. Insurers rely on independent, not in house, counsel to defend their policyholders' titles, hoping to avoid potential conflicts of interest, or claimed conflicts, between policyholders and themselves."[63]

The prospect of running up steep legal costs defending a title prompts insurers to settle claims when the cost is likely to exceed just paying the full insured amount. Insurers receive no credit against policy limits for defense costs, nor are there any limits to the number of claims an insurer must defend as long as the policy is in place.

5. No Right to Compensation Until Loss Occurs

Because a title policy is for indemnification, the insured seldom has a claim until there is proof of loss. An insured's claim for the removal of an easement or restriction of record only matures if and when it causes uncertainty about the owner's ability to use, develop or finance the property. Even then, the insurer has a *reasonable time to clear the defect.*

---

60. *See* ALTA, Homeowner's Policy of Title Insurance, 10/17/98, an extended coverage policy for homeowners, Paragraph 9, increasing policy limit by 10% in each of the first five years. A more recent version caps the insurer's liability at 125% of the original insured amount.

61. The insurer reserves "the option at any time of settling the claim or paying the amount of this policy in full." *Batdorf v. Transamerica Title Ins. Co. of Chicago Title.* 702 P.2d 1211, 1212, 41 Wash. App. 254, 257 (1985).

62. Some title policies affirm the insurer's option of paying the claim instead of defending the insured's title. Other policies appear to give the insured the benefit of both a legal defense of title and payment of insured losses by mentioning these remedies in the conjunctive: "all loss or damage not exceeding the amount of insurance stated herein and the costs and expenses of defending the title." *Chicago Title Ins. Co. v. Kent School Corp.*, 361 F. Supp. 2d 4, 8 (D. Conn. 2005).

63. Student Note, Protecting Title in Continental Europe and the United States, 7 Hastings Bus.L. J. 411 (Summer, 2011).

Statutes of Limitation. State statutes limit the time for bringing suits on title policies.[64] Statutes of limitations begin to run on potential claims only after there has been a loss, or an imminent threat of loss, and not from the date of discovery. However because of the uncertainty inherent in what counts as "an imminent threat of loss," the insured is best advised to disclose the defect to the insurer right away.[65]

The *Pro Tanto Clause*

Title insurers avoid paying twice on the same claim under a policy provision known as a *pro tanto* clause. Example: X buys property for $500,000 investing $100,000 in cash and taking title subject to a $400,000 mortgage. X's title proves defective—a total loss. The insurer pays $400,000 to the mortgagee and $100,000 to X, not $400,000 to the mortgagee and $500,000 to X.

Ordinarily, mortgagors are content to have title insurers pay off their mortgages. But suppose the property value fell to $400,000 and the balance due on the loan was $500,000. The borrower could end up with no property and a $100,000 unpaid debt.

E. The Difference between the Purchaser's and the Lender's Coverage

In the typical sales transaction, the same title insurer writes policies for both the purchaser and the purchaser's lender simultaneously at closing.

There are significant differences between lenders' and owners' policies though both policies guarantee against loss or damage from title defects, and promise to defend against adverse claims.

First, the buyer is insured fee ownership. The lender is insured a lien priority.[66] As long as the property has equity value, losses on lenders' policies are often minimal. Suppose the insured sale price was $500,000 with a $300,000 purchase money mortgage. The borrower is insured for $500,000 and the lender for $300,000. A title insurer that overlooked a $10,000 judgment lien would incur a $10,000 loss on an owner's policy but no loss at all if only the lender was insured.

Second, the borrower's policy terminates when the buyer sells.[67] The lender's policy terminates when the secured loan is repaid or discharged. The lender's coverage con-

---

64. The California limit is two years. Cal. Civ. Proc. § 339(1) (West 1982).

65. *Tabachnick v. Ticor Title Ins. Co.,* 29 Cal. Rptr. 2d 59 (1992) (The seller lied about the rights of a tenant in possession. The tenant had a forty-year recorded lease, which the buyer's title insurer neither disclosed nor excepted. After closing, the buyer learned of the tenant's interest and sued the seller for fraud. Only three years later did the buyer present a claim to his title insurer. He was too late. The New Jersey statute of limitations, two years, had expired).

66. A lender's first trust deed would have first priority, its second trust deed would have second priority, etc.

67. The insurance could continue if the buyer were later sued on deed warranties for title defects that existed at the date the policy became effective. It is highly improbable that insurers would have liability under grant deed covenants since these are only breached by the grantor and the policy excepts coverage for defects created by the insured. But there might be lurking liability under warranty deeds of which the grantor was unaware at the time of closing.

tinues if the lender becomes the owner of the security property through foreclosure or assigns the mortgage.[68]

Third, lenders usually obtain extended coverage against loss from the unrecorded rights of parties in possession, unrecorded easements and encroachments, and defects a survey would reveal. So, for instance, if the house was built on the wrong lot, the lender would be covered but the buyer would not. (Some buyers' policies sold for a premium cover this risk.)

Finally, insurers often provide endorsements for lenders that are unavailable to owners.

When title insurers evaluate and revise the terms of their policies, they work closely with lenders under the umbrella of the American Land Title Association. Title insurers appreciate the importance to their "bottom line" that lenders insist on residential title insurance.

Limitations to Lenders' Policy Coverage. Though ALTA is solicitous of lenders' opinions when promulgating policy language, title insurers rebuff lenders' claims for losses attributed to lenders' careless loan origination practices.

An example is of claims arising because the loan itself was bogus. Suppose a loan originator, maybe a mortgage broker, forges a borrower's signature on a note and deed of trust, or defrauds a borrower by never advancing the loan proceeds. Security interests are no better than the underlying debt, expressed in the adage "no debt, no mortgage." While title insurers can only verify whether the lien was executed and recorded, lenders are better positioned than title insurers to ascertain whether a borrower agreed to enter a secured loan, and whether the loan was actually funded.

Suppose an institutional lender buys a mortgage loan from a sleazy loan originator. The borrower defaults but prevents foreclosure persuading a court to set aside the forged or fraudulently obtained debt. The lender, experiencing a total loss, files a claim with its title insurer.

Under these circumstances, some title insurers take the position that according to the public land records, the deed of trust or mortgage looked OK. That is all the title insurer should be expected to insure. Title insurers insist that they are not in the debt authentication or collection business. Their mission is solely to determine the validity of the lien created, not to determine whether the debt is valid. They have no efficient

---

68. The mortgage assignee or foreclosure sale purchaser is only covered for defects arising under the assignor's policy, defects pre-dating the assignor's effective policy date. Further, there is a question about whether insurer defenses good against the originating lender would be good against the assignee. Suppose the mortgage lacks the insured priority because it is subordinate to an earlier lien created by the originating lender. Under the exclusion for defects created by the insured, the originating lender would not be entitled to compensation. Would the assignee? *Compare S. Title Ins. Co. v. Crow*, 278 So. 2d 294 (Fla. Dist. Ct. App. 1973) (assignee held entitled to recover since it acquired the lien without notice of the defect) *with Countrywide Homes, Inc. v. Lafonte.*, 2003 WL 1389089 (N.Y. Sup. Ct. 2003, unreported) (upholding insurer's denial of assignee's claim based on assignor's conduct).

means of determining off-record facts such as whether there are valid defenses to the borrower's underlying obligation on the debt.

Professor Roger Bernhardt finds this argument unconvincing. He explains: "All real estate professionals expect title insurance to cover the risk in an owner's policy that the estate in land ostensibly held by the insured was effectively conveyed to her through a chain of authentic and delivered deeds, even though the insurer has undoubtedly not actually investigated the validity of those underlying transactions. How is the burden of taking on that risk different when the policy covers the mortgage on the title rather than the title itself?"[69]

Despite the Professor's analysis, a California appellate court found otherwise and sided with the title insurer.[70]

F. Representing Insured Home Buyers Against Title Insurers

Usually, a title insurer's liability is capped by the insured amount. An exception is when the title insurer denies policy coverage in bad faith. Then, the insurer could be liable for: (a) reimbursing the insured its legal costs, (b) any damage proximately caused by its wrongful denial of a claim, (c) contract damages for breach of the implied covenant of good faith and fair dealing, (d) damages for intentional or negligent infliction of emotional distress, and (e) by statute in some states, actual and punitive damages.

In the case described next, buyers acquired a home on a large parcel intending to construct improvements for their children, including an in-ground backyard pool. Because of title defects the insurer neglected to uncover, they were not able to do this. Instead of admitting liability, the insurer contested it. Eventually, the insured homeowners prevailed in court.

As litigators know all too well, obtaining a favorable court judgment does not put money in the winning party's pocket. The following case depicts the role of a trial lawyer in transforming a favorable legal outcome into a financially meaningful one for his clients.

Crossman v. Yacubovich:[71] *The Story of a Title Dispute and Its Resolution*

The Crossmans Buy a Home. This story began on July 29, 2003, when Michael and Kimberly Crossman contracted to buy their dream house, located at 59 Shadow Ridge in St. Charles County, Missouri, for $160,900. The sellers were Peter and Sharon Yacubovich who acquired the house in 1994 for $88,500.

The three-bedroom, two-bath house attracted the Crossmans because of its large backyard. The sellers' listing broker even noted in her data sheet that other brokers

---

69. Roger Bernhardt, Title insurance and fraudulent loans: *First Am. Title Ins. Co. v X Warehouse Lending*, 2009, Digital Commons (last visited July 22, 2015), http://digitalcommons.law.ggu.edu/cgi/viewcontent.cgi?article=1404&context=pubs

70. *First American Title Ins. Co. v. XWarehouse Lending Corp.*, 177 Cal. App. 4th 106, 98 Cal. Rptr. 3d 801, 2009 Cal. App. LEXIS 1435 (Cal. App. 1st Dist. 2009).

71. 290 S.W.3d 775(Mo. App. Ct. 2009).

and agents "show the house to buyers looking for a big lot." The Crossmans "envisioned extending the deck, adding a pool, planting a garden, building a batting cage for their children, and fencing the yard for their dogs."

The Crossmans' Title Arrangements. To make sure they were acquiring good title and to handle their escrow and closing, the Crossmans hired Investors' Title Company. The company conducted a search of the public records, ordered a survey,[72] prepared a title commitment, and acted as an agent in obtaining a policy of title insurance for the Crossmans from Lawyers' Title.

The land description in Schedule A of their commitment was based on a recorded subdivision map: "Lot 33 of Shadow Creek, Plat Two," at plat book 21, page 55 of the St. Charles County Records. The Crossmans' policy contained numerous exceptions to coverage including one for "building lines and easements" according to the plat.

Bad News for The Crossmans: The Pipeline Easements. Soon after closing, a representative from Explorer Pipeline came through the neighborhood, removed nine trees from the Crossmans' property and warned them that a work shed in the backyard would have to be torn down.

The Crossmans learned that prior owners granted three easements in 1930, 1966 and 1971, to three different petroleum pipeline companies, traversing beneath roughly half of their property. The easement agreements conferred upon the pipeline companies unlimited rights of access, and specifically allowed the transportation of hazardous materials, including oil, through the pipelines. The easements prohibited the grantors or their successors from constructing anything permanent in the back yard that would interfere with access to those easements.

The Crossmans' lot was part of a 1979 subdivision and the developer/subdivider neglected to note these prior easements on the subdivision map. Because the title company relied on the subdivision map in researching the title, it failed to find the earlier recorded easements. Had the title company made a thorough search past 1979 through the St. Charles County land records, it would have found those easements.

The County offers online access to subscribers but online data only goes back to 1972. So the title company would have had to physically search the public records to find the easements, but did not bother to do this.

The Crossmans' Claim in Court. Instead of admitting its error, the title insurance company denied the Crossmans' claim based on a policy exception for "[b]uilding lines and easements according to the plat thereof recorded in Plat Book 21, Pages 55–56."

---

72. A "Surveyor's Real Property Report" or "spot survey" was ordered. "This is a location of improvements and cursory check for encroachments onto or from the subject property based on existing, but not confirmed, evidence. This does not constitute a boundary survey and is subject to any inaccuracies that a subsequent boundary survey might disclose. No property markers or corners will be set and it should not be used or relied upon for the establishment of any fence, structure, or other improvement. No warranty of any kind is extended therein to the present or future owner or occupant."

The Crossmans sued and the trial court granted the insurer's motion for summary judgment, and the Crossmans appealed. The trial court accepted the title insurer's assertion that the subdivision plat map mentioned the three easements. A more skeptical and energetic appellate court judge, Judge Mooney, took the time to examine the recorded plat map himself. He concluded that "the plat does not clearly, precisely, and unambiguously show the existence of multiple easements on the insured property." In a declaratory judgment, he found against the title insurer for having breached their insurance policy contract and for vexatious refusal to pay.

Judge Mooney had little regard for the title work in this case. It did not match up to the quality of work that the sellers' sellers received when they first acquired title. The Crossmans' sellers' title policy reported and excepted those three easements from coverage quite specifically. The Crossmans' title company just did not delve far back enough into the title records. It stopped searching when it came to the subdivision map, figuring, wrongly in this case, that the subdivider's surveyor would have noted any prior encumbrances on the map.

Developing a Strategy to Recover Compensation After Winning the Lawsuit. After the appellate victory on June 16, 2009, Gary Siegel, the attorney for the Crossmans, analyzed potential claims against (a) the sellers, (b) Investors Title Company, (c) Lawyers' Title Insurance Company, an affiliate of Old Republic, and (d) Topos Surveying and Engineering Company. Investors Title had done the title research, handled the closing, and also acted as Lawyers' Title's agent in selling the Crossmans a title insurance policy. Topos was the firm that Investors Title hired to survey the property for the Crossmans.

Seller Liability. The sellers had exposure under their general warranty deed for breach of a covenant against encumbrances, a covenant to warrant and defend, and a covenant of quiet enjoyment.

Additionally, there was evidence to suggest that the sellers actually knew about the easements and failed to disclose them.[73] Besides the exception to coverage of the easements in their title policy, they received an actual printed notice from one of the pipeline companies before listing their property for sale, indicating that it would be sending representatives out to the properties and asking homeowners to clear out foliage and remove structures that infringed upon their easement.[74] The sellers received that notice just before they listed their property for sale.

Though attorney Siegel appreciated that his clients had a strong case against the sellers, he perceived three problems with pursuing it vigorously. It would weaken his claims against the other defendants by giving them an argument that the sellers' misrepresentations and failures to disclose were intervening, intentional acts, not reasonably foreseeable. Further, and of obvious importance, there was no basis for recovering his substantial legal fees from the sellers.

---

73. Mr. and Mrs. Yacubovich both testified that they were not aware of the rights-of-ways that ran across the property when they entered into the contract to sell the property to the Crossmans.

74. Mr. Yacubovich testified that he did not "recall" receiving such a notice and that if he did, he "threw it away" assuming it was "junk mail."

Even more concerning, upon investigating the sellers' financial situation, attorney Siegel concluded that a judgment against them would not be collectable. They had very little equity in the house, no substantial assets besides the house, very limited income, they were approaching retirement and were considering the possibility of filing bankruptcy.[75]

Title Company and Title Insurer Liability. The title insurer argued that the buyers had actual and constructive notice of the pipeline easements because the easements had actually been recorded in favor of three separate pipeline companies in 1930, 1966 and 1971.

Attorney Siegel met this contention head on: requiring any home buyer to perform a title search, and second guess the search that it was paying its title insurer to perform, "runs contrary to public policy expectations of purchasers of title insurance policies, especially for purchasers of residential real property."

The appellate court agreed. The title company missed the pipeline easements in its apparently incomplete title search and should compensate the Crossmans for their loss instead of trying to foist the consequences of its ineptitude upon them.

The measure of damages was sticky. Title insurers have no liability just because a covered defect is shown to exist. An insured has no right to compensation under a title policy until the defect results in an actual loss. Further, the insurer's liability for a title defect is ordinarily limited to the insured amount of the policy—not to exceed the insured's actual loss.

In the Crossmans' situation, their actual loss would be measured by the diminution in value caused by the easement—$50,000 according to the Crossmans, and $15,000 according to the insurer's appraisal. As mentioned earlier, an insured can obtain substantial damages when an insurer denies coverage in bad faith. But it was hard to fault the insurer's initial denial of the claim as having been in bad faith after the trial court agreed with the insurer at the summary judgment stage. So much for Attorney Seigel's obtaining more than compensatory damages against the title insurer. So where were his legal fees to come from if not from the title insurer?

Surveyor Liability. The surveying company had some financial exposure because it overlooked stakes that the pipeline companies recently placed along its rights of way in the Crossmans' backyard. This oversight invited suspicion that perhaps the surveyor never actually made an on-site inspection. Despite the surveyor's vulnerability, its contract limited its liability to the cost of the survey.[76]

The Final Settlement. The Crossmans were particularly disturbed by the sellers' lack of candor, but having spent six years pursuing their claim, they realized that further litigation might not be productive for them. Eventually, the title insurer, surveyor,

---

75. Email from Mr. Seigel to author's research assistant, April 12, 2014.

76. The Title Order Form specified that the "spot survey" that was ordered " is subject to any inaccuracies" and "should not be used or relied upon.... No warranty of any kind is extended therein to the ... owner or occupant."

and the sellers each contributed something totaling about $75,000 ($15,000 for loss in value and $60,000 for attorneys' fees).

A Happy Ending for All: Instead of an in-ground swimming pool that would have infringed on the pipeline easements, the Crossmans built an above-ground pool in their backyard.

Questions

Question 1: *Shopping for Title Insurance.*

(a) Most home buyers negotiate the purchase price but do not shop for the best price for title insurance. What could explain this apparent anomaly?

(b) How can a home buyer be sure that the title insurer offering them a bargain rate has adequate financial resources to make good on its policies if the title is defective?

Question 2: *Preliminary Title Report.*

(a) Why is it necessary for a buyer to study the preliminary report or title commitment closely even in jurisdictions where the title insurers have no liability for errors and omissions in the preliminary report?

(b) What are the most compelling competing arguments concerning whether realty buyers and mortgage lenders should be entitled to rely on the description of title in a preliminary report or commitment, and hold the title insurer accountable for a negligent title search?

(c) When a prospective buyer contracts for an inspection of the physical condition of the house she has contracted to purchase, she can usually count on the inspector being willing to discuss any and all of the issues raised by its inspection report. But when a prospective home buyer has questions about the exceptions and exclusions in a preliminary title report or title commitment, title company lawyers and title searchers are going to be far less forthcoming in answering such questions. What could account for this?

Question 3: *Scope of Coverage. Off Record Risks.*

Title insurance covers the insured against defects appearing in the public records. Give examples of the three potentially costly off-record risks that as a prospective home buyer you would personally be most relieved to know are also covered?

Question 4: *Negotiating Coverage.*

The buyer of a restaurant strongly objects to an exception in the preliminary title report for a covenant barring the sale of alcoholic beverages, which was imposed eighty years ago and never enforced. What might a title insurer require of the seller as a condition to removing the exception?

Question 5: *Changing Ownership Without Losing Title Coverage.*

Ally Artist purchases an empty warehouse as an art gallery and wine bar. She obtained a title policy at the time of her acquisition. Now that the business has grown, she is worried about potential liability, having heard some horror stories of drunk patrons suing bar owners for their mishaps.

(a) Will she continue to be covered by her title policy if she transfers title of the real estate to a Limited Liability Company?

(b) Suppose she had taken title in a limited partnership, assuming unlimited liability as the general partner, while her investor became the limited partner because he wanted to avoid personal liability for partnership debts. Could she transfer her general partnership interest into a specially formed limited liability company without losing the benefit of her title insurance coverage?

Question 6: *Gap Coverage.*

(a) What is gap coverage?

(b) Why is it important to a real estate buyer or mortgagee?

Question 7: *Defects Known to or Assumed by the Insured.*

(a) A home buyer agrees to purchase subject to the seller's mortgage. Though the mortgage was properly recorded at the time the seller purchased the home many years ago, the buyer's title insurer had not excepted that mortgage from coverage. What policy language will the title insurer probably cite to justify denying liability to the buyer?

(b) A motorcycle gang has been hanging out for several years on vacant acreage that the owner has now sold to a buyer who purchased a title policy. Because the buyer observed the gang in action on the site, he insisted upon the seller paying extra for an extended coverage policy, insuring against loss by reason of any facts, rights, interests, or claims which are not shown by public record but which could be ascertained by an inspection of the land or by making inquiry of persons in possession thereof. The title insurer issued the policy with no exclusion for the gang's activities at the site. The buyer never mentioned to the title insurer his concerns about the gang. After closing, the buyer asked the gang to stop using the property. They are claiming a prescriptive easement or adverse possession. Is the title insurer liable for the costs of quieting or defending the buyer's title?

Question 8: *Donee's Rights Under a Title Policy.*

Since title policies exclude liability for losses that would not have occurred had the insured paid value, is there any point in cousin Miguel obtaining a title policy for the condo Aunt Teresa conveyed to him as a gift?

Question 9: *The Title Insurer's Options for Discharging Its Liability Under the Policy.*

(a) A buyer discovers that her title is subject to a lien for twice the amount of her purchase price, a properly recorded lien that the title insurer simply overlooked. Does she have the right to insist upon the insurer paying off the lien instead of just handing the insured a check for the policy amount?

(b) If there is room to dispute the legal validity of the lien, will the insurer be obligated to litigate, or can the insurer elect to pay the policy amount and not defend the title?

(c) The title insurer denies the claim for no particularly good reason, forcing the buyer to file suit. After a lengthy and distressing lawsuit in which the insurer defends its position vigorously and ultimately loses, would the insurer be limited in its recovery to the insured amount under the policy? If not, describe the sources and extent of the title insurer's potential exposure to liability.

Question 10: *Title Insurance Regulation, Fees and Expenses.*

In a 10-28-2006 article in Forbes magazine, Scott Woolley contended that title insurance was an oligopoly protected by state laws. Insurance regulators barred most general insurers from entering the title business. Title insurers routinely offered kickbacks to brokers for referrals with scant enforcement of federal and state statutes prohibiting such practices, and local governments were slow to transform their records into digital formats and make them available online. This enabled title insurers to extract excess profits. As proof of excess profits, he noted that policy premiums were rising steeply even as title insurer payouts on claims were steadily declining. *(Google: Scott Woolley, Title insurance).*

How could the title industry justify charging higher premiums for title coverage even as their pay-outs on claims were falling?

Question 11: *Defects An Inspection Would Reveal; Coverage Against Encroachments and Trespass.*

(a) The insured's concrete driveway is being damaged by the roots from honey lotus trees intruding from the neighboring property. Anyone familiar with this type of tree would know that it has extensive root systems that would be likely to compromise the driveway.

The insured has a premium homeowner's policy which insures against title defects that an inspection would reveal, and covers loss or damage from encroachments of the owner's property into neighboring terrain and any neighbor's encroachment into the insured's property. Is the driveway owner's title insurer liable?

(b) The insured acquired a house on a golf course. Their title policy covered defects an inspection would reveal.

After taking possession, they discovered that golf balls often landed in their yard, sometimes dented their garden wall and once even broke a second floor bedroom window.

The title was subject to recorded covenants, conditions and restrictions, which included an "easement for errant golf balls."

Neither the title commitment nor the title policy noted these CC&Rs as exceptions or exclusions to coverage. Is the title insurer liable to the homeowners for loss or damage caused by the stray golf balls?

Chapter 10

Real Estate Escrows and Closings[1]

Scope of the Chapter

A typical real estate contract begins with negotiations leading to buyer and seller entering a purchase and sale contract. When all goes well, it ends with a closing. Technically, a closing occurs at the precise moment buyers and sellers fulfill the contract promises they made to each other.

The seller's obligation to convey "marketable title" would typically be fulfilled by delivery of a title insurance policy and a notarized deed signed by the seller as grantor. The buyer and its mortgage lender would fulfill their obligations to pay the purchase price by remitting "good funds." In practice, the buyer and seller designate an intermediary acting as a closing agent to oversee completion of all the requisite conditions precedent to the closing.

The first part of this chapter is about the functions of these intermediaries. Depending on local custom and practice, the closing or escrow agent could be a title insurance company, an underwritten title company,[2] a bank or savings association,

---

1. The author is grateful for the advice and contributions made to this chapter by Danielle M. (Graf) Kitzes, Commerce Escrow Company; Robert Minsky, Commerce Escrow Company' and Rose Pothier, Attorney, Pothier & Associates, Santa Ana, California.

Va. Code Ann. §6.1-2.20 contains a good description of the scope of escrow, closing and settlement services: "'Escrow, closing or settlement services' means the administrative and clerical services required to carry out the terms of contracts affecting real estate. These services include, but are not limited to, placing orders for title insurance, receiving and issuing receipts for money received from the parties, ordering loan checks and payoffs, ordering surveys and inspections, preparing settlement statements, determining that all closing documents conform to the parties' contract requirements, setting the closing appointment, following up with the parties to ensure that the transaction progresses to closing, ascertaining that the lenders' instructions have been satisfied, conducting a closing conference at which the documents are executed, receiving and disbursing funds, completing form documents and instruments selected by and in accordance with instructions of the parties to the transaction, handling or arranging for the recording of documents, sending recorded documents to the lender, sending the recorded deed and the title policy to the buyer, and reporting federal income tax information for the real estate sale to the Internal Revenue Service."

2. An underwritten title company is one that has entered a contract with a title insurer that provides coverage against losses above a minimum deductible amount on policies that the underwritten title company issues. The underwritten company must comply with the title insurer's standards.

an attorney representing one or both parties, or a real estate broker. In southern California and a few western states, independent escrow agents are often chosen.[3]

The second part of the chapter is about closings: (1) the contents of an accounting known as a closing statement, and (2) post-closing liability for errors, omissions and fraud.

The concluding section is about the Real Estate Settlement and Procedures Act (RESPA). This federal law, now administered by the Consumer Financial Protection Bureau (CFPB),[4] enacted to restrain the costs of real estate financing and transfers, bars settlement service providers such as title insurers from paying kickbacks and referral fees to real estate brokers or others for steering clients to them. RESPA aims to eliminate kickbacks and referral fees because they "tend to increase unnecessarily the costs of certain settlement services."[5] Congress assumed, apparently, that if a title insurer paid a broker, say, $100 for each client referral, the insurer would find a way of tacking that $100 fee onto the cost of title insurance, one way or another.

I. The Escrow Agent

A. Functions

Escrow or closing agents represent both parties for a limited purpose, usually detailed in signed escrow instructions.

The Escrow Agent's Typical Check List of Things to Do[6]

1. Obtain identity information from both parties;

2. Obtain various reports required by the contract, including preliminary title reports, title policies, pest control and building inspections, and surveys;

3. Obtain "due diligence" waivers from buyers concerning the physical condition of the property and the title;

4. Request pay off demands from current lenders with releases to be recorded at closing;

5. Obtain escrow instructions and loan documents from buyer's lender;

6. Estimate, request and receive funds needed for closing and issue receipts for funds;

---

3. For a run down on the type of intermediary used state by state to process closings, see STEWART TITLE (last visited Feb. 15, 2016), https://www.stewart.com/content/dam/stewart/Microsites/International/PDFs/SISCO-1214-157-8%20US%20LawsCustoms%20Toolkit-NTS-REV2-A.pdf.

4. *See, e.g.*, CFPB Compliance Bulletin 2015-05, RESPA Compliance and Marketing Services Agreements, Oct. 8, 2015.

5. 12 U.S.C. §2601(b)(2). A consumer advocate points out that "80 to 92 percent of the premiums paid for title insurance go to middlemen—title and settlement agents, escrow agents and lawyers—who in turn often split their fees with affiliated realty and mortgage partners." REALTY TIMES, May 1, 2006, quoting J. Robert Hunter, representing Consumer Federation of America.

6. 2 CEB, CALIFORNIA REAL ESTATE SALES TRANSACTIONS §13.34 (3d ed. 1998).

7. Order documents (e.g., deeds, notes, deeds of trust, estoppel certificates, rent rolls, certificates of insurance, an affidavit that the seller is not a "foreign person" subject to the withholding of taxes under the Foreign Investment in Real Property Tax Act (FIRPTA), a certificate of good standing from the state in which a buyer or seller entity was formed, a resolution certified by an authorized officer of the entity confirming that all requisite actions have been taken to authorize entity participation in the transaction);

8. Obtain signatures of proper parties;

9. Compute pro-rations;

10. Arrange for prompt recordation of documents;

11. Collect and disburse funds;

12. Issue closing statement;

13. Report sale to IRS on form 1099-S.

What Escrow Agents Should Avoid

1. Preparing and modifying legal documents—such as quitclaim deeds, releases or affidavits, so as to be engaging in the unlawful practice of law.[7]

2. If a contract calls for a party's written authorization, not detecting an obvious forgery.[8]

3. Disbursing funds from escrow trust accounts on the basis of a trial court order before the appeal period runs.[9]

4. Disbursing funds before actual receipt. (The agent has a claim against the buyer for the flawed or fraudulent tender. But if the buyer is insolvent, the escrow agent will probably get stuck with the loss.)[10]

---

7. *See Bishop v. Jefferson Title Co. Inc.*, 28 P.3d 802, 107 Wash. App. 833 (2001) (Escrow agent inadvertently included language in seller's purchase money deed of trust obligating seller to assume obligation of existing deed of trust for buyer's benefit, not what the seller intended or instructed. In doing this, court held the escrow agent had engaged in the unauthorized practice of law and should be held to the same standard of professional conduct as an attorney.).

8. *Lee v. Escrow Consultants, Inc.*, 259 Cal. Rptr. 117 (Ct. App. 1989) (Seller forged buyer's signature to escrow instruction authorizing disbursement to seller of buyer's escrowed funds before closing. Escrow agent complied and was held liable to buyer for not following escrow instructions which required buyer's approval of disbursements.).

9. *Miller v. Craig*, 558 P.2d 984 (Ariz. Ct. App. 1976). The trial court judgment could be reversed on appeal and the agent would be liable for funds it paid out prematurely. A closing attorney gave the seller $5000 from an escrow account for a failure purchase and sale agreement. A trial court had awarded the seller specific performance. The sellers demanded the $5000, and the attorney gave it to them. Then, the buyers reversed the judgment on appeal, and the attorney was held to owe the buyers a refund of the $5000.

10. *Greenwald v. Chase Manhattan Mortgage Corp.*, 241 F.3d 76 (1st Cir. 2001). Law firm was acting as closing attorney in a sale of newly originated mortgage loans. Lender A originated the loans for sale to Chase, and was supposed to pay off existing loans on the security properties before selling the loan. The firm disbursed payments to pay off the liens before realizing that some of the checks from Lender A didn't cleared. Lender A was insolent and the law firm got stuck with the loss due to its premature payoff of the pre-existing liens.

Six Aspects of Escrow

1. An Illustration of the Limits of Escrow Agent Responsibility for Business Advice. The following summary of the facts in an often cited case is presented to demonstrate that the responsibilities of escrow agents are tethered strictly to their escrow instructions. Sellers contracted to sell their 350-acre chicken ranch for a total purchase price of $60,550, with $17,500 to be paid at or before closing, and the balance secured by a deed of trust due payable some time after the closing.

The sellers were to deed the property to the buyers at closing but were to receive a security interest in the property for the unpaid purchase price. The security interest took the form of a note signed by the buyers and a deed of trust that would be recorded.

With a bill of sale, the buyers were free to sell these items after the sale, and that is precisely what they did. They removed and resold the personal property that had been transferred to them by the bill of sale, and then defaulted on the deed of trust.

Here is where the problem arose—the sellers had told the escrow agent drafting the instructions that they did not intend to convey title to the personal property that accompanied the land until the buyers paid the full purchase price, not just the down payment. The personal property were items related to the use of the chicken farms, such as chicken brooders, pumps, and other items designed principally for raising chickens. The sellers understood that the buyers were going to have title and possession of the chicken farm when they made the down payment of $17,500, and executed a deed of trust for the balance of the purchase price. But they did not understand that with a bill of sale, the buyers could sell off all the personal property. Since the escrow instructions, contrary to what the sellers requested of the escrow agent, had explicitly called for them to provide a bill of sale at closing, title to the personal property was relinquished and the buyers had the right to sell the personal property. In affirming the long-standing rule that escrow agents are only responsible for carrying out the instructions of their principals and are not responsible for giving legal or business advice, or explaining the implications of the instructions to the parties to the escrow, the court observed: "It is unfortunate that the plaintiffs did not fully foresee the effect of the documents prepared at their request. However, the evidence is ample that the escrow instructions, objectively considered, controlled the rights of the parties."[11]

---

11. *Cunningham v. Security Title Ins. Co.*, 241 C.A.2d 626, 630 (1966). *See also Jafari v. FDIC*, 2 F. Supp. 3d 1125 (2014). Escrow agent had no liability to FDIC when paying off its lien while disregarding a request to provide opinion of counsel that the borrower would remain personally liable on the underlying debt in a pending bankruptcy proceeding. The FDIC was not a party to the escrow which was between no one except the buyer and seller. *But see Bowers v. Transamerica Title Ins. Co.*, 100 Wash. 2d 581, 675 P.2d 193 (Wash. 1983). Escrow agent held accountable to sellers for preparing an unsecured note from the buyer for $33,000 of the $45,000 purchase price. After closing, buyer borrowed $33,000 secured by the house, pocketed the money and filed for bankruptcy.

2. *Duty to Disclose Fraud in the Escrow*. In some situations, escrow agents may have to choose between safeguarding information received in confidence from a principal and disclosing material information to prevent fraud or a misrepresentation.[12]

An escrow agent facing this moral dilemma could simply withdraw from the transaction. State courts have reached different conclusions regarding the obligations of escrow agents to detect and disclose fraud in the escrow.[13] These decisions are controversial; escrow agents are supposed to be responsible solely for processing deals based on a literal reading of the instructions given them by the parties to the escrow. Escrow agents are not supposed to look past what it takes to close the deal on time. They barely have enough time to do that. But escrow agents also have an obligation to disclose all material matters to their principals, and both the buyer and the seller are the escrow agent's principals.[14]

Consider these situations:

(1) Seller A and Buyer B open an escrow for the sale of a 10-unit apartment house. B then contracts to sell the apartment house to C for $100,000 more than the A-B contract price, planning to use C's funds to pay A.

Should the escrow agent disclose to Seller A and C the existence of the companion escrows? While there is some disagreement about this, escrow agents are best advised to "blow the whistle" when the buyer is "flipping" the property to make a quick profit in a "double escrow."[15] Both A and C are depending on the other escrow to complete their transaction with B.

Although case law is thin on the subject, the escrow agent is probably best advised not to process the second escrow without the informed consent of both the seller in the first escrow and the buyer (and perhaps the buyer's lender) in the second escrow.

(2) The mortgage lender has received a copy of the purchase and sale agreement, verifying that the buyer's down payment is large enough to satisfy the lender's maximum 75% loan-to-value ratio. In escrow, seller and buyer modify escrow instructions to require that the escrow agent withhold a large part of the down payment and return

---

12. Wayne S. Bell & Summer B. Bakotich, *Surviving the Real Estate 'Escrow' Process in California*, 1 DRE.Ca.Gov 14 (last visited July 10, 2015), http://www.dre.ca.gov/files/pdf/Escrow_Info_Consumers .pdf.

13. *Burkons v. Ticor Title Ins. Co.*, 798 P.2d 1308, 1312–13 (Ariz. Ct. App. 1990). *See Shaheen v. Am. Title Ins. Co.*, 586 P.2d 1317, 120 Ariz. 505 (1978) (escrow agent had no duty to warn seller that deeds of trust were under secured); *Gordon v. N.M. Title Co.*, 421 P.2d 433, 77 N.M. 217 (1966) (no duty to investigate or report unfiled mechanics' liens); *Gebrayel v. Transamerica Title Ins. Co.*, 888 P.2d 83, 132 Or. App. 271 (1995) (no duty to inform buyer of not-of-record claim against property prior to closing).

14. Harry D. Miller & Marvin B. Starr, Current Law of California Real Estate § 5:23, at 449–50 (Bancroft-Whitney 2d ed. 1989).

15. In *Berry v. McLeod*, 604 P.2d 610 (Ariz. 1979), an Arizona court thought the escrow agent should have warned the seller that the seller's broker was buying the property through a dummy corporation, and reselling to the buyer in a double escrow. *See* Karen Lee Jacobsen, Note, *California Escrow Agents: A Duty to Disclose Known Fraud*, 17 Pac. L.J. 309 (1985) (applauding results in *Berry*).

it to the buyer after closing. The modified instructions disguise the kickback by labeling the withheld sum as compensation from the seller to the buyer for unspecified defects in the condition of the property. Does the escrow agent have a duty to inform the lender of the sellers' remittances to the buyer?

The mortgage lender was not even a party to the original escrow agreement which was only between buyer and seller. The mortgage lender and the escrow agent have no formal agreement linking them to each other directly. At most, the mortgage lender can claim to be a sub-agent of the escrow agent handling the transactions.

To be safe, the escrow agent would be best advised to seek the mortgage lender's specific approval of the remittances. But once she does this, the real estate broker is going to protest that the escrow agent had no business deciding whether the seller's payments to the buyer were reasonable costs of repair that the buyers would have had to make to cure property defects after the closing.

3. *Loan Sub-Escrows and Pay-Off Demands.* Properties are often sold or mortgaged that are subject to liens that the buyer or lender expects to be repaid and then released of record at closing. To make sure this happens, buyers and sellers need to instruct their escrow or closing agents accordingly.

In California, when the escrow agent handling a transaction is independent and possibly under-capitalized, lenders are often more comfortable entrusting loan proceeds to an underwritten title company. Escrow agents diverting to their personal bank account's funds advanced by a lender to pay off another lender's prior lien are a frequent source of fraud in real estate transactions. So the buyer's lender requires the buyer to set up a sub-escrow arrangement with an approved entity of the lender's own choosing to co-ordinate loan fund transfers. The designated agent is usually the same title company that has been instructed to oversee preparation of the lender's release.

Whether there is a sub-escrow or not, the escrow or closing agent will contact the holders of all existing liens and inquire how much they are demanding as a condition to releasing their security interest in the property being sold or mortgaged. These requests take the form of a *pay-off demand*. In the pay-off demand, the lienor details the sums it requires as the *quid pro quo* for signing the documentation necessary to release its lien to be recorded at closing. This demand is for a sum of money that includes principal, prepayment penalties, and interest to a specific date, and a per diem after that. Escrow agents have no obligation to double check the lender's math for accuracy as long as they have properly identified the loan that is to be repaid.

Pay-off demands sometimes erroneously exceed the amount of money that the borrower actually owes. Borrowers are supposed to figure this out by verifying the accuracy of the demanded sum. This can be a challenging computation to make as lenders seldom offer detailed breakdowns or explanations for the loan payoff amounts they demand.

Often, buyers and their mortgage lenders are expecting the proceeds of the new loan to repay all the existing debt on the property including federal and local tax liens. Mortgage lenders need to be sure the buyers' and sellers' escrow instructions made that clear. Otherwise, their escrow agent has no liability for not paying off all prior liens and securing their release by recordable documents.

You may wonder how it is possible to fulfill both the new lender's insistence on title insurance of a first lien once its funds have been used to repay existing mortgages, and the concurrent insistence of mortgagees to payment in full before they record releases of their liens. Well, it simply is not possible.

In California, the lender advancing money to pay off existing liens instructs its escrow agent to receive a written pay-off demand from all lien holders. The new lender's lien is recorded as soon as funds are wired according to the pay-off demands. A state statute[16] requires the paid-off lenders to record reconveyances or releases within 30 days.

4. Pro-Rations of Insurance and Property Taxes. Up to the moment of closing, the seller is responsible for property taxes, casualty insurance premiums, mortgage payments, and homeowners' dues. After closing, the buyer becomes responsible for these payments. Payment due dates would rarely be exactly the same for all of these, nor are they likely to be coterminous with the contract closing date. Therefore, the escrow agent needs to pro-rate the amounts that accrued during each party's period of ownership for each of these obligations.

There are two ways to do the math for loan pro-rations: (1) a 365-day year and actual days in each month (the actual method), or (2) a 360-day year, 30 days in a month (called the bank method). For property taxes, escrow agents usually choose the actual days method.

To start calculating the property tax pro ration, the closing or escrow agent determines the tax year over which each tax assessment accrues. Assume that in this jurisdiction the tax year is coterminous with the calendar year, January 1 through December 31.

Then, the "closer" needs to know the date on which the tax becomes due and payable without penalty. Most jurisdictions provide for installments, often twice a year. But for simplicity, assume that in this jurisdiction taxes are due on July 1 for the entire calendar year.

Next, the closer needs to know the annual tax bill for the subject property. For ease of computation, we will make it $3,650. To derive a per diem tax amount, divide the tax bill by a 365 (or 360) day year. That comes to $10 a day.

Suppose the closing is scheduled for December 1. The seller will owe taxes for the period from January 1 to November 30. The buyer will owe the property taxes from Dec 1 to Dec 31.

If the seller made the payment in July which would have covered the entire calendar year in which the taxes were paid, the buyer owes the seller a per diem payment measured by 31 x $10 = $310.

---

16. CAL. CIV. CODE § 2941. The mortgage lender who neglects to record the release or reconveyance within 30 days after its pay-off demand has been met is liable to the person affected by the violation for actual damages plus $1000.

If the seller did not pay the taxes on July 1, the tax assessor would be able to impose a tax lien and eventually foreclose the assessed property. Hence, the buyer would be liable for the taxes not paid in July. So the seller owes the buyer the taxes that accrued from Jan 1 to December 1, $10 x 334 days, $3,340. The closing or escrow agent will make the appropriate adjustments to each of their settlement statements.

5. *Payment of the Broker's Commission.* Real estate brokers prefer to be paid from sale proceeds at closing instead of having to depend on sellers paying commissions after the closing. In most states brokers have no automatic right to be paid from the seller's share of sale proceeds in escrow.[17] Real estate brokers are not usually parties to the escrow. Nor in most states are they regarded as having equitable liens against the sale proceeds or the property itself.[18]

Brokers would prefer not having to depend on the goodwill of sellers to pay the broker's commission after the seller receives the sale proceeds. So brokers draft their listing agreements, purchase and sale contracts and escrow instructions in such a way that the seller assigns the broker the right to be paid a commission by the escrow agent or closing attorney from sale proceeds concurrent with the closing, directly from the seller's share of escrowed sale proceeds. Sellers rarely object when asked for such an assignment in the listing agreement, even though by consenting, they relinquish the right to withhold payment of the broker's commission even for good cause.

Before paying the commission, the escrow agent will have an obligation under state licensing laws to make sure the broker was duly licensed at the time he or she performed the services for which the commission is being paid.[19]

6. *Matters Explicitly Made of No Concern to the Escrow Agent.* Escrow agents mark certain contract contingencies as "outside escrow," hoping to avoid becoming de facto mediators or arbitrators of disputes between the parties. For example, in a situation where the contract specifies: "Seller warrants to paint the house before closing," the escrow instructions could provide: "Escrow agent is to take no notice of whether the seller has painted the house. This matter is to be resolved by the parties outside escrow and is not a matter with which escrow is to be concerned." A buyer unhappy with the seller's paint job needs to specify other means for obtaining satisfaction from the seller, or to include a mutually agreed instruction that escrow is not to close until the buyer signs a statement that the seller has re-painted the house to buyer's satisfaction.

---

17. *First National Bank in Tucumcari v. Berger Briggs Real Estate & Insurance, Inc.*, 89 N.M. 185, 548 P.2d 863 (1976) (Broker is an unsecured creditor absent principal's creation by contract of a lien in favor of broker).

18. *See Contemporary Invs., Inc. v. Safeco Title Ins. Co.*, 193 Cal. Rptr. 822 (Ct. App. 1983) (Seller has the right unilaterally to cancel authorization to pay broker up to closing. Seller had not assigned funds to broker, nor had broker signed instruction ordering payment by escrow out of seller's sale proceeds.).

19. *Kangarlou v. Progressive Title Co., Inc.* 128 Cal. App. 4th 1174 (2005) (CAL. CIV. CODE § 1717 makes it a misdemeanor to pay a commission to an unlicensed broker).

B. Opening and Terminating an Escrow

Escrow Instructions. Escrow Instructions are prepared by the escrow officer and identify all of the terms of the escrow. To be valid, the instructions must be signed by all three parties—buyer, seller and agent.

Spoken escrow instructions are enforceable because they fall outside the Statute of Frauds, not being contracts for the sale of realty. Nonetheless, escrow agents strongly prefer written instructions. In some places, local practice calls for each party to sign its own escrow instructions. This is no problem where everyone is using the same form but inconsistencies can arise when they are not. The problem with joint instructions is loss of confidentiality. Buyers might not want the seller to know how they are financing the acquisition, and sellers might not want buyers to know about their creditors' or partners' rights. Some purchase and sale contract forms incorporate escrow instructions in the same document.

When Does Escrow Open? An escrow opens when at least one party deposits something (usually cash or a deed) *irrevocably* into the hands of an escrow agent, accompanied by instructions to deliver it to another person on specified conditions. During escrow, the agent holds documents and cash pursuant to the specified conditions of escrow. Typically, in escrow instructions accompanying a purchase and sale contract, the agent can only release funds or documents with the written approval of both parties.

Unilateral Withdrawal Is Permitted Until Escrow Opens. Sometimes, it becomes important to know the exact date when escrow opened and closed. Suppose the buyer decides to back out of the deal and wants her money returned. She has that right as long as the escrow agent is merely a stakeholder for the buyer—a *depositary* safeguarding the buyer's money. Once the buyer, the seller and the escrow agent sign irrevocable instructions, all three of them need to authorize the agent to return the buyer's funds.

Mutual Consent Is Required to Modify or Cancel After Escrow Opens. When one of the parties decides to terminate the escrow, the unwinding process begins with the escrow agent preparing cancellation instructions for all the parties to sign. Upon receipt of unanimous consent, the agent cancels, returns the deposit to the buyer, the deed to the seller and retains her cancellation fee.

Escrow instructions anticipate the possibility of irreconcilable differences. Some call for mediation or binding arbitration and, as a last resort, the escrow agent interpleading all the parties in a lawsuit.

Embezzlement Risk. When escrow agents go bad and embezzle funds or perpetrate ownership frauds by recording deeds prematurely, the risk of loss is borne by the party who was legally entitled to the funds or the deed at the moment of the fraud. The rationale is that the escrow agent represents both the buyer and seller, and has been designated by them jointly.

The buyer loses the money deposited in escrow if the escrow holder embezzles the money after escrow was opened but before all the conditions of escrow had been strictly performed. Once all the escrow conditions have been met, the seller bears the loss of the escrow agent taking off with the sale proceeds and the buyer bears the loss from the agent selling or mortgaging the property to a bona fide purchaser.

These rules apply only when neither party is at fault. The loss falls upon the party who causes or facilitates the embezzlement by delaying the closing or not taking action quickly after being alerted to the escrow agent's misconduct.

C. Choosing the Right Agent

Consumer advocates caution buyers and sellers not to choose their closing or escrow agent casually. Most spectacular real estate frauds could never have been launched without inattentive or corrupt closing agents.

Advice for Choosing an Agent:

(1) Don't rely solely on the broker in selecting an escrow agent without performing due diligence.

(2) Meet the agent before choosing one.

(3) Seek the advice of others about their experience with various closers.

(4) Obtain a copy of the agent's certificate of insurance to verify ample coverage for the transaction at hand.

(5) Avoid choosing an agent with business or personal ties to the other party. When everything goes smoothly, an agent's bias may not matter. But suppose the seller believes all the conditions of the contract have been satisfactorily performed, and the buyer does not. A truly neutral escrow holder will not release the funds and close the escrow until both parties sign a mutual consent statement. In the worst case, the escrow agent will interplead the parties and let a court decide.

(6) An online guide to escrow services prepared by the California Department of Real Estate cautions: "Check the license status and record of an escrow holder. You may be unknowingly working with, and entrusting your funds and documents to, an escrow that is not licensed, was previously revoked for unlawful activities, and/or has a record of disciplinary action for bad business practices."[20]

Regulation of Escrow Agents. In California, many agencies regulate closing or escrow agents depending on whether the agent is an attorney, a title company, a bank, a real estate broker or an independent escrow agent. Each of these is regulated separately. The California Department of Business Oversight (DBO) in the state Depart-

---

20. Wayne S. Bell & Summer B. Bakotich, *Surviving the Real Estate 'Escrow' Process in California*, 1 DRE.Ca.Gov 25 (last visited July 10, 2015), http://www.dre.ca.gov/files/pdf/Escrow_Info_Consumers.pdf.

ment of Corporations regulates independent escrow agents.[21] Real estate brokers are exempt from DBO regulations when acting as escrow agents in transactions where they represent one or both of the parties as a broker. In these situations, they are subject to the rules of their state broker licensing agency. Similarly, attorneys are exempt from DBO when closing transactions in which they represented one or both of the parties. They are subject to state bar regulations. Title companies acting as escrows are regulated by the California Department of Insurance. Bank regulators oversee banks performing escrow services.

II. Closings

Closings usually follow either of the two formats described in Chapter Two: (1) The New York style which features a closing conference attended by all the significant players in the transaction. (2) An escrow—western or California closing—through which buyers obtain title and sellers receive payment without a closing conference.[22] A third possibility is a hybrid closing in which the principals stay at home and all the documents and funds are remitted to the closing agent and exchanged in a meeting attended by their attorneys or other representatives.[23] A fourth option is for a non-attorney title agent to conduct a closing which the buyer and seller attend. Their attorneys may review documents in advance, and only appear at the closing if the additional expense is justified by the client's probable higher comfort level.[24]

A. Following the Money

Good Funds. The buyer's promise to pay would be fulfilled by the buyer's lender funding a loan and the buyer providing the balance due with "good funds." Some state statutory definitions of "good funds" allow wire transfers or cashiers' checks.[25]

---

21. In California, the Commissioner of Corporations licenses independent escrow agents. There are minimum bonding requirements. All deposited funds must be placed in a trust account except from execution or attachment for any claim against the escrow agent. Exempt from escrow licensing because they are regulated by other institutions are: banks and savings associations, title insurance companies, attorneys already representing one or more of the parties to the transaction, and brokers who are principals or listing or selling brokers in the transaction. *About the Escrow Law*, DBO.Ca.Gov (last visited July 10, 2015), http://www.dbo.ca.gov/Licensees/Escrow_Law/about.asp.

22. On the use of escrows generally, see Mann, *Escrows — Their Use and Value*, 1949 U. Ill. L.F. 398 (1949); William A. Ingrahm Jr., Note, *Escrow Agreements*, 8 Miami L.Q. 75 (1953).

23. *See* Rick Daley, Real Estate Development Law 311–312 (2011).

24. Donna M. More, Attorneys' Concerns in Real Property Sales Transactions, RPST FL-CLE 1, 1-7, § 1.8 (2013).

25. "What appears to be a wire transfer can turn out to be an ACH transfer ACH transactions and wire transfers are often confused with each other. They are both electronic transfers of money, but they are not the same.... Wire transfers are typically used for transferring large dollar amounts of funds between banks very quickly. In the United States, wire transfers are processed through the Federal Reserve Wire Network. The acronym ACH can stand for 'Automated Check Handling' or 'Au-

Others confer upon escrow agents the discretion of specifying what counts as "good funds." Often, purchase and sale contracts identify good funds.

Currently, many sellers and mortgage lenders will only accept wire transfers but not cashiers' checks. A cashier's check can be counterfeit,[26] and counterfeiters have been able to produce convincing forgeries of cashiers' checks. Cashiers' checks can be rescinded within three days. Once a counterfeit is detected, the check will be returned to the sender and any previously credited sums will be deducted from the escrow account.

Settlement Statement Defined. At a New York style closing, or soon after a western style closing, the escrow agent is expected to provide each party an accounting called a financial closing settlement statement that describes how proceeds were contributed and distributed in the transaction.[27] A party who detects accounting errors may legitimately raise objections even after the closing, though hunting down the overpaid party for a refund is much harder after the deal has been concluded.

Buyers and sellers each receive their own separate closing statements and have no right to view each other's closing statements. Participating lenders have a right to see all the statements.

Purchaser's Closing Statement. A purchaser's closing statement shows how the purchase price is being paid—possibly with cash from the buyer, new loan amounts supplied by a mortgage lender or a mortgage loan taken back by the seller, or through existing mortgage loans to remain on the property after closing.

The closing statement will detail the purchaser's incidental costs such as loan origination fees, the lender's attorney's fees, a share of the escrow fee, pro-rated property taxes, and miscellaneous expenses such as personal property that the purchaser has agreed to acquire from the seller at closing.

Seller's Closing Statement. The starting point in preparing the seller's closing statement is the contract purchase price plus any sums the buyer has agreed to pay for the seller's personal property. From this total, the closing agent subtracts:

(1) The amount of any liens the seller is obligated to repay as a condition to closing;

---

tomated Clearinghouse.' ACH transactions are electronic checks, and are used for processing lower dollar amount payments. They are processed in a manner is similar to that of paper checks, and do not travel directly from one bank to another. ACH transactions are processed through a clearinghouse that handles crediting and deducting accounts of the originating and paying banks. It typically takes one or two days to settle ACH transactions."

26. "The number of counterfeit cashier's checks deposited into banks has steadily increased in recent times. Much of this increase is attributed to the increase in private sales between individuals as facilitated by the Internet and on-line auctions. There also are inexpensive software programs that allow someone with a computer, a scanner and a good quality printer to 'create' a document that looks like a genuine check. Some counterfeits are doctored copies of genuine checks; other counterfeits are complete phonies. Even banks have trouble identifying genuine and counterfeit cashier's checks." *Sometimes Cashier's Checks Aren't as Good as Cash*, NHBusinessReview (last visited Feb. 19, 2016), http://www.nhbr.com/April-1-2005/Sometimes-cashiers-checks-arent-as-good-as-cash/.

27. Charles J. Jacobus & Bruce M. Harwood, Georgia Real Estate: An Introduction to the Profession 379 (1995).

(2) The lender's fees for allowing prepayment;

(3) An owner's title insurance policy;

(4) Pro-rated taxes and insurance premiums;

(5) The seller's share of the escrow fees;

(6) Local government recording fees and transfer taxes;

(7) The real estate broker's commission.[28]

Depending on the contract, the seller may also be responsible for termite reports and repairs, and other remedial work. Nothing prevents the buyer and seller from allocating any of these deductions by contract as they wish. The net sale proceeds are payable to the seller.

B. Unclaimed Funds Left in Escrow

Each year millions of dollars remain undisbursed in escrow accounts, sometimes because parties neglect to cash their checks, or because the escrow agent was unable to locate the seller. After a statutory period, these funds escheat[29] to the state under Unclaimed Property Acts.[30] Escrow agents and title insurers must remit unclaimed funds to the state after the statutory period or they face stiff fines and penalties for retaining these funds as their own.

III. The Real Estate Settlement and Procedures Act (RESPA)

RESPA was enacted in 1974 in response to an earlier study Congress had requested of HUD (Department of Housing and Urban Development) and the VA (Veterans Administration). That study showed mortgage borrowers were paying very high closing costs.

The list of closing costs is extensive, and refers to such items as title reports, credit reports, processing fees, appraisals, surveys, recording fees, pest inspection fees and local government tax stamps. For home loan borrowers willing to take the time to compare lender closing costs, the savings can be substantial. Such costs average 2–4% of the seller's gross sales price,[31] and come on top of real estate brokerage commissions, points and loan origination fees.

---

28. *Understanding Your Closing Statement—Part II*, HUD (last visited July 10, 2015), http://www.realestatescoop.net/?p=131.

29. The power of a state to acquire title to property for which there is no owner. Whether notice by publication gave property owners due process of law was challenged unsuccessfully in Taylor v. Yee, 780 F.3d 928 (9th Cir. 2015), cert. denied, 136 S. Ct. 929 (2016).

30. *See, e.g.,* Wyo. Stat. § 34-24-101 to -134 (Supp. 1995) (escrowed funds are subject to the act under which unclaimed property escheats after being held inactively for five years).

31. Mark Shroder, *The Value of the Sunshine Cure: The Efficacy of the RESPA Disclosure Strategy* (HUD Office of Policy Development and Research, July 17, 2000) (on file with author).

Surveys show that some borrowers end up paying a lot more than others for the same items. Los Angeles mortgage banker Steven Maizes encourages his clients to shop vigorously, particularly for escrow services. Firms performing escrow services in southern California compete vigorously and their fees can vary as much as 100% for handling comparable closings.

Loan Closing Cost Estimates and Disclosures. Borrowers shopping to reduce closing costs are assisted by the Real Estate Settlement and Procedures Act (RESPA). This law requires lenders making federally regulated mortgage loans[32] to deliver to borrowers a form detailing all the charges the borrower will incur in the course of closing the loan, these days before signing up for the loan.

The borrower has the chance to do some comparative shopping because RESPA requires home mortgage lenders to prepare a Loan Estimate of all the terms of the loan and incidental costs that borrowers will have to pay at closing. Formerly called a Good Faith Estimate (GFE).[33] The lender can charge a credit report fee but no other charges until the borrower receives the estimate and agrees to proceed with the loan. Later, at closing the borrower has the chance to match the estimate against the actual costs charged which are listed in a closing disclosure.[34]

While the estimated and disclosed actual costs do not have to match perfectly, consumers can compare them to see if they came reasonably close; otherwise, the lender could have been engaging in "bait and switch" tactics.[35] The statute however gave borrowers no cause of action for a lender failing to include a charge in the GFE. But banks and other regulated lenders are subject to examiners checking for RESPA compliance. Also, RESPA disclosures can be used as evidence in consumer claims based on common law fraud and deceptive trade practices when borrowers can prove that lenders deliberately misled them about what the closing costs would be.

RESPA's reliance on disclosure to reduce closing costs appears not to be working very well. The various fees charged for credit reports, appraisals, and title insurance have not changed in 30 years despite technological innovations that should have reduced those costs substantially.[36]

---

32. Most single-family mortgages qualify as "federally related"—originated by a federally regulated institution, one whose deposits are federally insured, or meant to be sold to a government sponsored entity. RESPA applies to most purchase loans, assumptions, refinances, property improvement loans, and equity lines of credit. 12 C.F.R. § 1024.2.

33. The responsibility for administering RESPA, formerly with HUD, was shifted by Congress to the Consumer Financial Protection Bureau (CFPB). HUD GFEs became CFPB loan estimates after Oct. 3, 2015.

34. 12 U.S.C. § 2603. The disclosure combines settlement cost information and Truth-in-Lending Act disclosures of the loan terms. *See* www.consumerfinance.gov/know-before-you-owe/compare/ (last visited 6/9/2016).

35. Debra Pogrund Stark et al., Dodd-Frank 2.0: Creating Interactive Home-Loan Disclosures to Enable Shrewd Consumer Decision-Making, 27 Loy. Consumer L. Rev. 45, 106 (2014), Germán A. Salazar, Mortgage Lending: New Regulations, New Causes of Action, 51–Mar Ariz. Att'y 18 (2015).

36. Jack Guttentag, *New Settlement Rules Needed*, Los Angeles Times, Jul. 28, 2002, at K5, col.1.

One reason is that lenders and real estate brokers often choose the title and escrow firms, and prefer to designate their own subsidiaries to perform these well-compensated services. Mortgage lenders require title insurance, and often select the title insurer and the title company that is to serve as the escrow agent in the transaction. Also, home buyers and sellers are not particularly adept at shopping closing costs. Third-party providers are known to resist cutting prices for individual consumers not likely to be repeat customers. "Competition by providers is directed to the lenders who select them, rather than to the borrowers who pay them."[37]

Kickback and Referral Fee Prohibition. RESPA declares: "No person shall give and no person shall accept any fee, kickback,[38] or other thing of value pursuant to any agreement or understanding, oral or otherwise, that business incident to or part of a settlement service involving a federally related mortgage loan shall be referred to any person."[39] Thus, service providers are barred from paying or accepting client referral or "steering" fees, kickbacks and unearned fees in the home buying process.

Under RESPA, title insurers, escrow agents and closing attorneys are barred from rewarding real estate brokers for client referrals, regardless of whether the inducement comes in the form of money, the assumption of debt or non-cash gifts.[40] A title insurer would be prohibited from making a cash payment to a broker per referral—even if the referred client paid no more than other consumers for title coverage.[41]

Penalties for kickbacks can be quite substantial and include criminal sanctions (up to one year in prison).[42] To illustrate, consider the case filed in the U.S. District Court in the Eastern District of New York against 13 attorneys who had established two affiliated title companies in which they were the major shareholders and from which they received referral fees. The attorneys agreed to pay $200,000 for the settlement of the RESPA allegations and to divest themselves of any interest in a title company for three years.[43]

RESPA Violations Persist. Individual violators and their employers who are successfully prosecuted risk heavy fines.[44]

---

37. Guttentag, *supra* note 36.

38. RESPA bars kickbacks which are any improper payments to obtain referrals of business.

39. John C. Weicher, Comment, *Policy First, Research Afterward—The History of RESPA*, 23 J. Real Est. Finan. and Econ. 297 (2001).

40. 12 U.S.C. §2607, §8. Appendix B to Part 3500 contains Illustrations of Requirements of RESPA. 24 C.F.R. §3500.14(b). Broker-to-broker referral fees are expressly exempted. Otherwise, split commissions in an MLS might be challengeable.

41. 24 C.F.R. §3500.14 (Nov. 2, 1992).

42. A major title insurer agreed to refund $24 million to consumers for kickbacks it had been making since 1997 to home builders, lenders and real estate agents. Associated Press, February 22, 2005.

43. Alan Rice & David Stemler, A.S. Pratt & Sons, *HUD's Crackdown on RESPA Violations Nets 13 New York Attorneys*, E-Mail News-Compliance, June 2003.

44. *See, e.g.*, Press Release, CFPB Takes Action Against Wells Fargo and JP Morgan Chase for Illegal Mortgage Kickbacks, Jan. 22, 2015. Banks to Pay $35.7 Million After Loan Officers Illegally Traded Referrals for Marketing Services. www.consumerfinance.gov/about-us/newsroom/cfpb-takes-action-against-wells-fargo-and-jpmorgan-chase-for-illegal-mortgage-kickbacks/ (last visited 6/9/2016).

Limits of RESPA's Reach. Commercial property buyers and sellers have only the common law and their own bargaining savvy to protect themselves since RESPA applies exclusively to home mortgage loans.

Markups. Often, banks and other lenders charge borrowers a "mark-up" fee on top of what the lender actually paid for a credit report, appraisal, or recordation of the mortgage. Three federal courts of appeals have read the anti-kickback provision of RESPA as *not* prohibiting a bank's markup of fees. Kickbacks are improper payments for business referrals. Markups involve no fee splitting among settlement service providers. They offset the bank's actual costs in identifying, contracting with, and overseeing service providers. A few courts have read the statute as barring the markups which are often huge compared to the underlying actual fee.[45]

Reasonable Compensation Allowed For Value of Services Rendered. RESPA allows reasonable payments to third parties for providing goods, services or facilities to homebuyers or home mortgage borrowers—even when those payments are made in connection with settlement services. Thus, an attorney for a buyer or seller could legitimately receive compensation from a title company for acting as a title agent. The attorney would have to perform core title agent services, such as "the evaluation of the title search to determine the insurability of the title, the clearance of underwriting objections, the actual issuance of the policy or policies on behalf of the title insurance company, and, where customary, issuance of the title commitment, and the conducting of the title search and closing."[46]

Congress delegated to HUD the delicate task of distinguishing reasonable payments from those made as kickbacks. In a policy statement, HUD explained that RESPA would be violated if a title insurer paid a closing attorney more than the reasonable value of the legal services the attorney had provided to the title insurer.[47] Critics point out that determining the appropriate fee for each of the many services involved in a real estate closing is a daunting task, and one that HUD has never attempted and probably never will.[48]

---

45. This is the disputed language: "No person shall give and no person shall accept any portion, split, or percentage of any charge made or received for the rendering of a real estate settlement service in connection with a transaction involving a federally related mortgage loan other than for services actually performed." 8(b), 12 U.S.C. § 2607(b). The dispute turns on how to interpret the "and" between the "give" and "accept" phrases of 8(b). To be a prohibited "kickback" under this sentence, must there be a fee split among two or more settlement service providers? Or would a lender merely charging a markup bring the charge within 8(b)? The issue is described in *McKell v. Washington Mut., Inc.*, 142 Cal. App. 4th 1457, 49 Cal. Rptr. 3d 227 (Cal. App. 2006). The landmark case holding that markups are not kickbacks under 8(b) is *Echevarria v. Chicago Title & Trust Co.*, 256 F.3d 623 (7th Cir. 2001).

46. 24 C.F.R. § 3500, App. B, ex. 4.

47. 12 U.S.C. § 2617(a); Statement of Policy 2001-1, issued pursuant to Section 19(a) of RESPA.

48. *See* Jack Guttentag, *Determining Fair Broker Charges*, LOS ANGELES TIMES, Oct. 7, 2001, at K5, col. 1. "HUD formulated the reasonable compensation rule but has never enforced it—probably because it can't figure out any way to do it.... Gathering the required data from brokers is far beyond HUD's capacity. It has never had more than four examiners enforcing all RESPA rules.... Furthermore, there are no generally accepted standards as to what constitutes 'reasonable compensation.'" Although

In truth, the issue would be far less contentious if service providers disclosed these relationships to their clients. A closing attorney, for example, could explain to a client-seller, "I received $1500 from the title company that we used for your transaction although they only pay me $1000 for the sort of title work I did for you when the work was done for a seller I did not refer to them." Or, "I receive reciprocal client referrals from the title company we used for your closing." An attorney not comfortable making such disclosures should probably be placed on the CFPB RESPA-Enforcement list.

The Controlled Business (Affiliated Firm) Rules. Large brokerage firms,[49] major homebuilders and some lenders manage to get around RESPA by forming or purchasing escrow agencies and title companies of their own and profiting from dividends or partnership distributions which are not characterized as illegal referral fees under RESPA. Firms are free to compensate their own employees on any basis including referral commissions although they cannot offer kickbacks to non-employees. This has led to some firms 'deputizing' independent contractors as nominal employees.

Federal regulations permit referrals among "controlled businesses" if: (1) the relationship among the firms is disclosed to the customer, (2) an estimate of charges is made by the controlled entity, (3) the customer is free to reject the use of the referred service and (4) the referring entity gets nothing for the referral except a return on its ownership interest.

Brokers slip the requisite disclosure forms into the hands of sellers and buyers who rarely object to the broker designating an escrow or title company affiliated with the broker's firm. As home buyers are coming to realize, the listing agent has no obligation to disclose whether affiliated firms charge more than non-affiliated firms providing identical services. The agent's obligation ends with disclosure of the affiliation. It is up to the home buyer to compare prices.

Brokerage firms that own title or escrow subsidiaries can funnel profits from those subsidiaries back into the brokerage firm. But RESPA would bar the brokerage firm from rewarding the individual brokers for each client they referred to the firm's title or escrow subsidiaries. Nonetheless, brokerage firms pay bonuses to office managers based on referrals, and offer sales agents informal incentives such as reimbursing some of their personal liability premiums for steering clients to the firm's title insurance and escrow companies.

---

written about mortgage brokerage charges, Professor Guttentag's observations would apply equally to other settlement costs.

49. Large brokerage firms are far more likely than small ones to offer related services in house such as mortgage brokerage and escrow. For instance, only 10% of brokerage firms offer mortgage services in house but 56% of residential brokers with more than 50 agents do so. Only 5% of residential brokerage firms offer escrow services but 23% of firms with more than 50 agents do. Peter F. Colwell & Charles M. Kahn, *The Economic Functions of Referrals and Referral Fees*, 23 J. REAL EST. FINAN. AND ECON. 267, 272 (2001), *citing* National Association of Realtors, *1999 Profile of Real Estate Firms*.

State and Common Law Regulation of Referral Fees. Many states promulgate their own regulations concerning referral fees. Some mirror the federal rules.[50] Others are more stringent. For instance, at the urging of the California Insurance Commissioner, California now requires any title insurance employee engaged in marketing to obtain from the insurance commissioner a certificate of registration (good for a term of three years).[51] The law explicitly bans title companies from luring title and escrow business with gifts or favors. The statute lists and outlaws virtually every conceivable 'goodie' a title insurer might give a broker, except for gifts with the title insurer's logo costing not more than $10. Violate the anti-kickback rule and the registrant's certificate could be revoked for a period of up to five years. Many executives in the larger title insurance firms strongly favor these restrictions. They give title insurance companies a good reason to reject the numerous requests that major clients seek for their favorite charities, social events, conferences and the like.

Contracting Against Undisclosed Kickbacks. Fiduciaries who receive referral fees without the prior consent of their principals are probably duty-bound by the common law of agency to turn over those fees to the principal.[52] For example, a real estate attorney who receives a fee for referring a real estate broker, title insurer or escrow agent to her clients should disclose the referral fee. Buyers and sellers whether of residential or commercial properties should insist on all of their agents warranting that they have neither paid nor received undisclosed fees in connection with the transaction or referrals related to it.[53]

Questions

Question 1: *Duties of an Escrow Agent.*

(a) In a particular transaction, the buyers and seller sign a purchase and sale contract but only the seller signs escrow instructions. Soon after the buyers deposit $15,000 as a down payment with their escrow agent, they suffer buyers' remorse, decide to back out of the deal, and ask the escrow agent to refund their $15,000. Under the law of agency what should the escrow agent do?

---

50. *See, e.g.*, CAL. FIN. CODE § 17420 (West 1999) (prohibiting the payment of commissions, fees, or other compensation for referral of escrow customers or accounts); CONN. GEN. STAT. ANN. § 20-320a (West 1999) (prohibiting brokers from receiving fees "for the referral of any buyer of real property to (1) an attorney-at-law ... or (2) any mortgage broker or mortgage lender....").

51. CAL. INS. CODE § 12404.

52. RESTATEMENT (SECOND) OF AGENCY § 382 requires fiduciaries "unless otherwise agreed" to account for "money or other things ... received or paid out on behalf of the principal." Section 388 requires an agent "unless otherwise agreed" to give all profits to the principal which the agent makes in connection with a transaction undertaken on behalf of the principal.

53. For realty sellers, a good starting point is the residential listing form prepared by the Minnesota Bar Association (which, it is said, Minnesota brokers are committed to using within 72 hours of hell freezing over): "You warrant and represent to Me and covenant that no fees, except as disclosed in this contract, will be paid by You to, or received by You from, any broker, real estate salesperson, banker, closing services company, title insurance company, or any other person, entity or controlled business arrangement."

(b) What should an escrow agent tell the seller in the above situation when he asks whether to sue or just cancel the deal?

(c) In another transaction, the buyer and seller each sign separate escrow instructions. The buyer adds an instruction that immediately following the closing, the escrow agent is to deed the property from the buyer to the listing broker. Later, the seller learns that the ostensible buyer was just acting as an intermediary for the listing broker who didn't want to risk having to reduce or waive her commission by disclosing that she was the buyer. Did the escrow agent owe a duty to disclose this instruction to the seller?

(d) In a third transaction, the escrow instructions call for the buyer to receive title free and clear of all liens and encumbrances except for one specifically identified lien — a new purchase money mortgage loan. Acting under a purchase and sale contract provision calling for buyer approval of the preliminary title report within five days of receipt, buyer tenders timely written approval to the escrow agent. The agent notices that Schedule B excludes from coverage a recorded lien for which the parties appear to have made no specific arrangement. The purchase price does not appear to have been reduced by the amount of the lien. Nothing in the contract obligates the buyer to assume or take subject to that lien. The agent finds it puzzling that the buyer never mentioned the lien. The seller tells the escrow agent not to worry about that lien if the buyer approves the preliminary title report without objecting to it. Does the escrow agent have an obligation to call the lien to the buyer's attention or just let sleeping dogs lie?

Question 2: *Allocating the Risk of Escrow Agent Malfeasance.*

Occasionally, escrow agents or closing attorneys abscond with funds buyers or lenders deposited with them to facilitate sale or loan closings. Under which of the following situations would the seller bear that loss if the escrow agent was uninsured and can't be found?

(a) The embezzlement of loan funds occurs after all other conditions of escrow have been met although the agent has yet to remit the final payment due to the seller.

(b) The embezzlement occurs during a 30-day delay in the closing which the buyer agreed to give the seller because she needed additional time to fund the pay-off of a judgment creditor's lien.

(c) The seller had agreed to complete some remedial termite repairs by closing but her contractor needed another week after closing to complete the work. The seller had agreed to leave $10,000 in escrow until the buyer certifies that he is satisfied with the work. Any savings is to be remitted to the seller. The parties sign a one week extension of the purchase and sale agreement. The escrow agent absconds with the $10,000 during that one week extension period. Who bears the loss — buyer or seller?

Question 3: *Closing Agent Responsibilities.*

Buyer and seller request escrow agent to modify the escrow instructions by charging the seller for $10,000 in closing costs and pro-rations of various kinds that the buyer had previously agreed to pay. They request that this re-allocation be made by the escrow agent outside of escrow after the closing. Is there any reason the escrow agent needs to disclose this modification to the buyer's mortgage lender?

Question 4: *Drafting Post-Closing Escrow Instructions.*

Seller agrees to make certain repairs after closing. To secure the seller's promised repairs, the escrow agent is required to withhold $75,000 of the purchase price until the buyers sign a release that they are satisfied with the repairs. The seller worries that the buyers may refuse to sign the release and force the seller to make further concessions or give up a portion of the cash to the buyers. Is there a way to word the instruction that does a better job of protecting a seller who makes the repairs in good faith and wants to be compensated fairly and promptly for the work without having to resort to mediation, arbitration or litigation?

Question 5: *Kickbacks Under RESPA.*

(a) In California, every home seller is required to deliver a Natural Hazard Disclosure Statement to the buyer before closing. Independent firms prepare these forms though title insurers are eager to enter the business. Would RESPA bar title insurers from giving any insurance policy purchaser a discount on the title policy for purchasing a Natural Hazard Disclosure Statement from the title insurer or an affiliated firm?

(b) Would title insurers be violating RESPA if an affiliated Natural Hazard Disclosure preparer sold individual Natural Hazard Disclosure Statements for half the usual price to brokers who customarily utilized the title insurer's policies?

Chapter 11

Terminating Failed Real Estate Contracts[1]

Scope of the Chapter

Some real estate contracts will never close as scheduled because the parties have a falling out. When they cannot resolve their differences through negotiation, they are left with these dispute resolution choices: mutual rescission, mediation, arbitration, litigation, and judicial reference. This chapter begins with a brief description and comparison of these options.

Then, we focus on the two kinds of remedies that courts can dispense: an award of money damages, or an order for the parties to specifically perform the purchase and sale contract.

Buyers filing suits for specific performance have the right to deter their sellers from selling or mortgaging free of the buyer's claim. They do this by placing in the public land records a *lis pendens*, a notice of the pending lawsuit. Buyers who win their suits for specific performance can enforce their judgment not only against the original seller but against anyone to whom the seller sells or mortgages the property after a *lis pendens* was recorded. Recording laws in every state subject anyone acquiring an interest in the seller's title to no greater rights than the seller had against the buyer.

In this chapter we also describe the measure of damages courts can impose for breach of real estate purchase and sale contracts. Because of the inherent difficulties of valuing real estate, buyers and sellers often specify a precise amount of money that a buyer who breached would owe the seller. The enforceability of such clauses—liquidated damage provisions—is the final topic covered in this chapter.

---

1. For their contributions to this chapter, the author is deeply indebted to Robert J. Odson, Partner, Shumener, Odson & Oh; Michael Newhouse, Buchalter Nemer; and Laine T. Wagenseller, Wagenseller Law Firm.

I. A Quick Comparison of Mutual Rescission, Litigation, Mediation, Arbitration and Judicial Reference

A. Definitions

Mutual Rescission. Rescission annuls the existing contract and restores the parties to their pre-contract positions. The buyer's rights under the contract are extinguished and the seller refunds any payments the buyer made — less agreed termination fee or "break up" fees, if they had contracted for any. Parties in a failed deal often favor mutual rescission because it allows them to get on with their lives with no lingering obligations. Ideally, the parties reach accord on a signed agreement, which serves both to cancel the escrow arrangement and terminate the contract.

A rescission agreement should specify whether the buyer gets a full refund of her deposit. Case outcomes on this point are mixed when the terminated contract made no mention of refunds upon termination. The agreement also needs to anticipate how to resolve the claims of other parties who participated in the now-terminated transaction. These participants could include real estate brokers, title insurers, escrow agents, and real estate attorneys. They may have spent time and money expecting to be paid at a closing that will no longer ever occur.

Litigation. Courts are "often clogged, costly, and unwieldy."[2] Litigation involves discovery, extensive motions practice, filing requirements, calendaring complications, delayed trial court dates, and cumbersome evidentiary rules. On the other hand, a willing buyer confronting a recalcitrant seller may have no other way except through a suit for specific performance to obtain title to a property she regards as special and irreplaceable.

Mediation. For disputants eager to shield their personal financial dealings from public view, arbitration and mediation share the advantage of a resolution outside the glare of publicity that could accompany a public trial. A mediator nudges compromise by guiding the disputants into realistically assessing the costs and uncertainties of the litigation option.[3]

Arbitration. Most arbitration agreements contemplate the arbitrator's decision being final, and they are. Arbitrated decisions are subject to only the most limited recourse to judicial review.

---

2. Jack M. Sabatino, *ADR as "Litigation Lite": Procedural and Evidentiary Norms Embedded Within Alternative Dispute Resolution*, 47 Emory L.J. 1289, 1349 (1998).

3. "Virtually every agreement for the purchase of real estate in California provides that the losing party in any litigation must reimburse the prevailing party for attorneys' fees. In most cases, however, these agreements also have an interesting twist. If the prevailing party pursues litigation after failing or refusing to go to mediation, then that party will forfeit his or her right to recover for attorneys' fees." Michael P. Carbone, *Settle Your Real Estate Dispute Early — And Save Big Money*, Mediation Strategies Blog (last visited July 10, 2015), http://www.mediate.com/mobile/article.cfm?id=5262.

In thoughtfully formulating an agreement to arbitrate, the parties can select the arbitrator, delineate the availability and parameters of discovery, decide whether the arbitrator's opinion must be in writing and be made according to law. Also, to a considerable extent they can prescribe the grounds for judicial appeal.

Arbitration usually ends up being "quicker and cheaper than court resolution, with its potential for protracted pretrial adversary bickering, extensive discovery, and multiple appeals."[4] But arbitration is not free. Arbitrators' fees can run into the tens of thousands of dollars.[5] Arbitrators charge by the hour or day and, as one attorney put it: "To be blunt, the arbitrator doesn't have a financial interest in streamlining the process."[6]

The form contracts used by mortgage lenders and home builders strongly favor arbitration to dodge trial by jury and avoid consumer class actions. Consumer advocates challenge these mandatory arbitration clauses. Mandatory arbitration precludes class actions, often the only feasible means of aggrieved consumers vindicating claims each of which is modest but taken together, justify the high costs of litigation.[7] In recognition of this, Fannie Mae and Freddie Mac, the nation's leading purchasers of home mortgage loans, will not purchase loans subject to mandatory arbitration that borrowers would unknowingly agree to when signing their mortgage documents.[8] In another swipe at mandatory arbitration, California courts have freed home buyers from mandatory arbitration provisions in the litigation of construction defect claims.[9]

Arbitration also precludes a buyer from recording a *lis pendens* to warn any informed subsequent purchaser or lender of the dispute.

Judicial Reference. Judicial reference is a form of binding arbitration with no jury trial. This technique calls for the parties to petition a court for an appointed referee to resolve their dispute as would a trial court, using the same rules of procedure and discovery. As with arbitration, the parties select their own referee, often a retired judge, or they ask the court to designate one.

The case remains within the judicial system. The referee's 'recommendation' is subject to review by the referring judge (after a comment period by the parties). The

---

4. *Ibid.*

5. Randall G. Block, *Arbitration in Real Property Transactions: Efficient, Cost Effective, Fair or None of the Above?*, 26 Ca. Real Prop. J. 40 (2008).

6. Pat Milhizer, *Commercial Arbitration Moves Beyond the Generic*, Chi. Law., Nov. 2006, at 10015 (quoting Chicago lawyer Ray G. Rezner).

7. Theodore Eisenberg, *Geoffrey P. Miller, and Emily Sherwin, Arbitration's Summer Soldiers: An Empirical Study of Arbitration Clauses in Consumer and Nonconsumer Contracts*, 41 U. Mich. J.L. Reform 871 (2008).

8. "They will purchase home mortgage loans with arbitration clauses worded so as to become null and void upon sale to FNMA." *Arbitration Clauses Blocked by Fannie Mae & Freddie Mac*, Realty Times (last visited July 18, 2015), http://realtytimes.com/rtpages/20040210_arbitration.htm.

9. *Villa Milano Homeowners Ass'n v. Il Davorge*, 84 Cal. App. 4th 819 (2000). *But see Basura v. U.S. Home Corp.*, 120 Cal. Rptr. 2d 328 (Ct. App. 2002) (holding that Federal Arbitration Act precludes state courts from denying enforcement of mandatory arbitration provisions in home builders' contracts with buyers).

judge within ten days then adopts or rejects the arbitrator's decision, after which the order is subject to appellate review like any other court order or judgment.[10]

B. Arbitrators Usually Have the Last Word, but Not Always

Courts tend to defer to arbitration awards and mediated settlement agreements— though "tolerance for fallibility has its limits,"[11] as was illustrated in *Burlage v. Superior Court of Ventura County.*[12]

This case arose because the sellers never disclosed that their swimming pool and a portion of their backyard encroached into an adjoining property, owned by a country club. An arbitrator had awarded $1,533, 320 to the purchaser, not far shy of the full purchase price, $1.75 million.

The arbitrator had accepted the damage estimates advanced by the buyers' expert witness: $250,000 in punitive damages, $552,750 in compensatory damages to relocate the pool plus the diminished value of the site, and $732,570 in attorneys' fees.

The award greatly exceeded the purchaser's actual loss because the purchaser's title insurer was able to negotiate a lot line adjustment with the country club for $10,950. Under that agreement, the size of the purchaser's parcel was actually increased, not diminished, as the purchasers obtained clear title to all of the land that had been encroaching into the country club property.

The arbitrator was well aware of the settlement but mistakenly believed that he could not take into account events that had occurred after escrow closed. The court vacated the arbitrator's award under a state statute requiring them to do so when a party's rights "were substantially prejudiced" by an arbitrator's refusal to hear material evidence.[13]

II. Measuring Damages for Breach of a Real Estate Purchase and Sale Contract

Damage remedies are money judgments to compensate the injured parties—with three components:

(1) Reliance: to reimburse "out of pocket" costs incurred by innocent parties in performing their contracts such as escrow fees, surveys, attorneys' fees or the costs of inspections;

---

10. William L. Stern, *Should Your California Agreements Contain a "Judicial Reference" Clause?*, MorrisonFoster (last visited June 10, 2015), http://www.mondaq.com/unitedstates/x/34460/ Consumer/Should+Your+California+Agreements+Contain+a+Judicial+Reference+Clause.

11. 178 Cal. App. 4th at 529 (2009).

12. *Id.* at 524 (2009). *See also* Julia Rabich, Sarah Stoner & Nancy A. Welsh, *Judicial Review of Arbitration Awards and Mediation Agreements: Tips for Sustaining Deference*, Disp. Resol. J., February– April 2012, at 48.

13. 178 Cal. App. 4th at 529.

(2) Restitution: to restore expenditures incurred by the non-breaching party that benefitted the breaching party such as a refund of deposited funds;[14]

(3) Compensatory Damages or Expectation Damages: to put the injured party in the same position as if the contract had been faithfully performed.

In most states, the measure of expectation damage under a real property contract is the difference between the contract price and the market value of the property on the date of breach.[15] In other words, buyers have suits for damages when sellers renege on contracts in which they short changed themselves by underpricing their own property; sellers have suits for damages when buyers renege on contracts in which they agreed to pay more than the property was worth.

III. Specific Performance

A. A Specific Performance Scenario

Specific performance is a decree ordering each of the parties to perform the contract precisely according to all its terms and conditions including the purchase price. This contrasts markedly from the uncertainty or outcomes in suits for contract damages where appraisers for the buyer and the seller duel against each other before a judge or jury. Specific performance is the remedy enabling a home buyer to acquire title to the house of her dreams or a commercial buyer to realize the profits she had anticipated from developing or operating the realty.

In practice, sellers are tempted to breach their contracts when market prices are on the rise, and buyers try to get out of their contracts when prices are falling.

Attorney Michael Newhouse prepared an analysis of options for his developer-clients called *Beyond Specific Performance: Recovering Your Damages Through Escrow, Following A Specific Performance Judgment.*[16] He wrote it for developers who had experienced being in escrow on a property that was perfect for their next development. But the seller backed out just before closing for no apparent reason except that their property values had been rising. In these circumstances, sellers are often looking to re-negotiate for a higher price. The developer weighs three choices:

(1) Accede to a price increase as the "cost of doing business."

(2) Let the deal go, get back the deposit, and move on to another property rather than spending time and legal fees forcing the sale.

(3) Sue for specific performance.

---

14. Restatement (Second) of Contracts § 344; John D. Calamari & Joseph M. Perillo, The Law of Contracts § 14.4 (4th ed. 1998).

15. In England and about half the U.S. states, if the seller's breach was due to unanticipated title defects, buyers were not entitled to expectation damages. California by statute mirrors a trend applying the same measure of damage rules to buyers and sellers.

16. Michael R. Newhouse, Esq., BuckhalterNemer, Feb. 4, 2015, on file with author.

In evaluating the choices, the developer will need to balance the possible settlement amount against the cost, time and emotional drain of litigation, the developer's alternate use of time and resources, and the predictable uncertainty (a "known unknown") of court outcomes.

Once the developer chooses to litigate, a suit for specific performance has considerable advantages over a suit for damages. A suit for money damages will only yield the developer the difference between the land purchase price and the value of the land at the date of the seller's breach, not the full profit potential of the completed development project. A developer's loss of potential profits from an unbuilt project are too speculative to be included as an element of allowable compensatory damages in a developer's suit against a breaching land seller.[17]

B. The Basics

"Specific Performance" is available where:

(1) The buyer has put the seller on notice of its demand that escrow close;

(2) The buyer has "substantially" performed its end of the bargain (e.g., paid its earnest deposit and cleared its contingencies, or has the ability to perform);

A buyer seeking specific performance who has not already paid or put into escrow the entire purchase price must demonstrate either an assured ability to perform at all times during the lawsuit or secure performance to "the satisfaction of the court."[18]

(3) The seller has not performed (e.g., refuses to close escrow);

(4) The purchase and sale agreement (PSA) essential terms are definite enough for a court to ascertain;

(5) The PSA is reasonable and fairly priced (e.g., the seller is not being unfairly taken advantage of);

Due to the remedy of specific performance having originated in English chancery courts, specific performance is an equitable remedy. This adds an additional prerequisite; specific performance is only available for contracts that are just and equitable. Where buyers have "clean hands," whose conduct in the transaction has been beyond reproach. And equity courts may refuse to enforce a purchase price or contract terms not deemed "fair, just and equitable."

(6) The terms of the requested "forced sale" are "substantially similar" to the terms of the PSA; and

(7) The buyer's "legal remedy" (i.e., simply getting a money judgment against the breaching seller) is inadequate.

Sellers demonstrate the inadequacy of money damages to obtain specific performance by pointing out that real estate assets are unique and therefore difficult to value.

---

17. William Lindsley, J.D., Alys Masek, J.D., and Nancy E. Yuenger, J.D., California Jurisprudence 3d (2015), § 82.

18. Cal. Civ. Code § 3386.

Real estate developers buying undeveloped land may also elect to sue for specific performance. They show the difficulty of estimating the ultimate sales prices that will be realized for their proposed projects, due to location, topography, soils, land use entitlement status or some combination of these.[19]

Attorney Newhouse recommends that the developer "focus on evidence establishing that the buyer specializes in acquiring the type of property at issue in the suit, and improving them for a specific purpose in the marketplace. The buyer should also make efforts to explain to the court that few properties of the type in question become available for sale, and that even fewer properties specifically fit the buyer's business model."

Winning A Specific Performance Lawsuit. Granting specific performance, a court will seek to put the parties in the same position as if the contract had been performed pursuant to its terms, a sale of the property at the price and terms agreed upon. Moreover, the victorious party will also be entitled to a judgment for the rents and profits from the time he was entitled to the conveyance under the contract. The buyer receives the promised title; the seller receives the agreed-upon contract price.

The court will consider an equitable accounting to calibrate damages as if the contract had been performed on time. For example, a buyer winning a suit for specific performance would be entitled to a credit for tenant rents while the property was tied up in litigation. Conversely, the owner will be credited with operating expenses including the mortgage, property taxes and insurance, during the litigation delay.[20] Alternatively, a seller who obtains specific performance may be able to choose between obtaining interest on the purchase money from the original date set for closing to the actual court-enforced closing date, or retaining the rents for the time period. Developers may be awarded compensation to off-set rising construction and development costs.[21]

Relinquishment by Contract. The right to specific performance can be relinquished by contract.[22] Sellers wanting to put their properties back on the market after a failed sale need the buyer's airtight waiver of specific performance embedded in their purchase and sale contract. Otherwise, buyers can put the seller's property in limbo by recording a *lis pendens.* This is an easy-to-file notice placed in the public land records to deter the seller from trying to sell or refinance the property until the underlying lawsuit is resolved.

---

19. *Stewart Dev. Co. v. Superior Court*, 166 Cal. Rptr. 450, 108 Cal. App. 3d 266 (1980). CAL. CIV. CODE § 3387 (West 1997) creates a presumption in favor of specific performance for realty buyers, a presumption that money damages are an inadequate remedy, conclusive for buyers contracting for a single family home they intend to occupy, rebuttable for all other realty buyers.

20. *Real Estate Litigation: Specific Performance*, WAGENSELLER LAW FIRM (last visited July 23, 2015), http://www.wagensellerlaw.com/articles/real-estate-litigation-specific-performance/.

21. *Bravo v. Buelow*, 168 Cal. App. 3d 208, 213, 215 (1985) (buyer credited $70,000 for increased construction costs of $20/sq. ft. resulting from delay); *Hennefer v. Butcher*, 182 Cal. App. 3d 492, 505 (1986) (increased development costs $150,000 offset from $1.05 million purchase price).

22. *See Doyle v. Ortega*, 872 P.2d 721 (Idaho 1994) (Buyer denied specific performance when seller breached; contract provided, in the event of seller's breach, the buyer's remedy was the right to a return of the deposit, the seller to pay legal, escrow, title and other costs).

Attorney Newhouse reports on an occasion when a client took his advice:

- *Our client, a developer and manager of high-end student housing properties around University of Southern California, among other areas, located a property they planned to add to their portfolio, remodel, and market as a rental.*

- *Escrow was entered into, at a fair market price, $860,000.00, and buyer tendered the required earnest deposit.*

- *However, once contingencies had expired, and closing was scheduled, the seller refused to sign closing documents unless the buyer agreed to raise the purchase price.*

- *In response we sent a written demand that seller close escrow, or face a specific performance lawsuit, including recovery of attorneys' fees and lost rents and profits, etc. due to the delay in performance.*

- *Seller still refused, and client filed suit seeking over $217,528.60 in escrow credits, including credits to pay off tax liens, attorneys' fees, increased construction costs, and lost rents due to the delay.*

- *Seller failed to timely respond to the suit. Following an entry of default, we successfully obtained a judgment awarding all damages sought in the form of closing credits based on provisions in the contract had the contract been performed voluntarily. This reduced the purchase price from $860,000 to $642,471.40.*

- *Furthermore, the judgment required the seller to execute the closing documents within 7 days. If seller refused, the clerk was ordered to execute the documents on seller's behalf.*

- *Seller failed to execute the closing documents, and the clerk of the court signed the closing documents on her behalf. This allowed escrow to close, and title to transfer to the Buyers.*

- *Buyers then remodeled the property, and it is now rented and occupied by USC students.*

C. *Lis Pendens* (Notice of a Pending Action)

Purpose. Lis pendens statutes are designed to preserve the status quo during litigation that could impact the title or possession to real property. The recorded notice contains the following information: the name of the plaintiff and defendant in the underlying lawsuit, the date and court where the action was filed, the object of the lawsuit, and a legal description of the property potentially affected by the lawsuit.[23] "The world" is put on constructive notice from the time the notice is placed in the public land records. Anyone who acquires an interest in the underlying property will take subject to the eventual outcome of the lawsuit, and risks forfeiting title or possession if the plaintiff prevails.

Even if the statutory notice is not filed, a buyer or lender with actual, inquiry or imputed notice of a pending lawsuit takes subject to the outcome.[24] Because the purpose of the statute is to provide notice, a subsequent purchaser with actual knowledge from off-record sources already has what the statute offers.

Practical Consequences. Technically, a notice of *lis pendens* does not prohibit the owner from selling or mortgaging the realty.[25] But no well informed buyer or mortgage lender is going to assume the risk of forfeiting their interest on the outcome of a lawsuit unless the property owner has made it worthwhile for them.

Sometimes, a seller might be in a position to negotiate title insurance coverage for a prospective buyer that specifically insures title regardless of the outcome of the underlying lawsuit for which the *lis pendens* was recorded. Usually, this occurs in situations where the seller is in a financial position to indemnify the title insurer.

A buyer might balk at the offer of insurable title, knowing that title insurers do not actually promise good titles, just compensation for loss or damage for a title defect. The title insurer's payment obligation is the lesser of the insured policy amount and the value of the property at the date of loss. Suppose a seller actually wants the property because of some unique feature or profitable development potential. Her title policy will not compensate for profit potential foregone or the unique "consumer surplus" value the property had for her.

Eligible and Ineligible Underlying Claims. To justify recording a *lis pendens*, the claimant in the underlying dispute must be seeking title or possession of the property identified in the "lis." The property owner can have a *lis pendens* set aside if filed for

---

23. In California, it is sufficient to give the case caption and a statement that the action affects the use or right of possession. *Compare* CAL. CODE OF CIV. PROC. § 405.2 (West 2004), *with* former § 409(a).

24. *Breeding v. NJH Enters., LLC*, 940 P.2d 502 (Okla. 1997) (Bank's lien against husband's homestead was subordinate to divorced wife's lien imposed in wife's appeal of divorce case. Bank knew the appeal was pending).

25. Judge David M. Gersten, *The Doctrine of Lis Pendens; No Need for a Balance*, 59 FLA. BAR J. 83 (1995).

an underlying claim that could be redressed with money damages, such as could a buyer's or tenant's suit for contract damages, or for a refund of liquidated damages.

Expungement. In tacit recognition that realty buyers can cloud sellers' titles without prior judicial review, state statutes have been enacted enabling property owners to petition for judicial relief in the form of posting a hefty bond or ordering the recorded *lis pendens* to be quashed or expunged from the public records. In California, the property owner also has the option of compelling the buyer to demonstrate in a "mini-trial" the likelihood that it will prevail on the merits in the underlying for specific performance.[26] Once a court has ordered a *lis pendens* to be expunged, the property owner is free to sell, mortgage or lease the property, and the buyer, mortgagee or lessee would be a purchaser in good faith, free of constructive notice or actual knowledge of the underlying claim that the *lis pendens* referenced.

IV. Liquidated Damages

A. The Case for Liquidated Damages

A liquidated damage clause is a contract provision by which the parties agree in advance to the amount of damages payable on a breach. Purchase and sale agreements in commercial and residential real estate alike often limit the breaching buyer's liability to a fixed liquidated damage sum.

"A primary goal of such clauses is to control risk. The buyer is willing to stipulate damages so that he will be liable for no more than the agreed amount, while the seller is ensuring that the buyer will be liable for no less."[27]

"A further purpose of liquidated damage clauses is avoidance of the litigation process altogether."[28] Litigation sidetracks buyers and sellers from focusing on their primary objectives for entering the transaction: the seller to sell and the buyer to acquire an acceptable property. Litigation outcomes are costly, uncertain and can leave out many of the actual damages that the non-breaching party would incur. For instance, suppose the seller was depending on the buyer performing and had committed to purchasing another property with the sale proceeds. The buyer's breach could hamper the seller's ability to complete the purchase of the "uplink" property, pushing the seller into breaching that contract while losing the benefit of it.

---

26. (1) "the court finds that the pleading on which the notice is based does not contain a real property claim"; or (2) "the court finds that the claimant has not established by a preponderance of the evidence the probable validity of the real property claim." CAL. CODE CIV. PROC. § 405.30.

27. Jeffrey B. Coopersmith, *Refocusing Liquidated Damages Law for Real Estate Contracts: Returning to the Historical Roots of the Penalty Doctrine*, 39 EMORY L.J. 267 (1990).

28. *Id.*

B. Liquidated Damages in Real Estate Purchase and Sale Contracts

Courts and legislatures have placed numerous formal limits on the use of liquidated damage clauses.

(1) In most jurisdictions, the parties need to have agreed to a liquidated damage provision in their contract.[29]

(2) Liquidated damage clauses are only permissible when actual damages would be difficult to calculate at the time of breach. This is seldom an issue in real estate contracts because real estate valuations are presumed to be difficult to forecast.

(3) Many courts decline to enforce liquidated damage sums that, on the day the contract was entered, were grossly disproportionate to any reasonable estimates of the probable losses a breach would cost the non-breaching party.

(4) Some courts impose a hindsight test, and decline to enforce any liquidated damage sum against a buyer that greatly exceeds the seller's actual loss at the date of breach or trial—typically measured by the seller's resale price.

Imagine the parties had contracted for a $100,000 liquidated damage sum on a purchase price of $1,000,000. The buyer breached. The market was rising, and the seller was able promptly to resell the house for $1,200,000. In many jurisdictions, courts would order the seller to refund the buyer's $100,000, explaining that the seller had no actual loss.

These same courts would probably balk at awarding the seller actual damages when the market was trending in the opposite direction and the seller's loss exceeded $100,000. This asymmetry in liquidated damage cases is evidenced by judicial refusal to enforce provisions giving sellers the option of choosing between the greater of liquidated or

---

29. In New York, a vendee who defaults on a real estate contract without lawful excuse cannot recover his or her down payment as long as a reviewing court deems the sum reasonable. Ten percent is the norm. Courts order refunds only upon a showing of disparity of bargaining power between the parties, fraud, duress, illegality or mutual mistake. *Lawrence v. Miller*, 86 N.Y. 131 (1881). Although New York courts have not explained why sellers should be able to keep down payments of 10% or less when buyers breach, one justification could be that this is an option price for the buyer having put a contractual "hold" on the seller's ability to sell the property.

The rule was affirmed in *Uzan v. 845 UN Ltd. Partnership*. In this case two Turkish billionaires sued developer Donald Trump to retrieve $8,000,000—25% of the $32,000,000 purchase price—on four condo units. They had refused to close on their contracts, jittery in the wake of the terrorist attack that brought down the World Trade Center twin towers September 11, 2001.

Their closing had been set for about six weeks later, October 19, 2001. Mr. Trump alleged no actual loss approaching $32,000,000. No matter. In New York, a buyer has no right to a refund of a deposit except on a convincing showing of disparity of bargaining power between the parties, duress, fraud, illegality or mutual mistake.

The Trump World Tower project website offered units on the 89th and 90th floors at prices in 2007 of $12, $13, and near $16 million, suggesting that despite the time-value of money, Trump may have profited from the buyers' breaches, especially after pocketing the 25% deposits.

actual damages. Courts reject these as illegal penalties, not true liquidated damage clauses because they do not offer buyers the comfort of fixed liability limits.[30]

Non-Refundable Deposits. In jurisdictions that limit sellers to charging defaulting buyers no more than their actual losses, courts could require sellers to refund deposits labelled non-refundable when, soon after the buyer breaches, the seller is able to close a deal with another buyer at a price higher than the breaching buyer had contracted to pay. For the seller to be entitled to retain the non-refundable deposit, it had to be drafted in compliance with the jurisdiction's norms for a valid liquidated damage clause.

Drafting "Reasonable" Liquidated Damage Provisions. Real estate litigators appreciate that courts and legislators struggle with the issue of how to determine when liquidated damage provisions are so harsh as to constitute impermissible penalties or forfeitures.

Ideally, real estate transactions attorneys could help by encouraging buyers and sellers to articulate how they settled on a particular liquidated damage sum.

(1) When the property is going to be off the market for any considerable period of time, sellers could tally an estimate of their probable holding costs: insurance, maintenance, mortgage interest payments and property taxes, minus fair rental or fair use value.

(2) A liquidated damage clause may also be priced as an option since the seller is not going to be able to enter another contract for a property already under contract.[31]

(3) Liquidated damage clauses in some commercial realty contracts achieve an element of transparency and fairness by pricing different types of breaches separately. For instance, a contractor or "build-to-suit" developer might be charged $1,000 per day if the project is not completed by a certain date. A retailer might contract to receive $5,000 per day for failure of the shopping center developer to deliver vacant possession by the closing date. A home or condo builder might contract for a fixed sum of $7,500 if the buyer breaches after the seller made certain improvements according to the buyer's specifi-

---

30. Jeffrey B. Coopersmith, *Refocusing Liquidated Damages Law for Real Estate Contracts: Returning to the Historical Roots of the Penalty Doctrine*, 39 Emory L.J. 267, 305 (1990).

31. *Mahoney v. Tingley*, 529 P.2d 1068, 86 Wash. 2d 95 (1975). In this case, the buyer's $200 deposit was denominated as liquidated damage in the deposit receipt. The seller claimed actual damages of $3,141.44. The court held the seller to the $200 cap, citing a case in which the buyer had been summarily refused a refund because the seller's actual damage was less than the liquidated damage sum. *City of Kinston v. Suddreth*, 146 S.E.2d 660, 266 N.C. 618 (1966). *See also Harris v. Dawson*, 388 A.2d 748 (Pa. 1978) (Clause construed as liquidated damage clause where $100 down-payment seller retained "either on account of the purchase money, or as compensation for the damages and expenses he has been put to in this behalf." Actual loss was $6,000.).

Only rarely do courts allow sellers to recover actual damages when their proven losses exceed the liquidated damage sum. One of those cases is *Cmty. Dev. Serv., Inc. v. Replacement Parts Mfg.*, 679 S.W.2d 721 (Tex. App. 1984) (Because the buyer would have forfeited a $160,000 deposit for the smallest breach, when the buyer breached, the seller was allowed to disregard the liquidated damage language in the contract, and obtain actual damages, a sum equal to the retained deposit plus an additional $71,820 in lost profits).

cations. Each of these elements of liquidated damage, if reasonable, is enforceable independently.[32]

California's Liquidated Damage Statute. In some states, liquidated damages in real estate contracts are presumptively valid only up to a specified percentage of the purchase price: 5% in Oklahoma, 3% in California.[33]

The three percent is presumed valid in California unless either the buyer can prove that the sum was unreasonably high[34] or the seller can justify a sum exceeding 3%. The presumption applies only if the sum has actually been paid.

The California statute makes the seller's 'actual loss' a factor in evaluating the validity of a liquidated damage provision. Extending to either party the prerogative of introducing evidence of a post-breach sales price if the sale occurs within six months of buyer's default. So, for example, a breaching buyer could claw back her forfeited liquidated damage payment if the seller, a month or two later, found a buyer who willingly paid far more than the breaching buyer had contracted to pay. Thus, in California, if the seller resells at a profit above the contract price within six months, the buyer can introduce evidence of that sale as proof that 3% overcompensated the seller.

Sellers forced to part with the property within six months at a price well below what the breaching buyer had promised to pay can introduce evidence of the resale as proof that a reserved sum above 3% was justified. Hence, the statute "still permits the application of a hindsight-based test for the reasonableness of the stipulated sum within the six-month time frame."[35] After six months, the seller's resale price has no bearing on her right to retain the liquidated damage sum or her obligation to return it.

The liability of the breaching seller for liquidated damages is not subject to the presumptive statutory ceiling of three percent. Instead, the breaching home seller's

---

32. *See, e.g., Olcott Lakeside Dev., Inc. v. Krueger,* 616 N.Y.S.2d 841 (1994) (Buyer had ordered homebuilder to customize house and then breached. Contract called for $10,000 as liquidated damage for breach and an additional $10,000 if buyers breached after customizing work was done. Both sums were collectible as liquidated damage.).

33. CAL. CIV. CODE § 1675 (West 1985). "(c) If the amount actually paid pursuant to the liquidated damages provision does not exceed 3 percent of the purchase price, the provision is valid to the extent that payment is actually made unless the buyer establishes that the amount is unreasonable as liquidated damages. (d) If the amount actually paid pursuant to the liquidated damages provision exceeds 3 percent of the purchase price, the provision is invalid unless the party seeking to uphold the provision establishes that the amount actually paid is reasonable as liquidated damages. (e) For the purposes of subdivisions (c) and (d), the reasonableness of an amount actually paid as liquidated damages shall be determined by taking into account both of the following: (1) The circumstances existing at the time the contract was made. (2) The price and other terms and circumstances of any subsequent sale or contract to sell and purchase the same property if the sale or contract is made within six months of the buyer's default."

34. The Law Revision Commission had recommended 5% but it was reduced to 3% as a concession to then Governor Pat Brown.

35. Coopersmith, *Refocusing Liquidated Damages Law for Real Estate Contracts: Returning to the Historical Roots of the Penalty Doctrine,* 39 EMORY L.J. 267, 296 (1990).

only protection against being held to an excessive liquidated damage sum is governed by California's general prohibition against forfeitures and penalties.[36]

Liquidated Damage Provisions in Commercial Real Estate Contracts. The 3% presumption applies only to residential sales, not to commercial deals. Nonetheless, the statute can be seen as creating an inference of legitimacy for liquidated damage clauses in commercial transactions not exceeding 3%.[37]

California has several statutes dealing directly with liquidated damage provisions in commercial transactions. One statute appears to endorse a freedom of contract norm regarding liquidated damages for the buyer's breach.[38] But a companion statute allows the buyer to repudiate the liquidated damage provision by establishing that it was "unreasonable."[39]

Specific Performance Remedy Not Barred by a Liquidated Damage Clause. A liquidated damage provision does not necessarily preclude either party from seeking specific performance.

Since the California statutory scheme for liquidated damages only pertains to breaching buyers, sellers cannot substitute a fixed liquidated damage sum as a substitute for their obligation to transfer title by specific performance. This is not much of a surprise considering the time honored legal norm that buyers are entitled to specific performance of realty contracts.

Buyers, though, might be surprised to learn that their liability for breach is not limited to a 3% deposit labeled liquidated damages.[40] Sellers could sue them for specific performance to pay the full contract price.

---

36. CAL. CIV. CODE § 1679 (West 1985).

37. *Hong v. Somerset Assocs.*, 207 Cal. Rptr. 597, 161 Cal. App. 3d 111 (1984) (Court upheld $25,000 as liquidated damages for purchasers' failure to conclude sale of 36-unit apartment complex at sale price of $1,325,000).

38. CAL. CIV. CODE § 1676 (West 1978) provides:

"Except as provided in Section 1675, a provision in a contract to purchase and sell real property liquidating the damages to the seller if the buyer fails to complete the purchase of the property is valid if it satisfies the requirements of Section 1677 and the requirements of subdivision (b) of Section 1671."

CAL. CIV. CODE § 1677 (West 1978) provides:

"A provision in a contract to purchase and sell real property liquidating the damages to the seller if the buyer fails to complete the purchase of the property is invalid unless: (a) The provision is separately signed and initialed by each party to the contract; and (b) If the provision is included in a printed contract, it is set out either in at least 10-point bold type or in contrasting red print in at least 8-point bold type."

39. *See* § 1676, which contains a cross-reference to § 1671(b). If sections 1676 and 1677 ensure that both parties were aware of and intended the consequences of a liquidated damages clause, perhaps allowing for a party to escape enforcement by showing "unreasonableness" is a way of protecting against substantive "unfairness" factors such as duress, fraud, and the like. If so, why not state this directly? It is difficult to see why the parties would stipulate an unreasonable amount in the absence of "unfairness" or the belief that the liquidated damages.

40. *See* CAL. CIV. CODE § 1680 (West 1978).

This unexpected result relates to a bifurcated system of remedies that dates back to the time in England when there were separate courts of law and equity. Law courts awarded damages. Only equity courts could grant specific performance.

Hence, property lawyers have long assumed that a liquidated damage clause ordinarily removes all of the non breaching party's other damage remedies but leaves intact the seller's right to specific performance.[41] It would be more in keeping with buyers' and sellers' expectations if the default rule made liquidated damages the seller's sole remedy for the buyer's breach unless the seller explicitly retained the right to specific performance.[42]

Until courts and legislatures appreciate why the default rule needs to be reversed, there are several ways that contracts can be drafted to address this problem. "[Buyer/seller] waives any right to specific performance of this agreement." Alternately, lawyers familiar with the legal history of separate law and equity courts might specify that "liquidated damages shall be the seller's sole remedy in law or equity."

Questions

Question 1: *To Sign the Arbitration Clause or Not?*

(a) Would you counsel a client selling or buying a home to agree to mediation, arbitration or both?

(b) As the real estate broker with a listing on the house, how would you explain to your client, the seller, why it was in his or her beat interest to initial the arbitration clause in the form purchase and sale agreement your association had prepared?

Question 2: *Specific Performance: Strategic Choices.*

(a) Why do you guess home sellers so rarely seek specific performance from breaching buyers?

(b) Would you advise a developer-client to seek specific performance for vacant land the buyer was refusing to sell just a few days before the scheduled closing date?

(c) Real estate brokerage forms usually contain liquidated damage provisions capping the liability of breaching buyers but not of breaching sellers. What reasoning do you imagine supports this asymmetry in brokers' minds?

Question 3: *Pre-Closing Release of Escrowed Funds and "No Recordation" Clause.*

The seller owns a 200-acre citrus grove in a rapidly subdividing area. The buyer is a land developer. They enter a purchase and sale agreement contingent on the buyer being able to obtain certain government approvals for a new subdivision. The buyer

---

41. *Compare Save-Way Drug Inc. v. Standard Inv. Co.*, 490 P.2d 1342 (Wash. Ct. App. 1971) ("earnest money shall be forfeited and this contract thereupon shall be of no further binding effect" held insufficient to bar specific performance), *with Martin v. Dillon*, 642 P.2d 1209 (Ore. 1992) (holding the opposite).

42. Jeffrey B. Coopersmith, *Refocusing Liquidated Damages Law for Real Estate Contracts: Returning to the Historical Roots of the Penalty Doctrine*, 39 Emory L.J. 267, 303 (1990).

deposits 10% of the purchase price of $500,000 with an escrow agent when the contract is signed.

The contract specifies that the buyer has six months from the date on which both parties signed the contract to deposit an additional $100,000 with the balance due at closing, ten months after the contract was first signed.

Alternately, the buyer can provide the seller with notice of the buyer's intent to terminate the contract any time before six months from the date that both parties signed the contract, and obtain a refund of the $50,000 initial deposit.

At the seller's request, the following "No Recordation" provision was included in the contract: "In no event shall this Agreement or any document or other memorandum related to the subject matter of this Agreement be recorded without the consent of Seller."

According to the terms of the contract, if the buyer fails to make the final payment, time is of the essence. The seller is entitled to retain $150,000 denominated as liquidated damages. This provision of the purchase and sale contract was initialed by the buyer and seller.

(a) The seller wants a provision to be included in the contract and the accompanying escrow instructions that once the buyer deposits the full $150,000, these funds should be remitted to the seller, either to be applied to the purchase price at closing, or as liquidated damages if the buyer fails to come up with the balance of the purchase price on or before the contract closing date. Can you imagine any reasonable basis for the buyer to object to such a provision?

(b) The buyer had advanced the $150,000 but had some difficulty raising the balance of the purchase price on time. At the end of six months from the initial contact date, the seller sent a notice to the buyer declaring that she would regard the contract as terminated if the buyer failed to come up with the balance of the purchase price within two weeks.

Four weeks after the seller sent that notice, the buyer tendered a cashier's check for $350,000 which the seller refused to accept, claiming that the contract had ended, and the seller was retaining $150,000 as liquidated damages. Do you see any reasonable basis for the buyer to obtain specific performance or a return of the $150,000?

(c) The buyer files a suit for specific performance and records a *lis pendens*. The seller files suit to expunge the *lis pendens* on the basis of the "No Recordation" provision. If you were the trial judge, how would you decide the seller's expungement motion, and why?

Question 4: *Lis pendens: Strategic Factors.*

(a) Suppose in a market in which house prices are rising rapidly, a seller refuses to honor a purchase and sale contract for her residence because she comes to believe she will garner a much higher price by putting the property back on the market. What strategic advantage could the buyer obtain by filing a suit for specific performance and recording a *lis pendens*?

(b) Why would the owner of a $400,000,000 office building be well advised to limit a potential buyer's purchase and sale contract remedies to liquidated damages, and specifically to bar specific performance?

Question 5: *The Case for Liquidated Damages.*

(a) What are the advantages of liquidated damages to a breaching home buyer over potential liability to the seller for specific performance or actual damages?

(b) Why are home sellers not usually better off reserving the right to actual damages from breaching buyers?

Question 6: *Liquidated Damages and the Actual Loss Rule.*

If you had to choose between the New York and California approaches to liquidated damages in residential purchase and sale agreements, which would you prefer and why?

Question 7: *The Interplay of Specific Performance and Liquidated Damages.*

O enters a non-binding letter of intent to sell three office buildings to P, as a portfolio sale of all three of O's buildings. For each of the three properties, O and P sign separate purchase and sale agreements. None of the agreements mentions that the three properties are being sold together. Each of the three purchase and sale agreements gives the buyer the right to specific performance. Each contract also liquidates any damage claims either party may have against the other to the amount of P's down payments — $250,000 per property.

Two of the buildings appreciate in value and are easy to purchase because the buyer can assume the seller's existing and highly favorable financing. The third building must be financed anew. Since the time when the purchase and sale contract was first entered, financing office building acquisitions has become far more costly and challenging. Also, the third building has lost its main tenant, and this loss has greatly reduced the building's value.

The purchase price of the two "good" buildings was $12,000,000 and $23,000,000. Each of those buildings is now worth a million dollars more ($13,000,000 and $24,000,000) due partly to the favorable financing and partly to some new tenancies. The contract price of the third building was $17,000,000. Presently, it would sell for $14,000,000 to an all cash buyer or $15,000,000 if the buyer could find a loan of no less than $12,000,000 at 7% for ten years.

P is about to close escrow with O on the first two buildings. P's contract with O for the third building has a financing contingency that won't expire until several weeks after the scheduled closings on the two buildings. O wants P to waive the financing contingency on the third building as a condition to closing on the first two. O contends that P was obligated to buy all three buildings or none of them. P wants to close on the two, and walk away from the third by invoking the financing contingency.

(a) If the court finds that P has the right to acquire two of the buildings without buying the third since the parties entered three separate agreements, is P better off seeking specific performance or liquidated damages for the first two?

(b) If you had drafted the purchase and sale agreement for P, would you have limited P's damages for O's breach to $250,000 for each property?

(c) If P convinces a trial court judge that O has repudiated the third contract, should P be entitled to $250,000 as liquidated damage? After all, O's breach will have saved P from a huge loss.

(d) If you had drafted the purchase and sale agreement for O, what provision would you have made — in hindsight — regarding specific performance and damages in each of the three separate contracts?

Chapter 12

An Introduction to Mortgage Lending[1]

Scope of the Chapter

This chapter introduces core concepts of mortgage lending and borrowing. Mortgage loans are important because most buyers of residential and commercial property acquire realty with mortgage loans, and the mortgage market is the single largest market for consumer financial products and services in the United States.

The Underwriting Process. We start by describing the basic information that mortgage lenders consider in deciding whether to make a mortgage loan and what to charge the borrower. A clear understanding of how lenders evaluate loan applications can be helpful to borrowers who anticipate seeking a mortgage loan for a home or commercial real estate acquisition, and want to plan ahead so that they will qualify for the loan they need.

Loan Terms. Then, we look at the main loan terms that will determine the borrowers' monthly payment levels and total outlays over the life of their mortgage loans: (1) the principal amount borrowed, (2) how quickly the principal is repaid (the amortization schedule and the loan maturity date), and (3) the interest rate and loan origination costs.

Mortgage Documentation. Next, we turn to the basic mortgage loan documents—the note and the mortgage or deed of trust. The note is an "IOU" in which the borrower agrees to repay the debt. In an accompanying mortgage or deed of trust, specific real estate is pledged as collateral that the lender may foreclose if the borrower defaults.

Security Impairment (Waste), Illegal Acts That Could Result in Forfeiture of Mortgage Property, Patriot Act Compliance, and Liability for Toxic and Hazardous Substances. The borrower has obligations that would justify the lender restraining the borrower's conduct or even foreclosing although the borrower is repaying the debt on time.

In this chapter we describe four such instances: (1) The borrower is "impairing the lender's security interest" in the property by damaging it (committing waste). (2)

---

1. In preparing this chapter, the author has benefitted from the observations of Jon Daurio, Mark J. Forbes, Reza Jahangiri, Derik Lewis, and Steven Maizes.

The borrower is conducting or allowing illegal acts on the property (e.g., producing or dealing in meth).[2] (3) The borrower is doing business with specially designated nationals and blocked persons in violation of the provisions of the Patriot Act (an anti-terrorism law) (e.g., renting the property to a money-launderer). (4) The borrower is releasing or allowing hazardous substances on the security property which could result in the property owner having to undertake and finance costly government-mandated clean-up efforts.

Following the Money: The Mortgage Loan Players, Loan Categories, and Securitization. Having examined the loan itself, our next topics are about "financial intermediation." The first aspect of financial intermediation is about how borrowers go about finding a loan, perhaps by approaching lenders directly or seeking assistance from mortgage bankers or mortgage brokers. We compare these alternatives.

The second aspect of financial intermediation is about the sources of capital. Savers can place their funds in depository or non-depository institutions, a distinction with significant implications for the types and riskiness of available mortgage financing. Some institutions retain the loans they originate within their own investment portfolios. Other institutions sell the loans they originate. (The distinction can matter to borrowers in ways that will become apparent in the next three chapters as we discuss prepayment, due on sale clauses, loan servicing, foreclosure and work-outs.)

To access funds from across the globe, mortgage lenders may sell their loans to firms that are adept at pooling borrower repayments to funnel into financial products acceptable to bond buyers. This process is called securitization. Through securitization, individual mortgage loans are pooled as collateral for mortgage-backed bonds that investors purchase for the right to receive a share of the cash flow that accumulates as borrowers repay their mortgage loans. The rather complex securitization trail is explained in this chapter as well.

Investors, including bond buyers, are sensitive to the credit risks they are taking when they advance money now for the right to receive future payments. The riskiness of mortgage backed bonds depends on whether mortgage borrowers repay their loans. Not all home mortgage loans are equally likely to be repaid. Obviously, mortgage bond investors are able to command higher rates of return for acquiring riskier bonds. In order to set the appropriate mortgage loan interest rate on a home loan or on a portfolio of home loans, home mortgages are divided into four risk categories: prime, subprime, jumbo and alt-A. The differences among them are described in this chapter.

---

2. "Meth labs are easily transportable and can be set up quickly and in most locations. Meth is commonly "cooked" in rental houses, garages, rented storage lockers, apartments or unoccupied homes. Meth labs can be set up on crop land or future home-building sites. The toxic residue left from cooking the illegal substance seeps into the soil and accumulates on walls, ceilings and furniture, with long-term health consequences." David DeDecker, Meth labs carry obligations for property owners, The Hastings Banner (Hastings, Michigan), June 18, 2016. http://hastingsbanner.com/meth-labs-carry-obligations-for-property-owners-p2198-86.htm(Last visited June 18, 2016.)

Structural shortcomings in the securitization process accounted for a great deal of the mortgage meltdown of 2008 that led to a global recession. In the concluding pages of this chapter, we recap the most often cited causes of this debacle. This is an important effort because assumptions about its causes will probably long influence the attitudes and behavior of home buyers, mortgage loan borrowers, mortgage lenders, bond investors and government regulators.

In passing, we comment on the unsuccessful law suits brought by homeowners who sought to hold their mortgage lenders accountable for engaging in the reckless mortgage lending practices that precipitated the collapse of US house prices.

I. The Underwriting Process

A. Primary Underwriting Factors

1. Residential Mortgage Underwriting

To estimate the chances of a borrower defaulting and the lender not being able to recoup its principal and interest, loan underwriters evaluate home loan applications by looking to the 'three C's': *capacity, credit reputation, and collateral.*[3]

Capacity. Capacity is usually measured by the borrower's Debt-to-Income (DTI) ratio, calculated by dividing the borrower's total recurring monthly debt by gross monthly income. The debt component of DTI is meant to be inclusive, and covers: (1) the borrower's "long-term" debt payments (any obligations that will continue for more than 10 months) and (2) the financial obligations that the borrower will incur with home ownership. Those obligations include principal and interest payments on the mortgage, real property taxes, and casualty insurance premiums.

Suppose a lender established a policy of not making loans to borrowers with a DTI ratio exceeding, say, 38%. A borrower with recurrent monthly debts of $3800 would only qualify for a loan if the borrower's monthly gross income was $10,000 or more. In recent decades, home mortgage loan originators have set the DTI bar at anywhere from 38% to 43%, and as high as 55% if there are compensating factors enhancing the borrower's credit-worthiness.

Traditionally, DTIs are calculated based on pre-tax income and exclude many normal living expenses, such as income and payroll taxes, food, clothing, home utilities, cell phones, home repairs and maintenance, auto and commute expenses, child care, retirement savings, and gym memberships.

---

3. Even applying the same standards, default and foreclosure rates of private securitized debt have been higher than those loans purchased by FNMA and FHLMC. Final Report of the National Commission on the Causes of the Financial and Economic Crisis in the United States, The Financial Crisis Inquiry Report, p. 219 (last visited, Jan. 2, 2016), https://books.google.com/books?id=QIKfTVrhNfMC&pg=PA219&lpg=PA219&dq=FICO+and+LTV+Ratios+Combined&source=bl&ots=mzcdW3TI4r&sig=VFykuehhiWIVWkaUooUxP_xujTQ&hl=en&sa=X&ved=0CEAQ6AEwBmoVChMIuMjZiYGEyQIVBimICh1SjwB2#v=onepage&q=FICO%20and%20LTV%20Ratios%20Combined&f=false.

Borrowers with very high incomes can be far better credit risks despite their relatively high DTIs. For example, a borrower with a 60% DTI who earns $500,000 a year will have $200,000 for discretionary spending.

Credit reputation. Loan underwriters usually measure credit reputation by the borrowers' automated credit scores.[4] Borrowers receive lower scores when they pay debts late, default or have filed bankruptcy, as do borrowers who max out their allowable credit lines.[5] Credit scores have proven to be highly predictive of default.[6]

Collateral. This is usually the ratio of the loan to the appraised value of the security property (LTV). The higher the borrower's down payment, the lower the borrower's risk of default. "Borrowers with a sizeable chunk of equity in a home are less likely to walk away when things get bad." Their ability to save up for a down payment may demonstrate budgeting skills that can be useful in averting defaults.[7] Also, house prices need to fall quite a bit before a borrower who made a large down payment and can no longer afford to pay the mortgage, will be unable to sell the house for at least some amount of net cash.

In estimating the probabilities of a borrower defaulting, it is important to distinguish between the original loan-to-value ratio, and the current LTV (CLTV) at any point in time. As long as a property owner's CLTV does not exceed the combined mortgage debt on the property, the owner who cannot afford to make mortgage payments has the option of cashing out by selling. Conversely, when property values fall so that the CLTV is well above the combined mortgage debt on the property, owners are more likely to default than when they had substantial equities in the property.

While increasing down payments substantially reduces the risk of default and the extent of a foreclosing lender's likely losses, a 3% down payment requirement would exclude six successful borrowers for every one foreclosure it prevented. Furthermore, the impact of a 10% down payment standard would be particularly acute for com-

---

4. "Several firms collect data on the payment histories of individuals from lending institutions and use sophisticated models to evaluate and quantify individual creditworthiness. The process results in a credit score, which is essentially a numerical grade of the credit history and creditworthiness of the borrower. There are three different credit-reporting firms that calculate credit scores: Experian (which markets the Experian/ Fair Isaac Risk Model), Transunion (which supports the Emperica model), and Equifax (whose model is known as Beacon). While each firm's credit scores are based on different data sets and scoring algorithms, the scores are generically referred to as FICO scores, since they are based on Fair Isaac's software and models. Underwriters typically purchase credit scores from all three credit bureaus, and apply the median figure to their analysis; in the event that only two scores are available, the lower of the two is used." Frank J Fabozzi, Anand K. Bhattacharya, and William S. Berliner, Mortgage Backed Securities (2d ed.2011), p. 6.

5. Laurence G. Taff, Investing in Mortgage Securities (2003).

6. A borrower with a 740 FICO score and only 3% down payment has, on average, a lower foreclosure rate than a borrower with a 660 FICO score and more than 20% down payment. Borrowers with FICO scores below 620 are twenty times more likely to enter foreclosure than borrowers with FICO scores above 660. *Ken Fears, Fannie and Freddie to Back Three Percent Down Loans Safely,* EconomistOutlook (last visited, Jan. 12, 2015), http://economistsoutlook.blogs.realtor.org/2014/11/12/fannie-and-freddie-to-back-3-down-loans-safely/

7. Peter Eavis, *Down Payment Rules Are At Heart of Mortgage Debate,* NY Times, April 24, 2013.

munities of color, as 60% of African-American and 50% of Latino borrowers who are currently successfully paying their mortgages would have been excluded from the mainstream mortgage market had such a requirement been in place.[8]

Are Borrowers Entitled to Hold the Lenders' Appraisers Liable for Faulty Appraisals? Lenders obtain appraisals to determine whether the value of the property that the borrower is offering as collateral for a mortgage loan falls within the range of the lender's acceptable loan to value ratio limits.

The appraiser may later be faulted for having under or over valued the property. Perhaps the appraiser failed to consider all of the available comparable properties in applying the comparable sales approach to value, maybe disregarding some recent sales, or failing to notice significant differences between the subject property and the chosen "comps."[9]

Borrowers can be misled by faulty appraisals, whether too high or too low. Too high, and the borrower risks paying more than a property is worth because the lender provides financing in reliance on the faulty appraisal, financing without which the buyer would have been unable to complete the purchase. Too low, and the lender rejects the borrower's request to finance what could have been a financially sound investment for the buyer.

In either situation, the lender who ordered the appraisal could hold the appraiser accountable on various legal theories including breach of contract and negligent misrepresentation. Generally, borrowers have no contract claims against appraisers since they have no contract with them even if the borrower paid for the lender's appraisal. Most agreements between lenders and appraisers explicitly specify that the appraisal is being prepared exclusively for the use of the lender.[10]

Borrowers could claim that the appraisal was a negligent misrepresentation. To validate such a claim, the borrower would need to prove that the lender intended for the borrower to rely on the appraisal in entering the loan agreement and the buyer did rely on it.[11] The starting point in analyzing this sort of claim is the Restatement (Second) of Torts § 552, "Information Negligently Supplied for the Guidance of Others."

---

8. Center for Responsible Lending, *The Negative Impact of a Government-Mandated 10 Percent Down Payment for Qualified Residential Mortgages* (QRM's) (last visited, Aug. 3, 2015).

(QRMs) [fn:http://www.responsiblelending.org/mortgage-lending/policy-legislation/regulators/QRM-10percent-issue-brief-Aug16-1-2.pdf]

9. A court described the way an appraiser dealt with "comps" who was conspiring with a sleazy "house flipper" to deceive lenders and FHA into financing houses for far more than they were worth." Hoffman identified the sales of three properties as comparable, two of which he emphasized because the properties were only two blocks away. One, the evidence showed, was larger than he reported-1, 830 sf. rather than 1,600 sf. It also had a fireplace and a modern kitchen, which the subject property did not have. Evidence showed that the second comparable was "in far superior condition than the subject property." Three other lower-price sales in the area were ignored." *Hoffman v. Stamper*, 867 A. 2d 276, 287 (2005).

10. Shelby D. Green, *Re-Appraising The Appraisers: Expanding Liability To Buyers And Borrowers In The Story Of The 2008 Financing Industry Crisis,*

11. Restatement Second, Torts § 552(2)(b). 25-DEC Prob. & Prop. 10

So, for instance, a developer had a purchase and sale contract to acquire property for a specific project, and sought financing. The lender's appraiser failed to notice that the property was directly above an earthquake fault, so that the property was practically useless. Unfortunately for the lender, the purchaser had already acquired the property, and the lender had made the development loan, before the error became apparent. The borrower sued the appraiser to no avail.

Here is how the court explained why it rejected the developer's negligent misrepresentation claim against the appraiser: "There was no loan contingency in the purchase agreement and the buyer had other means of determining suitability of the property and did not in fact rely on the appraisal. Moreover, the appraisers had not manifested an objective intention that the borrower could rely on the appraisal, and since the borrower was not an intended third party who could rely on the appraisal, there was no liability in the absence of privity with the appraisers."[12]

In a case with the opposite outcome, a mortgage broker routinely commissioned appraisals specifically to assist second mortgage loan investors to decide whether to purchase the loans based on the appraised values of the underlying properties. The appraiser knew that. An investor relying on the appraisal acquired a second mortgage on which the borrower defaulted almost immediately.

At that point, the second trust deed investor realized that the property had been grossly over-valued, and sued the appraiser. The investor was held entitled to sue the appraiser for negligent misrepresentation as a third party beneficiary of the mortgage broker's contract with the appraiser.[13]

An Arizona Homebuyer Was Able to Hold the Lender's Appraiser Liable When She Paid Too Much for Her House. In a landmark Arizona case, *Sage v. Blagg Appraisal Co., Ltd,.*[14] "Shari Sage made an offer to purchase a Scottsdale home for $605,200. The offer was written on a form Arizona Association of Realtors "Residential Resale Real Estate Purchase Contract" that provided that the buyer's obligation to complete the purchase was "contingent upon an appraisal of the Premises by an appraiser acceptable to the lender for at least the sales price." The contract further provided that Sage would reimburse the cost of the appraisal at closing. The appraisal, dated September 14, 2004, recited the livable area of the home as 2,440 square feet and estimated its market value to be $620,000.

A year and a half after she bought her home, Sage obtained another appraisal in connection with a refinancing. That appraisal stated that the livable area of the home

---

12. *Willemsen v. Mitrosilis*, 230 Cal. App. 4th 622, 629–632, 178 Cal. Rptr. 3d 735 (4th Dist. 2014).The above quote comes from Miller and Starr California Real Estate 4th, re-written by Karl e. Geier, 2 Cal. Real Est. §4:90 (4th ed.) (updated June, 2016).

13. *Soderberg v. McKinney*, 44 Cal. App. 4th 1760, 1768, 1771, 52 Cal. Rptr. 2d 635 (2d Dist. 1996)

14. 221 Ariz. 33, 209 P.3d 169 (2009).

was 1,871 square feet, 569 fewer square feet than stated in the Blagg appraisal. Sage then sued Blagg's company, alleging his appraisal negligently misrepresented the value of her home at the time of her purchase. Sage alleged that if Blagg's appraisal calculated the home's value based on the correct amount of livable space, she would have realized the home was then worth less than she had contracted to pay for it and would have exercised her right to cancel the deal."

In holding that Shari Sage could hold the appraiser liable, the court explained: "The limited duty imposed pursuant to Restatement § 552 in the circumstances we describe adds nothing to the substantive obligation an appraiser undertakes by accepting an engagement from a lender. Pursuant to that duty, the appraiser is obligated to perform the appraisal in a non-negligent fashion; the appraiser will owe the prospective homebuyer the same standard of care ... Our recognition of the duty owed by an appraiser to the buyer/borrower, moreover, is consistent with evolving industry standards that acknowledge that a buyer/borrower in fact relies on an appraisal prepared at the request of the lender.

Finally, adopting Blagg's contention that an appraiser retained by a lender owes no duty to the buyer/borrower would mean that a prospective homebuyer who seeks to rely on a pre-purchase appraisal must contract separately with an appraiser for that purpose. In the purchase in this case, as is not uncommon, the buyer was obligated to reimburse the cost of the appraisal ordered by the lender. Even if we were to assume such an arrangement were not the general rule, we see no reason to impose on the parties to a transaction the burden of paying twice for the same information simply so that the buyer may join the lender within the scope of the appraiser's duty of care. Public policy and common sense compel the conclusion that when a lender to which a prospective homebuyer has applied for a loan contracts for an appraisal of the home, the appraiser the lender hires owes a duty of due care not only to the lender but also to the homebuyer."[15]

Are Mortgage Loan Borrowers Entitled to Assume That Lender Approval of Their Credit Means They Can Afford the Loan? Perlas and Len Villacorta owned property on Drakes Circle in Discovery Bay. They sought to refinance the property with a home equity line of credit from GMAC Mortgage, LLC, secured by their real property. Their loan documents clearly showed that they would owe monthly payments of $2,601.54. They never had sufficient income to cover those payments, defaulted on

---

15. 221 Ariz. 33 39, 209 P.3d 169,175. Professor Dan Schecter raises important questions about this decision: "Could the appraiser obtain a waiver of this new duty to the purchaser? Would that waiver be reliably enforceable in a residential transaction? (I doubt it.) Since the appraiser is sometimes the agent of the lender, are lenders now at risk of vicarious liability for faulty appraisals? Can the appraiser be characterized as an independent contractor? Will this decision mean that appraisers will have to obtain additional insurance to cover the risk of liability to purchasers? In the wake of the current mortgage mess, we can expect to see many more disappointed homebuyers who seek to impose liability on allegedly negligent appraisers." Dan Schecter, *Purchaser May Recover for Negligent Appraisal, Even Though Appraiser Was Retained by a Mortgage Lender [Sage v. Blagg Appraisal Co., Ltd.* (Ariz. App. Div.)], 2009 Comm. Fin. News. 41 (2009).

the loan and were facing imminent foreclosure when they brought this suit to head off the foreclosure.[16]

The loan had been arranged through a consultant who, apparently, filled out a loan application on the borrowers' behalf which they never saw, reporting their income to be $114,000 a year. In fact, the borrowers contended that they had told the consultant over the phone that their annual income was $50,000 ($4,167 a month). It is hard to imagine that GMAC would have made that loan to Perlas and Len Villacorta with a DTI of 62.4%, had it known their actual monthly income (2,601/4,167=62.4%). It also strains credulity they thought this loan was one they could afford.

The borrowers sought to set aside the deed of trust on various grounds, including that they should have been able to assume they could afford the loan if the lender deemed them qualified to receive it.

In rejecting the borrowers' claim, the court observed that they had never alleged that the lender ever told them they had the ability to repay the loan. Further, the court explained: "a loan transaction is at arm's length and there is no fiduciary relationship between the borrower and lender … A lender is under no duty to determine the borrower's ability to repay the loan. The lender's efforts to determine the creditworthiness and ability to repay by a borrower are for the lender's protection, not the borrower's."[17]

The Federal Consumer Protection Bureau (CFPB),[18] Ability-to-Pay and the Qualified Mortgage.[19] In response to the mortgage crisis of 2008, Congress established the Federal Consumer Protection Bureau. Its mission includes replacing risky pre-crisis lending practices with safer ones. Precipitating the mortgage crisis, lenders made loans to many borrowers whose debt-to-income ratios exceeded earlier prevailing standards. To prevent a recurrence, the CFPB introduced an "ability-to-repay" rule requiring residential mortgage lenders to make a good-faith effort to determine whether borrowers possess the ability to repay their mortgage loans.[20]

---

16. 187 Cal.App.4th 429, 113 Cal.Rptr.3d 790 (2010).

17. 113 Cal.Rptr.3d 790, 796 (2010).

18. *Ability to Repay and Qualified Mortgage Standards Under the Truth in Lending Act (Regulation Z)*, Cfpb (last visited Jan. 13, 2016), http://www.consumerfinance.gov/regulations/ability-to-repay-and-qualified-mortgage-standards-under-the-truth-in-lending-act-regulation-z/

19. *See also* Ability-to-Repay and Qualified Mortgage Standards under the Truth in Lending Act, Final Rule, 78 Fed. Reg. 6408 (January 30, 2013), 12 C.F.R. § 1026 (January 1, 2014).

20. The Ability-to-Repay Rule, Regulation Z Section 1026.43, requires that a creditor make a "reasonable and good faith determination at or before consummation that the consumer will have a reasonable ability to repay the loan according to its terms." The creditor must follow underwriting requirements and verify the information by using reasonably relied upon third-party records. The rule applies to all residential mortgages including purchase loans, refinances, home equity loans, first liens, and subordinate liens. In short, if the creditor is making a loan secured by a principal residence, second or vacation home, condominium, or mobile or manufactured home, the creditor must verify the borrowers' ability to repay the loan. The section does not apply to commercial or business loans,

Under CFPB guidelines, 43% is the maximum debt-to-income home mortgage lenders should normally approve.[21] The CFPB recognizes a broad public and consumer interest in how residential mortgage lenders determine whether borrowers have the ability-to-repay ...

The CFPB has offered a "safe harbor" to mortgage lenders. They can escape liability for failing to ascertain a borrower's ability to repay when making "qualified mortgages."[22]

2. Commercial Mortgage Underwriting

Lenders underwriting income-producing property (such as an apartment house, shopping center, hotel, office building, distribution warehouse or parking lot) are anticipating that the loan will be repaid from the net operating income produced by the security property. Besides relying on the property's recent financial statements, lenders look to the track record and reputation of the sponsor.

Oversight. Commercial mortgage lenders keep a watchful eye on their borrowers' operations and cash flow as shown in periodic financial records and statements. They sometimes contract for the right to approve the owner's major leases, budgets, capital expenditures, reserves for capital replacements, and management company.

Hard and Soft Lock Box Accounts. As additional security, lenders may insist that borrowers place rents in a lock box. This is a special bank account that the lender controls. The tenants make their rental payments to this account. The mortgage lender distributes the project cash flow in this order: mortgage debt service is paid first, then operating expenses and the balance, if any, to the borrower. This arrangement is called a hard lockbox. Other lenders allow what is called a soft lock box which is only activated after the borrower defaults. Until then, the borrower collects and disburses the cash flow.

Commercial mortgage lenders apply three ratios in underwriting their loans: LTV, DSCR, and Debt Yield.

The Debt Service Coverage Ratio (DSCR aka DCR). The debt service coverage ratio, sometimes called debt coverage ratio, is the ratio of net operating income to debt service. Net Operating Income (NOI) is the amount of rent available to cover the payments of principal and interest on the mortgage. Debt service is the amount of periodic payments necessary to cover principal and interest due on the debt. Lenders insist on DSCRs well above the 'break even' point of 1.0. The more risk averse the lender, the higher the DSCR. Lenders know that rents can fall and expenses can

---

even if secured by a personal dwelling. It also does not apply to loans for timeshares, reverse mortgages, loan modifications, and temporary bridge loans.

21. http://www.consumerfinance.gov/askcfpb/1791/what-debt-income-ratio-why-43-debt-income-ratio-important.html (Last visited, 06/20.2016.).

22. *Ability to Repay and Qualified Mortgage Standards Under the Truth in Lending Act (Regulation Z)*, Cғᴘʙ (last visited Jan. 13, 2016), http://www.consumerfinance.gov/regulations/ability-to-repay-and-qualified-mortgage-standards-under-the-truth-in-lending-act-regulation-z/.

rise unexpectedly, diminishing NOI. So they base the loan amount on a sum the borrower could repay with less than 100% of the NOI.

A DSCR of 1.5 means that for every dollar of mortgage payments due, the borrower is expected to earn $1.50 in rent (after paying operating expenses). With $60,000 of NOI, and a DSCR of 1.5 the borrower can pay debt service of $40,000.

Debt Yield Ratio. This is NOI divided by the loan amount multiplied by 100%. It is more conservative than DSCR and an antidote to risk when interest rates are being kept low as a result of government intervention in the money markets. (Governments keep money cheap to encourage employment and investment at the expense of savings.)

Low interest rates on government debt restrain cap rates because equity investors tend to peg their returns to a spread or margin above government borrowing rates. With low cap rates, income-producing properties trade at high prices despite anemic net operating incomes. But when the time comes that interest rates rise, cap rates will follow, and the value of all equities could plummet, including commercial real estate, unless there are substantial increases in net operating income.

Imagine an office building with a steady or declining NOI of $100,000 a year. The lender had made a loan at an LTV of 80% at a time when the cap rate on buildings like this had been 5%. The building would have been worth $2,000,000 and the loan would have been for $1,600,000 (value = NOI/cap rate).

If cap rates were to rise to 10%, the value of the building would fall to $1,000,000, and the $1,600,000 loan would be far "underwater" with a debt yield ratio of 100,000/1,600,000= .0625 x 100, or 6.25%.

Typically, lenders insist upon a debt yield ratio of 10%. Using that metric, the lender under these facts would not have made a loan of more than $1,000,000.

II. Loan Terms

A. The Principal Amount Borrowed

The biggest determinant of a borrower's repayment obligation is the amount borrowed. But even on loans of the same principal amount, a borrower can end up with wildly different monthly payment levels and borrowing costs, depending on the borrower's interest rate, whether the rate was fixed or adjustable, loan closing costs, the amortization schedule, and the loan maturity date.

B. Amortization and the Loan Maturity Date

Lenders charge borrowers interest on the unpaid balance of their debts—the principal due. So the more quickly a loan is repaid, the less interest the borrower ends up paying on it. Interest payments not paid when due are added to the loan principal. Amortization refers to the repayment schedule, literally the death (mort) of the loan.

Full Amortization. Borrowers could make a series of periodic payments of interest and principal so that on the maturity date, the loan principal will have been fully repaid without the necessity of a balloon payment. This is called a fully amortized loan.

Partial Amortization. Some loans provide for periodic repayments of principal that would not fully repay the loan on the date it becomes due and payable (the loan maturity date). Commercial mortgage loans often call for partial amortization. Repayments of principal are required to be made as if the loan were not to be fully repaid until the end of 30 years. But the note calls for the loan to be repaid in full much sooner than that, typically at the end of five or ten years. Such loans would be called "30 due in 10" or "30 due in 5."

However, in order to avoid a payment default, the borrower must repay the mortgage on or before the due date. The borrower can do this by making a large "balloon" payment, refinancing the loan for an amount sufficient to repay the mortgage debt, or selling the property for a sum large enough to repay the loan.

Partial amortization has the advantage to the borrower of lower monthly payments than would be due on a fully amortized loan. The lender takes comfort in the fact that at least some of the loan principal is being repaid, reducing the size of the eventual balloon payment.

Negative Amortization. Negative amortization occurs when periodic payments (the "pay rate") fall short of the amount of interest due for that loan period. The loan principal increases with each deferred payment of interest as unpaid accrued interest is added to loan principal.

Negative amortization is a feature of adjustable rate loans with introductory 'teaser' interest rates set below the actual rate of interest accruing on the debt. These are called 'teaser' rate loans because they are designed to lure borrowers into signing up for loans with deceptively inviting low initial monthly payments. At some point, borrowers will be responsible for fully amortizing monthly payments plus accrued interest on the deferred loan principal payments.

Consider what happened to Roseanne Harriman. She invested $82,000 as a down payment to buy a home for herself and her disabled son.[23] With a FICO score of 758, she would have easily qualified for a thirty year, fixed rate, fully amortized mortgage loan. That is the loan she preferred and thought she had.

Instead, her mortgage broker arranged an adjustable rate loan with deep negative amortization. Roseanne's monthly payments only covered interest of one percent although the loan was accruing interest at a much higher rate. The unpaid interest payments were added to the principal amount she owed on her loan. These deferred interest payments increased the loan amount so much that after three years, her mortgage loan principal exceeded the $82,000 down payment she made.

Unfortunately for her, she had no recourse against the mortgage broker who steered her into this loan. Because she trusted him, she signed all the loan documents without

---

23. *Harriman v. Sunfield Financial, Inc.*, 2012 WL 7655970 (Cal. App. 1 Dist.) (Appellate Brief).

reading them. The documents accurately described the loan she actually received. Rendering a weak case hopeless, she filed suit only after expiration of the five-year statute of limitations for suits on a debt.

The Graduated Payment Mortgage (GPM).[24] In special situations, negative or deferred amortization can be sensible for some borrowers. The Federal Housing Agency (FHA) has a program, the Graduated Payment Mortgage (GMP), for first time home buyers whose incomes are expected to rise in five or ten years. This enables them to purchase a home with affordable monthly payments that will grow as their earnings increase. Doctors in residency programs or young lawyers expecting to become partners can use the cash they save by deferring repayments of principal to make affordable a home that otherwise would have been out of their price range for years.

The Reverse Mortgage. (Home Equity Conversion Mortgage — HECM).[25] The FHA insures mortgage lenders on loans made to homeowners 62 years of age or older, with valuable equities in their homes. This program enables them to borrow money either in a lump sum or a series of monthly payments, and not to repay any of the loan until they leave the home or pass away. Many elderly borrowers who are house rich and cash poor would not be able to borrow mortgage money but for the reverse mortgage because they have no income to support monthly payments. Overwhelmingly, retired home owners desire to stay in their houses, and the reverse mortgage makes this possible by allowing them to draw down the equity in their homes in their waning years. They can use an initial lump sum from the reverse mortgage loan to repay their existing mortgages, greatly reducing their monthly outlays. Then, they can live on the balance of the reverse mortgage loan paid out in monthly instalments.

Negative Amortization Loans for Developers. Negative amortization can also be useful to developers building or renovating income producing properties that have negative cash flow until the projects are completed and fully rented. An accommodating lender could set a low "pay rate" on the developer's loan until the net operating income from the apartment house, shopping center, or office building stabilizes at target levels and the project generates enough cash flow to pay the full interest due on the loan.[26]

No Amortization

(a) With no amortization, the borrower minimizes her monthly debt service payments but hugely increases her interest payments over the life of the loan.

(b) Interest payments on most home loans are deductible from the taxpayer's adjusted gross income. Interest on commercial loans is deductible as a business expense.[27]

---

24. 24 CFR 203.45.

25. 12 U.S. Code § 1715z–20.

26. Randy P. Orlik and Anthony Theop http://portal.hud.gov/hudportal/HUD?src=/hudprograms/gpmhilos, *The Promissory Note, CEB California Real Estate Finance Prac- tice:Strategies and Forms* (1st ed., January 2014 update), Section 3.12.

27. The point at which principal and interest payments are about an equal par of each monthly payment occurs after 24% of the life of the loan on a 15-year 6% loan and 81% of the life of the loan on a 30-year 12% loan.

Since repayments of principal are not deductible, tax conscious borrowers maximize their deductions when their loan payments consist entirely or mostly of interest payments.

'Interest only' (no amortization) loans disadvantage borrowers in various ways. Lenders charge higher interest rates on loans with no amortization. Borrowers forego the forced savings plan built into a fully amortizing loan. Also, the borrower pays more interest over the life of the loan since interest accrues on the unpaid loan balance. Eventually, the borrower will owe a lump sum at the loan maturity date and borrowers not able to pay it will be at risk of default if they cannot refinance or sell the house for more than the amount owing.

The Costs of Delayed Amortization. Consider the example of $180,000 financed either with a 30 or 15-year mortgage loan.

The interest rate on the 30-year loan will be 4% and on the 15-year loan, 3.25%. (The shorter-term loan carries a reduced interest rate.)

Over the life of the loan, a borrower amortizing principal over 30 years will make *interest* payments of *$129,240* vs. *$47,520* on the 15-year loan.

If we tack on the *principal and interest* payments, the total life of loan payments on the 30 year, fully amortized loan equal *$309,349* vs. *$227,520* on the 15-year loan.

By spreading out the payment obligation over 30 years, the borrower reduces monthly debt service considerably, from *$859.35* on the 30-year loan compared to a sum of *$1264.80* on the 15-year loan– a difference of *$405.45* per month.

The Qualified Mortgage (QM). The CFPB created "ability to repay" exceptions for Qualified Mortgages. These are mortgages with risky, costly features such as "negative amortization," "teaser rates," loan terms longer than 30 years, or high Debt-To-Income Ratios.[28]

C. Mortgage Interest Rates

These next few paragraphs are an introduction to the determinants of mortgage interest rates.

How Markets Set Mortgage Rates. Mortgage rates of interest generally track the rates of interest paid on U.S. government bonds[29] or the London Interbank Offered Rate (LIBOR) plus a spread. The spread reflects the fact that every mortgage loan has a greater risk of non-payment than a U.S. government bond, and less liquidity because U.S. government bonds are widely and quickly tradable. The spread compensates lenders for potential political risks such as unfavorable tax law changes for mortgage lenders or restrictive foreclosure policies. Spreads could also be needed to attract investors to buy obligations issued in any currency except U.S. dollars.

---

28. Sanford Shatz, *An Overview of the Consumer Financial Protection Bureau's Ability-to-Repay and Qualified Mortgages Rule*, *Business Law Today*, April 2013 (ABA).

29. This site is the Wall Street Journal comparative bond market data page. http://online.wsj.com/mdc/public/page/mdc_bonds.html.

Both interest rates and spreads fluctuate with investor anxieties in general and with specific loans — the credit worthiness of the borrower, the loan-to-value ratio, the amortization period, the maturity date, whether the rate is fixed or adjustable, and so on.

Bond values and interest rates move in opposite directions because as prevailing market rates of interest on bonds rise, bonds issued earlier at lower rates are proportionately worth less. Conversely, when bond interest rates fall, bonds issued earlier at higher rates are worth proportionately more.

This is a bit confusing at first, though ultimately understandable. Bonds are traded in highly competitive markets. Suppose the day after you purchase a one-year U.S. Treasury obligation for $5,000 paying 4% interest, market rates of interest fall to 2%. Bond investors would bid up the price of your bond to the point where they would be receiving approximately 2% on the sum they paid for your bond.

Rate Locks. *Rate locks protect borrowers against interest rates rising during the time it takes to underwrite and process their loan applications. A rate lock is the lender's promise made to the borrower, for a fee, that the interest rate and points on the loan will not change as long as the loan is closed within a prescribed period of days, usually metered in 15-day intervals up to 90 days. The rate lock fee is paid up-front, based on a percentage of the locked loan principal for commercial properties, or a flat fee for residential properties.*

If rates fall, rate locked borrowers could have saved the lock fee and gotten a more favorable interest rate if they had done absolutely nothing about rates. Lenders sometimes shave down the locked rate just a bit if they can.

To discourage borrowers from looking elsewhere for financing when interest rates decline below the locked rate, rate lock contracts (particularly for commercial properties) often obligate borrowers to pay 'break up' damages for not taking the loan. Damages are set to equal the present value of the difference between the locked rate and comparable market rates on the date the loan was to have closed.

Discount Points (Pre-Paid Interest). In some instances, borrowers agree to pay "discount points" (aka "points") as a form of pre-paid interest for a lower interest rate, which reduces their monthly payments. A point is one percentage of the loan amount. On a $100,000 loan, one point is $1000. One point typically lowers the interest rate by 1/8% to 1/4%. Whether paying points saves borrowers money depends on how long they keep their loans in place. A borrower who pays one point for an annual reduction of 1/4 of one percent will break even if she keeps the loan for four years.[30] Some borrowers require a reduction in the monthly payment amount to qualify for the loan.

The lender could add the points to the loan principal or deduct the points from the loan proceeds actually distributed at closing. Either way, the borrower will be paying interest on the points. Alternately, the borrower could pay the points up-front by writing a check for $1,000.

---

30. David Reed, *Should You Pay Discount Points? It Depends on How Long You Plan to Keep the Mortgage.* REALTOR.ORG (last visited Aug. 15, 2015),

In reality, many homeowners throw money away by buying down their rates. On average, most borrowers either refinance, or sell their home every six years and never fully realize the benefit of paying points.[31]

Consider this example: L is borrowing $200,000 amortized over 30 years to purchase a home. His lender is offering him either a 4% rate at 0 discount points, or a 3.75 % with 1 point ($200,000 x 1% =$2000). The 3.75% will lower his monthly payments by $28.50, but cost an additional $2000 in fees. Should he take the lower rate? It depends. It will take L about 70 months ($2000/$28.50) to recoup the cost of the point. If he sells or refinances his home before 70 months he will not fully recoup the cost of getting the lower rate.

The ARM/FRM Gamble. Borrowers may choose between mortgage loans with fixed or adjustable interest rates or a combination of the two. Borrowers on fixed rate debt enjoy payment predictability, as their monthly payments remain the same for the duration of the loan.

The interest due on an adjustable rate mortgage fluctuates according to an agreed index plus a fixed margin.[32] The formula is index + margin = ARM interest rate.[33]

ARMs are risky for borrowers whose incomes are unlikely to rise with interest rates.

Interest Rate Fluctuations: When ARMs Are Better and When Worse Than FRMs. The adjustable rate borrower will be better off than the fixed rate borrower when rates fall. Even then, many fixed rate borrowers will have the option of re-financing and prepaying their loans with a new mortgage written at the lower prevailing rates.

An adjustable rate borrower will experience rate increases when interest rates rise.

ARM Caps and Floors. There are three potential types of caps: limits on how much higher a single periodic payment can rise above the prior periodic payment; a limit on how high the interest rate can rise in a given year; and a limit on how high the interest rate can rise over the life of the loan.

With a life of loan cap, most borrowers could estimate whether they will be able to afford the maximum rate they might be charged in a worst-case situation. Suppose the adjustable interest rate is 6% and the life of loan cap is 3%. A borrower can calculate what the monthly payment would be at 9%, and decide whether that payment level would be sustainable with her future income prospects in mind. Without a life of loan cap, she could not possibly make such a determination.

---

31. Colin Robertson, *How Long Do You Plan to Keep Your Mortgage?* The Truth About Mortgage (last visited Aug. 15, 2015), http://www.thetruthaboutmortgage.com/how-long-do-you-plan-to-keep-your-mortgage/

32. Federal Reserve Board, Consumer Handbook on Adjustable Rate Mortgages. The various indices all tend to move in the same direction with slight but financially significant differences (last visited Aug. 15, 2015), http://files.consumerfinance.gov/f/201401_cfpb_booklet_charm.pdf).

33. Some researchers have suggested that the margin depends on how tight the caps are on the loan, the length of the rate adjustment frequency, the type of index used, the contract rate, the loan size, the up-front fees, and the call for prepayment and other options (*e.g.*, "due-on-sale" features). *See, e.g.*, Sa-Aadu & Sirmans, *The Pricing of Adjustable Rate Mortgage Contracts*, 2 J. Real Est. Fin. & Econ. 253 (1989).

Many ARMs contain a "floor" below which the interest rate cannot fall, no matter how deeply mortgage interest rates plummet. Borrowers beware: A considerable percentage of ARMs have floors but no caps. This means that borrowers are playing a 'heads-you-win, tails-I lose' game with their lenders. If rates fall below a certain level, the borrower will be paying an interest rate greater than prevailing market levels. If rates go up, the borrower's interest rate can rise limitlessly.

The Payment Option ARM and Negative Amortization. An Option ARM is an adjustable-rate mortgage (ARM) under which the borrower can elect among a variety of payment plans. (1) Paying an amount that covers both principal and interest. This is the only way that borrowers reduce the amount they owe on their mortgage debt with each payment. (2) Paying an amount that covers only the interest. Interest-only payments do not pay down any of the amount borrowed, the loan principal. (3) Paying a minimum (or limited) amount that does not even cover the accrued interest.

This third option is an introductory "teaser" rate, set well below the borrower's actual contract rate of interest under the note. As a consequence, the borrower's principal balance *increases* each month by the difference between the teaser rate and the contract rate. Rather than amortizing the loan with each monthly payment (as occurs with a standard mortgage loan), the principal amount that the borrower owes is growing and eroding the borrower's equity monthly. This is negative amortization.[34]

Lenders set a limit on the amount by which negative amortization can accrue, often as a percentage of the original loan amount, or a fixed dollar sum. After a period of negative amortization, the loan documents call for the borrower's monthly payment schedule to be re-calibrated so that at the new much higher monthly payment level, the borrower will have fully amortized the loan by the original scheduled maturity date.

Option ARM borrowers are prone to experiencing payment shock when their teaser rate periods expire, not having fully anticipated what was to come.

Why Borrowers Sometimes Prefer ARMs. Homebuyers prefer ARMs not because they regard themselves as more adept at being able to forecast future interest rate trends than mortgage lenders and investors. Financially literate borrowers tend to prefer fixed rate mortgages but sometimes select ARMs for the same reason that not so sophisticated borrowers choose adjustable rate mortgages. Because of the lower monthly payments on the ARM, they qualify to borrow larger loan amounts, enabling them to purchase properties they could not otherwise have acquired.

---

34. This opinion deals with a challenge based on whether the lender adequately disclosed an option ARM to the borrowers by providing copies of the note and other descriptive information but did not clearly caution the borrowers of the dire implications of the teaser rate on the eventual monthly payment levels they would be burdened with making to fully amortize their debts before maturity. *Boschma v. Home Loan Center*, Inc.,129 Ca. Rptr. 3d 874, 885 (2011).

Borrowers and lenders alike have a harder time computing borrower liability accurately on adjustable-rate loans than they do on fixed-rate loans.[35] Interest rates on hybrids usually fall somewhere in between fixed and adjustable rates.[36]

The hybrid is ideal for borrowers who want the security of a fixed rate but who anticipate selling or refinancing before the fixed rate becomes adjustable. The current favorite among adjustable rate borrowers is a hybrid that combines a short-term fixed rate mortgage with a long-term adjustable rate mortgage. "It might be quoted as a 5/1, meaning that for the first 5 years the note rate is fixed and thereafter it floats and is re-set once per year."[37] Monthly payments are set so that the loan principal would be completely repaid at the end of 30 years. But in year six the rate becomes adjustable.[38] A borrower who wants to be rid of the adjustable rate loan in year six and beyond can sell the property or refinance back into a fixed rate loan. In either a sale or refinance, the borrower's note could have imposed a steep prepayment premium for the borrower taking advantage of the privilege of paying off the old loan ahead of its stated maturity date.

Participating Mortgage Interest Rates. In a participating mortgage, the lender accepts a below market interest rate in return for a contingent share in the cash flows from operations and/or appreciation of the property. Used for income producing properties (offices, retail), the lender's share of operating income might be measured as a percentage of the security property's gross income (all receipts) or a percentage of net income (cash flow). The lender's share of appreciation could be calculated upon sale, refinancing, or appraisal at a set date. Participating mortgages come into play when inflation panic drives interest rates sky-high. Lenders are able to set minimum fixed rates at affordable levels without risking that their loans would become bad investments if rates rose precipitously.

D. The Truth-in-Lending Act (TILA) and the Real Estate Settlement Procedure Act (RESPA)

As mentioned in Chapter 10, RESPA was enacted in 1974 to help home mortgage borrowers economize on closing costs. TILA was enacted in 1968 to make comparative shopping for a home loan more manageable for borrowers. By promulgating authoritative definitions of key lending terms, TILA imposes a measure of uniformity — imperfect but better than any readily available alternatives — in the way lenders cal-

---

35. Paul Duke, *Adjustable-Rate Mortgage Errors Spark Concerns*, Wall St. J., Oct. 26, 1990, at A16. The alleged over-charges in most cases aren't huge–in the range of $500 to $1,000 over the life of the loan.

36. Peter E. Knight, *Convertible ARMs: A Loan for All Leasing?*, Bottomline, Jan. 1988, at 53.

37. Laurence G. Taff, Investing in Mortgage Securities (2002), p. 119.

38. N. Noel Fahey, *The Pluses and Misses of Adjustable-Rate Mortgages*, 3 FannieMae Papers (last visited Aug. 15, 2015), http://www.certifiedscripts.com/pdf/fanniemae.pdf. In Europe these hybrids are regarded as fixed rate loans.

culate and disclose to consumers the cost of credit.[39] The CFPB is responsible for the administration of both laws. It has now promulgated TILA-RESPA integrated loan estimate and closing document forms.[40]

The Cooling Off Period and the Right to Rescind. After signing closing documentation, borrowers enjoy a 'cooling off' period and a chance to 'shop' the loan because they can rescind without penalty anytime within three business days of being presented with a complete, substantially accurate disclosure statement. The three-day period extends to three years if the lender neglected to provide the required disclosures. These include detailed information on the borrower's right to rescind and instructions and forms regarding its exercise.

The three-day rescission period applies to certain credit transactions in which consumers pledge their homes as security for loans used for personal, family, or household purposes.[41] Except in a financial emergency, borrowers cannot be made to waive their right to rescind before the three days expires. However, the rescission right does not apply to purchase money home loans[42] or to the refinancing of such loans by the originating purchase money-lender.

E. Advice for Mortgage Loan Shoppers

Mortgage Rate Shopping: 10 Tips to Get a Better Deal by Colin Robertson.[43] Below are 10 tips aimed at helping you better navigate the shopping experience and ideally save some money.

1. Advertised mortgage rates generally include points

[See the latest mortgage rates from dozens of lenders, updated daily.]

You know those mortgage rates you see on TV, hear about on the radio, and view online. Well, most of the time they require you to pay mortgage points.

So if your loan amount is $200,000, and the rate is 3.75% with 1 point, you have to pay $2,000 to get that rate. And there may also be additional lender fees on top of that.

2. The lowest rate may not be the best

Most shoppers are probably looking for the lowest interest rate, but at what cost? The lowest rate may have steep fees and/or require discount points, which will push

---

39. 15 U.S.C. § 1601.

40. TILA-RESPA Integrated Disclosure Guide to the Loan Estimate and Closing.

41. *See Weber v. Langholz*, 46 Cal. Rptr. 2d 677 (Ct. App. 1995) (holding that TILA doesn't apply to loan used for investment purposes).

42. 15 U.S.C. § 1635(e)(1); 15 U.S.C. § 1602(w) (1988).

43. Colin Robertson is a former mortgage loan originator and currently the chief writer for TheTruthAboutMortgage.com, a mortgage blog focused on the consumer home loan experience (last visited Aug. 15, 2015), http://www.thetruthaboutmortgage.com/mortgage-rate-shopping-10-tips-to-get-a-better-deal/.

the APR higher and make the effective rate less desirable. Be sure you know exactly what is being charged for the rate provided to accurately determine if it's a good deal.

3. Compare the costs of the rate

Additionally, you need to compare the costs of doing the loan at the par rate, versus paying to buy down the rate. And it may be in your best interest to take a slightly higher rate to cover all your closing costs, especially if you're cash-poor or simply don't plan on staying in the home very long.

4. Compare different loan types

When comparing pricing, you should also look at different loan types, such as a 30-year vs. 15-year. If it's a small loan amount, you may be able to refinance to a lower rate and barely raise your monthly payment. For example, if you're currently in a 30-year loan at 6%, dropping the rate to 2.75% on a 15-year fixed won't bump your mortgage payment up a whole lot. And you'll save a ton in interest and own the home much sooner.

5. Watch out for bad recommendations

However, don't overextend yourself just because the bank or broker says you'll be able to pay off your mortgage in no time at all. They may recommend something that isn't really ideal for your situation, so do your research before shopping. You should have a good idea as to what program will work best for you, instead of blindly following the loan officer's opinion. It's not uncommon to be pitched an adjustable-rate mortgage when you're looking for a fixed loan, simply because the ultra-low rate and payment will sound enticing.

6. Consider banks, online lenders, credit unions, and brokers

I always recommend that you shop around as much as possible. This means comparing rates online, calling your local bank, a credit union, and contacting a handful of mortgage brokers. If you stop at just one or two quotes, you may miss out on a much better opportunity. Put simply, don't spend more time shopping for your new couch or stainless-steel refrigerator.

7. Research the companies

Shopping around will require doing some homework about the companies in question. When comparing their rates, also do research about the companies to ensure you're dealing with a legitimate, reliable lender. There are plenty of accessible reviews online that should make this process pretty simple.

8. Mind your credit

Understand that shopping around may require multiple credit pulls. This shouldn't hurt your credit so long as you shop within a certain period of time. In other words, it's okay to apply more than once, especially if it leads to a lower mortgage rate.

More importantly, do not apply for any other types of loans before or while shopping for a mortgage. The last thing you'd want is for a meaningless credit card application to take you out of the running completely.

9. Lock your rate

This is a biggie. Just because you found a good rate, or were quoted a great rate doesn't mean it's yours. You still need to lock the rate (if you're happy with it) and get the confirmation in writing. The loan also needs to fund. So if you're dealing with an unreliable lender who promises a rate, but can't actually close the loan, the rate means absolutely nothing.

10. Be patient

Take your time. This isn't a decision that should be taken lightly, so do your homework and consult with family, friends, co-workers, and whoever else may have your best interests in mind.

If a company is aggressively asking for your sensitive information, or trying to run your credit report right out of the gate, tell them you're just looking for a ballpark quote. Don't ever feel obligated to work with someone, especially if they're pushy.

III. Documentation: Notes, Deeds of Trust/Mortgages, and Guarantees

Borrowers are well advised to shop for the best loan rates and terms, and then to make sure the loan documents they sign conform precisely to the loan they thought they were receiving. Often, borrowers are presented with a huge pile of loan documents and pressured quickly to sign or initial for closing with not enough time to verify that the loan docs they are hurriedly signing conform to the loan they were promised. Borrowers beware! Courts routinely dismiss lawsuits filed by duped borrowers who signed loan documents relying on the outright lies of their lenders or brokers.

A. The Note

Borrowers sign a note evidencing receipt of loan proceeds and promising unconditionally to repay the debt. The note contains payment terms–the amount borrowed, the rate of interest, the time and place where payments are due, the maturity date, the amortization requirement, whether the note can be paid before its stated maturity date (prepayment), prepayment charges, and limitations on the right of the borrower to sell the property to an assuming grantee (the due-on-sale clause).

B. Mortgages and Deeds of Trust

A mortgage or deed of trust refers to the note but does not specify the loan terms. It is a document that encumbers real property by serving as collateral for the payment of the accompanying note or other obligation. Because it is an instrument that could affect title or possession to real property, it is recorded in the public land records. This results in anyone buying or lending against the property being "subject to" the lender's right to foreclose if there is a default on the accompanying note. Once the debt is repaid, the mortgage or deed of trust becomes a nullity since they were only pledged as collateral for the debt. Still, until these security interests are released of record, they cloud create doubt regarding the borrower's title since no subsequent purchaser or mortgagee can be sure the debt was paid off.

A Mortgagor Usually Is, But Need Not Be, the Note Obligor. The borrower and the mortgagor are usually one and the same. But owners sometimes pledge property as collateral for another's debt without intending to become personally liable on the debt. Such a property owner becomes a guarantor to the extent of the value of the collateral.

The Security Property Could Be Owned by More Than One Person. Suppose A and B own Blackacre. B wants to borrow money secured by the property to pay her tuition. A is willing to risk his interest in the security property to help B borrow money but does not want to be held personally liable if B's debt exceeds the value of the property. So A and B both sign the mortgage or deed of trust, but only B signs the note. The pledged collateral would be security for the borrower's promise to repay the loan. However, A as an accommodating property co-owner, would not become personally liable for repayment of B's debt.

Comparing Deeds of Trust to Mortgages. The differences between a deed of trust and a mortgage are formal and minimal. In fact, even where deeds of trust are the security instrument of choice, people in the real estate industry usually refer to them as mortgages.[44]

There are two parties to a mortgage:

(1) **Mortgagor = borrower**

(2) Mortgagee = lender

The mortgagor is the property owner who grants a lien in her property to the lender, the mortgagee, receiving the collateral. Once the mortgage debt is repaid, the purpose of the collateral has been served and the mortgage becomes a nullity. To clear the public land record of its lien, the mortgagee is supposed to execute a recordable 'satisfaction' of mortgage.

There are three parties to a Deed of Trust.

(1) **Beneficiary = lender.**

(2) Trustor = borrower.

(3) Trustee = third party appointed by lender.

---

44. C. Darrell Sooy and Morgan T. Jones III, *The Deed of Trust, in* CEB, California Real Estate Finance Practice, section 4.1 (2012 update).

The borrower grants the trustee title to the realty as collateral for the repayment of the obligation identified in the note, and empowers the beneficiary to order the trustee to sell the pledged property if necessary to repay the debt.

Judicial and Private Power of Sale Foreclosures. In some states, mortgage lenders can only foreclose by a judicially supervised sale. About thirty states allow private power of sale foreclosures. Judicial sales are costlier and more time consuming than privately conducted ones.

Lenders foreclosing by private power of sale must reserve those rights in the security instrument and must comply strictly with the notice and other provisions in the security instrument. They must also follow the procedures that states have enacted which govern private powers of sale in minute detail.

Foreclosure Sale Proceeds and Shortfalls. The foreclosure sale proceeds are credited against what the borrower owes the lender on the note secured by the deed of trust. Once the debt is paid or the foreclosure concluded, the trustee reconveys title to the trustor free of the deed of trust.

In states that allow private power of sale foreclosures, mortgagors can empower their mortgagees to conduct a private sale. Following the foreclosure sale, the mortgagee or the sheriff deeds the property to the winning bidder. The mortgagee executes and records a satisfaction of mortgage. This clears the foreclosed lien from the title; the foreclosure sale purchaser takes title free of the foreclosed liens and all other liens subordinate to it.

The mortgage foreclosure sale proceeds are applied first to cover the costs of the sale, and then to reimburse the foreclosing lender and other secured junior lienors. Any *surplus* is given to the foreclosed mortgagor. In situations where the unpaid balance of the foreclosed debt exceeds the foreclosure sale price, the shortfall is called a *deficiency.*

Recourse and Non-recourse Debt. Following the recent recession when many houses were foreclosed that were worth less than the mortgage loans placed against them, lenders began suing borrowers even though recovery rates were quite low.[45] A borrower who owed $300,000 on a mortgage loan after losing the house through foreclosure when it was worth $250,000, could be liable for a $50,000 deficiency judgment. Suppose that the foreclosing lender obtains a deficiency judgment following a foreclosure sale.

Is the lender empowered to garnish the borrower's wages, lien the borrower's bank accounts, obtain liens against other realty the debtor owns, and have those properties sold to pay the debt?[46] Yes for recourse debt; no for non-recourse debt.

---

45. Kimbriell Kelly, Lenders Seek Court Actions Against Homeowners Years After Foreclosure, Washington Post, June 15, 2013.

46. Stephanie Lane, *How Do Mortgage Lenders Collect Deficiecy Judgments?* Nolo (last visited Aug. 15, 2015), http://www.nolo.com/legal-encyclopedia/how-do-mortgage-lenders-collect-deficiency-judgments.html

"Virtually all home purchase money mortgage lenders use standard documents that are thought to impose recourse liability on home purchase mortgagors except where excluded or limited by state law."[47] Unless the note specifically disclaims personal liability, the default rule is that a debtor who signs a promise to pay a debt is personally liable. The only borrowers who are free of the looming disaster of deficiency liability are those entitled to the protection of one or another of the various types of state anti-deficiency laws.[48] Fewer than 14 states have anti-deficiency laws. California has all of the major anti-deficiency protections.[49]

As Professor John Mixon observed, virtually no home mortgagor who has not had extensive professional training or a prior foreclosure would even imagine the possibility of a hovering judgment lien after foreclosure. A cursory reading of the note recites that the borrower owes repayment. But the note also states that the deed of trust protects the note holder from possible losses which might result: "if I do not keep the promises which I make in this Note."[50] To most home mortgagors, if they even bother to read the Note, this might imply that they could get booted out of their homes if they did not pay the note holder what was due. But home loan borrowers might be surprised to learn that if the debt, as detailed in the note, is not repaid, they could also lose their wages, bank accounts, and other properties they own.

To avoid personal liability, the borrowers need nonrecourse clause; "neither the borrower nor any constituent partner of borrower shall be personally liable for the payment of any principal, interest or other sum evidenced by the Note or for any deficiency judgment that lender may obtain following foreclosure of the mortgage." This is the provision limiting the lender's sole recourse to the property encumbered by the mortgage and any other collateral given to secure the loan.

C. "Bad Boy" Guarantees As Carve outs of Commercial Non-Recourse Mortgage Debt

The Use of Entities in Commercial Realty Transactions. For many commercial properties, the nominal borrower is a special purpose entity (SPE), sometimes also known

---

47. John Mixon, Fannie Mae/ Freddie Mac Home Mortgage Documents Interpreted as Non-Recourse Debt (last visited Aug. 15, 2015), http://scholarlycommons.law.cwsl.edu/cgi/viewcontent.cgi?article=1069&context=cwlr

48. See generally, Cole F. Morgan, Judicial Treatment of California's Anti-Deficiency Legislation Section 580B: Is it Effective? 8 J. Bus. Entrepreneurship & L. 223 (2014) (Short sale seller held not liable for deficiency because the purchase money was non-recourse from the outset under Section 580B.

49. Amy Loftsgordon, *Deficiency Judgments After Foreclosure in California*, Nolo (last visited Aug. 15, 2015),

http://www.nolo.com/legal-encyclopedia/deficiency-judgments-after-foreclosure-california.html

50. Indeed, this linkage of the Note and the Deed of Trust could be interpreted as disqualifying the note as a negotiable instrument because it embodies more than an unconditional promise to pay money. It incorporates all the other promises the borrower made in the deed of trust regarding the security property.

as a special purpose vehicle (SPV).[51] The entity holds title to no other assets and has no other liabilities except the mortgaged realty. The SPE will be constrained by its operating agreement from engaging in any other business.[52] It has no direct ties to the individuals or the parent corporation who are actually the owners and operators of the larger deal making enterprise. If the "borrower" alone is liable on the note, the mortgage lender's only practical recourse is foreclosure of the mortgaged property. Mortgage lenders hope to preclude the creditors of individual LLC members from successfully pursuing claims to LLC assets by making clear that their loans to the LLC are non-recourse not just to the LLC but to its members we well.

Personal Guarantees in Commercial Real Estate Transactions. Lenders sometimes obtain personal guarantees from project sponsors or investors to deter them from engaging in opportunistic behavior that could deprive the mortgage lender of its legitimate priority to the cash flow from the security property. The lender will ask the principals to sign guarantees that amount to "bad boy carve outs" to non-recourse debt.

When the security property is owned by a single purpose LLC, here are typical examples of behavior for which individual LLC members might be personally liable:

(1) misrepresentation, fraud, or waste;

(2) any diversion of rents, insurance proceeds, condemnation awards, or other income except to pay debt service and operating costs; and

(3) any failure to pay real estate taxes, charges for materials or labor furnished for the property, or other items that might create a lien on the property.

Some lenders have much longer lists of carve outs to non-recourse liability for a particular mortgage loan.[53] These hold the promoter liable if the debtor entity (usually an LLC) files bankruptcy or becomes insolvent.

In negotiating over the carve out language, borrowers would prefer limiting their liability to intentional misrepresentations made in writing. They would also appreciate the lender notifying them of any breach and giving them an opportunity to cure before commencing formal legal action.

---

51. The Standard & Poor's guidelines define an SPE as "an entity which is unlikely to become insolvent as a result of its own activities and which is adequately insulated from the consequences of any related party's insolvency." Legal Criteria for U.S. Structured Finance Transactions, Ch. 3. (last visited Aug. 15, 2015), http://www2.standardandpoors.com/spf/pdf/fixedincome/ SF_legal_criteria_FINAL.pdfStandard & Poor's . See generally, Caryl V. Welborn, *The Role of Special Purpose LLCs and Other Entities in the World of Structured Finance: Ramifications for LLC Structuring*, VML0316 ALI-ABA 129 (2006).

52. "To mitigate the risk that the owner-lessor will become bankrupt or insolvent, the ownership entity often must be a bankruptcy remote, special purpose entity (SPE). Fitch Ratings requires the owner to agree not to commingle funds, to maintain separate books and records, to pay its own expenses, to not incur additional debt, and to do no other business other than hold the leased premises." Real Estate Investor's Deskbook § 5:112 (3d ed.).

53. Sarasek, *supra* note 14, at 367, 371.

IV. Mortgage Lenders Can Prohibit Security Impairment

There are well-established limits on the mortgage lender's right to interfere with the mortgagor's use and enjoyment of the security property since the only legitimate function of the mortgage or deed of trust is to secure repayment of the underlying debt. Allowable exceptions empower the mortgagee to take corrective action to halt mortgagor conduct that impairs the lender's security interest.

Material Adverse Changes. Commercial mortgage lenders would also want the option of declaring a loan due and payable following any material adverse changes in the financial positions of borrowers and guarantors. Lenders worry that a borrower losing money on one project may divert funds and effort from other projects, including the mortgaged property.

Borrower's counsel might prefer that the lender's right to declare the loan in default be limited to a material adverse change which "in the reasonable opinion of the lender acting in good faith, impairs its security or increases its risk."[54]

Four Security Impairing Events. This section describes four ways that borrowers could impair the value of the security: (1) committing waste, (2) committing crimes that could result in the forfeiture of the property to the government, (3) lending or leasing to persons or firms in violation of the Patriot Act, and (4) causing environmental degradation by producing, storing or transporting toxic and hazardous wastes.

A. Waste

Acts Potentially Constituting Waste by Mortgagors. Waste is the legal term used to characterize any act by which a person who holds a present possessory interest in real property wrongfully diminishes its value to the detriment of other owners. In this section our attention is on the doctrine of waste in mortgage law.

Security Impairment. Most courts deny mortgagees any relief for waste–no injunction, no receiver, no damages, no foreclosure–unless the lender proves security impairment.[55]

There is more than one way to define the term "security impairment." Mortgage lenders would prefer a definition that anything which reduces the value of the security property impairs its security interest. Mortgagors would prefer a definition that the lender's interest is unimpaired as long as the value of the security property

---

54. Saul J. Feldman, *Negotiaing and Drafting Commercial Loan Documents in the Current Lending Environment.*(last visited Aug. 15, 2015), http://www.feldmanrelaw.com/Negotiating-Docs.htm,

55. "It would be an unreasonable and unjustifiable rule if on every occasion that a mortgagor or trustor cut down a tree or removed an old shed ... he was compelled to accompany such act with proof that it did not render the mortgage security inadequate in order to forestall an acceleration of the maturity of the debt...." *Manke v. Prautsch*, 401 P.2d 680, 683 (Nev. 1965).

equals or exceeds the amount the borrower owes the lender on the secured debt. Alternately, security impairment could be defined as the original loan-to-value ratio, or a sum adequate to preserve the lender's original loan-to-value ratio when it made the loan.[56]

(1) Lack of Maintenance and Repair. The Restatement (Third) of Property (Mortgages) (1997) proclaims that mortgagors are accountable for making all reasonable repairs. Mortgagors would have no obligation to repair defects that existed at the time the property was mortgaged even if the defects were latent, or they knew about them and the mortgagee did not. Nor would mortgagors have any obligation to repair or reconstruct the damaged security property following natural disasters, such as earthquakes or fires. The mortgagor's failure to rebuild after a fire or other catastrophe is not waste—as long as the mortgagor did not cause the calamity.[57] Conversely, the lender could hold the borrower accountable for removing support beams just before the house collapsed in a mild earth tremor.

(2) Physical Destruction. A mortgagor who bulldozes a building with no thought of replacement has committed waste. These days, mortgagors would probably enjoy the leeway to demolish obsolete structures to make way for value-enhancing replacements. Consistent with preventing security impairment, a mortgagee could legitimately insist that the borrower take appropriate measures to assure completion. A mortgagor who demolishes the existing structure and commences construction without the necessary financing or building permits commits waste, as does a mortgagor who abandons an incomplete project.

(3) Removal of Fixtures. "Removing fixtures from the property constitutes waste of the real estate, when such removal causes a substantial reduction of the land's value. To remedy the removal, the mortgagee can use either replevin to recover the fixture or trover for its value. Several jurisdictions also provide the mortgagee with the remedy to assert a separate lien upon the removed property. A mortgagee does not have an action for waste against removal of fixtures or demolition of buildings, when such items are replaced with others of greater or equal value."[58]

When a mortgagor strips fixtures from the property on the eve of foreclosure to hawk at a garage sale, the mortgagee has the right to buy new fixtures as replacements.[59]

---

56. Patrick A. Randolph, Jr., *Mortgagee's Remedies for Waste*, 548 PLI/Real 577 (2008).

57. *See, e.g., Krone v. Goff*, 127 Cal. Rptr. 390, 53 Cal. App. 3d 191 (1995). When earthquake coverage is not required in mortgages and the borrower pays for coverage anyway, the borrower is free to use the proceeds of earthquake insurance as she likes, to rebuild or keep the money–even if the policy mistakenly names the lender as a beneficiary.

58. Patrick A. Randolph, Jr., *Mortgagee's Remedies for Waste*, 548 PLI/Real 577 (2008).

59. *See Bell v. First Columbus Nat'l Bank*, 493 So. 2d 964 (Miss. 1986). Here, the debtors held a garage sale five days before foreclosure, where they sold everything they could strip or tear out of the house. The court held them liable for the reasonable cost of repairing the 11-year-old house, even though old items had to be replaced with new, because the foreclosing lender had no sensible choice but to make the repairs in order to sell.

A borrower in default on a home mortgage was subject to a jail term for damaging mortgaged property so badly the foreclosing lender was unable to sell it.[60] The defaulting borrower demanded "$10,000 plus" as the price for leaving the property in good condition. The lender refused. Out of spite, the mortgagor and his aunt caused approximately $166,000 of damage to a home that had once been worth at least $705,000. They damaged it so badly, it became unsellable. The mortgagor and his aunt spray painted walls, tile, and carpet, and sledge-hammered plumbing pipes, outlets, walkways, the outdoor fireplace, and swimming pool and spa areas. They pulled out countertops, cabinets, appliances, drawers, doors, gates, air conditioners, speaker systems, chandeliers, light fixtures, banisters, exterior facades, and trees. The police found many of these items in the defendants' storage unit and on Craigslist where they were advertising them for sale.

(4) Non-Payment of Property Taxes and Rent Skimming. Generally, mortgagors commit economic waste if they are so delinquent in property taxes as to risk a tax lien foreclosure. Similarly, mortgagors could be personally liable for waste by diverting rental income into their own pockets instead of using it to make mortgage and property tax payments.[61] This is called rent skimming.[62]

Specific Mortgage Covenants. Typically, lenders do not depend on courts selecting creditor-friendly definitions of waste. They contract for the behavior they expect from borrowers, starting with affirmative covenants not to commit waste. Mortgagors also covenant to pay taxes, insure for the benefit of the lender, maintain the security property "in as good condition as when the mortgage loan was first entered," not to use or allow use of the property for illegal purposes, and not to pocket rents without paying the mortgage. The mortgagee's rights then depend on the construction and enforceability of these specific promises, and not on the application of judicial definitions of waste.

B. Risk of Forfeiture for Mortgagor's Illegal Acts

To combat crime and make sure crime does not pay, Congress and state legislatures empowered various government agencies to confiscate property used in a crime or

---

60. *People v. Acosta*, 226 Cal. App. 4th 108, 171 Cal. Rptr. 3d 774, (4th Dist. 2014). The legal issue in the case was whether Ca. Penal Code 502.5 was unconstitutionally vague and the court found that it was not. Professor Roger Bernhardt points out that "Nine months in jail may be a severe sanction for destroying mortgaged property, but I don't know how much good that does the lender, because revenge is not repayment."

61. *Nippon Credit Bank. Ltd. v. 133 N. Cal. Blvd.*, 103 Cal. Rptr. 2d 421, 86 Cal. App. 4th 486 (2001). The mortgagor, a multi-millionaire, withheld property tax payments from operating income in an unsuccessful effort to cajole the lender into re-negotiating the debt when the value of the security property plummeted during a deep real estate recession. The lender foreclosed and purchased the property for far less than the outstanding balance due on the mortgage. Then, the lender sued the borrower in tort for waste—nearly $400,000 in delinquent property taxes. The lender prevailed and obtained a punitive damage judgment against the borrower for $2,000,000.

62. Cal. Civ. Code § 890.

acquired with proceeds from an illegal activity. For instance, a drug dealer risks forfeiture of a home acquired with proceeds from the sale of contraband, or that was used as a base for illegal drug sales. Forfeiture may arise from a civil or criminal suit,[63] and the property may be seized even before the owner's conviction.

These controversial laws[64] have led many lenders to insert specific provisions in mortgages prohibiting borrowers from committing acts that could result in forfeiture of the security property. A purchaser or lender about to invest in property that is already subject to a forfeiture action will need title insurance to cover the forfeiture action risk, and possibly a court order approving the sale.

Federal and most state statutes create 'innocent owner' exemptions. Innocent owners are typically defined as those who can establish that the illegal acts were committed without their knowledge or consent. Mortgage lenders, even after taking possession following foreclosure, are entitled to raise the innocent owner defense,[65] have a constitutional right to compensation following the government's seizure of title wiping out the innocent mortgagee's security interest,[66] and are entitled to notice before seizure.

Mortgagees seeking to foreclose their liens free of the forfeiture must establish that the criminal activity took place after their mortgages were executed and recorded,[67] and that they were "reasonably without cause to believe" that the property was used in, or purchased with the proceeds of, illegal drug or RICO (Racketeer Influenced and Corrupt Organizations) activities.[68]

To be safe, a lender would probably have to take 'reasonable steps' to determine the legitimacy of the borrower's resources and intended use of the loan proceeds.[69]

---

63. J. Donald Cole & Robbie J. Dimon, *Risky Business: Dealing With Forfeiture Titles*, 12 Prob. & Prop. 8, 10 (1998).

64. Look at 'drug forfeiture' websites for police officials lauding the use of forfeiture sale proceeds to supplement drug enforcement agency budgets. For a critique of overzealous enforcement, resulting in injury and even death to innocent property owners, see the website of FEAR (Forfeiture Endangers American Rights).

65. *See U.S. v. Fed. Nat'l Mortgage Ass'n*, 946 F.2d 264 (4th Cir. 1991). However, state laws are constitutional even if they provide no 'innocent owner' defense to civil forfeiture. *Bennis v. Mich.*, 116 S.Ct. 994 (1996). Federal circuits differ on whether the innocent owner must prove lack of knowledge AND lack of consent (Ninth Circuit), or just lack of knowledge OR lack of consent (Second, Third, and Eleventh Circuits). James J. Brown, *Innocent Owners' Rights to Federally Forfeited Real Property*, 364 PLI/REAL 207 (1992).

66. *Shelden v. U.S.*, 7 F.3d 1022 (Fed. Cir.1993). (an innocent mortgagee has the right to compensation for a Fifth Amendment taking following an administrative forfeiture of the property that is the subject of the mortgage).

67. Even if the borrower's illegal activity pre-dated the recordation of the mortgage, the lender would still be entitled to foreclose if the government hadn't recorded a *lis pendens* in a forfeiture action before the recordation of the mortgage. In *U.S. v. Real Prop. at 2659 Roundhill Drive*, 194 F. 3d 1020 (9th Cir. 1999), the mortgagee foreclosed after the government had recorded its *lis pendens* in a forfeiture action but the mortgage had been recorded long before the filing of the government's lawsuit. The Ninth Circuit upheld the mortgagee's right to foreclose.

68. 18 U.S.C. §983d(3)(A)(ii).

69. H Michael D. Weiss, Note, *The Poor Tax Revisited: The Effects of Shifting the Burden of Investigating Drug Crimes to Lenders*, 70 Tex. L. Rev. 717 (1992).

Lenders with good cause can demand that borrowers provide assurance that they are not engaged in activities that could result in forfeiture of the security property. Under U.C.C. § 2-609, any party to a contract who comes to have "reasonable grounds for insecurity" about the other party's performance is entitled to demand "adequate assurance" of performance, and may even be required to make such a demand as a pre-condition to declaring a breach. But a mortgagor with a good defense to an underlying forfeiture action can probably ignore a lender's demand for adequate assurance.[70] A lender has no justiciable basis for insecurity just from lending mortgage money to borrowers reputed to be engaged in criminal activity unless the lender has good reason to believe the source of the borrower's down payment is tainted. A criminal complaint would probably not suffice;[71] a criminal conviction for money laundering would.

Despite being entitled to raise the innocent owner defense, forfeiture laws place mortgage lenders at risk. First, fighting a government agency to establish innocence can be costly, enervating and embarrassing. Governments can take years to resolve forfeiture disputes. Second, jurisdictions differ on whether the mortgagee can foreclose while a forfeiture action is pending. Third, the attorney general is probably entitled to recoup its costs as a first lien against foreclosure sale proceeds. If the foreclosure sales price fails to cover those costs plus the mortgage, the mortgagee loses.[72] Finally, the prevailing mortgagee will have a valid claim against the government for reasonable attorneys' fees and post-judgment interest but no other damages unless the seizure was made without reasonable cause. Add up all these factors, and it is easy to imagine the innocent lender ending up with insufficient funds to cover the debt from its delayed foreclosure sale at which the lender's lien was subordinate to the attorney general's lien for costs.

C. Compliance with Anti-Terrorism Laws

Implementing federal anti-terrorist laws and executive orders, the Office of Financial Assets Control (OFAC) of the U.S. Treasury Department has drawn a list of Specially Designated Nationals[73] and Blocked Persons suspected of being engaged in terrorist

---

70. Evan H. Krinick, *May A Bank Demand That A Borrower Provide 'Adequate Assurance' of Performance Under UCC Section 2-609 When the Government Threatens Forfeiture of the Bank's Collateral?*, 116 Banking L. J. 278 (1999). *See In re Martin Specialty Vehicles*, 87 B.R. 752 (Bankr. D. Mass. 1988) (Court denied Lender the right to accelerate delinquent loan when lender could have covered delinquency from funds in debtor's operating account. Lender's true reason for accelerating was that one of the borrowers was reputed to be a member of organized crime and lender was sensitive to recent publicity that it had engaged in money laundering.).

71. *See Normandy Realty Inc. v. Boyer*, 773 N.Y.S.2d 186 (2003) (Landlord seeking to evict tenant must establish by preponderance of evidence tenant's intentional use of premises for illegal purpose. No-knock search warrant and arrest weren't enough in this case.).

72. Damon G. Saltzburg, Note, *Real Property Forfeitures as a Weapon in the Government's War on Drugs: A Failure to Protect Innocent Ownership Rights*, 72 B.U. L. Rev. 217 (1992).

73. This list presently includes The Balkans, Burma, Cote d'Ivoire, Cuba, Iran, Liberia, North Korea, Sudan, Syria and Zimbabwe.

activity.[74] All U.S. persons (broadly defined) are barred from engaging in any transactions with specially designated nationals and blocked persons.[75]

Participants in a real estate transaction must exercise due diligence to ensure that the property involved is not owned directly or indirectly, or controlled by anyone on the OFAC's no-go lists.[76] In the past, dealmakers regarded as proprietary the names of the principals they represented. Now, they may be asked and expected to identify those principals.[77] Lawyers, too, representing lenders, buyers and sellers of real estate are required to make sure they are not involved in transactions with individuals on OFAC's no-go lists or with money-launderers.[78]

All financial institutions involved in real estate closings and settlements are also required to have programs in place to detect money-laundering which is widely done by criminal and terrorist organizations to hide their activities.[79]

To comply with these statutory mandates, lenders, hedge funds, equity funds, and individual entrepreneurs routinely require borrowers and investors to sign documents assuring that none of them, their owners, or tenants are on those lists or have been indicted or convicted under the anti-money laundering laws. Lenders expect to be informed of anyone affiliated with the investor, borrower or any tenant who has been "indicted, arraigned or custodially detained on charges involving money laundering or predicate crimes to money laundering." Borrowers also promise not to rent or do business with listed persons or entities, and not to re-pay their debts to a lender or entrepreneur with funds received from any tainted person or organization.

---

74. Executive Order No. 13224, 66 Fed. Reg. 49079 (Sept. 25, 2001). Timothy J. Boyce & Thomas C. Bogle, *Are You Doing Business with Osama?* 5 Prac. Real Est. Law. 25 (September 2004).

75. Andrew A. Lance, *Provisions in Real Estate Documents in Anticipation of Regulations under the USA Patriot Act*, 549 PLI/Real 19 (2008).

76. "Persons involved in real estate closings and settlements" are included in the Bank Secrecy Act's definition of financial institutions, adopted by the Patriot Act. Bank Secrecy Act, 31 U.S.C. § 5312(a)(2)(U) (2000). However, such persons are essentially exempted from the Bank Secrecy Act other than having to report cash transactions of $10,000 or more. Steven A. Teitelbaum et al., Anti-Terrorism Clauses in Commercial Real Estate Transactions, 25 No.2 Prac. Real Estate Law. 29, 31 (March 2009).

77. Kevin L. Shepherd, *The Usa Patriot Act: The Complexities Of Imposing Anti-Money Laundering Obligations On The Real Estate Industry*, 39 Real Prop. Prob. & Tr. J. 403 (2004).

78. See USA Patriot Act, 31 U.S.C.A. § 53.18; Executive Order 13224. https://www.treasury.gov/resource-center/sanctions/Programs/Documents/terror.pdf (Last visited 06/18/2016).

79. "Money laundering is the process of making illegally-gained proceeds (i.e. "dirty money") appear legal (i.e. "clean"). Typically, it involves three steps: placement, layering and integration. First, the illegitimate funds are furtively introduced into the legitimate financial system. Then, the money is moved around to create confusion, sometimes by wiring or transferring through numerous accounts. Finally, it is integrated into the financial system through additional transactions until the "dirty money" appears "clean." Money laundering can facilitate crimes such as drug trafficking and terrorism, and can adversely impact the global economy." https://www.fincen.gov/news_room/aml_history.html (Last visited 06/18/2016.)

D. Minimizing the Lender's Risk of Environmental Liability[80]

Owners' Limitless Liability for Environmental Clean Up Costs. Owners and operators of property have extensive obligations and financial exposure under various federal, state and local environmental laws, ordinances and regulations. Basically, these laws were enacted as homeowners were becoming aware of the severe health hazards they faced when schools and housing had been built on land previously contaminated by industrial wastes or when they relied on the use of well water from polluted aquifers.[81] The resulting legislation required the owners of polluted land or aquifers to remove the contaminants to the satisfaction of government agencies. If contaminants were not removed, federal agencies were empowered to do the work and bill the owner for it, imposing a lien upon the site to secure reimbursement.

Perhaps the best known of these laws is the federal Comprehensive Environmental Repose Compensation and Liability Act of 1980 (CERCLA). This law imposes liability on property owners for the release or presence of hazardous substances irrespective of the owner's culpability, causality or knowledge. Liability for clean-up costs can often exceed the owner's equity in the property. Under CERCLA, liability is strict (i.e., without regard to fault), retroactive (i.e., without regard to whether the toxic discharge was legal at the time it occurred), and joint and several (i.e., any owner can be held fully liable for the misdeeds of others although the statute creates a right of contribution).

Other environmental laws impose liability for the release of asbestos containing materials (ACMs) into the air and require the removal or containment of ACMs. Federal law requires owners of housing constructed prior to 1978 to disclose the risk of exposure to lead-based paint to potential residents or purchasers. A complete list of all environmental laws that impose liability on owners would go on for pages.

Why Clean Up Exposure Worries Lenders and What They Do About It. Laws imposing clean up liability for environmental contaminants concern lenders for three reasons: (1) compliance costs could deplete the financial ability of the borrower to repay the debt; (2) potential liability for compliance could diminish the value of the security property as bidders deduct compliance costs from their purchase offers; and (3) lenders who acquire possession either before or after foreclosure could become directly liable.

---

80. See Matthew H. Ahrens and David S. Langer, *Environmental Risks for Lenders Under Superfund: A Refresher for the Economic Downturn*, 3 Bloomberg Corporate Law J..482 (2008).

81. The most memorable example came from an elementary school and housing tract built in an area of upstate New York near a waste dump in the 'Love Canal.' Many 'Love Canal' websites depict this episode and the heroic efforts of a homemaker named Lois Marie Gibbs to call the nation's attention to the 'Love Canal' problem. Mrs. Gibb's efforts were memorialized in an ABC-TV 1982 movie starring Marsha Mason. This riveting tale was based on wild misinformation regarding the health risks of the Love Canal waste dump. Since the enactment of CERLA, billions have been spent remediating hazardous waste sites though they pose a negligible risk compared to the consequences of smoking cigarettes, bad diet and poor exercise habits. Timur Kuran and Cass R. Sunstein, *Availability Cascades and Risk Regulation*, 51 STAN. L. REV. 683, 697-98 (1999).

CERCLA amendments address the third concern in part by exempting any "person, who, without participating in the management of a facility, holds indicia of ownership primarily to protect his security interest in the facility."[82] As long as the borrower remains in possession, lenders have no liability unless they become 'owners or operators' by assuming decision-making control over environmental compliance or the entire operation. CERCLA exempts lenders, following foreclosure, who become owners by purchasing at their own foreclosure sales and operate the security property primarily to "preserve, protect or prepare" the facility for sale "at the earliest practicable, commercially reasonable time, on commercially reasonable terms."[83] Lenders would prefer a blanket exemption, but lawmakers refused to take the chance that categorically exempting lenders would open a major loophole in the law.

Cautious lenders try to distance themselves from any environmental risks by insisting upon 'clean' environmental site assessments both before making loans and again prior to acquiring title at foreclosure.

Lenders also prefer that borrowers qualify themselves under CERCLA as bona fide purchasers. Achieving this status frees borrowers from liability for hazardous and toxic waste spills pre dating their acquisition. To qualify, buyers must make all appropriate inquiries about the prior use of the property, typically through a Phase I Environmental Site Assessment Process and audit,[84] certifying the site to be free of toxic or hazardous material.[85] Some lenders only fund borrowers with BFP status.

Environmental insurance is available for commercial real estate lenders, and its use is growing so rapidly, some industry experts expect it eventually to be as popular as title insurance.[86] These policies make it feasible for lenders to finance ambitious re-use projects for contaminated military or industrial "brownfield" sites at otherwise prime locations.[87]

---

82. 42 U.S.C. § 9601(20)(A).

83. 42 U.S.C. § 9601(20)(E)(ii)(II). *See also* Baxter Dunaway, THE LAW OF DISTRESSED REAL ESTATE § 3.04 (1985-97).

84. *EPA, CERCLA, Brownfields and Lender Liability,* EPA.GOV (last visited Aug. 15, 2015). http://epa.gov/brownfields/aai/lenders_factsheet.pdf

85. See 70 FR 66070-01, 2005 WL 2847047 (F.R.) Defining 'all appropriate inquiries' to attain bona fide purchaser status under CERCLA. For Phase I audit standards see, American Society for Testing and Materials E1527 (1996). Phase I audits involve a site inspection, searching public and agency records for compliance with environmental laws on site or nearby and interviews with past site owners and occupants to determine whether past uses might have involved illegal discharges. The audit does not include soil borings, well installations or sample collection and analysis. However, environmental consultants have incentives to order further inquiry since they risk accountability for undiscovered pollutants and often stand to profit from doing or overseeing additional work.

86. Monika Cornell, *Environmental Insurance: An Option to a Phase I Environmental Site Assessment,* 18 R.E. FIN. J. 24, 25 (Winter 2003).

87. For a list of types of coverage available to lenders, see John W. Ames, *Toxins-Are-Us: Insurance Coverage for U.S. Trustees in Operating Chapter 11,* 1995 ABI JNL LEXIS 138 (Dec./Jan. 1996). *See generally* Janet M. Johnson, *For Real Estate Lawyers: A Practical Guide to Identifying and Managing Potential Environmental Hazards and Conditions Affecting Commercial Real Estate,* 32 REAL PROP., PROB. & TR. J. 619 (1998).

Environmental Indemnity. Lenders often require environmental indemnities from commercial mortgage loan borrowers. They seek the borrower's promise not to contaminate the property with hazardous or toxic wastes, obtain assurance that the borrower will comply with environmental laws relating to the use and occupancy of the property, that the borrower has not received any notice or advice from any government agency with respect to hazardous materials on the site, the property will be kept free of asbestos, and that the borrower will indemnify, defend, protect and hold the mortgage lender harmless from liability for any breach of warranties, representations, and covenants made in the indemnification agreement. The borrower's liability is explicitly made full recourse and not limited to the original or amortized loan amount.[88]

V. Following the Money in Mortgage Lending

A. The Primary Financial Players in Home Mortgage Markets

Capital Sources. Savings are funneled into residential and commercial mortgage loans from institutions defined either as depository or non-depository. The leading depository institutions are commercial banks, savings and loan associations, and credit unions. Non-depository institutions include life insurance companies, pension funds, real estate investment trusts, and private real estate funds. Because the U.S. government insures depositors' accounts in depository institutions up to certain dollar limits, U.S. taxpayers have been burdened with heavy losses when depository institutions lost billions on their improvident loans. To curb excessive risk-taking, government regulators oversee bank underwriting criteria of depository lenders.[89]

Mortgage Brokers. Mortgage brokers work independently as intermediaries bringing banks, mortgage lenders and borrowers together. They need to be licensed. Their job is to attract potential borrowers, and shop broadly in the mortgage market place to identify the best rates and terms for each of their borrowers. Mortgage brokers also have a duty to explain the loan terms and delineate the risks and risks to their borrowers.

Mortgage brokers are compensated by a fee based on the size of each of the loans they originate. Typically, the fee is 1% to 2% of the loan amount. Those fees can be paid by the borrower or the lender but not by both, under a federal law applicable to residential loans.

Mortgage Bankers. Mortgage bankers perform the same functions as mortgage brokers with one important difference. They have the capacity to originate loans from

---

88. Thomas C. Roberts and Gary York, The Environmental Indemnity, CEB, Real Estate Finance Practice, section 5 (2012 update).

89. *See, e.g.*, C.F.R. Title 12, Part 34: Real Estate Lending and Appraisals. See also, how non-depositary loan originators are subject to more stringent controls. John P. Kromer, and Heidi M. Bower, *The Safe Act's Unlevel Playing Field, Mortgage Banking* (last visited Aug. 15, 2015), http://www.buckleysandler.com/news-detail/the-safe-acts-unlevel-playing-field.

their own borrowed capital. Their goal is not to hold the loans they originate to maturity. Instead, they pledge them as collateral for capital supplied by warehouse lenders until they are able to sell the loans, usually to issuers of mortgage backed securities.

Warehouse Lenders. Warehouse lenders make short term loans to mortgage bankers to enable them to fund the mortgage loans they originate. Mortgage bankers sell the loans they originate, and use the sale proceeds to repay the warehouse lender's temporary advances. The warehouse lender releases its collateral interest in the loans upon being repaid.

Direct Mortgage Lenders. A direct mortgage lender is simply a bank or other lender with retail operations that work directly with borrowers to originate loans. Among the largest direct mortgage lenders are *Wells Fargo, JP Morgan Chase, Bank of America, Quicken Loans*, and *US Bancorp*. Direct mortgage lenders urge borrowers to deal directly with them instead of going to mortgage brokers or mortgage bankers to save having to pay the mortgage banker or broker fees, a cost that the direct lender absorbs.

Mortgage bankers and mortgage brokers are quick to point out that the bank will have included all of its costs of doing business in the loan origination fees it charges borrowers. Further, the broker or mortgage banker will shop the entire mortgage loan marketplace to find the loan most suitable for each of its clients. A direct lender will steer borrowers to the loan that is best for the bank.

In rebuttal, direct lenders could explain that mortgage interest rates are not set by direct lenders, mortgage brokers or mortgage bankers. Mortgage interest rates are determined in global secondary markets for US home mortgage loans since most residential mortgages are sold through a process known as securitization, described below. Basically, all three types of intermediaries — direct lenders, mortgage bankers and mortgage brokers — set their interest rates according to the same rates prevailing in the secondary mortgage market.

Direct lenders also have more flexibility in striking especially good mortgage deals with borrowers on home loans. They do this for borrowers whom they are eager to attract as customers, borrowers with substantial assets and in a position to direct further lucrative business to the bank.

Fiduciary Obligations: Direct Lenders, Mortgage Brokers, and Mortgage Bankers. The question of whether direct lenders, mortgage brokers or mortgage bankers owe their customers or clients a fiduciary duty of care can be framed this way: When the best deal for the borrower is not optimal for the broker, does the broker have a fiduciary duty to put the borrower's interest first?

Consider the ways in which, for example, the best loan for a mortgage broker to arrange would not necessarily be optimal for a prospective borrower. An obvious example would be when the broker earns a fatter fee for originating a more expensive loan than the borrower could otherwise obtain. Federal law now inhibits brokerage commissions from being based on the interest rates that the borrower pays.[90]

---

90. See 15 U.S.C. § 1639b(c) (Supp. IV 2010).

Another example is when the borrower's credit rating would qualify for a lower rate of interest than the loan which the mortgage broker arranges for the borrower without even mentioning the better alternate. This practice, too, is now curbed by federal law.[91]

Fuller v. First Franklin Financial Corporation. A horrific example of lenders and mortgage brokers allegedly engaging in predatory lending can be found in the case of *Fuller v. First Franklin Financial Corporation.*[92]

According to the lawyers representing them, the borrowers, first-time home buyers, sought a loan from Sacramento 1st Mortgage (SFM). The employee who dealt with them at SFM purported to be a mortgage broker but was unlicensed. He organized a loan of $435,000 on a home that was hugely over-appraised.

Drawing on the borrowers' pleadings, the court opinion explained: "The broker hired an appraiser to value the property that plaintiffs wanted to buy. Pursuant to a common scheme with First Franklin and SFM, the appraiser chose outdated sales of homes that were not truly comparable in value (having greater square footage, more rooms, and other added amenities), resulting in a significantly inflated appraisal of the subject property of which defendants were aware."[93] The "defendants" included both the mortgage brokerage firm and the lender—First Financial—that made the loan.

The mortgage broker arranged a very expensive loan for the borrowers, far more costly than what they could have qualified for. Again, the court draws from the borrowers' pleadings an explanation of the lender's motivations: "Pursuant to its business scheme, First Franklin ignored standard underwriting protocols—creating a high risk that plaintiffs and many others would face foreclosure under the loans and inflated home appraisals—in order to maximize its market share of loans, deflecting any risk to itself by selling off these so-called subprime mortgages to investors."[94] The plaintiffs also alleged that First Franklin agreed to remit an undisclosed kickback to SFM for securing the loan out of proceeds First Franklin received from plaintiffs.

The mortgage lender contended that it had no fiduciary obligation to the mortgage borrowers because it had no dealings with them other than to make a loan. Thus, it had no responsibility to describe the loan terms, or verify for the benefit of the borrowers that the appraisal was accurate. Nor did it have any obligation to inform the borrowers that they could have qualified for more favorable financing elsewhere. The appellate court agreed but noted that the borrowers' counsel had alleged that the lender was in cahoots with the mortgage brokerage firm in a business plan to arrange just such predatory loans as this one, and if these allegations proved true, the lender could be found vicariously liable for all of the misdeeds of its co-conspirator, the mortgage broker.

---

91. See 15 U.S.C. § 1403(c)(3)(A). (Prohibiting mortgage brokers from not arranging qualified mortgages for those who qualify for them.)

92. 216 Cal.App.4th 955 (2013).

93. 216 Cal.App.4th 955, 959 (2013).

94. 216 Cal. App. 4th 955, 961 (2013).

Fiduciary Duties: A Summary.

Banks are not their borrowers' fiduciaries. They have no binding legal obligation to find the best possible mortgage deal for each of their customers.[95] The borrower must ultimately decide whether the loan is suitable, subject to federal ability-to-repay and other CFPB guidelines. There are exceptions such as those mentioned in the Fuller case or when a direct lender promises a prospective borrower to find the best loan. Then, a principal-agency relationship is formed.

Mortgage loan brokers and mortgage loan bankers owe the same fiduciary duties and standard of conduct as real estate brokers, described in Chapter 3.

Nonetheless, borrower and lender obligations are not reciprocal. Borrowers are free to shop aggressively for the best possible loan term even while working with a mortgage broker, mortgage banker or direct lender.

Federal Housing Administration (FHA). The FHA insures the lender against defaults by the borrower. The program is financed by borrower-paid premiums, a percentage of the loan amount at closing and annual mortgage-insurance premiums calculated as a percentage of the remaining balance of the loan amount.

The FHA got hit hard by the mortgage meltdown. For the first time in its 79-year history it had to ask Congress for a $1.7 billion bailout to cover its projected losses for the fiscal year that ended September 30, 2013.[96]

Federal Home Loan Mortgage Corp (Freddie Mac) and Federal National Mortgage Association (Fannie Mae). Collectively, they are referred to as *Government Sponsored Enterprises*, GSEs.

Both of these entities buy home and multi-family mortgage loans, enabling lenders who originate mortgage loans to earn origination fees and quickly replenish their capital so that they can make new loans.

By pooling the payments of borrowers on hundreds of loans, and structuring the right to receive shares of those payments to meet the needs of various types of large investors, Fannie Mae and Freddie Mac make it possible for even the most risk averse pension funds, family trusts, and other capital sources to invest in home and multi-family mortgages.

In 2008, both Fannie Mae and Freddie Mac were facing imminent financial disaster as borrowers defaulted on their loans in unprecedented numbers while home prices nose-dived in many markets across the U.S. Pre-emptively, the GSEs were placed in government receivership. The huge cost to taxpayers of that takeover, and the structural weaknesses that contributed to the institutions' financial problems prompted policymakers to consider various alternatives for the government's future role in the sec-

---

95. *Smith v. Home Loan Funding Inc.*, 192 Cal. App. 4th 1331, 121 Cal.Rptr.3d 857 (2d Dist. 2011), as modified on denial of rehr'g (March 28, 2011).

96. Paul M.J. Suchecki, *Advantages and Disadvantages of FHA Mortgages, MYBANKTRACKER* (last visited, Jan. 12, 2016) http://www.mybanktracker.com/news/2014/01/29/fha-mortgages-advantages--disadvantages/

ondary market for residential mortgages. Meanwhile, these institutions have returned to solvency and profitability.

B. Categories of Home Loans

Home mortgage loans are popularly characterized as *prime, subprime, jumbo, and alt-A.*

Prime residential mortgages. "The majority of loans originated are underwritten to high credit standards, where the borrowers have strong employment and credit histories, income sufficient to pay the loans without compromising their credit worthiness, and substantial equity in the underlying property. These loans are broadly classified as prime loans, and have historically experienced relatively low incidences of delinquency and default."[97] Prime loans "are defined as mortgages for borrowers whose credit scores are 740 or higher; whose debt-to-income ratios are lower than average; and, whose mortgage features the standard amortization schedule common to a fixed-rate or an adjustable-rate mortgage." Bank and GSE definitions of prime vary from time to time, and at this moment are being relaxed by both types of institutions.[98]

"*Subprime* borrowers are burdened with low credit scores, high debt-to-income ratios, limited income and assets, possibly payment delinquencies, debt collection judgments and bankruptcies. Subprime borrowers pay higher interest rates than those offered by standard lenders. They also tend to be less financially knowledgeable and sophisticated and less comfortable dealing with banks. Subprime loan underwriting often utilized nontraditional measures to assess credit risk. Issuance of the product declined precipitously after 2006, when it became evident that the sector was plagued by poor underwriting, fraud, and an excessive reliance on rising home prices."[99]

"Underwriting standards in the subprime mortgage market vary from lender to lender and are not guided by secondary market standards as in the prime mortgage market. As a result, it is difficult for borrowers to determine whether or not a loan offered by a subprime lender is the best loan for which they qualify given their individual risk profiles."[100]

Jumbo loans exceed the maximum loans limits, also referred to as "non conforming." The GSEs make no attempt to promulgate underwriting standards for these

---

97. Frank J Fabozzi, Anand K. Bhattacharya,a nd William S. Berliner, *Mortgage Backed Securities* (2d ed.2011), p. 5.

98. Karen Weise, *Getting a Mortgage is Finally Getting Easier*, BLOOMBERG BUSINESS (last visited Jan. 10, 2016), http://www.bloomberg.com/bw/articles/2014-08-05/banks-relax-lending-standards-for-prime-mortgages

99. Frank J Fabozzi, Anand K. Bhattacharya, and William S. Berliner, Mortgage Backed Securities (2d ed.2011), p. 5.

100. Kenneth Temkin, Jennifer E. H. Johnson, Diane Levy, Subprime Markets, GSEs, and Risk-Based Pricing-Forward, (2002). http://www.huduser.gov/portal/Publications/pdf/subprime.pdf.

loans since they do not acquire them. Prime jumbo borrowers tend to have high incomes, high credit scores, greater invested equity (lower loan-to-value ratios), and tend to borrow on 30-year, fixed interest rate loans.

Alt-A (alternative-A) loans were once considered to be prime loans (the "A" refers to the A grade assigned by underwriting systems). They are made to borrowers whose credit scores tend to fall between the prime and subprime sector. These loans were made with incomplete documentation, without the two year's tax returns, W-2 forms and other indicia currently required. They were sometimes based solely on the borrower's self-declarations of income and earned the name "liar's loans." As with subprime loans, issuance of alt-A loans fell sharply with the post-2006 decline in home prices and mortgage credit performance.[101]

C. Securitization

1. Portfolio vs. Securitized Lending

Thirty years ago, banks and other lenders that made loans kept them on their balance sheets. They were called *portfolio lenders* because they held the loans they originated in their own portfolios.

Other lenders sell their loans or issue securities based on the income streams from those loans. As a percentage of all residential mortgage loans originated in the U.S., estimates are that as many as 80% may be securitized into Residential Mortgage Backed Securities (RMBS).[102] Only about 20% of commercial mortgage loans are securitized into Commercial Mortgage Back Securities (CMBS).[103]

2. Why Mortgage Lenders Sell Their Mortgage Loans

Most lenders sell their home mortgage loans. Here are some of the reasons:

(1) *Liquidity*. By selling its loans, the lender receives a lump sum payment equal or greater than the loan balance. Through securitization, loan originators have many more sources of funding than they could obtain through retail deposits and other conventional sources.

(2) *Fee Income*. Lenders make substantial fees originating mortgage loans. Selling the loans they originate enables them to replenish their coffers, pumping up their loan volume and reaping the fees from each new loan.

---

101. Frank J Fabozzi, Anand K. Bhattacharya, and William S. Berliner, *Mortgage Backed Securities* (2d ed.2011), p. 5.

102. Levitin, Adam J. and Wachter, Susan M., *The Commercial Real Estate Bubble*, Georgetown Law and Economics Research Paper No. 12-005; Harvard Business Law Review, Vol. 3, pp. 83, 91 (last visited Aug. 15, 2015), Available at SSRN: http://ssrn.com/abstract=1978264 or http://dx.doi.org/10.2139/ssrn.1978264

103. *Ibid.* at 92.

(3) *Avoiding Interest and Other Risks.* Most depository institutions pay depositors interest on their savings. Currently, interest rates are low due to weak demand and government intervention in the money markets. Historically, though, depository lenders experienced enormous outflows of deposits when market rates of interest rose sharply, and they were unable to compete for funds with money market funds because their deposits had been placed in long-term, fixed rates mortgage loans. The loan originator, holding its loans to maturity, also reduces the risk of borrowers defaulting.

In a competitive financing environment, securitization works to the advantage of mortgage loan borrowers as well by attracting billions into mortgage securities from investors worldwide. This lowers the cost and increases the availability of borrowed capital.

(4) *Profit on the Loan Sale.* Originating lenders also reap immediate profits by selling their loans to bond investors for a premium greater than the wholesale value of the right to receive mortgage payments.

3. The Securitization Participants

The cash flow from mortgage loans comes from ***borrowers***. The borrower may have worked with a ***mortgage broker, a mortgage banker,*** or a ***direct lender*** in arranging that loan. The loan will be funded by a ***mortgage lender***, perhaps a bank, savings association or credit union.

Securitization requires the aggregation or pooling of large numbers of mortgages because the process is expensive and there are huge economies of scale in it. A bond offering of mortgages would ideally be for $500,000,000 or more.

Loan originators might cooperate with an issuer such as a *Wall Street investment bank*, or sell their loans to a ***loan aggregator*** who will take it from there. An ***issuer*** complies with securities laws and assembles the documentation necessary to offer bonds secured by the revenues from the aggregated mortgage loans.

The ***mortgage loan originator*** transfers the mortgages to a specially formed entity, a ***depositor***.[104] The depositor insulates the ultimate bond investors from potential claims to the bonds that might be asserted by the originator's other creditors. In exchange for certificates, the depositor transfers the mortgage loans to a ***trust*** established for the sole purpose of holding mortgages for the benefit of investors. The depositor sells the certificates directly to mortgage investors or to broker-dealers who find investors for the certificates.

Mortgage investors rely on ***underwriters*** for assurance that the bonds are of the quality that the originators and issuers promised and that the investors expect. Mortgage investors' payments reimburse the loan originator and cover the costs of underwriting and marketing the mortgages as securities.

---

104. Bianca A. Russo, *Commercial Mortgage Securitization*, 899 PLI/COMM 355 (2008).

A lender could develop the staffing capacity to comply with securities laws and issue its own bonds to potential investors. Alternately, it could contract with a Wall Street investment-banking firm to act as the bond issuer.

Bond investors. Bond investors purchase rights to receive payments from borrowers repaying their mortgage loans. Bond buyers do not worry about credit risk when the underlying loans are FHA-insured, or acquired by a GSE that the bond market believes will act as if the underlying mortgages were government-guaranteed.

Bond buyers of privately securitized debt deal with credit risk by creating a senior-subordinate bond structure. The safest "tranche" or "slice" in the offering is held by the most senior class of bonds. The riskiest tranche is called the "first loss" piece because it will be the first to incur losses if loan collections are inadequate to repay all the classes of bondholders. Typically, investors in privately securitized bonds rely on advisors who are much influenced by the ratings of credit rating agencies.

Credit Rating Agencies. Before issuing mortgage-backed bonds, the issuer obtains ratings for each class of bonds from one or more credit rating agencies. These agencies decide the size of each tranche in the offering based on probability of a default and loss in worst-case scenarios.

The highest rating is reserved for bonds that the credit rating agency believes have default risks no greater than those of the highest rated corporate and government debt. Bond investors convinced that they are acquiring the right to a cash flow with virtually no risk of non-payment accept lower yields on their investment. This is good for bond issuers. Their revenues are based on mortgagors' monthly payments. The greater the spread between the weighted average payments that mortgagors make and the coupons that bond issuers must pay to attract bond investors, the more profitable the venture will be for those who put it together.

Loan Servicers will collect borrower payments monthly and remit them to the *trustee* of a specially formed *trust* who represents all the bondholders in a given offering. The trustee will make the funds available for distribution to bond investors.

Title to the notes and mortgages in the pool will be transferred many times en route from the loan originator maybe through the hands of a warehouse lender who financed the originator's loans to borrowers before selling the loans to an aggregator who transferred them to a depositor who finally conveyed them to the trustee for the bondholders.

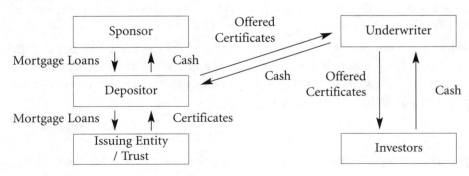

4. Structuring Securitized Debt Obligations

Collateralized Mortgage Obligation. A collateralized mortgage obligation (CMO) is a type of MBS in which the mortgages are put into separate pools with varying degrees of risk and maturities (tranches). Each tranche is sold as a separate security. CMOs are a type of *Collateralized Debt Obligation* (CDO).

Sequential Pay CMO. In a sequential pay CMO, issuers distribute cash flow to bondholders according to credit risk. Bondholders in the senior or A-rated tranches are paid first. Holders of subordinate ("B") rated tranches bear the brunt of the first losses if mortgagors default.

Tranching to Allocate Default Risk. Some investors might be worried about repayment and insist on purchasing only, say, two-thirds of the cash flow from the bonds in exchange for a smaller premium above what the mortgage borrowers were actually obligated to pay. Other investors might be willing to take their chances by standing last in the payment line if they could garner a larger share of the borrowers' actual cash flow.

Timing of Payouts. Some investors need their money sooner; others want to match the cash flow to obligations that will not mature for many years. Through "tranching," all these disparate preferences of bond investors can be accommodated for an appropriate price. For instance, banks and other depository institutions are usually seeking short term investments while life insurance companies and pension funds are looking for longer term investments to match their liabilities. So a CMO could have three tranches that mature in five, seven, and twenty years each.

A Stripped Mortgage-backed Security (SMBS). This is a type of CMO in which the interest and principal of the mortgage are separated into principal-only and interest-only bonds. A zero coupon bond is a bond that pays no interest. It is sold at a deep discount to its face value, and matures to its face value.

When interest rates fall sharply enough to make the costs of prepayment worthwhile for borrowers, they rush to prepay their existing loans so that they can re-finance at the lower prevailing rates. This is good for holders of principal only (PO) debt because mortgages are repaid at par (face value) while investors acquired their PO bonds at discounts based on normal projections of interest rate fluctuations. Conversely, the holders of interest only (IO) bonds lose out when the rate of prepayment exceeds bond market expectations. Borrowers owe no interest after their debts are extinguished.

Just the opposite happens when interest rates rise. Investors in IO strips are receiving rates of interest on their invested funds that are below current market rates. This reduces the value of their bonds proportionately. Because borrowers are paying what have become below market rates, they tend to retain their mortgages longer than if rates had remained constant or fallen. Rising interest rates cause prepayments to decelerate which increases the discount rate applied to cash flows and lowers the PO price.

Sponsor Reps and Warranties. The sponsor represents and warrants every aspect of the mortgage loans that it originates for eventual sale to the bond investors. These "reps and warranties" include loan-to-value ratios, the borrower's credit history, and the characteristics of the loan terms. The originators and sellers of these mortgage loans make warranties and representations concerning underwriting.

Upon discovery or notice of a breach in the reps and warranties, the Trustee representing the bondholders can demand that the Originator, Seller or Depositor within 90 days: cure the breach, repurchase the loan, substitute good collateral, or make an indemnification payment to the Trust for the benefit of the certificate holders. The breach must have materially and adversely impacted the value of the loan.[105]

5. A Recap of Often-Cited Causes of the U.S. Foreclosure Crisis

In 2007-2008, an avalanche of mortgage defaults and foreclosures in the U.S. triggered a global recession that continues to the date of this publication, nearly a decade later. A review of the proffered explanations for what sparked this debacle is important to students of mortgage finance and mortgage law because it will continue to influence private and government decision making in these fields for years to come.

- Home mortgage loans were originated and purchased worldwide in a belief that house prices would continue rising indefinitely as they had from 1970 to 2005.

- House price increases from 2000 to 2005 had been prompted by central banks in many countries lowering interest rates to avert a global recession They feared that a recession could be caused by the dual shock of a dotcom stock price collapse in 2000 and terrorists toppling the World Trade Center buildings in New York City, on September 11, 2001. (Currently, house prices are rising, also due to government-restrained interest rates.)

- Mortgage loan originators reduced lending standards because they were counting on buoyant house prices to keep defaults low and foreclosure losses minimal. As long as house prices were rising year to year, borrowers unable to make their mortgage payments just needed to call a broker and put their houses on the market to reap the rising equity values of their houses. Lenders could do the same by foreclosing on cash-poor borrowers too hopeful or hapless to face the inevitable.

- The riskier the borrower and the loan, the higher the interest rate that loan originators could charge. Originators were rewarded with fat commissions on risky loans. There were no mechanisms for clawing back commissions on loans that later went into default.

- Lending institutions had poor risk management techniques for calculating subsequent losses on risky loans written at high initial interest rates.

- Investors across the globe flooded Wall Street with cash to buy high-yielding U.S. mortgage backed securities. They blindly trusted in the integrity of U.S.

---

105. For a comprehensive discussion of the securitization process, a description of the misrepresentations, and a court's reasoned rejection of loan originator defenses to liability on their warranties and repurchase obligations, see *Finance Agency v. Nomura Holding America, Inc., et al.* CCH Federal Securities Law Reporter, 2014 WL 6792706 (C.C.H.).

home mortgage lending practices and were willfully indifferent to the risks of buying loans that had been made to high risk borrowers.

Global CDO Issuance

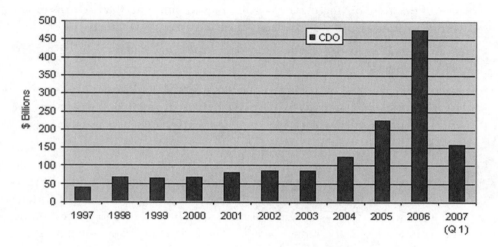

- Investors made little effort to evaluate the quality of the loans they were purchasing. Instead, they relied on the AAA ratings that SEC approved credit rating agencies placed on RMBS bonds, the same ratings they placed on U.S. Treasuries and the highest quality corporate debt. Amazingly, the rating agencies' models for assessing home mortgage risk neglected to account for the possibility of house price declines.

- Credit rating agencies are paid by bond issuers, not bond buyers, and earn commissions only on bonds that issuers can sell profitably. Basically, this usually means that rating agencies need to give AAA quality ratings on a large percentage of bonds in any given offering. The leading credit rating agencies are criticized widely for putting profits ahead of principle, as they routinely assigned high grades to low-quality debt securities. Their rationalization was that if they refused issuers their desired ratings, a competing credit agency would accommodate issuers to earn their business. According to a New York Times account of a recently completed SEC study, eight years after these companies were found to have engaged in dubious practices leading to the mortgage meltdown, not much has changed.[106]

- A culture of greed and cheating within lending institutions poisoned the underwriting process. Rampant fraud by borrowers on mortgage loan applications was often abetted by commission-hungry mortgage brokers, some of whom

---

106. http://globaleconomicanalysis.blogspot.com/2016/01/pigs-at-trough-rating-agencies-as.html.

showed borrowers how to fake loan applications to get the loans they wanted but could not afford.

• Loan underwriters and originators knew that if money was lost on the loans they made, it would come from the pockets of the bond buyers of securitized debt. (Often, they were mistaken because the investment branches of their own institutions were buying these risky offerings to pump up their returns on investments, unaware of just how risky their institution's own loans were.)

• If the originating lender still held the loan, its losses would often be covered by FHA insurance.

• Elected officials and government regulators nurtured and rejoiced in the liberalization of credit standards by the GSEs because it resulted in expanding the ranks of home owners especially among residents in low income areas.

• On September 15, 2008, Lehman Brothers filed for bankruptcy. With $639 billion in assets and $619 billion in debt, Lehman's demise intensified the crisis and contributed to $10 trillion in market capitalization from global equity markets in October 2008, the biggest monthly decline on record at the time. The ensuing defaults and foreclosures slowed consumer spending and led to a recession resulting in job losses and reduced wages. The Federal Reserve claimed it lacked the authority to bail out Lehman. It also miscalculated the disastrous impacts that resulted from the Lehman bankruptcy.

• Lately, researchers looking back have concluded that the huge losses were more attributable to falling house prices than to lax underwriting standards.[107]

Bank of America v. Superior Court:[108] *Do Home Buyers Hammered by Collapsing House Prices Have a Claim Against the Lenders Whose Deceitful Practices Precipitated the Housing Price and Mortgage Meltdown?*

This suit was brought by borrowers who had acquired their homes with loans from Countrywide Financial. They sued Bank of America because it had acquired Countrywide. "Countrywide Financial was one of the subprime lenders at the heart of the financial crisis; its predatory lending practices resulted in disgustingly large payouts for executives while sticking low-income borrowers with explosive mortgages they hadn't a hope of paying back. The New York Times' Gretchen Morgenson called Countrywide, 'Exhibit A for the lax and, until recently, highly lucrative lending that has

---

107. Fernando Fereira and Joseph Gyourko, *A New Look at the US Foreclosure Crisis: Panel Data Evidence of Prime and Subprime Borrowers from 1997 to 2012*, NATIONAL BUREAU OF ECONOMIC RESEARCH (last visited Aug. 15, 2015). http://www.nber.org/papers/w21261. Even so, only 18% of home owners with negative equities defaulted during the mortgage crisis]. See also, Palmer, Christopher, Why Did So Many Subprime Borrowers Default During the Crisis: Loose Credit or Plummeting Prices? (last visited, Jan. 12, 2016). Available at SSRN: http://ssrn.com/abstract=2665762 or http://dx.doi.org/10.2139/ssrn.2665762 (concluding that changing borrower and loan characteristic accounted for 40% of the defaults and declining house prices, the rest.)

108. 198 Cal.App.4th 862, 130 Cal.Rptr.3d 504 (2011).

turned a once-hot business ice cold and has touched off a housing crisis of historic proportions.'"[109]

They sued their mortgage lender, Countrywide, for "fraudulent concealment of an alleged scheme to bilk investors by selling them pooled mortgages at inflated values." [It] knew [the] scheme would lead to a liquidity crisis and grave damage to each Plaintiff's property value and thereby result in each Plaintiff's loss of the equity such Plaintiff invested in his house.

The borrowers who filed the suit lost millions in falling home prices. Their suit was based on two prongs. First, they argued that Countrywide had an obligation to them as borrowers, not to fraudulently conceal its nefarious lending practices. Second, those practices were precisely what led to the huge defaults by totally unqualified subprime borrowers and this was the root cause of falling house prices, the mortgage meltdown and the ensuing recession.

The *"unraveling of the Defendants' fraudulent scheme has materially depressed the price of real estate throughout California,* including the real estate owned by Plaintiffs, resulting in the losses to Plaintiffs."

The trial court was somewhat sympathetic to the borrowers' lawsuit: "if Mozilo (Countrywide CEO and co-founder) and his troops are intentionally inflating the value of all or much of American real estate, in order to generate more loans, in order to generate short-term profits and bonuses, and they know they are doing it, but choose not to tell their customers ... that they are being sucked into this maw; ... at least under my first theory of first principles [of tort] ... that duty might be recognized."

The appellate court saw it differently: On the issue of Countrywide's fraudulent concealment of its scandalous lending practices, the court observed: "The general duty is not to warn of the intent to commit wrongful acts, but to refrain from committing them. Guided by the above, we conclude that while Countrywide had a duty to refrain from committing fraud, it had no independent duty to disclose to its borrowers its alleged intent to defraud its investors by selling them mortgage pools at inflated values."

Responding to the issue of causation between Countrywide's concealment and the mortgage borrowers' losses, the appellate court concluded: "The defect in this allegation is that homeowners who did not obtain loans from Countrywide likewise suffered a decline in property values, a decline in their home equity, and reduced access to their home equity lines of credit. Irrespective of whether a homeowner obtained a loan from Countrywide, or obtained a loan through another lender, or whether a homeowner owned his or her home free and clear, all suffered a loss of home equity due to the generalized decline in home values. That being the case, there is no nexus

---

109. Sarah Jaffe, Countrywide Whistleblower reveals rampant mortgage fraud part of 'everyday business.'" http://www.rawstory.com/2012/07/countrywide-whistleblower-reveals-rampant-mortgage-fraud-part-of-everyday-business/ (Last visited 06/20/2016).

between the alleged fraudulent concealment by Countrywide and the economic harm which these plaintiffs/borrowers have suffered."[110]

Questions

Question 1: *Direct Mortgage Lender, Mortgage Broker or Mortgage Banker.*

Suppose you or a friend of yours is looking for a home mortgage loan. You could approach a direct mortgage lender, mortgage broker, or mortgage banker either in person or online. The text describes the differences. Do you see any reason to prefer one type over another, or would you canvass several loan sources regardless of whether they were direct lenders, mortgage bankers or mortgage brokers?

Question 2: *The Three Cs of Mortgage Loan Underwriting.*

(a) What information is required for each of the three Cs of home mortgage loan underwriting–capacity, credit reputation and collateral?

(b) If you were personally making a home mortgage loan to an individual you did not know, would you rely equally on each of the three Cs, or would you regard one or another of them as the most probative?

(c) As a borrower, how would you decide how much of a home mortgage loan you could afford? Would you rely mostly on the two ratios–housing and total debt to income?

(d) Apparently, between two borrowers with low down payments (for instance 10% of the purchase price), the one with the higher credit score is significantly less likely to default. How would you explain that?

(e) If you were advising a mortgage lender, would you advise the lender to organize its underwriting criteria to accommodate the data that borrowers with higher credit scores and low down payments seem to be less risky than borrowers with somewhat lower scores and higher down payments? How would the lenders implement your advice?

Question 3: *Underwriting, Default Rates and House Prices.*

One of the lessons of the mortgage default and foreclosure crisis of 2008 seems to be that house price trends matter much more than individual or property character-istics as predictors of defaults and losses for lenders. Why does this finding not com-pletely undermine CFPB efforts to stiffen "ability-to-repay" underwriting and the avoidance of any but "qualified mortgages"?

Question 4: *Amortization.*

(a) What is the difference between full, partial, no amortization and negative amortization?

(b) What is a balloon payment?

---

110. 198 Cal.App.4th 862, 873.

(c) What is the maturity date and the amortization period of a loan "20 due in 10"?

(d) Why would a borrower ever find such a loan advantageous?

(e) What could attract a lender to fund a loan partially amortized or "interest only?"

(f) A first time homebuyer is looking for an affordable "starter" home, hoping in time to trade up with rising personal income and, hopefully, rising property values. What would be the advantages and disadvantages of an interest only loan to this homebuyer?

(g) Describe briefly the ideal potential borrower for an FHA Graduated Payment Mortgage or a Reverse Mortgage (an FHA Home Equity Conversion Mortgage). Why is negative or no amortization sensible in these situations?

Question 5. *Adjustable or Fixed Rate Loans?*

(a) Why would any price-conscious homebuyer ever choose an adjustable rate loan at a time when fixed rate, 30-year mortgage loans were available at historically low interest rates?

(b) To a borrower who worries about whether she will be able to afford an adjustable rate loan, why is the life-of-loan cap more important than periodic annual caps?

Question 6. *Rate Locks.*

(a) When would a borrower be well advised to purchase a rate lock and when would such a purchase be a waste of money?

(b) Is there any good reason for a loan applicant to spend good money buying a rate lock on an adjustable rate loan? After all, the rate itself moves with market conditions.

Question 7: *Commercial Loan Underwriting. LTV, Debt Yield, DSCR.*

(a) What is the difference between Debt Yield and DSCR?

(b) Why do commercial lenders resort to three metrics in deciding whether to make their loans: loan-to-value ratios, debt service coverage ratios, and debt yield ratios? What does each one measure that the other two do not, and why would a commercial mortgage lender care?

Question 8: *Notes and Mortgages.*

(a) What is the difference in content between a note and a mortgage or deed of trust?

(b) Following payment in full or foreclosure of a previously recorded mortgage or deed of trust, what recorded document should a subsequent purchaser expect to see if the security instrument was a mortgage? A deed of trust?

Question 9: *The Mortgagor's Obligation to Repair Defects.*

What rationale could possibly support the Restatement (Third) of Property (Mortgages) position that mortgagors have no responsibility for repairing defects that existed at the time the mortgage was entered even though the mortgagor knew about the defects, the mortgagee did not, and the defects were latent?

Question 10: *Waste, Demolition and Redevelopment.*

A real estate developer acquires a large, two story space a few blocks from a thriving commercial area that is in bad condition, half vacant, and generating a net operating income of $100,000 a year. The developer had worked for a major discount clothing retailer, and knew the firm was seeking locations just like the one he acquired. He bought the land for $500,000 with personal funds and equity investments from family and friends.

Then, he signed the retailer to a 15-year lease at a rent that could easily amortize the $4,000,000 in renovation costs to meet the retailer's requirements as a condition of the retailer taking possession and commencing its obligations under the lease. The developer borrowed $4,000,000 from a bridge lender for a term of three years at an interest rate of 9% when prime commercial mortgage lending rates were 5%.

The loan was non-recourse. The "borrower" was a specially formed Limited Liability Company. But the developer signed a non-recourse carve-out guaranty to be personally liable for waste.

The developer managed to clear the building of tenants and demolished the structure. She drew plans and was about to apply for building permits when the retailer filed bankruptcy.

She will default on her bridge loan. Is she going to be held personally liable on the "bad boy" carve out for waste?

Question 11: *How Mortgage Lenders Limit Liability Under CERCLA.*

(a) What CERCLA risks do mortgage lenders take when they finance real estate developers building new projects on previously developed industrial sites that might have been subject to hazardous or toxic waste?

(b) How can mortgage lenders reduce those risks?

Question 12: *Mortgagees and the Drug Forfeiture Laws.*

A wealthy Brazilian national who lives in Uruguay, through her second cousin who is a Los Angeles real estate broker, acquires a run-down motel on Sunset Boulevard with a purchase money mortgage loan from Chase.

She hires a young man to manage the motel who was one of her son's friends at a Swiss boarding school. The purchaser rarely visits Los Angeles and never saw the motel. If she had observed the clientele coming and going from the motel for a while, she might have realized why it has a reputation in the neighborhood as a place of prostitution and drug sales.

The DEA seizes the motel in a sting operation. The young man who managed the hotel was earning $10,000 a month leasing space to several gang members who have been indicted for selling drugs, money laundering and other felonies.

The Chase mortgage prohibited illegal acts. Chase initiates a non-judicial foreclosure. The DEA claims the property through the drug forfeiture laws. Is Chase likely to free the motel from the DEA's forfeiture by contending that it is an innocent lender? Would the DEA be able to enjoin Chase from foreclosing non-judicially?

Question 13. *Securitization Issues.*

(a) Why would a commercial bank ever sell its safest and highest yielding home mortgage loans to an aggregator for eventual securitization?

(b) A bond investor fears that interest rates are going to be rising soon. Would that investor be attracted to IO or PO mortgage backed bonds?

(c) A commercial developer is a major mortgage borrower who appreciates the lower rates achievable on mortgage loans originated for eventual securitization. Her mortgage lender reserves the right of prior approval of major leases. Once the loan was securitized, approval delays by her loan servicer have occasionally caused her to lose a prime tenant because it took so long for her loan servicer to secure the lease approval. What provision should she negotiate to include the next time she borrows money from her mortgage lender of choice?

Chapter 13

Prepayment of Mortgage Loans

Scope of the Chapter

US capital markets offer borrowers a diverse menu of financing choices whether they are borrowing money to acquire real estate assets, or refinancing loans secured by real estate. They can select fixed or adjustable rate loans, loans with varying maturity dates up to 30 years, and varying obligations for repaying principal.

This rich menu of repayment options brings about diverse pools of cash flows appealing to an equally diverse universe of potential investors—ranging from some who seek a predictable fixed rate, short term repayment to others prepared to take the risks, and the higher returns, of investing in adjustable rate, long term mortgage loans.

The first question answered in this chapter is why borrowers, having chosen from an extensive menu of options regarding the duration and other terms of their mortgage loans, decide later to prepay their loans ahead of schedule, and how prepayment impacts borrowers and lenders.

Then, we answer the pivotal legal questions raised by prepayment. (1) Are there historic common law limitations on the borrower's right to prepay without the lender's consent? (2) If not, are there juridical limits on what lenders may charge borrowers for the privilege of prepayment, similar to the common law limitations against penalizing debtors who default?

Finally, we examine the contract provisions used by lenders to prevent, discourage or shift the actual costs of prepayment from themselves to their prepaying borrowers. These take the form of temporary lockouts, prepayment fees, yield maintenance and defeasance—all explained in the concluding pages of this chapter.

I. Why Prepayment Matters

A. Why Borrowers Decide to Prepay

Borrowers seek to prepay their existing mortgage loans, for many reasons, mainly these:

    (1) To facilitate a sale when relocating for one of the many reasons people move— to a domicile that better meets their household needs, or to be closer to a new job, maybe as part of an adjustment to a divorce or death in the family.

Buyers usually want to select their own lender and borrow on their own terms. So they will greatly prefer that the owner convey title 'free and clear' of all existing liens.[1] To accommodate, the seller will need to prepay its own mortgage so that the buyer's mortgage lender can have a first lien as security for its purchase money mortgage loan.

(2) Borrowers refinance their mortgages to take advantage of falling interest rates.[2]

(3) Buyers can extract the rising equity values of their properties by refinancing, as long as they can find a lender willing to lend a sum greater than necessary to prepay the existing mortgage, and the property owner is entitled to pocket the excess cash tax-free.

(4) Some borrowers seek to repay their mortgages sooner than they had originally contracted to repay the debt in order to reduce their total interest payments over the life of the loan. (This is sometimes called "curtailment.") "If, for example, a prepayment of just $50 is added to the first mortgage payment, that $50 is deducted from the principal balance remaining on the loan. That means that the borrower never pays a penny of interest on that $50.00—not for the next month, not for the next year, and not for the next 30 years."[3]

If a borrower has a $300,000 loan at a rate of 4% amortized over 30 years his principle and interest payment is $1432.25, and his total cost to payoff the loan over 30 years is $515,610 ($1432.25 x 360). If the same borrower were to pay $2219.06, he would pay off the loan in 15 years instead of 30, and his total cost to payoff the loan would be $399,430.80 ($2219.06 x 180). You see the difference? Making the 15 year payment saved the borrower roughly $115,000 in interest payments.

(5) Prepayment may arise from a default that leads to the lender foreclosing.

(6) Prepayment may result from the security property being destroyed by flood, fire or some other casualty.

B. Lenders' Attitudes Vary about Borrowers Prepaying Mortgage Loans

It is easy to understand why mortgage lenders bristle at late payments. But why do they object to borrowers repaying mortgage loans early?

---

1. Prepayment fees aren't regarded as restraints on alienation because they don't prevent the borrower from selling the security property. They only increase the borrower's cost of selling the security property when the buyer doesn't want to keep the existing loan in place. In setting the sales price, the provident borrower anticipates this expense.

2. For example, a study of all single-family home loans securitized by FHLMC (Freddie Mac), originated in 1984, showed that by 1987, 74.1% had been re-financed to take advantage of falling interest rates, 94.1 % by 1994. Jesse M. Abraham & H. Scott Theobald, *Commercial Mortgage Prepayments*, THE HANDBOOK OF COMMERCIAL MORTGAGE-BACKED SECURITIES 55, 57 (Fabozzi & Jacob eds., 1997).

3. Jay Romano, *The Benefits of Prepaying Mortgages*, NEW YORK TIMES (last visited Aug. 11, 2015), http://www.nytimes.com/1996/12/08/realestate/benefits-of-prepaying-mortgages.html

Here are some of the reasons.

(1) When borrowers prepay loans during periods of falling interest rates, their lenders will have little choice but to reinvest the prepaid sums at prevailing market rates. This will diminish the lender's cash flow from the mortgage portfolio and reduce the present value of the lender's entire loan portfolio.[4]

(2) Mortgage lenders lose far more money to prepayments than to defaults. In a study of 4.2 million FHA loans, two researchers discovered that interest rate losses to lenders following prepayment hugely exceeded losses due to default.[5]

(3) Borrowers who prepay to extract rising equity values from their properties are effectively increasing the lender's credit risk by increasing the loan to value ratios that existed before the prepayment.

(4) Many institutions engage in asset-liability management, acquiring assets with yields systematically calibrated to cover their anticipated future liabilities. Insurance companies, pension funds, university endowments, and family trusts all do this. Loan prepayments on mortgages prompted by falling interest rates compromise investor efforts to match cash flow from their assets and their projected liabilities.

Sometimes, mortgage lenders welcome prepayments. Here are some examples:

(1) Investors who purchased loans at deep discounts can turn tidy profits when borrowers prepay those loans at par.

(2) When borrowers prepay loans yielding lower than current market interest rates, their mortgage lender will benefit by reinvesting the prepaid money at prevailing rates.[6]

(3) Lenders who charge significant pre-paid interest (points) increase their effective yields when borrowers prepay sooner than anticipated.[7]

---

4. Megan W. Murray, Prepayment Premiums: Contracting for Future Financial Stability in the Commercial Lending Market, 96 Iowa L. Rev. 1037, 1046 (March, 2011).

5. $576 million compared to $12 million. Joseph R. Mason and Joshua Rosner, *Where Did the Risk Go? How Misapplied Bond Ratings Cause Mortgage Backed Securities and Collateralized Debt Obligations Market Disruptions* 54 (Hudson Institute, May 2007), online at http://www.hudson .org/files/publications/Hudson_Mortgage_Paper5_3_07.pdf (visited May 2013).

6. This is true of portfolio lenders, those who retain the loans they originate. As the text indicates just a few pages from now, the investors in securitized mortgages are generally more single-mindedly determined to maintain an uninterrupted cash flow from their mortgage investments and tend not to welcome prepayment even when they could reinvest prepaid sums in higher yielding securities or mortgages.

7. "For example, if one "discount point" (one percent of the amount of the loan) is charged on a loan with a face amount of $100,000, the lender will in fact disburse only $99,000 to the borrower. Nevertheless, if the borrower elects to prepay the loan before any amortization of the principal has occurred, the amount necessary to prepay is the $100,000 face amount. Thus the "points" have two effects: they increase the effective interest yield to the lender, and they produce additional revenue to the lender if prepayment occurs." See John M. Harris, Jr. & G. Stacy Sirmans, *Discount Points, Effective Yields, and Mortgage Prepayments,* 2 J. REAL EST. RES., Winter 1987, at 97.

Investors in Mortgage Backed Securities Can Trade Directly on Prepayment Speeds and Expectations. Investors in mortgage backed securities can elect to purchase tranches that are exclusively "principal only" (PO) or "interest only" (IO). The bond servicers collect monthly payments of principal and interest from mortgage borrowers, and the trustee for the bond holders divides these into principal payments which are transmitted to the PO bondholders and interest payments sent to IO strip purchasers.

"POs typically have long positive durations and rise in value when rates decline, while IOs generally have negative durations, increasing in price when rates rise. However, the critical driver of performance strips is prepayment expectations. POs perform well if prepayment speeds are fast, in the same way that returns would be enhanced if a zero-coupon bond were called prior to maturity at par. By contrast, IOs perform well if prepayment speeds are slow; they can be viewed as an annuity where the value increases the longer it remains outstanding."[8]

II. Prepayment Law

A. The Default Rule

The Majority Default Rule: No Presumptive Right to Prepay. Lenders are deemed to have the right to *perfect tender in time*, to absolutely bar prepayment, a rule that can be traced to an 1823 New York court opinion.[9] "The justification for this rule is that if the lender is forced to accept prepayment for which it did not bargain, it would be exposed to a lesser than anticipated rate of return, possibly adverse tax consequence and added reinvestment costs."[10]

A creditor could no more be compelled to accept payments before they are due, than a lender could compel a debtor to make payments in advance of the due date specified in the note unless the lender reserved a call option.[11] Lenders predicate their loan pricing on receipt of a predictable stream of payments over the life of the loan. Payment should be made exactly on schedule, neither early nor late. "A debtor has no more right to pay off the obligation prior to its maturity date than he does to pay it off after its maturity date."[12]

---

8. Frank J. Fabozzi, Anand K. Bhattacharya, William S. Berliner, Mortgage Backed Securities (2d ed. 2011), p.26.

9. *See Ellis v. Craig*, 7 Johns Ch. 7 (N.Y. 1823).

10. *Metro. Life Ins. Co. v. Promenade Towers Mut. Housing Corp.*, 581 A.2d 846, 850 (Md. Ct. Spec. App. 1990). Williams v. Fassler, 110 Cal. App. 3d 7(1980).

11. Frank Alexander, *Mortgage Prepayment: The Trial of Common Sense*, 72 CORNELL L. REV. 288, 317 (1987). Professor Alexander presents an interesting analysis and critique of the early case from which this rule was derived. *Id.* at 291.

12. *Williams v. Fassler*, 110 Cal. App. 3d 7(1980) (upholding 50% prepayment penalty because sellers taking back note and deed of trust would have incurred comparable tax liability if the debt were prepaid.).

B. The Drafting Burden Exception to the Default Rule

Lenders Must Explicitly Bar Prepayment in Many Jurisdictions or Borrowers May Prepay Without Penalty. Many courts have set the borrowers right to prepay as the default rule, only allowing lenders to bar prepayment if in the mortgage and the note, the lender clearly prohibits it.[13]

The courts justify requiring lenders to include a "no prepayment" provision in the promissory note because lenders draft the loan documents. They reason that few borrowers would know the perfect tender in time rule, be thinking about prepayment when they become borrowers, or infer that no mention of prepayment meant prepayment was prohibited without the lender's consent.[14] The Restatement (Third) of Property (Mortgage) § 6.1 (1997) supports this position.

A single sentence would suffice to ordain "perfect tender in time": "The borrower has no right to make payments in advance of when they fall due." Some lenders have drafted promissory notes that prohibit prepayment, reserve the right of the lender to allow prepayment in its sole and absolute discretion, and impose any prepayment fee the lender deems appropriate.

Ambiguities Regarding Prepayment Are Interpreted Against the Lender. Unless a lender has clearly barred prepayment in the note, some courts seize upon the slightest turn of phrase in the note to justify allowing prepayment. If the note calls for repayment of a monthly sum "on or before" a certain date, this phrase could support an argument that the parties meant to give the maker the right to discharge the note by prepayment.[15] Similarly, when the note contains a payment schedule that allows the borrower to pay a given sum "or more," courts take the "or more" to signal that the borrower can prepay as much of the debt as she prefers on the payment dates mentioned in the note.

---

13. John C. Murray, *Yield Maintenance Revisited: Prepayment Premium Provisions in Commercial Loan Documents*, First American (last visited Aug. 11, 2015), http://www.firstam.com/content.cfm?id=3026 (citing cases from Missouri, North Carolina and Pennsylvania adopting the minority view and from Alabama, California, Connecticut, Indiana, Maryland, Massachusetts, Missouri, Nebraska, Texas, West Virginia, and Washington following the majority view).

See, e.g., Dale Whitman, *Mortgage Prepayment Clauses: An Economic and Legal Analysis*, 40 U.C.L.A. L. Rev. 851, 858-59 (1993); Robert K. Baldwin, *Prepayment Penalties: A Survey and Suggestion*, 40 Vand. L. Rev. 409, 430-32 (1987), describing laws of Ohio, Missouri, Mississippi, Rhode Island, New York, Michigan and Virginia (allowing prepayment of residential loans after a period of years and limiting prepayment fees).

Courts have affirmed the pro-lender default rule in Alabama (1996), Kansas (1995), West Virginia (1995), Nebraska (1993), and Maryland (1990).

14. In Pennsylvania and Florida, borrowers have the right to prepay, absent express language in the note to the contrary. 41 Pa. Cons. Stat. Ann. §§ 101 to 405 (West 1999), Fla. Stat. Ann. § 697.06 (West 1994). On the other hand, the Tennessee legislature appears to have ratified the pro-lender common law presumption. Tenn. Code Ann. § 47-14-108 (2005) ("the privilege of prepayment of a loan ... shall be governed by contract between the parties").

15. Miller and Starr, 2 California Real Estate 222 (2d ed. 1989); *Garner v. Sisson Props.*, 31 S.E.2d 400 (Ga. 1944); *Latimer v. Grundy County Nat'l Bank*, 239 Ill. App. 3d 1000, 1002 (1993) (borrower had right to prepay because of phrase "if not sooner paid").

C. Absolute Prepayment Prohibitions Are Not Restraints on Alienation

'Lock-ins' and 'lock-outs' are the names of contract provisions that prohibit the borrower from making a prepayment during a specified period of time. "The clause is known by these alternate terms because it locks-in the loan payments and locks-out prepayment."[16]

Lock-ins can prevent borrowers from converting their real estate holdings into cash. Imagine a borrower who acquired property with a purchase money loan ten years earlier that the borrower is only a few years from repaying entirely. The property value has risen substantially. But as a practical matter, the borrower cannot sell the property unless the new buyer can acquire the property free and clear of the present first mortgage. Understandably, under circumstances like these, borrowers have challenged lock-ins as unreasonable restraints on alienation.

Uniformly, state courts have declared either that lock-ins are not restraints on alienation at all or that they are reasonable.[17] Here is how the Oregon Supreme Court explained it. "There is an expense attached to loaning money on real property, and it is an entirely legitimate aim of purveyors of credit to loan it for a length of time and at a rate of interest which guarantee a certain net return on the management of the money. This appears to us to be no less valuable an interest than that of defendants' in making liquid their equity for the purpose of using it elsewhere."[18]

Hard and Soft Lock-ins. These prohibitions come in versions called hard or soft. Soft lock-outs are targeted at borrowers refinancing to take advantage of falling interest rates but allow prepayment to facilitate a sale. Hard lock-outs apply even when the borrower is refinancing in order to sell the security property.

Hard lock-outs are commonly found in commercial real estate (CRE) loans with maturities of less than five years. CRE loans with durations of longer than five years are sometimes written with lock-outs that expire after the first three to five years.

Courts routinely enforce lock-out provisions except in bankruptcy courts where judges sometimes allow the bankrupt borrower to disregard a lock-out and prepay a delinquent loan when necessary to facilitate the borrower's confirmed reorganization plan.[19]

---

16. Scott Talkov, Exposing the Myth of Mortgage Prepayment Penalties in the Aftermath of River East, 44 Real Prop., Trust & Est. L J 587, 593 (Fall, 2009).

17. *See, e.g., Clover Square Assocs. v. Northwestern Mut. Life Ins. Co.*, 674 F. Supp. 1137, 1139 (D.N.J. 1987) (although lender's refusal to waive lockout hindered a sale, lockout was held a reasonable restraint on alienation).

18. *Hartford Life Ins. Co. v. Randall*, 283 Or. 297, 583 P.2d 1126, 1127 (Or.1978).

19. *Cont'l Sec. Corp. v. Shenandoah Nursing Home P'ship*, 188 B.R. 205, 214 (W.D. Va. 1995) (The loan was originated in 1990 with a lockout until 2001. The court allowed the debtor to prepay in 1994, declaring that the equitable power of a bankruptcy court to "fashion a reorganization plan almost certainly trumps a contract provision." Exacerbating the mortgagee's loss, the court denied compensatory damage because the lender had not reserved in the note a "backup" fee, applicable to prepayment despite the lockout.).

D. State and Federal Policies Favoring Homeowners' Option to Prepay

The freedom-of-contract rationales that support the lender side of the prepayment debate do not extend to home owner borrowers. Consumer advocates and federal regulators are convinced that just disclosing prepayment prohibitions and penalties to home owners is ineffectual because consumers are poorly positioned to assess the changes in their lives that could propel them to seek prepayment of their mortgage loans. "When you apply for an FHA loan as a new borrower, it's easy to assume that you'll stay in the same property for a long time—even for the entire course of your FHA mortgage. But life doesn't always work out that way. People get jobs in faraway cities, change their minds about the places they live or simply grow out of that first home. When that happens you may wish to sell the property and make a new application for an FHA home loan."[20]

National housing policy is also relevant in justifying regulatory protection of the home owner's prepayment prerogatives. The right to prepay mortgage debt would matter very little if real estate purchasers relied on short term lines of credit to finance their acquisitions and refinancing. But in the US, government policies strongly favor long-term, predictable financing and maximum flexibility to home owners so that they can borrow easily and adjust their financing situations to their changing needs. Home mortgage loans are freely prepayable at borrower's discretion if they are FHA insured, VA guaranteed, or acquired by FNMA or FHLMC.[21] Fannie Mae cannot purchase mortgage loans with prepayment penalties.[22] Under CFPB regulations, prepayment penalties are only allowed on fixed rate, "qualified mortgages" (Q.M.s). Q.M. criteria mandate no loan terms exceeding 30 years, no negative amortization, and no balloon payments.[23]

---

20. http://www.fha.com/fha_article?id=62

21. This is the prepayment provision in Fannie Mae Form 3200 for fixed rate mortgages: *"I have the right to make payments of Principal at any time before they are due. A payment of Principal only is known as a "Prepayment." When I make a Prepayment, I will tell the Note Holder in writing that I am doing so. I may not designate a payment as a Prepayment if I have not made all the monthly payments due under the Note.*

I may make a full Prepayment or partial Prepayments without paying a Prepayment charge. The Note Holder will use my Prepayments to reduce the amount of Principal that I owe under this Note. However, the Note Holder may apply my Prepayment to the accrued and unpaid interest on the Prepayment amount, before applying my Prepayment to reduce the Principal amount of the Note. If I make a partial Prepayment, there will be no changes in the due date or in the amount of my monthly payment unless the Note Holder agrees in writing to those changes." Multistate Fixed Rate Note, Fannie Mae (last visited Aug. 11, 2015), https://www.google.com/webhp?sourceid=chrome-instant&ion=1&espv=2&ie=UTF-8#q=FNMA+residential+form+prepayment

22. Fannie Mae, (last visited July 10, 2015), https://www.fannie.mae.com/content/announcement/se11306.pdf

23. Amy Loftsgordon, "When are Prepayment Penalties Allowed in New Mortgages?", http://www.nolo.com/legal-encyclopedia/when-are-prepayment-penalties-allowed-new-mortgages.html (Last visited: 06/12/2016).

These prepayment privileges are not free. In pricing loans, lenders take prepayment into account. Prime residential borrowers pay between one-fifth and one-half of a percentage point for loans that allow prepayment free of charge. Higher risk borrowers pay more.

Most often, commercial real estate loans contain some form of prepayment prohibition or exit fee.

III. Prepayment Disincentives

"Like bonds with call provisions, mortgages allowing prepayment at will are less valuable to investors. As a result, lenders seek to reduce the risk of prepayment through various financial disincentives in notes."[24] These fees are not direct restraints on alienation because they allow the borrower to sell or refinance mortgaged property though at a fee.

A. Sliding Scale Percentage Fees

Some prepayment penalties are based on sliding scales. The first two were designed for home loans; the second two, for commercial loans.

Six Months' Interest With 20% Fee in Any Year. This formula is very easy to calculate. The borrower owes six months' interest on the prepaid sum after deducting 20% of that amount. It is the oldest of prepayment fees, common to many home and multifamily mortgages.[25] The idea seems to have been that these fees compensate the lender for the time it needs to re-invest the prepaid loan proceeds and to cover the origination costs it may not have had time to recoup on the prepaid loan.

'3-2-1-0.' As mentioned above, prepayment penalties in home mortgage loans are greatly restricted under new regulations of the Consumer Financial Protection Bureau, through amendments to the Truth in Lending Act.

---

24. George Lefcoe, Prepayment Disincentives in Securitized Commercial Loans, 13 Probate an Property 6 (last visited July 10, 2015), http://www.americanbar.org/publications/probate_property_magazine_home/probate_1999_index/probate_sept_oct_1999_index/rppt_publications _magazine_1999_so99lefcoe.html

25. This formula was written into the 1971 FNMA/FHLMC single-family note. The formula later appeared in the regulations of the Federal Home Loan Bank Board governing allowable prepayment fees in the home loans of savings and loan associations. It is codified in Cal. Civ. Code § 2954.9(a)(1). A similar provision enacted by the New Mexico legislature, N.M. Stat. Ann. ' 56-8-30 was enforced in favor of the buyer of a "recreational" (second) residence in *Naumburg v. Pattison*, 711 P.2d 1287, 103 N.M. 649 (1985).

"The principal and accrued interest on any loan secured by a mortgage or deed of trust on owner-occupied residential real property containing only four units or less may be prepaid in whole or in part at any time but only a prepayment made within five years of the date of execution of such mortgage or deed of trust may be subject to a prepayment charge and then solely as herein set forth. An amount not exceeding 20 percent of the original principal amount may be prepaid in any 12-month period without penalty. A prepayment charge may be imposed on any amount prepaid in any 12-month period in excess of 20 percent of the original principal amount of the loan which charge shall not exceed an amount equal to the payment of six months' advance interest on the amount prepaid in excess of 20 percent of the original principal amount."

A prepayment penalty may not be imposed more than three years after the covered transaction is consummated and the maximum amount of the prepayment penalty is: (1) two percent of the outstanding principal balance during the first two years of the loan and; (2) one percent during the third year following consummation.[26]

4-4-3-3-2-2-1-0. This prepayment fee comes from a $20,500,000 loan secured by a multi-family dwelling made by JP Morgan Chase for seven years at a fixed rate of 3.5%. It calls for a prepayment penalty of 4% if prepaid in years seven or six, 3% if prepaid in years five or four, 2% if prepaid in years three or two, 1% if prepaid in year one, and no penalty if prepaid later than year seven.

Fixed fees are not about offsetting the mortgage lender's interest rate risk since they are the same whether the prepaid interest rate was higher, lower or the same as comparable market rates in the year of prepayment. Presumably, when the fixed fee is the same whenever it is prepaid, the fee is compensation for the transactions costs of the issuer or lender in originating a new loan.

Graduated fees that decline as the loan matures appear to be roughly calibrated to the lender's duration risk by shrinking the borrower's prepayment cost, the longer she defers prepaying. Suppose interest rates have fallen 1.5% since the borrower took out her $400,000 loan a year ago. She agreed to a prepayment fee of 4% of the prepaid balance in the first year of the loan, 3% in year two, 2% in year three, 1% in year four, and no prepayment in year five. Refinancing in year one, she retrieves her prepayment fee only by holding the loan nearly three years. She breaks even after two years, and realizes a net savings in year four because only then will the 1.5% in interest saved exceed the 1% prepayment fee.

B. Yield Maintenance (YM)

This type of prepayment fee appears in commercial real estate loans. In theory, yield maintenance clauses could be (and sometimes are) written so as precisely to align the borrower's costs of prepayment to the lender's prospective loss on reinvesting the prepaid sums.

Suppose a borrower prepays a loan with an interest rate lower than current interest rates on comparable loans. The borrower would add a sum of money to the prepay-

---

26. 12 CFR § 1026.43(a)(2). Taken together, the Dodd-Frank Act's amendments to TILA relating to prepayment penalties mean that most closed-end, dwelling-secured transactions: (1) May provide for a prepayment penalty only if the transaction is a fixed-rate, qualified mortgage that is neither high-cost nor higher-priced under §§ 1026.32 and 1026.35; (2) may not, even if permitted to provide for a prepayment penalty, charge the penalty more than three years following consummation or in an amount that exceeds two percent of the amount prepaid; and (3) may be required to limit any penalty even further to comply with the points and fees limitations for qualified mortgages, or to stay below the points and fees trigger for high-cost mortgages. Section 1026.43(g) now reflects these principles. http://www.consumerfinance.gov/eregulations/sxs/1026-43-g/2013-00736?from_version=2015-01321&fr_page=6547

ment that would exactly suffice to yield the lender the same total interest payment as it would have received had the borrower kept the loan to maturity.

Equitable formulas would compare the lender's 'original yield' to the 'current yield' it would receive on comparable investments. Some regional banks that retained mortgage loans in their own portfolios wrote YM provisions exactly like that.

Portfolio lenders would certainly have access to information about the interest rates they were charging on mortgage loans comparable to the ones being prepaid because they originated such loans themselves. But prepaying borrowers might challenge the lender deciding on its own which properties were truly comparable to the one being prepaid, a scenario leading to dueling appraisers, protracted disputes, and, possibly hefty litigation or arbitration costs.

While there is an advantage in the certainty of pegging the 'current yield' in a prepayment penalty formula to an easily ascertainable number, it over-compensates the lender to define the current yield as the rate paid on U.S. Treasuries of maturities comparable to the loan being prepaid. Treasury yields will always be lower than private mortgages of comparable duration although the spread between the two rates varies.

When interest rates on truly comparable loans have not changed at all, so the lender loses nothing on reinvesting prepaid sums, prepayment can cost the borrower plenty. Consider the example of a loan being prepaid one minute after origination. The borrower instantly prepays a freshly originated $10,000,000 loan, with a ten year maturity date, 8% interest rate at a time when U.S. Treasuries of comparable maturity were yielding 6.5%. Along with repayment of the $10,000,000, the borrower's prepayment fee would be $1,100,000 even though rates had changed not one time during the intervening minute[27] ($1,100,000 = $150,000 per year x ten years, discounted to present value).[28]

Of course, the mortgage lender will incur origination costs upon reinvesting prepaid sums—appraisals, title reports and the like. But these are passed along to the new borrower. To offset any costs of originating a new loan that are not going to be paid by the new borrower, most yield maintenance provisions entitle lenders to charge a minimum fee of 1% upon prepayment. This is sometimes justified by reference to administrative costs and lost interest during the time it takes to originate a new loan—although the lender would incur many of the same costs even if the loan were repaid at its stated maturity date.

---

27. Sam W. Galowitz, *The Myth of the Yield Maintenance Formula*, 15 R.E.F.J. 27, 29 (Fall 1999). Further, some yield maintenance formulas neglect to credit the borrower by discounting the lump sum payment the lender is receiving well ahead of schedule to present value.

28. "Commercial mortgage spreads over U.S. Treasuries have ranged from over + 250 basis points to + 75 basis points over the last 13 years." (1983-96), Galia Gichon, *The Whole Loan Commercial Mortgage Market*, THE HANDBOOK OF COMMERCIAL MORTGAGE-BACKED SECURITIES 41, 44 (Fabozzi & Jacob eds., 1997).

C. Defeasance[29]

Defeasance has become an important feature of loans included in Commercial Mortgage Backed Securities (CMBS) offerings. Typically, a CMBS offering has fewer than 100 loans ranging in size from a million to several hundred million dollars (a few of some of the more recent vintages tipping over $1 billion).[30]

Actually, defeasance does not prepay the underlying debt; the debt remains completely intact, and undisturbed. Defeasance involves a *substitution of security* for the debt. In place of the mortgage or deed of trust, the borrower assembles a portfolio of Treasury securities to secure the debt.[31] These Treasury bonds are assigned to a trustee who holds them for the benefit of the mortgage investors and disburses bond proceeds at the precise times and in the exact amounts as the borrower was obligated to make.

This arrangement is an accommodation between the owners of office buildings, shopping centers and other income-producing commercial real estate who want the ability to sell properties free of existing debt, and investors in Commercial Mortgage Backed Securities (CMBS) who seek uninterrupted cash flows on their bonds.

To see how defeasance works, consider this example. Suppose a borrower needs to replace an interest only $1,000,000 mortgage loan that yields 6% with a Treasury of comparable maturity that generates $60,000 of annual interest payments. To do this, the borrower will have to purchase Treasury obligations of approximately $1.5 million. At the mortgage loan maturity date, the borrower will be able to repay the $1 million mortgage loan in full and retrieve the extra $500,000 in Treasuries, called the 'residual'. But until then, the borrower has tied up $1.5 million of its own money in Treasuries to replace a $1 million mortgage obligation.

Matching US Treasury with mortgage obligations is expensive. It will require the services of an experienced bond trader because mortgage payments usually call for amortization and simple interest while Treasury interest is compounded annually with no amortization.

Prepaying borrowers will also incur substantial charges and processing fees, including a Certified Public Accountant's comfort letter that the cash flow from the substituted

---

29. Defeasance is modeled after an arrangement used by corporations to remove bonds from their books. In the corporate setting, funding the retirement of corporate bonds with Treasuries is called 'in substance' defeasance, to distinguish it from 'legal' defeasance, since the corporation's obligations to the bondholders remain in place although the bond obligation is removed from the corporation's books. When rates have risen enough that Treasury obligations can be purchased for less than the face value of the bond, the corporation recognizes earnings in the year of the purchase. This is good for executives whose compensation depends on earnings and for bondholders whose repayment is now, in effect, government-guaranteed. Share prices don't seem to suffer. James M. Johnson, Robert A. Pari & Leonard Rosenthal, *The Impact of In-Substance Defeasance on Bondholder and Shareholder Wealth*, 44 J. Fin. 1049 (1989).

30. D. Eric Remensperger, Bond Bombs, 32-JAN L.A. Law. 38 (January, 2010).

31. For a defeasance calculator see, LoopNet (last visited Aug. 11, 2015), http://www.loopnet.com/xNet/MainSite/LoopLender/Calculators.aspx?Calculator'defease

collateral will meet all scheduled mortgage payments on time, a legal opinion that the borrower has fully complied with all defeasance requirements, and the costs of forming a special purpose entity to act as the trustee for the lender, holding title to the U.S. Treasury bonds and remitting bond payments to the mortgagee.

FNMA is now making defeasance far easier than a conduit loan by creating its own residential mortgage backed security instead of requiring the borrower to pay high commission costs to buy a series of U.S. Treasury securities to replace the stream of mortgage payments.[32] The amount needed to purchase the security is known as the defeasance deposit, and it can be greater or less than the mortgage balance, depending upon interest rates at the time of defeasance.

IV. Doctrinal Challenges to Prepayment Fees

Borrowers challenging the validity of prepayment disincentives have not had much success overall but sometimes gained a bit of traction invoking these three legal theories: (A) prepayment fees are unreasonable liquidated damage clauses; (B) they are unreasonable under Bankruptcy Code Sec. 506(b);[33] or (C) inapplicable to *involuntary* prepayments.

A. Liquidated Damages

To prevent breach of contract penalties that greatly exceed the non-breaching party's likely loss, liquidated damages must be "reasonable in the light of the anticipated or actual loss caused by the breach."

Fixed fee arrangements apply even when the prepaid interest rate is lower than prevailing market rates so that the lender could actually increase its yield on the prepaid sum by reinvesting it at current market rates. The YM clause "systematically guarantees the lender the rewards of a higher yield commercial mortgage without the corresponding higher risks that would normally accompany such high-yield mortgages

---

32. "In a defeasance, the real estate collateral is replaced by a Fannie Mae security, and the real estate owner (the borrower) is replaced with a new entity that owns the security and is controlled by Fannie Mae. Fannie Mae defeasance is far easier than a conduit loan defeasance because Fannie Mae creates its own security instead of requiring the borrower to pay high commission costs to buy a series of U.S. Treasury securities to replace the stream of mortgage payments. The amount needed to purchase the security is known as the defeasance deposit, and it can be greater or less than the mortgage balance depending upon interest rates at the time of defeasance. http://redcapitalgroup.com/wp-content/uploads/2015/02/FNMA-TS-012_PrepaymentOptions.pdf

33. Under 11 U.S.C. 506(b) The secured creditor's claim for a prepayment penalty is treated as part of the secured claim if it represents a reasonable fee, cost or charge. If adjudged unreasonable, it is treated as unsecured. In the unusual case of the debtor's estate being large enough to pay all creditors' claims, whether secured and unsecured, the fee should be paid from the debtor's estate, subject to the limitation applicable to all creditor claims under 11 U.S.C. 502, that they be lawful under state law. *Gencarelli v. UPS Capital Business Credit*, 501 F.3d 1 (1st Cir. 2007).

since the lender will reinvest the prepayment in a similar mortgage and double-collect on the risk premium while avoiding the greater risk of borrower's non-payment."[34]

A few courts have applied liquidated damage rules to prepayment fee provisions but most courts have refused. They understand that although borrowers may not appreciate the significance of a prepayment provision because they do not consider the many circumstances in which they might want to prepay, borrowers do have choices, and lenders price their loans based on the choices the borrower makes when the loans are originated. Understandably, courts characterize a prepayment fee as a kind of option price for the lender indulging the borrower in selecting a loan different from the one it had first chosen.[35] Most courts have declined to cast a prepayment fee as a penalty for the borrower defaulting because the borrower has not defaulted; the borrower has elected a loan different from the than the one it had.

B. Bankruptcy Code Section 506(b)

Under this section of the Bankruptcy Code, secured creditors are allowed to recover any "reasonable fees, costs or charges provided for under the agreement." Some bankruptcy courts have agreed with borrowers who claimed that yield maintenance clauses overcompensated lenders by defining 'original yield' as the contract rate and 'current yield' as the rates paid for U.S. Treasury obligations.[36] They refuse to top off a senior mortgagee's repayment in full with a big prepayment fee that results in junior lienors and suppliers going unpaid.[37]

C. Challenges to Involuntary Prepayments

To this point we have been discussing voluntary prepayments. Sometimes, lenders claim a prepayment fee for a borrower's *involuntary* prepayment. Here are some examples:

---

34. Scott Talkov, Exposing the Myth of Mortgage Prepayment Penalties in the Aftermath of River East, 44 Real Prop., Trust & Est. L J 587, 591 (Fall, 2009).

35. *River East Plaza, L.L.C. v. Variable Annuity Life Ins. Co* ,498 F.3d 718 (7th Cir. 2007).

36. "The bankruptcy courts in various jurisdictions have differed as to whether the lender with an over secured claim should be entitled to a prepayment premium and whether the charge is reasonable under federal or state law." John C. Murray, *Enforcement of Prepayment-Premium Provisions in Mortgage Loan Documents* (2008). *Compare In re A.J. Lane & Co.*, 113 B.R. 821 (Bankr. D. Mass. 1990) (striking down fee based on 1% of prepaid balance prepayment fee as unreasonable liquidated damage), *with In re Schaumburg Hotel Owner Ltd.* 97 B.R. 943 (Bankr. N.D. Ill.,1989) (upholding fee of 10% of prepaid sum as reasonable liquidated damage) and *In re Vanderveer Estates Holdings, Inc.*, 283 B.R. 122 (Bkrtcy.E.D.N.Y.,2002) (upholding yield maintenance clause based on current Treasury rates.).

37. Alice Green, *To Fee or Not to Fee: Bankruptcy Courts' Struggle for Reasonableness in Prepayment Premiums*, 17 J. Bankr. L. & Prac. 1 Art. 1 (2008); Scott K. Charles, Emil A. Kleinhaus, *Prepayment Clauses in Bankruptcy*, 15 Am. Bankr. Inst. L. Rev. 537 (2007). "An oversecured lender should be entitled to include, as part of its claim, interest at the default rate on the debt and a prepayment." Courts have differed when the debtor is undersecured. John C. Murray, Bankruptcy Considerations: Validity and Enforceability of Prepayment Premium Provisions in Mortgage Loan Documents (July 2005).

(a) Government condemnation for public use of the security property, where the eminent domain proceeds are used to repay the mortgage debt;

(b) An insured casualty loss where the proceeds are used to repay the mortgage debt.

(c) A borrower's default on the basis of which the lender declares the entire debt due, and initiates foreclosure, adding the prepayment fee to a deficiency claim against the borrower.

Most courts allow lenders to enforce prepayment fees as long as there is clear language in the note covering the situation.[38] Similarly, courts have allowed lenders to enforce prepayment penalties triggered by the lender declaring all sums due after a borrower has defaulted, when the prepayment was written to apply: "whether said prepayment is voluntary or involuntary, including any prepayment effected by the holder's exercise of the Acceleration Clause."[39]

Court outcomes here are mixed. Some courts have declined to enforce a prepayment premium upon an involuntary acceleration not specifically covered in the loan documents.[40] Other courts have granted enforcement even in the absence of specific provision when the prepayment was lender accelerated.[41]

Borrowers feeling trapped in their loans might decide to force the lender's hand by defaulting to induce the lender to foreclose. Then, the borrower could bid the amount of the loan at the foreclosure sale, and reclaim title to the property, free of the mortgage. The borrower succeeding in this high-risk strategy depends on the lender electing to foreclose. But the lender could seek remedies other than foreclosure, including specific performance of the lock-out.

Questions

Question 1: *Why Borrowers Prepay?*

(a) Why do borrowers ever prepay?

(b) When do mortgage lenders welcome and when do they resist prepayment?

---

38. *Northwestern Mutual Life Ins. Co. V. Uniondale Realty Associates*, 816 N.Y.S. 2d 831 (Supreme Court, Nassau County, 2006)(Opinion contains the language that would legitimize a fee for involuntary prepayment. *But see* RESTATEMENT (THIRD) OF PROPERTY: MORTGAGES 6.3 (1997): the lender should not be permitted to charge a prepayment fee when an insured casualty loss or an eminent domain taking occurs, even if the mortgage documents provide for a fee."

39. Pacific Trust Company TTEE v. Fidelity Federal Savings & Loan Association, 184 Cal.App.3d 817 (1986).

40. *Tan v. California Fed. Sav. & Loan Assoc.*, 140 Cal. App. 3d 800, 824, 189 Cal Rptr. 775, 809 (1983)

41. *Mutual Life Ins. Co. of New York v. Hilander*, 403 N.W.2d 260, 264 (Ky. App. 1966) (upholding right of mortgagee to collect prepayment premium where mortgagor paid off mortgage, including prepayment premium under protest, in response to mortgagee's threat to accelerate defaulted loan, even though *3015 prepayment provision did not specifically mention involuntary prepayments); *West Portland Dev. Co. v. Ward Cook, Inc.*, 246 Ore. 67, 71, 424 P.2d 212, 214 (Or. 1967)

Question 2: *Practical Economics of Prepayment Prohibitions.*

(a) Describe situations in which lenders would welcome prepayment.

(b) When would most lenders resist prepayment if they could?

(c) Why would a borrower ever want to prepay a long-term fixed rate loan bearing an interest rate of 4% when the borrower would have to pay an interest rate of 7% currently on a comparable loan?

Question 3: *Lock-outs, Hard and Soft.*

When would prepayment be allowed by a soft lock-out but not a hard lock-out?

Question 4: *The Simple Math of Fixed Fees.*

(a) When is a prepaid lender likely to be undercompensated by a fixed fee formula?

(b) When is a prepaid lender likely to be overcompensated by a fixed fee formula?

Question 5: *Comparing Defeasance to Yield Maintenance.*

(a) Explain and compare the difference between yield maintenance and defeasance.

(b) For the borrower seeking to match assets and liabilities, which is usually preferable?

Question 6: *Prepayment Default Rule.*

A home buyer eager to prepay to take advantage of falling interest rates reads through the note and mortgage carefully and finds no mention at all of prepayment. Assuming no applicable statutes conferring prepayment rights, does this mean she has the right to prepay even without the lender's consent, or that she has no right to prepay?

Question 7: *Enforceability of Prepayment Penalties.*

How can courts justify upholding a yield maintenance or defeasance provision as a reasonable estimate of the lender's actual or anticipated loss as a result of the borrower prepaying?

Question 8: *A Bridge Lender's Prepayment Penalty.*

A lender that engages in making short term, risky loans agrees to lend a developer $15,000,000 — $5,000,000 to close escrow on a failing neighborhood shopping center, and $10,000,000 to refurbish the abandoned grocery store that was the most important tenant in the center before it failed. The developer is well known for these kinds of "turn around" deals. The loan would be non-recourse, for a term of ten months. The developer would have the option of extending the term for an additional six months. The interest rate is $150,000 per month.

There is a prepayment provision allowing the borrower to prepay the loan at any time by paying exactly the interest that the lender would have earned if the loan had been outstanding for ten months plus an exit fee of one month's interest. The note recites that this provision is not a penalty. It is a material inducement to the lender to make the loan, and represents a fair and equitable allocation of risk of loss between the parties. Is the prepayment provision likely to be overturned as an unenforceable penalty disguised as a liquidated damage clause?

Chapter 14

The Mortgage Lender's Right to Call the Loan Upon Sale of Mortgaged Property: The Due-on-Sale Clause

Scope of the Chapter

A property owner who takes out a mortgage loan has the right at common law to sell the property subject to the mortgage without the lender's prior knowledge or consent. This is only a default rule. The lender could add a provision to the note and the mortgage or deed of trust requiring its prior consent.

The consent requirement is called a due-on-sale clause, a provision by which mortgage lenders reserve the option of approving or rejecting the buyer to take over the seller's mortgage obligation. Rejection means that the seller needs to prepay the loan before title changes hands.

Here are the main questions raised and answered in this chapter:

(1) Why do buyers usually prefer to arrange their own financing, and when might they be interested in retaining their sellers' mortgages?

(2) What exactly does a due-on-sale clause provide?

(3) Can lenders withhold consent at will? What might they require in exchange for their consent?

(4) Why and how did the federal government insulate due-on-sale clauses from all potential legal challenges?

(5) What are exceptional circumstances under federal law when lenders have no choice but to allow buyers to retain their sellers' mortgages?

(6) What is the difference between a successor to the original borrower *assuming* the debt and taking *subject to* it?

(7) Would it ever be a good idea for a buyer, acquiring property subject to a prior recorded mortgage, to conceal the sale from the lender and why might they want to?

(8) Once a purchaser assumes a seller's mortgage, does the seller continue to be liable for the original debt if the purchaser defaults?

(9) What provisions might commercial realty property owners and lenders agree to include in a carefully negotiated due-on-sale clause to serve their respective interests when buyers assume the seller's mortgage?

(10) Can lenders use due-on-sale clauses to prohibit borrowers from incurring mortgage debts junior to theirs? Why would a senior lienor ever object to the borrower placing a junior lien on the property since a junior lien holder is another potential source of repayment for the senior mortgage?

I. When the Property Owner Sells Mortgaged Real Estate

A. Why Most Buyers Want Their Own Loans

Loan Terms. More often than not, realty buyers have no desire to retain their sellers' mortgages. They prefer a new mortgage loan on terms tailored to their own needs with a lender of their own choosing. Anticipating that their mortgage lender will insist upon having a first lien, buyers contract for title free and clear of all existing liens and encumbrances, necessitating the seller's mortgagee to sign a recordable satisfaction, signifying that the mortgage debt was repaid.

Down Payments and Loan-to-Value Ratios. Buyers are disinclined to keep the seller's mortgage in place when increasing property values would result in their having to make a larger down payment than if they opted for a new loan. Suppose the property was worth $1,000,000 years ago when the seller acquired it with a $700,000 purchase money mortgage loan, a loan-to-value ratio of 70%, and a down payment of *$300,000*. If the property is now worth $2,000,000, and the seller had repaid none of the loan principal, the buyer's down payment would be $600,000 on a new loan with a 70% loan-to-value ratio based on the $2,000,000 current value of the property.

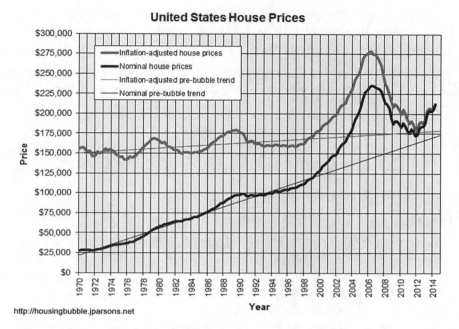

http://housingbubble.jparsons.net

B. When Buyers Could Prefer to Assume Their Seller's Mortgage Loans

Keeping a Below Market Interest Rate. Prevailing interest rates figure prominently in buyers' decisions to take over their seller's mortgage debts. Buyers prefer retaining their seller's loans when current rates are higher, and prefer a new mortgage loan when current rates are lower.

You can see from the chart below that 30-year fixed interest rates peaked in 1981. Since then, buyers seeking to assume their sellers' loans had to have reasons other than bargain interest rates for wanting to do so. If interest rates have now hit rock bottom and start to rise, sellers' loans are going to begin attracting buyers as they did in the late 1970s and early 1980s.

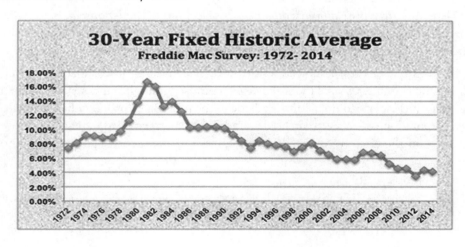

Credit Issues. Another reason buyers sometimes hope to keep their sellers' loans in place is when they have credit problems that could complicate their ability to arrange a new loan at affordable rates.

Avoiding Repayment Fees. The avoidance of steep prepayment penalties incentivizes some buyers and sellers of commercial property to try to retain the seller's mortgage financing.

II. The Content of a Due-on-Sale Clause

A. The Due-on-Sale Clause

Here is the standard due-on-sale clause:

> <u>**Transfer of the Property or a Beneficial Interest in Borrower.**</u> *If all or any part of the Property or any interest in it is sold or transferred (or if a beneficial interest in Borrower is sold or transferred and Borrower is not a natural person) without Lender's prior written consent, Lender may, at its option, require immediate payment in full of all sums secured by this Security Instrument. However, this option shall not be exercised by Lender if exercise is prohibited by federal law as of the date of this Security Instrument*

A Due on Sale Clause Does Not Prohibit or Invalidate a Sale. The lender has no right to impede any sale or transfer of the mortgaged property that the borrower wishes to make—after paying off the mortgage.

The Due-on-Sale Provision Is Optional, Waivable, Not Automatic.[1] Due-on-sale clauses always give lenders the option of waiver for two reasons. There could be times when lenders are willing to allow a buyer to assume the seller's debt and mortgage. In addition, a federal statute preempting state interference with lenders' due-on-sale clauses only applies to clauses worded as options. Worded differently, a due-on-sale clause might not survive a state law-based challenge, specifically, that due-on-sale clauses are unreasonable restraints on alienation (discussed later).

There Are Virtually No Limits on a Lender's Decision to Deny Consent. Because the due-on-sale clause places no explicit limitations on the lender's consent, courts have held that lenders need not offer any "reasonable" justification in denying consent.

In an early case on the subject, a borrower challenged as unreasonable a lender's raising the loan interest rate to market levels because under the circumstances of that transfer, the lender had no credit risk. Title to the mortgaged property had been held by a corporation with a sole shareholder, and was being transferred to that shareholder directly. So the effective ownership and control of the security property had not

---

1. The federal statute defines the term 'due-on-sale' clause to mean "a contract provision which authorizes a lender, at its option, to declare due and payable sums secured by the lender's security instrument if all or any part of the property, or an interest therein, securing the real property loan is sold or transferred without the lender's prior written consent." 12 U.S.C. §1701j-3(a)(1).

changed; the lender's security interest was as good as ever. But the court recognized that due-on-sale clauses are not just about giving lenders a way to limit their credit risks when the mortgaged property changes hands. These clauses also give lenders a chance to fulfill a legitimate business purpose by raising the borrower's interest rate to current market levels.[2]

Lender's Right to Levy a Prepayment Fee After Denial of the Borrower's Request to Assign. Some lenders routinely deny loan assumption requests, hoping the borrower will instead prepay, so they can collect a prepayment fee. Federal law protects homeowners against federally-regulated savings associations charging prepayment fees after the lender calls their loans pursuant to a due-on-sale clause.[3] A few state legislatures[4] and courts[5] have extended similar protections for homeowners.

Commercial mortgage lenders are free to charge their borrowers prepayment fees even when it was the lender that forced the borrower into a situation where it had no choice but to prepay. Due-on-sale clauses in commercial real estate mortgages usually specify that the borrower owes a prepayment fee regardless of how the loan became due and payable, even when the prepayment was involuntary because the lender accelerated the debt following a borrower default, whatever the reason for the default. However, in these "involuntary" prepayment situations, lenders have no right to prepayment fees unless the lender specifically contracted for them.[6]

B. Why and How the Federal Government Insulated Due-on-Sale Clauses from All Potential Legal Challenges

Federal Pre-emption of State Laws Restricting the Use of Due-on-Sale Clauses.

Due-on-sale clauses existed long before the 1970s but until then mortgage lenders rarely said "no" to an assumption request. In general, they were perfectly content to keep mortgage loans on their books as long as they were collecting what was due.

---

2. *Bonady Apartments, Inc. v. Columbia Banking Federal Sav. and Loan Ass'n*, 119 Misc. 2d 923, 465 N.Y.S.2d 150 (Sup 1983), aff'd as modified on other grounds, 99 A.D.2d 645, 472 N.Y.S.2d 221 (4th Dep't 1984).

3. 12 C.F.R. §591.5(b)(2)(I).

4. *See* CAL. CIV. CODE §2954.10 (West 1993). An accelerating obligee "may not claim, exact, or collect any charge, fee, or penalty, for any payment resulting from that acceleration." The statute allows lenders on loans other than those "secured by residential property ... containing four units or less" to enforce their borrowers' waivers of this statutory protection. But waivers after January 1, 1984, "shall be separately signed or initialed by the obligor and its enforcement shall be supported by evidence of a course of conduct by the obligee of individual weight to the consideration in that transaction for the waiver or agreement." *See also* N.Y. REAL PROP. LAW §254-a (McKinney 1989).

5. *In re LHD Realty Corp.*, 726 F.2d 327 (7th Cir. 1984) (prohibiting mortgagee from accelerating on a due-on-sale clause and concurrently levying a prepayment penalty).

6. John C. Murray, Enforceability of Mortgage Due- on- Sale Clauses—An Update (2015), p. 4. *http://www.americanbar.org/content/dam/aba/publishing/rpte_ereport/2015/2-March/enforceability _of_mortgage.authcheckdam.pdf; See also,* Miller & Starr, 5 Cal. Real Est. §13:127 (4th ed.); Robert G. Kimball and Steven M. Goldstein, Enforceability of Prepayment Fees by Commercial Lenders, 27-DEC Ariz. Att'y 12 (1990).

This changed dramatically during times of spiraling price inflation in 1969, 1973-74 and 1980-81.[7] As inflation surged, savers withdrew deposits from savings and loan associations—the main home mortgage financiers at that time—to place their funds in accounts with money market funds. Savings associations could not pay savers the rates that money market funds could offer because they invested in fixed-rate, long-term, low yielding home mortgage loans while money market funds invested in short-term government bonds and triple-A rated corporate debt. Before the recession, money market funds paid savers decent interest rates much higher than savings associations could pay. (Currently, they are paying almost nothing.)

Savings associations were starting to fail in the 1980s. Struggling to improve their cash flows, they began to enforce due-on-sale clauses by conditioning their consent on raising mortgage interest rates to current market levels. Judges understood this: "The 'due-on-sale' clause was a way of eliminating these low-yielding loans as soon as the property was sold, so that it could re-loan the money at current higher rates or negotiate a higher rate in the event the purchaser assumed the existing loan."[8]

Borrowers were distressed. A lender might increase a home mortgage loan written in 1970 at an interest rate of 8.5% to 14.5%-15%, in the early 1980s. These unaffordable rate hikes impaired the value of home equities and impeded home sales.

Homeowners sued, contending that due-on-sale clauses were unreasonable restraints on alienation. Borrowers won only a few of these state court lawsuits.[9] The U.S. Supreme Court held that federally chartered savings associations could enforce due-on-sale clauses free of state imposed limitations.[10] This would have put federally chartered thrifts at a competitive advantage against state chartered ones had Congress not intervened to legitimize all due-on-sale clauses.

The enforceability of due-on-sale clauses attracted Congressional attention because Congress wanted to avert the financial collapse of the savings and loan industry.[11] A collapse would have cost the federal government billions.

Garn-St. Germain Depository Institutions Act.[12] In 1982, Congress came to the aid of all mortgage lenders by enacting a law which broadly preempted most state

---

7. Brad DeLong, *The Inflation of the 1970s: Presentation Notes* (last visited Aug. 12, 2015), http://econ161.berkeley.edu/Econ_Articles/theinflationofthes.html

8. *Community Title Co v. Roosevelt Savings & Loan*, 670 S.W.2d 895 (Mo. App. 1984).

9. *Tucker v. Lassen Savings & Loan Association*, 12 Cal. 3d 629 (1974); *Wellenkamp v. Bank of America, 21 Cal. 3d 943 (1978). See* Grant S. Nelson & Dale A. Whitman, REAL ESTATE TRANSFER, FINANCE, AND DEVELOPMENT 460, text at nn. 5, 6 (4th ed. 1992); Richard C. Maxwell, *The Due-on-Sale Clause: Restraints on Alienation and Adhesion Theory in California*, 28 U.C.L.A. L. REV. 197 (1980).

10. *Fidelity Federal Savings and Loan Association v. De La Cuesta*, 458 U.S. 156 (1982).

11. The right to raise interest rates when houses sold had very little impact on the plight of savings associations. Ultimately, savings associations lost over $150 billion. Since most of their deposits were insured by the Federal Savings and Loan Insurance Corporation (FSLIC), and the losses exceeded the FSLIC reserves, U.S. taxpayers picked up the tab. The right to raise interest rates when houses sold had very little impact on the plight of savings associations.

12. 12 U.S.C. § 1701j-3 et seq. (1982).

law limitations on the exercise of due-on-sale clauses.[13] The Garn-St. Germain Act endowed lenders with the absolute right to enforce due-on-sale clauses in their sole discretion, except in certain limited situations involving home mortgage loans, described later.[14]

The federal law applied broadly to every "loan, mortgage, advance, or credit sale secured by a lien on real property."[15] This law protects every conceivable type of lender including individual sellers, banks and other institutions, and government entities.

C. The Exceptional Circumstances Under Federal Law When Lenders Have No Choice But to Allow Transferees to Retain Existing Mortgages

In the backlash to this legislation, Congress enacted a set of consumer-friendly exceptions, applicable only to liens secured on residential real property containing fewer than five dwelling units.[16]

(1) The creation of a lien or other encumbrance subordinate to the lender's security instrument which does not relate to a transfer of rights of occupancy in the property;[17]

This exception was quite important to commercial banks. They were eager to make home equity loans. 'Home equity' borrowers have already mortgaged their properties. So the home equity loan will be "subordinate to the [first mortgage] lender's security instrument." There was also a consumer rights aspect. Without this exception, homeowners would be denied access to one of their least expensive forms of consumer credit which they might need in order to finance medical emergencies, college tuition

---

13. Banking deregulation forced savings associations to compete with banks for savings deposits. But many savings associations didn't have the funds to compete. They had locked themselves into long-term, fixed rate home mortgage loans at rates of 7-10%. As inflation escalated mortgage rates to 15% and beyond, savings association were eager to increase their portfolio yields by terminating or raising the interest rate on the fixed rate loans in their portfolios. Since that time, savings associations have sought to reduce their interest rate risk by using adjustable rate mortgage loans and selling their fixed rate home mortgage loans shortly after origination.

14. "(1) Notwithstanding any provision of The Constitution or laws (including the judicial decisions) of any state to the contrary, a lender may ... enter into or enforce a contract containing a due-on-sale clause with respect to a real property loan. (2) Except as otherwise provided in subsection (d), the exercise of the lender of its option pursuant to such a clause shall be exclusively governed by the terms of the loan contract, and all rights and remedies of the borrower shall be fixed and governed by the contract." 12 U.S.C. § 1701j-3(b) (1996).

States could 'grandfather' contracts entered or mortgages assumed between the time of a state constitutional, statutory or judicial prohibition against due-on-sale clauses and three years after Garn-St. Germain's enactment, October 15, 1982. 12 U.S.C. § 1701j-3(c).

15. 12 U.S.C. § 1701j-3(d).

16. 12 U.S.C. § 1701j-3d.

17. Some borrowers thought to evade due-on-sale clauses through this exception by selling on installment sale contracts or contracts for deed and then retaining token possession. Federal regulators have made clear that this exception is inapplicable to installment sale contracts and contracts for deed. 12 C.F.R. § 591.2(b) (2001).

for their kids, or financing for a new business. Of course, this exception puts first mortgage lenders at risk because it denies them the right to limit a homeowner's total debt-to-income ratio (DTI) or Combined Loan-to-Value Ratio (CLTV) and the higher the DTI and CLTV, the greater the first mortgage lender's risk of its loan going into default.

(2) The creation of a purchase money security interest for household appliances;

This exception confirmed the rights of appliance vendors to obtain first liens on the appliances they financed.

(3) The granting of a leasehold interest of three years or less not containing an option to purchase;

Without this exception, homeowners who rented their houses for short periods of time without their lenders' prior approval could be forced to pay off their existing mortgage loans. But for this provision, a faculty member, for example, going on sabbatical, would have to secure the approval of her mortgage lender to lease the home for a period as short as a semester or a year.

(4) A transfer by devise, descent or operation of law on the death of a joint tenant or tenant by the entirety;

Without this exception, if a husband and wife held title as joint tenants with right of survivorship, and one of them died, the lender could declare the loan due and payable.[18]

(5) A transfer to a relative resulting from the death of a borrower;

Without this exception, the lender could declare the loan due and payable if a father passed away, leaving his house to his daughter.

(6) A transfer where the spouse or children of the borrower become an owner of the property;

(7) A transfer resulting from a decree of dissolution of marriage, legal separation agreement or from an incidental property settlement agreement, by which the spouse of the borrower becomes an owner of the property;

(8) A transfer into an *inter vivos* trust in which the borrower is and remains a beneficiary and which does not relate to a transfer of rights of occupancy in the property; or

(9) Any other transfer or disposition described in regulations prescribed by the Federal Home Loan Bank Board.[19]

Is Lender Consent Required For Any of These Exceptions? In explaining its rationale for these exceptions, a Senate committee cited hardship situations involving involuntary transfers resulting from death, marriage dissolution and the needs of families

---

18. Sarah Bolling Mancini and Alys Cohen, *Surviving the Borrower: Assumption, Modification, and Access to Mortgage Information After a Death or Divorce,* 43 PEPPERDINE LAW REVIEW (forthcoming 2016).

19. 12 U.S.C. § 1701j-3(d).

to take out second mortgages to send a child to college or finance home improvements. Congress concluded that it would be unfair and inappropriate for a lender to block the new homeowner's assumption of the existing mortgage in any of these circumstances. Hence, for transfers falling within one of the Garn-St. Germain exceptions, mortgage lenders are absolutely prohibited from enforcing their due-on-sale clauses.[20]

Death, Divorce and Loan Assumptions. To appreciate fully the implications of these exceptions upon death or divorce, consider this example: A and B are married. For over a decade they have resided in the same house that A acquired before the couple first met. To finance purchasing the house, A, a successful casting director, had obtained a 30-year, fixed rate mortgage. B was a studio musician with fluctuating earnings. A passed away two months ago, leaving everything including the house to B.

B wants to stay in the house, and feels that she will be able to manage the mortgage payments one way or another, perhaps with the help of family and friends or by selling some of the assets A left to her.

The note and deed of trust on the purchase money mortgage enabling A to buy the house had been signed by A but not by B. A paid most of their expenses and was the major income earner of the pair. The lender has reviewed B's credit situation, and does not believe B qualifies for the loan

Does B have a right to compel the lender to allow her to become an assuming grantee of A's mortgage under Garn-St. Germain whether the lender consents or not?

Suppose the same facts except that A is alive and well but A and B recently divorced. Their settlement agreement gives B title to the house. A wants the bank to remove her from title. Rather than doing that, the lender would prefer for the existing loan to be repaid in full at once. A and B are not interested in trying to obtain a new mortgage. They want the loan transferred to B who is willing to sign an agreement assuming personal liability for the debt, as long as the lender releases A from liability. Under Garn-St. German, does the lender have any lawful choice in the matter? This is the sort of situation where A and B may need legal assistance because many bank officials are unaware of the exceptions to Garn-St. Germaine that are applicable to this situation.

D. Due-on-Sale Clauses That Commercial Realty Lenders and Borrowers Can Live With

The Statutory Exceptions Do Not Apply to Commercial Loans. None of these exceptions apply to loans secured by commercial property.

Legislators rarely confer the benefits of consumer protection laws upon commercial borrowers because they are deemed competent to negotiate their own loan terms.

---

20. Sarah Bolling Mancini and Alys Cohen, *Surviving the Borrower: Assumption, Modification, and Access to Mortgage Information After a Death or Divorce*, 43 Pepperdine Law Review, text at footnotes 122-124 (forthcoming 2016).

Hence, lenders can reserve the option in commercial loans to declare a loan immediately due and payable upon a change in title or possession or the borrower taking out a junior lien.

Applicability of Due-on-Sale Clause When the Borrower Is an Entity; Change of Control Provisions. It has become common for mortgage due-on-sale clauses to contain a "change of control" provision requiring the lender's consent for "direct or indirect" changes in the equity ownership, control or management structure of the mortgagor. Quite often, ownership of the mortgaged property is vested in a special purpose entity (SPE) that owns only the security property, and holds title in a specially formed limited liability company, corporation, or a limited partnership. When ownership is vested like that, a prospective buyer would have the option of purchasing the real estate asset indirectly by acquiring ownership of the entity that holds title. To prevent such transfers from taking place without the lender's consent, most due-on-sale clauses require the lender's consent "if a beneficial interest in Borrower is sold or transferred and Borrower is not a natural person."[21]

This would preclude, for example, any one of the ten members of an LLC that owned an office building from selling or transferring his or her own interest without the lender's consent. This could discourage investors from advancing capital for entities with multiple owners. Often, commercial borrowers and lenders agree to a less restrictive limitation under which the lender's consent is only needed for changes in majority control of the entity,[22] a specified lesser percentage (the provision quoted below allows transfers of up to 25%), or transfers or sales of their interest by named major sponsors or developers on whose talents and resources the lender was principally relying. Provisions like these have become fairly common.[23]

Highlights of a Portfolio Lender's Due-on-Sale Clause. Here are highlights of the features of a due-on-sale clause used by a Los Angeles bank in a long-term mortgage loan secured by a multi-family project.

(1) The lender's consent to a sale, transfer or other conveyance will not be unreasonably withheld provided the request for consent is accompanied by the customary information and application the bank requires at the time of the request, the lender may consider the factors it usually applies for loan assumption requests, the loan and the borrower meet the lender's usual underwriting, regulatory, legal and related requirements at the time.

---

21. This provision might not be covered by the federal pre-emption, leaving its actions open to challenge in a state court. John C. Murray, Enforceability of Mortgage Due- on- Sale Clauses — An Update (2015), p. 10.

22. *See, e.g.*, FHLMC Multifamily Deed of Trust, Assignment of Rents and Security Agreement (Virginia), Version 01-2/15/97: "If borrower is a limited partnership, transfer of a general partnership interest or transfer of limited partnership interest in borrower that would reduce initial owners to less than 51% of all limited partnership shares." A similar 51% rule applies if borrower is a limited liability company, corporation or trust.

23. John C. Murray, Due-On-Sale Clauses: Can They Still Be Challenged?, SP 2002 ALI-ABA 1865 (2008).

(2) The lender may specifically evaluate the financial responsibility, structure, and real estate operations experience of any proposed transferee.

(3) There are no defaults on the loan.

(4) The borrower agrees to pay various prescribed fees including lender's reasonable attorneys' fees and document preparation fees.

(5) The proposed transferee signs an agreement assuming liability under the note, and provides such financing statements and other documents as the lender may require.

(6) The borrower and guarantors, if any, pledge to remain liable on their obligations until the lender releases them from liability in lender's sole discretion.

(7) Certain transfers are freely permitted. These include a transfer of up to 25% of the equity interests, transfers by devise, decent, or operation of law as a result of the death of any person, and transfers for estate planning purposes.

(8) None of the entities or persons liable for repayment of the note shall be released from liability.

(9) If the borrower is an entity, lender is making the loan based on the continued existence, control and ownership of that entity. Borrower will not alter the name, jurisdiction, organization, structure, ownership or control of that entity without the lender's prior consent and will do all things necessary to maintain its continued existence and its continuous right to carry on its business.

The Anomaly of a Lender's Agreement Not to Withhold Consent Unreasonably. The provision quoted above also required that the lender exercise its consent reasonably, not to withhold consent unreasonably. Not defining "reasonable" or "unreasonable" can be a fertile source of future dispute.

One court held that a due-on-sale clause that the lender could only invoke "reasonably" was too uncertain, indefinite, and vague to be enforced because it provided no guidelines for what would count as a "reasonable" basis for the lender denying consent.[24] Generally, the lender wants to satisfy itself that the new owner is as competent, honest, and financially secure as the one it is replacing.

On whether a lender can condition consent on its increasing the interest rate to current market levels, most courts have decided that would be reasonable.[25] A few have decided otherwise.[26] To be on the safe side, a due-on-sale clause requiring the

---

24. *Patel v. Gingrey,* 196 Ga. App. 203, 205-06 (1990).

25. *See, e.g., Torgerson-Forstrom H.I. of Willmar, Inc. v. Olmstead Fed. Sav. & Loan Ass'n,* 339 N.W.2d 901 (Minn. 1983) (as condition to approving assumption, lender increasing loan amount by 2% to current market level of 11 3/8% held reasonable under due-on-sale clause that lender would not unreasonably withhold consent to buyer assuming original obligor's note).

26. John C. Murray, *Due-on-Sale Clauses: Can They Still Be Challenged?,* 17 PRAC. REAL EST. LAWYER 7, 11 (July 2001); *Newman v. Troy Sav. Bank,* 64 F.2d 52 (5th Cir. 1981) (transfer fee of one percent held unreasonable when no language in mortgage authorized an assumption fee).

lender's reasonable consent will specify an increased interest rate or a transfer fee as reasonable.[27]

III. Transfers of Existing Mortgages

A. The Assumption Process

Lenders Are Free to Apply Their Customary Underwriting Standards in Deciding Whether to Allow the Buyer to Assume the Seller's Loan. When realty buyers wish to assume their seller's mortgages or deeds of trust, they condition their obligation to acquire the property on their receiving the consent of the seller's lender, usually as part of the escrow or closing process.

Generally, in deciding whether to allow a loan to be assumed, lenders are free to apply their customary underwriting procedures, and often do, requiring a loan application from the buyer, a property appraisal to make sure the loan is within current loan-to-value ratio standards, a credit report, and similar documentation.

In exchange for granting approval, lenders levy origination fees to cover the costs of the paperwork, increase below market interest rates to current market levels (or sometimes a bit more), and update the loan terms to its current standards.

Commercial Loans. For the buyer and seller, the process is always "a trip to the dentist," according to real estate broker Kevin Shannon. If all goes well, the lender issues a conditional approval letter based on its scrutiny and approval of the various closing documents and exhibits.[28]

Commercial mortgage lenders will often withhold consent unless they are satisfied that the current net operating income from the property is within the parameters of their current debt service coverage ratios (DSCR). In addition, they may increase borrower reserve requirements if they believe the reserves are inadequate for replacing major components of the project such as elevators, roofing, and HVAC systems.

There are no judicially enforceable time limits on how long a mortgage lender can take to make its decision of whether to grant or deny the borrower's request, even though a delay could cause the buyer or seller to lose their right to enforce their purchase and sale contract for exceeding a "time of the essence" performance deadline in the current contract.

The mortgage lender could go farther and insist on personal guarantees of the debt from the principals acquiring the property, increase reserve requirements to cover anticipated major replacements of building components, or even institute a *"lock box."*

---

27. John C. Murray, *Enforceability of Mortgage Due-On-Sale Clauses-An Update*, AMERICAN BAR. ORG, 1, 6-8 (last visited Aug. 12, 2015), http://www.americanbar.org/content/dam/aba/publishing/rpte_ereport/2015/2-March/enforceability_of_mortgage.authcheckdam.pdf

28. CMSA/MBA Assumption Task Force Report, October 2007. Once the borrower has submitted all the requisite documents (this takes on average 38 days), the assumption is typically approved within 30 days.

(A lock box is an arrangement for all the rents to be placed into a lender-controlled account from which the lender first disburses its loan payments to itself, then pays all verified operating expenses, and finally remits what is left to the borrower.)

Residential Loans. Sometimes, lenders may institute impound accounts which obligate buyers to include, along with their monthly mortgage payments, pro-rated sums out of which the lender will pay property taxes and insurance premiums on the borrower's behalf when these obligations fall due.

Lenders also insist upon grantees signing agreements promising personally to repay the debt. These are called assumption agreements. Once an assumption agreement is executed, lenders customarily provide a written release of the original borrower from any personal liability under the note and deed of trust.

Formalities. The formalities necessary for the buyer to become an assuming grantee vary from state to state. In most jurisdictions, including New York and California, the agreement to assume must be in writing. New York also requires that the writing state the amount assumed, and the writing be signed and acknowledged at the time of the conveyance.[29]

In California, the assumption agreement must be signed by the assuming grantee or appear in the conveyance itself (which is not signed, ordinarily, by the grantee).[30]

Even in the absence of a writing, courts will usually admit parol evidence to establish that an assumption was truly intended, although some courts require "clear and convincing" evidence of it.[31] Oral promises to pay debts fall outside the Statute of Frauds and are admissible in court despite the parol evidence rule.

B. The Difference Between a Successor Assuming the Debt and Taking Subject to It

When a buyer acquires realty with full knowledge of an existing mortgage lien, either by virtue of actual knowledge or constructive notice via the public land records, she is said to take title "subject to" the mortgage.

The penalty for not keeping up mortgage payments could be foreclosure and eventual eviction. This is because in the security instrument–whether a mortgage or deed of trust–the secured lender will have reserved the right to declare all the debt due and payable if there is a default in any of the loan terms, and will also have reserved the right to initiate foreclosure if the borrower does not repay the full balance due on the entire accelerated debt.

The note contains all the financial details—the amount borrowed, the interest rate, the amortization period, and so on. The deed of trust only references the note; it does not re-state any of the payment terms. It pertains to the security property, its

---

29. N.Y. Gen. Oblig. Law § 5-705 (McKinney 2001).
30. Cal. Civ. Code § 1624(a)(6) (West 1998).
31. *Cassidy v. Bonitatibus*, 497 A.2d 1018, 5 Conn. App. 240 (1985).

maintenance, the payment of property taxes, and the right of the lender to foreclose if there is a default on the note.

A grantee who acquires title "subject to" the mortgage does not sign the note, and has hence not agreed to repay the mortgage debt personally.

A grantee assumes the debt by signing the note, or promising the seller that she will repay the debt. Even if the grantee (the buyer) only makes the promise of payment to the grantor (the seller), the lender has the right to enforce that promise. The grantee has become the primary obligor by promising to pay off the grantor's mortgage debt. Because the grantor remains liable to the lender on the original note, the grantor is a surety until the debt is paid.

The practical difference between an assuming grantee and a "subject to" grantee pertains to deficiency liability. A deficiency occurs when the mortgage lender is still owed money after applying the proceeds from a foreclosure sale to the repayment of the debt.

Suppose the grantee stops paying the debt when the lender is still owed $400,000. Eventually, the lender will foreclose, and the property will be sold at public auction. Later, the lender can initiate a procedure to eject the grantee from the property.

Lenders can bid the debts they are owed at a foreclosure sale. If the lender bids $400,000 for the property, by definition there is no deficiency.

If the lender stands aside, and a third party places the highest bid of, say, $300,000, there will be a $100,000 deficiency. The lender will then be in a position to obtain a judgment against an assuming grantee for $100,000. (The lender could attempt to collect on its own or hire a collection agency.)

Beware of Becoming a 'Subject to' Grantee Without the Mortgagee's Consent. Promoters of 'get rich quick in real estate' schemes tout 'subject to' buying and assure their audiences that they don't need the mortgage lender's prior approval. Nor do they need to submit a loan application and meet the credit lender's standards for loan approval. They will incur no loan closing costs, and these transactions won't impact their credit ratings because they are not assuming the loans.[32]

Other bloggers encourage buyers not to worry too much about due-on-sale clauses because the sanctions for violation are not that serious.

They make their case like this: There is no "due on sale" jail. Transferring title to a property secured by a due-on-sale mortgage is not illegal. There is no federal or state law which makes it a crime to violate a due-on-sale clause.

"If the lender discovers the transfer, it may at its option, declare a default, and call the loan due and payable. If the loan is not fully repaid, the lender has the option of

---

32. Matthew S. Chan, The TurnKey Investor's 'Subject to' Mortgage Handbook (last visited Aug. 12, 2015), www.turnkeyinvesting.com

commencing foreclosure proceedings. So the real question is: Are you willing to take a property subject to a mortgage containing a 'due on sale' clause with the risk of getting caught?"[33]

There is a pretty good chance that the lender will learn that the property has been sold without its consent. Mortgage lenders have many ways to learn about a sale the mortgagor and the mortgagor's grantee are trying to hide. The easiest way is when the seller's deed is recorded. Mortgage lenders hire title companies and other service providers to inform them of any changes in ownership of properties on which they hold mortgages.

Lenders will also be informed when the seller's insurance policy is cancelled or the name of the insured is changed. Mortgage lenders are named as the co-insured on these policies and keep close watch over them. Insurance companies will report to the lender any change in the name of the insured, or any premium delinquency. If the monthly mortgage payments come from anyone except the original obligor on the note, the loan servicer could sound an alarm.

A grantee who does not insist upon recording its deeds is unusually trusting or completely naïve to allow title to remain in the grantors' name, to make their monthly mortgage loan checks payable to their grantors, and trust their grantors to promptly remit those payments from their own personal accounts on their grantees' behalf.

As if this were not enough, conspiring to violate a lender's due-on-sale clause can constitute common law fraud and is a statutory infringement in some states. Brokers advising buyers and sellers to evade these clauses have been sanctioned by statute and regulators in some states.

From a Blogger on Bigger Pockets: "I wanted to share a recent experience. I recently received a letter from one of my lenders (Flagstar bank) calling out a deed transfer I made around 2-3 years ago. I transferred a deed via quitclaim from my name into an LLC. The loan was secured in my name as it was one of my first 4 Fannie loans. They noticed that I had added my LLC to my insurance. They first demanded that my insurance carrier change the named insured back into my name. Then I received a letter invoking the due on sale clause with a copy of the deed. They are giving me 30 days to transfer it back from the LLC into my name and change the insurance accordingly. They will not accept mortgage payments in the meantime.

I've made every payment on time with no issues. All you hear is that the bank will never call the due on sale clause. Well it does happen."[34]

---

33. William Bronchick, *How to Beat the Due On Sale Clause*, CREONLINE (last visited Nov. 8th, 2015), http://www.creonline.com/beat-the-due-on-sale-clause.html

34. Serge S, *Due On Sale Clause Was Called By Bank*, BIGGERPOCKETS.COM (last visited Nov. 8th, 2015), https://www.biggerpockets.com/forums/311/topics/183825-due-on-sale-clause-was-called-by-bank

C. Personal Liability of Assuming Grantee Whose Grantor Was Not Personally Liable

Suppose that A sells property to B, extracting a promise from B to 'assume and agree to pay' A's mortgage obligation. That would make sense if A were personally liable on the note. As a matter of common law, A would be a surety for B if A had been personally liable for the mortgage debt. But consider the case in which A's loan was a nonrecourse loan. Could the mortgage lender hold B personally liable for a deficiency as an assuming grantee if A had no stake in whether B defaulted?

Some courts have answered this question with a resounding 'no' — California and New York among them. They figure that A just made a mistake in requiring B to repay a debt for which A had no personal liability. Enforcing B's promise to A would confer a pure windfall on the lender, absent proof of specific consideration for B's assumption of liability.

Other courts, probably in the majority, see in the A to B sale itself ample consideration for B's promise to pay the mortgage debt. A might have extracted that promise from B to honor an on-going relationship with the lender and safeguard A's reputation as a person who always makes sure his debts are paid whether legally obligated to pay them or not. Courts hold B liable, explaining: "A person should do that which he or she promises to do."[35]

In these jurisdictions, even if the original obligor possessed a good defense against the originating lender, the assuming grantee would be denied the right to invoke that defense–including fraud or duress perpetrated by the lender in making the loan. Similarly, courts in these jurisdictions would deny an assuming grantee the benefit of the grantor's nonrecourse status in defending against the lender's claim for a deficiency.

D. Personal Liability of the Seller (Grantor) After Deeding the Property

The Seller Becomes the Buyer's Surety Absent a Release from the Lender or if the Buyer Had Signed a Nonrecourse Note. Most borrowers will have obligated themselves to repay the debt by signing a note acknowledging the receipt or benefit of the borrowed funds and promising to repay. The obligor remains liable for payment even after selling the security property unless discharged by the mortgage lender.

By well-established judicial precedent, grantees are only secondarily liable to pay the lender if the grantee defaults. It will usually come as a surprise when a mortgage lender contacts a former borrower with whom the lender last had contact many years ago, and requests payment on a mortgage secured by a home the original home borrower sold so long ago they can hardly remember their buyer's name.

---

35. *Somers v. Avant*, 261 S.E.2d 334, 336, 244 Ga. 460, 463 (1979). *See also* Restatement (Third) of Property, Mortgages, § 5.1 (c)(1) (1997) ("Mortgagees rights against transferee ... exist whether or not the transferor is personally liable on the obligation secured by the mortgage.").

Grantees, when they signed their original mortgage and note, may have lived in a state where a deficiency judgment would have been allowed for the type of mortgage loan they obtained, for example, a purchase money loan taken by the seller. Then, they relocated to a state where a seller making a purchase money loan would be barred from pursuing a deficiency claim against them. Their rights in this situation would probably be governed by the laws of the state where the security property is located, and where they resided at the time they incurred the mortgage debt.

Equitable Subrogation. Prudent grantors insist that mortgage lenders formally release them of any obligation on mortgage debts once the mortgage lender enters an agreement with a grantee to assume the debt.

Suppose the seller never obtained a release and decided to pay off the debt for her own grantee. By the doctrine of equitable subrogation, the seller would then acquire the lender's rights against the grantee to sue on the note, foreclose or both. The seller also has a good legal claim against the grantee directly for reimbursement or, in some states, for a court ordering the grantee to pay the debt directly to the lender (called exoneration).

E. Personal Liability of the Successive Grantees After Deeding the Property

Imagine a situation in which property subject to a mortgage is sold by A to B and then by B to C. A and B assumed the loan. C took subject to it, defaulted and filed bankruptcy.

The foreclosing lender was still owed money on the debt, having received less than the unpaid balance due on the mortgage. The lender sought a deficiency.

Since C was never personally liable on the debt and is bankrupt, the mortgagee eyes A and B as possible payees. Both of them had assumed the debt. Does the mortgagee have the option of pursuing either or both of them? Are A and B co-sureties, jointly and severally liable?

This was the question the court answered persuasively in *Swanson v. Krenik.*[36] The court explained that personal liability for the mortgage debt falls to grantees in the inverse order by which they assumed the debt. Hence, B becomes liable for what C doesn't pay. And A is only a surety for B, but not for the debts of C. There is an easy-to- follow logic at work here. After all, B made the decision to sell to C. A had no say in the matter, "no real influence over their grantee's decision to convey the property to a second grantee, or over the selection of that grantee."[37]

In a carefully executed commercial realty transaction, the same result would be fashioned by B obtaining a promise of indemnification from C, and A, a promise of indemnification from B.

---

36. 868 P.2d 297 (Alaska 1994).
37. 868 P. 2d at 300-301.

IV. The Right of the Lender to Prevent the Borrower from further Encumbering the Security Property

Due-on-Encumbrance Clause Defined. A due-on-encumbrance clause gives the lender the right to declare the entire unpaid balance of the debt due and payable if the borrower takes out a loan secured by the same property without the lender's prior written consent.

When loan documents only contain a due-on-sale clause, but make no mention of 'encumbrances,' lenders argue that a 'sale' includes an encumbrance since the very point of any security instrument is to give the lender the right to sell the property in the event of default. On the other hand, borrowers argue that lenders should be required to reserve that right expressly, and not be able to piggyback an implied due-on-encumbrance prohibition into a standard due-on-sale clause.

Federal Due-on-Encumbrance Preemption for Homeowners Does Not Extend to Commercial Borrowers. As we saw in the first of the exceptions to due-on-sale enforceability in the Garn-St. Germain Depository Institutions Act, Congress voted to protect homeowners by prohibiting lenders from declaring their mortgages due and payable if a borrower created a lien or encumbrance subordinate to theirs but figured commercial borrowers could look out for themselves. "Most lawyers believe this confirms that the Act permits enforcement of due on encumbrance clauses covering commercial property but the language of the Act is not clear."[38]

Why Senior Lienors Could Object to Junior Lien Debt. At first glance it is hard to see why a senior lender would object to a borrower taking on junior secured debt. The junior lender becomes an additional potential source of repayment to avert a foreclosure of the senior lien which would wipe out the junior lienor's security interest. Anyway, borrowers denied the right to incur secured debt could borrow unsecured credit. This will be more costly and thus could actually increase the senior lienor's ultimate credit risk by over burdening the mortgagor.

Consider the situation of a homeowner who seeks to raise cash for a small business. She could borrow against a second mortgage on the equity in her house at a rate of interest of 8% or run up the charges on her credit cards at 18%. Her debt-to-income ratio will be far greater when she borrowers at 18%, thus increasing the chance that she will default across the board on all her loans.

Ironically, in good times when real estate values are on the rise, many first mortgage lenders see no problem with their borrowers taking on junior secured debt. Sometimes, they are eager to make those risky loans themselves to increase their yields.

Generally, though, mortgage lenders are wary of debtors taking on junior secured debt. A borrower's equity stake in the mortgaged property is reduced commensurately

---

38. Alan Wayte, *Selected Issues in the Negotiation of Real Estate Financing Documents*, SN001 ALI-ABA 1041 (2007).

as is the commercial property owner's incentive to 'mind the store' instead of focusing their attention on projects in which they still have substantial equity stakes.

Further, mortgage investors in bonds backed by senior mortgages are quite sensitive to a borrower's combined loan-to-value ratio—just as they are concerned about a borrower's total debt-to-income ratio, not just the amount of the first lien. A borrower who is about to lose her property because she cannot afford to make payments on her first and second mortgages is likely to default on both.

Legal Complications of Junior Liens for Senior Lienors. Legally, there are many ways in which a junior lienor can impact the rights of a senior mortgagee:

(1) If the junior mortgagee files bankruptcy, this will automatically result in the senior mortgage lender not being able to enforce its rights without the prior consent of the bankruptcy court.

(2) The junior mortgagee's vote in favor of a bankrupt debtor's reorganization plan could be decisive in forcing the plan upon an unwilling senior mortgagee.

(3) A foreclosing junior mortgagee could inadvertently discharge a tenant of its lease.

(4) If the borrower neglected to pay property taxes and insurance premiums as all mortgages and deeds of trust require mortgagors to do, the junior lienor might decide to avert the senior mortgage lender foreclosing by making those payments on the mortgagor's behalf. To the extent a junior lienor makes those payments on the borrower's behalf, the junior lienor would have a lien against the property that is superior to the lien of the senior mortgagee.

(5) Refinancing becomes more difficult if the junior lienor will not subordinate to the refinanced first lien.

(6) The junior lienor may have a first lien on improvements made after the first mortgage was recorded but before the junior lien became effective.

(7) To head off an imminent foreclosure resulting from a declining rent roll, the senior lienor may need the junior lienor's approval to relax the borrower's loan obligations, or consent to the senior lienor adding to its senior loan additional funds it is willing to advance for a refurbishment.

Credit Agencies, Junior Liens and Intercreditor Agreements. Credit rating agencies which evaluate securitized mortgage obligations disapprove of borrowers incurring junior lien financing. Bond ratings are based on the likelihood of default which rises as borrowers have less "skin in the game" (equity) to lose. Rating agencies are very sensitive to "combined" loan-to-value ratios that take into account junior liens. In rating commercial mortgage backed securities, they consider the combined mortgage indebtedness relative to the value of the security property and the debt service coverage ratios on all secured debt. They also look for documentation that the junior lienor had pledged not to terminate any leases without the senior lender's prior consent.[39]

---

39. Patricia Frobes & Frank Crance, *Anticipating the Future in Loan Documentation*, 18 Prac. Real Est. Lawyer 41, 55 (March 2002).

Typically, the creditors of a common debtor allocate among themselves credit risks, consequences of default and bankruptcy through intercreditor agreements.[40] In these agreements, junior lienors are pressed to surrender many of their rights and remedies following the debtor's default or bankruptcy. They also promise to be bound by extensions and modifications of the senior debt, and to receive no payments and enforce no rights without the senior lienor's prior consent. In exchange, the junior lienor will seek the right to notice if the mortgagor defaults on the senior lien, and the opportunity to cure the default and purchase the senior debt.[41]

Questions

Question 1: *Why Buyers of Mortgaged Property Ever Want to Assume the Seller's Loan.*

Most realty purchasers arrange their own acquisition financing. Why are some buyers eager to keep the seller's financing in place while other purchasers prefer to start from scratch obtaining their own loans?

Question 2: *Factors that Buyers and Sellers Consider in Deciding Whether the Buyer Should Assume the Seller's Mortgage.*

In March, 2014, Seller acquired a condo for $240,000, paying $40,000 down and obtaining a $200,000 mortgage loan, fixed rate interest, fully amortized, 30-year maturity at 3.95%. Four years later, February, 2018, the buyer contracted to sell the condo for $300,000. Prevailing mortgage interest rates on fixed rate, fully amortized loans had risen to 7.6%.

(a) Would it be a good idea for the buyer to assume or take subject to the seller's loan?

(b) If so, would the buyer be well advised to learn whether the seller's note and mortgage had a due-on-sale clause?

(c) Would it be good or bad news for the buyer if there were no due-on-sale clause in the seller's note and deed of trust?

(d) What would the lender probably require before granting consent for the buyer to assume the seller's loan under a due on sale clause?

Question 3: *Mortgage Lenders and Assuming Grantees.*

(a) Why do most mortgage lenders balk at the prospect of their borrowers being free to sell the security property without their consent?

---

40. George H. Singer, *The Lender's Guide to Second-Lien Financing*, Banking Law Journal 199–200 (last visited Aug. 11 2015), http://www.lindquist.com/files/Publication/0611cf1d-72f4-4b32-a5ec-00d521026e0f/Presentation/PublicationAttachment/964a8361-687c-47a5-aa66-0726c43fe20c/The%20Lenders%20Guide%20to%20Second%20Lien%20Financing.pdf

41. A popular structural variant for a senior-subordinate loan scenario for large commercial loans is the A/B Note. Two promissory notes with a single borrower are secured by the same deed of trust or mortgage. The senior note is meant to be securitized and the subordinate B note to be sold to a third party. The lenders' rights including the allocation of loan payments are detailed in an A/B Co-Lender Agreement. Both loans are usually serviced by the A note holder. See David M Linder and Hilary M. Roxburgh, *B Note Purchases*, SM100 ALI-ABA 585 (2007).

(b) What rationale could there be for the common law default rule that buyers have the right to sell the security property subject to the mortgage without the lender's prior consent? The lender made the loan on the understanding that the original borrower signing the note would be the one obligated to repay it, and that original borrower remains personally liable to repay the debt.

Question 4: *The Lender's Remedy Under a Due-on-Sale Clause.*

(a) What remedy does the lender typically reserve under a due-on-sale clause if a borrower transfers an interest in the security property without the lender's prior consent?

(b) If a lender agrees to be "reasonable" in denying consent to a loan assumption request, what specific items should the lender include in the drafted due-on-sale clause to be sure it can properly underwrite the loan, modify the loan terms to current norms, and levy fees sufficient to recoup its costs.

Question 5: *The Implication for the Buyer of Assuming the Seller's Debt.*

B buys a house from A for $250,000, and assumes A's loan. A's loan balance on the date of sale is $175,000. Two years later, B sells to C who also assumes the unpaid balance on A's loan, now $171,000. C loses his job and defaults on the loan. A's lender forecloses. The balance of the debt is $170,000 at the date of foreclosure. At the foreclosure sale the highest bid is:

(1) *$190,000*

(2) $150,000

(a) In which of these situations will C find himself worse off for having 'assumed' instead of taken 'subject to' the debt?

(b) Does A have any exposure here, and, if so, is there anything A can do about it?

(c) Suppose that C had assumed A's note though B had taken title 'subject to' it. Would C be personally liable on the A note even though B had not been?

Question 6: *LLCs and the Due-on-Sale Clause.*

(a) If title to a mortgaged warehouse was held by a specially formed single member LLC, would a typical FNMA/FHLMC form due-on-sale clause in the mortgage, read literally, prevent an LLC member from selling its membership interest in the LLC without the mortgagee's prior written consent?

(b) A blogger recently wrote: "I have 4 rental properties financed through 3 different mortgage companies. 2 of the 3 told me today that they would call the mortgage due if I transfer the property to an LLC." What advice would you offer the blogger based on your reading of the standard due-on-sale clause?

Question 7: *Federal Regulatory Limitations on the Use of Due-on-Sale Provisions.*

(a) A faculty member on sabbatical leases his house for a year. Does the federal statute permit the lender to enforce a due-on-sale clause and declare the entire debt due and payable because of the one-year lease?

(b) What if the lease came with an option to buy at the end of the year?[42]

(c) Parents get a divorce. Mom gets title to the house. Dad, retired, gets title to what had been their vacation house. Lender learns dad is no longer on title to the primary residence, and demands Mom pay the full loan balance. Can the lender lawfully do this?

(d) Husband dies and leaves his share of the security property, a 10-unit apartment house, to his wife. Is she subject to a due-on-sale acceleration?

(e) Homeowner takes out a home equity loan. May the mortgagee holding a first mortgage on her house exercise a due-on-sale acceleration?

(f) The owner of a 30-unit apartment house takes out a loan secured by a second mortgage. Can the owner's first mortgagee invoke a due-on-sale clause and accelerate?

(g) An investor in distress properties convinces a defaulting homeowner to avoid the credit impairment and embarrassment of an imminent foreclosure by conveying legal title to the investor in trust for the benefit of the borrower, so that the investor can attempt to market the property before the borrower's interest is lost through foreclosure. Is this transaction protected from due-on-sale acceleration?

Question 8: *Due-on-Encumbrance Clauses.*

(a) What three little words could be inserted into a standard due-on-sale clause to make clear that the clause would apply if the debtor further encumbered the already mortgaged property?

(b) Why do you suppose Congress freed homeowners to obtain junior lien financing without the consent of their senior lienors and did not extend the same privilege to commercial realty borrowers?

(c) What objections could a senior lienor of commercial rental realty ever have to one of its successful owner retail operators obtaining junior lien financing?

(d) An investor buys AAA rated residential mortgage backed bonds. The underlying assets are 300 mortgages each secured by first liens on houses worth $1,000,000 or more, with initial loan-to-value ratios no greater than 70%. Why would the bond investors or the credit rating agency that had conferred the AAA rating care if one or more of the borrowers obtained second mortgages?

---

42. *See Auernheimer v. Metzen*, 780 P.2d 796, 98 Or. App. 722 (1989) (an option was held to be a transfer when granted). Nelson and Whitman question the result: "Can this be correct? Is an option an interest in land?" Nelson & Whitman, *supra* note 21, at 471. Such disputes seldom arise, according to real estate columnist Robert J. Bruss. When asked by a reader if entering into a lease with an option to buy would "trigger the mortgage due-on-sale clause," Mr. Bruss replied: I've never heard of a lender enforcing a due-on-sale clause just because the property owner signs a lease-option with a tenant. How would the lender learn you entered into a lease-option? It just doesn't happen if the mortgage payments are made on time." Los Angeles Times, March 21, 2004, p. K5, col. 1.

Chapter 15

Mortgage Foreclosure[1]

Scope of the Chapter

Because the quintessential remedy of secured creditors is foreclosure, this chapter on mortgage foreclosure begins by analyzing the differences between secured and unsecured debt. We contrast the remedial options of an unsecured creditor to those available to a lender secured by a mortgage or deed of trust.

Then we turn to the way that residential and commercial real estate is financed to identify the position of the mortgage lender among the different types of debt and equity used to finance real estate. These relationships are depicted by what is known as a capital stack.[2] Typically the safest position in the capital stack is occupied by mortgage lenders because they have to right by foreclosing to remove all other claims to property pledged as security for a real estate venture.

The process of foreclosure is bounded by the terms of the mortgage or deed of trust being foreclosed, state statutes, and common law norms. We outline this process step-by-step.

The interests of junior lienors are wiped out by a senior mortgagee lender foreclosing. A section of the chapter describes the predicament and options available to a junior lienor when a borrower defaults on an obligation secured by a senior mortgage.

Then, we consider how a landlord's mortgage lender's foreclosure impacts tenants' leases. Does the foreclosure terminate the lease? Tenants often enter agreements with their landlord's mortgage lenders to answer this question in documents called Subordination and Non-Disturbance Agreements (SNDA), defined this section.

There are various ways for mortgage lenders and defaulting borrowers to avert often disruptive and costly foreclosures. These include loan modifications, forbearance, short sales, work-outs, and deeds in lieu of foreclosure, compared in a section on alternatives to foreclosure.

---

1. The author is grateful to the following who appeared in USC law classes as guest experts on mortgage lending and foreclosure and whose observations contributed to the material in this chapter: Brian Angel, Steve Dailey, Jon Daurio Derik Lewis, Ryan McBride, Kevin Miller, Rowan Sbaiti, Jesse Sharf, David Sotolov, Brian Weinhart, Pamela Westhoff, and Jan Zemanek.
2. http://recappartners.co/the-capital-stack/ (Last visited 06/23/2016).

The concluding section is about the ways of investing in distress real estate and mortgage loans in default.

I. Personal Judgments

Unsecured Creditors and Debt Collection. To compare the difference between the remedies of unsecured and unsecured creditors when debtors default, consider how unsecured creditors collect on bad debts, say, a credit card issuer. Suppose a card holder missed a couple of monthly payments. The issuer will probably begin by calling the card holder, with follow-up calls continuing for 90 days or so. Next, the issuer will send demand letters. Often, credit card issuers sell unpaid debts to collection agencies. The collection agency will try phone calls and demand letters, too, typically more aggressive than the credit card issuer. The debtor may be able to negotiate a settlement at a lower amount than the full debt, sometimes even for pennies on the dollar, payable in a lump sum or installments. That failing, at some point, the issuer or the collection agency could file suit. Unless the debtor asserts a good defense, the suit will end with the collection agency or creditor obtaining a court judgment ordering the debtor to pay up.

Under the The Fair Debt Collection Practices Act (FDCPA), debt collectors must begin the collection process by making an accurate statement of the amount owed and offer to validate or prove the accuracy of the creditor's claim within 30 days. If they neglect to do this, debtors have the right to make a Demand for Validation of Debt. The collector must then offer the debtor proof of the creditor's claim before proceeding with its collection effort.

The FDCPA was designed to curb misleading and harassing practices by debt collectors. Any consumer debtor who owes money on a credit card, personal loan, or home mortgage is entitled to be treated fairly and without harassment. Under the statute, the debtor has certain protections concerning how and when the creditor can contact the debtor, and what the creditor can and cannot say.

The FDCPA applies to debt collectors, though not to original creditors or mortgage servicers who were collecting payments on the loan before default. Nor does the statue apply to actions by foreclosing trustees or landlords evicting tenants who are not classified as debt collectors under this law.

Securing an Unsecured Lien. With a court-issued judgment against the debtor in hand, unless the debtor pays up or the creditor and debtor work out a settlement, the creditor or collection agency will need to "execute on the judgment."[3] To do this, they need to identify specific debtor-owned assets that could include bank accounts, wages, real or personal property. The court will require the debtor to provide a Statement of Assets.

---

3. Ralph Warner, Collecting From a Judgment Debtor: Wage Garnishment, Property Liens, and Bank Account Levys. http://www.nolo.com/legal-encyclopedia/free-books/small-claims-book/chapter24-6.html (Last visited 06/25/2016).

If those assets include a bank account, the creditor will obtain a court order instructing an officer of the court (for example, the sheriff) to levy (seize) debtor property by making demand upon an appropriate official at the bank. The levy compels the bank to transfer assets from the debtor's deposited funds to the creditor, subject to certain statutory limits. Also, in most states, the creditor can "garnish" the debtor's wages through a court order served on the debtor's employer to remit a portion of the debtor's wages to the creditor, also limited by a percentage, usually less than 25%, of the debtor's net wages.

Judgment creditors may impose liens on the debtor's personal and real property. Procedures for perfecting these liens vary by state.[4] In California, the creditor obtains a lien on the debtor's *personal property* by filing a Notice of Judgment Lien with the California Secretary of State.[5] The creditor perfects a lien against any *real property* the debtor owns or acquires by obtaining an abstract of the judgment against the debtor from the court that issued it, and then recording that abstract in any county where the debtor owns or later acquires property.[6]

The creditor's previously unsecured judgment becomes secured at the moment that the creditor records an abstract of the judgment with the county recorder. Collecting upon that lien does not necessarily involve much effort or expense if the creditor is patient. The reason is simply this. If ever the debtor attempts to sell or finance the property, any buyer or mortgage lender would insist upon all liens against the debtor's real property being released of record. The escrow agent or attorney processing the transaction will seek the creditor's signed release in exchange for the judgment being paid. Otherwise, the creditor's judgment would be superior to the buyer's or lender's interests in the debtor's real property, having been recorded before they acquired their interests in the debtor's real property.[7]

Timing Is the Difference Between the Rights of Secured and Unsecured Creditors. Returning to our credit card example, assume that the card holder owns a house and

---

4. For a state-by-state list of real property lien procedures, see https://www.nolo.com/legal-encyclopedia/collect-court-judgment-with-real-30038.html (Last visited 06/25/2016).

5. Cal. Civ. Proc. §§ 697.510-697.670.

6. Cal. Civ. Proc. § 697.310. (a) Except as otherwise provided by statute, a judgment lien on real property is created under this section by recording an abstract of a money judgment with the county recorder.

(b) Unless the money judgment is satisfied or the judgment lien is released, subject to Section 683.180 (renewal of judgment), a judgment lien created under this section continues until 10 years from the date of entry of the judgment.

7. *Diamond Heights Village Ass'n, Inc. v. Financial Freedom Senior Funding Corp.*, 196 Cal. App. 4th 290, 302–303, 126 Cal. Rptr. 3d 673 (1st Dist. 2011). A homeowner's association obtained a default judgment against a condo unit owner for unpaid maintenance assessments. Its attempts to foreclose its lien were frustrated by the debtor repeatedly filing bankruptcy petitions. Eventually, the debtor obtained a reverse mortgage secured by the condo. The mortgagee took free of the HOA's abstract of judgment, having had neither actual nor constructive notice of the judgment because the HOA had never recorded it.

the creditor would prefer being paid now instead of not having to wait for the debtor to sell or refinance the house.

By following state-mandated procedures, the creditor can "foreclose." This process takes many months and requires a good deal of paperwork on the creditor's part.[8] The creditor begins by obtaining a court-issued writ of execution for the sheriff to sell the debtor's house.

The timing of lien priorities matters greatly because the sale proceeds will be distributed to lien creditors in order of priority, including mortgage lenders who recorded before the judgment creditor recorded its abstract of judgment. The liens of judgment creditors who never bothered to record their abstracts of judgment will date back to when the sheriff places a Writ of Levy in the public land records where the property is located.

Mortgage Lender Deficiency Judgments. In most states, not only do mortgage lenders have the right to foreclose. They have the option of obtaining personal judgments against borrowers. "In what are known as recourse states, if the lender forecloses and the foreclosure sale does not yield an amount sufficient to cover the borrower's outstanding debt balance, the lender may file for a deficiency judgment against the borrower to make-up the difference."[9] For instance, of the 4,500,000 foreclosures that took place in 2011, lenders could obtain deficiency judgments in 64.5% of the cases, saddling them with debts that could last a life-time.[10]

California has the most extensive panoply of laws protecting home buyers against lenders pursuing deficiency claims. Lenders must foreclose before taking any other action to collect the mortgage debt. A lender who sues the borrower personally on the debt before foreclosing loses the right to foreclose on the security property.[11] Also, if the property owner obtained the loan to acquire the mortgaged property, the mortgage lender is barred by statute from obtaining a deficiency judgment.[12] After foreclosing in California by non-judicial sale, lenders cannot obtain deficiency judgments.[13]

The Policy Arguments For and Against Allowing Deficiency Judgments. Here are some of the arguments made by advocates opposed to mortgage lenders being able

---

8. For the process by which a creditor can have the debtor's real estate sold to satisfy the judgment, see California Courts, Collect from the Debtor's Property. http://www.courts.ca.gov/11190.htm (last visited 06/28/2016.)

9. Kristen Barnes, *Pennies On The Dollar": Reallocating Risk And Deficiency Judgment Liability,* University of Akron: Ohio's Polytechnic University IdeaExchange@UAkron (Last visited 06/22/2016).

10. See Jessica Silver-Greenberg, *House is Gone but Debt Lives On,* WALL ST. J., Oct. 1, 2011, at A1.

11. CAL. CIV. PROC. CODE §726(A). "There can be but one form of action for the recovery of any debt or the enforcement of any right secured by mortgage upon real property."

12. CAL. CIV. PROC. CODE §580 (b). 580b. The statute bars deficiency judgments by lenders secured by one-to-four family dwellings occupied by the buyer, or by the re-financing of these mortgage loans. It bars deficiency judgments on any seller-financed mortgages or deeds of trust on all real property.

13. CAL. CIV. PROC. CODE §580 (d).

to sue borrowers personally, instead of just being able to foreclose: (1) Mortgage lenders are better able to evaluate and price the risks of the market than borrowers; (2) Mortgage lenders are more capable than borrowers of absorbing losses on loan defaults and foreclosures; (3) Mortgage lenders sometimes overvalue house prices and fabricate data regarding borrowers' abilities to repay;[14] (5) Most defaults result from life circumstances beyond the borrower's control such as illness, job loss, and declining house prices; (6) Pursuing home owners for deficiencies is likely to push some of them into filing bankruptcy which is unlikely to yield much cash for the mortgage lender and devastating for other creditors;[15] (7) In fact, Lenders rarely seek deficiency judgments even in states that allow them, because the legal costs of collection almost always far exceed what lenders actually net from these efforts.

Deficiency collections are sparse because borrowers will have drained their bank accounts, maxed out on their credit card debt, sold any truly marketable personal property they owned, and. Perhaps, hidden or attempted to hide everything else before risking the loss of their homes by defaulting on their mortgages.[16]

On the other side of the debate, proponents of deficiency judgments fear that debtors would be more inclined to walk away from their mortgage obligations if they could do so with impunity, especially where they could have afforded to pay their mortgage loans. The threat of deficiency liability is a deterrent to default and without it, lenders would experience greater losses, tighten loan standards, and increase interest rates, adversely impacting all potential borrowers.[17]

II. The Capital Stack

A convenient way to think about the various sources of capital invested in a real estate transaction is to envision them as being layered in a stack one on top of the other, the riskiest layer shown at the top of the stack, and the most secure interest at the base.

A. The Residential Capital Stack

In residential transactions, the capital stack is quite simple, consisting of two or, at most, three layers—a senior mortgage and the owner's equity. Assuming a $400,000

---

14. 66 So. Car. L. Rev. 243, 246 (2014).

15. Baran Bulkat, I'm Behind on My Mortgage.Can Chapter 13 Help Me Catch Up? https://www.nolo.com/legal-encyclopedia/behind-my-mortgage-chapter-13-help-me-catch-up.html (Last visited, 06/25/2016).

16. Melissa B. Jacoby, Daniel T. McCue, Eric S. Belsky, *In or Out of Mortgage Trouble? A Study of Bankrupt Homeowners*, 85 Am. Bankr. L.J. 291, 292 (2011) ("in the two years prior to bankruptcy, roughly half of our homeowner sample had not missed a single mortgage payment in that period.").

17. See generally, Judy Gedge, *Should Deficiency Judgments Be Banned? Teaching Materials Designed To Promote An Informed Student Debate*, 19 J.L. Bus. & Eth. 65 (Winter, 2013).

purchase price with a $100,000 down payment from the borrower and a $300,000 mortgage loan, the borrower equity of $100,000 would be at the top of the capital stack, and the $300,000 mortgage debt at the bottom.[18]

Maybe the home buyer needs to secure additional funds to close the gap between the senior mortgagee's maximum loan to value ratio and the amount of cash the buyer can raise for a down payment.

The home seller is sometimes willing to become a junior lienor by agreeing to take back a note and purchase a money mortgage secured by the house in order to facilitate the sale.

Purchase money "seconds" are subordinate to the buyer's senior or first mortgage loan, and superior to all subsequent claims against the security property unless the junior lienor agrees to a subordinated lien priority.

A three-tiered $500,000 home-purchase capital stack, for example, at the top would have the borrower's down payment of $150,000 (the equity), followed by the junior debt (the seller's purchase money mortgage or deed of trust) for $75,000, and at the bottom, the senior mortgage debt of $275,000.

Not all "seconds" are used to finance home purchases. Home owners sometimes borrow money to make home improvements or for other uses, from starting a small business to paying tuition for their children or grandchildren. Mortgage lenders, including banks, are comfortable making these loans as long as the value of the home exceeds by a safe margin the combined loans of the senior mortgage and the new loan. These are often called HELOC (Home Equity Lines of Credit) mortgages.

B. Commercial Real Estate Loans

Commercial capital stacks are often multi-layered, and depicted as pyramids. Here is a commercial real estate lending capital stack drawn in early 2016 for a particular type of transaction.

The percentages shown to the right of each layer will tend to vary greatly based on money market fundamentals at the time, the type of project, its location, the promoters and other participants, and real estate supply and demand for the project.

---

18. https://www.crowdstreet.com/education/article/understanding-capital-stack/ (Last visited 06/23/2016).

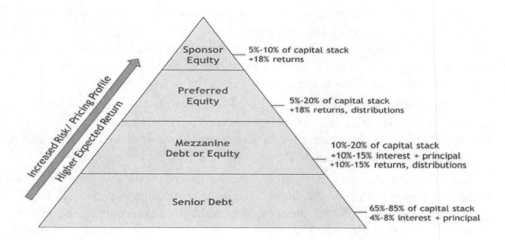

Project Sponsor's Perspective. Investors expect sponsors to demonstrate sufficient confidence in their own deals to place funds in their projects, to have "skin in the game." Beyond that, sponsors construct their capital stacks by balancing the weighted cost of capital[19] against the increased say that investors will insist upon having in project management and decision making as their share of the at-risk capital rises. A large percentage of her own cash in the deal cushions the promoter against the possibility of being forced out of the venture entirely. A lower percentage from the promoter means more from other equity investors. To compensate for the greater risk if the deal fails, they will expect a commensurately larger share of the cash flow and, perhaps, greater managerial prerogatives as well.

Investor's Perspective. Basically, the structure of the stack determines the investor's place within that structure, how and when the investor will get paid and whether the investor has the ability to take control of the underlying property if things go badly.

The Equity Owner. The term "equity" or "sponsor equity" is the riskiest position in any capital stack. It represents the value of the asset after subtracting all the liabilities against it. These would include senior and junior mortgages, mezzanine debt and preferred equity.

"Sponsor equity" is often held in a joint venture negotiated between project promoters and their investors.

Their respective rights to cash flow from the project are memorialized in "waterfalls" that prescribe the exact order in which each of them is entitled to the cash flow from the project.

---

19. "A sponsor's job is to work the numbers and find the ideal combination of financing sources." http://www.inman.com/2016/02/09/work-capital-stack-investment-property-financing/ (Last visited 06/23/2016).

Typically, the promoter defers its compensation until the joint venture money partner receives a specified return of and on its investment. Payments are made from net operating income—income after operating expenses including property taxes and insurance. These payments will be subordinate to the obligations of everyone in the capital stack nested below the sponsor equity.

The Place of Senior, Junior and A-B Note Holders in the Commercial Real Estate Capital Stack. The senior mortgagee is shown in the safest location, at the base of the capital stack. A senior mortgagee's foreclosure would wipe out the security interests in the real estate of any claimants above it, starting with junior mortgagees.[20]

The A-B Loan Structure. In Chapter Five, we described the A-B loan structure which is currently found in many loans originated for inclusion in commercial mortgage backed securities (CMBS). Recall that in the A-B loan structure, the borrower signs two separate notes, each to a designated lender based on distinct loan terms. A single deed of trust or mortgage on the same real estate asset secures both notes. The A-B arrangement belongs at the bottom of the capital stack in the same layer as the senior mortgage because the B Note holder subordinates its rights to the A-note holder.

Mezzanine Debt and Preferred Equity in the Capital Stack.[21] The two layers of risk occupying the space between the senior secured mortgage and the joint venture equity are *Mezzanine Debt* and *Preferred Equity*. Project sponsors look to preferred equity and mezzanine debt arrangements to fill gaps in the requisite equity capital at the lowest blended total cost of financing the project.

Typical Provisions in Preferred Equity. Preferred equity arrangements come in "hard" and "soft" variations. "Hard" terms are like loans, entitling the preferred equity investor to monthly "interest," a fixed maturity date for loan repayment, a default rate of "interest," late payment penalties, and if the borrower defaults, the option of taking over the management and control of the project.

"Soft" arrangements are true equity contingent on the project generating positive cash flow sufficient to pay operating expenses and sums owed on senior secured debt.

Investors in hard and soft preferred equity interests often negotiate to receive a share of operating profits and of value appreciation from a sale or refinancing.

Typical Mezzanine Loan Terms. The concept of mezzanine financing has long been a mainstay of corporate finance, and is now a well-established niche in real estate financing.[22] Typically, mezz borrowers pledge interest payments to mezz lenders as a

---

20. For a good introduction to second trust deed investing, see Jan B. Brzeski, *Trust Deed Investing FAQ*, ARIXACAPITAL (last visited Jan. 10, 2016), http://www.arixacapital.com/investor-resources/trust-deed-investing-faq/

21. Robert J. Sullivan and Adrian D. Boddie, *Hunting For the Perfect Subordinate Debt Tool? Mezzanine Financing and Preferred Equity Financing: Suitable Ammunition,* 30 Real Estate Finance J. 6(Fall Winter 2014).

22. Corporate mezzanine loans are typically secured by senior subordinated debt, convertible subordinated debt or redeemable preferred stock. "While there are no hard and fast rules for optimizing a company's capital structure, companies that are ahead of the curve use an efficient combination of senior debt, mezzanine debt, and equity capital to minimize their true cost of capital." Corry Silbernagel

percentage of the amount loaned, at fixed or floating rates. Mezzanine financing might fill the sponsor's need for capital. It is usually riskier and hence more expensive than senior debt (closer to the top of the pyramid).[23]

Enforcement Rights of Mezz Lenders and Preferred Equity Investors. Unlike senior and junior mortgagees, neither mezzanine lenders nor preferred equity investors have direct liens on the underlying property. A specially formed LLC holds title to the underlying property. That LLC could be owned by all the investors in the capital stack (a one-tier structure), or the investors could be members in another LLC that is formed exclusively to be the owner of the title-holding LLC (a two-tiered structure). The de facto owners of the real estate pledge their LLC memberships as security for the mezzanine loan and the preferred equity investment contract.

The mezz lender's security interest is the right to acquire those membership interests in the LLC. Because LLC membership interests are personal property, not real property, mezzanine lenders enforce their right to foreclose under article 9 of the UCC (Uniform Commercial Code) in a "commercially reasonable sale."[24] This nonjudicial remedy has proven to be efficient and effective. Often, the mezz lender ends up owning the LLC as the only bidder at the carefully orchestrated "commercially reasonable sale." Suitable buyers are not lining up for a chance to bid on defaulted LLC membership interests.

Preferred equity investors do not have market-tested norms comparable to those of mezz lenders foreclosing under the UCC. They must resort to idiosyncratic remedies based on the particular terms of their joint venture contracts. Nonetheless, they usually end up in the same position as the mezz lender, taking over the management and ownership of the defaulting LLC.

After exercising their respective remedies, mezz lenders usually oust the mezz borrower completely from any decision making role in the LLC while preferred equity investors often find themselves sharing ownership prerogatives with the former owners who failed to fulfill the promises they made to their preferred equity co-venturers.

The Due on Sale Clause and the Intercreditor Agreement. A due-on-sale clause in most senior mortgage loans empowers the mortgagee to declare the mortgage loan

---

and Davis Vaitkunas, Mezzanine Finance (Bond Capital). http://pages.stern.nyu.edu/~igiddy/articles/Mezzanine_Finance_Explained.pdf (Last visited March 13 (2016). They are typically secured by senior subordinated debt, convertible subordinated debt or redeemable preferred stock. "While there are no hard and fast rules for optimizing a company's capital structure, companies that are ahead of the curve use an efficient combination of senior debt, mezzanine debt, and equity capital to minimize their true cost of capital."

23. *Mezzanine Financing Basics and The Intercreditor Agreement*, PROPERTYMETRICS (last visited Mar. 22, 2016), http://www.propertymetrics.com/blog/2015/07/23/mezzanine-financing-basics-and-the-intercreditor-agreement

24. Jeffrey J. Temple, *Mezzanine Loan Foreclosure*, NEW YORK LAW JOURNAL (last visited Mar. 21, 2016), http://www.mofo.com/~/media/Files/Resources/Publications/2007/03/Mezzanine%20Loan%20Foreclosure/Files/Mezzanine%20Loan%20Foreclosure/FileAttachment/070312NYLawJournal.pdf

immediately due and payable if a majority of stakeholders in the ownership entity—the borrower LLC—change hands without the mortgagee's prior written consent. So the entrepreneur who wishes to put together a capital stack of three or more layers to finance a real estate asset will seek pre approval rights from senior mortgage lenders for mezz lenders and preferred equity investors, or to identify the criteria by which the mortgage lender would grant approval.

Senior Debt: The Mortgage Lender at the Bottom of the Stack. *"It's not a bad thing to be on the bottom when it comes to the capital stack. Why? Because the bottom layer is home to the most senior debt, meaning investors here are more senior to everyone above them in the stack.*

So what does that mean? If the property performs well and generates cash flows that are sufficient to pay periodic debt service payments (interest and sometimes principal as well), it's pretty simple—debt holders get their full periodic payment before any other capital contributors are paid. When the property is sold, it's again the senior debt holders that are paid first, getting their outstanding principal and any accrued interest back.

But what happens if the property is underperforming and debt service payments are not met? In case of an uncured default, senior debt holders typically have the right to initiate a foreclosure process, take ownership of the property, and liquidate it. Once again, they will be the first in line to receive any amounts due to them once the property is sold.

Not surprisingly, senior debt investors enjoy the lowest return in the capital stack, as they have first access to cash flows and the collateral, putting them at the lowest risk in the stack."[25]

III. Defaults

A. Defaults on Residential Mortgage Loans

Monetary Defaults. A monetary default starts with the mortgagor not making timely payments of principal and interest. Overwhelmingly, foreclosures are avoided if the value of the security property exceeds the mortgage debt.[26] The property owner has the option of salvaging the equity value by selling the property before the mortgage lender initiates foreclosure. With a high enough sales price, the seller can pay off the mortgage loan and keep what is left after paying the costs of sale.

---

25. https://www.realtymogul.com/resource-center/articles/demystifying-the-capital-stack (Last visited 06/23/2016).

26. "Research has shown that a negative equity position is a necessary condition for mortgage default, although a second trigger, like a shock to the borrower's monthly income or expenses, is generally required for a foreclosure to occur." Jun Zhu, Jared Janowiak, Lu Ji, Kadiri Karamoni and Douglas McManus, *The Effect of Mortgage Payment Reduction on Default: Evidence from the Home Affordable Refinance Program* 43 Real Est. Economics 1035 (Wiinter, 2015). CoreLogic estimated that as of year-end 2009, 11.3 million residential properties—representing 24% of all residential properties with mortgages—were in a negative equity position.

Non-monetary Defaults. Not all defaults are about money owed directly to the lender. Examples of *non-monetary defaults* could include not paying property taxes, or maintaining casualty insurance coverage for the benefit of the mortgage lender, a mortgagor's failure to maintain the property in "reasonable repair," constructing a home improvement in violation of local building or zoning codes, or using Airbnb. "Homeowners who make a practice of using Airbnb may unknowingly be violating their mortgage agreements by converting the property into in essence a rental property."[27]

Strategic Defaults. A strategic default occurs when a property who could have afforded mortgage payments stops making them. These sorts of defaults became quite common when house prices slumped in the mortgage meltdown of 2008. The incidence of strategic defaults rose on properties with mortgage debts that exceeded the value of their properties by 25% or more and was counter to all previous mortgage lending experience.

The following chart shows the devastating impact on home owners' equities of declining house prices from 2005 to 2008. Note the sharp rebound from 2012 to 2015. Buyers who acquired their houses at prevailing price levels from 2008 to 2012 were well rewarded when values rose sharply between 2012 and 2015.

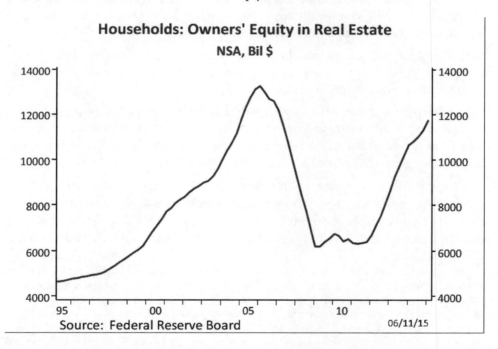

Are Strategic Defaults a Good Idea for Borrowers? California debtor's rights attorney Stephen Elias, in a Foreclosure Survival Guide,[28] advised homeowners to make a dispassionate economic analysis before deciding whether to default.

---

27. https://www.lexisnexis.com/legalnewsroom/real-estate/b/real-estate-law-blog/archive/2014/09/08/airbnb-rentals-raise-thorny-legal-issues.aspx?Redirected=true (Last visited 07/04/2016).

28. 9 Stephen Elias, The Foreclosure Survival Guide (Nolo.2011), p. 45.

Start by estimating whether the property is financially "under water" based on its current market value. Then, subtract the mortgage balance due, other liens against the house, and add the costs of sale. Even if the owner had no remaining equity value in the house, real estate values are often quite volatile, and owners should closely examine the prospects for a local price recovery.[29]

Property owners are sometimes able to find comparable space without changing neighborhoods, at rents one-third to one-half the costs of home ownership. But consumer attorney Elias counseled defaulting owners to stay put and not walk away, so they could benefit from free possession as long as possible. Typically, in California, this would be from six months to a year, maybe longer.

Attorney Elias cautioned mortgagors considering a strategic default to save the money they would have spent on mortgage payments, not squander it, and seek professional advice concerning the possibility of personal liability for any deficiency if the sales price at the foreclosure sale came up short of the mortgage debt they owed.

The strategic defaulters will sometimes incur federal income tax liability since debts forgiven can be classified as income called "forgiveness of indebtedness income"[30] under the Internal Revenue Code unless the debtor is insolvent. This potential source of tax liability is based on the difference between what they owed on their mortgage loans less the value of the houses they lost to foreclosure.

Before defaulting, mortgagors also should weigh the impacts on their future credit, though credit impairment does not last forever. After seven years, foreclosures and most negative credit events are forgotten.[31]

Are Strategic Defaults Morally Defensible? Academic views on strategic defaults vary. In a standard mortgage-loan document, the borrower promises to repay the amount borrowed plus interest. The promise is absolute, not contingent on repayment being no longer convenient or advantageous for the borrower.

George Brenkert, a professor of business ethics at Georgetown University, believes that "borrowers who can pay—and weren't deceived by the lender about the nature of the loan—have a moral responsibility to keep paying. It would be disastrous for the economy if Americans concluded they were free to walk away from such commitments."

---

29. Lucia Mutikani, *U.S. home sales rebound signals strong spring selling season,* Reuters, April 20, 2015. http://www.reuters.com/article/us-usa-economy-idUSKCN0XH1P3(Last visited 06/30/2016). "Many of the economic forces that helped trigger recovery in affluent and middle-class communities aren't working in lower-income communities.... Negative equity preys on the less affluent." Joe Light, *Why the U.S. Housing Recovery Is Leaving Poorer Neighborhoods Behind,* Wall. St. J.(06/23/2015.) http://www.wsj.com/articles/in-u-s-poorer-areas-have-yet-to-see-housing-rebound-1435091711 (Last visited 06/30/2016).

30. IRS, Topic 431: *Cancelled Debt—Is It Taxable or Not?* Irs.gov (last visited Mar. 21, 2016), https://www.irs.gov/taxtopics/tc431.html

31. "For those who lost their homes in the early years of the crisis, credit scores are improving as the black marks drop away, improving their ability to borrow again. This could have widespread implications for the U.S. economy, including a boost in demand for mortgages in the coming years." Anna Maria Andriotis Laura Kusistos and Joe Light, *After Foreclosures, Home Buyers Are Back,* Wall St Journal, April 8, 2015.

In rebuttal, John Courson, chief executive of the Mortgage Bankers Association, a trade group, contends: "It isn't just a matter of the borrower's personal interest. Defaults hurt neighborhoods by lowering property values," he says, adding, "What about the message they will send to their family and their kids and their friends?"[32]

A different view on strategic defaults was advanced by Professor Brent White, an associate law professor at the University of Arizona. He contended that homeowners should make the decision on whether to keep paying based on their own interests, "unclouded by unnecessary guilt or shame." White believes that borrowers should shed feelings of shame or guilt and exaggerated fears of the practical consequences.[33] "Walking away may be the most financially responsible choice if it allows one to meet one's unsecured credit obligations or provide for the future economic stability of one's family."[34]

B. Defaults on Commercial Loans

1. Who Is the "Borrower" in a Commercial Real Estate Mortgage Loan? The Preference for Single-Asset, Limited Liability Borrowers

As mentioned earlier, in commercial real estate transactions, lenders often prefer that the "borrower" not be an individual but rather that it be a "special purpose entity," typically a limited liability company (LLC). This may seem odd since if the borrower is an LLC, the individual members of the LLC have no liability for repaying the mortgage debt.

There are several reasons why lenders are comfortable with LLCs as borrowers. For starters, lenders underwrite their loans based on the assumption that the mortgage loan is going to be repaid solely from the net operating income of the security property. Mortgage lenders insist upon ample documentation that keeps anyone else — other creditors or the equity owners — from tampering with the rents until the money owed on the mortgage loan is paid first each month, along with property taxes and insurance premiums.

Mortgage lenders prefer the borrower to be a "bankruptcy remote" entity with no other assets except the mortgaged property. If more than one property is owned by the same LLC, all of the properties will become assets in the LLC's bankruptcy. A bankruptcy filing results in a temporary automatic stay of the lender's right to enforce its lien. In order to foreclose, the lender will have to petition the Bankruptcy Court for relief from the automatic stay. Special relief from the automatic stay is available where the bankrupt debtor is a single asset real estate entity.[35] So a mortgage lender

---

32. James R. Hagerty and Nick Timiraos, *Debtor's Dilemma: Pay the Mortgage or Walk Away?* WALL ST. J. (last visited Mar. 21, 2016), http://www.wsj.com/articles/SB126100260600594531

33. Brent T. White, *Underwater and Not Walking Away: Shame, Fear and the Social Management of the Housing Crises,* Arizona Legal Studies Discussion Paper No. 09-35 (October 2009).

34. White at p. 52.

35. "Single asset real estate (SARE) debtors are subject to special provisions of the Bankruptcy Code that limit the protections otherwise applicable to ordinary chapter 11 debtors. In particular, if

that has underwritten a loan on the basis of the net operating income produced by one particular real estate asset—anything from a fourplex to a regional shopping center, wants to cordon off that asset in a specially formed entity, usually an LLC, that holds title to no other properties.

2. Non-Monetary Defaults in Commercial Loans

Commercial mortgage loans are replete with provisions that could lead to non-monetary defaults. Lenders often reserve the right to approve the borrower's major leases, additional secured debt, or the sale of the mortgaged property. Borrowers covenant to abide by applicable laws, ordinances, and recorded covenants, conditions and restrictions. They commit to furnish financial statements periodically. When lenders contemplate mortgage loans being repaid solely from a project's net operating income, and not by the sponsor personally, the loan could be declared in default if the ratio of net operating income to debt service fell below a stated minimum. Lenders often condition loans on the borrowing entity's financial condition not deteriorating.

C. Mortgage Loan Servicing

CMBS AND RMBS Loan Servicers.[36] Loans that end up being included in a Commercial Mortgage Backed Security (CMBS) or Residential Mortgage Back Security (RMBS) will be serviced by two distinct entities in a dual-servicer structure.

Master Servicers. There will be a master servicer for overseeing the day-to-day routine of collecting payments from mortgagors, remitting payments to the trustees for the investors in the mortgage-backed bonds, maintaining loan file records, detailing loan balance and payment changes, periodically reporting to investors, guarantors and trustees, processing lien releases and responding to requests for pay-off demands.

Master servicers gather the periodic operating statements and rent rolls that mortgagors are obligated to provide, inspect the mortgaged properties, maintain loan pay-

---

a single asset real estate debtor does not begin making monthly payments to secured creditors, section 362(d)(3) of the Bankruptcy Code directs bankruptcy courts to grant relief from the automatic stay to allow secured creditors to institute actions against the debtor unless, within ninety days of the commencement of the bankruptcy case (or thirty days after the court determines that the debtor is a single asset real estate entity, whichever is later) "the debtor has filed a plan of reorganization that has a reasonable possibility of being confirmed within a reasonable time." Doron Kenter, *SARE Tactics: Placeholder Plans May Not Suffice to Protect a Single Asset Real Estate Debtor from Losing Chapter 11 Protections*, BANKRUPTCYBLOG (last visited Mar. 21, 2016), http://business-finance-restructuring .weil.com/chapter-11-plans/sare-tactics-placeholder-plans-may-not-suffice-to-protect-a-single-asset-real-estate-debtor-from-losing-chapter-11-protections/

36. Stewart McQueen, Gennady A. Gorel, and Chris Van Heerdon, *An Investor's Guide to The Pooling and Servicing Agreement*, DECHERTLLP (last visited Jan. 10, 2016), https://www.dechert.com/ files/Publication/1d980804-1044-4746-858a-187bbe66d005/Presentation/PublicationAttachment/ 6833e68e-763a-4dde-8bc3-1ca51e4e6106/An%20Investor%E2%80%99s%20Guide%20to%20 The%20Pooling%20and%20Servicing%20Agreement%20-%20June%202013.pdf

ment records, make sure the properties are insured, and keep track of property tax payments.

Special Servicers. The special servicer takes over when borrowers stop making payments, as loans become non-performing. In home loans, special servicers initiate contact with the borrower to determine the reason for non-payment, identify loss mitigation options and collect the paperwork for it, refer the file for foreclosure, short sale, or deed-in-lieu, and maintain foreclosed property in compliance with local housing and building codes.

In commercial loans, the special servicer is responsible for dealing with difficult situations—loans more than 60 days delinquent or in imminent default, borrowers in receivership, bankruptcy or insolvency, situations like that.

The special servicer is typically required to be an established banking, mortgage financing, or mortgage servicing institution that maintains certain credit rating. Both the master servicer and the special servicer are required to act in the best interests of the certificate holders. However, compensation arrangements for mortgage servicers create some built-in conflicts between servicers and the investors they are pledged to serve.[37]

The Mortgage Loan Servicing Fiasco and the 2007 Real Estate Recession. Loan servicers entered multi-year contracts based on fees that had not been set in contemplation of anything like the foreclosure avalanche that started in 2007 which is depicted in the graph below. Loan servicing fees derive largely from a small percentage of loan collections, largely automated, with huge economies of scale, and quite profitable as long as borrowers pay on time. But servicing income declines rapidly with rising defaults; and organizing loan modifications and workouts is expensive for loan servicers who did not price it into their contracts.

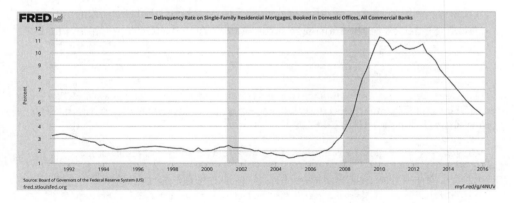

---

37. Adam J. Levitin and Tara Twomey, *Mortgage Servicing,* 28 YALE J. ON REG. 1 (2011). "Servicers' compensation structures create a principal-agent conflict between them and MBS investors. Servicers have no stake in the performance of mortgage loans, so they do not share investors' interest in maximizing the net present value of the loan. Instead, servicers' decision of whether to foreclose or modify a loan is based on their own cost and income structure, which is skewed toward foreclosure."

Basically, "homeowners who found themselves in trouble during the Great Recession could not get an effective shot at saving their home, were improperly shuffled through the foreclosure process with false documents, and were stolen from up and down the line."[38]

In a complaint against one of the worst performing servicers, the Federal Consumer Financial Protection Bureau (CFBP) alleged that the mortgage servicer OCWEN (now bankrupt)

"charged borrowers more than stipulated in the mortgage contract;

forced homeowners to buy unnecessary insurance policies;

charged borrowers unauthorized fees;

lied in response to borrower complaints about excessive and unauthorized fees;

lied about loan modification services when borrowers requested them;

misplaced documents and ignored loan modification applications, causing homeowners to slip into foreclosure;

illegally denied eligible borrowers a loan modification, then lied about the reasons why."[39]

Based on abusive servicing practices similar to those mentioned in the above list, a National Mortgage Settlement was entered in February 2012, by 49 states, the District of Columbia, and the federal government, on the one hand, and the country's five largest mortgage servicers, on the other. It provided for over $50 billion in relief for distressed borrowers and in payments to the government entities. Soon thereafter, the big banks who paid that huge settlement sold their mortgage servicing rights to firms like Ocwen.

"This game of Whac-a-Mole, with customer accounts passed around from one rogue business to another like a hot potato, shows that the problem lies with the design of the mortgage servicing industry itself, not the individual companies."[40]

---

38. David Dayen, *Another Slap on the Wrist for a Company That Abused Homeowners* (12/20/2013). https://newrepublic.com/article/116010/ocwen-mortgage-fraud-settlement-servicer-fined-home owner-abuse (Last visited 07/01/2016).

39. *Ibid.*

40. *Ibid.* An international accounting firm summarized the structural problems facing mortgage servicers:

- Low dollar, high volume transactions with limited control checks
- Touched by multiple departments causing lack of data integrity and ownership
- Governed by complex and evolving judicial, legislative, regulatory and investor require-ments that define prohibitions on borrower assessment and reimbursement
- Reimbursed via complex claim processes with significant manual interactions
- Impacted by data quality issues that are often exacerbated by servicing transfers

PwC, Servicing Fees and Advances: Show Me the Money (10/2014). https://www.pwc.com/us/en/ consumer-finance/publications/assets/pwc-servicing-advance-white-paper.pdf (Last visited 07/01/ 2016).

To see the sorts of practices that prompted so much public outrage against loan servicers, consider the following case.

Servicing Agent Errors and Omission: **Wright v. Litton Loan Servicing.**[41] A defaulting borrower who claimed that the lender cheated her was telling the truth. With the help of a community legal services attorney, Andrea Wright was able to prove that she refinanced her home mortgage through a mortgage company in 1998 for $33,600, at an adjustable rate minimum of 13.875% that could rise as high as 20.375%. The originating lender, a mortgage company, sold the loan three days later to a bank. After fifteen months, Andrea Wright became unable to make her payments and filed for chapter 13 bankruptcy protection.

In the bankruptcy proceedings, she alleged and proved a number of statutory violations by the originating lender. She reached a vindicating settlement approved by the Bankruptcy Court.

(1) the principal amount of the mortgage was reduced to $25,894;

(2) the rate of interest was fixed at 8%;

(3) the mortgage was to be amortized at the rate of $190.66 per month for a 30-year period; and

(4) the bank paid plaintiff's counsel fees.

Surprisingly, Andrea Wright's legal troubles were not yet over and actually worsened two years later after Litton Loan Servicing began collecting her monthly payments. By that time, the loan had been sold to Wells Fargo Bank of Minnesota acting as trustee for a group of investors. No one had bothered to tell Wells Fargo or its servicer, Litton, about the Bankruptcy Court settlement that had so dramatically altered the terms of the original note.

For 29 months Litton neglected to adjust its records and continued to demand of the borrower more money than she owed. Compounding its errors, Litton attempted to overbill the borrower significantly for escrow accounts, and claimed to be owed $40,917.12 in unspecified fees.

Attempting to straighten things out, the borrower did everything she could think of. She sent letters, copies of the settlement agreement, account records, phone calls ... all to no avail.

Even after Andrea Wright's legal aid attorney faxed a letter to the servicer explaining the situation, Litton took 28 months to correct its records.

Eventually, Litton initiated foreclosure, and the borrower brought suit under the Federal Debt Collection Practices Act (FDCPA) and state consumer protection laws.

The court found that Litton violated the FDCPA[42] by sending twenty separate letters demanding amounts not due and misinforming the debtor of the cost of cure.

---

41. Not Reported in F.Supp.2d, 2006 WL 891030 (E.D.Pa. 2006).

42. 15 USC § 1692 et. Seq. https://www.ftc.gov/enforcement/rules/rulemaking-regulatory-reform-proceedings/fair-debt-collection-practices-act-text (Last visited March 23, 2016).

As a result, the court awarded $2,000 under the FDCPA and treble damages under state law. To compensate for her emotional distress, anxiety, fear of losing her home, loss of sleep, and frustration as a result of the defendant's conduct, the court awarded her $25,000.

The servicer's sole witness had no explanation for how these egregious billing errors occurred or why it would take over two years to correct the firm's records. Unfortunately, errors like these are all too common.[43]

Possible Changes and Reforms in Mortgage Servicing. The CFPB has become the federal regulator for mortgage servicing, implementing Dodd-Frank, RESPA and TILA requirements, coordinating its efforts with other federal and state agencies, imposing rigorous performance, reporting and accounting standards on servicers, and pursuing successful claims against errant servicers.[44]

CFPB settlements of legal disputes with 16 of the nation's largest servicers are generating structural reforms within these firms, internal quality controls and audits, policies for default and foreclosure management, timelines to ensure prompt response to consumer requests, clear definitions for loss mitigation procedures, designated single-point-of-contact (SPOC) customer service, and monitoring and disclosure of all foreclosure process fees.

There will almost certainly be changes in servicer compensation, mirroring the significantly larger costs to servicers of dealing with non-performing loans. But these discussions and reforms are occurring when the mortgage loan servicers who survived the recession are benefiting from the strong tail winds of a housing market largely recovered from recession lows that has been gaining momentum month-by-month since January, 2010.[45]

The U.S. Department of Housing and Urban Development (HUD) has posted a description online, detailing the responsibilities of home mortgage servicers.[46]

Many states are enacting new licensing requirements for mortgage loan servicers, record keeping and communication norms, fee restrictions, increasing pre-foreclosure timing and notice requirements, instituting mandatory foreclosure mediation, and requiring servicers to provide borrowers with information about mortgage relief options.[47]

---

43. Kurt Eggert, Limiting Abuse and Opportunism by Mortgage Servicers, 15 HOUSING POLICY DEBATE 753 (2004).

44. Press release, CFPB, State Authorities Order Ocwen to Provide $2 Billion in Relief to Homeowners for Servicing Wrongs (Dec 13, 2013). https://www.google.com/webhp?sourceid=chrome-instant&ion=1&espv=2&ie=UTF-8#q=CFPB+mortgage+servicing (Last visited 06/30/2016). OCWEN has since filed bankruptcy.

45. Stuart I. Quinn and Faith A. Schwartz, Mortgage Servicing: Foundation for a Sound Housing Market (Corelogic, October, 2014), page 6-9.

46. *Your Rights and the Responsibilities of the Mortgage Servicer*, HUD.Gov (last visited Mar. 21, 2016), http://portal.hud.gov/hudportal/HUD?src=/program_offices/housing/ramh/res/rightsmtgesrvcr

47. Nanci L. Weissgold and Morey Barnes Yost, *Foreclosure Laws Continue To Complicate Mortgage Loanservicing And Lengthen The Foreclosure Process*, 67-APR DISP. RESOL. J. 62 (February-April 2012).

IV. Foreclosure

A. Why Is Foreclosure By Sale Required by Law?

What Is Foreclosure? The term "foreclosure" refers to the right of a mortgagee or deed of trust beneficiary to compel the sale of a real estate asset to repay a specific debt. With limited exceptions, state laws require that the debtor's rights in the security property can only be terminated at a public sale open to all bidders. The purpose is to preserve any equity value that the borrower may still have in the property, a norm enshrined in 17th century English equity jurisprudence.

Who Gets Foreclosure Sale Proceeds? The foreclosure sale proceeds are credited first against the costs of sale, and then paid to the holders of the debt being foreclosed, next to junior lienors. The balance, if any, called "the surplus," is given to the borrower. This is how the borrower retains the equity value of the property—if there is any.

Are Foreclosure Sales Really Worth the Cost or Just a Waste of Money? The foreclosure sale process has been challenged as imposing inefficient delays and costs on the mortgage lending business. When the property is worth more than the debt, the borrower just needs to put the house on the market. Why go through the charade of a foreclosure sale when there is no homeowner equity to protect?

The answer is that many property owners do not react rationally under the stress of losing their houses. Some are experiencing an incapacitating illness or consumed in caring for a family member who is ill or dying. Others are mentally incompetent, caught in the midst of domestic strife, embroiled in a dispute with a co-owner or partner, facing overwhelming and unmanageable financial obligations, or so stressed out as to be incapacitated. They procrastinate; maybe they simply do not realize that they could sell their houses for more than the balance due on their mortgages. Anyway, once they have missed a few mortgage payments, and the lender has recorded a notice of default, potential buyers are going to back away.

Why Are Foreclosure Sales Particularly Important to Junior Lienors? Another reason for requiring foreclosure by sale is protect junior lienors. As a matter of law, their security interests in the foreclosed property are terminated. They become entitled to foreclosure sale proceeds on those rare occasions when the property is worth more than the senior mortgage debt being foreclosed. Investors in second trust deeds or mortgages—and there are lots of them, could sensibly show up to bid on the foreclosed property even when the owner had no reason to do so.

Do the numbers. Suppose the property is worth $400,000, the senior mortgagee is owned $350,000 and the second mortgage is for $100,000. The owner has no equity since the combined liens exceed the value of the house by $50,000. But if the second mortgage investor allows its interest to be terminated by the foreclosing lender making a "credit" bid, it will have lost $50,000 that it could have salvaged by bidding $350,001, and then selling the house for its market value of $350,000.

Why Are Foreclosure Sales Advertised So Ineffectually? Foreclosure sales are not well advertised and rarely draw large numbers of bidders. Neither courts conducting judicial sales nor trustees holding nonjudicial sales are required to make sure these sales yield "fair market value." Those who are charged with conducting foreclosure sales do not list their properties with real estate brokers or advertise in big circulation newspapers. Notice by publication is required but satisfied with a brief legal notice placed in any "newspaper of record."[48] No more is required than that, and the avoidance of collusive practices.

The statutory notices rarely reach regular buyers in the real estate market. Publication is in "newspapers of record," not online or in the Sunday newspaper real estate pages. Only the mortgagee's representative is likely to show up at a foreclosure sale, and perhaps a small group of speculators looking to buy at bargain prices.[49] Those provisions are meant to alert the borrower being foreclosed and junior lienors of the imminent foreclosure sale, not to entice a crowd of eager bidders.

Why the Credit Bid? Anyway, why should the foreclosing lender go all out to pump up the foreclosure sales price? The foreclosing lender will almost always be the winning bidder. It has a huge competitive advantage besides its familiarity with the foreclosed property. Instead of paying all cash on the spot, the foreclosing lender receives a credit toward its bid in the amount of the debt or foreclosure judgment. It is allowed to bid the amount owed on the mortgage, a "credit" bid. This avoids the circularity of the lender bidding cash, handing the cash to the sheriff or trustee conducting the sale, and their handing it back to the lender as the high bidder at the sale. Everyone else has to pay cash on the line.

Why Is It Not in the Best Interest of a Foreclosing Lender to Encourage Competitive Bidding at the Foreclosure Sale? Mostly likely, the property was not worth more than the amount owed or the borrower would have listed it with a broker and sold it.

In those situations where the property is really worth more than the balance due on the foreclosed debt, once the lender obtains title to the property as the winning bidder, it can decide the most prudent way to sell the property. If the lender incurs that expense prior to the sale, any competing bidder willing to pay one dollar more than the lender's "credit" bid is probably going to end up with the property because most lenders are not geared up to be real estate property entrepreneurs, and some lenders (like banks) are greatly limited by their regulators in the real estate equities they can hold.

Strict Foreclosure. Strict foreclosure is the alternative to foreclosure by sale. It is a court decree terminating the mortgagor's interest in the security property without a

---

48. *BFP v. Resolution Trust Corp.*, 511 U.S. 531 (1994). Former property owners in Ch. 11 bankruptcy challenged a nonjudicial foreclosure sales price as not having brought "reasonable equivalent value" under the Bankruptcy Code, 11 U.S.C. § 548(a)(2). A majority of the Supreme Court held that as long as the foreclosure sale met statutory standards, the "forced sale" price was all the Code required.

49. Robert A. Glaves, *The Controversy Over Section 548 Of The Bankruptcy Code In The Mortgage Arena: Making The Case For A Federal Statute Reforming The Foreclosure Process*, 23 J. MARSHALL L. REV. 683, 690-692 (1990.)

foreclosure sale. It is in common use only in Connecticut, Illinois and Vermont.[50] Even in these states, courts may order appraisals to be sure the value of the security property does not exceed the mortgage loan balance.

This is important because, otherwise, if the value of the security property exceeded the mortgage debt owed, the lender foreclosing without a sale would be overcompensated by pocketing the surplus.

In any event, courts in these "strict foreclosure" states have the option of requiring a judicial sale if they deem it necessary to safeguard the mortgagor from being stripped of equity value.[51]

On occasion, other states allow mortgagees to obtain decrees of strict foreclosure, but only in situations in which the lender seeks to cure technical defects in a previously conducted foreclosure sale proceeding.

B. Three Milestones in the California Non-Judicial Foreclosure Sale Process

All non-judicial foreclosure processes have milestones like California's—A notice of default, notice of sale, and trustee's deed upon sale. State statutes vary greatly in the details or timing and the extent to which courts will intervene to safeguard borrowers' interests. All of these laws are meant to slow down the time from the borrower's first missed payment and the lender's ousting the borrower from title and possession.

Before recording or filing a notice of default or notice of sale, a California statute requires mortgage servicers to substantiate the borrower's debt by reviewing competent and reliable evidence the borrower's default and the lender's right to foreclose, including the borrower's loan status and loan information.[52]

---

50. G. Nelson & D. Whitman, REAL ESTATE FINANCE LAW 504-505 (2d ed. 1985).

51. Under our law, an action for strict foreclosure is brought by a mortgagee who, holding legal title, seeks not to enforce a forfeiture but rather to foreclose an equity of redemption unless the mortgagor satisfies the debt on or before his law day. *Barclays Bank of N.Y. v. Ivler*, 565 A.2d 252, 253 (Conn. App. Ct. 1989). Once the mortgagor fails to pay the debt in full on law day (*i.e.*, the last day for redemption set by the courts), the debtor's interest in the property is extinguished. *Amresco v. New England II, L.P. v. Colossale*, 774 A.2d 1083, 63 Conn. App. 49 (2001) (mortgagee sought strict foreclosure upon five lots covered by blanket encumbrance but mortgagor convinced trial court to restrict foreclosure to two parcels because their value, combined with additional cash from the debtor, equaled the debt); *Fid. Trust Co. v. Irick*, 538 A.2d 1027, 206 Conn. 484 (1988) (strict foreclosure unavailable where there is equity value in the security property).

Nineteen other states recognize its use under limited circumstances. It is available when the mortgaged land is clearly insufficient to pay the debt.

At common law, to close out the borrower's equity without the bother of a foreclosure sale, the lender had to forego a deficiency judgment. Richard B. Powell & Patrick J. Rohan, 3 POWELL ON REAL PROPERTY 37-346 to 37-347 (1987). However, in Connecticut and Vermont strict foreclosure of a mortgage satisfies the mortgage debt only to the extent of the value of the property at the time of foreclosure. Accordingly, actions were allowed for deficiencies following strict foreclosure. *Hammond v. Stiles*, 567 A.2d 444, 446 (Me. 1989).

52. CAL. CIV. CODE § 2924.17.

1. Notice of Default

In California, the first formal move towards foreclosure is the preparation and circulation of a statutory Notice of Default.[53] The notice is recorded. The lender must also provide a mailed copy (registered or certified) to the borrower at the borrower's address listed in the note. It is up to the borrower to inform the lender or the lender's trustee of any address change. The lender can hold the foreclosure sale no earlier than 90 days after the Notice of Default (plus the time for providing notice of sale). Later is OK unless the delay disadvantages the mortgagor.

The Notice of Default informs the borrower that foreclosure is imminent, declares the price of curing the default and reinstating the loan, and advises the borrower to seek the advice of an attorney. Anyone looking for distressed properties can arrange to receive copies of recorded Notices of Default by area.[54] Anyone can record a Request for Notice of Default and Notice of Sale for a specific property.[55]

After the Notice of Default is recorded, any prospective buyer takes title subject to the lender's foreclosure sale. A buyer purchasing from the defaulting seller forfeits title to the winning bidder at the lender's foreclosure sale.

2. Notice of Sale

Foreclosing lenders in California are required by statute to inform the debtor and the general public of the time and place of the pending foreclosure sale. This notice must be posted conspicuously on the property, sent by registered or certified mail to the debtor and all others who requested it, and recorded in the public land records.

Foreclosing lenders are also required to publish in a local newspaper of general circulation no less than three times at least 20 days before the sale. (A notice published August 15, 22 and 29 would meet that standard even though only 14 days elapsed between the first and last publication.)[56]

3. Trustees' Deed Upon Sale

Nonjudicial sale foreclosures in California are held in a public place, often the steps of the courthouse or recorder's office, and the property is auctioned to the highest bidder.

---

53. Cal. Civ. CODE 2924. In response to the subprime mortgage crisis, the legislature enacted Cal. Civ. Code 2923.5 requiring lenders, before sending out a Notice of Default, to notify, meet and consult with defaulting home owners to discuss options to foreclosure. The statute details the requisite due diligence combination of mailed and telephone notices and their timing. The law only applies to loans made between January 1, 2003 and December 31, 2007 and terminates on January 1, 2013 unless extended.

54. Two of the most popular are Foreclosures.com and RealtyTrac.com.

55. Cal. Civ. Code 2924 (b). A copy of the request form can be found at http://www.fidelitytitle.net/Uploads/38/22/13822/Gallery/Request%20for%20Notice.pdf (Last visited 07/01/2016),

56. *Hotchkiss v. Darling*, 20 P. 2d 343 (4th Dist. 1933).

The foreclosure sale terminates ("forecloses") the owner's interest in the security property. The winning bidder at the sale becomes the new owner of the foreclosed property. After a nonjudicial sale, the high bidder receives a trustee's deed upon sale (TDUS), or after a judicial foreclosure sale, a deed issued by the court, or signed by the sheriff and confirmed by the court after a judicially ordered sheriff's auction of the security property.

In California, within fifteen days of the sale, the trustee is supposed to prepare and record a trustee's deed upon sale. According to the statute, the recorded notice relates back to 8 AM on the day the sale was held. Normally, a purchaser at the foreclosure sale will enjoy priority over a competing lienor whose interest was perfected before the actual moment of the sale but after 8 AM on the date of sale. Usually this is of no legal significance because the competing lienor would have been on constructive notice of the sale from the time the Notice of Default had been recorded. But in the case of a bankruptcy petition, the federal bankruptcy law automatically stays all creditor enforcement activities including foreclosures, at the precise moment the bankruptcy petition is filed.[57]

C. Timing and Costs for the Foreclosing Mortgage Lender from Default to Eviction

Timing. A California lender could possibly foreclose nonjudicially within six months, maybe a bit less, from the day the borrower first missed a mortgage payment to the day the property was sold at foreclosure. This would be a stretch under current law. A more realistic scenario would be ten to eleven months for a nonjudicial sale. The process could take three years for a judicial sale, longer if borrowers defend.

Some of the delay is due to California's Homeowner's Bill of Rights. This law requires lenders personally to contact defaulting borrowers and maintain a line of communication with them to avoid foreclosure if at all possible.

The pace of the foreclosure process also depends somewhat on how busy loan servicers are, and whether lenders are eager to add to their portfolio of foreclosed real estate properties.

Costs. Lenders and servicers begin incurring costs as soon as a borrower stops making mortgage payments.[58] Most likely, defaulting borrowers would also have stopped paying property taxes, casualty insurance premiums, and maintenance costs. The lender will need to pay these bills as well as legal and court fees, fees for foreclosure notices, auctioneers, and title insurance.

---

57. *In re Sandor*, 198 B.R. 326 (Bkrtcy.S. D. Cal. 1996). A foreclosure sale is invalid if conducted after the moment the bankruptcy petition is filed.

58. Policy Paper, May 28, 2008. © Mortgage Bankers Association May 2008. All Rights Reserve, THE WALL STREET JOURNAL (last visited Aug. 15, 2015), http://www.wsj.com/articles/after-foreclo sures-home-buyers-are-back-1428538655Foreclosure

Once the lender has taken title through a foreclosure auction or sale, it has to prepare and market the home for sale. These expenses can be significant, accounting for over 40 percent of foreclosure-related gross losses.

D. Acceleration, Equitable, Redemption, Cure, Reinstatement and Statutory Redemption

1. Acceleration

An *acceleration* clause in a note, deed of trust or mortgage gives the lender the right to declare the entire debt due and payable following a monetary default. Before acceleration, borrowers can cure defaults and reinstate their loans by making up the missed payments.

Why Lenders Accelerate. The right to accelerate is important to the lender because without it, the lender would be required to file a separate suit after each missed payment. Not accelerating, the lender would have to file suit monthly as payments fell due.

When Borrowers Are Relieved from Acceleration for Monetary Defaults. Borrowers may be allowed to halt the foreclosure process by just making up their missed payments, and not having to repay the entire loan amount, if: (1) a common court allows it; (2) a lender accepts it; (3) a statute grants them the right to reinstate; (4) the loan documents allow reinstatement; or (5) they file a Chapter 13 bankruptcy proceeding and a bankruptcy court allows it.

Waiver and Estoppel. Lenders can end up forfeiting their right to accelerate by a pattern of accepting late payments without forewarning borrowers that late payments will no longer be acceptable.

Many mortgages contain anti-waiver provisions that the lender accepting a late payment is not a waiver of its right to insist on timely payment in the future. Courts often disregard these clauses in the borrower's favor,[59] and will hold lenders to oral or written assurances that a late payment would unwind the acceleration.

---

59. *Kreiss Potassium Phosphate Co. v. Knight*, 124 So. 751, 98 Fla. 1004 (1929). *Cf. McGowan v. Pasol*, 605 S.W.2d 728, 732 (Tex. App. 1980) (After affirming trial court's decision that lender had no right to foreclose because of a late payment when lender had often accepted late payments in the past, the appellate court explained: Ordinarily, acceptance of past due installments on a note waives only the option to accelerate on the past defaults and does not waive the option to declare the balance due on the note for future defaults.... However, where, as is the case here, the holder of the note has accepted late payments on numerous occasions in the past, he is precluded from accelerating the maturity of an installment note because of a single late payment unless he has, prior to the late payment for which default is claimed, notified the maker that in the future he will not accept late payments.... Even though the January, 1977, note contained a waiver of notice of acceleration provision, it did not provide for automatic acceleration in the event of default, nor did it provide that the holder's failure to exercise the option to accelerate upon default would not constitute a waiver of exercise of the same right upon any subsequent default.). *See generally* Robert R. Rosenthal, *The Role of Courts of Equity in Preventing Acceleration Predicated Upon a Mortgagor's Inadvertent Default*, 22 Syracuse L. Rev. 897 (1971). (even with advance warning the lender may not be able to accelerate in some states where courts deem acceleration a disproportionately harsh remedy for a minor payment delay).

The Mailbox Rule. Mortgage borrowers claiming the check was lost in the mail are out of luck. The "mailbox rule" that documents are presumed effective when post-marked, or on the date mailed, applies to offer and acceptance, tax returns and court filings, but not to the payment of debt. However, when a borrower always mails payments to the lender, and a check is truly lost in the mail, courts often imply waiver of actual delivery as long as the borrower, once notified, promptly tenders the missed payment.[60]

When Borrowers Are Relieved from Non-Monetary Defaults. Borrowers willing to incur the costs and uncertainties of litigation may find arguments to support their petitions to enjoin the lender from accelerating for non-monetary defaults.

Some of those alleged defaults involve questions of fact, for instance, whether the borrower's lax maintenance really constitutes "waste" or whether too frequent Airbnb rentals converts an owner-occupant into an innkeeper, violating "an owner occupant" requirement in the mortgage loan documents.[61]

Further, the lender will have to demonstrate that the borrower's conduct threatens the lender's "security interest."[62] Of the many possible definitions of "security interest," the lender will contend that any diminution in the value of the property is impairing. The borrower will counter that as long as the disputed conduct did not demonstrably reduce the value of the property below the loan balance due, it was not an impairment justifying foreclosure.

Only an alleged breach that is "material" justifies foreclosure. "A non-monetary default (failure to maintain the property, failure to provide financial statements, etc.) may not be a material default."[63]

2. Equitable Redemption

This term refers to a prerogative that English chancery courts granted mortgagors to pay their debts in full after the debt had matured, even if they were a bit late.[64] By our current norms of consumer protection, this may not seem like much of a concession. But it represented a significant debtor protection in the 17th century.

The mortgagee was regarded as the owner as a matter of law unless the debtor paid the full amount of the debt precisely on time called the law day. This was centuries

---

60. *Kerin v. Udolf*, 334 A.2d 434, 165 Conn. 264 (1973).

61. NK "http://massrealestatelawblog.com/2014/07/24/airbnb-rentals-raise-thorny-legal-issues/ "http://massrealestatelawblog.com/2014/07/24/airbnb-rentals-raise-thorny-legal-issues/ (Last visited 07/05/20160.

62. "The justification for the right to accelerate is to protect the beneficiary from actions by the trustor that jeopardize or impair the beneficiary's security." 5 Cal. Real Est. § 13:168 (4th ed.)

63. Stephen B. Yoken, *Foreclosure on Real Property in Nevada* (National Business Institute Seminar April 16, 2009).(Last visited 07/04/2016). https://www.swlaw.com/assets/pdf/publications/2009/04/ 16/Foreclosure-on-Real-Property-in-Nevada_9515502_1.pdf

64. Charles J. Reid Jr., *The Seventeenth-Century Revolution in the English Land Law*, 43 Clev. St. L. Rev. 221 (1995) (last visited Mar. 21, 2016), available at http://engagedscholarship.csuohio.edu/ clevstlrev/vol43/iss2/4

before the days of escrow agents and wire transfers. The mortgagor had to hand over cash or its equivalent to the creditor. Sometimes, mortgagors were late—but not necessarily because they lacked the funds. Quite often, the value of the property exceeded the amount of the debt. English land prices often spiked upward, especially during times of rampant inflation. Cunning creditors hid or went abroad on "law day," and having not been paid strictly on time, returned to declare themselves absolute owners of the debtor's estate.

Law courts sided with mortgage lenders but by the 17th century equity courts were allowing mortgagors to repay their debts late—within a judicially determined "reasonable" time. This right to pay late came to be known as the *equity of redemption*. This is how the word "equity" came to be used to describe the value of the owner's interest in the security property. Debtors paying late could be quite unfair to creditors. Creditors could never be sure how late was too late. "Late" could sometimes be a matter of years.

So mortgage lenders began to initiate suits as soon as mortgagors defaulted, seeking courts to set a "drop dead" date beyond which the borrower would have forfeited any claim to regain title. Thus was born the foreclosure law suit!

Mortgage lenders saw judicial foreclosure as a last resort, expensive and tedious.[65] Lenders were not allowed to keep the land and call themselves even. They had to sell the land, and were allowed only to keep so much of the sale proceeds as were left after deducting their costs of sale and the amount the debtor owed. Any surplus belonged to the mortgagor.

Mortgage lenders began contracting in their loan agreements for the right, if the mortgagor defaulted, to sell the security property on their own, free of judicial supervision,[66] a right to a private power of sale which Parliament eventually confirmed.[67] In situations where lenders brought foreclosure actions ahead of selling the realty, occasionally, English equity courts began to order sales of foreclosed property on their own. Thus, we can find in English practice the origins of both nonjudicial and judicial foreclosure sales. Courts favored foreclosure by sale for the same reason they allowed tardy borrowers to pay late: to make sure the borrower received any surplus value from the security property after payment of the mortgage debt.[68]

3. Loan Provisions Allowing Cure and Reinstatement

Most borrowers, having defaulted on their mortgages, are in no position to prepay the entire mortgage debt; equitable redemption was a right they seldom possessed the means to exercise.[69]

---

65. Frederick Pollock, THE LAND LAWS 128 (1896, republished in 2000).

66. Ibid. See also, James Geoffrey Dunham, *In Defense of Strict Foreclosure: A Legal and Economic Analysis of Mortgage Foreclosure*, 36 So. CAR. L. REV. 461 (1985).

67. Edgar Noble Durfee and Delmar W. Doddridge, *Redemption from Foreclosure Sale: The Uniform Mortgage Act*, 23 MICH. L. REV.825, 827 (1925).

68. Morris G. Shanker, *Will Mortgage Law Survive?*, 54 CASE W. RES. L. REV. 69 (2003).

69. 59 C.J.S. MORTGAGES ' 516 (database updated June 2004).

The borrower can learn the exact amount needed to cure the default as well as a good-through date for the amount due by requesting a reinstatement quote or reinstatement letter. The quote will include:

- all of the back and current payments now due

- any applicable late fees

- the cost of any property inspections

- the attorney/trustee fees and costs for the foreclosure procedure

- other expenses incurred to preserve and protect the lender's interest in the property, and

- often, a recording fee for the notice of cancellation of the sale.

In the U.S., reinstatement free of acceleration is embedded in most residential mortgage loans. For instance, the FNMA/FHLMC single family form requires that the lender cannot start the foreclosure process without first sending the borrower a notice allowing a 30-day grace period during which to cure the default.[70] The form can omit these provisions only when state law offers mortgagors more generous protections against acceleration.

Statutes in many states allow reinstatement free of acceleration.[71] Some apply only when the security property is the mortgagor's residence,[72] but most apply to all mortgages. The requisite time for cure ranges from the moment before the foreclosure sale commences to a period 90 days earlier than that.[73]

The California foreclosure statute gives the borrower up to five days before the sale to cure the default. But the trustee conducting the foreclosure on behalf of the lender (the trust deed beneficiary) has the option of accepting the borrower's payment curing the default as late as a nanosecond before the foreclosure sale commenced.[74]

Once the borrower cures the default, the lender is required to dismiss the foreclosure proceeding, and, within 21 days of reinstatement, execute and deliver a notice to the

---

70. If I am in default, the Note Holder may send me a written notice telling me that if I do not pay the overdue amount by a certain date, the Note Holder may require me to pay immediately the full amount of Principal which has not been paid and all the interest that I owe on that amount. That date must be at least 30 days after the date on which the notice is mailed to me. Clause 6C, Multi-Family Note (last visited Aug. 15, 2015), http://www.goodmanlaw.com/pdf/fnma-nte.pdf

71. Ariz. Rev. Stat. Ann. ' 33-813 (1956); Cal. Civ. Code ' 2924c (West Supp. 1983); Ill. Ann. Stat. ch. 95, para. 57 (Smith-Hurd Supp. 1983-84); Minn. Stat. Ann. ' 580.30 (West Supp. 1983); Miss. Code Ann. ' 89-1-59 (Supp. 1982); Neb. Rev. Stat. ' 76-1012 (1981); Pa. Stat. Ann. tit. 41, ' 404 (Purdon Supp. 1983-84); Utah Code Ann. ' 57-1-31 (1981); Wash. Rev. Code Ann. ' 61.24.090 (1974).

72. Texas Prop. Code Ann. ' 51.002 (d) (Vernon 1995).

73. Minn. Stat. Ann. 580.30 (West 2000) allows reinstatement at any time before the sale of the premises. N.D. Cent. Code 32-19-28 (2003) allows 30 days from service of notice before foreclosure. In Illinois the commercial mortgagor has 90 days before foreclosure sale to cure. 735 Ill. Comp. Stat. 5/15-1602 (2004).

74. *Finucane v. Union Planters Bank, N.A.*, 732 N.E.2d 175 (Ind. Ct. App. 2000).

trustee rescinding the declaration of default. The trustee should record the notice of reinstatement no later than 30 days afterward.

Some states limit the frequency with which a mortgagor can avail itself of forbearance.[75] Other states discourage mortgagors from defaulting repeatedly by permitting the lender to assess its reasonable costs and attorneys' fees each time the mortgagor cures a default.

4. Statutory Redemption

Definition. Foreclosure terminates the borrower's *equitable* right of redemption. That was the historic purpose of foreclosure.

Statutory redemption laws in 33 states allow the foreclosed debtor to re-purchase the security property from the foreclosure sale purchaser, usually at the foreclosure sales price. Legislators know that bidding at foreclosure sales is rarely robust. This way, borrowers can get back their property is the foreclosure sale was too much of a bargain for the winning bidder. (Foreclosed borrowers don't need cash to benefit from these laws; they can assign their statutory rights of redemption.)

The Policy Debate. The policy debate over the wisdom of statutory redemption turns on whether redemption increases or decreases the amounts bid at foreclosure sales. Advocates of statutory redemption thought it would discourage bidders from offering too little at foreclosure sales. Others contend that it probably has the opposite effect since it discourages bidders from paying full value because they do not receive title to the property until the redemption period ends. Nonetheless, borrowers utilize their rights under these laws often enough to demonstrate that they have some utility.[76]

The Redemption Price. Predominantly, states require the foreclosed borrower to pay the foreclosure sales price, plus accrued interest and certain allowable costs. In a few states, the borrower redeems by paying the foreclosed debt, plus interest, if the foreclosing lender bought the property at foreclosure.

Redemption Time Periods. The redemption period ranges from a few months to as long as 18 months, sometimes depending on the type of property involved. Owner-occupants and farmers tend to get more time.

California sets the period at one year if the lender, foreclosing by judicial sale, seeks a deficiency judgment, three months if the foreclosure sales price equals or exceeds the debt, and zero if the lender renounces the chance of a deficiency before the sale.

---

75. [S]uch relief shall not be again available to the mortgagor under the same mortgage for a period of five years from the date of dismissal of such foreclosure. 735 ILL. COMP. STAT. ' 5/15-1602 (2004).

76. Patrick B. Bauer, *Statutory Redemption Reconsidered: The* Operation *of Iowa's Redemption Statute in Two Counties Between 1881 and 1980,* 70 IOWA L. REV. 363, 412 (1985): Within the century as a whole, Iowa's redemption statute was used to rectify price inadequacy in slightly more than one of every ten mortgage foreclosure sales and in almost three of every ten judgment execution sales.

Type of Sale from Which Redemption Is Possible. Some states, Minnesota for one, allow redemption from either a judicial or nonjudicial foreclosure. In other states, it is available for one or the other but not both; in Missouri, only from a nonjudicial foreclosure, in Washington, Utah and California only from judicial foreclosure.

Right to Possession During the Redemption Period. In most states the borrower retains the right to possession during the redemption period giving them a roof over their heads while they try to scrape up the means of redeeming.

During this time, the foreclosure sale purchaser has only a future interest, usually evidenced by a certificate of sale, contingent on the redemption right not being exercised. They receive a deed only when the redemption period has ended and the right has lapsed. The uncertain outcome and the long wait surely discourages potential bidders.

Obligations of Borrowers in Possession During Redemption Period. When borrowers remain in possession during protracted redemption periods, foreclosing lenders fear inadequate maintenance, maybe even property damage or destruction, loss of rent and interest.

Some states address this by specifying standards. Colorado, for instance, requires borrowers to keep the premises in repair, use reasonable diligence to continue to keep the premises yielding an adequate income, pay current taxes, and keep the premises insured for the protection of the holder of the certificate of purchase.[77] Failure constitutes waste under the statute.

Effect of Borrower's Redemption on Extinguished Junior Liens. In most states, the borrower's redemption revives any junior liens erased by the foreclosure sale. But in California, the redeeming borrower takes title free of junior liens, presumably as an added incentive for junior lienors to bid at the foreclosure sale so the sale brings the best possible price.[78]

Of course, the junior lienor whose lien is extinguished by the senior lienor foreclosing, like any other unsecured creditor, can sue the borrower personally on the unpaid note. Once the junior lienor obtains a judgment, that judgment can attach to the property which the borrower acquired by redemption, subject to intervening liens. So if the value of the property rises, or if the statutory redemption price was below market value, the junior lienor may be able to recover some or all of the debt at the end of the day.

---

77. COLO. REV. STAT. 38-38-602 (2000). California allows the foreclosure sale purchaser to collect and hold rents and profits from the property or charge the debtor the fair use value if the debtor elects to remain in possession, to enter the property to make repairs and obtain a court order restraining waste. But if redemption is exercised, the foreclosure sale purchaser must account to the redeeming party for rents and profits received during the redemption period. CAL. CIV. PROC. CODE ' 729.000 et seq. (West 1980).

78. Oddly enough, junior liens are revived in California when the mortgagor purchases at the senior lienor's foreclosure sale. The author has no explanation for why the redeeming mortgagor should take title free of junior liens but not the purchasing mortgagor.

E. Foreclosure Sales: Judicial and Non-Judicial

1. Differences Between Judicial and Power of Sale Procedures

Generally, foreclosure by public auction is the rule in the U.S., for which there are two formats: *judicial and power of sale (nonjudicial)*.[79] All states allow *judicial foreclosure*. This involves a lawsuit resulting in a decree authorizing a public official, usually the sheriff, to sell the property at public auction.

A majority of states also permit *power of sale (nonjudicial foreclosure)*.[80] These sales are conducted by the foreclosing lender or by a trustee that the lender designates under a deed of trust.

Professional trustees, appointed by the lender, oversee all aspects of the sale, meeting the notice requirements, conduct the sale, and then issuing a Trustee's Deed upon Sale (TDUS) to the winning bidder.

The lender can only exercise this right by specific reference in its security instrument.[81]

Federal statutes authorize the Department of Housing and Urban Development (HUD) to foreclose its residential mortgages multi-family and one-to-four-unit dwellings by nonjudicial sale.[82]

The biggest difference between judicial and nonjudicial foreclosures is that judicial sales start with a lawsuit that is almost always filed by an attorney. A lawsuit ends typically with a court judgment directing sale of the property and appointment of an officer to conduct the sale, a Writ of Sale, a Notice of Levy and Notice of Sale. The levying public officer executes, records and serves the levy. Notice is mailed and served to occupants of the property, posted and advertised as required by statute. The sale is held. Following the sale, the designated trustee issues a deed, the Trustee's Deed Upon Sale (TDUS) or a certificate of sale if the property is subject to redemption (discussed later). A TDUS contains no covenants or warranties.

Routinely, when a deed of trust is originated, the mortgage lender names one of its own employees or a title insurance company to serve as the nominal trustee. These

---

79. For a clear description of one state's judicial and nonjudicial foreclosure processes, *see* Monica Amis Wittrock, *Residential Liens and Foreclosures (Oklahoma Focus)*, 51 OKLA. L. REV. 269 (1998).

80. RESTATEMENT (THIRD) OF PROPERTY *(Mortgages)* at 575 (1997). A state-by-state list appears in Baxter Dunaway, THE LAW OF DISTRESSED REAL ESTATE App. 9A (Clark Boardman Callaghan 1989).

81. Should a California lawyer representing a borrower in a loan secured by California real estate say anything when she observes that the lender's lawyer, from New York, has neglected to reserve the right of power of sale foreclosure in the deed of trust? In New York, mortgages are foreclosed judicially. In California, most deeds of trust are foreclosed by nonjudicial sale assuming the power is reserved in the deed of trust. But some New York lawyers don't know that, just as some California lawyers don't realize the legal hazards of foreclosing by power of sale in New York.

82. *See generally* Patrick A. Randolph, Jr., *The New Federal Foreclosure Laws*, 49 OKLA L. REV. 123 (1996); Ann M. Burkhart, *Real Estate Practice in the Twenty-First Century*, 72 MO. L. REV. 1031 (2007).

trustees do nothing as long as the loan is in good standing. Once the lender decides to foreclose upon a defaulting debtor's interest,[83] it will substitute a new trustee, typically a private firm which specializes in conducting foreclosures. Some law firms oversee this kind of work but most trustee firms operate independent of lawyers.

Statutes prescribe the form and procedure for posting, publishing, recording and mailing the notice of intent to sell and the notice of sale. Unlike judicial proceedings, there is no requirement for personal service of process. Mailed notices suffice. Statutes also prescribe the rules governing conduct of the sale. In most states, sales may be conducted by anyone chosen by the trustee or beneficiary. There is no need to wait for a place on the sheriff's schedule, as there is with a judicially ordered sale.

Theoretically, the trustee is supposed to act as a common agent of borrower and lender. That was why courts and legislatures went along with the idea of privately conducted sales in the first place. In practice, the lender designates the trustee. In order to assure fairness to the borrower, statutes and state court decisions impose norms of "good faith" and neutrality upon trustees.[84]

Whether lender-appointed trustees fetch higher prices than courts or sheriffs may be disputed. But nonjudicial foreclosures save lenders the cost of court proceedings, and the process is much quicker.

2. Possible Borrower Defenses Against Judicial and Non-Judicial Sales

Borrowers sometimes interpose defenses to foreclosure. In judicial foreclosure, these become part of the borrower's responsive pleadings. In a nonjudicial foreclosure sale, the borrower needs to petition a court in order to challenge a foreclosure sale, either before or after the sale.

---

83. There is no need to designate a trustee at all until commencement of the foreclosure process since the recordation of the deed of trust won't be affected by the absence of a named trustee. Subsequent purchasers and creditors of the security property will be charged with constructive notice anyway as long as the beneficiary and trustor are properly identified. *Bisbee v. Sec. Nat'l Bank & Trust Co.*, 754 P. 2d 1135, 157 Ariz. 31(1988).

84. *See*, e.g., West's Revised Code of Washington Annotated 61.24.010: (3) The trustee or successor trustee shall have no fiduciary duty or fiduciary obligation to the grantor or other persons having an interest in the property subject to the deed of trust.(4) The trustee or successor trustee has a duty of good faith to the borrower, beneficiary, and grantor.

The state of Colorado dispatches with even the appearance of collusion between the foreclosing trustee and the mortgage lender by empowering an official called the public trustee to oversee all power of sale foreclosures within its borders. Willis Carpenter, *A Brief History of Colorado's Public Trustee System (1894-2002)*, 31 Colo. Law. 67 (Feb. 2002).

In Michigan, nonjudicial sales are allowed as long as the mortgage contains a power of sale provision. The sale is conducted by the sheriff after the lender complies with statutory provisions regarding notice by advertising. http://www.nolo.com/legal-encyclopedia/summary-michigans-foreclosure-laws.html (Last visited 06/24/2016).).

Lenders go too far down the road of self-dealing by allowing one of their own employees or partners to conduct the sale and then purchasing the property at their own sale, unless they are in a state that explicitly allows this as several states have done T.M. Claauretie, *State Foreclosure Laws, Risk Shifting, and the Private Mortgage Insurance Industry*, 56 J. Risk and Insur. 544 (1989).

The most commonly asserted defenses to foreclosure are:

- The borrower never defaulted; the servicing agent simply credited the wrong account with the payments.

- The lender miscalculated the sums due;

- No valid lien existed against the property because the borrower's signature was forged;

- In originating the loan the lender or mortgage broker neglected to take into account the suitability of the loan in light of the borrower's limited financial means, or falsified the borrower's loan application to show more income and assets than the borrower had;[85]

- The foreclosing lender or trustee failed to name all interested parties;

- The foreclosing lender or trustee failed to comply in detail with notice and other procedural requirements of state foreclosure law that resulted in demonstrable harm to the borrower;[86]

- The foreclosure sale price was grossly inadequate, and was tainted by irregularity, unfairness or fraud;[87]

- A grossly inadequate foreclosure sales price was attributable to a procedural defect in the sale;[88]

---

85. A mortgage fraud blog describes a trial November 25, 2008, in which a mortgage broker James Sparks testified that he modified the borrower's loan application to show an income high enough to support the lender's required loan to value ratio, Mortgage Fraud Blog (last visited Aug. 14, 2015), http://www.mortgagefraudblog.com/index.php/weblog/comments/pair_indicted_in_los_angeles_foreclosure_rescue_scheme/

86. Certain types of notice defects can be fatal though most are not. For instance, the notice of sale could have inaccurately described the property being sold by omitting a portion of it. The portion of the property that was omitted from the notice of sale will be excluded from the property sold. "A nonjudicial foreclosure sale is presumed to have been conducted regularly and fairly; one attacking the sale must overcome this common law presumption by pleading and proving an improper procedure and the resulting prejudice." Knapp v. Doherty, 123 Cal.App.4th 76, 20 Cal.Rptr.3d 1 (2004). In this case, the borrower received notice of sale earlierless than the statutory requisite of 90 days after the notice of default but nine days earlier than the statute required the trustee to send notice of sale. In fact, the sale did not actually take place until a year later. The borrower never bid at the sale, and the property was sold to a third party bidder.

87. Molly F. Jacobson-Greany, *Setting Aside Nonjudicial Foreclosure Sales: Extending the Rule to Cover Both Intrinsic and Extrinsic Fraud or Unfairness*, 23 Emory Bankr. Dev. J. 139, 154 (2006). See, *e.g, Johnson v. Jefferson Standard Life Ins. Co.*, 429 P.2d 474, 5 Ariz. App. 587 (1967). The high bidder paid $5,000 for property worth $73,000. The sale was set aside because the deputy sheriff had failed to read the notice of sale at the county courthouse, and the mortgagee arrived eight minutes late with an offer of $56,228.

88. Court opinions and Restatement (Third) of Property Restatement (Third) of Property (Mortgages) § 8.3 (1997), condone setting aside a regularly conducted foreclosure sale when the price is grossly inadequate.

Courts seldom do. Courts recognize that property sold at foreclosure seldom brings the same price as property sold at leisure and pursuant to normal marketing techniques. They also realize that setting aside these sales too easily would be more likely to reduce incentives to bid at the sales

- The originating lender violated the Truth in Lending Act and/or the Real Estate Settlement Procedures Act;[89]

- The original transaction was fraudulent and the lender financing it owed a duty to the seller to discover this;[90]

- The mortgagee misrepresented the value of the property;[91]

- The mortgagee exercised so much control over the property, it became an unwitting partner or joint venturer, and partners and joint venturers are barred from foreclosing against each other;[92]

---

than to induce foreclosing lenders to spend good money advertising those sales. After all, borrowers with valuable equities could list their properties for sale with a broker before they go into default, or even afterward.

An extreme example of a court refusing to set aside a foreclosure sale for gross inadequacy of price arose in California not long ago. A judgment creditor had initiated proceedings resulting in a judicially supervised sheriff's sale of the borrower's property. Stuck in traffic, the creditor's bidder was a couple of minutes late for the sale. The high bid had been $2,000. The creditor had planned to bid $6.5 million for the property, estimated to be worth between six and ten million dollars. A California appellate court refused to set aside the sale in the face of a statute, that a judicial foreclosure is "absolute and may not be set aside for any reason." *Amalgamated Bank v. Superior Court*, 149 Cal. App. 4th 1003, 57 Cal. Rptr. 3d 686 (2007).

A few cases have hinged on the basis of it. For one of those few, see *Pisano v. Tupper*, 591 N.Y.S.2d 888, 188 App. Div. 2d 991 (1992) (sale price of $5,000 for $80,000 farm held so grossly inadequate that it shocks the conscience of the court). The Restatement endorses a 20% benchmark for actionable price inadequacy.

When inadequacy of price is combined with sale irregularities, courts are inclined to set aside the sale. In Texas, for example, a court will not set aside a winning bid, even one that is well below fair market value at the date of sale, unless the sale procedures were seriously flawed, the sale price was grossly inadequate and there was a causal connection between the procedural defect in the sale and the grossly inadequate selling price. Motten v. Chase Home Fin., 831 F. Supp. 2d 988, 994 (S.D. Tex. 2011) (applying Texas law); Anna Kalinina, Grossly Inadequate Procedure; Non-Judicial Foreclosure in Texas, 65 Baylor L. Rev. 1061, 1074 (2013).

89. Nearly every residential mortgage loan has TILA and/or RESPA violations which can be used as leverage in negotiations, or litigated, McFarlin & Guerts, LLP (last visited Aug. 14, 2015), http://www.mcfarlinlaw.com/

90. *Mathurin v. Lost & Found Recovery, LLC,*19 Misc.3d 756, 854 N.Y.S.2d 629 (N.Y. Supp 2008).

Plaintiffs couldn't afford payments on their mortgage and were persuaded to deed the property to the impecunious nominee of a foreclosure rescue scam artist, and take back a lease-purchase option. The con artist promised the plaintiff homeowners that it would obtain a new loan on more favorable terms and re-convey title back to the plaintiffs after a year. Instead, the con artist conveyed title to a straw buyer and refinanced plaintiff's loan for $133,000 more than the balance on that mortgage. The straw buyer promptly defaulted on the mortgage. Plaintiffs sued to enjoin the refinancing mortgagee's foreclosure. The court allowed plaintiffs to proceed to trial to prove that the bank that made the refi loan owed a duty to them as sellers to learn that they had been duped by a crook who had engaged in many of these illicit deals, arranging loans for buyers with no capacity or intent to repay the debts.

91. Robin Paul Malloy, *Lender Liability for Negligent Real Estate Appraisals*, 1984 U. Ill. L. Rev. 53 (1984).

92. Lender liability claims arise when lenders exercise extraordinary control over the borrower's business practices or breach promises concerning forbearance. For a list of useful lender precautions, see Joshua Stein, *Troubled Loans: Overview, Options and Strategy* ,549 PLI/Real 267 (2008).

- The mortgagor tendered partial performance and the mortgagee seemed to have accepted it;[93]
- The foreclosing mortgagee is not the original mortgagee and cannot establish an uninterrupted chain of ownership of the note from its inception;[94]
- The trustee foreclosing under a deed of trust cannot demonstrate that it was instructed to foreclose by the original beneficiary or its assignee holding the note.

3. Borrower Defenses to Foreclosure Based on Flawed Mortgage Loan Transfer Procedures: Show Me the Note and Proof of the Mortgage Assignment

We turn to the last two items on the above list. They resulted from the inept documentation that many participants in mortgage securitization routinely used as they transferred mortgage loans from originators to bond investors.

Here, we answer these questions:

(1) Ideally, how should the present holder of a mortgage loan document or authenticate its right to enforce the borrower's original obligation when it is not the original lender?

(2) Why have so many lenders been unable to provide this basic documentation when borrowers request it on the eve of foreclosure?

(3) Should borrowers be able to delay or prevent foreclosures initiated by lenders incapable of evidencing a flawless paper trail showing how they came to the present owners of the mortgage loan?

The Perfect Paper Trail for Mortgage Loan Assignments. Ideally, the foreclosing entity should be able to produce:

(1) a purchase agreement for the note and mortgage with the loan specifically identified along with the date of the sale transaction;

(2) physical possession of the original note, best of all endorsed to the holder either on the back of the note or by an endorsement firmly attached to the note ("an allonge");[95]

---

93. Stuart M. Saft, *Borrowers' Defenses to Mortgage Foreclosures*, 7 REAL EST. FIN. J. 5 (Fall 1991); Kathleen Agan Knox, *Procedures to Delay Real Property Foreclosures*, 23 W. ST. U. L. REV. 303 (1996).

94. By statute and case law in a growing number of states a foreclosing mortgage holder must prove that it has a recorded chain of assignments from the original mortgagee. See, e.g., Cal. Civ. Code § 2924(a)(6) (Borrower is entitled to see written evidence that the foreclosing entity is the holder of the beneficial interest in the deed of trust, the original trustee, or the substituted trustee or designated agent of the trust deed holder.); *Bayview Loan Servicing, L.L.C. v. Nelson*, 890 N.E.2d 940 (Ill.App.2008). Foreclosure defense attorneys are well aware of this defense and inform borrowers: The right to payment depends, with limited exceptions, upon the foreclosing lender's actual possession of the note. The property owner's first line of defense is show me the note, not a copy, but the original, and show how the foreclosing lender has come to the right to payment under the note (by proper endorsement or assignment.) From the website of M. W. Roth, a California foreclosure defense attorney (last visited Aug.15,2015), http://www.mwroth.com/foreclosuredefense.html. (Last visited 06/22/2016).

95. § 3-104(a) of the Uniform Commercial Code (UCC). Also, under § 3-301 of the UCC, the right to enforcement of a note lies with the holder of a note and nonholders in possession of a note.

(3) a copy of the original mortgage or deed of trust and of each assignment of it;

(4) evidence of the time and date when the mortgage or deed of trust was first recorded. Copies of all assignments of mortgages, stamped with the time and date when each of them was recorded in the public land records.[96] (State laws vary on whether assignments of mortgages or deeds of trust need to be recorded as a pre-condition to foreclosure.)[97]

The Documentation Problem. A mortgage lender before initiating foreclosure should have in its possession the mortgage borrower's original note and accompanying mortgage or deed of trust. A foreclosing lender that did not originate the loan should be able to produce the note signed by the original debtor and endorsed to itself, along with an assignment of the deed of trust.

Had a loan changed hands more than once, the present owner should be able to trace the ownership trail of the note and mortgage, just as a homeowner could trace its title back to a grant from the sovereign, or for a shorter but generally acceptable period of time.

In the universe of securitized loans, the original lender sold the note signed by the borrower, along with the accompanying deed of trust or mortgage, to a loan aggregator who sold the debt to an issuer of mortgage backed bonds who would transfer title to a trustee for the bond holders, who would authorize a document custodian to take possession of the paperwork and contract with a loan servicer to collect and, if necessary, foreclose.

Notes are transferred by delivery (physical possession) and endorsed to "bearer" or to a designated assignee. For the note purchaser to be a holder in due course, free of certain defenses the borrower might have had against the originating lender, the note had to meet certain tests of "negotiability" and be physically delivered to the ultimate note purchaser, made payable to bearer or endorsed to a specific note buyer.

Section 3-301 also permits a party to enforce a mortgage note if the note has been lost, stolen or destroyed. However, in these instances, the party that seeks to enforce the note must prove that it has the right to enforce the note, commonly established by a lost document affidavit.

96. "Recording is necessary to establish the mortgagee's priority relative to the claims of other parties to the property securing the borrower's note. It is evident enough that deeds of trust themselves ought to be recorded, to ensure that subsequent potential purchasers and encumbrancers of the property have notice of them and thereby take their proper place in line when claims against the land need to be ranked: Grantees want to be assured their titles are marketable and lenders to be assured that their liens have priority." Bernhardt, Roger, "The Uncertain Requirement for Recording Assignments of Deeds of Trust" (2011). Publications. Paper 461. http://digitalcommons.law.ggu.edu/pubs/461.An assignment that is not recorded when the loan is assigned is worthless in terms of providing transparency to borrowers...." Dale Whitman, *What We Have Learned From The Mortgage Crisis About Transferring Mortgage Loans,* 49 REAL PROP TRUST & ESTATE LJ 1, 55 (Spring 2014).

97. In California, the assignment of the mortgage would need to be recorded before it was foreclosed but an assignment of the deed of trust would not be. See *Calvo v HSBC Bank* (2011) 199 Cal. App. 4th 118, 130 Cal. Rptr. 3d 815 (2011). "A promissory note is a negotiable instrument the lender may sell without notice to the borrower. The deed of trust, moreover, is inseparable from the note it secures, and follows it even without a separate assignment." *Yvanova v New Century Mortgage Corp.* 62 C4th 919, 927(2016). A mortgage is security for a debt, and becomes worthless once the debt is repaid. (Last visited 06/26/2016).

Court Outcomes. Courts have reached conflicting outcomes on what counts as a procedural shortcoming, and whether borrowers should have standing to challenge these procedural shortcomings in record keeping.[98] As mentioned earlier, because of the volume of foreclosures, many banks systematically failed to follow basic procedural safeguards, particularly from 2008 to 2011. Notably, in the 2012 settlement for $26 billion of the suit by the federal government and 49 states against banks and mortgage servicers, aggrieved former homeowners were given the opportunity to sue the banks if they alleged that they had lost their homes because of these improper procedures.[99]

Even when borrowers are granted standing to challenge foreclosures as procedurally flawed, they will have to show that the foreclosing mortgagee or trustee really did not own the loan on the date it initiated or authorized the commencement of foreclosure. Most of the glitches raised in litigated cases would not suffice.[100]

The only benefit defaulting borrowers reap from these skirmishes over flawed paperwork would be protracted periods of rent-free possession while the lender or loan servicer corrected their paperwork.

Procedural challenges to the foreclosing lender's missing or tardy paperwork should not be confused with those cases in which borrowers contended that they were not in default, were overcharged, or never owed the sums in the first place. In cases like these, courts expect lenders to produce probative evidence supporting their petitions.[101] Errors like these make foreclosures void. A foreclosing lender not producing an unbroken chain of endorsements of the note from the original holder to itself, render a sale voidable rather than void. Bare legal title passes to the foreclosure sale purchaser, subject to the right to set the sale aside by those injured by the defective foreclosure, such as the true owner of the note if the foreclosing lender did not.

Courts granting borrowers standing to challenge flawed documentation do not bar the foreclosing lender from returning to court later with a better prepared case. Decisions granting borrowers the right to sue are not *res judicata*. Courts dismiss these procedural skirmishes "without prejudice," entitling the lender or mortgage servicer to re-file once its paperwork is in order.

"While courts rarely explain the reasoning behind this aversion, it seems to arise from a reflexive belief that such an outcome would be unjust. Courts are therefore

---

98. Alan M. White, *Losing The Paper—Mortgage Assignments, Note Transfers And Consumer Protection*, 24 Loy. Consumer L. Rev. 468 (2012).

99. Goldie Sommer, *The Secret of the Short Sale*, 16 No. 12 Westlaw Journal Bank & Lender Liability 2 (2010).

100. Richard E. Gottlieb, James M. Golden, Brett J. Natarelli, *The Foreclosure Firestorm: "Robo-Signing" Allegations Have More Bark Than Bite*,67 Bus. Law. 649 (Feb. 2012).

See *Livonia Property Holdings, LLC v. 12840-12976 Farmington Rd. Holdings, LLC*, 717 F. Supp. 2d 724, 737 (E.D. Mich. 2010) (holding that a "litigant who is not a party to an assignment lacks standing to challenge that assignment").

101. *Glarum v. LaSalle Bank Nat'l Ass'n*, 83 So. 3d 780, 783 (Fla. Dist. Ct. App. 2011).

quick to sidestep well-established principles of res judicata in favor of ad hoc measures meant to protect banks against the specter of 'free houses.'"[102]

According to three student commentators who examined the issue, there would be substantial advantages to courts not giving lenders a second chance to re-file an illegitimate or rushed suit. Homeowners would have more time up front to regain their financial footing and negotiate a modification or repayment plan. "Courts' adhesion to traditional res judicata principles in the foreclosure process would have the added benefit of making negotiated settlements with borrowers more appealing to banks."[103]

4. Setting Aside Completed Foreclosure Sales to Bona Fide Purchasers

Foreclosing lenders are often the purchasers at their own foreclosure sales. One reason is that they are allowed to bid the amount of the debt. This avoids the circuity of the lender as purchaser writing a check to the trustee conducting the sale, and then having the trustee remit the funds back to the lender. Hence, it is often the situation that when a court invalidates a completed foreclosure sale, no one but the foreclosing lender is involved. But equities change when a foreclosed borrower attempts to regain title from a bona fide purchaser.

The bona fide purchaser has relied on the integrity of the foreclosure process, was certainly not responsible for any procedural shortcomings, raised money to cover the cost of the purchase, may well have made plans regarding the use of the property following foreclosure, and may even have taken possession before the borrower filed suit to set aside the sale.

V. The Junior Lienor

A. Lien Priorities

Foreclosure not only erases the borrower's equity of redemption, it also eliminates any interests the borrower created after the foreclosed mortgage was first recorded. These "wiped out" interests include junior mortgage liens, recorded judgments of general creditors, easements and leases.

In legal jargon, the borrower is said to have transferred to the junior lienor a portion of the equity of redemption subject to earlier liens. Since a foreclosure by the earlier lienholder would wipe out the borrower's interest in the security property, such a foreclosure would also terminate any liens created by the borrower after the first one.

Though the junior lienor's security interest would be dissipated by a senior lienor's foreclosure sale, the borrower remains personally liable to the junior lienor unless the loan had been made on a nonrecourse basis.

---

102. Megan Wachspress, Jessie Agatstein, Christian Mott, *In Defense Of "Free Houses,"* 125 Yale L.J. 1115, 1126-27 (2016).

103. Megan Wachspress, Jessie Agatstein, Christian Mott, *In Defense Of "Free Houses,"* 125 Yale L.J. 1115, 1127 (2016).

Conversely, a junior lienor's foreclosure leaves senior liens intact. A winning bidder at the junior lienor's foreclosure sale takes title subject to those liens.

Generally, junior lienors have no right to force lienors senior to them to join in their foreclosure sales. Of course, with the consent of a senior lienor, a junior lienor could foreclose for both of them. In this situation, the senior would be entitled to first crack at the foreclosure sale proceeds.[104]

B. The Junior Lienor's Options When the Senior Lienor Initiates Foreclosure

Los Angeles real estate attorney Steven Dailey describes the options that a junior lienor has once a senior mortgagee initiates foreclosure:

(1) cure the default on the senior lien;

(2) initiate foreclosure of the junior lien;

(3) redeem the senior lien which would give the junior lienor the rights that the senior lienor had;

(4) negotiate a purchase of the senior lienor from its holder;

(5) bid at the foreclosure sale;

(6) wait to see if the senior lienor's foreclosure sale produces a surplus;

(7) if the senior lienor's foreclosure sale does not produce a sum sufficient to repay the junior lien debt, seek a deficiency judgment by suing the borrower personally.[105]

Trustee or Litigation Guarantees. To be sure of notifying everyone who requested or should have received notice of the default and sale, the trustee or foreclosing attorney orders from a title company a report called a Trustee Sale or Litigation Guarantee. The title insurer guarantees that the company has identified all parties with recorded interests in the property and all who have recorded requests of notice.

The title insurer will seek to limit its contractual liability to refunding its fee for the policy, leaving the trustee or lender to bear any loss occasioned by the omission of a party entitled to notice. The alert lender will accept no such liability limit and will insist that the title insurer guarantee its report to the greater of the value of the trust deed being foreclosed or the value of the foreclosed property.[106] The trustee wants the

---

104. *Shaikh v. Burwell*, 412 S.E. 2d 924, 331 N.C. 555 (Ct. App. 1992), review denied, 418 S.E.2d 667 (N.C. 1992) (Vendors had taken back a secured note subordinate to the purchaser's first mortgage. When the purchaser defaulted on both mortgages, the vendors foreclosed after obtaining the consent of the senior lienor to include its debt in the sale. The sale trustee announced that at the sale. The trustee properly allocated proceeds first to the foreclosing vendors, then to the first mortgagee.).

105. Some states, California included, bar mortgage lenders foreclosing non-judicially from seeking post-sale deficiency judgments. Cal. Code Civ. Proc. 580(d). But a junior lienor is free to seek a deficiency after its security interest is wiped out by a senior lienor foreclosing.

106. The lender should not accept a trustee sale guarantee policy which limits recovery to the amount of the lien being foreclosed because the foreclosing trustee may be liable to an omitted junior

title insurer to fully compensate any party it fails to properly notify of the foreclosure sale since it relied on the title insurer's flawed list of those entitled to notice.

C. Impact of Failure to Join Junior Lienor in Senior Lienor's Foreclosure Sale

1. When Junior Lienors Are Not Made Parties to a Judicial Foreclosure Action

A judicial foreclosure seeks to close out the borrower's equity of redemption. As a result, the prime and indispensable defendant to be served is the borrower. But foreclosure also has the ancillary purpose of removing from title any liens or interests junior in priority to the foreclosing mortgage. To accomplish this end, several necessary parties must be served, including the holders of all junior interests of record or any persons known to have unrecorded interests in the property. *The claims of parties not notified survive the foreclosure decree.*[107]

2. When Junior Lienors Receive No Notification of Nonjudicial Sales

Now, let us consider the position of the junior lienor not notified of a senior lienor's nonjudicial sale foreclosure. Notice of a power of sale foreclosure parallels service of process in a judicial sale. But few courts will extend constitutional due process protections to junior lienors omitted from nonjudicial sales. The omitted lienor's remedies depend on state law and the provisions of the mortgage pertaining to notice of foreclosure.

In about half the states, mortgagees foreclosing nonjudicially have no obligation at all to notify junior lienors.[108] End of story. An omitted junior lienor may have a tort claim against the trustee or title insurer whose error led to the lack of notice if the foreclosed property had any remaining equity value.

Failure to provide statutory notice has the effect of making the sale voidable in three states.[109] A statute in the state of Washington extends to junior lienors omitted from nonjudicial sale foreclosures the identical remedies they would have had if not served notice of a judicial sale.[110] In states requiring notification of junior lienors, the junior lienor may have to record a request of notice in order to obtain meaningful relief.

---

lienor for the value of the property at the date of the foreclosure sale less the amount of the highest bid. In a recent case, a senior lien of $20,000 was foreclosed. The title insurer failed to inform the foreclosing trustee of a junior lienor owed $210,000. The value of the property at foreclosure was $120,000, but a third party won with a bid of $20,000. Later, the junior lienor claimed it had been damaged to the extent of $100,000 by not having received notice of the senior lienor's foreclosure sale.

107. *See, e.g., Como, Inc. v. Carson Square, Inc.,* 648 N.E.2d 1247 (Ind. Ct. App. 1995) (Interest of shopping center tenant not named and served as defendant, survived foreclosure of senior mortgage. When the mortgagee sold the center, purchaser was bound by the lease as well.).

108. Grant A. Nelson & Dale A. Whitman, *Reforming Foreclosure: The Uniform Nonjudicial Foreclosure Act,* 53 Duke L. J. 1399, 1470-71 (2004).

109. *Id.* at 1475-76.

110. Wash. Rev. Code Ann. ʹ 61.24.040 (IX)(7) (West 2004).

Notice defects in nonjudicial sales are sometimes deemed cured by state statutes. Some statutes declare proper notice to be a rebuttable presumption of a concluded sale. Such a requirement implies nothing more than that the plaintiff, the omitted junior lienor, bears the burden of proof. Other states enshrine as conclusive, but only for *bona fide* foreclosure sale purchasers, recitals in the trustees deed that all notice requirements were met. (A *bona fide* purchaser is one who paid value and did not actually know of the defective notice.) Some states completely safeguard the validity of nonjudicial foreclosure titles by ordaining as conclusive a recital in the trustees deed that all procedural requirements were met.

3. Resolving Claims of the Omitted Junior Lienor

A foreclosing mortgagee may be able to convince an omitted junior lienor to sign a release, satisfaction or reconveyance when the senior lien exceeds the value of the foreclosed realty. After all, if the foreclosed realty has no value above the sum owed the first mortgagee, the junior lienor has nothing to gain by protesting the lack of notice. Even if the junior lienor won't sign a release voluntarily, the senior lienor might be able to convince a court to grant a decree of strict foreclosure based on the lack of equity in the foreclosed property.

In the opposite circumstance, when the value of the foreclosed realty exceeds the sum owed the senior lienor, the senior could pay off the junior lien, or convene a new foreclosure sale. Alternately, the junior could offer to pay off the senior lien in exchange for title to the foreclosed realty. A junior lienor wrongfully excluded from a judicial sale could petition a court to foreclose subject to a revived senior debt.

Another option would be for the junior lienor to seek compensation in the amount of any surplus value from the party whose negligence resulted in the junior's having been omitted from the sale. In such an action, the plaintiff must prove that it was damaged by the lack of notice. In most cases, unless the lack of notice led to an unusually low sale price, damages should not be awarded.[111]

VI. Tenants and the Landlord's Mortgagee: The SNDA

Suppose that a landlord is in financial difficulty and cannot make mortgage payments. What is the status of a tenant following the mortgage lender's foreclosure?

Tenant and Mortgage Lender Lien Priorities. The recording laws are the starting point for determining the rights of a tenant following a mortgage foreclosure. A tenant's lease that pre-dates the foreclosed mortgage survives the foreclosure as long as the lender had notice of it by virtue of the tenant being in possession or having recorded its lease. Conversely, if the mortgage or deed of trust was recorded first, the foreclosing lender has the right to terminate the lease.

---

111. *See* Joseph L. Hoffman, Comment, *Court Actions Contesting the Nonjudicial Foreclosure of Deeds of Trust in Washington*, 59 Wash. L. Rev. 323, 339-40 (1984).

In some states with judicial foreclosure, a "pick and choose" rule comes into play. In these states, the foreclosing lender who wants to terminate a tenant's lease serves the tenant with a complaint in its foreclosure suit. A foreclosing lender who wants to keep the lease in place just does not join the tenant in the foreclosure suit.

Commercial Leases: The Lender's Preferred Options. Many mortgage lenders find it unacceptable that commercial leases, if recorded before the foreclosed deed of trust or mortgage, would be forced upon either the lender or the foreclosure sale purchaser, had they preferred to terminate the lease.

Although when making its loan, the mortgage lender reviewed and approved the lease, mortgage lenders are not clairvoyant. If the time ever comes when they foreclose, they want to reserve the option of keeping favorable leases and terminating unfavorable ones.[112]

In California, lenders can achieve this result by electing to subordinate the mortgage to the lease prior to foreclosure if the lease details the mortgage lender's right of an "election to subordinate."[113]

The Tenant's Preferred Options. The tenant would want the same choice, to stay or go, if the mortgage lender forecloses. "For the tenant, the consequences of a mortgage foreclosure could be disastrous. He faces the prospect of losing his lease or being permitted to remain only under terms and conditions dictated by the lender."[114] A well-positioned tenant might be able to convince the landlord to grant an option to the tenant in the lease to terminate the lease upon foreclosure unless the mortgage lender and tenant execute a mutually acceptable nondisturbance agreement.

If the lease were there before the mortgage, the mortgage lender would take subject to such a provision. If the lease were entered after the mortgage was in place, the mortgage lender would need to agree to subordinate its mortgage to the tenant's lease. There are nationally recognized tenants with credit ratings and customer loyalty strong enough to sway mortgage lenders to agree.

Subordination, Non-disturbance and Attornment Agreements (SNDA). Tenants and mortgage lenders often abrogate these default rules by contracting with each other. Through direct negotiation between them, the tenant agrees to subordinate its interest in the lease to the mortgagee. This eliminates the tenant's right to remain in place following foreclosure even if the tenant was there first. In return, the mortgagee agrees not to disturb the tenant's rights under the lease as long as the tenant does not default on the lease. Also, the tenant promises to accept the mortgage lender or its successor as the new landlord. This is called "attornment."

These arrangements are embodied in Subordination, Attornment and Non-disturbance Agreements (SNDA). Major mortgage lenders and national credit-worthy

---

112. Patricia J. Frobes and David S. Kitchen, *The Priority of Liens and Leases*, 15 Cal. Real Prop. J. 1 (Fall 1997).

113. Joel R. Hall, Negotiating Nondisturbance Agreements, SX024 ALI-CLE 963 (2016).

114. Joel R. Hall, Negotiating Nondisturbance Agreements, SX024 ALI-CLE 963 (2016).

tenants each insist upon their own form lease provisions which will reference their own version of an SNDA. Generally, each of them aspires to the unilateral right of keeping or terminating the lease upon foreclosure. Which prevails depends on whether the tenant or the mortgage lender is more important to the landlord.

If neither of them is positioned strongly enough to dictate the outcome completely, the typical SNDA is drafted to retain the lease. After all, this is what would happen if the landlord sold the property voluntarily, or if the mortgage default was resolved not through foreclosure but by the landlord executing a deed in lieu of foreclosure for the mortgage lender.

Negotiating Additional Lease Provisions as Part of the SNDA. When the mortgage lender has its way, it will want to add provisions on these topics:

1. A tenant's waiver of claims against the lender for landlord defaults that occurred under the lease prior to foreclosure;

2. A tenant's waiver of any rights against the lender to rent offsets or defenses that the tenant may have against any prior landlord;

3. An agreement that the tenant will give the lender notice of any default under the lease and will permit the lender some additional time to cure the default;

4. A prohibition against any assignment or subleasing without the lender's prior written consent;

5. A statement that the lender is not bound by rent previously paid to the prior landlord;

6. A statement that the lender will not be responsible to return any security posted with the prior landlord unless actually received by the lender; and

7. A statement that the lender will not be bound by lease amendments and rent reductions made without the lender's prior approval.[115]

8. A statement that the lender will not be liable for completion of the tenant improvements (expenditures to improve the tenant's premises) at the commencement of the term or upon renewal of the lease that the landlord promised as a condition of the lease. (Some lenders accept this as a lending risk.)

9. "A lender may seek to modify rent concessions, the stipulated rent that is effective upon a renewal, and items which have been excluded from operating expense increases such as increase in property taxes resulting from a transfer of the property if it concludes that these concessions are not market."[116]

As one real estate transactions lawyer puts it: "There is no area of loan documentation and due diligence which is more costly, protracted and contentious than ne-

---

115. Thomas C. Homburger and Lawrence A. Eiben, *Who's On First-Protecting The Commercial Mortgage Lender*, 36 REAL PROP. PROB. & TR. J. 411, 424 (Fall, 2001).

116. Alan J. Robin, *Lenders And Leases And The Evolving Use Of Subordination, Nondisturbance, And Attornment Agreements*, SM012 ALI-ABA 955 (2007).

gotiating Nondisturbance Agreements (especially where there are terms of the lease that a lender seeks to have modified following a foreclosure)."[117]

VII. Alternatives to Foreclosure

A. Private Sale

In Rising Markets Borrowers Avoid Default by Selling or Refinancing. During times when real estate values are on the rise and interest rates are stable or declining, borrowers struggling to make their mortgage payments on time can avoid defaulting by selling their homes. During years when house prices are increasing, this is a winning strategy for borrowers in financial trouble. In the U.S. from 2001 to 2006, as house prices soared in most U.S. cities, delinquency and foreclosure rates fell to all- time lows even among high risk borrowers.[118] This contributed to the eventual foreclosure debacle because loan originators, credit rating agencies and purchasers of mortgage backed securities were lulled into complacency and underestimated how default rates among subprime borrowers would soar once house prices began to erode in early 2006. Foreclosure rates shot up.

B. Short Sale

Short Sale Defined. When values have fallen so that the house is worth less than the mortgage loan, and the borrower lacks the resources to continue making payments on the loan, the borrower may attempt to persuade the lender to release its mortgage lien in exchange for the net proceeds of a sale at the current fair market value of the property. "In a short sale, the proceeds from the transaction are less than the amount the seller needs to pay the mortgage debt and the costs of selling. For this deal to close, everyone who is owed money must agree to take less — or possibly no money at all. That makes short sales complex transactions that move slowly and often fall through."[119]

Pros and Cons. For the property owner, a short sale means losing the house under stressful circumstances. Sellers thinking about a short sale have often "experienced some significant financial hardship such as the death of a wage earner, divorce, health issues, or loss of employment that has resulted in their loans becoming delinquent. Facing foreclosure and damaged credit, and possibly still unemployed, the seller may have been told that a short sale is the only real option available to them when in fact

---

117. Alan J. Robin, *Lenders And Leases And The Evolving Use Of Subordination, Nondisturbance, And Attornment Agreements,* SM012 ALI-ABA 955 (2007).

118. Ferrell, Allen, Bethel Jennifer E. And Hu, Gang, *Legal and Economic Issues in Subprime Litigation.* HARVARD LAW AND ECONOMICS DISCUSSION PAPER, No. 612, P. 25. (last visited Aug. 15, 2015), Available at SSRN:http://ssrn.com/abstract=1096582.

119. Jennie Phipps, *How to Navigate a Short Sale.Bankrate,* BANKRATE.COM (last visited Aug. 12, 2015), http://www.bankrate.com/finance/real-estate/how-to-navigate-a-short-sale-1.aspx

that is not actually true."[120] Other options could include a loan modification, forbearance, refinancing, deed in lieu of foreclosure, a consent foreclosure, and bankruptcy.

On the plus side, a short sale avoids the seller having a foreclosure on his or her credit record, and can often be achieved with a release from deficiency liability either from the lender or by law.[121]

A short sale often nets the mortgage lender more than would have received by selling the property after foreclosing because it saves the costs of foreclosing and marketing the property, the lost revenue on the sale proceeds during the much lengthier foreclosure process, and the expense of putting the house in decent shape after occupancy by a borrower facing eviction following foreclosure.

Further, lenders obtain credit towards their share of the $26 billion National Mortgage Settlement for the debts they forego in a short sale. This simultaneously eases the pressure on them to grant loan modifications based on principal reductions, their least favored form of mortgage debt relief.[122]

The Process. Short sales are necessarily contingent on lender approval. So the listing agreement and purchase and sale contract need to forewarn brokers and prospective buyers that any sale is going to be "contingent on lender approval."

To obtain that approval, the seller and broker need evidence of the seller's financial inability to continue paying the mortgage, and the fairness of the proposed selling price. Lenders have long lists of required documentation including seller financial statements, pay stubs, and tax returns along with an appraisal or a broker's opinion of value of the mortgaged property.

Once the seller receives and accepts an offer from a qualified buyer, lenders take time before responding to a request for consent. In recognition of this, lawyers handling short sales recommend steep down payments that morph into liquidated damages to keep impatient buyers in the deal for a 60 to 90 day lender review period.

Early completion of the buyer's inspections and appraisal are also a good idea, though buyers are understandably reluctant to pay for them before the lender has approved the short sale offer price.[123] But if the inspection uncovers defects that the financially strapped seller declines to cure, the buyer may hold out for an estimated cost-of-cure reduction in the contract price. Suppose the lender had already approved a contract price of $400,000 when the mortgage balance had been $500,000. And after inspection, the buyer wants to reduce the price by an additional $25,000 for a

---

120. Philip J. Vacco, *Surviving a Short Sale:Guidelines for a Rewarding Short Sale Experience*, 27-APR Prob. & Prop. 40, 41 (2013).

121. CAL. CIV. PROC. CODE § 580 (e) bars deficiencies where there is a "deed of trust or mortgage for a dwelling of not more than four units" if "the trustor or mortgagor sells the dwelling for a sale price less than the remaining amount of the indebtedness outstanding at the time of sale, in accordance with the written consent of the holder of the deed of trust or mortgage."

122. Jessica Ziehler, *The 2012 Mortgage Settlement With Large Banks*. 32 Rev. Banking & Fin. L. 286, 294 (2013).

123. Philip J. Vacco, *Surviving a Short Sale*, 27-APR Prob. & Prop. 40 (2013).

new roof. Better to have waited to see if this would happen before having submitted a proposed contract price to the lender for approval.

Short sales often falter, even after the mortgage lender approves the sales price, when a junior lien holder refuses to release its lien without charging a substantial fee even while recognizing that its lien could be wiped out by a senior lienor foreclosing or a seller filing bankruptcy.

Short Sale Fraud. "Short sale fraud occurs when someone deliberately misrepresents a fact or omits a fact in order to induce a lender, investor, or insurer to agree to a short sale that it would not have approved if it had known the truth."[124]

Mortgage lenders are rightly wary of short sales because real estate brokers, sellers and potential buyers have an incentive to collude among themselves to cheat the mortgage lender by underpricing the house, and then selling it for its full value, free of the mortgage lender's lien.

Short sale fraud comes in two basic forms. The buyer can pay cash to the seller "under the table." Or they can arrange a sale to a "straw" buyer from whom the seller will re-acquire title to the property directly or through a surrogate entity in order to sell it for a higher price to a purchaser already waiting in the wings or yet to be found.

United States v. Gendason et al.[125] A loan officer at a Florida-based mortgage lender with the help of three co-conspirators were able to identify borrowers 62 years or older interested in re-financing their existing mortgages with reverse mortgage loans. Preparing loan applications on behalf of these borrowers, the loan officer over-valued their houses, and managed to convince a reverse mortgage lender to advance $2.5 million of FHA insured mortgage loans. The reverse mortgage loans were each contingent on its mortgage being a first lien. So the loan proceeds were meant to pay off existing mortgages.

To avoid having to pay the full balance due on each of these existing mortgage loans, the loan officer and his three accomplices created sham sales of each of the houses at prices well below the amounts due on the existing loans. They succeeded in persuading each lender to accept the sales price as payment in full for each house on which it had a mortgage. This netted the co-conspirators about $1,000,000.

The US Department of Justice filed criminal charges against them, and they were given jail terms ranging from two to five years, and fined $1, 654, 805.36.[126]

C. Forbearance

Debt Service Shortfalls. "Under a forbearance agreement, the servicer (or lender) agrees to reduce or suspend the borrower's mortgage payments for a period of time. In exchange, the borrower promises to start making the full payment at the end of

---

124. *Short Sale Fraud: Three Scams to Avoid.* https://www.nolo.com/legal-encyclopedia/short-sale-fraud-three-scams-33440.html (Last visited 07/01/2016).

125. No. 11-CR-60145, plea agreement filed (S.D. Fla. Aug. 19, 2011).

126. United States Attorney's Office , Southern District of Florida, *Loan Officer And Title Agent Sentenced For $2.5 Million Reverse Mortgage And Loan Modification Scheme* (Nov.3, 2011).

the forbearance period, plus an extra amount to pay down the missed payments. Forbearance is most common when someone is laid off or called to active military duty for a relatively short period of time and cannot make any payments now but will likely be able to catch up soon."[127]

A borrower wishing to stay put, despite having missed some monthly payments, could seek forbearance. This is a delay or deferral of the mortgagor's obligations. Suppose, for instance, that the borrower owes $5,000 in back payments. Instead of being forced to pay the entire debt at once or face foreclosure, the lender might forbear.

Forbearance could take the form of a workout agreement in which the borrower made up the $5,000 in missed payments by adding $500 per month to her payments for the next 10 months. As long as the borrower can afford the higher monthly payments, forbearance keeps the borrower in the house and buys the borrower time to refinance or sell.

Missed Maturity Dates: Extend and Pretend. If the loan maturity date were fast approaching, instead of declaring a default and foreclosing, the original mortgage lender might be amenable to extending the maturity date in a move sometimes called "extend and pretend." Under this form of forbearance, the lender *extends* the maturity date and *pretends* that the value of the security property complies with the lender's current loan to value ratio requirements, suspecting it may not.

D. Loan Modifications

What Is a Loan Modification? Loan modifications are entirely different from forbearance. Instead of deferring payments due on the original obligation, loan modifications result in a reduced and more affordable monthly payment, hopefully an amount the borrower can afford. A *loan modification* agreement, sometimes called a recasting, is a change from the original loan terms.

Legal Requirements for a Loan Modification. *"A modification agreement is an amendment to the terms of a contract. Therefore, in order to be legally binding, the modification agreement must possess all of the elements of a contract.*

Modification agreements involving mortgage loans have additional requirements.

Because they title to real property, they must:

(a) be in writing;

(b) name the lender, borrower and trustee;

(c) recite the consideration;

(d) describe the land securing the debt and comply with the statute of frauds;

(e) be executed under seal;

(f) expressly continue the original agreement rather than terminating it;

---

127. Stephen Elias, *Avoiding Foreclosure: Basic Workout Options From Your Lender.* http://www.nolo.com/legal-encyclopedia/free-books/foreclosure-book/chapter4-6.html (Last visited 07/01/2016.)

(g) provide for endorsers, guarantors or others who may be secondarily liable; and

(f) be delivered and accepted."[128]

Types of Modifications. The types of modifications that may be on offer vary from one lender to the next. Among the possibilities, the lender could extend the loan payback (amortization) period (usually to 40 years), defer principal payments (usually at zero interest), or reduce the interest rate temporarily or permanently.

Income producing property that is heavily mortgaged may not produce enough income to service the debt, due to declining rents, increasing expenses, or both. A temporary solution could be for the lender to extend principal repayments or even reduce the interest "pay rate" below the accrued interest on the loan. In exchange, the lender would probably expect the borrower to relinquish control of the cash flow by agreeing to a "lock box" arrangement, calling for tenants to deposit their rents into a bank account controlled by the lender.

In "underwater" situations where the mortgage debt exceeds the current market value of the property, borrowers prefer a reduction in the principal loan amount of the debt to a reasonable percentage of the current fair market value of the property (e.g., 80%). The chance that financially strapped borrowers will default again increases greatly when loan modifications do not actually reduce the amount of the monthly payment obligation.[129]

Principal reductions are hugely effective in curbing strategic defaults by financially distressed homeowners. But lenders rarely offer them. "That's because lenders are naturally loath to forgo money that's owed to them and may be restricted by contractual obligations to investors who own mortgage-backed securities." Also, they are fearful of triggering a stampede of borrowers demanding loan modifications to reduce what they owe to the current market value of the house even if they could afford to make their current payments.[130]

Accommodating Creditors Might Reserve Some Upside as the Quid Pro Quo. Mortgagees, in exchange for interest rate or principal reductions, sometimes insist upon a share of the borrower's future equity value upon sale or refinancing.[131]

---

128. Legal memorandum from John H. Small and Jeffrey E. Oleynik, 01/29/2009. https://www.ncbankers.org/uploads/File/Legal/vol__41__no__01.pdf (Last visited, 07/01/2016.)

129. "Any modification that reduces total payment and interest (P&I) reduces the likelihood of subsequent re-default and foreclosure. Modifications that increase the loan principal- primarily through capitalized interest and fees- are more likely to fail, even while controlling for changes in P&I." Schmeiser, *Maximilian D. and Gross, Matthew B., The Determinants of Subprime Mortgage Performance Following a Loan Modification* (November 17, 2015). Journal of Real Estate Finance and Economics, Vol. 52, No. 1, 2016. Available at SSRN: http://ssrn.com/abstract=2692216

130. This is why Oklahoma, Fannie Mae, and Freddie Mac refused to join the National Mortgage Settlement. See Review of Options Available for Underwater Borrowers and Principal Forgiveness, FED. HOUSING & FIN. AGENCY 13, http://www.fhfa.gov/webfiles/24108/PF_FHFApaper73112.pdf.(Last visited 06/03/2016.)

131. FHA insurance is available for refinancing the mortgage debts of troubled borrowers. Borrowers reducing their mortgage debt must surrender a share of equity and equity appreciation to HUD under the Housing and Economic Recovery Act of 2008, 122 Stat. 2654.

Costs and Benefits. The potential benefits and costs of these programs are well known. During a crisis, mortgage debt relief can prevent foreclosures and the attendant losses that for both borrowers and lenders. Avoiding foreclosures also benefits neighborhoods—unsightly lawns and poorly maintained houses, prices spiraling downward, squatters and drug dealers taking over vacant houses.[132] Debt relief could also boost consumption and employment.[133] Borrowers retain title, protect their reputations, enhance the changes of their being able to borrow again, and avoid tax liabilities that are sometimes incident to foreclosure.

An unanticipated cost of government-sponsored modification efforts were the large number of unscrupulous individuals who extracted fees from anxious home owners, promising to assist them in obtaining loan modifications and who did nothing but pocket fees they obtained by fraud and misrepresentations.[134]

Modifications Are Financially Easier for Investors to Grant Who Purchased Non-performing Loans at Deep Discounts Than for Loan Originators.

The lenders who originate loans are often very reluctant to recognize their losses by granting loan modifications, especially modifications that reduce the amount of principal repayment due on the loan. Admitting mistakes is never easy, and accepting repayment for a sum far less than the loan balance due would signal a potential weakness in the entire portfolio of comparable loans the lender still carried on its books.

Investors in nonperforming loans buy at deep discounts. An investor who purchased a loan at 60% of its face could grant a modification up to 40% of the original loan amount without suffering a loss of its invested capital. Simply by reducing the borrower's obligation to an affordable level, the investor might be able to turn a nonperforming loan into a performing one.

Rights of Junior Lienors When Senior Loans Are Modified Without Their Consent. Mortgage lenders, agreeing to modify the terms of a loan, often prepare and then

---

132. "A foreclosure decreases the value of surrounding homes, so communities that experience many foreclosures may see declining property values, making it difficult for residents to build home equity. Foreclosures increase the supply of available homes in a neighborhood and tend to reduce the pool of potential buyers, both of which put negative pressure on home values. According to MIT, the value of a home drops by 1 percent, on average, if it is within roughly 250 feet of a foreclosure. Foreclosed homes can also fall into a state of disrepair while unoccupied, causing their values to drop sharply." http://people.opposingviews.com/effects-foreclosures-communities-7813.html (Last visited March 23, 2016).

133. Mayer, Christopher J. and Morrison, Edward R. and Piskorski, Tomasz and Gupta, Arpit, *Mortgage Modification and Strategic Behavior: Evidence from a Legal Settlement with Countrywide* (October 11, 2012). Columbia Law and Economics Working Paper No. 404; Kreisman Working Papers Series in Housing Law and Policy No. 4. (last visited Aug. 15, 2015), Available at SSRN: http://ssrn.com/abstract=1836451 or http://dx.doi.org/10.2139/ssrn.1836451 © 2011 by Christopher J. Mayer, Edward Morrison, Tomasz Piskorski, and Arpit Gupta.

134. Two Plead Guilty in $18.5 Million Mortgage Scheme: More than 8,000 Homeowners Victimized Across the Country, SigTarp.Gov (last visited Jan. 10, 2016), https://www.sigtarp.gov/Press%20Releases/Abghari_Romano_Press_Release.pdf

record loan amendments. Suppose the borrower encumbered the property with another lien after the subsequently modified mortgage loan was recorded but before the modification was granted. Would that lienor's claim against the security property be superior subject to the loan as modified?

For example, a homeowner borrows $200,000 to buy a house secured by recorded Mortgage A. Then, the homeowner borrows $500,000 secured by Mortgage B, a Home Equity Line of Credit (HELOC). Soon thereafter, struggling through a particularly hard time, the homeowner negotiates a modification of Mortgage A — temporarily reducing the interest rate. The modification is recorded as Mortgage C. Is Mortgage B superior or subordinate to Mortgage C?

The junior lienor B is subordinate to C, unless (B) can show how the C modification materially prejudiced its recovering the sums due on its loan, or the value of its security interest.[135] Hence, a reduction of the interest rate or the principal amount due on the senior mortgage would be harmless to the junior lienor. An increased interest rate would not be. The result of an increased interest rate would be a split priority. Up to the original interest rate, the modified loan would be superior. Beyond that, it would be subordinate to the earlier mortgage.

A mortgage lender can enshrine its lien priority with language that all those claiming interests in the security property subsequently derived through the borrower are deemed to consent to any future modifications, extensions, amendments or alterations of the senior mortgage.[136]

Work Outs. Commercial real estate lenders are often willing to negotiate modifications known as workout arrangements. Workouts allow the *de facto* owner to remain as the project operator.

Workout arrangements vary. The lender agrees to forego debt payments for a while, renegotiates to extend the amortization period, defers a maturity date when the loan was fully due and payable, reduces the interest rate, or exchanges some or all of the debt for equity — a share of operating income or potential gain on sale.

When market values are depressed, and the value of the property is less than the loan balance, the lender must be convinced that the default was not precipitated by the borrower's incompetence, ineptitude or dishonesty. Lenders accede only when convinced the borrower possesses the determination and skill to turn the project around, is competent and trustworthy, and no one could do better at managing what has become a difficult financial bind. They are more amenable to workouts with borrowers have a good management team, deep knowledge of the marketplace, excellent relationships with local governments and tenants, accurate records, and feasible plans for improving matters.

---

135. The Restatement (Third) of Property (Mortgages) §7.3(b) (1997).

136. The Restatement (Third) of Property (Mortgages) §7.3(c) (1997). The Restatement curbs the prior lender's potential monopoly position by allowing the borrower to promulgate a "cut off" notice beyond which the prior mortgage would be subordinated.

Lenders are particularly receptive to workouts requested by borrowers who offer as a *quid pro quo* cash to pay down the loan in exchange for a loan extension to head off a rapidly approaching loan maturity date.

In addition, a borrower might propose to provide periodic reporting or give the lender either greater control over the cash proceeds from the real estate, a one-time principal reduction payment, a cash deposit to cover future enforcement costs, reimbursement of lender costs already incurred, or deletion of undesirable deal terms, such as transfer restrictions or confidentiality requirements.[137]

Why Workouts and Modifications Are Difficult to Achieve Securitized Loans. Workouts and deeds in lieu of foreclosure become particularly challenging to negotiate when mortgage loans are securitized. The loan originator no longer owns the mortgages. A trustee holds title for the various tranches of bondholders, and pays them according to the terms of their bonds, as long as mortgagors continue making their payments on time. Those payments are made through a master servicer, tied to the bondholders by the explicit terms detailed in a lengthy Loan Pooling and Servicing Agreement (PSA). The master servicer has no responsibility for dealing with delinquent loans. Typically, once a borrower misses payments for 60 days, the master servicer turns over the file to a special servicer for collection.

Under the terms of many PSAs, special servicers have broad discretion "to reduce the payment amounts, change the payment terms, forebear in the enforcement of any rights, extend the maturity date or do similar things to work out a problem loan."[138] Those extraordinary powers are qualified. They can only be exercised if the loan is in default or imminent risk of default, the modifications leave intact the pass through tax status of the bonds, and the *"modification or amendment would increase on a net present value basis the recovery to the bondholders."*[139] PSAs seldom specified whether this meant that the modification had to maximize the net present value of all tranches of bondholders, taken together, or of each tranche considered individually.

Deciding how best to deal with a default situation, special servicers quite often need to choose between attempting a workout or initiating foreclosure expeditiously. Special servicers cannot easily prove whether the net present value of bondholder interests would somehow be greater under one or the other option.

There is no need for the special servicer to prove anything to anyone if all of the investors are in agreement about whether the value of the security property is on the rise or declining. If everyone agrees that the property value is poised to rise, delaying foreclosure for a workout will probably benefit all the bondholders regardless of whether they hold senior or subordinate bonds. Conversely, where the overwhelming consensus among the bondholders and their representatives is that the market is in freefall, expeditious foreclosure will look like the way to go. But investors often disagree about the direction that valuations are going to take. This not only makes for lively

---

137. Joshua Stein, *Troubled Loans: Overview, Options and Strategy*, 536 PLI/Real 11, 38 (2007).
138. William G. Murray, Jr., *Workouts in the Twenty First Century*, SL100 ALI-ABA 287 (2006).
139. *Ibid.*

real estate markets; it also engenders heated debates among the various classes of bondholders.

Usually, the lender maximizes net cash flow by foreclosing unless the borrower comes up with a stunning and irresistible plan for reversing the project's downturn. Even then, not all tranche positions will be impacted alike.

Modifying securitized loans can invite challenges by the holders of various tranches because a modification that benefits one tranche could disadvantage others. For instance, foreclosure might be averted by a reduction of the interest rate on a securitized mortgage loan. This could harm the AAA tranche holders if the mortgage pool was capable of generating enough income to cover payments due the most senior tranche of investors. But if that modification averted foreclosure, it could greatly benefit the holders of lower rated tranches facing a wipe out in the event many mortgages in the pool went into foreclosure.

Fear of litigation by the various tranche holders deters some special servicers from even thinking about modifying mortgage loans without the consent of all classes of bondholders. Some PSAs call for majority approval, some require super majority approval, and others demand nothing less than bondholder unanimity.

E. Deeds in Lieu of Foreclosure

In form, a deed in lieu of foreclosure is identical in form to any other type of deed although the borrower accedes to give it precisely to head off an imminent foreclosure.[140] Borrowers agree to sign deeds in lieu of foreclosure when they have little or no equity in the security property, no expectation of the property appreciating in the foreseeable future, and little chance of staving off foreclosure by reinstatement or refinancing.

With a deed in lieu, lenders save the legal and administrative expenses of foreclosure—ten percent of the loan balance, possibly more. Borrowers facing foreclosure become sloppy housekeepers, careless managers, and thereby depress the value of the security property before the lender has a chance to reach it. The lender can stem any further deterioration of the collateral by taking over the property in as little as a day. A protracted foreclosure would only demoralize the employees and independent contractors responsible for operating and maintaining the property. By accepting a deed in lieu, the lender reassures these service providers of its intention to maintain the property as a going concern, and obtains the cooperation of the delinquent borrower in assuring an orderly transition from the borrower's management team to the lender's.

Tangible benefits for borrowers could take the form of a negotiated debt reduction or forgiveness, a complete discharge of personal liability, and often a one-time cash payment. Deeds in lieu of foreclosure save the embarrassment and emotional strain of a protracted foreclosure, and stanch the flow of red ink if the property was pro-

---

140. D. Barlow Burke, REAL ESTATE TRANSACTIONS 319 (Little, Brown, 1993).

ducing less revenue than it cost to own. The default won't necessarily show up on the borrower's credit report and, if it does, a deed in lieu of foreclosure will look better than a foreclosure.

Lenders accepting a deed in lieu of foreclosure are taking some risks: (1) they assume all the burdens of ownership; (2) the claims of junior lienors may ripen into senior liens once the senior lienor trades in its mortgage or deed of trust for fee ownership; and (3) borrowers may later decide they were wrongfully short-changed out of a valuable ownership interest.

1. Risks of Ownership

Lenders are exposed to the same risks of ownership in accepting a deed in lieu that they would assume as property purchasers because once the deed is executed, they become the title owners. At a minimum they will need a title search to reveal liens placed on the property after their mortgage was first recorded, a physical inspection for conditions that could result in personal injury or property damage claims, and an environmental audit for hazardous substance contamination (CERCLA liability).

Lenders resist taking title to properties with hazardous wastes, in non-compliance with the construction requirements of the Americans with Disabilities Act (ADA), vulnerable to outstanding tort and contract claims, money-losing franchise deals not readily terminable, or with zoning and building code violations. Competent lenders anticipate these possibilities and perform the same exacting due diligence before accepting a deed in lieu as knowledgeable buyers perform before acquiring any unfamiliar asset.

2. Claims of Junior Lienors

The Spurious Application of the Doctrine of Merger. Junior liens of record will still cloud titles until released by a recorded document signed by the junior lienor. Junior lienors usually know this and appreciate the nuisance value of their holding out for some cash, even if the value of the security property is worth less than the senior mortgage.

To improve the status of their claim, a junior lienor might invoke the doctrine of merger. The doctrine of merger specifies: "If two estates in the same property shall unite in the same person in his individual capacity, the lesser estate shall be merged in the greater."[141] The argument is superficially plausible because lenders usually record a release, satisfaction or reconveyance of the mortgage along with the deed in lieu. The junior lienor will contend that by accepting a deed in lieu of foreclosure, the lender's senior mortgage merged (disappeared) in the deed in lieu. By prevailing on this claim, the junior lien would elevate its status to that of a senior lien.

---

141. Ga. Code Ann. § 44-6-2 (2004).

Although courts occasionally agree,[142] most courts reject the merger argument,[143] and allow a revival of the senior lender for a sufficient period of time to permit the senior lienor to foreclose its first lien, thereby wiping out the junior lien. In this scenario, the junior lienor receives the same rights it would have had before the deed in lieu was signed–the right to bid at the senior mortgagee's foreclosure sale, and maybe the right to redeem the senior lien.

Courts would be saved the trouble of dealing with the merger doctrine in these formalistic ways if Restatement (Third) of Property (Mortgages) (1997) § 8.5 were followed. The Restatement abolishes merger as it applies to mortgages or the enforceability of a mortgage obligation. As Professor Ann M. Burkhart has convincingly argued, "The primary issue in each case is whether the lender in fact would be enriched unjustly if it were permitted to enforce the debt."[144] Case outcomes should not depend on archaic blunderbuss of the doctrine of merger.

Professor Michael Madison offers several expedient ways for the senior lender to protect itself from junior lien claims based on merger when the senior lienor accepts a deed in lieu: (1) have the borrower convey the property to a subsidiary or nominee of the lender; (2) place a standard anti-merger clause in the deed proclaiming that all of the lender's loan documents are to remain in full force and effect; (3) don't extinguish the debt, retain the note and security interest, and prepare a separate agreement for the borrower containing a covenant not to sue.

Other Creditors' Claims. Lenders planning to operate the security property may have little choice but to pay the borrower's debts to trade or construction contractors in order to keep them on the job. "The lender should not give the borrower a full 'release of liability,' if third parties have outstanding claims, arising from the borrower's operation of the property, for which the lender does not wish to be solely responsible."[145]

In dealing with any lenders but particularly with federally regulated lenders, borrowers take needless risks to rely solely the undocumented say-so of whoever claims to be representing the lender in negotiating the deed in lieu. They need any settlement agreement (or commitment to settle) to be "approved by the board of directors of the depository institution or its loan committee." By law, the approval also needs to be reflected in the minutes of the board or committee. Otherwise, the settlement is vulnerable to subsequent review and avoidance by an FDIC receiver.[146]

Fraudulent Conveyances, 'Reasonably Equivalent Value,' UFTA, UFCA.

Junior lienors have another basis for challenging a deed in lieu of foreclosure by a mortgagor to a senior mortgagee. The Uniform Fraudulent Transfer Act (recently

---

142. *Janus Props. v. First Fla. Bank,* 546 So. 2d 785 (Fla. Dist. Ct. App. 1989).

143. *BGJ, Inc., II v. First Ave. Inv. Corp.,* 520 N.W.2d 508 (Minn. Ct. App. 1994) (citing 2 JONES ON MORTGAGES § 1109 (8th ed.)).

144. Ann M. Burkhart, *Freeing Mortgages of Merger,* 40 VAND. L. REV. 283, 382 (1987).

145. *Ibid.*

146. *Ibid.*

renamed, with minor changes, as the Uniform Voidable Transactions Act (UVTA)[147]) exposes deeds to the risk of rescission if the mortgagor or affected creditors can prove that the extinguished debt was worth less than the fair market value of the property transferred.[148]

The deed in lieu is also challengeable as a fraudulent conveyance under Uniform Fraudulent Conveyancing Acts (UFCA) if the debtor received less than equivalent value, and the deed delayed, hindered or defrauded creditors such as the junior lienor.[149]

F. Deeds Absolute and the Prohibition of Clogs on the Equity of Redemption

Sometimes, mortgage lenders have attempted to deny borrowers the protection of foreclosure by sale by disguising security interests as deeds absolute. They have the borrower execute a deed of the property to the lender, and place the deed in the hands of an escrow agent with instructions to record the deed upon the lender notifying the escrow agent that the borrower has defaulted on its promises to the lender. To put the borrower's fears to rest that the lender plans to keep the property as its own even if the borrower repays the debt, the lender promises in the deed, orally or in a separate writing, to re-convey title to the borrower once the debt is repaid on time. Alternatively, the lender could grant the borrower a written option to repurchase, the option price being the borrower's repayment of the debt.

The borrower would have no reason to challenge this arrangement if the lender keeps its promise to reconvey the property once the borrower has repaid the debt. Unless the lender tries to keep the property as his own, claiming ownership by virtue of the deed ostensibly granting title to him, the borrower would have no need of the various safeguards and protections of mortgage law: reinstatement, notice of acceleration, equitable redemption, notice of default, a foreclosure sale, the surplus if any from the foreclosure sale, statutory redemption and statutory or court imposed protections against deficiency judgments.

Only if the borrower defaults or the lender reneges would the borrower need to petition a court to re-characterize the deed absolute executed at the time of loan origination as an *equitable mortgage*.[150]

---

147. *See* Unif. Voidable Transactions Act Task Force of the Bus. Law Section of the Pa. Bar Ass'n, *Report on the Amendments to the Fraudulent Transfer Act (to be known as the Pennsylvania Voidable Transactions Act)*, 86 Pa. Bar Ass'n Q. 83 (2015). These state statutes are also similar to the earlier Uniform Fraudulent Conveyance Act ("UFCA") dating back to 1918, versions of which still apply in Maryland and New York

148. Md. Code Ann., Com. Law § 15-201; N.Y. Debt. & Cred. Law § 270.

149. See John C.Murray, *Deeds in Lieu of Foreclosure: Practical and Legal Considerations*, 26 Real Prop., Prob. & Tr. J, 459 (Fall 1991).

150. Borrower waivers of rights made following a default are discussed in chapter 23 on workouts. For an explanation of why courts are more tolerant of post-origination waivers of the right of equitable redemption, than waivers entered at the point of loan origination, See Marshall E. Tracht, Renegotiation and Secured Credit, 52 Vand. L. Rev. 599 (1999).

In litigation, the borrower will derisively label the deed absolute as an *impermissible clog on the equity of redemption*. (Think of clogged drains, Professor Grant Nelson suggests, impediments to the borrower reclaiming the security property by paying off the debt).[151] The borrower's right to relief dates back to English chancery courts where many of the present-day assortments of mortgagor protections originated.[152]

For the borrower, the challenge will be to convince a court that a document formally denominated a deed was actually a disguised mortgage. A deed, absolute in form, is presumed in law to be what it looks like. The legal starting point is that documents are what they appear to be. In the absence of a showing of fraud, mistake, ignorance or undue influence, the burden is on one seeking to establish a deed absolute as a mortgage to overcome this presumption by clear, unequivocal and convincing evidence.[153]

Currently, borrowers' attorneys are having some success utilizing the equitable mortgage concept to protect homeowners from pernicious schemes by self-proclaimed foreclosure consultants. In a typical scam, the con artist promises a homeowner facing foreclosure to refinance the owner's existing mortgage on more favorable terms if only the owner deeds the property to the con artist or a nominee. The consultant will tell the owner that the transfer of title is necessary to enable the consultant to use its good credit to facilitate the refinancing of the home owner's existing mortgage.

Often, the consultant pays the homeowner several thousand dollars for signing the deed. The con artist enters a lease of the home back to the owners. The lease comes with an outsized option price inflated to richly reward the consultant's efforts in the improbable event that the homeowner ever accumulates enough cash to exercise the option. The consultant refinances the mortgage, pockets personally any surplus above the amount necessary to pay off the home owner's existing mortgage, and disappears. This transaction strips the owners of any equity value they may have had in the property.

To reclaim their title, the former owners will be burdened with proving that the deed absolute was fraudulently induced, but not only that. The mortgage lender actually knew or should have realized a scam was taking place. Since the former owners

---

151. Professor Simpson uses another metaphor: The sense of clog here is of a piece of wood attached to an animal or even person to restrain movement. A.W.B. Simpson, A History of the Land Law 245 (2d ed. 1986).

152. A.W.B. Simpson, A History of the Land Law 246 (2d ed. 1986).

153. Bernstein v. New Beginnings Trustee, LLC, 988 So.2d 90 (Fla. App. 2008). Re-characterization disputes raise questions of fact. Courts look at all the circumstances surrounding the deal to uncover the parties' intent. Among factors frequently mentioned in case reports are: (1) the prior relationship of the parties, whether they started out as buyer and seller or debtor and creditor; (2) whether the sales or lease option price approximated full market value or the lesser percentage customary in mortgage lending; and (3) whether the borrower incurred an obligation, legal or practical, to repay or exercise the option. The Restatement (Third) of Property (Mortgages) 3.2 and 3.3 recognizes that the obligation need not be the personal liability of any person. The threatened loss of a valuable equity suffices to support a claim of equitable mortgage.

remained in possession as tenants, the lender could have asked them why the continued living there after deeding title to someone else. Had he bothered to ask, they would have explained the situation. Their legal argument is that the deed with the lease-purchase option was a clog on their equity of redemption because it was a disguised equitable mortgage, only terminable by foreclosure.[154]

VIII. Acquiring Distressed Debts or Properties

Someone interested in acquiring distressed properties has four choices: (A) buy directly from the mortgagor in default, before foreclosure; (B) purchase the defaulted note from the lender or special servicer; (C) bid for the property at the lender's fore-closure sale; (D) following foreclosure, buy from the lender directly. Foreclosed property held by lenders is called Real Estate Owned (REO).[155]

A. Purchasing the Equity Directly from an Owner in Default

In situations where the property is worth more than the combined secured debts against it, President Alexis McGee of Foreclosures.com says, "The best deals are buying from the owner before the foreclosure, the minute the notice of default is filed." Purchasers might beat the rush by contacting owners after their first or second delinquency, before the lender has recorded a Notice of Default. But this information is not made public; buyers would need access to the lender's records.

Financially challenged owners with properties worth more than the liens against them would get the best price for their homes by listing them with a broker before missing a loan payment. Many do precisely this. But some debtors suffer long periods of denial and inaction, and never get around to listing their homes for sale until it is far too late.

Some investors may see an opportunity in homes where the owners have fallen behind in mortgage payments but whose homes are worth considerably more than the mortgage-loan balance. Such investors meet owners in this situation, hoping to convince them to sell their equities for small sums. The investor's pitch includes a promise to cure the default, rent the house to the former owner, and then sell it back once he or she can afford to repurchase.

Some investors lack the personality and the stomach for negotiating with home-owners in distress. "A lot of times they'll slam the door in your face," said one buyer of distressed residential properties, "but sometimes you can convince them that you can help them walk away less scathed than if the bank forecloses on them." Attorney

---

154. Essex Property Services, Inc. v. Wood, 246 N.J. Super. 487, 587 A.2d 1337 (N.J.Super.L.1991).
155. There is even a website specializing in REO information called REO.com

Generals in many states keep a watchful eye for foreclosure investor piranhas misleading homeowners into selling their houses for paltry sums.[156]

Buying distressed property takes a thick wallet because the purchaser acquires title subject to all the mortgage debt against it. To head off losing the property to foreclosure, the spec buyer needs to advance funds out of pocket to keep the seller's mortgage payments current.

Under a due-on-sale clause, the buyer may need the lender's consent to keep the loan in place. The lender, as a *quid pro quo* for granting consent, may require the spec buyer to become personally liable on the debt or pay an increased interest rate. Financially strapped homeowners often allow the property to drift into disrepair; spec buyers will need to invest cash to fix up the place before trying to sell it.

Prospective buyers of distressed property should make sure that the property is worth more than the seller owes in mortgage payments, and not subject to back property taxes.

Spec buying of distressed properties is no fool's paradise. Sometimes, buyers misjudge house price trends, buy into a rapidly declining market, and lose thousands of dollars in the bargain, never managing to recoup all their costs. Their outlays include the price they paid the seller, the money spent for repairs, and property taxes, insurance, maintenance and mortgage payments.

You hear little about distressed sale buyers' losing money on their deals because, like most investors, boasting about their winnings is far more pleasurable than bemoaning their losses.

B. Purchasing Defaulted (Nonperforming) Notes from the Lender or a Special Servicer

Surprising, perhaps, to people unfamiliar with the active trading that occurs for nonperforming loans, there are lively markets for bad debts. While it is easy to understand why lenders and bondholders might want to unload loans in default, who wants to pay good money for them? But mortgage investor Jon Daurio has the answer: "There is no such thing as a bad loan; there is only bad loan pricing, a function of whether the mortgage investor correctly predicted the default rate and loss severity of the purchased loans." In short, a loan secured by real property usually has some value even if that value is less than the balance due on the defaulted mortgage. Without a doubt, nonperforming loans sell at discounts from the balance due on them. Investor gains accrue to those with the right answer to the big question: "how much less"?

The value of nonperforming notes can depend on the procedural hurdles to foreclosure in the jurisdiction where the security property is located, on whether the

---

156. James R. Hagerty, *Last Resort: Slower Home Sales Open Up a Market for Some Investors The Threat of Foreclosure Feeds a Real-Estate Niche That Thrives on Hard Luck How to Be a White Knight*, WALL STREET JOURNAL, May 30, 2006.

paperwork is in order, the notes are all available and endorsed to the present assignees, and each of the accompanying deeds of trust or mortgages matches up with an accompanying notes. Another consideration is the type or condition of the property. Notes are more difficult to sell on types of property that require intensive management, such as an assisted living facility or a hotel. Environmental contamination of the site to be foreclosed will deepen the discount because of the liability and cleanup cost risks.

Similarly, notes will sell at discounts secured by property owner in construction or with significant repairs needed.[157]

C. Purchasing at a Foreclosure Sale

Because lenders are not particularly adept at debt collection, some are willing to sell defaulted mortgage loans at deep discounts before foreclosure. Investors who buy nonperforming loans are left with the messy business of foreclosing or attempting to modify the loan, perhaps by reducing the balance due, based on realistic estimates of the home's current value so that the defaulting home owner may be able to afford payments on the new, much lower mortgage debt.[158]

At foreclosure sales, astute or lucky bidders can sometimes buy property at prices well below market value.[159]

Buying at a foreclosure sale is definitely not an activity for the faint of heart. Most of the property sold at foreclosure sales is not worth as much as the debt foreclosed. These are usually all cash sales, in California by cashier's check. (Bidders bring one check to cover the minimum bid, and checks in additional denominations to cover overbids.)

Buyers take the title and the property 'as is.' Foreclosing trustees are only obliged at common law to disclose material latent defects they actually know about. This is especially risky because bidders seldom gain access to the house beforehand. They have to rely on a drive-by look that does not necessarily reveal the condition inside. These houses are often in bad condition; defaulting homeowners tend not to be enthusiastic about maintaining houses in good condition from which they face eviction. Distraught debtors sometimes damage property, remove lighting and plumbing fixtures, and tear out entire kitchens during pending foreclosure actions.

---

157. Beverly J. Quail and Joseph E. Lubinski, *Real Estate Law: How Borrowers Should Deal with Special Servicers*, vol. 30, ABA GP Solo., AmericanBar.Org (last visited Mar. 21, 2016), http://www.americanbar.org/publications/gp_solo/2013/may_june/real_estate_law_how_borrowers_should_deal_special_servicers.html.

158. John F. Wasik, Discounted Mortgage Notes Can Stop Foreclosures, Bloomberg.com (last visited Aug. 15, 2015), http://www.bloomberg.com/apps/news?pid=20601039&sid=a_z7EHhoDVFQ&refer=columnist_wasik

159. Kate Murphy, Finding Bargains (and Headaches) at Foreclosure Sales, New York Times, Aug. 7, 2005, Section 3, col 1.

Foreclosing lenders are reluctant to share appraisal or environmental information in their files concerning the property. Such information may not have been confirmed and they are wary of being held accountable for errors and omissions.

Adding a further element of uncertainty, many scheduled foreclosure sales are postponed at the last minute as borrowers and lenders haggle to strike a workout accord, or the owner attempts a last minute sale.[160] To avoid wasted effort, experienced foreclosure sale bidders conduct their due diligence just a day or two before the sale. It would not pay them to research properties scheduled for foreclosure much sooner. In their hurried last minute push for information, errors are likely.

Foreclosing lenders provide absolutely no title warranties nor are the trustees or sheriffs conducting the sale under any obligation to inform bidders whether lien being foreclosed is a first mortgage. A winning bidder at the foreclosure auction sale takes title free of all liens junior to the one being foreclosed, and subject to all liens senior to the one being foreclosed. Bidders need to find a way of obtaining reliable title information on their own. Courts decline to set aside foreclosure sales because the high bidder mistakenly believed she was bidding on a first lien when in fact the foreclosed lien was but a second or third mortgage. Having to pay off an unanticipated senior lien could sour what otherwise would have been a sweet deal for the foreclosure sale purchaser. For this reason, knowledgeable bidders commission a pre-sale title report.[161]

A winning bidder confronts another obstacle if someone is living in the foreclosed property. Foreclosing trustees make no promise that the property will be vacant after they deed it to the foreclosure sale purchaser. Upon taking title, the foreclosure sale purchaser could beseech the occupant to leave, offer cash for a prompt and peaceful departure, and, if all else fails, file an unlawful detainer action for quiet possession.[162]

---

160. *Klem v. Washington Mutual Bank,* 176 Wash.2d 771, 295 P.3d 1179 (2013). A homeowner lost her house through foreclosure that was worth $235,000 for a default of $75,000. The homeowner suffered from dementia and was represented by a guardian. The guardian marketed the house. After the foreclosing trustee had scheduled a foreclosure sale, the guardian found a buyer willing to pay $235,000. She requested that the trustee postpone the sale 30 days to give her time to close. The trustee refused because it never postponed sales without the lender's prior approval and the lender had not responded to the trustee's question about whether to postpone. At the sale, the winning bidder paid $1 more than the amount due on the debt ($83,000 by then). They sold the house soon after for $235,000. The guardian sued and won a judgment against the trustee for $151,912.33 under the Washington Consumer Protection Act. (This was the difference between the forced sales price and contract price which was also the fair market value at the date of the sale.) The Washington Supreme Court concluded that the trustee should have used its own judgment and acted in the best interest of the borrower and the lender, in deciding whether to postpone the sale. Not doing so was an unfair trade practice.

161. *In re Niland,* 825 F. 2d 801 (5th Cir. 1987) (Debtor set aside foreclosure sale held by judgment creditor because under Texas law, the creditor's lien was subordinate to owner's homestead interest in the foreclosed property.) One exception is if the debtor is so slow to challenge the foreclosure sale as to be equitably estopped from ever doing so.

162. For all residential properties in California, including apartment houses, lenders must notify all property occupants of the pending foreclosure sale, by posting and mail, CAL CIV. CODE 2924.8,

Mortgage lenders who purchase at their own foreclosure sales can sometimes resell profitably.[163] But most foreclosing lenders end up collecting less than two-thirds of the principal balance due with significant variation by region, property type, year of foreclosure, loan to value ratio, debt service coverage ratio and size of loan.

For those foreclosed properties with sizable equities, sales can be well attended and bidding lively. Institutional lenders shy away from becoming speculators in distressed property. That line of work requires skills few bankers possess. Other bidders know this and start the bidding at no more than $1 above the mortgage lender's opening bid.

Bidding is often dominated by a handful of individuals who make a living in the acquisition of distressed residential and small commercial properties. Courts sometimes have referred to professional foreclosure sale bidders as the forty thieves and have on occasion denied them *bona fide* purchaser status.[164]

Sometimes professional bidders huddle and select only one of them to bid on properties with substantial equities that are about to be foreclosed. Then, they split a quick resale profit with each other. Agreements like this to *chill the bidding* are barred by statute and common law,[165] and constitute felonies. They persist anyway because they are hard to prove and highly profitable.

Institutional Bidders Entered the Home Foreclosure Market. Traditionally, local bidders had been the main professionals at foreclosure sales. But they were joined, starting in the 2008 real estate recession, by a new set of foreclosure sale entrants: private equity firms, hedge funds, real estate investment trusts and other institutional investors. These players spent more than $20 billion acquiring as many as 200,000 homes from 2012 to 2014. One example was Blackstone, a private equity firm. It was spending more than $100 million a week investing $8 billion to buy 43,000 homes

---

and provide pre-eviction notice of no less than 60 days from the date of foreclosure. CAL CIV. CODE 1161b.

163. Steven Wechsler, *Through the Looking Glass: Foreclosure by Sale as De Facto Strict Foreclosure An Empirical Study of Mortgage Foreclosure and Subsequent Resale,* 76 CORNELL L. REV. 850 (1985).

164. *Estate of Yates,* 32 Cal. Rptr. 2d 53, 25 Cal. App. 4th 51 (1994) (Court set aside a sale for procedural irregularity after experienced speculator made the winning bid in an amount substantially below market value of the foreclosed property. Speculator was characterized as not a *bona fide* purchaser); *Melendrez v. D & I Inv., Inc.,* 26 Cal. Rptr. 3d 413, 127 Cal. App. 4th 1238 (2005) (Court characterized experienced speculator as *bona fide* purchaser and refused to set aside foreclosure sale. Winning bid was $197,100 and market value estimated at $317,000 to $380,000.).

165. *Lo v. Jensen,* 106 Cal. Rptr. 2d 443, 88 Cal. App. 4th 1093 (2001) (At foreclosure sale of condo unit conducted by homeowners' association after unit owner failed to pay association fees, two frequent foreclosure sale bidders joined forces to bid and buy on a 50/50 basis. Their wining bid on an unencumbered condo they appraised at $150,000-160,000 was just over $5,000 the amount of the debt. The court allowed the unit owner to set aside the sale upon reimbursing the winning bidder the amount of its bid.). CAL. CIV. CODE ' 2924h(g) (West 1993) bars payment of consideration for not bidding or for any effort to fix or restrain bidding.

in 14 cities.[166] Others include Colony Capital, Cerberus Capital, and Fortress Investment Group (through subsidiary, Nationstar).

As sophisticated investors, they realized that with declining house prices in many cities, it was possible to acquire houses at such low prices that money could be made renting them out. Millions of former homeowners foreclosed out of their houses were headed for the rental market. So were millennials, deferring marriage until their 30s or later, deeply in debt on student loans, wary of mortgage loans and mortgage lenders, and not at all convinced that houses were the best investments, having witnessed rapidly falling house prices.

In the chart below, observe that rents climbed steadily from 1990 to 2014 while house prices took a sharp fall from 2008 to 2012, the years that major private equity firms were actively bidding for houses at foreclosure sales.[167]

Private equity firms acquiring houses at distress prices during the slump could make decent returns converting them into rentals, finance their purchases by securitizing their housing portfolios, and eventually sell off their portfolios as house prices spiked upward.

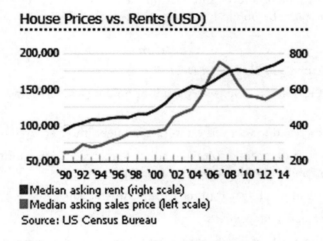

House Prices vs. Rents (USD)

■ Median asking rent (right scale)
■ Median asking sales price (left scale)
Source: US Census Bureau

D. Buying R.E.O. from the Foreclosing Lender

Lenders will have listed their REO properties with real estate brokers or perhaps hired a public auctioneer to sell the property on its behalf. Lenders unload foreclosed property quickly because it is not producing income and making matters worse, bank regulators demand that hefty reserves be kept on hand to cover potential losses on foreclosed property.

---

166. Bloomberg Business, *Blackstone's Homebuying Binge Ends As Prices Surge*, Bloomberg.Com (last visited Jan. 10, 2016), http://www.bloomberg.com/news/articles/2014-03-14/blackstone-s-home-buying-binge-ends-as-prices-surge-mortgages#media-2

167. Mixed Symbols in the U.S. Housing Market, GlobalPropertyGuide (last visited Jan. 10, 2016), http://www.globalpropertyguide.com/North-America/United-States/Price-History

Occasionally, mortgage lenders negotiate terms with potential buyers of foreclosed property before they foreclose. This is a bad idea because the foreclosed borrower could legitimately claim that the pre-sale negotiation removed the prospective buyer's incentive to bid at the foreclosure sale, in effect, "chilling" the bidding. Instead, foreclosing lenders should wait until after acquiring title before negotiating to sell the foreclosed realty.

REO departments sell assets directly, usually in bulk, to favorite customers, list properties with select real estate brokers or contract with professional auctioneers to market the property.

Especially in times of market uncertainty, public auctions have the advantage of accelerating the time from listing to sale.[168] Auctioneers advertise widely especially for sellers willing to pay the advertising bill, hold several open houses for potential bidders before the sale date, arrange for institutional financing and title insurance, and comply with state disclosure laws. For their services auctioneers typically charge 10% of the gross sales price compared to the customary 5-6% brokerage fees.[169] Bidders usually have 45 to 60 days for due diligence before the sale, read title reports and conduct inspections with no assurance of submitting the winning bid. Lenders hope some buyers catch auction fever and heat up the bidding.[170] About one in five U.S. home sales took place by public auction in 2005.[171]

Questions

Question 1: *Secured and Unsecured Debt.*

(a) What is the difference between a creditor holding a secured and an unsecured debt?

(b) How does a creditor convert an unsecured debt into a secured one?

(c) Why is it important for a secured creditor to record evidence of its security interest such as an abstract of judgment or a deed of trust?

(d) Why are debtors obligated to repay unrecorded debts?

Question 2: *Deficiency Judgements.*

(a) What is the practical significance to home mortgage borrowers and lenders of the following statute?

Arizona Revised Statutes § 33-729A provides: "[If a mortgage has been given on property used as a single family or two-family home on a parcel of up to 2 acres and] the proceeds of the mortgaged real property sold [in the foreclosure process] are insufficient to satisfy the judgment [for the amount due on the mortgage loan], the

---

168. Steven L. Good and Celeste M. Hammond, *Real Estate Auctions Legal Concerns for an Increasingly Preferred Method of Selling Real Property,* 40 REAL PROP. PROB. & TR. J. 765 (2006).

169. James R. Hagerty and Michael Corkery, Slowing home market propels auctions into fast track, WALL STREET JOURNAL, Aug. 27, 2006.

170. *Ibid.*

171. Paul Owers, Houses Going, Going, Gone! More Sellers Turn to Auctions, SOUTH FLORIDA SUN-SENTINEL, June 18, 2006.

judgment may not otherwise be satisfied out of other property of the judgment debtor, notwithstanding any agreement to the contrary."

(b) Do you anti-deficiency laws are, on the whole, a good or bad idea?

Question 3: *The Foreclosure Process.*

(a) Explain briefly the differences between judicial and nonjudicial foreclosure, as you would to a friend who was in business school, has just lost her job, and cannot meet her monthly home mortgage payments.

(b) What do each of these documents accomplish for the borrower and the lender: (1) notice of default; (2) notice of sale; (3) notice of acceleration.

(c) What advice would you give a friend thinking of a 'strategic default' on an 'underwater' house who could rent a comparable house at half the price?

(d) Do you regard a 'strategic default' as morally defensible?

(e) What are the practical consequences, pro and con, of a strategic default?

(f) Clearly, strategic defaults could be avoided if lenders were willing to grant principal reductions to preserve the lender's loan to value ratio—but not to exceed current market value levels. Why are lenders so unwilling to modify loans in default by granting principal reductions, even though it could save them the enormous costs of foreclosures?

(g) Why are the purchasers of non-performing loans at steep discounts more inclined to grant loan modifications by reducing the loan balance due to current market value?

Question 4: *The Special Purpose Entity.*

(a) Why are commercial real estate lenders often insistent on the mortgaged property being held by a special purpose entity that has no other assets or liabilities?

(b) The consequence is that the "borrower" is likely to be an LLC whose members have no liability for the entity's debts. How does the mortgage lender benefit from releasing from personal liability the very individuals responsible for the success or failure of the venture that the lender has made possible with its loan?

(c) Rick Li owns three shopping centers. All three shopping centers are located in neighborhoods with large Asian-American populations. Two are anchored by grocery stores specializing in serving an Asian consumer base. A poorly performing grocery store that had anchored the third center is closing. Mr. Li needs a short-term loan to re-position that third center along the lines of his two successful ones. For Mr. Li's re-positioning loan, who should sign the note and deed of trust as the 'borrower'? Would Mr. Li and his lender prefer 'the borrower' to be:

(1) Mr. Li personally?

(2) A separately formed LLC holding title to the third center (the one needing renovation)?

(3) The existing LLC that holds title to all three of the centers?

(d) The mortgage lender might want "cross collateralization," a provision added to the mortgages on the two thriving locations, that these centers are additional security for the mortgage loan on the third center. Would this be pretty much the same, or not much different, from having the existing LLC hold title to all three of the centers?

Question 5: *Why Are Commercial Entrepreneurs Forgiven for Failed Projects?*

The past financial calamities of commercial real estate entrepreneurs who know how to create large-scale projects are often quickly forgotten. An example of this was evident in the real estate roller coaster career of former attorney turned developer Ian Bruce Eichner. In the 1990s, he developed and lost several NYC signature high-rise office projects: Cityspire to the Bank of Nova Scotia and 1540 Broadway to bankruptcy. Then, in 2008, Eichner's $4 billion Cosmopolitan hotel-condo project in Las Vegas could not be refinanced upon completion, and construction lender Deutsche Bank foreclosed and eventually sold it to Blackstone at a huge loss, for less than $2 billion.

Despite all these setbacks his commercial real estate lenders and partners experienced, Eichner is currently developing a 64-story condo tower in mid-town Manhattan and a 32-story condo tower in Harlem.[172] Commercial developers with the talent and capacity to construct complex projects are not held personally accountable for the ups and downs of real estate market values.

Why do you suppose sophisticated commercial real estate lenders continue to finance promoters of spectacularly disastrous projects when a defaulting homeowner will not be eligible for another home mortgage loan for years?

Question 6: *Monetary and Non-monetary Defaults.*

The basic purpose of mortgage law is to make sure the mortgagee does not cheat the mortgagor out of more than the amount due on the loan. Clearly, monetary defaults relate to the mortgage lender's financial stake. But non-monetary defaults are more elusive to appraise. Also, they could result in a precipitous foreclosure even though the value of the security property exceeded the debt, and the default caused no direct monetary loss to the lender.

Would you be sympathetic to a mortgagor seeking a court injunction to prevent foreclosure for a non-monetary default? One example could be a borrower experiencing a material adverse change in its financial situation due to eroding market conditions at other locations. Another could be the failure of the borrower to maintain a Debt Service Coverage Ratio of 1:2 at the security property because a major tenant went bankrupt and the space is presently vacant and on the rental market.

Question 7: *Reinstatement, Equitable Redemption and Statutory Redemption.*

In a notice of intent to accelerate, a mortgage lender informs a defaulting borrower she has 30 days to make up her last three monthly mortgage payments, all past due, totaling $3,150, including allowable costs. She owes $100,000 on the mortgage loan. At foreclosure, the winning bidder pays $85,000.

(a) What is the price of reinstatement?

---

172. Ian Bruce Eichner, Wɪᴋɪᴘᴇᴅɪᴀ (last visited Aug. 16, 2015), https://en.wikipedia.org/wiki/Ian_Bruce_Eichner

(b) What will it cost the borrower to exercise her right of equitable redemption?

(c) What will the borrower or a junior lienor have to pay for statutory redemption?

Question 8: *Why Not Strict Foreclosure?*

(a) If you were to compare the amounts due on foreclosed mortgages with the winning bids at foreclosure sales, you would discover that only rarely does the winning bid exceed the foreclosed debt. Most of the time, the only bidder is the mortgage lender bidding exactly the amount due on the debt. Yet, foreclosure sales add hugely to the losses that lenders incur when they foreclose — typically, losses equal 30% of the amount due. Then why do you suppose more states have not embraced "strict foreclosure," a process that allows lenders to petition the court for title to the security property without a foreclosure sale?

(b) An imaginative mortgage expert has an idea for offering property owners the equivalent of mortgage financing at a much lower price. Instead of a note and deed of trust, the borrower deeds the property to the lender and the lender leases the property back to the borrower with an option to buy at the end of thirty years. The lease payments are calibrated to be the same as mortgage payments would have been. The lease and the option terminate if the borrower misses a payment. The lender's yield is lower than what a typical interest payment would have been on a mortgage — reduced by the difference between what a foreclosure by sale would have cost a lender, and the costs of a summary eviction if the tenant defaults. The borrower defaults at the end of the second year. The lender initiates a summary eviction. Does the borrower/lessee have a good defense to the eviction?

Question 9: *The Validity of a Mortgagee's Lien Subject to a Purchase Option.*

When Uncle Sal sold his vacation beach house to Niece Laura for $500,000, they both knew the property was worth much more than that. So she had no problem acceding to Uncle Sal's request that she give Nephew Ricardo an option to buy the house for $200,000 if she sold the house any time in the ensuing decade. Uncle Sal was a title insurance underwriter, and insisted that the option be duly recorded.

A year after Sal deeded the house to Laura, she borrowed $850,000 secured by a deed of trust on the house to invest in a tech start-up that she was sure would become a "unicorn."[173] The unicorn bubbled into bankruptcy, Laura's investment became worthless, she also lost her personal savings in the failed venture, and she has defaulted on her mortgage loan.

Her lender has initiated foreclosure. The lender's title insurance policy never excepted Ricardo's option from title coverage.

Laura has kept Ricardo up to date on her situation. After consulting with Uncle Sal, they believe this might be a good time for Ricardo to exercise his option. He has

---

173. "They're called "unicorns" — private companies valued at $1 billion or more. The billion-dollar technology startup was once the stuff of myth. Today they're seemingly everywhere, backed by a bull market and a new generation of disruptive technology." http://fortune.com/unicorns/ (Last visited March 23, 2016.)

tendered Laura a written notice to that effect and has placed $200,000 in an escrow account. His escrow instructions authorize the agent to transfer the funds to Laura in exchange for a deed from her as soon as the escrow agent can obtain a policy of title insurance for Ricardo, confirming his ownership free of the mortgage. The agent concurrently is to transfer the $200,000 to the foreclosing mortgage lender with Laura's consent, conditioned on the lender executing a recordable reconveyance of the deed of trust and a release protecting Laura against any personal liability on the note and deed of trust.

If the escrow agent is unable to procure the requested title policy for Ricardo, or a reconveyance and release signed from the lender along with Laura's written consent, Ricardo has authorized the agent to interplead the mortgage lender, Laura and Ricardo to unravel their respective rights and priorities based on the current situation.

Sal, being in the title insurance business, considered the possibility of whether Laura had an obligation to inform the lender's title insurer of Ricardo's option. He has decided she does not because the option was duly recorded. This had two consequences. The mortgage lender is not a bona fide purchaser under the recording laws since it had constructive notice of Ricardo's interest. And the title insurer was derelict for not having checked the public records carefully enough to find Ricardo's recorded option from Sal.

What are the rights of Laura, Ricardo and the mortgage lender to the property and the $200,000?

Question 10: *A Junior Lienor's Options.*

A second trust deed investor made a loan of $150,000 secured by a deed of trust on a fourplex. Each unit is about 1100 square feet. The property was subject to a first deed of trust for $400,000 made by an individual investor. That loan is coming due in three months. The property was built in 1954 and needs updating — electrical, plumbing, roofing. It is renting for $1.50 per square foot where newly built units rent for $2.50 per square foot. The owner was going to use the second trust deed money to improve the property but became ill, has been unable to work, and has missed two consecutive months of payments on both mortgages.

(a) What options are available to the holder of the second deed of trust?

(b) What advice would you offer on what she should do once the first trust deed holder sends out a Notice of Default, which is imminent?

Question 11: *Rights of An Omitted Junior Lienor.*

(a) You have a friend who occasionally purchases second deeds of trust on houses owned by individuals who rent them out. What options are available to her if she receives a notice of default from the holder of a first mortgage that it will soon foreclose?

(b) She recently learned that one of her properties was foreclosed by a senior lienor who never notified her of the foreclosure sale. What questions would you ask before offering an opinion about whether she should do anything about it?

Question 12: *Tenants' Status Following Foreclosure.*

Mortgage lenders financing hotels often require that the hotel developer enter a franchise agreement[174] with a name hotel brand and a hotel management agreement with an experienced firm.

The mortgage lender providing hotel financing would want to be sure that if there was default on the loan, and it had to foreclose, that there would be no sudden disruption in the hotel operation. It would want to assess for itself the cause of the default. Was it caused by general market conditions beyond the control of the hotel operator, or was the default due to the hotel owner having chosen the wrong brand, or inept management?

Depending on the conclusions reached by the mortgage lender or a subsequent bidder on the hotel property, the lender or bidder would want the option of retaining, terminating or renegotiating the hotel owner's franchise and hotel management agreements.

Which of the following best provides that option?

(A) If the mortgage is recorded before the franchise agreement, upon the mortgage lender's foreclosure, the franchise agreement or hotel management agreement would be terminated. The mortgage lender would then have the option of entering new agreements with the same brand or operator if it chose.

(B) If the franchise agreement or the hotel management contract were recorded before the mortgage, the mortgagee's foreclosure would not disturb these arrangements and the purchaser at the foreclosure sale would replace the owner under those agreements.

(C) If the franchisor or hotel management company subordinated their interests to the mortgage, and promised to attorn on the condition that the foreclosure sale purchaser agreed to a non-disturbance promise following foreclosure, this would give the lender or its successor the option to retain or terminate.

(D) The mortgage lender would accomplish its goal if the franchisor or hotel management company subordinated their interests to the mortgage, they agreed to attorn to the mortgage lender or its successor, and the mortgage lender promised not to disturb those agreements as long as the franchisor or the management company was not in default under them.

Question 13. *Alternatives to Foreclosure.*

(a) Which of the alternatives to foreclosure keep a defaulting home owner in the house?

---

174. A franchise is a licensing agreement by which a hotel is operated under a particular brand, or 'flag.' Brands help hotels attract patrons, manage reservation systems, assist in guiding management practices, and with national merchandising and uniform standards throughout the chain.

(b) Which of the alternatives best suits a borrower who can afford the mortgage payments and would like to retain ownership but is considering defaulting because the mortgage balance exceeds the present market value of the house?

(c) Why do mortgage lenders generally prefer short sales to loan modifications reducing the loan balance to the current market value of the security property?

Question 14. *Mortgage Modification Provisions.*

A mortgagor had acquired her home with a purchase money mortgage loan for 80% of her $300,000 purchase price, $240,000. Her interest rate at the time was 7%, interest only for three years, a fixed rate for 30 years with amortization to commence at the end of year three sufficient to repay the debt at the end of the original loan term of 30 years.

Exactly two years later, she borrowed $50,000 to invest in a media-tech start-up. This loan was secured by a deed of trust at a fixed interest rate of 9%, interest only, due and payable in three years.

Meanwhile, she quit her salaried position as a special assistant to a bank vice president in order to work in the start-up full time. The start-up is not generating enough money for her to meet her mortgage obligations. She has defaulted on both her loans. The house is presently worth $250,000.

Her senior mortgagee is willing to modify her loan by reducing the interest rate to 4.5% but only if it can reduce the loan term to five years while maintaining the 30-year amortization schedule. The mortgagor will owe a balloon payment when the modified loan becomes due and payable at the end of five years.

(a) The second trust deed lender seeks to establish its priority as a first lien because the modification materially increases its risk. Is this true?

(b) Does it make any difference that the senior mortgage has no provision in it that the mortgagor and her successors are deemed to consent to any future modifications, extensions, amendments or alterations of the senior mortgage?

Question 15: *Buying Distress Property.*

From the perspective of an investor seeking to profit from the purchase of distressed realty, compare: (1) buying from a defaulting owner before foreclosure either before or after recordation of a notice of default, (2) purchasing at the mortgagee's foreclosure sale, or (3) buying from the mortgagee after the lender acquires title at its own foreclosure and listing the property for sale with either (a) a real estate broker or (b) a public auction house.

Index

(References are to pages.)